The Sunday Telegraph

# GOOD WINE GUIDE 1998

ROBERT JOSEPH

DORLING KINDERSLEY
LONDON • NEW YORK • SYDNEY • MOSCOW

A Dorling Kindersley Book

Editor Robert Joseph
Deputy Editor Anna Griffith
Associate Editor Jonathan Goodall
Editorial Assistants Hilary Lumsden,
Dominic Kelly.
Editorial Production Gill Pitts

Typeset by RJ Publishing Services
Film outputting bureau: Personality UK
Printed and bound in Great Britain by Jarrold Book Printing,
Thetford, Norfolk

First published in 1983 by The Sunday Telegraph


Visit us on the World Wide Web at
http://www.robert-joseph.com
and http://www.dk.com



A CIP catalogue record is available from the British Library.

ISBN 0-7513-0460-3

# Contents

# INTRODUCTION

Welcome to the 13th edition of a very different kind of wine guide. The *Sunday Telegraph Good Wine Guide* is really three books in one. In the first section – the *Basics* – you will find all the grounding you need to get through a dinner party among wine buffs, as well as guidance on styles, flavours, vintages and the most compatible marriages between hundreds of wines and dishes.

The following section – the *A–Z* – is an encyclopedia of some 2,500 wines, terms, regions and producers that will enable you to find your way as easily through the intricacies of an auctioneer's catalogue as around the wine shelves of a supermarket. Unlike any other encyclopedia of its kind, the A–Z goes on to recommend currently available vintages and examples that show off specific wines and winemakers at their best.

This year, for the first time, the *A–Z* also tells you how to pronounce the names of all those wines. So, with the book to hand, you will never have to pause before ordering a bottle of Ngatarawa from New Zealand or Beaulieu Napa Valley Cabernet (it's ***boh-lyoo*** by the way, not ***boh-lyuh*** as a French-speaker might reasonably expect you to pronounce it).

Having chosen your wine, you won't have to search to find a decent merchant from whom to buy it. Simply turn to the third section of the book – the *UK Merchants* – where you will find details of over 200 British stockists, ranging from quirky one-man-bands and City traditionalists to wine clubs, mail-order specialists, high street chains and supermarkets.

Taken as a whole, the *guide* should, (as a reviewer wrote of a previous edition), be the 'only wine book you need' when choosing, buying or drinking wine in 1998.

This year's *Guide* owes its existence to a number of people. Editorial assistants Hilary Lumsden and Dominic Kelly; sub-editor Gill Pitt; associate editor Jonathan Goodall; and, most particularly, Anna Griffith, my deputy editor, were all crucial. At Dorling Kindersley, I have to thank Fay Franklin, Vivien Crump, Ingrid Vienings, and Emily Hatchwell, who had the task of checking every dot and comma. Giles Kime and Shoshana Goldberg, my colleagues at the *Sunday Telegraph*; and Susan Vumbach Low, Casilda Grigg and Damian Riley-Smith at *WINE* Magazine were as indulgent as ever. All of these people share any credit for this book; the criticism should fall on my shoulders alone.

# The Basics

# NEWS

## CHANGING TIMES

Every so often, if you look very carefully and keep an open mind, it may just be possible to catch a glimpse of the future. Twenty years ago, a skilful or unusually gifted prophet might, for instance, have predicted the current success of wines from New World countries and regions like Australia, Chile and California – but, as I recall from conversations at the time, it was a rare European winemaker who would even have found room in his brain for the thought. Back then, most Burgundians and Bordelais thought their counterparts in the Barossa, Maipo and Napa Valleys an irritating irrelevance. The ambitious wines produced by these Johnny-come-latelies might score highly in blind tastings, but they would never really compare with a top class claret or Burgundy.

Today, that kind of pig-headed chauvinism is on a par with a belief in the flatness of the earth and the divine right of kings. There is no longer any denying that great wine can be made in all sorts of previously unsuspected places, and that perfectly decent stuff can be produced in such countries as Canada and Uruguay.

**Appellation Spring**

As vines are planted from one side of the globe to the other, however, two opposing trends are gradually becoming apparent. On the one hand, there is the inexorable move towards a European-influenced cocktail of regional pride and marketing hype that I like to call appellationism.

There are, of course, plenty of young regions with a valid claim to a separate identity. Coonawarra in Australia and Malborough in New Zealand, for example, make wines that are recognizable 'blind' in a line-up of bottles from other places. But what about the patches of land that enjoy precisely the same red soil and climate a few miles up the road from Coonawarra that aren't allowed to use this hallowed name on their label? And even if Marlborough makes great, distinctive Sauvignon Blanc, who's to say that its Chardonnay might not be best used in blends with wine made from the same grape in Gisborne – another region altogether?

This kind of argument, however, is an anathema to the more precious appellationists. The French authorities, for example, outlaw the addition of even a drop of Bergerac to a vat of wine made from the same grape varieties a few kilometres down the road in Bordeaux. Californian rules are slightly less strict, but plenty of producers throw up their hands in apartheid-like horror at the very idea of wines from Napa sharing the same bottle as the fruit of grapes grown on the other side of the hills in Sonoma.

**Blends and means**

In the opposite corner, however, there are the vinous liberals who – to put it baldly – care a lot less about precisely where a wine comes from than the way it tastes. The winemakers of Champagne and the port houses of the Douro use the blending vat as one of their most valuable tools. Neither Dom Pérignon nor Dow's 1994 vintage port, for instance, comes from a single vineyard or village; both benefit from the winemakers having respectively had a range of individual Champagnes and ports with which to play mix-and-match.

In Australia, cross-regional blending is commonplace. Penfolds' Grange – undeniably one of the world's greatest wines – is a mixture of grapes grown in various parts of the state of South Australia. All sorts of other tasty but more modestly-priced wines describe themselves merely as being from 'South East Australia', a region that covers some 90% of the vineyards on the continent.

**Heading West**

Several laterally-minded Californians have extended the logic of this line of thinking a little further. When big-name wine producers like Mondavi and Monterey Vineyards found that there were insufficent locally-grown Merlot grapes to satisfy the growing demand for their wines made from this variety, they simply went shopping overseas. Southern France, they discovered, had plenty of Merlot. All they had to do was to turn it into wine, ship it back home and bottle it with almost precisely the same labels as the Californian Merlots so popular with their customers. A few eyebrows may have been raised at the small print stating that the imported wine came from the 'Languedoc Region' rather than the west coast of the US. As far as I am aware, however, the switch was acheived without anyone shouting 'foul'.

This kind of – what some might call cynical, others might term astute – behaviour is far from limited to California. In Bangkok, I came across bottles of white wine from a well-known German wine company. The labels were covered with the familiar Gothic script and I naturally assumed them to be full of wine from the Rhine of Mosel. On closer inspection, the wine turned out to have been made in the the former Soviet republic of Moldova, which is not – to the best of my knowledge – part of Germany.

Is this the trend for the future? Just as we buy Volkswagens that have been manufactured in South America or Eastern Europe and some of the cheaper Japanese hi-fis that have been assembled in Britain, we could well become increasingly happy to drink stylistic 'brands' of wine rather than examples of particular regions that vary according to the producer and vintage.

### Where's it all going?

Setting aside the question of where wines are made, one of the areas of interest in 1997 focused on where they were drunk. Back in 1978, most of the world's more basic wine was consumed within a few hundred miles of where the grapes were grown. In countries where there were no – or few – vineyards, wine was still an occasional pleasure, and was often restricted to the finer fare that was the preserve of the wealthy who stocked their cellars from specialist merchants.

Fast forward twenty years and the picture has been transformed completely. Today, astonishing as it may seem to outsiders, in countries like France, Italy and Spain, where wine was once more commonly drunk than water, its consumption is in danger of becoming a minority activity. Young southern Europeans saw wine drinking as the kind of thing their parents did – and have accordingly decided that it was not for them.

This trend, coupled with the growing success of affordably-priced wines from the New World, is worrying for traditional producers of stuff like Muscadet and dry white Bordeaux, who are already sitting on cellars of unsold wine. In twenty years time, when Brussels has given up subsidizing inefficient European farming, thousands of winegrowers in regions like these may simply have had to give up growing grapes.

### Oriental sweet and sour

The greatest hope for the survival of these wines may well lie overseas, in countries where people are only beginning to discover wine. When we look back at 1997, I think it could be remembered as the year when the wine world as a whole suddenly began to notice the wine drinking potential of the Far East.

In a momentary distraction from the business of reintegrating Hong Kong into the rest of China, the Beijing authorities quietly announced their offical preference for wine as a national drink. Grapes, it was decreed, unlike the grain and rice used for other alcoholic drinks, are not a staple food that could be used to feed hungry citizens.

Local entrepreneurs have been ready to turn a profit out of supporting the official pro-wine line. The Karaoke bars in Shanghai and Beijing are apparently full of Chinese whose favourite tipple of the moment is Mouton-Cadet blended half-and-half with Sprite lemonade. Gallic purists may wince at the thought; I'd perversely argue that this could be an ideal way to drink the mean-flavoured basic Bordeaux of recent poor vintages. Maybe they should try serving it to some of those young French non-drinkers.

Elsewhere in Asia, huge quantites of rather pricier claret is being enjoyed 'straight'. A few British wine merchants have been successfully selling fine wine to rich Asians for years, but until 1997 no one had even begun to suggest that wine drinkers in places like Taiwan, Singapore and Hong Kong might really influence the way the rest of us drink. The giddy activity surrounding the 1995 and 1996 top Bordeaux when they were first released 'en primeur' (i.e. in the barrel) was, however, largely fuelled by Asians, many of whom bought their wine through traditional London merchants.

Those buyers were also in evidence at Christie's and Sotheby's auctions in 1997, contributing, for example, to the lunatic bidding at the sale of Sir Andrew Lloyd Webber's cellar. With a little help from rich enthusiasts in Scandinavia, Germany and the US, they are increasingly pricing fine Bordeaux out of its traditional markets.

Anyone doubting just how popular top class wine is becoming in the Far East should take a look at the duty-free shop in Singapore's Changi Airport, where I discovered shelves packed with clarets of which most wine lovers merely dream. Is it any coincidence that it was the owners of that shop, the French giant LVMH, who, in 1997, sought to buy Château d'Yquem, producer of the world's most expensive white wine?

Sauternes is of course an established classic wine. Until now, the idea of anyone creating a 'new' top-flight Bordeaux château was only a little more likely than that of a new planet being discovered lurking near the moon. But over the last few years we have seen the arrival of three instant success stories: Château Le Pin, Valandraud and, in 1997, La Mondotte. These all share four characteristics. They are all made principally from the Merlot grape; they are produced in tiny quantities; they have all been snapped up by buyers in Asia, and were sold for prices that leave their producers reeling in surprise.

### All that glitters

As the new buyers become steadily more influential, and as new ways of buying and trading wine – principally over the internet – take hold, we could encounter all sorts of other phenomena. As a final note, I would warn of the growing incidence of forged bottles and labels. In 1997, as the international wine press disclosed details of a batch of fake Champagne that was allegedly linked to the KWV, South Africa's biggest wine company, I came across four separate stories of bottles of illustrious claret that turned out to be fakes. For a wine drinker, as the Chinese say, these are interesting times.

# Tasting & Buying

## Spoiled for Choice

Buying wine today has become wonderfully – and horribly – like buying a gallon of paint. Just as the paint manufacturer's helpful chart can become daunting with its endless shades of subtly different white, the number of bottles and the information available on the supermarket shelves can make you want to give up and reach for the one that is most familiar, or most favourably priced.

If you're not a wine buff, why should you know the differences in flavour to be found in wines made from the same grape in Mâcon in France, Maipo in Chile and Marlborough in New Zealand? Often, the merchant has helpfully provided descriptive terms to help you to imagine the flavour of the stuff in the bottle. But, these too can merely add to the confusion. Do you want the one that 'tastes of strawberries or raspberries', the 'refreshingly dry', or the 'crisp, lemony white'?

Over the next few pages, I can't promise to clear a six-lane highway through this jungle but, with luck, I shall give you a path to follow with rather more confidence when you are choosing a wine, and one from which you can stray to explore for yourself.

### The Label

Wine labels should reveal the country or region where the wine was made (see page 16). Nowadays, a growing proportion is sold by its grape variety (see page 36). Both region and grape, however, offer only partial guidance as to what you are likely to find when you pull the cork.

Bear in mind the following:

1) Official terms such as Appellation Contrôlée, Grand or Premier Cru, Qualitätswein and Reserva are as trustworthy as official pronouncements by politicians.
2) Unofficial terms such as Reserve Personnel are, likewise, as trustworthy as unofficial pronouncements by the producer of any other commodity.
3) Knowing that a wine comes from a particular region is often like knowing nothing more about a person than where they were born; it provides no guarantee of how good the wine will be. Nor, how it will have been made (though there are often

local rules). There will be nothing to tell you, for instance, whether a Chablis is oaked or not; nor, more annoyingly, will an Alsace or a Vouvray always reveal its sweetness on the label.

4) Beware of falling into the trap of trusting a 'big name' region to make better wine than a supposedly lesser one. Rotten wines come out of Nuits-St-Georges, the Napa Valley, Margaux and Rioja – as well as just about every other region.

5) Don't expect wines from the same grape variety to taste the same wherever the grape is grown: a Chardonnay from South Africa might taste far drier than one from California and less fruity than one from Australia. The precise flavour and style will depend on the producer.

6) Just because a producer makes a good wine in one place, don't trust him to make others either there or elsewhere. For example, the team at Lafite Rothschild are responsible for the dire Los Vascos white in Chile; while some of Robert Mondavi's inexpensive Woodbridge wines bear no relation to the quality of his Reserve wines.

7) The fact that there is a château on a wine label has no bearing on the quality of the contents.

8) Nor does the boast that the wine is bottled at said château.

9) Nineteenth-century medals look pretty on a label; they say nothing about the quality of the 20th-century stuff in the bottle.

10) Price provides some guidance to a wine's quality: a very expensive bottle may be apalling, but it's unlikely that a very cheap one will be better than basic.

## A WAY WITH WORDS

Before going any further, I'm afraid that there's no alternative to returning to the thorny question of the language you are going to use to describe your impressions.

You could of course dispense with descriptive words altogether, as one distinguished visitor did when he visited Bordeaux 170 years ago. Château Margaux was, he noted 'a wine of fine flavour – but not of equal body'. Lafite, on the other hand, had 'less flavour than the former but more body – an equality of flavour and body'. As for Latour, well, that had 'more body than flavour', while Haut-Brion was merely 'a wine of fine flavour'. George Washington may have been a great president, but he was evidently not the ideal person from whom to learn the subtle differences between the flavours of four of the world's most famous wines.

Michelangelo, on the other hand, was quite ready to apply his artistry to the white wine of San Gimignano in Tuscany, of which he said 'it kisses, licks, bites, thrusts and stings...' Earlier still, in the 12th century, one Alexander Neckham described a wine he particularly liked as 'sweet-tasted as an almond, creeping like a squirrel, leaping like a roebuck, delicate as fine silk and colder than crystal', while contemporary pundits routinely refer to wines as having 'gobs of fruit' and tasting of 'kumquats and suede'.

So, there's nothing new in outlandish expressions for wine; each country and each generation simply comes up with its own vocabulary. Some descriptions, such as the likening to gooseberry and asparagus of wines made from the Sauvignon Blanc, are both historically and internationally well established – and can be justified by scientific analysis, which confirms that the same aromatic chemical compound is found in the fruit, vegetable and wine.

No one knows why the Gewürztraminer should produce wines that smell and taste of lychees, or why reds made from the Grenache should be recognisably peppery, but they are. And recognising those hallmark smells and flavours can be very handy if ever you have to guess a wine's identity.

Then there are straightforward descriptions that could apply to almost anything we eat or drink. Wines can be fresh or stale, clean or dirty. If they are acidic, or overfull of tannin, they will be 'hard'; a 'soft' wine, by contrast might be easier to drink, but boring.

There are other less evocative terms. While a downright watery wine is 'dilute' or 'thin', subtle ones are called 'elegant'. A red or white whose flavour is hard to discern is described as 'dumb'.

Whatever the style of a wine, the quality it is supposed to have, is 'balance'. A sweet white, for example, needs enough acidity to keep it from cloying. No one will ever enjoy a wine that is too fruity, too dry, too oaky, or too *anything*.

The flavour that lingers in your mouth long after you have swallowed or spat it out is known as the 'finish'. Wines whose flavour – pleasant or unpleasant – hangs around, are described as 'long'; those whose flavour disappears quickly are 'short'.

Finally, there is 'complex', the word that is used to justify why one wine costs ten times more than another. A complex wine is like a well-scored symphony, while a simpler one could be compared to a melody picked out on a single instrument.

## TASTING

Wine tasting is surrounded by mystery and mystique. And it shouldn't be – because all it really consists of is paying attention to the stuff in the glass, whether you're in the formal environment of a wine tasting, or taking a sip of the house white in your local wine bar. In fact, apart from spitting (which calls for unusually tolerant wine bars) there's really no difference in the way you actually do the tasting.

Every time you taste a wine, you will, above all, be deciding whether or not you like it. Beyond that, you may also be judging whether you reckon it to be a good example of what it claims to be. A bottle of Champagne costs a lot more than basic Spanish fizz, so it should taste recognisably different. Some do, some don't.

## See

The appearance of a wine can tell you quite a lot about it. Assuming that it isn't cloudy (in which case you should send it straight back), it will reveal its age and may give some hint of the grape and origin. Some grapes, like Burgundy's Pinot Noir, makes naturally paler wines than, say Bordeaux's Cabernet Sauvignon; wines from warmer regions tend to have deeper colours. Tilt the glass away from you over a piece of white paper and look at the rim of the liquid. The more watery and brown it is, the older the wine (Beaujolais Nouveau will be violet through and through).

## Swirl

Vigorously swirl the wine around the glass for a moment or so to release any reluctant smells.

## Sniff

You sniff a wine before tasting it for the same reason that you sniff a carton of milk before pouring its contents into your tea. The smell can tell you more about a wine than anything else. If you don't believe me, just try tasting anything while holding your nose, or while you've got a cold. When sniffing, concentrate on whether the wine seems fresh and clean, and on any particular smells that indicate how the wine is likely to taste.

What are your first impressions? Is the wine fruity, and, if so, which fruit does it remind you of? Does it have the characteristic vanilla smell of a wine that has been fermented and/or matured in new oak barrels? Is it spicy? Or herbaceous? Sweet or dry? Rich or lean?

## Sip

Take a small mouthful and – this takes practice – suck air between your teeth and through the liquid. Look in a mirror while you're doing this: if your mouth looks like a cat's bottom and sounds like a child trying to suck the last few drops of Coca Cola through a straw, then you're doing it right. Hold the wine in your mouth for a little longer to release as much of its flavour as possible.

Focus on the flavour. Ask yourself the same questions about whether it tastes sweet, dry, fruity, spicy, herbaceous. Is there just one flavour, or do several contribute to a 'complex' overall effect?

Apart from the flavour, concentrate on the texture of the wine. Some wines – Chardonnay, for example – are mouth-coatingly buttery, while others – e.g. Gewürztraminer – can seem to be almost oily. Muscadet is a good example of a wine with a texture that is closer to that of water.

Reds, too, vary in texture, some seeming tough and tannic enough to make the inside of one cheek want to kiss the inside of the other. Traditionalists were tolerant of that tannin, believing it necessary to a wine's longevity. More modern winemakers, including the men and women responsible for the best estates in Bordeaux and Burgundy, take a different view. For them, there is a difference between the harsh tannin and the 'fine' (non-aggressive) tannin to be found in wine carefully made from ripe grapes. A modern Bordeaux often has as much tannin as old-fashioned examples – but is far easier to taste and drink.

### Spit

The only reason for spitting a wine out – unless it is actively repellent – is quite simply to maintain a measure of sobriety at the end of a lengthy tasting. I still have the notes I took during a long banquet in Burgundy at which there were dozens of great wines and not even the remotest chance to do anything but swallow. The descriptions of the first few are perfectly legible; the thirtieth apparently tasted 'very xgblorefjy'. If all you are interested in is the taste, not spitting is an indulgence; you ought to have got 90% of the flavour while the wine was in your mouth.

Pause for a moment or two after spitting the wine out. Is the flavour still there? How does what you are experiencing now compare with the taste you had in your mouth? Some wines have a surprisingly unpleasant aftertaste; others have flavours that linger deliciously.

## SHOULD I SEND IT BACK?

Wines are subject to all sorts of faults, though far less than they were even as recently as a decade ago.

### Acid

All wines, like all fruit and vegetables, contain a certain amount of acidity. Without it they would go very stale very quickly. Wines made from unripe grapes will, however, taste unpalatably 'green' and like unripe apples or plums – or like chewing leaves or grass.

### Bitter

Bitterness is quite a different thing. On occasion, especially in Italy, a touch of bitterness may not only be forgivable, it may even be an integral part of a wine's character, as in the case of Amarone reds. Of course, the Italians like Campari too. Even so, a little bitterness goes a very long way.

## Cloudy

Wine should be transparent. The only excuse for cloudiness is in a wine like an old Burgundy whose deposit has been shaken up.

## Corked

People often complain that a bottle is 'corked' when they find a few crumbs of cork floating on the surface. In fact, genuinely corked wines have a musty smell and flavour that comes from a mould in the cork. Some corks are mouldier, and their wines mustier, than others, but all corked wines become nastier the longer they are exposed to oxygen. Between 3–8% of bottles of wines are corked. Screw caps and plastic corks are a far better bet.

## Crystals

Not a fault, but included because people often think there is something wrong with a white wine if there is a layer of fine white crystals in the bottom of the bottle. They are just tartrates that fall naturally.

## Maderised/Oxidised

Madeira is fortified wine from the island of the same name that has been intentionally exposed to the air and heated in a special oven. Maderised wine is unfortified stuff from anywhere, which has been accidentally subjected to warmth and air. The difference between the two is that Madeira is delicious, extraordinary, nutty, tangy stuff, while maderised wine simply tastes like cheap, stale dry sherry.

Oxidised is a broader term, referring to wine that has been exposed to the air – or made from grapes that have cooked in the sun. The taste is reminiscent of poor sherry or vinegar – or both.

## Sulphur (SO2/H2S)

Sulphur dioxide is almost universally used as a protection against the bacteria that would oxidise (qv) a wine. In excess, as sulphur dioxide, it will be smelled when you sniff the wine and may make you cough or sneeze. Even worse, though, is hydrogen sulphide and *mercaptans*, its associated sulphur compounds, which are created when sulphur dioxide combines with the wine. Wines with hydrogen sulphide smell of rotten eggs, while mercaptans reek of all sorts of nastiness, ranging from rancid garlic to burning rubber. If you think you have found these characteristics, pop a copper coin into your glass. It may clear the problem up completely.

## Vinegary/Volatile

Volatile acidity is present in all wines, but only in small proportions. In excess – usually the result of careless winemaking – what can be a pleasant component (like a touch of balsamic vinegar in a sauce) tastes downright vinegary.

# COUNTRIES

## WHERE IN THE WORLD?

Despite the plethora of bottles whose labels bear the name of the same grape variety, the country and region in which a wine is made – with its climate, traditions and local taste – still largely dictate the style of the stuff that ends up in your glass. In the next few pages, we'll take a whirlwind tour of the wine world, which should give you a clearer idea of what to expect from all of the most significant winemaking nations. (For more information on grapes, terms and regions, see the A–Z, which starts on page 83).

## AUSTRALIA

**Reading the label:** Late harvest/noble harvest – *sweet*. Show Reserve – *top-of-the-range wine, usually with more oak*. Tokay – *Australian name for the Muscadelle grape, used for rich liqueur wines*. Verdelho – *Madeira grape used for limey dry wines*. Mataro – *Mourvèdre*. Shiraz – *Syrah*. Tarrango – *local success story, fresh, fruity and Beaujolais-like*.

Twenty or so years ago, Australian wines were the butt of a Monty Python sketch. Today, they are the reliable vinous equivalent of Japanese hi-fi and cameras. It is hard to explain quite how this switch happened, but I would attribute much of the credit to the taste the Australians themselves have developed for wine. Having a populace that treats wine the way many Americans treat milk or beer has helped to provide the impetus for two of the best wine schools in the world – and for a circuit of fiercely fought competitions in which even the humblest wines battle to win medals.

Another strength has been the spirit of exploration which led to the establishment of regions like the Barossa and Hunter Valleys, and which is now fuelling the enthusiastic planting of vines in previously unknown places, such as Orange, Robe, Mount Benson, Young and Pemberton.

Remember these names; they are already appearing on a new generation of subtler, Australian reds and whites that will make some of today's stars look like clod-hoppers. And look out too for unconventional blends of grape varieties, as well as delicious new flavours none of us has ever tasted. Australia is the only region or

country to have drawn up a master plan for world wine domination within 25 years. Judged by what's been achieved so far, I think the Aussies may well be on track to achieving their ambitions.

## AUSTRIA

**Reading the label:** Ausbruch – *late harvested, between Beerenauslese and Trockenbeerenauslese*. Erzeugerabfullung – *estate-bottled.* Schilfwein – *literally, 'reed wine', made from grapes dried on mats.*

Forget the anti-freeze scandal of a decade ago. Today, Austrian winemakers are riding high, with brilliant, late-harvest wines (including some wonderfully weird sweet reds – don't knock 'em till you've tried 'em), dry whites and increasingly impressive reds.

## CANADA

**Reading the label:** VQA (Vintners Quality Alliance) – *local designation seeking to guarantee quality and local provenance.*

The Icewines are the stars here, though Chardonnays are fast improving and progress is also being made with reds made from the Pinot Noir and Merlot.

## Eastern Europe

Some parts of Eastern Europe are coming to terms with life under capitalism a lot more successfully than others, but throughout the region, winemaking is improving by fits and starts.

### Bulgaria

The pioneer of good Iron Curtain reds, Bulgaria remains a reliable source of ripe Cabernet Sauvignon and Merlot, as well as creditable examples of the earthy local Mavrud. Whites are getting better too, thanks largely to the efforts of visiting Australian winemakers.

### Hungary

Still probably best known for its red Bull's Blood, Hungary's strongest card today lies in the Tokajis, the best of which are being made by foreign investors. Reds are improving, as are cheap and cheerful Australian-style Sauvignons and Chardonnays.

### Romania, Moldova and Former Yugoslavia

It is too early to see whether the new Yugoslav republics can export as many bottles of wine as used to go out under the Laski Rizling label, but Romania produces decent if atypical Pinot Noirs, while Moldova's strength lies in whites.

## England and Wales

British winemakers are doubly handicapped by an unhelpful climate and by governments of both political hues that give almost none of the help on offer to their counterparts elsewhere in Europe. Even so, the vineyards of England and Wales are steadily developing a potential for using recently developed German grape varieties to make world-class wine. Best of the bunch so far are dry Loire-style whites, high-quality, late-harvest wines and good fizz. There are reds too, but these are only really of curiosity value and are likely to remain so until global warming takes effect.

## France

**Reading the label:** Appellation Contrôlée (or AOC) – *designation referring to the region and style of what are supposedly France's better wines.* Blanc de Blancs – *white wine made from white grapes.* Blanc de Noirs – *white wine made from black grapes.* Cave – *cellar.* Cave des Vignerons de – *usually a co-operative.* Cépage – *grape variety.* Château – *wine estate.* Chêne – *oak barrels, as in Fûts de Chêne.* Clos – *(historically) walled vineyard.* Côte(s)/Coteaux – *hillside.* Crémant – *sparkling.* Cuvée – *a specific blend.* Demi-sec – *medium sweet.* Domaine – *wine estate.* Doux –

sweet. Grand Cru – *higher quality, or specific vineyards*. Gris – *pale rosé, as in Vin Gris*. Jeunes Vignes – *young vines (often ineligible to produce Appellation Contrôlée wine.)* Méthode Classique – *used to indicate the Champagne method of making sparkling wine*. Millésime – *year or vintage*. Mis en Bouteille au Château/Domaine – *bottled at the estate*. Moëlleux – *sweet*. Monopole – *a vineyard owned by a single producer*. Mousseux – *sparkling*. Négoçiant (Eleveur) – *a merchant who buys, matures, bottles and sells wine*. Pétillant – *lightly sparkling*. Premier Cru – *'first growth', a quality designation that varies from area to area*. Propriétaire (Récoltant) – *vineyard owner/manager*. Reserve (Personelle) – *legally meaningless phrase*. Sur Lie – *aged on the lees (dead yeast)*. VDQS (Vin Délimité de Qualité Superieur) – *perpetually "soon-to-be-abolished" official designation for wines which are better than Vin de Pays but not good enough for Appellation Contrôlée*. Vieilles Vignes – *old vines (could be any age from 20–80), should indicate higher quality*. Villages – *supposedly best part of a larger region, as in Beaujolais or Côtes du Rhône Villages*. Vin de Pays – *wine with regional character*. Vin de Table – *basic table wine. Stupid rules mean that these wines are banned from mentioning their provenance, grape varieties or vintage on their labels*.

## FRANCE

Still the benchmark, or set of benchmarks, against which winemakers in other countries test themselves. This is the place to find Chardonnay in its finest oaked (white Burgundy) and unoaked (traditional Chablis) styles; Sauvignon (from Sancerre and Pouilly Fumé in the Loire, and in blends with the Sémillon, Bordeaux); Cabernet Sauvignon and Merlot (claret); Pinot Noir (red Burgundy and Champagne); Riesling, Gewürztraminer and Pinots Blanc and Gris (Alsace). The Chenin Blanc still fares better in the Loire than anywhere else and, despite their successes in Australia, the Syrah (aka Shiraz) and Grenache are still at their finest in the Rhône.

France's problem remains the unpredictability of the climate in most of its best regions, and the unreliability of far too many of its winemakers, who are often happy to coast along on the reputation of the region in which they happen to work.

## ALSACE

**Reading the label:** Selection de Grains Nobles – *lusciously sweet wine made from grapes affected by Noble Rot.* Vendange Tardive – *late harvested.* Edelzwicker – *blend of white grapes, usually Pinot Blanc and Sylvaner.*

Often underrated, and confused with German wines from the other side of the Rhine, Alsace deserves to be more popular. Its odd assortment of grapes make wonderfully rich, spicy wine, both in their customary dry and more unusual, late-harvest styles. This is my bet to follow the success of its spicy red counterparts in the Rhône.

## BORDEAUX

**Reading the label:** Chai – *cellar.* Cru Bourgeois – *level beneath Cru Classé but possibly of similar quality.* Cru Classé – *'Classed Growth', a wine featured in the 1855 classification of the Médoc and Graves, provides no guarantee of current quality.* Grand Cru/Grand Cru Classé – *confusing terms, especially in St. Emilion, where the former is allocated annually on the basis of a sometimes less-than-arduous tasting, while the latter is reassessed every decade.*

According to most wine atlases, Bordeaux is one large region (with an annual production twice as large as Australia) broken up into a set of sub-districts. In reality, as the most recent vintages have shown, it makes more sense to think of the region as a group of high-quality vineyards, surrounded by a huge area rarely capable of much better than mediocre fare.

At the top of the quality tree are the red wines made by the best producers in the villages of St. Estèphe, Pauillac, St. Julien, Moulis and Margaux in the Médoc to the north of Bordeaux, and in Pomerol and St. Emilion to the east; the reds and whites of the

Pessac Léognan region of the Graves to the south of the city, and the luscious sweet wines of Sauternes and Barsac. But watch out for good, supposedly lesser appellations here, such as Fronsac and Côte des Francs.

## Burgundy

**Reading the label:** Hospices de Beaune – *wines made and sold at auction by the charitable Hospices de Beaune.* Passetoutgrains – *a blend of Gamay and Pinot Noir.* Tasteviné – *a special label for wines that have passed a tasting by the Confrèrie des Chevaliers de Tastevin.*

The heartland of the Pinot Noir and the Chardonnay, this is the region that produces such wines as Chablis, Nuits St. Georges, Gevrey-Chambertin, Beaune, Meursault, Puligny-Montrachet, Mâcon Villages, Pouilly Fuissé and Beaujolais. According to the official quality pyramid, the best wines come from the Grands

Crus vineyards; next are the Premiers Crus, followed by plain village wines and, last of all, basic Bourgogne Rouge or Blanc.

Unfortunately, despite the simplicity of the system, it can be tough to find a good bottle. The problem lies in the number of individual producers who make their own wines with varying measures of luck and skill. The region's merchants are as variable in their quality as the growers. As a rule, therefore, place your trust in a supposedly humble wine from a reliable producer, rather than a pricier Premier or Grand Cru from one with lower standards.

## CHAMPAGNE

**Reading the label:** Blanc de Blancs – *white wine from white grapes, pure Chardonnay*. Blancs de Noirs – *white wine made from black grapes*. Brut Sauvage/Zéro – *bone dry*. Extra-Dry – *(surprisingly) sweeter than Brut*. Grand Cru – *from a top-quality vineyard*. Négoçiant-manipulant (NM) – *buyer and blender of wines*. Non-Vintage – *a blend of wines usually based on wine of a single vintage*. Récoltant manipulant (RM) – *individual estate*.

The world's most famous man-made luxury? At its best, the sparkling wine made in the Champagne region to the east of Paris still leaves all imitators standing. Nowhere else achieves the blend of biscuity richness and subtle fruit that is to be found in any top-class Champagne. Beware cheap Champagne, however, and poór wine from big-name Champagne houses who should know better.

## LOIRE

**Reading the label:** Moëlleux – *sweet.* Sur Lie – *on its lees (dead yeast), usually only applied to Muscadet.* Côt – *local name for the Malbec.*

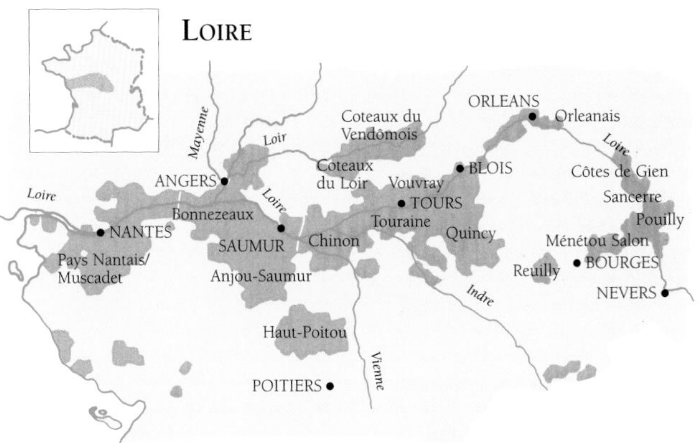


From Muscadet on the Atlantic coast to Sancerre and Pouilly Fumé at the other end of the river, this is one of the best places in the world to seek out fresh, dry white wine. There are some delicious sweet whites too, made from the Chenin Blanc at Vouvray, Quarts de Chaume and Bonezeaux, some fresh fizz in Saumur, and some crunchily blackcurranty reds from Chinon and Bourgeuil.

As elsewhere, buy with care. This is a region of regularly shoddy winemaking and widespread sulphur dioxide abuse, which gives far too many bottles – particularly the late-harvest, sweet ones – an unpleasantly "woolly" character. Although when good wines are found they are truely excellent.

## RHONE

**Reading the label:** Vin Doux Naturel – *fortified wine, such as Muscat de Beaumes de Venise.* Côtes du Rhône Villages – *wine from one of a number of better sited villages in the overall Côtes du Rhône appellation, and thus, supposedly finer wine than plain Côtes du Rhône*

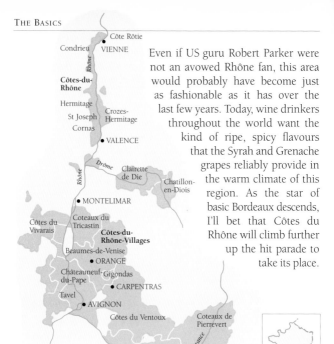

Even if US guru Robert Parker were not an avowed Rhône fan, this area would probably have become just as fashionable as it has over the last few years. Today, wine drinkers throughout the world want the kind of ripe, spicy flavours that the Syrah and Grenache grapes reliably provide in the warm climate of this region. As the star of basic Bordeaux descends, I'll bet that Côtes du Rhône will climb further up the hit parade to take its place.

**RHONE**

## THE SOUTH WEST

> **Reading the label:** Perlé or Perlant – *gently sparkling, used in one of the styles of Gaillac.*

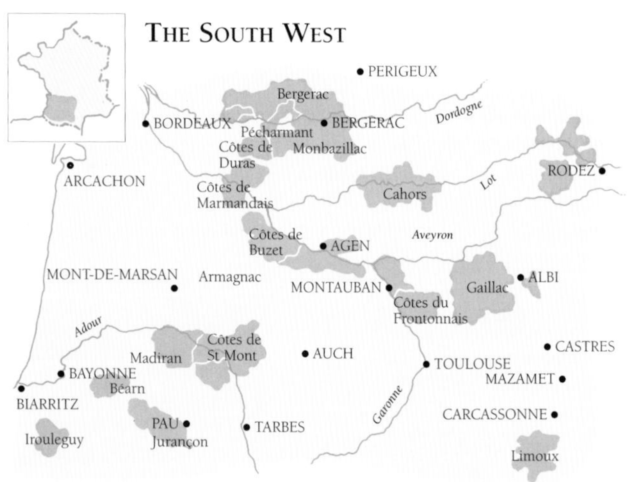

The conservative corner of France, heading inland from Bordeaux. This is the place to find wines like Jurançon, in its sweet and dry form, Gaillac, Cahors and Madiran. Once upon a time these wines, though famous among French wine buffs, were often old-fashioned in the worst sense of the term.

Today, a new wave of winemakers is learning how to extract unsuspected fruit flavours from grapes like the Gros and Petit Manseng, the Tannat, the Mauzac and the Malbec. These wines are worth the detour for anyone bored with the ubiquitous Cabernet Sauvignon and Chardonnay and dissatisfied with poor quality claret.

## THE SOUTH

**Reading the label:** Vin de Pays d'Oc – *a country wine from the Languedoc region. Often some of the best stuff in the region.* Rancio – *woody, slightly volatile character in Banyuls and other fortified wines that have been aged in the barrel.*

### LANGUEDOC-ROUSSILLON

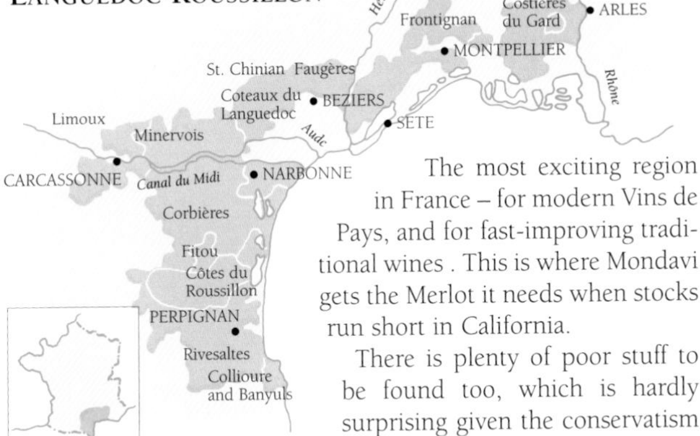


The most exciting region in France – for modern Vins de Pays, and for fast-improving traditional wines . This is where Mondavi gets the Merlot it needs when stocks run short in California.

There is plenty of poor stuff to be found too, which is hardly surprising given the conservatism of a region which produces 10% of the world's wine. Even so, the combination of an ideal climate and some increasingly dynamic winemaking (including with foreign investment) is steadily raising the quality of wines like Fitou, Corbières, Minervois and Côtes de Roussillon, as well as other, lesser-known classics, such as Cassis, Bandol, Banyuls and Collioure.

## EASTERN FRANCE

**Reading the label:** Vin de Paille – *sweet, golden wine from grapes dried on straw mats.* Vin Jaune – *sherry-like, slightly oxidised wine.*

Savoie's zingy wines are often only thought of as skiing-fare, but, like Arbois' nutty, sherry-style whites, they are characterfully different, and made from grape varieties that are grown nowhere else.

# GERMANY

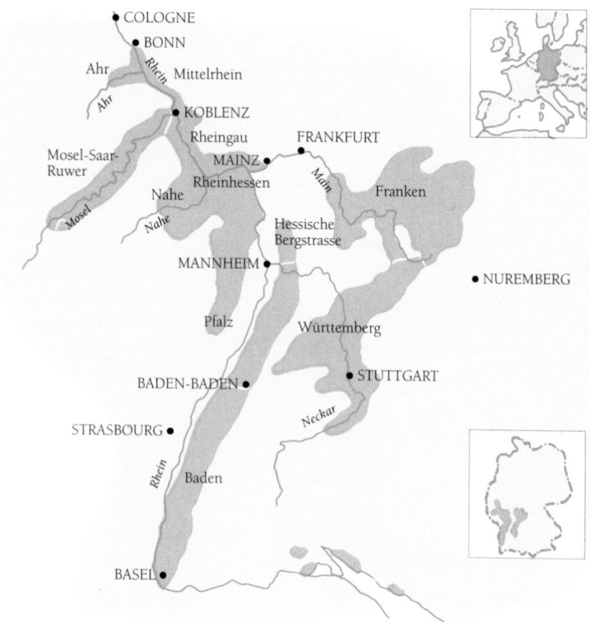


**Reading the label:** Amtliche Prüfungsnummer (AP number) – *official identification number*. Auslese – *sweet wine from selected grapes above a certain ripeness level*. Beerenauslese – *luscious, sweet wines from selected, ripe grapes (Beeren), hopefully affected by Botrytis*. Erzeugerabfüllung – *bottled by the grower/estate*. Halbtrocken – *off-dry*. Hock – *English name for Rhine wines*. Kabinett – *first step in German quality ladder, for wines which fulfil a certain natural sweetness*. Kellerei/kellerabfüllung – *cellar/producer/estate-bottled*. Landwein – *a relatively recent quality designation – the equivalent of a French Vin De Pays*. QbA (Qualitätswein bestimmter Anbaugebiet) – *basic quality German wine, meeting certain standards*. QmP (Qualitätswein mit Prädikat) – *QbA wine with 'special qualities' subject to (not very) rigorous testing. The QmP blanket designation is broken into five sweetness rungs, from Kabinett to Trockenbeerenauslesen plus Eiswein*. Schloss – *literally 'castle', the equivalent of Château, designating a vineyard or estate*. Sekt – *very basic, sparkling wine*. Spätlese – *second step in the QmP scale, late-harvested grapes, a notch drier than Auslese*. Staatsweingut – *state-owned wine estate*. Tafelwein – *table wine, only the prefix 'Deutscher' guarantees German origin*. Trocken – *dry*. Trockenbeerenauslese – *wine from selected dried grapes which are usually Botrytis-affected*. Weingut – *estate*. Weinkellerei – *cellar or winery*.

Germany's wine industry is a curiously polarised affair. On the one hand there is the torrent of poorly-made sugar water with which the Germans have annually slaked millions of Britons' thirst for cheap white wine. And on the other, there are the serious examples of the Riesling grape, which leave the rest of the world standing.

For real quality in Germany, look for Mosel Rieslings from producers like Dr Loosen and Richter, wines from the Rhine from new-wave winemakers such as Künstler, Müller Catoir and Kurt Darting, not to mention the occasional successful red from Karl Lingenfelder. Avoid Trocken Kabinett wines from northern Germany unless you want the tartar and enamel removing from your teeth.

## ITALY

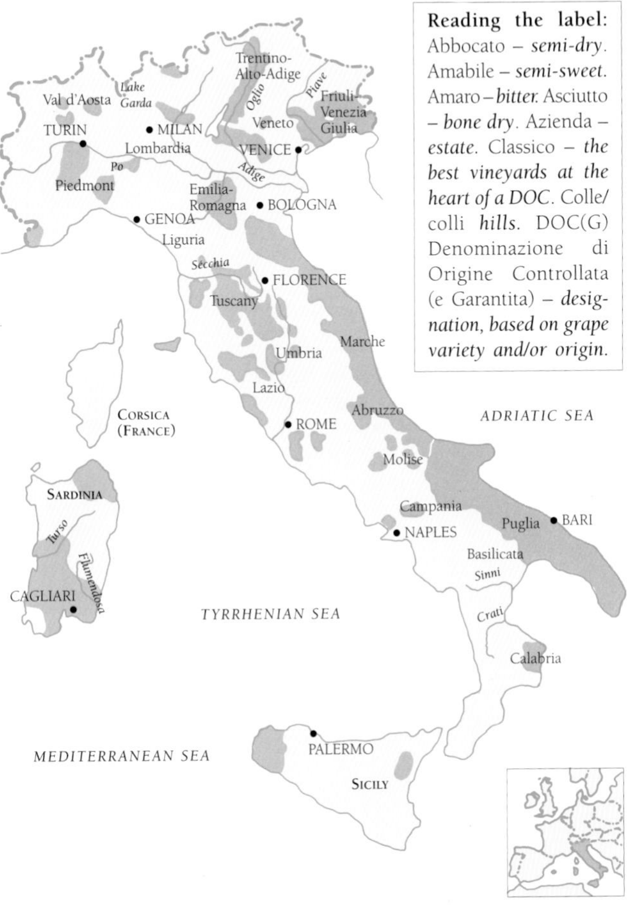


**Reading the label:** Abbocato – *semi-dry*. Amabile – *semi-sweet*. Amaro – *bitter*. Asciutto – *bone dry*. Azienda – *estate*. Classico – *the best vineyards at the heart of a DOC*. Colle/colli *hills*. DOC(G) Denominazione di Origine Controllata (e Garantita) – *designation, based on grape variety and/or origin*.

Dolce – *sweet*. Frizzante – *semi-sparkling*. IGT, Indicazione Geograficha Tipica – *questionable new designation for quality Vino da Tavola*. Imbottigliato all'origine – *estate-bottled*. Liquoroso – *rich, sweet*. Passito – *raisiny wine made from sun-dried grapes*. Recioto – *strong, sweet (unless designated Amarone)*. Vino da Tavola – *table wine that does not fit into the DOC system. Includes basic stuff as well as some of Italy's top wines. To be replaced for the latter by* IGT.

Three facts about Italy. 1) It is more a set of regions than a single country. 2) Few Italians comply for long with laws they find inconvenient. 3) Style is often valued more highly than content. Taken together, these make for one of the world's most confusing wine–producing countries. Individual producers all do their own thing, using indigenous and imported grape varieties and designer bottles and labels in ways that leave Euro-legislators – and humble wine drinkers – exhilarated and exasperated in equal measure.

## NEW ZEALAND

A great vintage in 1997 followed the decent one in 1996, which had finally brought an end to a series of very tricky harvests. New Zealand now has plenty of gooseberryish Sauvignon Blancs, Chardonnays and innovative Rieslings and Gewürztraminers, as well as some of its best ever reds.

Hawkes Bay seems to be the most consistent region for reds, while Gisborne, Marlborough, Auckland and Martinborough share the honours for white (though the latter has had some successes with the Pinot Noir).

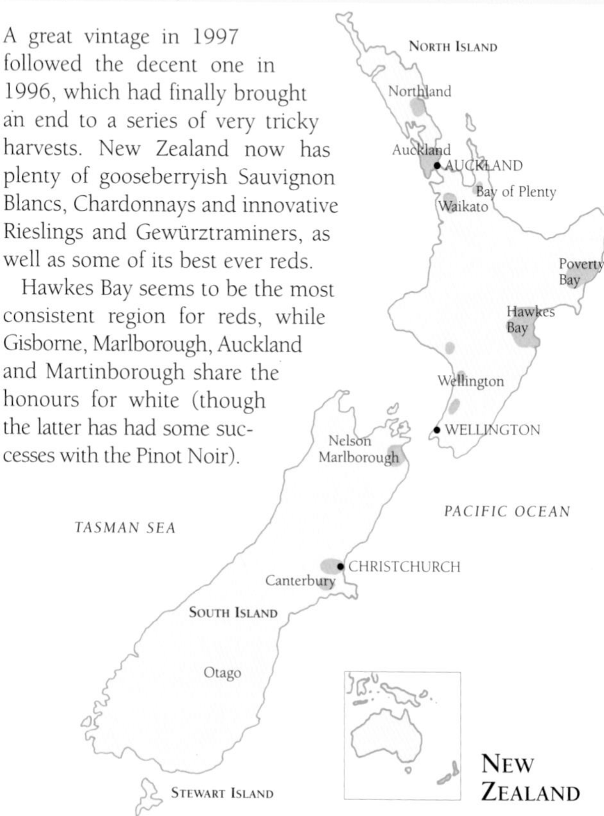

## NORTH AFRICA

Islamic fundamentalism has done little to encourage winemaking of any description in North Africa. Even so, Algeria, Morocco and Tunisia can all offer full-flavoured, old-fashioned reds that will probably delight people who liked Burgundy when it routinely included a dollop of Algerian blackstrap.

## PORTUGAL

**Reading the label:** Adega – *winery*. Branco – *white*. Colheita – *vintage*. Engarrafado na origem – *estate-bottled*. Garrafeira – *a vintage-dated wine with a little more alcohol and minimum ageing requirements*. Quinta – *vineyard or estate*. Reserva – *wine from a top-quality vintage, made from riper grapes than the standard requirement*. Velho – *old*. Vinho de Mesa – *table wine*.

Like Italy, Portugal has grapes grown nowhere else in the world. Unlike Italy, however, until recently the Portuguese had done little to persuade foreigners of the quality of these varieties.

But now, thanks to two Australian winemakers, Peter Bright and David Baverstock, and the efforts of dynamic, innovative Portuguse producers like Luis Pato in Bairrada, we are beginning to see what the native grapes can produce.

Try any of Pato's Bairradas, Bright's new-wave Douro reds and Baverstock's tasty Quinta do Crasto red wines from the Douro.

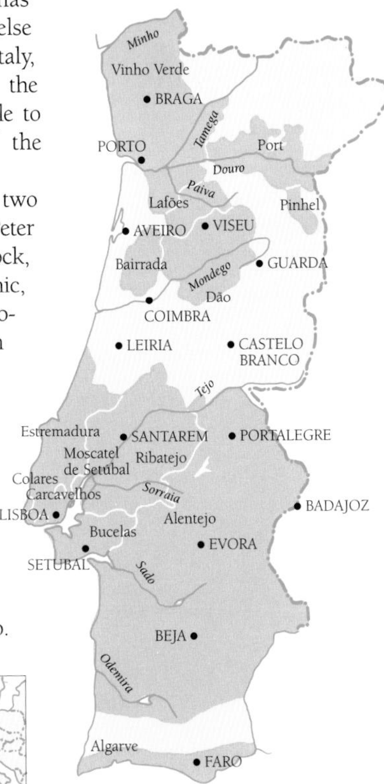


PORTUGAL

# SOUTH AFRICA

**Reading the label:** Cap Classique – *South African term for Champagne-method sparklers*. Cultivar – *grape variety*. Edel laat-oes – *noble late harvest*. Edelkeur – *'noble rot', a fungus affecting grapes and producing sweet wine*. Gekweek, gemaak en gebottel op – *estate-bottled.* Landgoedwyn – *estate wine*. Laat-oos – *late harvest*. Oesjaar – *vintage*. Steen – *local name for Chenin Blanc*.

Despite some of the oldest vineyards in the New World, some major philosophical changes are needed before the Cape can field a truly world-class team of bottles. The problem – recognised by visitors from Bordeaux and Australia – lies in green flavours that stem from an unwillingness to allow the grapes to ripen properly. Mulderbosch, Thelema, Plaisir de Merle, Vergelegen and Fairview show what can be done, while Kanonkop and Vriesenhof support the cause for South Africa's own spicy red grape, the Pinotage.

For the moment though, late-harvest and sparkling wines remain South Africa's strongest suit.

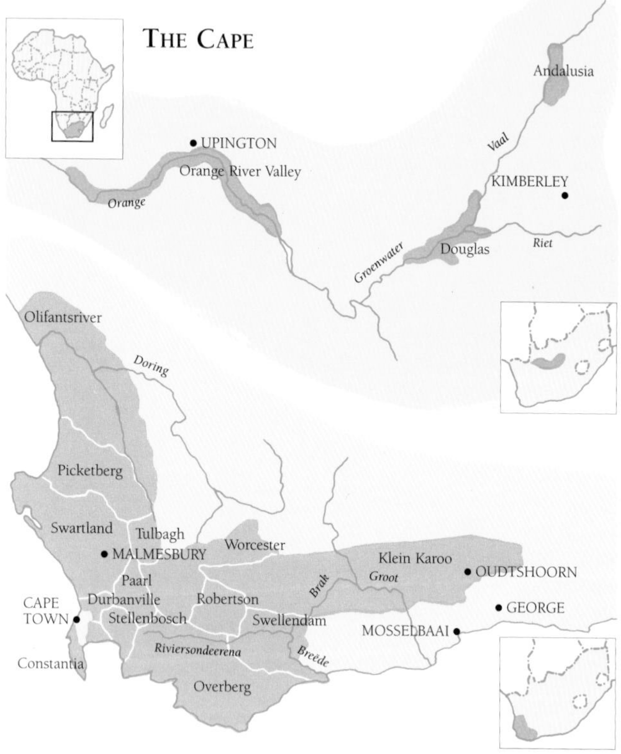

# SOUTH AMERICA

## ARGENTINA

**Reading the label:** Malbec – *spicy red grape*. Torrontes – *unusual grapey white.*

As it closes up on Chile, this is a country to watch. The stuff to look for now is the grapey but dry white Torrontes and some good Cabernet. Also check out the spicy reds made from the Malbec, a variety once widely grown in Bordeaux and still used in the Loire.

## CHILE

**Reading the label:** Envasado en Origen – *estate-bottled.* Carmenaire/Grand Vidure – *grape variety once used in Bordeaux but no longer found there.*

Arguably the most exciting wine-producing country in the world, thanks to a combination of ideal conditions (vintages are very consistent), skilled local winemaking and plentiful investment. The most successful grape at present is the Merlot, but the Cabernet, Chardonnay, Pinot Noir and Sauvignon, can all display a combination of ripe fruit and subtlety often absent in the New World.

# SOUTH EASTERN EUROPE

## GREECE

Finally casting off its image as purveyor of Europe's worst wines, Greece is beginning to rediscover the potential of a set of highly characterful grape varieties. It will take time before many of the new-wave wines reach the outside world, but producers like C. Lazaridi, Gentlini and Hatzimichalis are set for international success.

## CYPRUS

Still associated with cheap sherry-substitute and dull wine, but things are changing. Look out for the traditional rich Commandaria.

## TURKEY

Still lurching out of the vinous dark ages, Turkey has yet to offer the world red or white wines that non-Turks are likely to relish.

## LEBANON

Château Musar has survived all the tribulations of the last few years, keeping Lebanon on the map as a wine-producing country.

## ISRAEL

Once a source of truly appalling wine, Israel can now boast world-class Cabernet and Muscat, from the Yarden winery in the Golan Heights. The big Carmel winery now produces acceptable wines too and has shrugged off the dismal offerings of the past.

# SPAIN

**Reading the label:** Abocado – *semi-dry*. Año – *year.* Bodega – *winery or wine cellar.* Cava – *Champagne-method sparkling wine*. Criado y Embotellado (por) – *grown and bottled (by)*. Crianza – *aged in wood,* DO(Ca) (Denominacion de Origen (Califacada) – *Spain's quality designation, based on regional style, with a newly-introduced higher level* (Califacada) *to indicate superior quality*. Elaborado y Anejado Por – *made and aged for.* Gran Reserva – *a quality wine aged for a designated number of years in wood; more than for an ordinary Reserva*. Joven – *young wine, specially made for early consumption*. Reserva – *official designation for wine that has been aged for a specific period*. Sin Crianza – *not aged in wood*. Vendemia – *harvest or vintage*. Vino de Mesa – *table wine.* Vino de la Tierra – *new designation similar to the French 'Vin de Pays'.*

Spain used to be relied on for a certain style of highly predictable wine: soft, oaky reds with flavours of strawberry and vanilla, and whites that were either light, dry and unmemorable (Marqués de Caceres Rioja Blanco), oaky and old – fashioned (traditional Marqués

de Murrieta Rioja), or sweet and grapey (Moscatel de Valencia). Suddenly, however, like a car whose driver has suddenly found an extra gear, Spainish wines have begun to leap ahead – into often largely uncharted territory. The first region to hail the revolution was the Penedés, where Miguel Torres made a speciality of using traditional and imported grape varieties.

Others have overtaken Torres, in regions like Somontano, Rueda and Navarra. And in Rioja itself experiments are quietly going on to see whether the Cabernet Sauvignon can improve the flavour of this traditional wine. There are traditionalists who would prefer all this pioneering business to stop, but the wine genie is out of the Spanish bottle and there seems little chance of anyone forcing it back inside again.

## SWITZERLAND

**Reading the label**: Gutedel, Perlan, Fendant – *local name for the Chasselas*. Grand Cru – *top designation which varies from one canton to the next*. Süssdruck – *off-dry, red wine*.

Ferociously expensive for non-Swiss wine drinkers, but recommendable wines on their own terms. This is one of the only places the Chasselas produces anything even remotely memorable. (Incidentally, Switzerland is also the only country I know that has largely switched from corks to screw-caps, so you're unlikely to get a nasty, musty bottle.

# USA

**Reading the label:** Blush – *rosé.* Champagne – *any sparkling wine.* Fumé – *oak-aged white wine, especially Sauvignon (Blanc Fumé).* Meritage – *popular, if pretentious, name for a Bordeaux blend (white or red).* Vinted – *made by (a vintner, or winemaker).* White (Grenache, Zinfandel, etc) – *next thing they'll be calling it 'wine of colour'. Here, 'white' actually refers to the unfashionable rosé, slightly pink wines, sometimes also referred to as 'blush'.*

## CALIFORNIA

These are busy days for the best-known winemaking state of the Union. After 20 years of almost single-minded devotion to the Chardonnay and Cabernet and to the Napa Valley, the focus has broadened to take in a wider range of grapes (particularly Italian and Rhône varieties) and regions (Sonoma, Santa Barbara, especially for Pinot Noir, plus San Luis Obispo, Santa Cruz, Mendocino and Monterey).

Within the Napa Valley too, where vineyards are being replanted in the wake of the damage caused by the phylloxera louse, there is growing acknowledgement that some sub-regions produce better wines than others. Carneros is already famous for its Pinot Noir, Chardonnay and Oakville, while Rutherford and Stag's Leap are known for their Cabernet. But do try other worthwhile areas, such as Mount Veeder and Howell Mountain.

## THE PACIFIC NORTHWEST

Outside California, head north to Oregon for some of the best Pinot Noirs in the US (at a hefty price) and improving, but rarely earth-shattering Chardonnays, Rieslings and Pinot Gris. Washington State has some Pinot too, on the cooler, rainy west of the Cascade mountains. On the east, the irrigated vineyards produce great Sauvignon and Riesling, as well as top-flight Chardonnay, Cabernet and a particularly good Merlot.

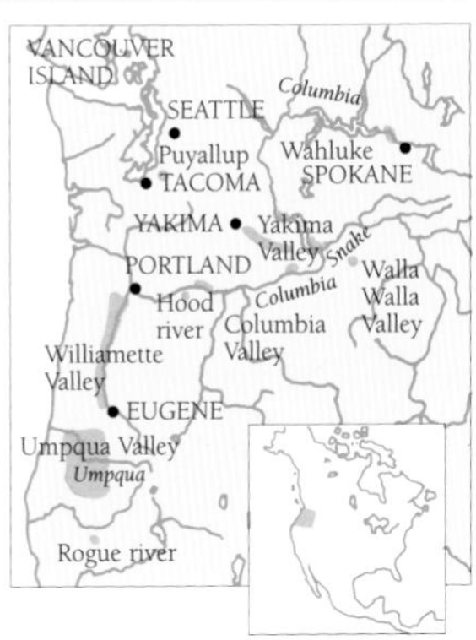


## NEW YORK AND OTHER STATES

Once the source of dire 'Chablis' and 'Champagne', New York State is now producing worthwhile wines, particularly in the micro-climate of Long Island, where the Merlot is thriving. The Finger Lakes are patchier but worth visiting, especially for the Rieslings and cool-climate Chardonnays. Elsewhere, Virginia, Missouri, Texas, Maryland and even Arizona are all producing wines to compete with California and indeed some of the best that Europe can offer.

# THE GRAPES

## BLENDS OR SINGLE VARIETIES?

Some wines are made from single grape varieties – e.g. red or white Burgundy, Sancerre, German Riesling and Barolo – while others, such as red or white Bordeaux, port and Châteauneuf du Pape, are blends of two or more types of grape. Champagne can fall into either camp, as can New World so called 'varietal' wines which, though labelled as 'Chardonnay', 'Cabernet Sauvignon', etc. can, depending on local rules, contain up to 25% of other grape varieties. Blends are not, per se, superior to single varietals – or vice versa.

## WHITE WINE GRAPES

### CHARDONNAY

Ubiquitous but hard to define. In Burgundy and in the best Californians (Kistler, Sonoma Cutrer) it tastes of butter and hazelnuts; lesser New World efforts are sweet and simple. Australians range from oaky tropical fruit juice to subtle, buttery pineapple (Petaluma and Leeuwin). New Zealand's efforts are tropical too, but lighter and fresher (Te Mata, Cloudy Bay). Elsewhere, Chile is beginning to hit the mark, unlike South Africa where most examples taste unripe. In Europe look around southern France, Italy, and now Spain, but beware of watery cheaper versions.

### CHENIN BLANC

A Loire variety that produces fresh fizz, and both dry and lusciously sweet, honeyed wines – together with stuff that tastes like unripe apples and, when over-sulphured, old socks. Most Californian Chenins are semi-sweet and ordinary. South Africans call the grape the Steen, and sometimes get it right – as occasionally do the Australians (at Moondah Brook) and the New Zealanders (Millton).

### GEWÜRZTRAMINER

Outrageous stuff that smells of parma violets and tastes of lychees. At its best in Alsace, both dry and sweet, as a Vendange Tardive or Selection de Grains Nobles (Zind-Humbrecht, Schlumberger). Try examples from Germany and north-east Italy too.

## MARSANNE

A classic flowery, lemony variety used in the Rhône in wines like Hermitage (from producers like Guigal), and in Australia – especially in Goulburn in Victoria (Chateau Tahbilk and Mitchelton); in southern France (in Vin de Pays d'Oc blends such as La Pérousse and from Mas de Daumas Gassac) and in innovative wines from California. At its best young or after five or six years.

## MUSCAT

The only variety whose wines actually taste as though they are made of grapes, rather than some other kind of fruit or vegetable. In Alsace, southern France and north-east Italy it is used to make dry wines. Generally, though, it performs best as fizz (Moscatos, and Asti Spumantes from Italy and Clairette de Die Tradition from France) and as sweet fortified wine. Look out for Beaumes de Venise and Rivesaltes in southern France, Moscatel de Setúbal in Portugal, Moscatel de Valencia in Spain and Christmas puddingy Liqueur Muscat in Australia (Morris, Chambers, Yalumba).

## PINOT BLANC/PINOT BIANCO

As rich as Chardonnay, but with less fruit. At its best in Alsace where it develops a lovely cashew nut flavour. When well handled it can also do well in Italy, where it is known as Pinot Bianco (Jermann), and Germany, where it is the Weissburgunder. Most Californian Pinot Blancs are really made from the duller Melon de Bourgogne of Muscadet fame.

## PINOT GRIS

An up-and-coming Alsace variety also known as Tokay but unrelated to any of the world's other Tokays. Its wines can be spicy, and appear in both sweet and dry versions. In Italy it is called Pinot Grigio and in Germany Grauerburgunder. Look for New World examples from Oregon (Eyrie), California and New Zealand.

## RIESLING

For purists this, not the Chardonnay, is the king of white varieties. Misunderstood – and often mispronounced as Rice-ling rather then Rees-ling – it carries the can for huge quantities of cheap German wine made from quite different grapes. At its best, it makes dry and sweet grapey, appley, limey wines that develop a spicy 'petrolly' character with age. The best examples come from Germany, in the Mosel (Dr Loosen) and Rhine (but beware of aggressively dry – *Trocken* – tooth-enamel removers), Alsace (Zind-Humbrecht), Washington State (Kiona) and Australia (Tim Adams). Don't confuse with the unrelated Laski, Lutomer, Welsch, Emerald or White Riesling.

## SAUVIGNON/FUMÉ BLANC

The grape of Loire wines such as Sancerre, Pouilly Fumé and white Bordeaux, where it is often blended with the Sémillon. This gooseberryish variety now performs brilliantly in Marlborough in New Zealand (where the flavours can include asparagus and pea-pods) and increasingly well in South Africa (Thelema, Mulderbosch) and Australia (Shaw & Smith, Cullens). Chile has some good examples (from Casablanca) – and also some poor ones, made from a different variety called the Sauvignonasse. In the US, Washington State can get it right, but in California, it is usually horribly sweet or overburdened by the flavour of oak. (Oaked versions here and elsewhere are usually labelled Fumé Blanc.) Only the best ones improve after the first couple of years.

## SÉMILLON

A distinctive, peachy variety with only two successful homes. In Bordeaux, usually in blends with the Sauvignon Blanc, it produces sublime dry Graves and sweet Sauternes – and over-sulphured stuff that tastes like old dishcloths. In Australia there are brilliant, long-lived dry wines which are made purely from Semillon in the Hunter Valley (often unoaked) and Barossa Valley (usually oaked). Good 'noble' late-harvest examples have also been produced in Riverina. Elsewhere in Australia the grape is sometimes blended with Chardonnay, a cocktail which has proved popular in California (in Geyser Peak's Semchard).

## SYLVANER

A characterful grape that is more or less restricted to Alsace and Franken in Germany, the Sylvaner has a recognisably 'earthy' character that is quite at odds with most modern wines. Crossing the Sylvaner with the Riesling, incidentally, produced the Müller-Thurgau, the 'catty' variety that has taken over so many of Germany's vineyards in recent years.

## VIOGNIER

Now a cult grape, the Viognier was once more or less confined to the small appellations of Condrieu and Château Grillet in the Rhône, where good examples showed off its extraordinary perfumed, peach blossomy character, albeit at a high price. Today, however, it has been successfully grown in the supposedly 'lesser' French regions of the Ardèche and Languedoc-Roussillon, in California, where it is made with loving care (and over-generous exposure to oak barrels), and in Australia (Heggies Vineyard). While more affordable examples are welcome, this remains one of the world's trickier grape varieties to grow, make and buy as a finished wine.

# RED WINE GRAPES

## BARBERA

A widely grown variety in Italy, and at its best in Piemonte. The keynote is a wild berryish flavour that reminds me pleasantly of cheesecake. Increasingly successful in blends with Nebbiolo and Cabernet. Making inroads into California and Australia.

## CABERNET SAUVIGNON

A remarkable success story, historically associated with the great red wines of the Médoc and Graves (where it is blended with the Merlot) and, more recently, with some of the best reds from the New World, especially California, Chile and Australia. Eastern Europe has good value examples (Bulgaria), as does southern France (Vin de Pays). Spain is rapidly climbing aboard (in the Penedès, Navarra and – though this is kept quiet – Rioja). The hallmark to look for is blackcurrant, though unripe versions (Bordeaux from poorer producers and poorer years, and all too many examples from South Africa) taste like a blend of weeds and green peppers. There are some impressive Italian Cabernets, especially from starry estates in Tuscany, though these always taste more distinctively Italian than of the grape. Good New World Cabernets can smell and taste of fresh mint, but with time, like the best Bordeaux, these can develop a rich, leathery 'cigar box' character.

## GRENACHE/GARNACHA

Pepper – freshly ground black pepper – is the distinguishing flavour, sometimes with the fruity tang of boiled sweets. At home in Côtes du Rhône and Châteauneuf-du-Pape (where it is often blended with other varieties), it is also frequently found in Spain (as the Garnacha) in blends with the Tempranillo. It only performs well when producers don't try to grow too many grapes per acre. Seek out 'Old Vine' or 'bush' examples from Australia.

## MERLOT

The most widely planted variety in Bordeaux and Languedoc Roussillon. In Bordeaux it is used, (often almost unblended), in Pomerol, where wines can taste of ripe plums and spice, and in St Emilion, where the least successful wines show the Merlot's less lovable side: they taste dull and earthy. Wherever it is made, the Merlot should produce softer wines than the Cabernet Sauvignon, though in California, where there are some good examples, Duckhorn used to make an uncharacteristically tough one. Elsewhere, Washington State, Chile and (when the grapes are ripe) New Zealand are other places to look, along with Italy and (occasionally) Eastern Europe.

## NEBBIOLO/SPANNA

The red wine grape of Barolo and Barbaresco – the great wines of Piemonte. Traditionally these wines were heavily tannic and impenetrable, even after a long sojourn in old oak barrels; modern versions have a lovely cherry and rose-petally character, often with the sweet vanilla of *new* oak casks.

## PINOT NOIR

The recognisable flavours are of wild raspberry, plum and sometimes liquorice. The grape of all red Burgundy, and a major component of white and pink Champagne, the Pinot Noir has, until recently, produced few great wines elsewhere despite some heroic efforts. In other regions of France, it is used to make red and pink Sancerre (often disappointing, almost always over-priced), as well as very variable reds in Alsace and Germany (where it is called Spätburgunder). Italy makes a few good examples (as Pinot Nero), but for the best modern efforts, look to California – especially Carneros (from people like Saintsbury) and Santa Barbara (Au Bon Climat) – and also Oregon (Domaine Drouhin), Australia (Coldstream Hills), New Zealand (Martinborough), Chile (Cono Sur, Valdivieso) and South Africa (Hamilton Russell).

## PINOTAGE

Once only found in South Africa and New Zealand, this cross between the Pinot Noir and a spicy Rhône variety called the Cinsault is now more or less restricted to the former. Good examples are deliciously berryish when young and age into rich, gamey-spicy maturity. Sadly, until recently, these have been rare, and too many have tasted simultaneously green, earthy and dull. Kanonkop is a good exception to the rule.

## SANGIOVESE

The grape of Chianti, Brunello di Montalcino and of a host of starry Vino da Tavola wines in Italy, not to mention 'new wave' Italian-style wines in California. The recognisable flavour is of sweet tobacco, wild herbs and berries.

## SYRAH/SHIRAZ

The extraordinary spicy, brambly grape of the great wines of the Northern Rhône (Hermitage, Cornas, etc) and the best reds of Australia (e.g. Henschke Hill of Grace and Penfolds Grange), where it is also blended with the Cabernet Sauvignon (just as it once was in Bordeaux). Elsewhere in Europe the Marques de Griñon has made a great example in Spain, while Isole e Olena have made an unofficial one in Tuscany.

### TEMPRANILLO

Known under all sorts of names around Spain, including Cencibel (in Navarra) and Tinto Fino (in Ribeira del Duero), the grape gives Spanish reds their recognisable strawberryish character. Often blended with the Garnacha, it works well with Cabernet Sauvignon.

### ZINFANDEL

California's 'own', related to the Italian Primitivo. In California, it makes rich, spicy, blueberryish reds (see Ridge Vineyards) and ports and, when blended with sweet Muscat, sweet pink 'White Zinfandel'. Outside California, Cape Mentelle makes a good example in Western Australia and Delheim a floral one in South Africa.

## OTHER GRAPES

### WHITE

**Albariño/Alvarinho** Floral. Grown in Spain and Portugal.
**Aligoté** Lean Burgundy grape.
**Arneis** Perfumed variety in Piemonte.
**Colombard** Appley, but undistinguished; grown in south-west France, California and Australia.
**Grüner Veltliner** Limey. Restricted to Austria and Eastern Europe.
**Müller-Thurgau/Rivaner** 'Catty'. Grown in Germany and England.
**Scheurebe** Grapefruity grape in Germany.
**Torrontes** Grapey, Muscat-like variety of Argentina.
**Ugni Blanc/Trebbiano** Basic grape of south-west France and Italy.
**Verdejo** Interesting Spanish variety of Rueda.
**Verdelho** Limey variety in Madeira and table wine in Australia.
**Viura** Widely planted, so-so Spanish variety.
**Welschriesling** Basic. Best in late-harvest Austrians.

### RED

**Cabernet-Franc** Kid brother of Cabernet Sauvignon, grown alongside it in Bordeaux and by itself in the Loire and Italy.
**Cinsault** Spicy Rhône variety; best in blends.
**Dolcetto** Cherryish Piemonte grape.
**Dornfelder** Successful juicy variety in Germany.
**Gamay** The Beaujolais grape; less successful in the Loire and Gaillac.
**Malbec/Côt** Once in Bordeaux blends; now Cahors, Loire, Argentina.
**Mourvèdre (Mataro)** Spicy Rhône grape; good in California and Australia, but can be hard and 'metallic'.
**Petite-Sirah** Spicy; thrives in California and Mexico. Known as Durif in Australia.
**Tannat** Tough variety of Madiran and Uruguay.

# STYLES

## STYLE COUNSEL

In simple terms, wine can be separated into one or more of a few easily recognisable styles: red, white and pink; still and sparkling; sweet and dry; light and fortified. To say that the contents of a bottle are red and dry does little, however, to convey the way a wine tastes. It could be a fruity Beaujolais, a mature Rioja with the sweet vanilla flavour of the oak barrels in which it was matured, a blueberryish California Zinfandel, or a tough young Bordeaux.

Knowing the geographic origin of a wine and the grape can of course give a clearer idea of what it is like, but it won't tell you everything. The human touch is as important in wine as it is in the kitchen. Some chefs like to assemble often quite eclectic flavours while others prefer a more conservative range of ingredients. The wine world is similarly riven between producers who focus on obvious fruit flavours, and winemakers, in France for example, who talk about the *goût de terroir* – the taste of the earth or soil.

In a world that is increasingly given to instant sensations, it is perhaps unsurprising that it is the fruit-lovers rather than the friends of the earthy flavour who are currently in the ascendent.

### NEW WORLD/OLD WORLD

Until recently, these two winemaking philosophies could be broadly defined as belonging to the New and Old World. Places like California and Australia made wine that was approachably delicious when compared with the more serious wine being produced in Europe, which demanded time and food.

Life is never quite that cut-and-dried, however. Today, there are Bordeaux châteaux that are taking a decidedly New World approach and South Africans who take a pride in making wine as resolutely tough and old-fashioned as a Bordeaux of a hundred years ago.

#### Flying Winemakers

One phenomenon that has contributed to these changes in philosophy, has been the 'flying winemakers' – young Antipodeans who, like hired guns, are contracted to travel the world making wine wherever they go. Today, you can choose between a white Loire produced by a Frenchman – or one from the next vineyard that bears the evident fruity fingerprint of Australian-rules winemaking.

### Fruit of Knowledge

European old-hands like to claim that the Australians use some kind of alchemy to obtain those fruity flavours. In fact, their secret lies in the care they take over every step in the winemaking process. Picking the grapes when they are ripe (rather than too early); preventing them from cooking beneath the midday sun (as often happens in Europe while work stops for lunch); pumping the juice through pipes that have been cleaned daily rather than at each end of a three-week harvest; fermenting at a cool temperature (overheated vats can cost a wine its freshness), and storing and bottling it carefully, will help a wine made from even the dullest grape variety to taste fruitier.

## COME HITHER

If the New Worlders want their wines to taste of fruit, they are – apart from some of those South Africans and a few diehard Californians – just as keen to make wine that can be drunk young. To achieve this, they take care not to squeeze the red grapes too hard, so as not to extract bitter, hard tannins, and they try to avoid their white wines being too evidently acidic.

Traditionalists claim that wines made this way do not age as well as their efforts. It is too early to say whether this is true in the long term, but there is no question that the newer wave red Bordeaux of, say 1985, have consistently given more people more pleasure since they were first released, than the supposedly greater 1970 vintage, whose wines remained dauntingly hard throughout their lifetime. A wine does not have to be undrinkable in its youth to develop into something that's good to drink later on; indeed wines that start out tasting unbalanced tend to go on tasting that way.

## SPOTTING THE WOOD FROM THE TREES

Another thing that sets many new wave wines apart has nothing to do with grapes. Wines have been matured in oak barrels since Roman times, and traditionally new barrels were only bought to replace old ones that had begun to fall apart. Old casks have little to offer in the way of flavour but, for the first two or three years of their lives, new ones have a recognisable vanilla-caramel character which comes from the way the staves are bent over flames. It has taken winemakers a long time to discover the contribution the vanilla can make to the finished wine; indeed new casks were often rinsed out with dilute ammonia to remove it. Today, however, producers take the choice of forest, cooper and charring (light, medium or heavy 'toast') as seriously as the quality of their grapes.

Oak-mania began when top Bordeaux châteaux began to spend the income from the great vintages of the 1940s on replacements for their old barrels. In Burgundy in the 1970s, after an entire vintage was thought to have been spoiled by old barrels, the illustrious

Hospices de Beaune decreed that each harvest would go exclusively into new ones. Over the last 25 years, top producers and would-be top producers internationally have introduced at least a proportion of new oak, while even the makers of cheaper wine have found that dunking giant 'teabags' filled with small oak chips into wine vats could add some of that vanilla flavour too.

If you like oak, you should find it in top flight Bordeaux and Burgundy (red and white), Spanish wines labelled as Crianza, Reserva or Gran Reserva and Italians whose labels use the French term 'Barrique'. French wines that say they have been '*Elévé en fût de Chêne*' will generally taste oaky, but in some cases, this expression is merely used sneakily by a producer whose oak barrels are older than he is. Australian 'Show Reserve' will tend to be oaky, as will Reserve and 'Barrel Select' wines here from anywhere in the New World, as well as wines describing themselves as 'Fumé Blanc'.

## RED WINES – FRUITS, SPICE AND . . . COLD TEA

If you enjoy your red wines soft and juicily fruity, the styles to look for are Burgundy and other wines made from the Pinot Noir; Rioja and Navarra from Spain, inexpensive Australians, Pomerol, good St. Emilion from Bordeaux, and Merlots from almost anywhere. Look too for Nouveau, Novello and Joven (young wines).

### The Kitchen Cupboard

Some grapes, such as the Sangiovese in Italy, are not so much fruity as herby, while the Syrah/Shiraz of the Rhône and Australia, the peppery Grenache and – sometimes – the Zinfandel and Pinotage can all be surprisingly spicy.

### Some Like it Tough

Some places reliably produce traditional, cold-tea tannic wine. Most basic recent Bordeaux and all but a few wines from St. Estèphe and Listrac in Bordeaux are a good bet, as are most older-style wines from Piedmont, reds from Duckhorn and Dunn in California and most South Africans. As a rule, the Cabernet Sauvignon will make tougher wines than the Merlot or Pinot Noir.

## WHITE WINES – HONEY AND LEMON

If dry wines with unashamedly fruity flavours are what you want, try Muscat, the Torrontes in Argentina, basic Riesling and Chardonnay and New World and Southern French Sauvignon Blanc.

### Non Fruit

For more neutral styles, go for Soave or Frascati from Italy, Muscadet, Grenache Blanc and most traditional wines from Spain and Southern France.

### Riches Galore

The combination of richness and fruit is to be found in white Burgundy, better dry white Bordeaux and in Chardonnays, Semillons and oaked Sauvignon (Fumé) wines from the New World.

### Aromatherapy

Some perfumed, spicy, grapes, like the Gewürztraminer, are frankly aromatic. The Tokay-Pinot Gris, the Gewürztraminer's neighbour in Alsace fits the bill, as do the Viognier in France, the Arneis in Italy, the Albariño in Spain and the Grüner Veltliner in Austria.

### Middle of the Road

Today, people want wine that is – or says it is – either dry or positively sweet. The Loire can get honeyed semi-sweet wine right. Otherwise, head for Germany and Kabinett and Spätlese wines.

### Pure Hedonism

Sweet wine is making a comeback as people rebel against the health fascism that sought to outlaw such pleasures. The first places to look are Bordeaux, the Loire (Moelleux), Alsace (Vendange Tardive or Sélection des Grains Nobles); Germany (Auslese, Beerenauslese Trockenbeerenauslese); Austria (Ausbruch); the New World (Late Harvest and Noble Late Harvest); and Hungary (Tokaji 6 Puttonyos).

All of these wines should not only taste sweet, but have enough fresh acidity to prevent them from being in the least cloying. Also, they should have the additional, characteristic dried-apricot flavour that comes from grapes that have been allowed to be affected by a benevolent fungus known as ***botrytis*** or ***noble rot***.

Other sweet wines such as Muscat de Beaumes de Venise are fortified with brandy to raise their strength to 15% or so. These wines can be luscious too, but they never have the flavour of ***noble rot***.

## PINK

Tread carefully. Provence and the Rhône should offer peppery-dry rosé just as the Loire and Bordeaux should have wines that taste deliciously of blackcurrant. Sadly, many taste dull and stale. Still, they are a better bet than California's dire sweet 'White' or 'Blush' rosé. Look for the most recent vintage and the most vibrant colour.

## SPARKLING

Fizz comes in various styles too. If you find Champagne too dry, but don't want a frankly sweet grapey fizz like Asti Spumante or France's Clairette de Die 'Tradition', try a fruity New World fizz like the Cuvée Napa from California or Seaview from Australia. If you don't like that fruitiness, try traditional Cava from Spain, Prosecco from Italy and Blanquette de Limoux from France.

# STORING

## STARTING A CELLAR

Not so long ago, when winemaking was less sophisticated and there were fewer ways to counter tricky vintages, there were two kinds of wines: the basic stuff to drink straight away, and the cream of the crop that was left in the barrel and/or bottle to age. So, a good wine was an old wine. And vice versa. Young wine and old wine had as much in common as hamburgers and *haute cuisine*.

Today, just as fast food now includes delicious sushi, there are brilliant wines that never improve beyond the first few years after the harvest, and are none the worse for that. On the other hand, some wines – German Riesling, fine claret and top Australian Shiraz, for example – by their very nature, still repay a few years' patience.

Unfortunately, identifying when each particular wine is likely to be at its best is very tricky. The 1947 Mouton Rothschild will last beyond the millennium – long after the 1987 has popped its vinous clogs. Like human beings, wines can evolve unpredictably. Some fail to live up to their early promise; others are late developers, while some go through odd phases when they temporarily seem to lose their appeal. On balance though, I would rather drink a wine that is a little too young, than one that has lost its fruit.

### THE RESTING PLACE

While many of us – myself included – live in homes that are ill-suited for storing wine, one can often find an unused fireplace or a space beneath the stairs that offers wine what it wants: a constant temperature of around 7–10°C (never lower than 5°C nor more than 20°C), reasonable humidity (install a cheap humidifier or leave a sponge in a bowl of water), sufficient ventilation to avoid a musty atmosphere and, ideally, an absence of vibration (wines stored beneath railway arches – or beds – age faster). Alternatively, invest in a fridge-like Eurocave that guarantees perfect conditions (see page 254 for stockists) – or even adapt an old freezer.

### RACKS

Purpose-built racks can be bought 'by the hole', and cut to fit awkwardly shaped bits of wall (see page 254 for suppliers). Square chimney pots can be used too. If you have plenty of space, you could, for example, simply allocate a set of racks to red Burgundy, another to white, and a third to Californian wines. Unfortunately, though, even the best laid-out cellar plans fall apart when a gift of six cases of Australian Shiraz suddenly has to be squeezed into a part of the cellar with space enough for just two. Give each hole in the rack a cross-referenced identity, from A1 at the top left to, say, Z100 at the bottom right. As bottles arrive, they can then be put in any available hole, and their address noted in a cellar book.

## CELLAR BOOKS

Some people like leather-covered cellar books; I prefer my computer (Filemaker Pro or Microsoft Excel). Ideally, keep a regularly updated record of when and where you obtained each wine, what it cost and how each bottle tasted (is it improving or drying out?). If you worry about such things, you could also use it to be sure to serve a wine buff something different each time.

## TO DRINK OR KEEP?

A guide to which corks to pop soon and which bottles to treasure:

### Drink as Soon as Possible

Most wine at under £5, particularly Muscadet, Vins de Pays, white Bordeaux; Nouveau/Novello/Joven reds; Bardolino, Valpolicella; light Italian whites; most Sauvignon Blanc; almost all rosé.

### Less than 5 Years

Petit-Château Bordeaux and Cru Bourgeois, and lesser Cru Classés clarets from poorer vintages; basic Alsace, Burgundy and better Beaujolais; Chianti, Barbera, basic Spanish reds; good mid-quality Germans, English wines, cheaper New World Chardonnays; all but the finest Sauvignons; basic Chilean and Australian reds.

### 5-10 Years

Most Cru Bourgeois Bordeaux from good years; better châteaux from lesser vintages; all but the best red and white Burgundy and Pinot and Chardonnay from elsewhere; middle-quality Rhônes, southern-French higher flyers; good German, Alsace, dry Loire and white Bordeaux; Portuguese reds, California and Washington State; South African, Chilean and New Zealand Merlots.

### Over 10 Years

Top class Bordeaux, Rhône, Burgundy and sweet Loire from ripe years; top flight German Late Harvest, Italian Vino da Tavola and Barolo; best Australian Shiraz, Cabernet, Rieslings; and Semillon; and California Cabernet.

# SERVING

## THE RULES OF THE GAME

'The art in using wine is to produce the greatest possible quantity of present gladness, without any future depression'.
*The Gentleman's Table Guide, 1873*

A century ago, Englishmen used to add ice to claret and – in winter – a hint of spice. Today, Chinese wine drinkers apparently prefer their Mouton Cadet with a dash of Sprite. And why not? I'm sure the lemonade would do many a skinny Bordeaux a world of good. As with food and sex, it's worth questioning accepted rules – especially when they vary between cultures. Have no fear, the advice that follows is all based on common sense and experience – and offered only to help you to decide how you enjoy serving and drinking wine.

### SOME LIKE IT HOT

Particular styles of wine, like types of food, taste better at particular temperatures. Warm Champagne is as appetising as warm strawberries. Outside British pubs, though, white wine and fizz are more often served too cold than too hot. Paradoxically, it is the reds that suffer most from being drunk too warm. Few of the people who serve wines at 'room temperature' recall that, when that term was coined, there wasn't a lot of central heating. Be ready to chill a fruity red by putting the bottle in a bucket of ice and water for five to ten minutes before serving.

#### Red Wine

When choosing the temperature for a red, focus on the flavour of the wine. Tough wines are best slightly warmer. This is a guide:

**1)** Beaujolais and other fruity reds: 10–13°C (an hour in the fridge).
**2)** Younger red Burgundy and Rhônes and older Bordeaux, Chianti, younger Rioja, New World Grenache and Pinotage: 14–16°C.
**3)** Older Burgundy; tannic young Bordeaux and Rhônes; Zinfandel, bigger Cabernet Sauvignon, Merlot and Shiraz; Barolo, and other bigger Italian and Spanish reds: 16–18°C.

#### Rosé

Rosé should be chilled at 12–13°C, or for five to ten minutes in a bucket of ice and water.

### White Wine

The cooler the wine, the less it will smell or taste. Subtler, richer wines deserve to be drunk a little warmer.

**1)** Lighter sweeter wines and everyday fizz: 4–8°C (two or three hours in the fridge or 10–15 minutes in ice and water).

**2)** Fuller-bodied, aromatic, drier, semi-dry, lusciously sweet whites; Champagne, simpler Sauvignons and Chardonnays: 8–11°C.

**3)** Richer dry wines: Burgundy, California Chardonnay: 12–13°C.

## THE PERFECT OUTCOME

The Screwpull is still the most reliable way to get a cork out of a bottles. The 'waiter's friend' is the next best thing; otherwise choose a corkscrew that comes in the form of a wire spiral rather than one that looks like a large screw.

## WHICH GLASSES?

On occasions when no other glass was available I have enjoyed great wine from a tooth mug. To be honest, though, I suspect I'd have got more out of the experience if something a little more stylish had come to hand. Glasses should be narrower across the rim than the bowl. Red ones should be bigger than white. If you like bubbles in your fizz, serve it in a flute rather than a saucer from which they will swiftly escape. Dartington Crystal, Schott and Riedel are among a number of companies that now produce attractive glasses that are specially designed to bring out the best in particular styles of wine.

## TO BREATHE OR NOT TO BREATHE?

Some reds have an unwelcome gungy deposit; some red and white wines may benefit from the aeration of being poured into a decanter or another bottle. But don't decant every red wine you encounter. A tannic young claret, Cabernet or Italian red may soften to reveal unexpected flavours, but an old Burgundy or Rioja will have very little deposit, and may be too light-bodied to gain from decanting.

Stand the bottle for up to a day before decanting it. Pour it very slowly, in front of a torch or candle, watching for the first signs of the deposit. Coffee filters suit those with less steady hands.

## ORDER OF SERVICE

The rules say that white wines and youth respectively precede red wines and age; dry goes before sweet (most of us prefer our main course before the pudding); the lighter the wine, the earlier. But what if the red Loire is lighter-bodied than the white Burgundy? Can the claret follow the Sauternes that you are offering with the foie gras? Ignore the absolutes but bear in mind the common sense that lies behind them. Work gently up the scale of fullness, 'flavoursomeness' and quality, rather than swinging wildly between styles.

# INVESTING

## LIQUID ASSETS

On a single day in April 1997, the value of the 1996 Haut-Brion rose from 300 to 600 French francs per bottle, as merchants worldwide scrambled for it. If the excitement surrounding the 1995 vintage took everyone by surprise, the welcome for the 1996 wines was little short of astonishing. Prices of the top wines rose by as much as 50%.

Both vintages benefitted from the fervour of new converts in places like Taiwan, Singapore, Hong Kong and Thailand. While buyers from all these countries visited Bordeaux bearing loaded cheque-books, many preferred to allow British merchants to do their buying for them – which explains why far more wine was sold to the UK than was actually bought to be drunk by Britons.

### VALUE FOR MONEY?

The key questions, of course, are whether the vintage is worth its high prices, and will the wine bubble burst? To my mind, the top wines such as Margaux, Haut-Brion, Lafite and Léoville Las Cases really are exceptionally good – and unusual in the classic delicacy of their flavours. Asking whether they are value for money is a little like posing the same question about a Ferrari or a box at the opera. If people are prepared to pay these prices, for the moment at least, they are what the wine is worth. As for whether the Asians, Germans, Scandinavians and Americans are all about to become bored with wine, I'd guess that the answer is 'not yet'.

With the exception of a few Pomerols with a tiny production and a cult following, the wines whose value has grown have almost all been the blue chips – names that will ring bells among even the most casual Bordeaux drinker. There was no point in buying little-known clarets in 1995 or 1996; but nor was there real financial justification for investing heavily in wines from California, none of whose prices are rising at the rate of the best of Bordeaux.

### THE RULES

**1)** The popularity and value of any wine can vary from one country to another. **2)** Wines are not like works of art; they don't last forever, so be ready to see their value fall. **3)** Tread carefully among untried wines and among offerings from the New World. The prices of the recently created Châteaux Valandraud and le Pin may have risen dramatically, as may that of Penfolds Grange from Australia. These, however, are the exceptions to the rule that long-established, big name, top vintage Bordeaux are still the best target. **4)** When buying *en primeur*, deal with financially solid merchants. **5)** At auction, favour wines that are known to have been carefully cellared. **6)** Store your wines carefully and securely – in your own cellar or elsewhere. **7)** Follow your wine's progress; read critics' comments and watch auction prices. **8)** Beware of falling reputations: the 1975 Bordeaux came after a series of poor vintages and sold at high prices; within a decade they had been eclipsed by the 1970 and 1982 vintages, and today are on few people's shopping lists. The 1974 Californian Cabernets, once heavily hyped, are now similarly questioned. The following wines are worth investing in:

## FRANCE

### Bordeaux

Châteaux l'Angélus, Ausone, Cheval Blanc, Cos d'Estournel, Ducru-Beaucaillou, Eglise-Clinet, Figeac, Grand-Puy-Lacoste, Gruaud-Larose, Haut-Brion, Lafite, Lafleur, Latour, Léoville Barton, Léoville Las Cases, Lynch Bages, Margaux, la Mission-Haut-Brion, la Mondotte, Montrose, Mouton-Rothschild, Palmer, Pétrus, Pichon Lalande, Pichon Longueville, le Pin, Valandraud. Vintages: 1982, 1983 (for Margaux), 1985, 1986, 1988, 1989, 1990, 1995, 1996.

### Burgundy

Drouhin Marquis de Laguiche, Gros Frères, Hospices de Beaune (from *négociants* such as Drouhin, or Jadot), Méo-Camuzet, Romanée-Conti (la Tâche, Romanée-Conti), Lafon, Leroy, de Vogüé.

### Rhône

Chapoutier, Chave, Guigal (top wines), Jaboulet Aîné 'La Chapelle'.

## PORTUGAL (PORT)

Cockburns, Dow, Fonseca, Grahams, Noval, Taylors, Warre.

## CALIFORNIA

Beaulieu Private Reserve, Diamond Creek, Dominus, Duckhorn, Dunn Howell Mountain, Grace Family, Heitz Martha's Vineyard, (varied in the late 1980s and early 1990s), Matanzas Creek, Robert Mondavi Reserve, Opus One, Ridge, Spottswoode, Stag's Leap.

## AUSTRALIA

Jim Barry 'The Armagh', Henschke Hill of Grace and Mount Edelstone, Leeuwin Chardonnay, Penfolds Grange and Bin 707, Petaluma Cabernet, Wynns 'John Riddoch', Virgin Hills, Yarra Yering.

# VINTAGES

## TIME WILL TELL

A decade or so ago, a vintage chart was thought to be as necessary for the enjoyment of wine as a corkscrew and a glass. But that was in the days when wine of any quality was produced in only a dozen or so places, in years when the climate was just right. Man had yet to devise ways – physical, chemical and organic – of combatting pests and disease that used to spoil wine with dreadful regularity.

Really disastrous vintages are a rarity now. Though frost can cut production, every year the most skilled and the luckiest producers in almost every region manage to make drinkable wines. Some places, however, are naturally more prone to tricky vintages than others. Northern Europe, for example, suffers more from unreliable sun and untimely rain than more southerly regions, let alone the warm, irrigated vineyards of Australia and the Americas.

A dependable climate does not necessarily make for better wine, however. Just as plants often bloom best in tough conditions, grapes develop more interesting flavours in what is known as a "marginal" climate – which is why New World producers are busily seeking out cooler, higher altitude sites in which to plant their vines.

### IT'S AN ILL WIND

Some producers can buck the trend of a climatically poor year – by luckily picking before the rainstorms, carefully discarding rotten grapes, or even using new techniques to concentrate the flavour of a rain-diluted crop. In years like these, well-situated areas within larger regions can, in any case, make better wines than their neighbours. So, *Grand* and *Premier Cru* vineyards in France, for example, owe their prestige partly to the way their grapes ripen. The difference in quality between regions can, however, also be attributed to the types of grapes that are grown. Bordeaux had a rotten vintage for red wine in 1967, but a great one for Sauternes. Similarly, there are vintages where, for example, the St Emilion and Pomerol châteaux have already picked their Merlot grapes in perfect conditions before rainstorms arrive to ruin the prospects of their counterparts' later-ripening Cabernet Sauvignon in the Médoc, only a few miles away.

The following pages suggest regions and wines for the most significant vintages of this century.

# THE LAST FIVE YEARS

## 1997 (SOUTHERN HEMISPHERE)

Top class in Australia, New Zealand and Chile with fine reds from patient South African producers who allowed their grapes to ripen.

## 1996

Despite a poor start to the growing season in Europe, this proved to be an unexpectedly fine, classic vintage for the better châteaux of the Médoc, Graves and Sauternes (though less so in Pomerol). There were great red and white Burgundies and Loires and vintage-quality Champagnes. Alsace and the Rhône were patchier, while Germany's successes were often at Kabinett and Spätlese level. Italy, Spain and Portugal all made good wines, but little of truly exceptional quality. California got over a tricky growing season to produce some top class reds and whites. It was a good year for New Zealand and Australia. Less so for South Africa.

## 1995

A generally good rather than great year for Bordeaux, though the best châteaux made impressive wines. White Burgundy, red Loire, Rhône, Alsace and Italy are well worth buying, while Spanish reds from Rioja and Ribera del Duero excellent. The German harvest was tiny, but fine. There was a good vintage in Australia and the best in years for New Zealand, South Africa, North and South America.

## 1994

Bordeaux had little of great quality. For the best wines, look to Pomerol and St Emilion and the good-to-very-good whites. Excellent for vintage port and Portuguese table wines. Average-to-good in Italy, with some excellent wines from Austria and Germany. Alsace, though, was only average, as was the Loire, but the Rhône was variable with the best wines coming from the North. It was a fair year for Burgundy, great for California, unusually poor for Chile and New Zealand, but good to very good for Australia and South Africa.

## 1993

Bordeaux made light but delicate reds for early drinking. A poor year in Portugal, below average in Spain, and very variable in Italy and Austria. There is excellent Tokaji, very worthwhile Alsace and Loires (red and white), and reasonable Rhônes. Red Burgundy is good (though currently tough), and whites almost as good as 1992. A good year in South Africa and New Zealand; fair, though variable, in Australia.

## 1992

A poor, rainy year in Bordeaux, but Champagne is good and white Burgundy brilliant. Taylors and Fonseca produced great vintage port. Spanish, Portuguese and Italian wines were mediocre. Alsace, Loire, Rhône, red Burgundy and California were average to good while Australia and New Zealand were only patchy.

## 1991

Poor and uneven, yields badly cut by frost in Western France. Bordeaux is decent at best. Northern Rhône is a better bet. The best year for Vintage Port since 1985. Little of note from Italy, Burgundy, the Loire, Alsace or Austria, but Spain, South Africa, California, New Zealand and Australia all had a good vintage.

## 1990

A year for great long-lasting claret, rich dry whites and stunningly concentrated Sauternes. Superb for Madeira, excellent for Champagne, Australian and Californian reds. Spain had a good year for reds, especially from the Duero. Great Barolo and good Chianti, stunning Austrian wines, superb German Rieslings and Alsace and Loire whites, wonderful red Rhônes and Burgundy.

## 1985-1989

**1989** Top-class, juicy ripe red and good white Bordeaux and Champagne. Stunning German wines (from Kabinett to TBA) and excellent Alsace. Outstanding Loires (especally red), good red and superb white Rhône, good red Burgundy. **1988** Excellent, well-structured claret, average dry whites but exquisite Sauternes; fine Champagne, long-lasting Italian reds, Tokaji, German, Alsace, Loire reds and sweet whites, good red and white Rhône and excellent red Burgundy (though only average whites). **1987** Fading Bordeaux. Spanish reds are excellent, especially from Penedès. **1986** Powerful, long-lasting claret, good dry white and Sauternes, Australian reds, Austrian whites (Auslese to TBA); white Burgundy. **1985** Californian reds, claret, Vintage Port, Champagne, Spanish and Italian reds, Alsace and sweet Loire; red Rhône, Burgundy.

## 1980-1985

**1984** South African reds, Australian reds and Rieslings. **1983** claret, red Rhône, Portuguese reds, Sauternes, Madeira, Vintage Port, Tokaji, Sweet Austrians, Alsace. **1982** Claret, Champagne, Australian reds, Portuguese reds, Spanish reds, Italian reds, red and white Burgundy and Rhône. **1981** Champagne, Alsace. **1980** Californian and Australian Cabernets; Madeira, vintage port, Portuguese reds.

## 1970-1979

**1979** Champagne, Sassicaia, Sweet Austrians. **1978** Red and white Rhône, Portuguese reds, Bordeaux and Burgundy, Barolo, Tuscan and Loire reds. **1977** Port, sweet Austrians. **1976** Champagne, Loire reds and sweet whites; sweet Germans, Alsace, Sauternes. **1975** Top claret and port, Rioja, Eiswein, Sauternes, Grange. **1974** Californian and Portuguese reds. **1973** Napa Cabernet, sweet Austrians. **1972** Tokaji. **1971** Bordeaux (Merlot) and Burgundy, Champagne, Portuguese reds, Barolo and Tuscan reds; sweet Austrians, Germans, Alsace; red Rhône, Grange. **1970** Port, Napa Cabernet, red Bordeaux, Champagne, Rioja, Musar.

## 1960-1969

**1969** Sweet Austrians, Red Rhône, Burgundy. **1968** Madeira, Rioja, Tokaji. **1967** Sauternes, Tuscan reds, Châteauneuf-du-Pape, German TBA. **1966** Port, red and white Burgundy, Champagne, Portuguese reds, claret, Australian Shiraz, Musar. **1965** Barca Vehla. **1964** Claret, Tokaji, Champagne, Barca Vehla, Vega Sicilia, Rioja, sweet Loire, red Rhône. **1963** Vintage port, Tokaji. **1962** Champagne, top Bordeaux and Burgundy, Rioja, Australian Cabernet and Shiraz. **1961** Claret, Sauternes, Champagne, Brunello, Barolo, sweet Austrians, Alsace, red Rhône. **1960** Port, top claret.

## 1950-1959

**1959** Claret, Sauternes, Champagne, Tokaji; sweet Austrians, Germans, Loire and Alsace; red Rhône and Burgundy. **1958** Barolo. **1957** Madeira, Vega Sicilia, Chianti, Tokaji. **1956** Yquem. **1955** Claret, Sauternes, port, Champagne, Brunello, Grange. **1954** Madeira. **1953** Claret, Tokaji, Champagne, Vega Sicilia, Sweet Germans, Côte Rôtie, red and white Burgundy. **1952** Claret, Madeira, Champagne, Barolo, Tokaji, red Rhône, red and white Burgundy. **1951** Terrible everywhere. **1950** Madeira.

## 1940-1949

**1949** Red and white Bordeaux, Champagne, Tokaji, sweet Germans; red Rhône and Burgundy. **1948** Port, Vega Sicilia. **1947** Bordeaux and Burgundy, port, Champagne, Tokaji, sweet Loire. **1946** Armagnac. **1945** Brunello, Port, Bordeaux, Champagne; Chianti, sweet Germans, Alsace, red Rhônes and Burgundy. **1944.** Madeira, Port. **1943** Champagne, red Burgundy. **1942** Port, Rioja, Vega Sicilia. **1941** Madeira, Sauternes. **1940** Madeira.

## ANNIVERSARY WINES

**1938** Madeira. **1928** Alsace, red and white Bordeaux and Burgundy, Loire. **1918** Armagnac. **1908** Port. **1898** Very top claret, Madeira. For examples, contact the Antique Wine Co. 01827 830 707

# WINE & HEALTH

## WINE AND HEALTH

"Drink a glass of wine after your soup.
And you steal a rouble from your doctor."

*Russian proverb*

Despite the efforts of the anti-alcohol lobbyists, scientists are steadily proving that the folklorists' belief in wine was not misplaced.

### GREAT WHITE HOPE

After the seemingly endless series of reports of the special 'healthful' qualities of red wine, this year brought good news for Chardonnay fans. According to the Allied Dunbar national fitness survey – the most comprehensive ever to be held in Britain – white wine can be just as good at reducing blood pressure and heart disease as red.

### WINE AND HEART DISEASE

Wine seems to combat heart disease in two ways. People who daily drink up to half a litre of red have higher levels of HDL – 'good' cholesterol which escorts 'bad' cholesterol away from the artery walls and to the liver where it is destroyed. (In women the HDL levels rise after just one glass; men need to drink more to get the effect). An antifungal compound called Resveratrol naturally found in wine, has also been found to lower the total cholesterol levels of rats.

### WINE AND DIGESTION

Wine of both colours also helps to counter both constipation and diarrhoea, while white wine in particular stimulates the urinary functions. Wine has also been shown to kill cholera bacteria and to combat typhoid and trichinella, the poisonous compound in 'bad' pork. Surprisingly, leading researcher Dr Heinrich Kliewe actually recommends moderate amounts of wine as an accompaniment to some antibiotics. The wine apparently does not work against these drugs and can help to counteract some of their side effects.

### WINE AND VITAMINS

According to Dr Heinrich Kliewe, red wine contains 'almost all the minerals and trace elements ... in two multivitamin preparations'.

## WINE AND AGEING

Elderly, moderate drinkers are less prone to disability and mentally fitter than both heavier and lighter drinkers. This may be due to the trace mineral boron, which helps older women maintain higher levels of oestrogen, which in turn enables them to absorb calcium. Wine is also believed to give some protection against Alzheimer's Disease.

## WINE AND VIRUSES

According to Dr Jack Konowalchuk and Joan Speirs of Canada's Bureau of Microbial Hazards, the polyphenols in tannic red wine are effective against such viruses as cold sores and possibly even the supposedly incurable genital Herpes 2. Dr Konowalchuk's cold sore research was, it has to be said, carried out using wine concentrate.

## WINE AND PREGNANCY

Despite the fears it arouses, Fetal Alcohol Syndrome is rare outside the poorest inner cities of the US. In 1997, the UK Royal College of Obstetricians and Gynaecologists reported that up to 15 units of alcohol per week should do no harm to a fetus.

## WINE AND CALORIES

There is no difference in calories between a Muscadet or a claret. (around 110). Sweeter, but less alcoholic Liebfraumilch has about 79. A Stanford University survey suggests that the action of the wine on the metabolism somehow makes its calories less fattening.

## HANGOVERS

All alcohol – especially vintage port – is hangover-fare. The only way to avoid this fate is to drink plenty of water before going to bed.

## WINE AND CANCER

Alcohol has been linked to rare occurrences of mouth and throat cancer – but only among smokers. Red wine is rich in gallic acid, an acknowledged anticarcinogenic, and wine's role in reducing stress has been associated with a lower incidence of certain forms of cancer.

## WINE AND MIGRAINE

Red wine, like chocolate, can inhibit an enzyme called phenosulphotransferase-P, or PST-P, which naturally detoxifies all sorts of bacteria in the gut. An absence of PST-P is linked to migraine.

## WINE AND ASTHMA

Wines that are heavily dosed with sulphur dioxide (used to combat bacteria in most dried, bottled and canned foods) can trigger asthma attacks. New World and organic wines have lower sulphur levels.

# FOOD & WINE

## MATCHMAKING FOR BEGINNERS

One of the most daunting aspects of wine has always been the traditional obsession with serving precisely the right wine with any particular dish – of only ever drinking red with meat and white with fish or shellfish.

It may be reassuring to learn that some of these time-honoured rules are just plain wrong. In Portugal, for example, the fishermen love to wash their sardines and salt cod down with a glass or two of harsh red wine. In Burgundy too, they not only drink local red wine with trout – they even poach the fish in it.

On the other hand, the idea that a platter of cheese is somehow incomplete without a bottle of red wine can be exploded in an instant. Just take a mouthful of claret immediately after eating a little goat's cheese. The wine will taste metallic and unpleasant, for the simple reason that the creaminess of the cheese reacts badly with the tannin – the toughness – in the wine. A fresh, dry white would be far more successful (its acidity would cut through the fat), while the claret would be shown to its best advantage alongside a harder, stronger cheese such as a Cheddar or a Parmesan.

Even such an obvious pairing as beef and Bordeaux fails the test of an objective tasting. The protein of the meat makes all but the fruitiest wines taste even tougher than they really are.

However, there is also the other side of the coin, where, like people who are happier in a couple than separately, some combinations of food and wine simply seem to work.

### A SENSE OF BALANCE

There is no real mystery about the business of matching foods and wines. Some flavours and textures are compatible, and some are not. You might not want to eat strawberry mousse with your chicken casserole; on the other hand, apple sauce can do wonders for roast pork.

The key to spotting which marriages are made in heaven and which are modelled on those of the younger members of the British royal family, lies in identifying the dominant characteristics of what is on the plate and what is in the glass – and learning which are likely to complement each other, either through their similarities or through their differences.

## LIKELY COMBINATIONS

It is not difficult to define particular types of food and wine, and to guess at how they are likely to get on. A buttery sauce is happier with something tangily acidic, like a crisp Sauvignon Blanc, rather than a rich buttery Chardonnay. A subtly poached fish won't appreciate a fruit-packed New World white, and you won't do pheasant pie any favours by pulling the cork on a delicate red.

## WHAT TO AVOID

Some foods and their characteristics, though, make life difficult for almost any drink. Sweetness, for example, in a fruity sauce served with a savoury dish seems to strip some of the fruitier flavours out of a wine. This may not matter if the stuff in your glass is a blackcurranty New World Cabernet Sauvignon, but it's bad news if it is a bone dry white or a tough red with no fruit to spare.

Cream is tricky too. Try fresh strawberries with Champagne – delicious; now add a little whipped cream to the equation and see what a nasty flavour you will have created. Creamy sauces can have the same effect on a wine.

Spices are problematical, thanks to the physical sensation of eating them rather than any particular flavour. A wine won't seem nasty after a mouthful of chilli sauce; it will simply lose its fruity flavour and taste of nothing at all. On the other hand, some foods, such as ginger, chocolate, grapefruit and melon, like some of your spikier friends, can be downright difficult to get along with.

## ALWAYS WORTH A TRY

Some condiments actually bring out the best in wines. Sprinkling a little freshly ground pepper onto your meat or pasta can accentuate the flavour of a wine, just as it can with a sauce. Squeezing a fresh lemon onto your fish will reduce the apparent acidity of a white wine – a useful tip if you have inadvertently bought a case or two of tooth-strippingly dry German white or Muscadet. And, just as lemon can help to liven up a dull sauce, it will also help to make a dull white wine such as a basic Burgundy or a Soave taste more interesting – by neutralising the acidity in the wine, allowing its other flavours to make themselves apparent. Mustard performs a similar miracle when it is eaten with beef, somehow nullifying the effect of the meat protein on the wine.

## MARRIAGE GUIDANCE

In the following pages, I have suggested wines to go with a wide range of dishes and ingredients, taking the dominant flavour as the keypoint. Don't treat any of this advice as gospel – use it instead as a launchpad for your own food and wine experiments.

**Almond** Liqueur Muscats, or Beaumes de Venise.
  **Trout with Almonds** Bianco di Custoza, Pinot Blanc.
**Anchovies**
  **Salted Anchovies** Rioja red or white, Manzanilla or Fino sherry.
  **Fresh Anchovy (Boquerones)** Albariño, Vinho Verde, Aligoté.
  **Salade Niçoise** Muscadet, Vinho Verde or Beaujolais.
  **Tapenade** Dry sherry or Madeira.
**Aniseed** Dry white.
**Apple**
  **Apple Pie or Strudel** Austrian off-dry white.
  **Apple Sauce** Riesling (dry or off-dry).
  **Blackberry and Apple Pie** Late Harvest Riesling, Vouvray demi-sec.
  **Roast Pork with Apple Sauce** Off-dry Vouvray or Riesling.
  **Waldorf Salad** Dry Madeira.
**Apricot** Late Harvest Sémillon or Riesling, Jurançon Moelleux.
**Artichoke** White Rhône.
  **Artichoke Soup** Loire white (dry), Pinot Gris.
**Asparagus**
  **Asparagus Soup** Fresh dry whites, Sauvignon Blanc.
**Aubergines**
  **Ratatouille** Bulgarian red, Chianti, simple Rhône or Provence red, Portuguese reds, New Zealand Sauvignon Blanc.
  **Stuffed Aubergines** Beefy, spicy reds like Bandol, Zinfandel, a good Southern Rhône or a full-bodied Italian.
**Avocado**
  **Avocado with Prawns** Champagne, Riesling Kabinett, Sauvignon, Pinot Gris, Australian Chardonnay.
  **Avocado Vinaigrette** Unoaked Chardonnay – Chablis.

# B

**Bacon** Rich Pinot Gris or Alsace Riesling.
  **Bacon with Marinated Scallops** Fino sherry or mature Riesling, Shiraz-based Australians, Zinfandel from the States, or a heavy Cape red.
  **Warm Bacon Salad** New World Sauvignon Blanc, California Fumé Blanc, or a good Pouilly Fumé.
**Banana**
  **Flambéed Banana with Rum** Jurançon, Tokaji, Pedro Ximénez sherry, rum.
  **Banoffee Pie** Sweet Tokaji.
**Barbecue Sauce** Inexpensive off-dry white, or a simple fruity Cabernet.
  **Spare Ribs with Barbecue Sauce** Fruity Australian Shiraz, Grenache or Zinfandel, spicy Côtes du Rhône from a ripe vintage, or an off-dry white.
**Basil** Slightly sweet Chardonnay (ie Californian, commercial Australian).
  **Pasta in Pesto Sauce** New Zealand Sauvignon Blanc, Valpolicella.
**Beans**
  **Bean Salad** Spanish reds such as Rioja Reserva, Rueda, or New Zealand Sauvignon.
  **Bean Stew** Chunky Portuguese or Spanish reds.
  **Cassoulet** Serious white Rhône, Marsanne or Roussanne, or reds including Grenache and Syrah from the Rhône, crunchy Italian reds or Zinfandel.
  **Ribollita (Tuscan Bean Soup)** Red Lambrusco, or more serious Chianti.

**Beef**

**Beef with Green Peppers in Black Bean Sauce** Off-dry German Riesling, or characterful dry white like white Rhône or Marsanne.

**Beef with Spring Onions and Ginger** Off-dry German Riesling; one of the more serious Beaujolais crus.

**Beef Stew** Pomerol or St. Emilion, good Northern Rhône like Crozes-Hermitage, Shiraz or Pinot Noir from the New World.

**Beef Stroganoff** Tough beefy reds like Amarone, Brunello di Montalcino, Barolo, Côte Rotie or really ripe Zinfandel.

**Beef Wellington** Top Burgundy, Châteauneuf-du-Pape.

**Beefburger** Tasty country reds, Italian or Southern French Corbières.

**Boeuf Bourguignon** Australian Bordeaux-style, Barolo, or other robust reds with sweet fruit.

**Boiled Beef and Carrots** Bordeaux Rouge, Valpolicella Classico, Australian Shiraz.

**Bresaola (air dried beef)** Beaujolais, Barbera and tasty reds from the Languedoc.

**Carpaccio of Beef** Chardonnay, Champagñe, Cabernet Franc and other Loire reds, Pomerol.

**Chilli Con Carne** Robust fruity reds, Beaujolais Crus, Barbera or Valpolicella, spicy reds like Zinfandel or Pinotage.

**Corned Beef Hash** Spicily characterful reds from the Rhône or Southern France.

**Daube of Beef** Cheap Southern Rhône reds or Côtes du Rhône.

**Goulash** Eastern European red, Bulgarian Cabernet or Mavrud, Hungarian Kadarka or Aussie Shiraz.

**Meatballs** Spicy, rich reds from the Rhône, Zinfandel, Pinotage and Portuguese reds.

**Panang Neuk (Beef in Peanut Curry)** New World Chardonnay, New Zealand Sauvignon Blanc, or a spicy aromatic white Rhône.

**Rare Chargrilled Beef** Something sweetly ripe and flavoursome, but not too tannic. Try Chilean Merlot.

**Roast Beef** Côte Rôtie, good Burgundy.

**Salt Beef** Loire reds from Gamay or Cabernet Franc.

**Steak** Pinot Noir and Merlot from the New World, Australian Shiraz, Châteauneuf-du-Pape, good ripe Burgundy.

**Steak with Dijon Mustard** Bordeaux, Cabernet Sauvignon from the New World, or Australian Shiraz.

**Steak and Kidney Pie/Pudding** Bordeaux, Australian Cabernet Sauvignon, Southern Rhône reds or Rioja.

**Steak au Poivre** Cabernet Sauvignon, Chianti, Rhône reds, Shiraz or Rioja.

**Steak Tartare** Bourgogne Blanc, fruity reds, light on tannin; Beaujolais, Bardolino, etc, or traditionally vodka.

**Thai Beef Salad** New Zealand or South African Sauvignon Blanc, Gewürztraminer, Pinot Blanc.

**Beer**

**Carbonnade à la Flamande** Cheap Southern Rhône or Valpolicella.

**Beetroot**

**Borscht** Rich, dry Alsace Pinot Gris, Pinot Blanc or Pinot Grigio.

**Black Bean Sauce**

**Beef with Green Peppers in Black Bean Sauce** Off-dry German Riesling, or characterful dry white like white Rhône or Marsanne.

**Blackberry**

**Blackberry and Apple Pie** Late Harvest Riesling, Vouvray demi-sec.

**Black cherry**

**Black Forest Gâteau** Fortified Muscat, Schnapps or Kirsch.

**Blackcurrant**

**Blackcurrant Cheesecake** Sweet, grapey dessert wines.

**Blackcurrant Mousse** Sweet or sweet sparkling wines.

**Summer Pudding** Late Harvest Riesling, German or Alsace.

**Black Pudding** Chablis, New Zealand Chardonnay; Zinfandel or Barolo.

**Brandy**

**Christmas Pudding** Australian Liqueur Muscat, tawny port, rich (sweet) Champagne, Tokaji.

**Crepes Suzette** Asti Spumante, Orange Muscat, Champagne cocktails.

**Bream (freshwater)** Chablis or other unoaked Chardonnay.

**Bream (sea)** White Rhône, Sancerre.

**Brie** Sancerre or New Zealand Sauvignon.

**Brill** Dry white, Soave, Albariño, Vinho Verde.

**Broccoli**

**Broccoli and Cheese Soup** Slightly sweet sherry – Amontillado or Oloroso.

**Butter**

**Béarnaise Sauce** Good dry Riesling.

**Beurre Blanc** Champagne Blanc de Blancs, Dry Vinho Verde.

**Chicken Kiev** Chablis, Aligoté or Italian dry white.

**Butternut Squash**

**Butternut Soup** Aromatic Alsace Gewurztraminer.

# C

**Cabbage**

**Stuffed Cabbage** East European Cabernet.

**Cajun Spices** Cru Beaujolais.

**Gumbo** Zinfandel or maybe beer.

**Capers** Sauvignon Blanc.

**Skate with Black Butter** Crisply acidic whites like Muscadet or Chablis.

**Tartare Sauce** Crisply fresh whites like Sauvignon.

**Caramel**

**Caramelized Oranges** Asti Spumante, Sauternes.

**Creme Caramel** Aromatic sweet white – Muscat or Gewurztraminer Vendange Tardive.

**Carp** Franken Sylvaner, Dry Jurançon, Hungarian Furmint.

**Carrot**

**Carrot and Orange Soup** Madeira or perhaps an Amontillado sherry.

**Carrot and Coriander Soup** Aromatic dry Muscat, Argentine Torrontes.

**Cashew Nuts** Pinot Blanc.

**Chicken with Cashew Nuts** Rich aromatic white, Pinot Gris or Muscat.

**Cauliflower**

**Cauliflower Cheese** Fresh crisp Côtes de Gascogne white, Pinot Grigio, softly plummy Chilean Merlot or young, unoaked Rioja.

**Caviar** Champagne or chilled vodka.

**Celery**

**Celery Soup** Off-dry Riesling

**Cheddar (Mature)** Good Bordeaux, South African Cabernet, port.

**Cheese (general – see individual entries)**

**Broccoli and Cheese Soup** Slightly sweet sherry (Amontillado or Oloroso).

**Cauliflower Cheese** Freshly crisp, simple Côtes de Gascogne white, Pinot Grigio, softly plummy Chilean Merlot or young, unoaked Rioja.

**Cheeseburger** Sweetly fruity, oaky reds – Aussie Shiraz, Rioja.

**Cheese Fondue** Swiss white or Vin de Savoie.

**Cheese Platter** Match wines to cheeses, taking care not to put too tannic a red with too creamy a cheese. Burgundy cheeses demand fine Burgundy, Munster is best paired with Alsace Gewurztraminer.

**Cheese Sauce (Mornay)** Oaky Chardonnay.

**Courgette Gratin** Good dry Chenin from Vouvray or South Africa.

**Cream Cheese, Crème Fraîche, Mozzarella, Mascarpone** Fresh, light, dry whites – Frascati, Pinot Grigio.

**Raclette** Swiss white, or Vin de Savoie.

**Cheesecake** Australian Botrytised Semillon.
**Cherry** Valpolicella, Recioto della Valpolicella, Dolcetto.
**Roast Duck with Cherry Sauce** Barbera, Dolcetto or Barolo.
**Chestnut**
**Roast Turkey with Chestnut Stuffing** Côtes du Rhône, Merlot, or soft and mature Burgundy.
**Chicken**
**Chicken with Bamboo Shoots and Water Chestnuts** Dry German, New World Riesling.
**Barbecued Chicken** Rich and tasty white, Chardonnay.
**Chicken Casserole** Mid-weight Rhône such as Crozes-Hermitage or Lirac.
**Chicken Chasseur** Off-dry Riesling.
**Chicken & Ham Pie** Good Beaujolais.
**Chicken Kiev** Chablis, Aligoté or Italian dry white.
**Chicken Pie** White Bordeaux, simple Chardonnay or light Italian white.
**Chicken Soup** Soave, Orvieto or Pinot Blanc.
**Chicken Vol-au-Vents** White Bordeaux.
**Cock-a-Leekie** Dry New World white, simple red Rhône.
**Coq au Vin** Shiraz-based New World reds, red Burgundy.
**Coronation Chicken** Gewürztraminer, dry aromatic English; fresh Chinon.
**Cream of Chicken Soup** Big, dry, unoaked white (Chablis, Pinot Blanc).
**Devilled Chicken** Australian Shiraz.
**Fricassée** Unoaked Chardonnay.
**Lemon Chicken** Muscadet, Chablis or basic Bourgogne Blanc.
**Poached Chicken** Beaujolais, Valpolicella.
**Roast/Grilled Chicken** Reds or whites, though nothing too heavy – Burgundy is good, as is Barbera, though Soave will do just as well.
**Roast/Grilled Chicken with Bread Sauce** Côtes du Rhône or herby Provençal reds.
**Roast/Grilled Chicken with Sage and Onion Stuffing** Italian reds, especially Chianti, soft, plummy Merlots and sweetly fruity Rioja.
**Roast/Grilled Chicken with Tarragon** Dry Chenin (Vouvray or perhaps a good South African).
**Saltimbocca (Escalope with mozzarella and ham)** Flavoursome, dry Italian whites, Lugana, Bianco di Custoza, Orvieto.
**Smoked Chicken** Oaky Chardonnay, Australian Marsanne or Fumé Blanc.
**Southern Fried Chicken** White Bordeaux, Muscadet, Barbera, light Zinfandel.
**Tandoori Chicken** White Bordeaux, New Zealand Sauvignon Blanc.
**Chicken Liver** Softly fruity, fairly light reds including Beaujolais, Italian Cabernet or Merlot, or perhaps an Oregon Pinot Noir.
**Chicken Liver Paté** Most of the above reds plus Vouvray Moelleux, Monbazillac or Amontillado sherry.
**Chilli** Cheap wine or cold lager.
**Chilli Con Carne** Robust fruity reds, Beaujolais crus, Barbera or Valpolicella, spicy reds like Zinfandel or Pinotage.
**Hot and Sour Soup** Crisply aromatic English white, Baden Dry.
**Szechuan-Style** Dry aromatic whites, Alsace Pinot Gris, Riesling, Grenache Rosé, beer.
**Thai Beef Salad** New Zealand or South African Sauvignon Blanc, Gewürztraminer, Pinot Blanc.
**Chinese (general)** Aromatic white (Gewürztraminer, Pinot Gris, English).
**Chives** Sauvignon Blanc.
**Chocolate** Orange Muscat, Moscatel de Valencia.
**Black Forest Gâteau** Fortified Muscat, Schnapps or Kirsch.
**Chocolate Cake** Beaumes de Venise, Bual or Malmsey Madeira, Orange Muscat, sweet German or fine Champagne.
**Chocolate Profiteroles with Cream** Muscat de Rivesaltes.
**Chocolate Roulade** German or Austrian Eiswein.
**Dark Chocolate Mousse** Sweet Black Muscat or other Muscat-based wines.
**Milk Chocolate Mousse** Moscato d'Asti.

**Chorizo (pork)** Red or white Rioja, Navarra, Manzanilla sherry.
**Cider**
**Rabbit in Cider** Muscadet, demi-sec Vouvray, cider or Calvados.
**Cinnamon** Riesling Spätlese, Muscat.
**Clams** Chablis or Sauvignon Blanc.
**Clam Chowder** Dry white such as Côtes de Gascogne, Amontillado sherry or Madeira.
**Spaghetti Vongole** Pinot Bianco or Lugana.
**Cockles** Muscadet, Gros Plant, Aligoté, dry Vinho Verde.
**Coconut (milk)** California Chardonnay.
**Green Curry** Big-flavoured New World whites or Pinot Blanc from Alsace.
**Cod** Unoaked Chardonnay, good white Burgundy, dry Loire Chenin.
**Cod in Crumb Bake** Lugana, Pinot Bianco, Pinot Blanc.
**Salt Cod (Bacalhão de Gomes)** Classically Portuguese red or white – Vinho Verde or Bairrada reds.
**Smoked Cod** Vinho Verde.
**Cod's Roe (smoked)** Well-oaked New World Chardonnay.
**Taramasalata** Oaked Chardonnay or Fumé Blanc.
**Coffee**
**Coffee Gâteau** Asti Spumante.
**Coffee Mousse** Asti Spumante, Liqueur Muscat.
**Tiramisu** Sweet fortified Muscat, Vin Santo, Torcolato.
**Cognac**
**Steak au Poivre** Cabernet Sauvignon, Chianti, Rhône reds, Shiraz, Rioja.
**Coriander**
**Carrot and Coriander Soup** Aromatic dry Muscat.
**Coriander Leaf** Dry or off-dry English white.
**Coriander Seed** Dry, herby Northern Italian whites.
**Courgette**
**Courgette Gratin** Good dry Chenin from Vouvray or South Africa.
**Couscous** Spicy Shiraz, North African reds or earthy Southern French Minervois.
**Crab** Chablis, Sauvignon Blanc, New World Chardonnay.
**Crab Bisque** Chablis, Pinot Gris or dry sherry.
**Crab Paté** Crisp dry whites – Baden Dry or Soave.
**Crab and Sweetcorn Soup** Sancerre, other Sauvignon Blanc.
**Dressed Crab** Chablis or Mâcon Chardonnay
**Cranberry**
**Roast Turkey with Cranberry and Orange Stuffing** Richly fruity reds like Shiraz from Australia, Zinfandel or modern Rioja.
**Crayfish**
**Freshwater Crayfish** South African Sauvignon, Meursault.
**Salad of Crayfish Tails with Dill** Rich South African Chenin blends or crisp Sauvignon, white Rhône.
**Cream** When dominant, not good with wine, particularly tannic reds.
**Tagiatelle Carbonara** Pinot Grigio or a fresh red, such as Bardolino or Beaujolais.
**Cucumber**
**Cucumber Soup** Dry Madeira.
**Cumin** Soave, Lugana.
**Curry**
**Beef in Peanut Curry** New World Chardonnay, spicy aromatic white Rhône.
**Coronation Chicken** Gewürztraminer, dry aromatic English wine or a fresh Chinon.
**Curried Turkey** New World Chardonnay.
**Curried Beef** Beefy, spicy reds; Barolo, Châteauneuf-du-Pape and Shiraz/Cabernet or off-dry aromatic whites – Gewürztraminer, Pinot Gris. Or try some Indian sparkling wine or cold Cobra lager.
**Tandoori Chicken** White Bordeaux, New Zealand Sauvignon Blanc.
**Thai Green Chicken Curry** Big New World whites or Pinot Blanc from Alsace.

# D

**Dill** Sauvignon Blanc.
  **Gravadlax** Ice cold vodka, Pinot Gris or Akvavit.
**Dover Sole** Sancerre, good Chablis, unoaked Chardonnay.
**Dried Fruit** Sweet sherry, tawny port.
  **Bread and Butter Pudding** Barsac or Sauternes, Monbazillac or Jurançon.
  **Christmas Pudding** Muscat de Beaumes de Venise, or Eiswein.
  **Mince Pie** Rich, late harvest wine or botrytis-affected Sémillon.
**Duck** Pinot Noir from Burgundy, California or Oregon, or perhaps an off-dry German Riesling.
  **Cassoulet** Serious white Rhônes, Marsanne or Roussanne, or try reds including Grenache and Syrah from the Rhône, crunchy Italian reds or Zinfandel.
  **Confit de Canard** Alsace Pinot Gris or a crisp red like Barbera.
  **Duck Paté** Chianti or other juicy, herby red, Amontillado sherry.
  **Duck Paté with Orange** Riesling or Rioja.
  **Peking Duck** Rice Wine, Alsace Riesling, Pinot Gris.
  **Roast Duck** Big fruity reds like Aussie Cabernet, a ripe Nebbiolo or Zinfandel.
  **Roast Duck with Cherry Sauce** Barbera, Dolcetto or Barolo.
  **Roast Duck with Orange Sauce** Loire red or, surprisingly, a sweet white like Vouvray demi-sec.
  **Smoked Duck** Californian Chardonnay or Fumé Blanc.
**Duck Liver**
  **Foie Gras de Canard** Champagne, Late Harvest Gewürztraminer or Riesling, Sauternes.

# E

**Eel**
  **Jellied Eels** A pint of stout.
  **Smoked Eel** Pale dry sherry, simple, fresh white Burgundy.
**Egg**
  **Baked Eggs** Bordeaux Blanc, Côtes de Gascogne or other simple white, young fruity red
  **Crème Brulée** Jurançon Moelleux, Tokaji.
  **Eggs Benedict** Unoaked Chardonnay, Blanc de Blancs, fizz, Bucks Fizz or Bloody Mary.
  **Eggs Florentine** Unoaked Chardonnay, Pinot Blanc, Aligoté, Sémillon.
  **Omelettes** Cheap Beaujolais, Bardolino.
  **Tortilla** Young juicy Spanish reds and fresher whites from La Mancha or Rueda.

# F

**Fennel** Sauvignon Blanc.
**Fig** Liqueur Muscat.
**Frankfurter** Côtes du Rhône or Budweiser.

**Fish (general – see individual entries)**

**Bouillabaisse** Red or white Côtes du Rhône, dry rosé from Provence, California Fumé Blanc, Marsanne or Verdicchio.

**Cumberland Fish Pie** California Chardonnay, Alsace Pinot Gris, Sauvignon Blanc.

**Fish and Chips** Most fairly simple, crisply acidic dry whites (white Bordeaux, Sauvignon Blanc) or maybe a rosé.

**Fish Cakes** White Bordeaux, Chilean Chardonnay.

**Fish Soup** Manzanilla, Chablis, Muscadet.

**Kedgeree** Aligoté, crisp Sauvignon.

**Mediterranean Fish Soup** Provençal reds and rosés, Tavel, Côtes du Rhône, Vin de Pays d'Oc.

**Seafood Salad** Soave, Pinot Grigio, Muscadet, or a lightly oaked Chardonnay.

**Sushi** Saké.

**Foie Gras (see Duck and Goose Liver)**

**Fruit (general – see individual entries)**

**Fresh Fruit Salad** Moscato d'Asti, Riesling Beerenauslese or Vouvray Moelleux.

**Fruit Flan** Vouvray Moëlleux, Alsace Riesling Vendange Tardive.

**Summer Pudding** Late Harvest Riesling, German or Alsace.

# G

**Game (general – see individual entries)**

**Cold Game** Fruity Northern Italian Reds – Barbera or Dolcetto, good Beaujolais or light Burgundy.

**Roast Game** Big reds, such as Brunello di Montalcino, old Barolo, good Burgundy.

**Well-hung Game** Old Barolo or Barbaresco, mature Hermitage, Côte Rôtie or Châteauneuf-du-Pape, fine Burgundy.

**Game Pie** Beefy reds, Southern French, Rhône, Australian Shiraz or South African Pinotage.

**Garlic**

**Aïoli** A wide range of wines go well including white Rioja, Provence rosé, California Pinot Noir.

**Gazpacho** Fino Sherry, white Rioja.

**Garlic Sausage** Red Rioja, Bandol, Côtes du Rhône.

**Houmous** French dry white.

**Raw Garlic** Rosé.

**Roast Lamb with Garlic and Rosemary** Earthy soft reds like, Californian Petite Sirah, Rioja or Zinfandel.

**Roast/Grilled Chicken with Garlic** Oaky Chardonnay or red Rioja.

**Snails with Garlic Butter** Aligoté and light white Burgundy or perhaps a red Gamay de Touraine.

**Ginger** Gewürztraminer or Riesling.

**Beef with Onions and Ginger** Off-dry German Riesling; one of the more serious Beaujolais crus.

**Chicken with Ginger** White Rhône, Gewürztraminer.

**Goat's Cheese** Sancerre, New World Sauvignon, Pinot Blanc.

**Grilled Goat's Cheese** Loire reds.

**Goose** A good Rhône red like Hermitage, Côte Rôtie, or a crisp Barbera, Pinot Noir from Burgundy, California or Oregon, or perhaps an off-dry German Riesling.

**Confit d'Oie** Best Sauternes, Monbazillac.

**Goose Liver**

**Foie Gras** Best Sauternes, Monbazillac.

**Gooseberry**
- **Gooseberry Fool** Quarts de Chaume.
- **Gooseberry Pie** Sweet Madeira, Austrian Trockenbeerenauslese.

**Grapefruit** Sweet Madeira or sherry.

**Grouse**
- **Roast Grouse** Hermitage, robust Burgundy or good mature claret.

**Guinea Fowl** Old Burgundy, Cornas, Gamay de Touraine, St Emilion.

# H

**Haddock** White Bordeaux, Chardonnay, Pinot Blanc.
- **Mousse of Smoked Haddock** Top white Burgundy.
- **Smoked Haddock** Fino sherry or oaky Chardonnay.

**Hake** Soave, Sauvignon Blanc.

**Halibut** White Bordeaux, Muscadet.
- **Smoked Halibut** Oaky Spanish white/Australian Chardonnay, white Bordeaux.

**Ham**
- **Boiled/Roasted/Grilled/Fried Ham** Beaujolais-Villages, Gamay de Touraine, slightly sweet German white, Tuscan red, lightish Cabernet (eg Chilean), Alsace Pinot Gris or Muscat.
- **Braised Ham with Lentils** Light, fruity Beaujolais, other Gamay, Côtes du Rhône.
- **Chicken & Ham Pie** Good Beaujolais.
- **Honey-Roast Ham** Riesling.
- **Oak-Smoked Ham** Oaky Spanish reds.
- **Parma Ham** Try a dry Lambrusco, Tempranillo Joven, or Gamay de Touraine.
- **Pea and Ham Soup** Beaujolais.

**Hare**
- **Hare Casserole** Good Beaujolais Cru or, for a stronger flavour, try an Australian red.
- **Jugged Hare** Argentinian reds, tough Italians like Amarone, Barolo and Barbaresco, inky reds from Bandol or the Rhône.

**Hazelnut** Vin Santo, Liqueur Muscat.
- **Warm Bacon, Hazelnut and Sorrel Salad** New World Sauvignon Blanc, California Fumé Blanc, or a good Pouilly Fumé.

**Herbs (see individual entries)**

**Herring**
- **Fresh Herrings** Sauvignon Blanc, Muscadet, Frascati or cider.
- **Roll-Mop Herring** Savoie, Vinho Verde, Akvavit, cold lager.
- **Salt Herring** White Portuguese.
- **Sprats** Muscadet, Vinho Verde.

**Honey** Tokaji.
- **Baklava** Moscatel de Setúbal.

**Horseradish**
- **Roast Beef with Horseradish** California Pinot Noir or mature Burgundy.

**Houmous** French dry whites.

# I

**Ice Cream** Too cold and sweet for most wines. Try Marsala or Pedro Ximénez.

**Indian (general)** Gewürztraminer (spicy dishes); New World Chardonnay (creamy/yoghurt dishes); New Zealand Sauvignon Blanc (Tandoori).

# J

**Japanese barbecue sauce**

**Teriyaki** Spicy reds like Zinfandel or Portuguese reds.

**John Dory** Good white Burgundy or Aussie Chardonnay.

**Juniper**

**Pork Casserole** Mid-weight, earthy reds like Minervois, Navarra or Montepulciano d'Abruzzo.

**Venison Casserole** Shiraz-based Australians, Zinfandel from the States, or a heavy Cape red.

# K

**Kidney**

**Lambs' Kidney** Rich spicy reds – Barolo, Cabernet Sauvignon, Rioja reserva.

**Steak and Kidney Pie/Pudding** Bordeaux, Australian Cabernet Sauvignon, Southern Rhône reds or Rioja.

**Kipper** New World Chardonnay or a good Fino sherry; a nice cup of tea.

# L

**Lamb**

**Cassoulet** Serious white Rhône, Marsanne or Roussanne, or reds including Grenache and Syrah from the Rhône, crunchy Italian reds or Zinfandel.

**Casserole** Rich and warm Cabernet-based reds from France or Californian Zinfandel.

**Cutlets or Chops** Cru Bourgeois Bordeaux, Chilean Cabernet.

**Haggis** Côtes du Roussillon, Spanish reds, Malt Whisky.

**Irish Stew** A good simple South American or Eastern European Cabernet works best.

**Kebabs** Sweetly ripe Australian Cabernet/Shiraz.

**Kleftiko (Lamb Shanks baked with Thyme)** Greek red.

**Lancashire Hotpot** Robust country red – Cahors, Fitou.

**Moussaka** Crunchy Northern Italian reds (Barbera, Dolcetto, etc), Beaujolais, Pinotage, Zinfandel, or try some good Greek wine from a modern producer.

**Roast Lamb** Bordeaux, New Zealand Cabernet Sauvignon, Cahors, Rioja reservas, reds from Chile.

**Roast Lamb with Thyme** Try a New Zealand Cabernet Sauvignon or Bourgeuil

**Shepherd's Pie** Barbera, Cabernet Sauvignon, Minervois.

**Langoustine** Muscadet, Soave, South African Sauvignon.

**Leek**

**Cock-a-Leekie** Dry New World white, simple red Rhône.

**Leek and Potato Soup** Dry whites, Côtes de Gascogne.

**Onion/Leek Tart** Alsace Gewurztraminer, New World Riesling, good Chablis.

**Vichysoisse** Dry whites, Chablis, Bordeaux Blanc.

**Lemon**
**Lemon Cheesecake** Moscato d'Asti.
**Lemon Chicken** Muscadet, Chablis or basic Bourgogne Blanc.
**Lemon Meringue Pie** Malmsey Madeira.
**Lemon Tart** Sweet Austrian and German wines.
**Lemon Zest** Sweet fortified Muscats.
**Lemon grass** New Zealand Sauvignon, Sancerre, Viognier.
**Lemon Sole** Chardonnay.
**Lentils** Earthy country wines, Côtes du Rhône.
**Chicken Dhansak** Sémillon or New Zealand Sauvignon.
**Dal Soup** Try Soave or Pinot Bianco.
**Lime** Australian Verdelho, Grüner Veltliner, Fürmint.
**Kaffir Lime Leaves (in Thai Green Curry, etc)** Big-flavoured New World whites or Pinot Blanc from Alsace.
**Thai Beef Salad** New Zealand or South African Sauvignon Blanc, Gewürztraminer, Pinot Blanc.
**Liver**
**Calves' Liver** Good Italian Cabernet, Merlot or mature Chianti.
**Fegato alla Veneziana** Nebbiolo, Zinfandel or Petite Sirah.
**Lambs' Liver** Chianti, Aussie Shiraz or Merlot.
**Liver and Bacon** Côtes du Rhône, Zinfandel, Pinotage.
**Lobster** Good white Burgundy.
**Lobster Bisque** Grenache rosé, fresh German white, Chassagne-Montrachet, dry Amontillado.
**Lobster in a Rich Sauce** Champagne, Chablis, fine white Burgundy, good white Bordeaux.
**Lobster Salad** Champagne, Chablis, German or Alsace Riesling.
**Lobster Thermidor** Rich beefy Côtes du Rhône, oaky Chardonnay, or a good deep-coloured rosé from Southern France.

# M

**Mackerel** Best with Vinho Verde, Albariño, Sancerre and New Zealand Sauvignon.
**Smoked Mackerel** Bourgogne Aligoté, Alsace Pinot Gris.
**Smoked Mackerel Paté** Sparkling Vouvray, Muscadet.
**Mallard** Côte Rôtie, Ribera del Duero or Zinfandel.
**Mango** Best eaten in the bath with a bottle of Champagne.
**Marjoram** Provençal reds.
**Marsala**
**Chops in Marsala Sauce** Australian Marsanne or Verdelho.
**Zabaglione** Marsala, or a sweet Muscat.
**Mascarpone**
**Tiramisu** Sweet fortified Muscat, Vin Santo, Torcolato.
**Meat (general – see individual entries)**
**Cold Meats** Juicy, fruity reds, low in tannin i.e. Beaujolais, Côtes du Rhône, etc.
**Consommé** Medium/Amontillado sherry.
**Meat Paté** Beaujolais, Fumé Blanc, lesser white Burgundy.
**Mixed Grill** Versatile uncomplicated red – Aussie Shiraz, Rioja, Bulgarian Cabernet.
**Pasta in Meat Sauce** Chianti, Bordeaux Rouge.
**Melon** Tawny port, sweet Madeira or sherry, Quarts de Chaume, late harvest Riesling.
**Mincemeat**
**Mince Pie** Complemented by rich, late harvest wine or botrytis-affected Sémillon.

**Mint** Beaujolais, young Pinot Noir, or try a New Zealand or Australian Riesling.

**Thai Beef Salad** New Zealand or South African Sauvignon Blanc, Gewürztraminer, Pinot Blanc.

**Monkfish** A light fruity red such as Bardolino, Valpolicella, La Mancha Joven, or most Chardonnays.

**Mushroom** Merlot-based reds, good Northern Rhône, top Piedmontese reds.

**Mushroom Soup** Bordeaux Blanc, Côte de Gasgogne.

**Mushrooms à la Greque** Sauvignon, fresh, modern Greek white.

**Risotto with Fungi porcini** Top-notch Piedmontese reds – mature Barbera or Barbaresco, Barbera, earthy Southern French reds.

**Stuffed Mushrooms** Chenin Blanc, Sylvaner.

**Wild Mushrooms** Nebbiolo, good Bordeaux.

**Mussels** Sauvignon Blanc, light Chardonnay, Muscadet Sur Lie.

**Moules Marinières** Bordeaux Blanc or Muscadet Sur Lie.

**New Zealand Green-Lipped Mussels** New Zealand Sauvignon Blanc.

**Mustard**

**Devilled Chicken** Australian Shiraz.

**Dijon Mustard** Beaujolais.

**English Wholegrain Mustard** Beaujolais, Valpolicella.

**French Mustard** White Bordeaux.

**Rabbit with Mustard** Franken wine or Czech Pilsner beer.

**Steak with Dijon Mustard** Cabernet Sauvignon from the New World, or Australian Shiraz.

# N

**Nectarine** Sweet German Riesling.

**Nutmeg** Rioja, Aussie Shiraz, or for sweet dishes, Australian Late Harvest Semillon.

**Nuts** Amontillado sherry, Vin Santo and Tokaji.

# O

**Octopus** Rueda white, or a fresh modern Greek white.

**Olives** Dry sherry, Muscadet.

**Salade Niçoise** Muscadet, Vinho Verde or Beaujolais.

**Tapenade** Dry sherry or Madeira.

**Onion**

**Caramelized Onions** Shiraz-based Australians, Zinfandel from the States, or a heavy Cape red.

**French Onion Soup** Sauvignon Blanc, Aligoté, white Bordeaux.

**Onion/Leek Tart** Alsace Gewurztraminer, New World Riesling or a good Chablis.

**Orange**

**Caramelized Oranges** Asti Spumante, Sauternes.

**Carrot and Orange Soup** Madeira or perhaps an Amontillado sherry.

**Crepes Suzette** Sweet Champagne, Moscato d'Asti.

**Orange Zest** Dry Muscat, Amontillado sherry.

**Roast Duck with Orange Sauce** Loire red, or surprisingly a sweet white like Vouvray demi-sec.

**Oregano** Provençal reds, red Lambrusco, or more serious Chianti.

**Oxtail** Australian Cabernet, good Bordeaux.

**Oyster sauce**

**Beef and Mangetout in Oyster Sauce** Crisp dry whites like Muscadet, or a Northern Italian Lugana or Pinot Bianco, white Rhône, Gewürztraminer.

**Oysters** Champagne, Chablis or other crisp dry white.

# P

**Paprika**

**Goulash** Eastern European red, Bulgarian Cabernet or Mavrud, Hungarian Kadarka or Aussie Shiraz.

**Parmesan** Salice Salentino, Valpolicella.

**Baked Chicken Parmesan with Basil** Chenin Blanc, Riesling.

**Tagiatelle Carbonara** Pinot Grigio or a fresh red Bardolino or Beaujolais.

**Parsley** Dry Italian whites – Bianco di Custoza, Nebbiolo or Barbera.

**Parsley Sauce** Pinot Grigio, Hungarian Fürmint, lightly oaked Cardonnay.

**Trout with Lemon Parsley Butter** Hunter Valley Semillon, New World Riesling.

**Partridge**

**Roast Partridge** Australian Shiraz, Gevrey-Chambertin, Pomerol or St. Emilion.

**Pasta**

**Lasagne** Valpolicella, Barbera, Teroldego, Australian Verdelho or Sauvignon.

**Pasta with a Seafood Sauce** Soave, Sancerre.

**Pasta with Meat Sauce** Chianti, Bordeaux Rouge.

**Pasta with Pesto Sauce** New Zealand Sauvignon Blanc, Valpolicella.

**Ravioli with Spinach and Ricotta** Pinot Bianco/Grigio, Cabernet d'Anjou.

**Spaghetti with Tomato Sauce** Californian Cabernet, Zinfandel, Chianti.

**Spaghetti Vongole** Pinto Bianco, Lugano.

**Spinach/Pasta Bakes** Soft, fruity Italian reds – Bardolino, Lambrusco or rich tasty whites.

**Tagliatelle Carbonara** Pinot Grigio or a fresh red Bardolino or Beaujolais.

**Peach** Sweet German Riesling.

**Peaches in Wine** Riesling Auslese, Riesling / Gewurztraminer Vendange Tardive, sweet Vouvray.

**Peanuts**

**Beef in Peanut Curry** New World Chardonnay, or a spicy aromatic white Rhône.

**Satay** Gewürztraminer.

**Pepper (corns)**

**Steak au Poivre** Cabernet Sauvignon, Chianti, Rhône reds, Shiraz or a Rioja.

**Peppers (fresh green, red)** New Zealand Cabernet, Loire reds, crisp Sauvignon Blanc, Beaujolais, Tuscan red.

**Peppers (yellow)** Fruity Italian reds, Valpolicella, etc.

**Stuffed Peppers** Hungrian red – Bulls Blood, Chianti or spicy Rhône reds.

**Pheasant** Top-class red Burgundy, good American Pinot Noir, mature Hermitage.

**Pheasant Casserole** Top class red Burgundy, mature Hermitage.

**Pheasant Paté** Côtes du Rhône, Alsace Pinot Blanc

**Pigeon** Good red Burgundy; rich Southern Rhône. Chianti also goes well.

**Warm Pigeon Breasts on Salad** Merlot-based Bordeaux or Cabernet Rosé.

**Pike** Eastern European white.

**Pine Nuts**

**Pesto Sauce** New Zealand Sauvignon Blanc, Valpolicella.

**Plaice** White Burgundy, South American Chardonnay, Sauvignon Blanc.

**Plum**

**Plum Pie** Trockenbeerenauslese, Côteaux du Layon.

**Pork**

**Cassoulet** Serious white Rhône, Marsanne or Roussanne, or reds including Grenache and Syrah from the Rhône, crunchy Italian reds or Zinfandel.

**Pork Casserole** Mid-weight, earthy reds like Minervois, Navarra or Montepulciano d'Abruzzo.

**Pork Casserole with Tomatoes** Chablis, Côtes du Rhône

**Pork Pie** Spicy reds, Shiraz, Grenache.

**Pork Rillettes** Pinot Blanc d'Alsace, Menetou-Salon Rouge.

**Pork Sausages** Spicy Rhône reds, Barbera.

**Pork and Sage Sausages** Barbera, Côtes du Rhône.

**Pork Spare Ribs** Zinfandel, Aussie Shiraz.

**Roast Pork** Rioja reserva, New World Pinot Noir, dry Vouvray.

**Roast Pork with Apple Sauce** Off-dry Vouvray or Riesling.

**Saucisson Sec** Barbera, Cabernet Franc, Alsace Pinot Blanc.

**Spare Ribs with Barbecue Sauce** Fruity Australian Shiraz, Grenache or Zinfandel, spicy Côtes du Rhône from a ripe vintage, or an off-dry white.

**Szechuan-Style Pork** Dry aromatic whites, Alsace Pinot Gris, Riesling, Grenache Rosé, beer.

**Prawns** White Bordeaux, dry Australian Riesling, Gavi.

**Avocado with Prawns** Champagne, Riesling Kabinett, Sauvignon, Pinot Gris, Australian Chardonnay.

**Prawn Cocktail** Light fruity whites – German Riesling.

**Prawn Vol-au-Vents** White Bordeaux, Muscadet.

**Thai Prawns** Gewürztraminer, dry aromatic Riesling or New Zealand Sauvignon Blanc.

**Prunes** Australian Late Harvest Semillon.

**Pork with Prunes and Cream** Sweet Chenin-based wines or good Mosel Spätlese.

**Rabbit in Red Wine with Prunes** Good mature Chinon or other Loire red.

# Q

**Quail** Light red Burgundy, full-flavoured white Spanish wines.

**Quince** Lugana.

**Braised Venison with Quince Jelly.** Rich and fruity Australian or Chilean reds, good ripe Spanish Rioja, or a Southern French red.

# R

**Rabbit** Tasty, simple young Rhône, red, white or rosé.

**Rabbit Casserole** New World Pinot Noir or mature Châteauneuf-du-Pape.

**Rabbit Casserole with tomato** Aussie Shiraz, Portuguese red or Cahors.

**Rabbit in Cider** Muscadet, demi-sec Vouvray, cider or Calvados.

**Rabbit with Mustard** Franken wine or Czech Pilsner beer.

**Rabbit in Red Wine with Prunes** Good mature Chinon or other Loire red.

**Raspberries** New World Late Harvest Riesling or Champagne, Beaujolais, demi-sec Champagne.

**Raspberry Fool** Vouvray Moelleux.

**Summer Pudding** Late Harvest Riesling, German or Alsace.

**Raspberry Vinegar** Full-bodied Pinot Noir.

**Warm Bacon and Sorrel Salad** New World Sauvignon Blanc, California Fumé Blanc, or a good Pouilly Fumé.

**Redcurrant**

**Cumberland Sauce** Rioja, Australian Shiraz.

**Red Mullet** Dry rosé, New World Chardonnay, Sauvignon Blanc.

**Rhubarb**

**Rhubarb Pie** Moscato d'Asti, Alsace or Austrian Late Harvest Riesling.

**Rice**

**Rice Pudding** Monbazillac, sweet Muscat.

**Risotto with Fungi Porcini** Top-notch Piedmontese reds – mature Barbera or Barbaresco, young Barbera, Chianti, smoky Rhône reds.

**Rocket** Lugana, Pinot Blanc.

**Roquefort** The classic match is Sauternes – sweet wine goes very well with strong, creamy blue cheese.

**Rosemary** Light red Burgundy or Pinot Noir.

**Roast Lamb with Garlic and Rosemary** Earthy soft reds like California Petite Sirah, Rioja or Zinfandel.

**Rum**

**Flambéed Banana with Rum** Jurançon, Tokaji, Pedro Ximénez sherry, rum.

# S

**Saffron** Dry whites especially Chardonnay.

**Bass in Saffron Sauce** Riesling (German, Australian or Austrian), Viognier.

**Paella with Seafood** White Penedés, unoaked Rioja, Navarra, Provence rosé.

**Sage** Chianti, or country reds from the Languedoc.

**Pork and Sage Sausages** Barbera, Côtes du Rhône.

**Roast Chicken, Goose or Turkey with Sage and Onion Stuffing** Italian reds, especially Chianti, soft, plummy Merlots, sweetly fruity Rioja and brambly Zinfandel.

**Salami** Good beefy Mediterranean rosé, Sardinian red, Rhône red, Zinfandel, drily aromatic Hungarian white.

**Salmon**

**Carpaccio of Salmon** Cabernet Franc, Chardonnay. Australian reds, red Loire, Portuguese reds, Puligny-Montrachet.

**Gravadlax** Ice cold vodka, Pinot Gris or Akvavit.

**Poached Salmon** Chablis, good white Burgundy, other Chardonnay, Alsace Muscat, white Bordeaux.

**Poached Salmon with Hollandaise.** Muscat, Riesling, good Chardonnay.

**Salmon Paté** Best white Burgundy.

**Salmon Trout** Light Pinot Noir from the Loire, New Zealand, good dry unoaked Chardonnay, Chablis, etc.

**Sardines** Fresh Muscadet, Vinho Verde, very light and fruity reds such as Loire, Gamay.

**Scallops** Chablis and other unoaked Chardonnay

**Coquilles St-Jacques** White Burgundy.

**Marinated Scallops with Bacon** Fino sherry or mature Riesling.

**Scallops Mornay** White Burgundy, Riesling Spätlese.

**Sea bass** Good white Burgundy.

**Bass in Saffron Sauce** Riesling (German, Austrian or Australian), Viognier.

**Seafood (general – see individual entries)**

**Paella with Seafood** White Penedés, unoaked Rioja, Navarra, Provence Rosé.

**Pasta with a Seafood Sauce** Soave, Sancerre.

**Platter of Seafood** Sancerre, Muscadet.

**Seafood Salad** Soave, Pinot Grigio, Muscadet, lightly oaked Chardonnay.

**Sesame Seeds.** Oaked Chardonnay.

**Shrimps** Albariño, Sancerre, New World Sauvignon, Arneis.

**Potted Shrimps** New World Chardonnay, Marsanne.

**Skate** Bordeaux white, Côtes de Gascogne, Pinot Bianco.
**Smoked Salmon** Chablis, Alsace Pinot Gris, white Bordeaux.
**Avocado and Smoked Salmon** Lightly oaked Chardonnay.
**Smoked Salmon Paté** English oaked Fumé Blanc; New Zealand Chardonnay.
**Smoked Trout**
**Smoked Trout Paté** Good white Burgundy.
**Snapper** Australian or South African dry white.
**Sorbet** Like ice cream, too cold/sweet for most wines. Try fortified Muscats.
**Sorrel** Dry Loire Chenin or Sauvignon Blanc.
**Warm Bacon and Sorrel Salad** New World Sauvignon Blanc, California Fumé Blanc, or a good Pouilly Fumé.
**Soy sauce** Zinfandel or Australian Verdelho.
**Spinach** Pinot Grigio, Lugana.
**Eggs Florentine** Unoaked Chardonnay, Pinot Blanc, Aligoté, Sémillon.
**Ravioli with Spinach and Ricotta** Pinot Bianco/Grigio, Cabernet d'Anjou.
**Spinach/Pasta Bakes** Soft, fruity Italian reds (Bardolino, Lambrusco); rich whites.
**Spring Rolls** Pinot Gris, Gewürztraminer or other aromatic whites.
**Squid** Gamay de Touraine, Greek or Spanish white.
**Squid in Batter** Crisp and neutral dry white – Muscadet.
**Squid in Ink** Nebbiolo or Barbera.
**Stilton** Tawny port.
**Strawberry – no Cream** Surprisingly, red Rioja, Burgundy (or other young Pinot Noir), especially if the berries are marinaded. More conventionally, sweet Muscats or fizzy Moscato.
**Strawberries and Cream** Vouvray Moelleux, Monbazillac.
**Strawberry Meringue** Late Harvest Riesling.
**Strawberry Mousse** Sweet or fortified Muscat.
**Swede** Alsace Pinot Gris, unoaked Chablis.
**Sweet and Sour dishes (general)** Gewürztraminer or beer.
**Sweetbreads** Lightly oaked Chardonnay, Chablis, Pouilly-Fuissé, or light red Bordeaux.
**Sweetbread in Mushroom, Butter and Cream sauce** Southern French whites, Vin de Pays, Chardonnay.
**Sweetcorn** Rich and ripe whites – California Chardonnay.
**Corn on the Cob** Light fruity whites – German Riesling.
**Sweetcorn Soup with Chicken** Chilean Sauvignon, Southern French whites, Soave, Chilean Merlot.
**Sweetcorn Soup with Crab** Sancerre, other Sauvignon Blanc.

# T

**Taramasalata** Oaked Chardonnay or English Fumé Blanc.
**Tarragon** White Menetou-Salon or South African Sauvignon Blanc.
**Roast/grilled Chicken with Tarragon** Dry Chenin Blanc, Vouvray, South African whites.
**Thyme** Ripe and fruity Provençal reds, Rioja, Northern Italian whites.
**Roast Lamb with Thyme** New Zealand Cabernet Sauvignon, Bourgeuil.
**Toffee** Moscatel de Setúbal, Eiswein.
**Banoffee Pie** Sweet Tokaji.
**Tomato**
**Gazpacho** Fino sherry, white Rioja.
**Pasta in a Tomato Sauce** Californian Cabernet, Zinfandel, Chianti.
**Pizza** Barbera, Aussie Shiraz or Zinfandel.
**Pork Casserole with Tomatoes** Chablis, Côtes du Rhône.
**Tomato Ketchup** Aussie Shiraz, Californian Zinfandel, Beaujolais.
**Tomato Soup** Sauvignon Blanc.

**Tongue** Rich and tasty reds from Southern France and Italy.
**Tripe** Earthy French country red, Minervois, Cahors, Fitou.
**Trout** Pinot Blanc, Chablis.
**Smoked Trout** Bourgogne Aligoté, Gewürztraminer, Pinot Gris.
**Trout with Almonds** Bianco di Custoza, Pinot Blanc.
**Trout with Lemon Parsley Butter** Hunter Valley Semillon, New World Riesling.
**Truffles** Red Burgundy, old Rioja, Barolo, Hermitage.
**Tuna**
**Carpaccio of Tuna** Australian Chardonnay, red Loire, Beaujolais.
**Fresh Tuna** Alsace Pinot Gris, Australian Chardonnay, Beaujolais.
**Tinned Tuna** New World dry, fruity whites, Côtes de Gascogne.
**Turbot** Best white Burgundy, top California or Australian Chardonnay.
**Turkey**
**Roast Turkey** Beaujolais light Burgundy and quite rich or off-dry whites.
**Roast Turkey with Chestnut Stuffing** Côtes du Rhône, Merlot, or soft and mature Burgundy.

**Vanilla** Liqueur Muscat.
**Crème Brulée** Jurançon Moelleux, Tokaji.
**Custard** Monbazillac, sweet Vouvray.
**Veal**
**Blanquette de Veau** Aromatic, spicy whites from Alsace.
**Roast veal** Light Italian whites, Pinot Bianco, etc, or fairly light reds – Spanish or Loire.
**Saltimbocca (Escalope with Mozzarella and Ham)** Flavoursome, dry Italian whites, Lugana, Bianco di Custoza, Orvieto.
**Wienerschnitzel** Austrian or Hungarian white – Grüner Veltliner, Pinot Blanc.
**Vegetable Soup** Most full but unoaked dry whites like Pinot Blanc, or uncomplicated rustic reds such as Corbières.
**Vegetable Terrine** Good New World Chardonnay.
**Venison** Pinotage, Châteauneuf-du-Pape, mature Hermitage, Côte Rôtie; mature Burgundy, earthy Italian reds (Barolo, Brunello di Montalcino).
**Venison Casserole** Shiraz-based Australians, American Zinfandel, Cape red.
**Vinegar**
**Choucroute Garnie** White Alsace (Riesling, Pinot Blanc, Pinot Gris), or Italian Pinot Grigio. For red, try a Beaujolais.
**Sauerkraut** Pilsner beer.
**Vinegar – Balsamic** Recioto della Valpolicella.

**Walnut** Tawny port, sweet Madeira.
**Watercress**
**Watercress Soup** Aromatic dry Riesling (Alsace or Australia).
**Whelks** Vinho Verde, crisp Loire whites.
**Whitebait** Fino sherry, Spanish red/white (Garnacha, Tempranillo), Soave.
**Woodcock** Fine Cru Classé Bordeaux; good Graves; gamey old Pinot Noir.
**Worcestershire Sauce**
**Devilled Chicken** Australian Shiraz.

# A PERSONAL SELECTION

Of the thousands of wines I have tasted this year, these, for various reasons, are some of my favourites. Prices are rounded to the nearest pound. (For stockists, see page 239.)

## RED WINES FOR UNDER £5

**NV Dom. Cigogne** £3 (Victoria Wine, see page 253) Just when you begin to think that the wine world is all mapped out, along comes this characterful berryish young wine from Morocco.

**1992 Etchart Cabernet Sauvignon** £5 (Thresher, see page 252) Juicy, blackcurranty Cabernet to prove that Argentina can compete with Chile and Australia.

**1996 Sliven Young Vatted Cabernet** £3 (Safeway, see page 251) A Bulgarian bargain, packed with crunchy fruit. Great for parties.

**1994 Cathedral Cellars Merlot** £3 (Gordon & McPhail, see page 245) Evidence of improving winemaking from South Africa's biggest winery. Good, plummy Merlot.

**1996 Viña La Palma Merlot** £4 (Waitrose, see page 254) From La Rosa, one of Chile's names to watch, this is a lovely plummy, mulberryish wine with a hint of spice.

**1995 Piccini Chianti Classico Riserva** £4 (Asda, see page 240) Modern Chianti, with plenty of fruit to go with its characteristic flavours of herbs and tobacco.

**1996 Dr Abbott's Shiraz** £5 (Victoria Wine, see page 253) A tasty, smoky Australian-made wine with an Aussie-sounding name from Languedoc Roussillon in France. What is the world coming to?

**1996 Bright Brothers Douro Red** £5 (Thresher, see page 252) Another Australia-European, this time showing off the dark blueberrish flavours of the Douro in Portugal.

**1996 Peter Lehmann Barossa Valley Grenache** £5 (The Co-operative, see page 243) Rich, spicy, peppery wine from one of the best-value producers in Australia.

**1996 Vin de Crète** £4 (Sainsbury, see page 251) Juicy, modern party wine from Greece, the country you thought could make only Restina and 'Domestos'.

**1995 Four Rivers Cabernet** £5 (Eldridge Pope, see page 244) Sweet, herbaceous, minty wine with ripe blackberry fruit makes this an excellent Chilean alternative to claret.

## Red wines for under £10

**1995 Maglieri McLaren Vale Shiraz** £7 (Tesco, see page 252) Great, intense, berryish wine from an up-and-coming winery in the McLaren Vale, one of Australia's most interesting regions.

**1995 Jacana Ridge Reserve Pinotage** £10 (Safeway, see page 251) Hugh Ryman's Aussie winemakers in South Africa have fully exploited the plummy, spicy potential of this often disappointing variety.

**1996 Brouilly J-P Selles** £7 (Somerfield, see page 252) Boiled sweets and bananas, with a bit of dark chocolate. Beaujolais at its best.

**Valdivieso Caballo Loco No 1** £10 (Waitrose, see page 254) An extraordinary, inventive Chilean success: a rich, complex summer pudding blend of Bordeaux grape varieties and vintages.

**1995 Plaisir de Merle Cabernet Sauvignon** £10 (Majestic, see page 248) Rich, blackcurranty wine with sweet oak made in new South African winery by Paul Pontallier of Château Margaux.

**1995 Te Mata Estate Cabernet/Merlot** £9 (Edward Sheldon, see page 251) Intense, subtly oaked blackcurrant and blueberryish wine from New Zealand's top red producer.

**1995 Cosme Palacio** £6 (Waitrose, see page 254) Top class, flavoursome, strawberryish Rioja, made with the help of Bordeaux superstar, Michel Rolland.

**1991 Ch. Beau Site, Bordeaux** £10 (Cellars Direct, see page 242) Gently classy maturing claret at a very fair price.

**1993 Penfolds Bin 407** £8 (Unwins, see page 253) Stylish Australian Cabernet, with flavours of blackcurrant pastilles and sweet vanilla oak.

**1995 Carmen Grande Vidure** £6 (Oddbins, see page 249) A chance from Chile to taste the smoky-spicy, berryish Carmenère grape that once played a major part in Bordeaux.

**1995 Dom. Hatzimichalis Cabernet** £8 (Greek Wine Centre, see page 245) From Greece's one world-class winemaker, this great, deep, dark wine tastes of blueberries and sweet oak.

**1995 Fetzer Valley Oaks Cabernet** £6 (Waitrose, see page 254) Lovely ripe, rich Californian wine with bags of blackcurrant.

**1996 Coldstream Hills Pinot Noir** £10 (Oddbins, see page 249) Made by Australia's leading wine critic, this is a serious, raspberryish, New World alternative to red Burgundy.

**1995 Faugeres Les Jardins** £6 (Adnams, see page 240) Classy Southern French red, combining rich fruit with a hint of game.

**1996 Dom. Richaud Côtes du Rhône Villages** £7 (Hoults, see page 247) Served blind, this peppery, spicy stuff would pass for a wine selling at twice this price.

## Red wines for special occasions

**1994 Umani Ronchi Pelago** £17 (Noel Young Wines, see page 255) Ultra-classy modern Italian, proving that the Marches can compete with the best of Tuscany.

**1982 Ch. Caronne St Gemme** £22 (Nicolas, see page 249) Defying the critics who thought this vintage in Bordeaux too good to be true, this Cru Bourgeois is lovely subtle, cedary stuff.

**1990 Psaume Pomerol** £19 (Nicolas, see page 249) Made by Christian Moueix of Petrus and Dominus, this is great modern Pomerol from a really ripe year. Gorgeous, spicy and rich.

**1989 Jacaranda Ridge Cabernet** £18 (Unwins, see page 253) Gorgeous, blackcurranty Cabernet with spicy oak. Big, but not a blockbuster.

**1993 Opus One** £65 (Harvey Nichols, see page 246) A pricy but delicious blend of Californian and Bordeaux expertise. Intensely blackcurranty, with a lovely lingering finish.

**E & E Pepper Shiraz** £23 (Edward Sheldon, see page 251) Coming up on the inside to challenge Australia's greatest Shirazes, this is lovely spicy, smoky stuff.

**1995 Font de Michelle Châteauneuf-du-Pape** £12 (Bottoms Up, see page 241) Freshly ground pepper on strawberries. Good young Châteauneuf at its best.

**1993 Marimar Torres Pinot Noir** £16 (Pallant Wines, see page 249) While Miguel Torres has been making wine in Spain and Chile, his sister has produced some great wine in California.

**1993 Côtes du Rosa – Joseph Swan** £10 (Raeburn Fine Wines, see page 250) A brillant blend of berries and spice from a great little California winery.

**1995 Clos de l'Arlot, Nuits St Georges, Forets St Georges** £22 (Anthony Byrne, see page 242) Beauifully made Burgundy with flavours of raspberries and black cherries.

**1994 Caymus Cabernet Sauvignon** £18 (Direct Wines, see page 243) Top class, ultra-blackcurranty Californian wine with flavour to spare.

**1994 Barbera d'Alba Vignasse Del Pozzo R Voerzio** £16 (Valvona & Crolla, see page 253) Wild berries galore, plus some sweet new oak. Piedmont at its most exciting.

**1988 Santa Rita Casa Real** £11 (Oddbins, see page 249) Chile's top red wine. Glorious, intense, blackcurranty stuff.

**1992 Umathum Von Stein St Laurent** £17 (T.&W. Wines, see page 252) Lovely raspberryish wine made from the St Laurent, Austria's delicious answer to Pinot Noir.

**1985 Domaine de Chevalier** £35 (Oddbins, see page 249) A perfect example of a subtle red Graves that is just beginning to show signs of cherryish and cedary maturity.

## White wine for under £5

**1996 Moyston Unoaked Chardonnay** £5 (Great Northern Wine Company, see page 245) Australian white wines are not all packed with the flavour of new oak barrels, as this pineappley effort proves.

**Tenterden Estate Dry** £5 (Tesco, see page 252) An unusually successful – and fairly priced – English wine with a mouth-watering flavour to compete with dry wines from the Loire.

**1995 Magryede Oaked Pinot Gris** £4 (Oddbins, see page 249) An unusual combination of this spicy grape variety with vanilla oak. The shape of the future from Hungary?

**1996 Amethytos Fumé** £5 (Greek Wine Centre, see page 245) The label says "a wine of Drama". That's the region in Greece where this fresh, oaky, aspargussy Sauvignon was made.

**1996 Domaine Salices Sauvignon** £5 (Oddbins, see page 249) The combination of Australian expertise and the climate of Southern France are paying off well. Subtly gooseberryish.

**1996 La Domeque Tête De Cuvée Vieilles Vignes.** £5 (Asda, see page 240) Subtly aromatic wine from Languedoc Roussillon, made by blending Muscat with the other white grape varieties of the Rhône.

**1996 Waterside White** £5 (Safeway, see page 251) A flavoursome appley exception to the rule of lightweight, anonymous-tasting South African whites.

**1996 River Route Pinot Grigio** £3 (The Co-operative, see page 243) Modern, fresh, Italian-style white from Romania, with a mixture of pears and spice.

**1996 Casa Leona Chardonnay** £4 (Marks & Spencer, see page 248) Great, subtly fruit-salady wine from one of the best wineries in Chile.

**1996 Oxford Landing Chardonnay** £5 (Majestic, see page 248) Unabashed Aussie Chardonnay, with flavours of fruit salad and sweet oak. A delicious mouthful.

**1996 Arniston Bay Chenin Blanc/Chardonnay** £4 (Thresher, see page 252) Good easy-going appley, melony stuff, showing the new wave of wine-making in South Africa.

**1996 Philipe de Baudin Sauvignon** £5 (Sainsbury, see page 251) A consistent gooseberrish winner, made by a subsidiary of the Australian giant, BRL Hardy, in Southern France.

**1996 Trio Chardonnay** £5 (Thresher, see page 252) Another Chilean success from superstar winemaker Ignacio Recabaren. Lovely tropical wine.

**1996 Chardonnay Cuvée Australienne** £4 (Majestic, see page 248) A prime example of new and old world wine-making in Languedoc Rousillon.

## WHITE WINE FOR UNDER £10

**1996 Arneis delle Langhe, Alasia** £7 (Valvona & Crolla, see page 253) Lovely spicy, floral wine from one of the most characterful grape varieties in north-west Italy.

**1994 Chablis 'Cuvée la Chablisienne'** £8 (Great Northern Wine Co, see page 245) Classic white Burgundy, combining butter and steel, but without the usual note of oaky vanilla.

**1994 Orlando St Hilary Chardonnay** £8 (D Byrne, see page 242) New-wave Aussie Chardonnay, with the fruit and oak in perfect balance.

**1996 Montes Alpha Special Cuvée Chardonnay** £9 (Hedley Wright, see page 246) Rich, buttery but really classy wine from one of the top producers in Chile.

**1996 Pra Soave Classico** £7 (Booths of Stockport, see page 241) If you thought Soave was dull stuff to quaff in pizzerias, this almondy single-vineyard example could change your life.

**1996 Ch. de Lancyre 'La Rouvière'** £8 (Tesco, see page 252) Creamy, gently spicy modern wine from Southern France.

**1996 Villa Maria Reserve Sauvignon Blanc** £10 (Wine Rack, see page 255) New Zealand Sauvignon with style. Gooseberries with fresh whipped cream!

**1996 Dom. Pinard Sancerre** £9 (Anthony Byrne, see page 242) Beautifully made wine from one of the most reliable producers in Sancerre. Steel and ripe, appley fruit.

**1994 Lingenfelder Freinsheimer Riesling Halbstrocken** £8 (James Nicholson, see page 249) Subtly off-dry, with beautiful Riesling appley fruit and a hint of spice.

**1996 Vouvray Sec, Champalou** £7 (Just-in-Case, see page 247) Ripe honeyed-yet-dry Chenin Blanc from a star winemaker.

**1994 Grans Fassian Riesling Piesporter Goldtröpchen** £6 (Spar, see page 252) Bargain of the year? Proof anyway that this much-abused name can appear on pure appley-peary wine.

**1994 Casablanca Santa Isabel Estate Chardonnay** £9 (Moreno Wine Importers, see page 248) From Chile's newest, most exciting white wine region. Pure peachy Chardonnay.

**1995 Ch. du Seuil Graves Sec** £10 (Direct Wines, see page 243) Beautifully made peachy, gooseberryish, subtly oaked wine from a British-owned château.

**1995 St. Véran, Dom. des Valanges** £8 (Berry Bros & Rudd, see page 241) A fine example of Southern Burgundy. Creamy, with hazelnut richness.

**1995 Albariño Pazo De Barrantes** £10 (Holland Park Wine Co., see page 247) Lovely floral-spicy wine from the north-west of Spain.

## WHITE WINES FOR SPECIAL OCCASIONS

**1995 Gewurztraminer 'Himbourg' Dom. Zind-Humbrecht** £18 (Anthony Byrne, see page 242) A perfect, lycheeish example of this grape. Made by a master craftsman.

**1995 Meursault, les Narvaux, Pierre Morey** £19 (Howard Ripley, see page 250) Perfect modern Burgundy with hazelnuts and really subtle oak.

**1995 Meursault Clos de la Barre** £26 (Morris & Verdin, see page 249) An impeccably buttery yet restrained example of this appellation. Worth keeping.

**1995 Petaluma Chardonnay** £12 (Oddbins, see page 249) Arguably the most consistent Australian Chardonnay, and certainly the one that best bridges the gap between Old and New Worlds.

**1996 Te Mata Elston Chardonnay** £13 (Adnams, see page 240) New Zealand Chardonnay at its subtlest and classiest. Guava and buttered nuts.

**1994 E&J Gallo Sonoma Stefani Vineyard Chardonnay** £12 (Selfridges, see page 251) A fine Chardonnay from E&J Gallo would have been unimaginable a few years ago. This one is good melony, oaky stuff.

**1995 Torres Milmanda** £15 (Majestic, see page 248) Lovely rich, peachy Chardonnay from Spain with perfectly balanced oak.

### LATE HARVEST

**1989 Dom. Koehly Gewurztraminer Grand Cru Altenberg Vendanges Tardives** £20 (Hedley Wright, see page 246) Perfect, floral wine with honeyed richness.

**1990 Ch. Loubans Ste Croix du Mont** £17 (Lay & Wheeler, see page 247) Lovely honeyed, apricotty wine to beat many a Sauternes.

**1995 Ch. des Charmes Late Harvest Riesling** £9 (Great Northern Wine Co., see page 245) A top-class Canadian example of rich, appley wine.

**1979 Beerenauslese Burgstadt, Dürnstein, Freie Weingartener Wachau** £9 half (John Harvey, see page 246) Wonderful, concentrated, peachy wine from Austria.

**1995 Denbies Late Harvest** £6 half (Oddbins, see page 249) A pretty, peachy, well balanced wine from Surrey.

**1993 Blue Label Aszu 5 Putts, Royal Tokaji Wine Co.** £20 half (Lea & Sandeman, see page 248) Old English marmalade! One of the great flavours of the world.

**1990 Vouvray Moëlleux 'le Haut Lieu', Huët** £29 (Waitrose, see page 254) Honey and baked apples. Lovely wine from a master of the style.

## PINK, SPARKLING AND FORTIFIED

### ROSÉ

**1996 Paradines, Dom. Henry** £6 (Adnams, see page 240) Distinctive, fresh berryish wine from Southern France.

**1995 Château de Marsannay Rosé** £10 (Nicolas, see page 249) A rare chance to taste pink wine from Burgundy. Rich and raspberryish.

### FIZZ

**Hunters Miru Miru** £13 (Majestic, see page 248) Creamy, rich New Zealand wine with lovely Chardonnay pineapple flavours.

**Albert Etienne** £13 (Safeway, see page 251) One of the most reliable own-label Champagnes on the market.

**1993 Croser** £12 (Oddbins, see page 249) Probably the best New World fizz I've had all year. Made by Australian wine guru, Brian Croser.

**1989 Veuve Clicquot** £32 (Victoria Wine, see page 253) Big, concentrated Champagne. Enjoy now or keep for the Millennium.

**Brown Brothers Pinot Noir & Chardonnay** £11 (Unwins, see page 253) One of Australia's best-known producers has suddenly mastered fizz. Lovely subtly, fruity stuff.

**Alfred Gratien Champagne** £20 (Sainsbury, see page 251) Good value, traditional, Champagne from a little-known producer.

**Moët & Chandon Brut Impérial** £20 (Thresher, see page 252) The best-known, and currently one of the best.

### FORTIFIED

**Sandeman Royal Corregidor Rare Rich Oloroso** £10 (Oddbins, see page 249) Great, intense, dark, dry, raisiny sherry – the way the Spaniards love it.

**Gonzalez Byass Noë** £20 (Oddbins, see page 249) Brilliant molasses-like stuff to sip at or to pour over good vanilla ice cream.

**1989 Ramos Pinto Late Bottled Vintage Port** £12 (Haynes, Hanson & Clarke, see page 246) An unusually classy example of this style. Plummy and rich.

**1985 Churchill's Vintage Port** £26 (Smedley Vintners, see page 252) Classic maturing vintage port with plenty of further potential.

**Stanton & Killeen Rutherglen Muscat** £6 (Sandiway Wine Co., see page 251) Lovely liquid Dundee cake and Christmas pud.

**Blandy's Ten-Year-Old Malmsey** £16 (Waitrose, see page 254) Marmalade, walnuts and figs are the flavours here. Rich yet refreshing.

# A–Z *of* Wine

## HOW TO READ THE ENTRIES

*Names of wines are accompanied by a glass symbol (🍷); grape varieties by a bunch of grapes (🍇). Wine regions appear in a green band.*

*Words that have their own entry elsewhere in the A–Z appear in italics.*

*Poor vintages are not listed. Good vintages, ready to drink now, are featured in bold; good vintages that will improve with keeping are in green.*

🍷 **Ch. l'Angélus** [lon jay-loos] (*St. Emilion Grand Cru Classé, Bordeaux,* France) Lovely, plummy *St .Emilion* to watch: classy, if sometimes too showily oaked. The *Second Label* Carillon d'Angélus is also well worth seeking out. 79 82 **83 85 86 87** 88 89 90 92 93 94 95 96 ☆☆☆☆☆ **1990 ££££** ☆☆☆ **1991 £££**

*Throughout this section, examples are given of recommended producers and wines which represent the best examples of the region, style or maker.*

*Recommended wines are accompanied by stars.*
*☆☆☆☆☆ = outstanding in their style*
*☆☆☆☆ = excellent in their style*

*Prices are indicated, using the following symbols:*

| | |
|---|---|
| **£** | *Under £5* |
| **££** | *£5–10* |
| **£££** | *£10–20* |
| **££££** | *Over £20* |

## PRONUNCIATION GUIDE

All but the most common words are followed by square [ ] brackets, which enclose pronunciation guides. These use the 'sounding-out' phonetic method, with the accented syllable (if there is one) indicated by capital letters. For example, **Spätlese** is pronounced as *SHPAYT-Lay-Zuh.* The basic sounds employed in this book's pronunciations are as follows:

| | | | |
|---|---|---|---|
| **a** as in **can** | **ah** as in **father** | **ay** as in **day** | **ur** as in **turn** |
| **ch** as in **church** | **kh** as in **loch** | **y** as in **yes** | **zh** as in **vision** |
| **ee** as in **see** | **eh** as in **get** | **g** as in **game** | **i** as in **pie** |
| **ih** as in **if** | **j** as in **gin** | **k** as in **cat** | **o** as in **hot** |
| **oh** as in **soap** | **oo** as in **food** | **ow** as in **cow** | **uh** as in **up** |

Foreign sounds: eu is like a cross between oo and a; an italicised n or m is silent and the preceding vowel sounds nasal; an ñ is like an n, followed by a y (as in Bourgogne); an italicsed r sounds like a cross between r and w; rr sounds like a rolled r.

*Abboccato* [ah-boh-kah-toh] (Italy) Semi-dry.
*Abfüller/Abfüllung* [ab-few-ler/ Ab-few-lerng] (Germany) Bottler/bottled by.
*Abocado* [ah-boh-KAH-doh] (Spain) Semi-dry.

**Abruzzi/zzo** [ah-broot-zee/zoh] (Italy) Region on the east coast, with often dull *Trebbiano* whites and fast-improving *Montepulciano* reds. **Barone Cornacchia; Cantina Tollo.**

*AC* (France) See *Appellation Contrôlée.*

🍷 **Acacia** [a-kay-shah] (*Carneros,* California) One of California's best producers of *Chardonnay* and *Pinot Noir.* Under the same ownership as the similarly excellent *Chalone, Edna Valley* and *Carmenet.* ☆☆☆☆ **1995 Carneros Chardonnay £££**

*Acetic acid* [ah-see-tihk] This volatile acid (CH3COOH) features in tiny proportions in all wines. Careless winemaking can result in wine being turned into acetic acid, a substance most people know as vinegar.

***Acidity*** Naturally occuring (*tartaric* and *malic*) acids in the grapes are vital to contributing freshness and also help to preserve the wine while it ages. In cool regions, the malic is often converted to lactic by a natural process known as malolactic fermentation, which gives the wines a buttery texture and flavour. In hotter countries (and sometimes cooler ones) the acid level may (not always legally) be adjusted by adding *tartaric* and *citric* acid.

**Aconcagua Valley** [ah-kon-kar-gwah] (*Central Valley*, Chile) Region noted for blackcurranty *Cabernet Sauvignon*. The sub-region is *Casablanca*. Grapes from both are used by many Chilean producers. ***Errazuriz***.

**Tim Adams** (*Clare Valley*, Australia) Highly successful producer of *Riesling*, rich, peachy *Semillon* and deep-flavoured *Shiraz* and now the intense peppery Fergus. ☆☆☆☆☆ **1995 Aberfeldy £££**

***Adega*** [ah-day-gah] (Portugal) Winery – equivalent to Spanish *Bodega*.

**Adelaide Hills** [ah-dur-layd] (*South Australia*) Cool, high-altitude region, long known for top-class, lean *Riesling* and *Semillon*; now more famous for *Sauvignon Blanc* and *Chardonnay* from *Ashton Hills*, *Petaluma* and *Shaw & Smith, Pinot Noir*, and sparkling wine such as *Croser*. See also the new region of *Lenswood*. ***Henschke; Mountadam; Heggies.***

**Weingut Graf Adelmann** [graf-eh-del-man] (*Wurttemberg*, Germany) One of the region's best estates, making good red wines from grapes such as the *Trollinger*, Lemberger and Urban. Look for Brüssele'r Spitze wines.

**Age** [ah-khay] (*Rioja*, Spain) Big, modern, highly commercial winery.

**Aglianico** [ah-lee-AH-nee-koh] (Italy) Thick-skinned grape grown by the Ancient Greeks but now more or less restricted to Southern Italy, where it produces dark, hefty *Taurasi* and *Aglianico del Vulture*.

**Aglianico del Vulture** [ah-lee-AH-nee-koh del vool-TOO-reh] (*Basilicata*, Italy) Tannic, liquoricey-chocolatey blockbusters made on the hills of an extinct volcano. **D'Angelo; Casele.**

***Agricola vitivinicola*** (Italy) Wine estate.

**Aguja** [ah-khoo-ha] (*Leon*, Spain) Rare, so-called 'needle' wines, whose slight spritz comes from adding ripe grapes to the fermented wine.

**Ahr** [ahr] (Germany) Northernmost *Anbaugebiet*, making light, red wines.

**Airén** [i-REHN] (Spain) The world's most planted variety. Dull and fortunately more or less restricted to the hot, dry region of La Mancha.

**Ajaccio** [ah-JAK-see-yoh] (*Corsica*, France) One of Corsica's many questionable *Appellations*. The tangily intense reds and oaked whites from *Comte Peraldi* are better than mere holiday fare. **Gie Les Rameaux**.

**Albana di Romagna** [ahl-BAH-nah dee roh-MAN-yah] (*Emilia-Romagna*, Italy) Improving but traditionally dull white wine which, for political reasons, was made Italy's first white *DOCG*, thus making a mockery of the whole Italian system of denominations.

**Albariño** [ahl-BAH-ree-nyoh] (*Galicia*, Spain) The Spanish name for the Portuguese *Alvarinho* grape variety, and the peachy-spicy wine that is made from it in *Rias Baixas, Galicia*. Arguably Spain's best, most interesting, white. **Valdamor; de Barrantes.**

***Alcohol*** Now increasingly the health-conscious person's drug of choice, this is the magic ingredient that first encouraged man to muck around with fizzy grape juice. This simple compound, technically known as ethanol, is formed by the action of yeast on sugar during fermentation, and is responsible for wine's popularity, its balance, preservation and ageability.

**Aleatico** [ah-lay-AH-tee-koh] (Italy) Red grape producing sweet, *Muscat*-style, often fortified wines. Gives name to DOCs A. di Puglia and A. di Gradoli.

**Alella** [ah-LEH-yah] (*Catalonia*, Spain) *DO* district producing better whites (from grapes including the *Xarel-lo)* than reds. ☆☆☆ **1995 Marqués de Alella Clássico £££**

**Alenquer** [ah-lehn-KEHR] (*Oeste*, Portugal) Coolish region producing good reds from the *Periquita* grape and *Muscat*-style whites from the *Fernão Pires*. There are also increasingly successful efforts from some of France's familiar varietals.

**Alentejo** [ah-lehn-TAY-joh] (Portugal) Up-and-coming province north of the Algarve, with good red *Borba*. Australian-born *David Baverstock* produces juicy, red *Esperâo; JM da Fonseca* makes Morgado de Reguengo; and *Peter Bright*, another Aussie, produces the award-winning Tinta da Anfora plus other good examples at J.P. Vinhos. **Borba; Redondo**.

**Alexander Valley** (*Sonoma*, California) Appellation in which *Simi, Jordan, Murphy Goode* and *Geyser Peak* are based. Good for approachable reds. Reds: **86** 89 **90** 91 92 **94** 95 95 96 White: **91 92** 94 95 96

**Algeria** Old-fashioned, mostly red wines made by state-run cooperatives.

**Caves Aliança** [ah-lee-an-sah] (Portugal) Reliable, modern *Bairrada*, *Douro* and better-than-average *Dão*. ☆☆☆ **1994 Dão Particular ££**

**Alicante** (*Valencia*, Spain) Hot region producing generally dull stuff apart from the sweetly honeyed *Moscatels* that appreciate the heat.

**Alicante-Bouschet** [al-ee-KONT- boo-SHAY] Unusual dark-skinned and fleshed grapes traditionally used (usually illegally) for dyeing pallid reds made from nobler fare. *Rockford* uses it to make a good rosé.

**Aligoté** [Al-lee-GOH-tay] (*Burgundy*, France) The region's lesser white grape, making dry, sometimes sharp wine that is traditionally mixed with *cassis* for *Kir*. With loving care and a touch of oak it can imitate basic *Bourgogne* Blanc, especially in the village of *Bouzeron*. Highly-regarded in Eastern Europe. **Aubert de Vilaine, la Digoine.**

**Alion** [ah-lee-yon] (*Ribera del Duero*, Spain) Instantly successful new venture by the owners of *Vega Sicilia*, with oakier, fruitier, more modern wines. ☆☆☆☆☆ **1991 Reserva £££**

**All Saints** (*Rutherglen*, Australia) Good producer of *Liqueur Muscat*, *Tokay* and *Late Harvest* wines.

**Allegrini** [ah-leh-GREE-nee] (*Veneto*, Italy) Go-ahead top-class producer of single-vineyard *Valpolicella* and *Soave*. ☆☆☆☆ **1993 Valpolicella Classico la Grola £££**

**Thierry Allemand** [al-mo*n*] (*Rhône*, France) Producer of classic, concentrated single-vineyard *Cornas* from a tiny 2.5-ha (6-acre) estate. ☆☆☆☆ **1994 Cuvée Reynard £££**

***Allier*** [a-lee-yay] (France) Spicy oak favoured by makers of white wine.

***Almacenista*** [al-mah-theh-nee-stah] (*Jerez*, Spain) Fine old unblended Sherry from a single *Solera* – the *sherry* equivalent of a single malt whisky. ***Lustau***.

**Almansa** [ahl-MAN-suh] (Spain) Warm region noted for softish reds which can be almost black, thanks to the red juice of the grapes used.

**Aloxe-Corton** [a-loss kawr-ton] (*Burgundy*, France) *Côte de Beaune* commune with slow-maturing, majestic, sometimes tough, uninspiring reds (including the *Grand Cru Corton*) and potentially sublime whites (including *Corton Charlemagne*). Invariably pricy *Louis Latour's* whites can be fine. White: **79 85 86** 87 **88** 89 **90 92** 95. Red: **78 85** 86 87 **88 89 90** 92 95 96 **Arnoux; Bonneau du Martray; Drouhin; Jadot; Leflaive; Tollot-Beaut.**

**Alsace** [al-sas] (France) Northerly region whose warm micro-climate enables producers to make riper-tasting wines than their counterparts across the Rhine. Wines are named after the grapes – *Pinot Noir, Gewürztraminer, Riesling, Tokay/Pinot Gris, Pinot Blanc* (known as Pinot d'Alsace), *Sylvaner* and (rarely) *Muscat* In the right hands, the 50 or so *Grand Cru* vineyards should yield better wines. *Late Harvest* off-dry wines are labelled *Vendange Tardive* and *Sélection des Grains Nobles*. References to *Reserve* and Selection Personnelle often mean nothing. **76 79 81** 83 85 86 88 89 90 93 94 95 ***Albert Boxler; Ernest J & F Burn; Jean-Pierre Dirler; Dopff au Moulin; Hugel; Josmeyer; Albert Mann; Mittnacht-Klack; Ostertag; Schlumberger; Charles Schleret; Trimbach; Zind Humbrecht.***

**Elio Altare** [Ehl-lee-yoh al-TAh-ray] (*Piedmont*, Italy) The genial Svengali-like leader of the *Barolo* revolution and inspirer of *Clerico* and *Roberto Voerzio*, who now run him a very close race. ☆☆☆ **1992 Barolo £££**

**Altesino** [al-TEH-see-noh] (*Tuscany*, Italy) First class producers of *Brunello di Montalcino*, oaky *Vino da Tavola Cabernet* ('Palazzo') and *Sangiovese* ('Altesi'). ☆☆☆☆☆ **1990 Brunello di Montalcino Montosoli ££££**

**Alto-Adige** [ahl-toh ah-dee-jay] (Italy) Aka Italian Tyrol and Sudtirol. *DOC* for a range of mainly white wines, often from Germanic grape varieties; also light and fruity reds from the *Lagrein* and Vernatsch. Not living up to its promise of the early 1980's, when it was considered one of the most exciting regions in Europe. ***Alois Lageder; Tiefenbrunner;*** **Viticoltori Alto Adige.**

**Alvarinho** [ahl-vah-reen-yoh] (Portugal) White grape aka *Albariño*; at its lemony best in *Vinho Verde* and in the *DO* Alvarinho de Monção.

***Amabile*** [am-MAH-bee-lay] (Italy) Semi-sweet.

**Amador County** [am-uh-dor] (California) Intensely-flavoured, old-fashioned *Zinfandel*. Look for Amador Foothills Winery's old-vine *Zinfandels* and top-of-the-range stuff from *Sutter Home* and *Monteviña*. Red: **86 87 88** 89 **90** 91 92 94 95 White: **91 92** 94 95 96

***Amarone*** [ah-mah-ROH-neh] (*Veneto*, Italy) Literally 'bitter'; used particularly to describe *Recioto*. Best known as *Amarone della Valpolicella*. ***Quintarelli, Tedeschi; Allegrini.***

**Amberley Estate** [am-buhr-lee] (*Western Australia*) Young estate with a good *Semillon* and *Cabernet-Merlot* blend.

**Bodegas Amézola de la Mora** [ah-meh-THOH-lah deh lah MAW-rah] (*Rioja*, Spain) Eight-year-old estate producing unusually classy red *Rioja*.

**Amiral de Beychevelle** [beh-shuh-vel] (*Bordeaux*, France) *Second Label* of *Ch. Beychevelle*.

**Amity** [am-mi-tee] (*Oregon*, USA) Producer of quality *Pinot Noir*.

***Amontillado*** [am-mon-tee-yah-doh] (*Jerez*, Spain) Literally 'like Montilla'. In Britain, this is traditionally a pretty basic medium-sweet Sherry; in Spain, however, it is fascinating dry, nutty wine. ***Lustau, Gonzalez Byass.***

- **Robert Ampeau** [om-poh ] (*Burgundy*, France) *Meursault* grower with good *Savigny-les-Beaune* and *Volnay*. ☆☆☆☆ **1985 Savigny-les-Beaune Lavières ££££** ☆☆☆☆☆ **1992 Volnay Santenots ££££**

***Amtliche Prufüngsnummer*** [am-tlish-eh proof-oong-znoomer] (Germany) Official identification number supposedly relating to quality. (In fact, to earn one, wines merely have to have scored 1.5 out of 5 in a blind tasting). Appears on all *QbA/QmP* wines.

***Anbaugebiet*** [ahn-bow-geh-beet] (Germany) Term for 11 large regions (e.g. *Rheingau*). *QbA* and *QmP* wines must include the name of their *Anbaugebiet* on their labels.

**Anderson Valley** (*Mendocino*, California) Small, cool area, good for white and sparkling wines including the excellent *Scharffenberger* and *Roederer*. Do not confuse with the less impressive Anderson Valley, *New Mexico*. Red: **86 87 88** 89 **90** 91 92 94 95 96 White: **86 91 92** 94 95 96

- **Pierre André** [on-dray] (*Rhône*, France) Good, little-known producer of organic *Châteauneuf du Pape*.
- **Ch. l'Angélus** [lon jay-loos] (*St. Emilion Grand Cru Classé, Bordeaux*, France) Flying high since the late 1980's, this is a lovely, plummy *St Emilion* to watch: classy, if sometimes too showily oaked. The *Second Label* Carillon d'Angélus is also well worth seeking out. **79** 82 **83 85 86 87** 88 89 90 92 93 94 95 96 ☆☆☆☆☆ **1990 ££££**
- **Anghelu Ruju** [an-jeh-loo roo-yoo] (*Sardinia*, Italy) Intensely nutty-raisiny, port'n-lemony wine made by *Sella & Mosca* from dried *Cannonau* grapes. ☆☆☆☆ **1981 Sella and Mosca ££**
- **Ch. d' Angludet** [don gloo-day] (*Cru Bourgeois, Margaux, Bordeaux*, France) Made by *Peter Sichel*, classy cassis-flavoured, if slightly earthy, wine that can generally be drunk young but is worth waiting for. 70 **76 78** 79 80 **81 82 83 85** 86 87 88 89 90 91 92 93 94 95 96 ☆☆☆ **1995 £££**
- **Angoves** [an-gohvs ] (*Padthaway*, Australia) *Murray River* producer with improving, inexpensive *Chardonnay* and *Cabernet*. ☆☆☆ **1995 Kanarie Creek Cabernet Sauvignon £**
- **Weingut Paul Anheuser** [an-hoy-zur] (*Nahe*, Germany) One of the most stalwart supporters of the *Trocken* movement, and a strong proponent of the *Riesling*, this excellent estate is also unusually successful with its *Rulander* and *Pinot Noir*. ☆☆☆☆ **1993 Kreuznacher Monchberg ££**
- **Anjou** [on-joo] (*Loire*, France) Dry and *Demi-Sec* whites, mostly from *Chenin Blanc*, with up to 20% *Chardonnay* or *Sauvignon*. The rosé is almost always awful but there are good, light reds. Look for Anjou-Villages in which *Gamay* is not permitted. In Anjou area, there are smaller, more specific ACs, most importantly *Savennières* and *Coteaux du Layon*. Red: **88** 89 90 95 96 White: **88 89 90** 94 95 96 Sweet White: **76 83 85 88 89** 90 94 95 96 **Ch. du Breuil; Dom. du Closel; V de V Leberton; Richou**.

***Annata*** [ahn-NAH-tah] (Italy) *Vintage*.

***Año*** [An-Yoh] (Spain) Year, preceded by a figure – e.g. 5 – which indicates the wine's age at the time of bottling. Banned by the EU since 1986.

- **Roberto Anselmi** [an-sehl-mee] (*Veneto*, Italy) Source of *Soave Classico* wines that are exceptions to the generally dismal rule, as well as some extremely serious sweet examples. ☆☆☆ **1995 I Capitelli Recioto Di Soave £££**
- **Antinori** [an-tee-NOR-ree] (*Tuscany*, Italy) Pioneer merchant-producer who has improved the quality of *Chianti*, with examples such as Villa Antinori and Pèppoli, while at the same time spearheading the *Super-Tuscan* revolution with superb wines like *Tignanello, Sassicaia* and *Solaia*. ☆☆☆☆☆ **1994 Castello della Sala Cervaro ££** ☆☆☆☆ **1993 Solaia ££££**

***AOC*** (France) See *Appellation Contrôlée*.

***AP*** (Germany) See *Amtliche Prüfungsnummer*.

***Appellation Contrôlée (AC/AOC)*** [AH-pehl-lah-see-o*n* ko*n* TROH-lay] (France) Increasingly questioned designation for 'top quality' wine: guarantees origin, grape varieties and method of production – and in theory, quality, though tradition and vested interest combine to allow some pretty appalling wines to receive the rubber stamp.

**Aprémont** [ah-pray-mo*n*] (Eastern France) Floral, slightly *Petillant* white from skiing region. **Cave Cooperative "le Vigneron Savoyard" ☆☆☆ 1996 Ch. d'Aprémont ££**

**Apulia** [ah-pool-ee-yah] (Italy) See *Puglia*.

**Aquileia** [ah-kwee-LAY-ah] (*Friuli-Venezia Giulia*, Italy) *DOC* for easy-going, single-variety wines. The *Refosco* can be plummily refreshing. **Ca'Bolani and Corvignano Cooperatives.**

**Ararimu** [ah-rah-REE-moo] (*Auckland*, New Zealand) See *Matua Valley*.

**Arbin** [ahr-ba*n*] (*Savoie*, France) Red wine made from Mondeuse grapes. Somehow tastes best after a day's skiing rather than after work.

**Arbois** [ahr-bwah] (Eastern France) *AC* region. with light reds from *Trousseau* and *Pinot Noir* and dry whites from the Savagnin and *Chardonnay*. Look out for the sherry-like *Vin Jaune* and fizz. **☆☆☆ 1990 Savagnin, Fruitière Vinicole d'Arbois ££**

**Ch. d' Arche** [dahrsh] (*Sauternes Deuxième Cru*, *Bordeaux*, France) Greatly improved, but still slightly patchy. 81 82 **83** 85 **86 88 89** 90 93 94 95.

**Viña Ardanza** [veen-yah ahr-dan-thah] (*Rioja*, Spain) Fairly full-bodied red made with a high proportion (40per cent) of *Grenache*; good, oaky white, too. **☆☆☆☆ 1989 Rioja Tinto Reserva ££**

**d'Arenberg** [dar-ren-burg] (*McLaren Vale*, Australia) Excellent up-and-coming producer with impressive sweet and dry table wines and especially dazzling fortifieds. **☆☆☆☆☆ 1995 The Dead Arm, Shiraz £££**

**Argentina** The world's fourth biggest wine-producing nation makes *Cabernet* and *Merlot*, often with a touch more backbone than the Chileans, as well as unusually successful spicy *Malbec, Chardonnays* and also grapey whites from the *Muscat*-like *Torrontes*. **Catena; Luigi Bosca; Esmeralda; Etchart; Norton; Trapiche; Weinert.**

**Tenuta di Argiano** [teh-noo-tah dee ahr-zhee-ahn-noh] (*Tuscany*, Italy) Instant success story, with top-class vineyards, and lovely juicy reds. **☆☆☆☆☆ 1991 Brunello di Montalcino ££££**

**Argyle** (*Oregon*, USA) Classy fizz and still wines from *Brian Croser* (of *Petaluma*). **☆☆☆☆ 1993 Argyle Brut £££**

**Ch. d'Arlay** [dahr-lay] (*Jura*, France) Reliable producer of nutty *Vin Jaune* and light, earthy-raspberry *Pinot Noir*.

**Dom. de l'Arlot** [dur-lahr-loh] (*Burgundy*, France) Brilliant, recently constituted *Nuits St Georges* estate. Lovely, purely defined, modern reds and a rare example of white *Nuits St Georges*. **☆☆☆☆☆ 1994 Nuits St Georges Clos de l'Arlot £££ ☆☆☆☆ 1994 Les Fôrets Nuits St Georges ££**

**Ch. d'Armailhac** [darh-MI-yak] (*Pauillac 5th Growth, Bordeaux*, France). Same stable as *Mouton Rothschild*, and increasingly showing similar rich flavours. **78** 79 81 **82** 83 85 **86** 87 88 89 90 92 93 **94** 95 96 **☆☆☆☆ 1990 ££££**

**Dom. du Comte Armand** [komt-arh-mon] (*Burgundy*, France) Only one wine – the exceptional *Pommard* Clos des Epenaux. ☆☆☆☆ **1995 Pommard 1er Cru Clos des Epeneaux ££**

**Arneis** [ahr-nay-ees] (*Piedmont*, Italy) Spicy, white; makes good young, unoaked wine. ***Voerzio; Bava.***

**Ch. l' Arrosée,** [lah-roh-say] (*St. Emilion Grand Cru Classé, Bordeaux*, France) Small, well-sited property with fruity intense wines. **61** 79 81 **82** 83 **85 86** 87 88 89 90 93 **94** 95 ☆☆☆☆ **1990 ££££**

**Arrowfield** (*Hunter Valley*, Australia) Producer of ripe, full-flavoured *Chardonnay* and some good tawny.

**Arrowood** (*Sonoma Valley*, California) Excellent *Chardonnay* and *Cabernet* from the former winemaker of *Ch. St Jean*. ☆☆☆☆ **1993 White Riesling Late Harvest Russian River Valley Oak Meadow ££££**

**Arroyo** [uh-ROY-oh] (*Ribera del Duero*, Spain) A name to watch: flavoursome reds. ☆☆☆☆ **1991 Mesoneros de Castilla ££**

**Arruda** [ahr-ROO-dah] (*Oeste*, Portugal) Inexpensive *Beaujolais*-style reds.

**Giacomo Ascheri** [ash-SHEH-ree] (*Piedmont*, Italy) New-wave producer. Impressive single-vineyard, tobacco 'n' berry wines, also Nebbiolo and Freisa del Langhe. ☆☆☆☆ **1991 Barolo Vigna Farina £££**

***Asciutto*** [ah-shoo-toh] (Italy) Dry.

**Asenovgrad** [ass-seh-nov-grad] (Bulgaria) Demarcated northern wine region with rich, plummy reds from *Cabernet Sauvignon, Merlot* and *Mavrud*. ☆☆☆ **Asenovgrad Mavrud Reserve £**

**Ashton Hills** (*Adelaide Hills*, Australia) Small up-and-coming winery producing some subtle, increasingly creditable *Chardonnay*. ☆☆☆☆ **1992 Cabernet Merlot ££**

***Assemblage*** [ah-sehm-blahj] (France) The art of blending wine from different grape varieties. Associated with *Bordeaux* and *Champagne*.

**Assmanhausen** [ass-mahn-how-zehn] (*Rheingau*, Germany) If you like sweet *Pinot Noir*, this is the place.

**Asti** (*Piedmont*, Italy) Town famous for sparkling *Spumante*, lighter *Moscato d'Asti* and red *Barbera d'Asti*. Red: 82 **85 88** 89 90 **93 94** 95 White: 96 ***Fontannafreda Martini, Bersano***.

***Astringent*** Mouth-puckering. Associated with young red wine. See *Tannin*.

***Aszu*** [ah-soo] (*Hungary*) The sweet syrup made from dried and (about 10–15 per cent) 'nobly rotten' grapes (see *Botrytis)* used to sweeten *Tokaji*.

**Ata Rangi** [ah-tah ran-gee] (*Martinborough*, New Zealand) Inspiring small estate with high-quality *Pinot Noir* and New Zealand's only successful *Shiraz*. ☆☆☆☆ **1996 Pinot Noir £££**

**Au Bon Climat** [oh bon klee-Mat] (*Santa Barbara*, California) Top-quality producer of characterful and flavoursome *Pinot Noir* and classy *Chardonnay*. ☆☆☆ **1995 Chardonnay £££**

**Dom. des Aubuisières** [day Soh-bwee-see-yehr] (*Loire*, France) *Vouvray* domaine producing impeccable wines, which range all the way from richly dry to lusciously sweet. ☆☆☆☆ **1995 Vouvray Demi-Sec Cuvée Cyrielle ££**

**Auckland** (New Zealand) An all-embracing designation which once comprised over 25 per cent of the country's vineyards. Auckland is often wrongly derided by Marlborophiles who have failed to notice just how good the wines of *Kumeu River* can be, as can those produced by *Goldwater Estate*. *Matua Valley* is one of the larger producers.

**Aude** [ohd] (South-West France) Prolific département traditionally producing much ordinary wine. Now *Corbières* and *Fitou* are improving as are the *Vins de Pays*, thanks to plantings of new grapes (such as the *Viognier*) and the efforts of go-ahead firms like *Skalli Fortant de France* and *Val d'Orbieu*.

***Ausbruch*** [ows-brook] (Austria) Term for rich *Botrytis* wines which are sweeter than *Beerenauslesen* but less sweet than *Trockenbeerenauslesen*.

***Auslese*** [ows-lay-zuh] (Germany) Mostly sweet wine from selected ripe grapes usually affected by *Botrytis*. Third rung on the *QmP* ladder.

**Ch. Ausone** [oh-zohn] (*St. Emilion Premier Grand Cru Classé, Bordeaux*, France) Pretender to the crown of top *St. Emilion*, this estate which owes its name to the Roman occupation, can produce complex claret, but rarely the fruit-driven blockbusters of the 1990s. This may explain why, in 1995, the winemaking was taken over by *Michel Rolland*. **76 78** 79 81 **82 83** 85 **86** 87 88 89 90 92 93 94 95 96 ☆☆☆☆☆ **1990 ££££**

**Austria** Home of all sorts of whites, ranging from dry *Sauvignon Blancs*, greengagey *Grüner Veltliners* and ripe *Rieslings* to luscious *Late Harvest*. Reds are less successful, but the lightly fruity *Pinot-Noir*-like *St Laurents* are worth seeking out. ***Alois Kracher; Willi Opitz; Wachau***.

**Auxerrois** [oh-sehr-wah] (France) Named after the main town in northern *Burgundy*, this is the Alsatians' term for a fairly dull local variety that may be related to the *Sylvaner Melon de Bourgogne* or *Chardonnay*. South Africa's winemakers learned about it involuntarily when cuttings were smuggled into the Cape and planted there under the misapprehension that they were Chardonnay. (Were they intentionally sold a pup? I wonder). In *Luxembourg* it is the name for the *Luxembourg Pinot Gris*.

**Auxey-Duresses** [oh-say doo-ress] (*Burgundy*, France) Beautiful *Côtes de Beaune* village best known for its buttery whites but producing greater quantities of raspberryish, if often quite rustic, reds. A slow developer. ***Robert Ampeau; Michel Prunier; Olivier Leflaive; Guy Roulot.***

*AVA* (US) Acronym for American Viticultural Areas, a recent and somewhat controversial attempt to develop an American *Appellation* system. It makes sense in smaller appellations like Mount Veeder; less so in larger, more heterogenous ones like Napa.

**Quinta da Aveleda** (*Vinho Verde*, Portugal) Famous estate producing disappointing dry *Vinho Verde*.

**Avelsbach** [ahr-vel-sarkh] (*Mosel*, Germany) *Ruwer* village producing delicate, light-bodied wines. Qba/Kab/Spät: **85 86 88** 89 90 **91** 92 **93 94** 95 96 Aus/Beeren/Tba: **83** 85 88 89 90 91 92 **93 94** 95

**Avignonesi** [ahr-veen-yon-nay-see] (*Tuscany*, Italy) Ultra-classy producer of *Vino Nobile di Montepulciano*, *Super-Tuscans* such as Grifi, a pure *Merlot* likened by an American critic to Italy's *Pétrus*. There are also serious *Chardonnay* and *Sauvignon* whites – plus an unusually good *Vin Santo*. ☆☆☆☆ **1993 Vino Nobile di Montepulciano ££**

**Ayala** [ay-yah-lah] (*Champagne*, France) Underrated producer which takes its name from the village of Ay. ☆☆☆☆ **NV Brut £££**

**Ayl** [ihl] (*Mosel*, Germany) Distinguished *Saar* village producing steely wines. Qba/Kab/Spät: **86 88 89** 90 **91** 92 **93 94** 95 96 Aus/Beeren/Tba: **83** 85 88 89 90 91 92 **93 94** 95

***Azienda*** [a-see-en-dah] (Italy) Estate.

# B

🍷 **Babich** [ba-bitch] (*Henderson*, New Zealand) The rich 'Irongate' *Chardonnay* is the prize wine here, but the *Sauvignon Blanc* is good too. The reds improve with every vintage. ☆☆☆ **1996 Hawkes Bay Sauvignon Blanc ££**

🍷 **Quinta da Bacalhôa** [dah ba-keh-yow] (*Setúbal*, Portugal) The good and innovative *Cabernet-Merlot* made by *Peter Bright* at JP Vinhos. ☆☆☆ **1994 ££**

🍇 **Bacchus** [ba-kuhs] White grape. A *Müller-Thurgau-Riesling* cross, making light, flowery wine. ***Denbies; Tenterden***

🍷 **Dom. Denis Bachelet** [dur-nee bash-lay] (*Burgundy*, France) Classy, small *Gevrey Chambertin* estate with cherryish wines that are as good young as with five or six years of age. ☆☆☆☆ **1995 Charmes Chambertin ££££**

🍷 **Backsberg Estate** [bax-burg] (*Paarl*, South Africa) *Chardonnay* pioneer, with good, quite Burgundian versions. ☆☆☆ **1995 Chardonnay ££**

**Bad Durkheim** [baht duhr-kime] (*Pfalz*, Germany) Chief *Pfalz* town, producing some of the region's finest whites, plus some reds. Qba/Kab/Spät: **85 86 88 89** 90 **91** 92 **93 94** 95 96 Aus/Beeren/Tba: **83** 85 88 89 90 91 92 **93 94** 95 96 ***Kurt Darting.***

**Bad Kreuznach** [baht kroyts-nahkh] (*Nahe*, Germany) This is the chief and finest wine town of the region, giving its name to the entire lower *Nahe*. ***Paul Anheuser.***

**Badacsony** [bah-dah-chaw-nyih] (*Hungary*) Wine region renowned for full-flavoured whites.

🍷 **Baden** [bah-duhn] (Germany) Warm southern region of Germany, with ripe grapes to make dry (*trocken*) wines. Some of these – including the ubiquitous 'Baden Dry' – are good, as are some of the *Pinot Noirs*.

🍷 **Baden Winzerkeller (ZBW)** [bah-den vin-zehr-keh-luhr-rih] (*Baden*, Germany) Huge co-op whose reliability has done much to set *Baden* apart from the rest of Germany.

🍷 **Badia a Coltibuono** [bah-dee-yah ah kohl-tee-bwoh-noh] (*Tuscany*, Italy) Brilliant producer of *Chianti*, pure *Sangiovese* and *Chardonnay*. Renowned for mature releases. ☆☆☆☆ **1982 Chianti Classico Riserva £££**

🍇 **Baga** [bah-gah] (*Bairrada*, Portugal) Spicily fruity red grape variety – used in *Bairrada*. ☆☆☆☆ **1994 Bright Brothers Vinho Regional Beiras ££**

🍷 **Ch. Bahans-Haut-Brion** [bah-on oh-bree-on] (*Graves, Bordeaux*, France) The *Second Wine* of *Ch. Haut Brion*. Red: 82 83 85 **86** 87 88 **89** 90 92 93 94 95 ☆☆☆☆ **1990 ££££**

🍷 **Bailey's** (*Victoria*, Australia) Traditional, good *Liqueur Muscat* and hefty, old-fashioned *Shiraz*. Current wines are a little more subtle but still pack a punch. ☆☆☆☆ **1994: 1920's Block Shiraz £££**

🍷 **Bairrada** [bi-rah-dah] (Portugal) *DO* region south of Oporto, traditionally making dull whites and tough reds. Revolutionary producers like *Sogrape, Luis Pato* and *Alianca* are proving what can be done. Look for spicy, blackberryish reds; creamy whites. **85 88 90 91 92 93 94** 95 96

**Baja California** [bah-hah] (*Mexico*) The part of *Mexico* abutting the Californian border, probably best known for exporting illegal aliens and importing adventurous Californians and hippies in search of a good time. Also a successful, though little known, wine region; home to *L.A. Cetto*.

***Balance*** Harmony of fruitiness, *acidity, alcohol* and *tannin*. Balance can develop with age but should be evident in youth, even when, through *acidity* or *tannin* for example, wines may appear difficult to taste.

**Balaton** [bah-la-ton] (*Hungary*) Wine region frequented by flying wine-makers producing fair-quality reds and whites. ☆☆☆ **1995 Chapel Hill Barrique Fermented Chardonnay ££**

**Anton Balbach** [an-ton bahl-barkh] (*Rheinhessen*, Germany) Potentially one of the best producers in the *Erden* region – especially for *Late Harvest* wines. ☆☆☆☆☆ **1989 Niersteiner Pettenthal Riesling Beerenauslese ££££**

**Bodegas Balbás** [bal-bash] (*Ribera del Duero*, Spain) Small producer of juicy *Tempranillo* reds, using uncrushed grapes and also *Bordeaux*-style *Cabernet* blends and a lively rosé. ☆☆☆☆ **1995 Tradicíon ££**

**Ch. Balestard-la-Tonnelle** [bah-les-star lah ton-nell] (*St. Emilion Grand Cru Classé, Bordeaux*, France) Good, quite traditional *St. Emilion* built to last. 81 83 85 **86** 87 **88** 89 90 93 94 95

**Balgownie Estate** [bal-GOW-nee] (*Geelong*, Australia) One of Victoria's most reliable producers of lovely, intense, blackcurranty *Cabernet* in *Bendigo*. *Chardonnays* are big and old-fashioned and *Pinot Noirs* are improving. ☆☆☆☆ **1992 Cabernet Sauvignon, Bendigo £££**

**Bandol** [bon-dohl] (*Provence*, France) Traditional *Mourvèdre*-influenced plummy, herby reds, and improving whites. ☆☆☆☆☆ **1995 Château de Pibarnon £££**

**Villa Banfi** [veel-lah ban-fee] (Tuscany, Italy) US-owned producer with a range of improving *Brunello* and *Vini da Tavola*. ☆☆☆☆☆ **1992 Brunello di Montalcino £££**

**Bannockburn** (*Geelong*, Australia) Gary Farr uses his experience making wines at *Dom. Dujac* in *Burgundy* to produce concentrated, toughish *Pinot Noir* at home. The *Chardonnay* is good, if slightly big for its boots, and the *Bordeaux* blends are impressive too. ***Dom. Tempier; Ch. Vannieres.*** ☆☆☆☆ **1992 Pinot Noir, Geelong ££**

**Banyuls** [bon-yools] (*Provence*, France) France's answer to *Tawny port*. Fortified, *Grenache*-based, *Vin Doux Naturel*, ranging from off-dry to lusciously sweet. The *Rancio* style is rather more like *Madeira*. ☆☆☆☆ **1979 Select Vieux L'Etoile ££££ 1992 Rubis, Dom. de Baillaury ££**

**Antonio Barbadillo** [bahr-bah-deel-yoh] (*Jerez*, Spain) Great producer of *Fino* and *Manzanilla*. ☆☆☆☆ **Solera Manzanilla ££**

**Barbaresco** [bahr-bah-ress-koh] (*Piedmont*, Italy) *DOCG* red from the *Nebbiolo* grape, with spicy fruit plus depth and complexity. Traditionally approachable earlier (three to five years) than neighbouring *Barolo* but, in the hands of *Angelo Gaja* – and in the best vineyards– potentially of almost as high a quality. 78 79 82 **85 88** 89 90 **93 94** 95. **Castello di Nieve; Alfredo Prunotto.**

**Barbera** [Bar-Beh-Rah] (*Piedmont*, Italy) Grape making fruity, spicy, characterful wine (e.g. B. d'Alba and B. d'Asti), usually with a flavour reminiscent of cheesecake with raisins. Now in *California*, *Mexico* and (at *Brown Bros*) Australia. ☆☆☆☆ **Enzo Boglietti Barbara d'Alba ££**

🍷 **Barca Velha** [bahr-kah vayl-yah] (*Douro*, Portugal) Portugal's most famous red, made from port varieties by *Ferreira*. It's tough stuff this, but plummy enough to be worth keeping – and paying for. Also look out for Reserva Especial released in more difficult years. ☆☆☆☆ **1983 Ferreirinha ££££**

🍷 **Bardolino** [bar-doh-lee-noh] (*Veneto*, Italy) Light and unusually approachable for a traditional *DOC* Italian red. Also comes as Chiaretto Rosé. Commercial versions are often dull but at best are Italy's answer to *Beaujolais*. Best drunk young unless from an exceptional producer. ***Boscaini; Masi; Portalupi*** ☆☆☆ **1996 La Sorte Chiaretto Classico ££**

🍷 **Gilles Barge** [bahzh] (*Rhône*, France) Son of Pierre who won an international reputation for his fine, classic Côte Rôtie. Gilles, who now runs the estate, has also shown his skill with St. Joseph.

🍷 **Guy de Barjac** [gee dur-bar-jak] (*Rhône*, France) A master of the *Syrah* grape, producing some of the best – and most stylish – *Cornas* around.

🍷 **Barolo** [bah-ROH-loh] (*Piedmont*, Italy) Noblest of *DOCG* reds, made from *Nebbiolo*. Old-fashioned versions are undrinkably dry and tannic when young but, from a good producer and year, can last and develop extraordinary complexity. Modern versions are ready earlier. 78 79 82 **85 88** 89 90 **93 94** 95 ***Mascarello; Aldo Conterno; Borgogno; Clerico Roberto Voerzio; Elio Altare, Fontanafredda.***

🍷 **Baron de Ley** [Bah-Rohn Duh Lay] (*Rioja*, Spain) Small *Rioja* estate whose wines, partly aged in French oak, take several years to 'come round'. He is also experimenting with a Cabernet-based Table Wine: sounds interesting. ☆☆☆ **1991 Rioja Reserva ££**

**Barossa Valley** [bah-ros suh] (Australia) Big, warm region north-east of Adelaide which is famous for traditional *Shiraz*, 'ports' and *Rieslings* which age to oily richness. *Chardonnay* and *Cabernet* have moved in more recently, and the former makes subtler, classier wines in the increasingly popular higher altitude vineyards of the *Eden Valley* and *Adelaide Hills* ***Basedow; Grant Burge; Krondorf; Rockford; Melton; Penfolds; Peter Lehmann; Wolf Blass.*** ☆☆☆☆ **1995 Heritage Wines Chardonnay ££**

🍷 **Barossa Valley Estate** (*Barossa Valley*, Australia) Top end of BRL Hardy's wine portfolio with good old-vine *Barossa* reds. ☆☆☆☆☆ **1993 Ebeneezer Cabernet £££**

***Barrique*** [ba-reek] French barrel, particularly in *Bordeaux*, holding 225 litres. Term used in Italy to denote (new) barrel ageing.

🍷 **Jim Barry** (*Clare Valley*, Australia) Producer of the dazzling, spicy, mulberryish Armagh *Shiraz*. ☆☆☆☆☆ **1992 The Armagh ££££**

🍷 **Barsac** [bahr-sak] (*Bordeaux*, France) *AC* neighbour of *Sauternes* with similar, though not quite so rich, *Sauvignon Sémillon* dessert wines. 70 **71 73** 76 83 85 86 88 89 90 95 ***Ch. Climens; Doisy-Dubroca; Ch. Coutet; Doisy-Daëne.***

🍷 **De Bartoli** [day bahr-toh-lee] (*Sicily*, Italy) If you want to drink *Marsala* rather than use it in cooking, this is the name to remember. The raisiny Bukkuram, made from *Passito Muscat* grapes, is an alternative delight. ☆☆☆☆ **1990 Josephine Doré ££**

🍷 **Barton & Guestier** [bahr-ton ay geht-tee-yay] (*Bordeaux*, France) Highly commercial *Bordeaux* shipper. ☆☆☆ **1994 Ch. Magnol ££**

🍷 **Barwang** [bahr-wang] (*New South Wales*, Australia) Label for exciting cool-climate wines produced in newly-planted vineyards near Young in eastern New South Wales. ☆☆☆☆ **1995 Cabernet Sauvignon ££**

🍷 **Basedows** [baz-zeh-dohs] (South Australia) Producer of big, concentrated *Shiraz* and *Cabernet* and ultra-rich *Semillon* and *Chardonnays*. ☆☆☆☆ 1996 Barossa Chardonnay ££

**Basilicata** [bah-see-lee-kah-tah] (Italy) Southern wine region chiefly known for *Aglianico del Vulture* and some improving *Vini da Tavola*. ☆☆☆☆ 1993 Connetto Rosso d'Angelo £££

🍷 **Bass Philip** (*Victoria* Australia) South Gippsland pioneer who is arguably making Australia's best, most Burgundy-like Pinot Noir. ☆☆☆☆ 1995 Pinot £££

🍷 **Von Bassermann-Jordan** [fon bas-suhr-man johr-dun] (*Pfalz*, Germany) A highly traditional producer often using the fruit of its brilliant vineyards to produce *Trocken Rieslings* with far more ripeness than is often to be found in this style. ☆☆☆☆ 1991 Forster Kirchenstuck ££

🍇 **Bastardo** [bas-tahr-doh] (Portugal) Red grape used widely in *port* and previously in *Madeira*, where there are a few wonderful bottles left; Shakespeare refers to a wine called 'Brown Bastard'.

🍷 **Ch. Bastor-Lamontagne** [bas-tohr-lam-mon-tañ] (*Sauternes*, *Bordeaux*, France) Remarkably reliable, classy *Sauternes*; surprisingly inexpensive alternative to the big-name properties. 82 **83** 85 86 88 89 90 **94** 95 96

🍷 **Ch. Batailley** [bat-tih-yay] (*Pauillac 5th Growth, Bordeaux*, France) Approachable, quite modern tobacco cassis cedar claret with more class than its price might lead one to expect. 70 78 79 **82 83 85** 86 87 **88** 89 90 94 95 96 ☆☆☆☆ 1993 Ch. Batailley £££

🍷 **Bâtard-Montrachet** [bat-tahr mon-rah-shay] (*Burgundy*, France) biscuity-rich white *Grand Cru* shared between *Chassagne* and *Puligny-Montrachet*. Wines are often very fine; always expensive. ***Jean-Noel Gagnard; Vincent Leflaivre; Ramonet; Etienne Sauzet.***

🍷 **Beni di Batasiolo** [bay-nee dee bat-tah-see-oh-loh] (*Piedmont*, Italy) Producer of top-class *Barolo*, impressive cherryish *Dolcetto*, intense berryish *Brachetto*, and a subtle *Chardonnay*. ☆☆☆☆☆ 1995 Brachetto del Piemonte ££

🍷 **Dom. des Baumard** [day boh-marh] (*Loire*, France) Best producer of *Quarts de Chaume* ☆☆☆☆ 1990 Quarts de Chaume ££££

🍷 **Bava** [bah-vah] (*Piedmont*, Italy) Innovative producer making good *Moscato Barbera* and reviving indigenous grapes such as the rarely grown raspberryish *Ruche* and the *Erbaluce*. ☆☆☆☆ 1994 Alteserre ££ ☆☆☆☆ 1990 Stradivario Barbera d'Asti ££

🍷 **Ch. Beau-Séjour (-Bécot)** [boh-say-zhoor bay-koh] (*St. Emilion Grand Cru Classé, Bordeaux*, France) Reinstated in 1996 after a decade of demotion. Now making good – if not superlative – wine. 75 **82** 83 85 **86** 88 89 90 92 93 94 95 96

🍷 **Ch. Beau-Site** [boh-seet] (*St. Estèphe Cru Bourgeois, Bordeaux*, France). Benchmark *St. Estèphe* in the same stable as *Ch. Batailley*. 75 78 **82** 83 85 **86** 87 88 89 90 92 93 96

🍷 **Ch. de Beaucastel** [boh-kas-tel] (*Rhône*, France) The top estate in *Châteauneuf-du-Pape* using organic methods to produce richly gamey, long-lived, spicy reds, and rare but fine creamy-spicy whites. ☆☆☆☆ 1994 Châteauneuf du Pape £££ ☆☆☆☆☆ Beaucastel Homage à Joseph Perrin ££££ ☆☆☆☆☆ Lirac La Mordorée ££

🍷 **Beaujolais** [boh-juh-lay] (*Burgundy*, France) Light, fruity red from the *Gamay*, good chilled and for early drinking. Beaujolais-Villages is better, and the 10 Crus better still. With age, these can taste like (fairly ordinary) *Burgundy*. *Beaujolais Villages; Morgon; Chenas; Brouilly; Côte de Brouilly; Julienas; Fleurie; Régnié; St Amour; Chiroubles.*

**Beaujolais Blanc** (*Burgundy*, France) From the Chardonnay, rarely seen under this name. Commonly sold as *St Véran*. **Charmet; Tête.**

**Beaujolais-Villages** (*Burgundy*, France) From the north of the region, fuller-flavoured and more alcoholic than plain *Beaujolais*, though not necessarily from one of the named *Cru* Villages. **Duboeuf; Pivot; Large.**

**Beaulieu Vineyard** [bohl-yoo] (*Napa Valley*, California) Historic winery that has suffered at the hands of its multinational owners. The Georges de Latour Private Reserve *Cabernet* can be impressive and keeps well, and recent vintages of *Beautour* have improved – possibly thanks to the efforts of the late, great Andre Tchelistcheff. Other wines are memorably and unworthily ordinary. ☆☆☆☆ **1994 Cabernet Sauvignon Napa Valley Georges de Latour Private Reserve ££**

**Beaumes de Venise** [bohm duh vuh-neez] (*Rhône*, France) *Côtes du Rhône* village producing spicy dry reds and better-known sweet, grapey fortified *Vin Doux Naturel* from the *Muscat*. **Chapoutier ££**

**Ch. Beaumont** [boh-mon] (*Haut-Médoc Cru Bourgeois, Bordeaux*, France) High-flying wine with intense fruit and well handled oak. **82** 85 **86** 88 **89** **90** 92 **93** 94 95 96

**Beaune** [bohn] (*Burgundy*, France) Large, reliable commune for soft, raspberry-and-rose-petal *Pinot Noir* with plenty of *Premier Crus*, but strangely no *Grands Crus*. The walled city is the site of the famous *Hospices* charity auction. Reds are best from *Michel Prunier*, *Louis Jadot*; also (very rare) whites made with great success by *Joseph Drouhin*.

**Ch. Beauregard** [boh-ruh-gahr] (*Pomerol*, *Bordeaux*, France) Going against the grain of today's intense plummy *Pomerols*, but none the worse for that. **82** 83 85 86 87 88 89 90 92 93 **94** 95

**Ch. Beauséjour-Duffau-Lagarosse** [boh-say-zhoor doo-foh lag-Gahr-Ros] (*St. Emilion Premier Grand Cru Classé, Bordeaux*, France) Traditional wine for those who like their *St. Emilions* to be quite tough and tannic. 82 83 85 86 88 89 90 92 93 94 95 96 ☆☆☆☆ **1989 ££££**

**Cave de Beblenheim** [beb-len-hihm] (*Alsace*, France) Reliable across-the-board cooperative. ☆☆☆☆ **1995 Gewürztraminer ££**

**JB Becker** (*Rheingau*, Germany) One of Germany's few successful producers of ripe, classy *Pinot Noir* (here known as *Spätburgunder*). ☆☆☆☆ **1992 Eltviler Rheinberg Riesling, Auslese ££**

***Beerenauslese*** [behr-Ren-Ows-Lay-Zuh] (Austria/Germany) Sweet wines from selected, ripe grapes (Beeren), hopefully affected by *Botrytis*.

**Bekaa Valley** [Bik-Kahr] (Lebanon) War-torn region in which *Serge Hochar* grows the grapes for his *Ch. Musar* wines.

**Ch. de Bel-Air** [Bel-Ehr] (*Lalande-de-Pomerol*, *Bordeaux*, France) Impressive property making wines to make some *Pomerols* blush. 82 85 86 88 **89** 90 92 **94** 95 96

**Ch. Bel-Orme-Tronquoy-de-Lalande** [Bel-Orm-Tron-Kwah-duh-La-Lond] (*Haut-Médoc Grand Bourgeois, Bordeaux*, France) Traditional estate with generally old-fashioned wines. **82** 83 85 86 88 89 **90** 92 94 95 96

**Ch. Belair** [bel-lehr] (*St. Emilion Premier Grand Cru Classé, Bordeaux*, France) *Ch. Ausone*'s stablemate – lighter in style, but still a classy, long-lived *St. Emilion*. Red: 73 78 **79** **82** **83** **85** **86** 88 89 90 94 95 96 ☆☆☆☆ **1990 ££££**

**Albert Belle** [bel] (*Rhône* France) An estate that has only just begun to bottle its own excellent red and – oaky – white Hermitage.

🍷 **Bellet** [bel-lay] (*Provence*, France) Tiny *AC* behind Nice producing fairly good red, white and rosé from local grapes including the Rolle, the *Braquet* and the *Folle Noir.* (Excessively) pricey and rarely seen in the UK.

**Bendigo** [ben-dig-goh] (*Victoria*, Australia) Warm region producing big-boned, long-lasting reds with intense berry fruit.. ***Balgownie; Jasper Hill; Passing Clouds; Mountain Ida.***

***Bentonite*** [Ben-Ton-Nite] Type of clay with extraordinary properties, as a clarifying agent to remove proteins from wine before bottling, so avoiding the subsequent development of a protein haze in the bottle. Popular as a non-animal-derived *fining* material.

🍷 **Benziger** [ben-zig-ger] (*Sonoma*, California) Classy wines at the top end of the *Glen Ellen* range. ☆☆☆☆ **1994 Cabernet Vintner's Selection ££**

🍷 **Berberana** [behr-behr-rah nah] (*Rioja*, Spain) Increasingly dynamic producer of a range of fruitier young-drinking styles, as well as the improving Carta de Plata and Carta de Oro *Rioja*s, plus sparkling Marquès de Monistrol and the excellent *Marquès de Griñon* range. ☆☆☆☆ **1995 Marquès de Griñon Syrah ££**

***Bereich*** [beh-ri-kh] (Germany) Vineyard area, subdivision of an *Anbaugebiet*. On its own indicates simple *QbA* wine, eg *Niersteiner.* Finer wines are followed by the name of a (smaller) *Grosslage*; better ones by that of an individual vineyard.

🍷 **Bergerac** [behr-jur-rak] (France) Lighter, often good-value alternative to basic claret or dry white *Bordeaux*, revolutionised in the 1980s by *Ch. de la Jaubertie*. Fine, sweet *Monbazillac* is made here, too. ☆☆☆☆ **1995 Château Tour des Gendres Bergerac Moulins des Dames ££**

🍷 **Bergkelder** [berg-kel-dur] (*Cape*, South Africa) Huge firm that still matures and bottles wines for such top-class *Cape* estates as *Meerlust*, which, like its counterparts in *Bordeaux* and *California*, really ought to bottle their own. Even so, the Bergkelder's own *Stellenryck* wines are worth watching out for; the cheaper Fleur du Cap range is likeable enough and *Pongracz* fizz is first class. ☆☆☆☆ **1993 La Motte Millennium ££**

🍷 **Beringer Vineyards** [ber-rin-jer] (*Napa Valley*, California) Big Swiss-owned producer notable for two *Cabernets* (Knights Valley and Private Reserve) and increasingly impressive Burgundy-like *Chardonnay* ☆☆☆☆☆ **1995 Chardonnay Napa Valley Private Reserve £££**

**Bernkastel** [berhrn-kah-stel] (*Mosel*, Germany) Town and area on the *Mittelmosel* and source of some of the finest *Riesling* (like the famous Bernkasteler Doktor), along with a lake of poor-quality stuff. QbA/Kab/Spät: **85 86 88 89 90** 91 92 **93 94** 95 96 Aus/Beeren/TBA: **83 85** 88 89 90 91 92 **93 94** 95 96 **Deinhard; Dr Loosen; Dr Thanisch; Von Kesselstadt.**

🍷 **Berri Renmano** [Ber-Ree Ren-Mah-Noh] (*Riverland*, Australia) The controlling force behind the giant *BRL Hardy*, controlling quality brands like *Thomas Hardy*, *Château Reynella* and *Houghton*. Under its own name, though, it is better known for inexpensive reds and whites.

🍷 **Dom Bertagna** [behr-tan-ya] (*Vougeot*, France) Recently improved estate notable for offering the rare (relatively) affordable *Premier Cru* Vougeot alongside its own version of the easier-to-find *Clos Vougeot Grand Cru*.

🍷 **Best's Great Western** (Victoria, Australia) Under-appreciated winery in *Great Western* making delicious, concentrated *Shiraz* from old vines, attractive *Cabernet*, *Dolcetto*, *Colombard* and rich *Chardonnay*. ☆☆☆☆☆ **1994 Great Western Dolcetto ££**

🍷 **Bethany** [beth-than-nee] (*Barossa Valley*, Australia) Impressive small producer of knockout *Shiraz*. ☆☆☆☆☆ **1995 Shiraz £££**

🍷 **Dom. Henri Beurdin** [bur-dan] (*Loire*, France) White and rosé from *Reuilly*. ☆☆☆ **1995 Reuilly Blanc ££**

🍷 **Ch. Beychevelle** [bay-shur-vel] (*St. Julien 4th Growth*, *Bordeaux*, France) An over-performing *Fourth Growth* benefitting from ownership by an insurance giant. Typical *St Julien* with lots of cigar-box character. The *Second Label* Amiral de Beychevelle can be a worthwhile buy. Red: **70** 78 **82** 83 85 86 87 88 89 90 91 92 **94** 95 96 ☆☆☆☆☆ **1985 ££££**

🍷 **Léon Beyer** [bay-ur] (*Alsace*, France) Serious producer of lean, long-lived wines. ☆☆☆ **1993 Gewürztraminer ££**

🍷 **Beyerskloof** [bay-yurs-kloof] (*Stellenbosch*, South Africa) Newish venture, with Beyers Truter (of *Kanonkop*) aiming to produce South Africa's top *Cabernet* and *Stellenbosch Pinotage*. ☆☆☆☆ **1995 Pinotage ££**

🍷 **Bianco di Custoza** [bee-yan-koh dee koos-toh-zah] (*Veneto*, Italy) Widely exported *DOC*. A reliable, crisp, light white from a blend of grapes. A better-value alternative to most basic *Soave*. ***Portalupi; Tedeschi; Zenato*** ☆☆☆ **1996 Cavalchina ££**

🍷 **Maison Albert Bichot** [bee-shoh] (*Burgundy*, France) Big *Negociant* in *Beaune* with excellent *Chablis* and *Vosne-Romanée*, plus a range of perfectly adequate wines sold under a plethora of other labels. ☆☆☆☆ **1995 Chablis Grand Cru Vaudésir £££**

🍷 **Biddenden** [BID-den-den] (Kent, England) Maker of the wines from the usual range of Germanic grapes, but showing supreme mastery in this country of the peachy *Ortega*. ☆☆☆ **1995 Ortega £**

🍷 **Bienvenue-Batard-Montrachet** [bee-yen-veh-noo bat-tahr mo*n* ra-rhay] (*Burgundy*, France) Fine white Burgundy vineyard with potentially gorgeous, biscuity wines – at a price. ☆☆☆☆ **1995 Domaine Leflaive ££££**

🍷 **Weingut Josef Biffar** [bif-fah] (*Pfalz*, Germany). *Deidesheim* estate that is on a roll at the moment with its richly spicy wines. ☆☆☆☆ **1995 Spätlese Pfalz Deideshiemer Grainhübel ££**

🍷 **Billecart-Salmon** [beel-kah*r* sal-mo*n*] (*Champagne*, France) Wine drinkers fizz, great with food. Possibly the region's best all-rounder for quality and value. The one *Champagne* house whose subtle but decidedly ageable non-vintage, *vintage* and rosé I buy without hesitation. Superlative. ☆☆☆☆☆ **Champagne Brut £££**

🍷 **Billiot** [bil-lee-yoh] (*Champagne*, France) Impressive small producer with classy rich fizz. ☆☆☆☆ **Cuvée de Reserve NV £££**

**Bingen** [bing-urn] (*Rheinhessen*, Germany) Village giving its name to a *Rheinhessen Bereich* that includes a number of well-known *Grosslage*.
QbA/Kab/Spät: **85** 86 **88 89 90** 91 92 **93** 94 95 96
Aus/Beeren/TBA: **83 85** 88 89 90 91 92 **93 94** 95 96

**Binissalem** [bin-nee-sah-lem] (*Mallorca*, Spain) The holiday island is proud of its demarcated region, though why, it's hard to say. José Ferrer's and Jaime Mesquida's wines are the best of the bunch.

🍷 **Biondi-Santi** [bee-yon-dee san-tee] (*Tuscany*, Italy) Big-name property making asbsurdly expensive *Brunello di Montalcino* that can also be bought – after a period of vertical storage at room temperature – at the local trattoria. ☆☆☆ **1977 Brunello Di Montalcino ££££**

***Biscuity*** Flavour of biscuits (eg Digestive or Rich Tea) often associated with the *Chardonnay* grape, particularly in *Champagne* and top-class mature *Burgundy*, or with the yeast that fermented the wine.

🍷 **Dom. Simon Bize** [beez] (*Burgundy*, France) Intense, long-lived and good-value wines produced in *Savigny-Lès-Beaune*. ☆☆☆☆ **1995 Savigny-Les-Beaune Aux Grands Liards £££**

**Blaauwklippen** [blow-klip-pen] (*Stellenbosch*, South Africa) Large estate, veering between commercial and top quality. The *Cabernet* and *Zinfandel* are the strong cards. ☆☆☆ **1995 Zinfandel ££**

**Black Muscat** Grown chiefly as a table grape; also produces very mediocre wine – except that made at the *Quady* winery in California. ☆☆☆☆ **Elysium ££**

**Blagny** [blan-yee] (*Burgundy*, France) Tiny source of good, unsubtle red (sold as Blagny) and potentially top-class white (sold as *Meursault, Puligny-Montrachet,* Blagny, Hameau de Blagny or la Pièce sous le Bois). 78 80 83 **85** 86 87 **88 89 90** 92 95 96 ***Robert Ampeau; Thierry Matrot.***

**Blain-Gagnard** [blan gan-yahr] (*Burgundy*, France) Excellent producer of creamy, modern *Chassagne-Montrachet*. ☆☆☆☆☆ **1992 Bâtard-Montrachet ££££**

***Blanc de Blancs*** [blon dur blon] A white wine, made from white grapes – hardly worth mentioning except in the case of Champagne, where *Pinot Noir*, a black grape, usually makes up 30–70 per cent of the blend. In this case, Blancs de Blancs is pure *Chardonnay*. ☆☆☆☆☆**1990 Pol Roger Chardonnay ££££**

***Blanc de Noirs*** [blon dur nwahrr] A white (or frequently very slightly pink-tinged wine) made from red grapes by taking off the free-run juice, before pressing to minimise the uptake of red pigments from the skin. ☆☆☆☆☆ **Duval-Leroy Fleur de Champagne £££**

**Paul Blanck** [blank] (*Alsace*, France) Top-class *Alsace* domaine, specialising in single cru 'terroir' orientated wines. ☆☆☆☆ **1996 Pinot d'Alsace £££**

**Blandy's** [blan-deez] (*Madeira*, Portugal) Brand owned by the Madeira Wine Company and named after the sailor who began the production of fortified wine here. Brilliant old wines. ☆☆☆☆ **5 Year Old Pale Dry Sercial £££**

**Blanquette de Limoux** [blon ket dur lee-moo] (*Midi*, France) *Méthode Champenoise* sparkler, which, when good, is appley and clean. Best when made with a generous dose of *Chardonnay,* as the local *Mauzac* tends to give it an earthy flavour with age. ☆☆☆ **François de Secade ££ Aimery Co-operative.**

**Wolf Blass** (*Barossa Valley*, Australia) German immigrant who prides himself on making immediately attractive 'sexy' (his term) reds and whites, by blending wines from different regions of *South Australia* and allowing them plentiful contact with new oak. ☆☆☆☆ **1994 President's Selection Shiraz £££**

**Blauburgunder** [blow-boor-goon-durh] (Austria) The name the Austrians give their light, often sharp *Pinot Noir.*

**Blauer Portugieser** [blow-urh por-too-gay-suhr] (Germany) Red grape used in Germany and Austria to make light, pale wine.

**Blaufrankisch** [blow-fran-kish] (Austria) Berryish grape used to make wines that compete with the red wines of the Loire. ☆☆☆ **1995 Tinhof Neusiedlersee £££**

***Bocksbeutel*** [box-boy-tuhl] (*Franken*, Germany) The famous flask-shaped bottle of *Franken*.

**Bockstein** [bok-stihn] (*Mosel*, Germany) A vineyard in the village of *Ockfen*.

***Bodega*** [bod-day-gah] (Spain) Winery or wine cellar; producer.

**Bodegas y Bebidas** [bod-day-gas ee beh-bee-das] (Spain) One of Spain's most dynamic wine companies, and maker of Campo Viejo.

***Body*** Usually used as 'full-bodied', meaning a wine with mouth-filling flavours and probably a fairly high alcohol content.

**Jean-Marc Boillot** [bwah-yoh] (*Burgundy*, France) Small *Pommard* domaine run by the son of the winemaker at *Olivier Leflaive* with good examples from neighbouring villages. ☆☆☆☆ **1995 Meursault 1er Cru Charmes £££**

🍷 **Jean-Claude Boisset** [bwah-say] (*Burgundy*, France) Fast-growing *négociant* which now owns the excellent *Jaffelin négociant*, plus the previously dull but now much improved *Bouchard Aîné*. ☆☆☆ **1996 Bourgogne Blanc Charles de France ££**

🍷 **Boisson-Vadot** [bwah-son va-doh] (*Burgundy*, France) Classy, small *Meursault* domaine. ☆☆☆☆☆ **1992 Meursault Genevrières ££££**

🍷 **Bolla** [bol-lah] (*Veneto*, Italy) Producer of plentiful, adequate *Valpolicella* and *Soave*, and of smaller quantities of impressive single vineyard wines like its Jago and Creso. ☆☆☆☆ **1990 Amarone Classico della Valpolicella £££**

🍷 **Bollinger** [bol-an-jay] (*Champagne*, France) Great, family-owned firm at *Ay*, whose wines need age. The luscious and rare *Vieilles Vignes* is made from pre-*Phylloxera* vines, while the nutty *RD* was the first late-disgorged *Champagne* to hit the market. ☆☆☆☆ **1990 Champagne Grande Année ££££**

**Bommes** [bom] (*Bordeaux*, France) *Sauternes* commune and village containing several *Premiers Crus* such as *la Tour Blanche, Lafaurie-Peyrauguey, Rabaud-Promis* and *Rayne Vigneau*. 70 **71 75** 76 83 85 86 88 89 90 95 96

🍷 **Ch. le Bon-Pasteur** [bon-pas-stuhr] (*Pomerol, Bordeaux*, France) The impressive private estate of *Michel Rolland*, who acts as consultant – and helps to make fruit-driven wines – for half his neighbours, as well as producers in almost every other wine-growing region in the universe. 70 75 76 **82** 83 **85 86** 87 **88** 89 90 92 93 94 95 96 ☆☆☆☆ **1993 £££**

🍷 **Henri Bonneau** [bon-noh] (*Rhône* France) *Chateauneuf du Pape* producer with two special cuvées – 'Marie Beurrier' and 'des Celestins' – and a cult following.

🍷 **Dom. Bonneau du Martray** [bon-noh doo mahr-tray] (*Burgundy*, France) Largest grower of *Corton-Charlemagne* and a reliable producer thereof. Also produces a classy red *Grand Cru Corton*. ☆☆☆☆☆ **1993 Corton Charlemagne ££££**

🍷 **Ch. Bonnet** [bon-nay] (*Bordeaux*, France) Top-quality *Entre-Deux-Mers* château whose wines are made by *Jacques Lurton*.

🍷 **F Bonnet** [bon-nay] (*Champagne*, France) Reliable, little-known producer with good wines under its own and customers' names. ☆☆☆☆ **Blanc de Blancs Champagne Brut £££**

🍷 **Bonnezaux** [bonn-zoh] (*Loire*, France) Within the *Coteaux du Layon*, this is one of the world's greatest sweet wine producing areas, though the wines are often over-sulphured. **76** 83 **85** 86 **88 89** 90 94 95 ***René Renou.*** ☆☆☆☆ **Château de Fesles 'La Chapelle' £££**

🍷 **Bonny Doon Vineyard** (*Santa Cruz*, California) Randall Grahm, the original 'Rhône Ranger', has an affection for Italian varieties, which is increasingly evident in a range of characterful red, dry and *Late Harvest* whites. ☆☆☆☆☆ **1996 Ca'del Solo Il Pescatore.**

**Borba** [Bohr-Bah] (*Alentejo*, Portugal) See *Alentejo*.

🍷 **Bordeaux** [bor-doh] (France) Largest (supposedly) quality wine region in France, producing reds, rosés and deep pink *Clairets* from *Cabernet Sauvignon, Cabernet Franc, Petit Verdot*, and *Merlot*, and dry and sweet whites from (principally) blends of *Sémillon* and *Sauvignon*. *Bordeaux Supérieur* denotes (relatively) riper grapes. Dry whites from regions like the *Médoc* and *Sauternes*, where they are not part of the mainstream activity, are sold as *Bordeaux* Blanc, so even the efforts by Châteaux *Yquem, Margaux*, and *Lynch Bages* are sold under the same label as the most basic supermarket blended white. See *Graves, Médoc, Pomerol, St. Emilion*, etc.

**Borgogno** [baw-gon-yoh] (*Piedmont*, Italy) Resolutely old-fashioned *Barolo* producer whose wines develop a sweet, tobaccoey richness with age. In their youth, though, they're often not a lot of fun. ☆☆☆☆ **1985 Barolo ££££**

**De Bortoli** [baw-tol-lee] (*Riverina*, Australia) Fast-developing firm (following its move into the *Yarra Valley)* which startled the world by making a Botrytised, peachy, honeyed *Semillon* which beats *Ch. Yquem* in blind tastings – and by making it in the unfashionable *Riverina*. ☆☆☆☆ **1992 Cabernet Merlot Yarra Valley ££**

**Bodega Luigi Bosca** [bos-kah] (*Mendoza*, Argentina) Top-class producer, with good *Sauvignons* and *Cabernets*. ☆☆☆☆ **1995 Chardonnay ££**

**Boscaini** [bos-kah-yee-nee] (*Veneto*, Italy) Innovative producer linked to *Masi* and making better-than-average *Valpolicella* and *Soave*.

**Boschendal Estate** [bosh-shen-dahl] (*Cape*, South Africa) Modern winery producing some of the *Cape's* best fizz and fast-improving whites. ☆☆☆ **1996 Lightly Wooded Chardonnay ££**

**Ca' del Bosco** [kah-del-bos-koh] (*Lombardy*, Italy) Classic, if pricy *Barrique*-aged *Cabernet/Merlot* blends, fine *Chardonnay* and good *Pinot Bianco/Pinot Noir/Chardonnay Méthode Champenoise* Franciacorta, from perfectionist producer Maurizio Zanella. ☆☆☆☆☆ **1990 Maurizio Zanella ££££** ☆☆☆☆ **Franciacorta Brut NV £££**

**Ch. le Boscq** [bosk] (*St. Estèphe Cru Bourgeois, Bordeaux*, France) Improving property that excels in good vintages, but tends to make tough wines in lesser ones. 82 83 85 86 87 88 **89** 90 92 93 95

**Les Bosquet des Papes** [bos-kay day pap] (*Rhône* France) Serious *Chateauneuf du Pape* producer, making wines that last.

***Botrytis*** [boh-tri-tiss] Botrytis cinerea, a fungal infection that attacks and shrivels grapes, evaporating their water and concentrating their sweetness. Vital to *Sauternes* and the finer German and Austrian sweet wines. See *Sauternes, Trockenbeerenauslese, Tokaji*.

***Bottle-fermented*** Commonly found on the labels of US sparkling wines to indicate the *Méthode Champenoise*, and gaining wider currency. Beware, though – it can indicate inferior 'transfer method' wines.

**Bouchard Aîné** [boo-shahrr day-nay] (*Burgundy*, France) For a long time, an unimpressive merchant, but recently taken over by *Boisset* and now under the winemaking control of the excellent Bernard Repolt of *Jaffelin*.

**Bouchard Finlayson** [boo-shard] (*Walker Bay*, South Africa) Serious small-scale joint venture between Peter Finlayson (brother of Walter at *Glen Carlou)* and Paul Bouchard, formerly of *Bouchard Ainé* in France. Wines are made from some of South Africa's best cool-climate fruit (including grapes from *Elgin*). ☆☆☆ **1996 Sauvignon Blanc ££**

**Bouchard Père & Fils** [boo-shahrr pehrr ay fees] (*Burgundy*, France) Traditional merchant with some great vineyards. Recently bought by the *Champagne* house of *Henriot*, who appear to be more quality-conscious than the Bouchard family. At present, the best wines are the *Beaunes*, especially the Beaune de l'Enfant Jesus and the La Romanée from *Vosne-Romanée*. ☆☆☆ **1994 Beaune Vigne de l'Enfant Jésus £££**

***Bouquet*** Overall smell, often made up of several separate aromas. Used by Anglo-Saxon enthusiasts more often than by professionals.

**Ch. Bourgneuf** [boor-nurf] (*Pomerol, Bordeaux*, France) Rising star with rich, plummy, *Merlot* fruit. 81 82 83 **85** 86 88 **89** 90 95 ☆☆☆☆☆ **1990 £££**

***Bourgogne*** [boorr-goyñ] (*Burgundy*, France) French for *Burgundy*.

**Bourgueil** [boorr-goyy] (*Loire*, France) Red *AC* in the *Touraine*, producing crisp, grassy-blackcurranty 100 per cent *Cabernet Franc* wines that can age well in good years. Look for *Pierre-Jacques Druet*. **78 81 88 89 90** 95 ☆☆☆ **1996 Les Cent Boisselées ££** ☆☆☆ **1995 Domaine de la Chevalerie ££**

**Ch. Bouscaut** [boos-koh] (*Pessac-Léognan*, *Bordeaux*, France) Good, rather than great *Graves* property; better white than red. ☆☆☆☆ **1990 Blanc, Pessac-Léognan £££**

**J Boutari** [boo-tah-ree] (*Greece*) One of the most reliable names in Greece, producing good traditional red wines in Nemea and Naoussa ☆☆☆ **1995 Nemea ££**

**Bouvet-Ladubay** [boo-vay lad-doo-bay] (*Loire*, France) Producer of good *Loire* fizz and better *Saumur Champigny* reds. ☆☆☆ **1995 Saumur Rubis Rouge £££**

**Bouvier** [boo-vee-yay] (Austria) Characterless variety used to produce tasty but mostly simple *Late Harvest* wines.

**Bouzeron** [booz-rron] (*Burgundy*, France) Village in the *Côte Chalonnaise*, principally known for *Aligoté* which is supposedly at its best here. ☆☆☆☆☆ **1996 Aligoté Aubert de Villaine ££**

**Bouzy Rouge** [boo-zee roozh] (*Champagne*, France) Sideline of a black grape village: an often thin-bodied, rare and overpriced red wine which, despite what they say, rarely ages. 89 90 94 ☆☆☆ **Gosset ££££**

**Bowen Estate** [boh-wen] (*Coonawarra*, Australia) An early *Coonawarra* pioneer proving that the region can be as good for *Shiraz* as for *Cabernet*. ☆☆☆☆ **1994 Cabernet Sauvignon £££**

**Domaines Boyar** [boy-yahr] (*Bulgaria*) Privatised producers, especially in the *Suhindol* region, – selling increasingly impressive 'Reserve' reds under the Lovico label. Other wines are less reliably recommendable. ☆☆☆☆ **1990 Lambol Special Reserve Cabernet Sauvignon ££**

**Ch. Boyd-Cantenac** [boyd-kon-teh-nak] (*Margaux 3rd Growth*, *Bordeaux*, France) A third growth generally performing at the level of a fifth – or less. 78 **82 83 85 86** 88 89 90 93 **94** 96

**Brachetto d'Acqui** [brah-KET-toh dak-wee] (*Piedmont*, Italy) Eccentric Muscatty red grape. Often *frizzante*. ***Beni di Batasiolo.***

**Ch. Branaire-Ducru** [brah-nehr doo-kroo] (*Saint-Julien 4th Growth*, *Bordeaux*, France) A revival in the 1980s for this fourth-growth *St. Julien* estate. Red 75 79 81 **82** 83 85 86 87 88 **89 90** 91 92 93 95 ☆☆☆☆ **1985 ££££**

**Brand's Laira** [lay-rah] (*Coonawarra*, Australia) Traditional producer, much improved since its purchase by *McWilliams*. Delving into the world of *Pinot Noir* and sparkling *Grenache* Rosé.

**Ch. Brane-Cantenac** [brahn kon teh-nak] (*Margaux 2nd Growth*, *Bordeaux*, France) Perennial under-achieving *Margaux*, whose *Second Label*, the discouragingly named Ch. Notton, can be a worthwhile buy. Red: 75 78 79 81 82 83 85 **86** 87 88 89 90 95 **96** ☆☆☆ **1985 ££££**

**Braquet** [brah-ket] (*Midi*, France) Grape variety used in *Bellet*.

**Brauneberg** [brow-nuh-behrg] (*Mosel*, Germany) Village best known in the UK for the *Juffer* vineyard. ☆☆☆☆ **1993 Brauneberger Juffer Kabinett, Weingut Max Ferd Richter ££££**

**Brazil** Country in which large quantities of fairly light-bodied wines are produced in a region close to Puerto Allegre, where it tends to rain at harvest time. Large amounts of (unexceptional) *Zinfandel* have been shipped north to the US, however, and Australian flying winemaker *John Worontschak* has made some passable cheap wine. The Palomas vineyard on the Uruguayan border has a state-of-the-art winery and a good climate. The wines have yet to reflect those advantages, however.

**Breaky Bottom** (Sussex, England) One of Britain's best, whose *Seyval Blanc* rivals dry wines made in the *Loire* from supposedly finer grape varieties. ☆☆☆**1994 oaked Fumé ££**

**Marc Bredif** [bray-deef] *(Loire,* France) Big, and quite variable Loire producer, with still and sparkling wine, including some first class *Vouvray.* ☆☆☆ **Bredif Brut NV ££**

**Weingut Georg Breuer** [broy-yer] (*Rheingau*, Germany) Innovative producer with classy *Rieslings* and high quality *Rülander.*

**Bricco Manzoni** [bree-koh man-tzoh-nee] (*Piedmont*, Italy) Non-*DOC* oaky red blend of *Nebbiolo* and *Barbera* grapes grown on vines which could produce *Barolo* from *Monforte* vineyards; see *Altesino*. A wine that is drinkable young. ☆☆☆☆ **1990 Valentino Migliorini £££**

**Bridgehampton** (*Long Island*, USA) Producer of first class *Merlot* and *Chardonnay* to worry a Californian.

**Bridgewater Mill** (*Adelaide Hills*, Australia) More modest sister winery to the highly regarded *Petaluma,* using grapes from other sources as well as their own. ☆☆☆ **1994 Shiraz ££**

**Peter Bright** Australian-born Peter Bright of the *JP Vinhos* winery makes top-class Portuguese wines, including Tinta da Anfora and Quinta da Bacalhoa, plus a growing range in countries such as Spain and Chile, made under the Bright Brothers label. ☆☆☆ **1996 Campo dos Frados Chardonnay ££** ☆☆☆☆ **1996 Bright Brothers Baga ££**

**Bristol Cream** (*Jerez*, Spain) see *Harvey's*.

**Jean-Marc Brocard** [broh-kahrr] (*Burgundy*, France) Classy *Chablis* producer with well-defined individual vineyard wines, also producing unusually good Aligoté. ☆☆☆☆ **1994 Chablis Premier Cru Beauregard ££**

**Brokenwood** (*Hunter Valley*, Australia) Starry source of great *Semillon, Shiraz* and even (unusually for the *Hunter Valley) Cabernet*. ☆☆☆☆ **1994 Shiraz ££**

**Brouilly** [broo-yee] (*Burgundy*, France) Largest of the ten *Beaujolais Crus* producing pure, fruity *Gamay..* 85 87 **88 89** 90 **91** 93 94 ***Pierre Cotton.*** ☆☆☆ **1995 Château des Tours ££**

**Ch. Broustet** [broo-stay] (*Barsac Deuxième Cru*, *Bordeaux*, France) Rich, quite old-fashioned, well-oaked *Barsac* 2ème *Cru. 70* **71 75** *76* 83 85 86 88 89 90 95 96

**Brown Brothers** (*Victoria*, Australia) Family-owned and *Victoria*-focused winery with a penchant for exploring new wine regions and grapes. The wines are reliably good, though for real excitement, you should look to the *Shiraz and* the *Liqueur Muscat* (following the purchase of the old All Saints winery in *Rutherglen)*. The Orange Muscat and Flora remains a delicious mouthful of liquid marmalade, the *Tarrango* is a good alternative to *Beaujolais,* and the sparkling wine is a new success. ☆☆☆☆ **1992 Shiraz ££**

**Weingut Dr Becker Brüder** [bek-ker broo-dur] (*Rheinhessen*, Germany) Known in Germany for *Trocken Rieslings*, but a good source of *Late Harvest* wines and well-made *Scheurebe*.

**Bruisyard Vineyard** [broos-syard] (England) High-quality vineyard in Suffolk. ☆☆☆ **1990 Müller-Thurgau ££**

**Alain Brumont** [broo-mon] (South-West France) *Madiran* modernist with top-class reds under the Montus and Bouscassé labels, plus stunning banana-ish *Late Harvest Pacherenc de Vic Bilh* called Brumaire. ☆☆☆ **1995 Ch. Bouscassé ££**

**Le Brun de Neuville** [bruhn duh nuh-veel] (*Champagne*, France) Good, little-known producer with classy vintage and excellent rosé and *Blanc de Blancs*. ☆☆☆ **Champagne Rosé Brut £££**

**Willi Bründlmayer** [broodl-mi-yurh] (Austria) Oaked *Chardonnay* and *Pinots* of every kind, *Grüner Veltliner* and even a fairish shot at *Cabernet*. This is one of Austria's rising stars. ☆☆☆ **1995 Grüner Veltliner, Ried Lamm ££**

**Lucien & Andre Brunel** [broo-nel] (*Rhône* France) The Brunels' 'Les Caillous' produces a very good example of traditional, built-to-last *Châteauneuf du Pape*.

**Brunello di Montalcino** [broo-nell-oh dee mon-tahl-chee-noh] (*Tuscany*, Italy) Prestigious *DOCG* red from a *Sangiovese* clone. 78 79 81 82 85 88 90 94 95 *Altesino; Argiano; Villa Banfi; Tenuta Caparzo;* Talenti; Val di Suga.

***Brut*** [Broot] Dry, particularly of *Champagne* and sparkling wines. Brut nature/sauvage/zéro are even drier, while '*Extra-Sec*' is perversely applied to (slightly) sweeter fizz.

**Bual** [Bwahl] (*Madeira*) Grape producing soft, nutty wine – wonderful with cheese. ☆☆☆☆☆ Blandy's 10 Year Old Malmsey £££

**Buçaco Palace Hotel** [boo-sah-koh] (Portugal) Red and white wines made from grapes grown in *Bairrada* and *Dão*, which last forever but cannot be bought outside the Disneyesque Hotel itself.

**Bucelas** [boo-sel-las] (Portugal) *DO* area near Lisbon, best known for its intensely coloured, aromatic, bone-dry white wines. *Caves Velhas*.

**Buena Vista** [bway-nah vihs-tah] (*Carneros*, California) One of the biggest estates in *Carneros*, this is an improving producer of Californian *Chardonnay, Pinot Noir* and *Cabernet*. Look out for Reserve wines.

**Bugey** [boo-jay] (*Savoie*, France) *Savoie* district producing a variety of wines, including spicy white Roussette de Bugey, from the grape of that name.

**Reichsrat von Buhl** [rihk-srat fon bool] (*Pfalz*, Germany) One of the area's best estates, due partly to vineyards like the *Forster Jesuitengarten*. See *Forst*.

**Buitenverwachting** [biht-turn-fur-vak-turng] (*Constantia*, South Africa) Enjoying a revival since the early 1980s, this show-piece organic winery of *Constantia* is making particularly tasty organic whites. ☆☆☆ 1996 Chardonnay ££

**Bulgaria** Developing since the advent of privatisation and *Flying Winemakers*. Even so, Bulgaria's reputation still relies on its country wines, Cabernet Sauvignons and Merlots; there are no real examples of wines worth pulling out for a special occasion. *Mavrud* is the traditional red variety. 81 83 84 85 86 87 89 90 92 94 *Dom Boyar.* ☆☆☆ 1991 Twin Peaks Cabernet Sauvignon Rousse £

***Bull's Blood*** (*Eger*, Hungary) The gutsy red wine, aka Egri Bikaver, which gave defenders the strength to fight off Turkish invaders, is mostly anaemic stuff now, but privatisation has wrought some improvement. ☆☆ 1994 Egervin Vineyard Co.££

**Buller** (*Rutherglen*, Australia) Makers of sometimes excellent fortified wines.

**Burdon** (*Jerez*, Spain) The brand used by *Luis Caballero* for his top-class range of *sherries*. *Lustau*.

**Grant Burge** (*Barossa Valley*, Australia) Dynamic producer and – since 1993 – owner of *Basedows*. ☆☆☆☆ 1993 Shadnach Cabernet Sauvignon. £££

**Burgenland** [boor-gen-lund] (Austria) Wine region bordering *Hungary*, climatically ideal for fine, sweet *Auslese* and *Beerenauslese*. ☆☆☆☆ 1991 Helmut Lang Sämling 88 £££

**Weinkellerei Burgenland** [vihn-kel-ler-rih boor-gen-lund] (*Neusiedlersee*, Austria) Cooperative with top-class *Late Harvest* wines. ☆☆☆☆ 1991 Ruster Trockenbeerenauslese ££

**Alain Burguet** [al-lan boor-gay] (*Burgundy*, France) One-man domaine which proves how good plain *Gevrey Chambertin* can be without heavy doses of new oak. Look for his *Vieilles Vignes*. ☆☆☆☆ 1995 Bourgogne Vieilles Vignes £££

**Burgundy** (France) Home to *Pinot Noir* and *Chardonnay*; wines range from banal to sublime, but are never cheap. See *Chablis, Côte de Nuits, Côte de Beaune, Mâconnais, Beaujolais* and individual villages.

**Leo Buring** [byoo-ring] (*South Australia*) One of the many labels used by the *Penfolds* group, specialising in whites. and mature Shiraz's.

**Weingut Dr Bürklin-Wolf** [boor-klin-volf] (*Pfalz*, Germany) Impressive estate with great organic *Riesling* vineyards.

**Ernest J. & F. Burn** [boorn] (*Alsace* France) Classy estate focusing on making the most of their vines in the Goldert Grand Cru. Great traditional Gewurztraminer, Riesling and Muscat.

***Buttery*** Rich fat smell often found in good *Chardonnay* (often as a result of *malolactic fermentation)* or in wine that has been left on its *Lees*.

**Buxy (Cave des Vignerons de)** [book-see] (*Burgundy*, France) Cooperative with fair-value oaked Bourgogne Rouge and Montagny Premier Cru. ☆☆☆ **1995 Mercurey Les Montots ££**

**Buzbag** [buz-bag] (*Turkey*) Rich, dry red wine. Rarely well-made and often oxidised.

**Byron Vineyard** [bih-ron] (California) Impressive *Santa Barbara* winery with investment from *Mondavi*, and a fine line in *Pinots* and *Chardonnays*. ☆☆☆☆ **1995 Pinot Noir Santa Barbara Reserve £££**

# C

**Luis Caballero** [loo-Is cab-ih-yer-roh] (*Jerez*, Spain) Quality sherry producer responsible for the *Burdon* range; also owns *Lustau*. ☆☆☆☆

**Château La Cabanne** [la ca-ban] (*Pomerol, Bordeaux*, France) Up-and-coming *Pomerol* property. Red: 79 81 **82** 83 85 86 87 88 89 90 92 93 94

**Cabardès** [cab-bahr-des] (*South-West France*) Up-and-coming region north of Carcassonne using traditional Southern and *Bordeaux* varieties to produce good, if rustic, reds.

**Cabernet d'Anjou/de Saumur** [cab-behr-nay don-joo / dur soh-moor] (*Loire*, France) Light, fresh, grassy, blackcurranty rosés, typical of their grape, the *Cabernet Franc*. 78 81 83 **85** 86 **88 89 90** 95 ☆☆☆ **1995 Saumur Champigny Le Valvert ££**

**Cabernet Franc** [ka-behr-nay fron] Kid brother of *Cabernet Sauvignon*; blackcurranty, but more leafy. Best in the *Loire*, Italy, and increasingly in Australia and partnering *Cabernet Sauvignon* and particularly *Merlot* in *St. Emilion*. See *Chinon* and *Trentino*. ☆☆☆☆ **1995 Tim Knapstein 'The Franc' ££**

**Cabernet Sauvignon** [ka-ber-nay soh-vin-yon] The great red grape of *Bordeaux*, where it is blended with *Merlot* and other varieties. Despite increasing competition from the Merlot, still by far the most successful red varietal, grown in every reasonably warm winemaking country. See *Bordeaux, Coonawarra, Chile, Napa*, etc.

**Marqués de Cáceres** [mahr-kehs day cath-thay-res] (*Rioja*, Spain) Modern French-influenced *Bodega* making fresh tasting wines. A good, if anonymous, new-style white has been joined by a promising, oak-fermented version and a recommendable rosé (*Rosado*), plus a grapy Muscat style white. ☆☆☆ **1996 Satinela ££**

**Ch. Cadet-Piola** [ka-day pee-yoh-lah] (*St. Emilion Grand Cru Classé*, *Bordeaux*, France) Not always the producer of the classiest wines, but most are made to last, with concentrated fruit and tannin to spare. 82 **83 85** 86 87 88 89 90 92 93 95 ☆☆☆☆ **1993 £££**

**Cadillac** [kad-dee-yak] (*Bordeaux*, France) Sweet but rarely luscious (non-*Botrytis*) old-fashioned *Sémillon* and *Sauvignon* whites for drinking young and well-chilled. Ch. Fayau is the only really recommendable wine. Its *Yquem*-style label is pretty smart too. **83** 86 **88 89 90** 94 95 96

**Cafayate** [ka-fah-yeh-tay] (Argentina) See *Etchart*.

**Cahors** [kah-orr] (*South-West*, France) 'Rustic' *Bordeaux*-like reds produced mainly from the local *Tannat* and the Cot (*Malbec*). Some examples are frankly *Beaujolais*-like while others are tannic, and quite full-bodied, though far lighter than they were in the days when people spoke of 'the black wines of Cahors'. ☆☆☆☆ **1994 Ch. St. Pierre de Cenac ££**

**Ch. Caillou** [kih-yoo] (*Barsac Deuxième Cru Classé, Bordeaux*, France) Good, but rather simple wine – at its best in 1988 and 1990. 75 76 78 81 82 83 85 86 87 88 89 90 94 95 96

**Cairanne** [keh-ran] (*Rhône*, France) Named *Côtes du Rhône* village known for good, peppery reds. 76 78 **82 83 85 88** 89 90 91 95 96 ☆☆☆☆ **1996 Domaine Richaud ££**

**Calabria** [kah-lah-bree-ah] (Italy) The 'toe' of the Italian boot, making *Cirò* from the local *Gaglioppo* reds and *Greco* whites. *Cabernet* and *Chardonnay* are promising, too, especially those made by Librandi.

**Calem** [kah-lin] (*Duoro*, Portugal) Quality-conscious, small, Portuguese-owned producer with a British winemaker. The speciality *Colheita* tawnies are among the best of their kind. ☆☆☆☆ **1960 Colheita ££££**

**Calera Wine Co.** [ka-lehr-uh] (*Santa Benito*, California) Maker of some of California's best *Pinot Noir* from individual vineyards such as Jensen, Mills, Reed and Selleck. The *Chardonnay* and *Viognier* are pretty special, too. ☆☆☆☆ **1994 Pinot Noir Reserve ££**

**California** (USA) Major wine-producing area of the US. See *Napa, Sonoma, Santa Barbara, Amador, Mendocino,* etc, plus individual wineries. Red: 84 **85** 86 87 **90 91** 92 93 95 White: **85 90 91** 92 95 96

**Viña Caliterra** [kal-lee-tay-rah] (*Curico*, Chile) High-quality sister company of Errazuriz, founded as a joint venture with *Franciscan*, which is now doing their own thing at *Veramonte*. Now a 50-50 partner with *Mondavi*. ☆☆☆**1995 Cabernet Sauvignon Riserva ££**

**Ch. Calon-Segur** [kal-lon say-goor] (*St. Estèphe 3rd Growth, Bordeaux*, France) Traditional *St. Estèphe* that hasn't always lived up to its 3rd Growth status, but made a stunning 1995. 78 79 **82** 83 **85** 86 87 **88** 89 90 91 93 94 95 96 ☆☆☆☆ **1993 £££**

**Quinta da Camarate** [kin-tah dah kam-mah-rah-tay] (*Estremadura*, Portugal) Attractive *Cabernet Sauvignon*-based red from *J.M. da Fonseca*. ☆☆☆ **1995**

**Ch. Camensac** [kam-mon-sak] (*Haut-Médoc 5th Growth, Bordeaux*, France) Improving property following investment in 1994. 81 **82** 85 **86** 87 88 89 90 91 92 93 94 95 96 ☆☆☆☆ **1993 £££**

**Campania** [kahm-pan-nyah] (Italy) Region surrounding Naples, known for *Taurasi, Lacryma Christi* and *Greco di Tufo and wines from Mastroberadino.*

**Campbells** (*Rutherglen*, Australia) Classic producer of fortified wines and rich, concentrated reds. ☆☆☆☆ **Old Rutherglen Muscat ££**

**Campillo** [kam-pee-yoh] (*Rioja*, Spain) A small estate producing *Rioja* made purely from *Tempranillo*, showing what this grape can do. The white is less impressive. ☆☆☆ **1990 Riserva ££**

🍷 **Bodegas Campo Viejo** [kam-poh vyay-hoh] (*Rioja*, Spain) A go-ahead, often underrated *Bodega* whose *Reserva* and *Gran Reserva* are full of rich fruit. Albor, the unoaked red (pure *Tempranillo)* and white (*Viura*) are first-class examples of modern Spanish winemaking. ☆☆☆☆ **1992 Reserva ££**

**Canada** Surprising friends and foes alike, British Columbia and, more specifically, *Ontario* are producing good *Chardonnay, Riesling*, improving *Pinot Noirs* and intense *Ice wines*, usually from the *Vidal* grape.

🍷 **Canard Duchêne** [kan-nah doo-shayn] (*Champagne*, France) Improving subsidiary of *Veuve Clicquot*. ☆☆☆☆ **1990 Brut £££**

🍷 **Cánepa** [hoh-say can-ňay-pah] (Chile) Good rather than great winery, making progress with *Chardonnays* and *Rieslings* as well as reds. ☆☆☆☆ **1997 Chardonnay ££**

🍇 **Cannonau** [kan-non-now] (*Sardinia*, Italy) An Italian red clone of the *Grenache*, producing a variety of wine styles from sweet to dry, mostly in *Sardinia*.

🍷 **Cannonau di Sardegna** [kan-non-now dee sahr-den-yah] (*Sardinia*, Italy) Heady, robust, dry-to-sweet, *DOC* red made from the *Cannonau* grape. ☆☆☆☆ **1994 Argiolas Costera ££**

🍷 **Ch. Canon** [kan-non] (*St Emilion Premier Grand Cru Classé, Bordeaux*, France) First rate property, whose subtle wines are wonderful examples of the *St. Emilion* at their best. Worth seeking out in difficult vintages. **82** 83 **85 86** 87 88 89 90 92 93 94 95 96 ☆☆☆☆ **1990 ££££**

🍷 **Ch. Canon** [kan-non] (*Canon-Fronsac, Bordeaux*, France) Small property in *Canon Fronsac* owned by Christian *Moueix*. 82 83 85 **86** 88 89 90 93 95 ☆☆☆ **1993 £££**

🍷 **Ch. Canon de Brem** [kan-non dur brem] (*Canon-Fronsac, Bordeaux*, France) A very good *Moueix*-run *Fronsac* property. Red: 81 **82** 83 85 86 88 89 90 92 93 95 ☆☆☆ **1993 ££**

**Canon Fronsac** [kah-non fron-sak] (*Bordeaux*, France) Small *AC* bordering on *Pomerol*, with attractive plummy, *Merlot*-based reds from increasingly good value, if rustic, *Petits Châteaux*. **82 83 85** *86* **88 89** 90 *94* 95 ☆☆☆ **1994 Ch. Roumagnac ££**

🍷 **Ch. Canon-la-Gaffelière** [kan-non lah gaf-fel-yehr] (*St. Emilion Grand Cru Classé, Bordeaux*, France) High-flying estate following a purchase by quality-conscious Austrians, who, in 1996, created the instant superstar *la Mondotte*. 82 83 85 **86** 87 88 89 90 92 93 94 95

🍷 **Ch. Canon-Moueix** [kan-non mwex] (*Canon-Fronsac, Bordeaux*, France) A stylish addition to the *Moueix* empire in *Canon-Fronsac*. 82 83 85 86 87 88 89 90 92 93 94 95 ☆☆☆ **1995 ££**

🍷 **Ch. Cantemerle** [kont-mehrl] (*Haut-Médoc 5th Growth, Bordeaux*, France) A *Cru Classé* situated outside the main villages of the *Médoc*. Classy, perfumed wine with bags of blackcurrant fruit. Red: **61** 78 81 82 **83** 85 87 88 89 90 92 93 95 ☆☆☆☆ **1992 ££**

**Cantenac** [kont-nak] (*Bordeaux*, France) *Commune* within the *Appellation* of *Margaux* whose Châteaux include *Palmer*. **78** 79 81 **82** 83 **85 86** 88 89 90 94 95 96

🍷 **Ch. Cantenac-Brown** [kont-nak brown] (*Margaux 3rd Growth, Bordeaux*, France) Improving from its previously disappointing state. 70 78 79 81 82 83 85 **86** 87 88 89 90 93 94 95 ☆☆☆ **1993 ££**

**Canterbury** (New Zealand) Despite early success with *Pinot Noir* by *St. Helena*, this cool area of the South Island is best suited to highly aromatic *Riesling, Pinot Blanc* and *Chablis*-like *Chardonnay*. ***Giesen;*** **Daniel Schuster; St Helena;** ***Waipara Springs.***

*Cantina (Sociale)* [kan-tee-nuh soh-chee-yah-lay] (Italy) Winery (cooperative).

*Cap Classique* [kap-klas-seek] (South Africa) Now that the term '*Méthode Champenoise*' has unreasonably been outlawed, Cap Classique is the phrase developed by the South Africans to describe their *Champagne*-method sparklers.

🍷 **Ch. Cap-de-Mourlin** [kap-dur-mer-lan] (*St. Emilion Grand Cru Classé, Bordeaux*, France) Until 1983 when they were amalgamated, there were, confusingly, two different châteaux with this name. Good mid-range stuff. **79** 81 **82 83** 85 86 88 89 90 93 ☆☆☆☆ **1988 ££**

🍷 **Caparzo** [ka-pahrt-zoh] (*Tuscany* Italy) Classy, *Brunello di Montalcino* estate producing wines that age well. ☆☆☆☆ **1988 £££**

**Cape** (South Africa) All of the vineyard areas of South Africa are located in the Western Cape, most of them within an hour or two from Capetown. See under ***Stellenbosch, Paarl, Franschhoek, Walker Bay, Robertson, Tulbagh, Worcester*** etc. Red: **82 84** 86 **87** 89 **91 92** 93 94 95 White: **87 91** 92 93 94 95

🍷 **Cape Mentelle** [men-tel] (*Margaret River*, Western Australia) Brilliant French-owned winery, founded, like *Cloudy Bay*, by David Hoehnen. Impressive *Semillon-Sauvignon, Shiraz, Cabernet* and, remarkably, a wild, berryish *Zinfandel*, to shame many a Californian. ☆☆☆☆ **1996 Semillon Sauvignon Blanc ££**

🍷 **Capel Vale** [kay-puhl vayl] (West, Australia) Just to the north of the borders of *Margaret River*. A good source of *Riesling, Gewürztraminers* and improving reds such as the Baudin blend. ☆☆☆☆ **1995 Capel Vale Shiraz ££**

🍷 **Villa di Capezzana** [kap-pay-tzah-nah] (*Tuscany*, Italy) Conte Ugo Contini Bonacossi not only deserves credit for getting *Carmignano* its *DOCG*, he also helped to promote the notion of *Cabernet* and *Sangiovese* as compatible bedfellows, helping to open the door for all those priceless – and pricy – *Super-Tuscans*. ☆☆☆ **1993 Ghiaie della Furba. £££**

*Capsule* The sheath covering the cork. Once lead, now plastic, or a type of tin. In the case of new wave 'flanged' bottles, however, it is noticeable by its transparency or absence.

🍷 **Caramany** [kah-ram-man-nee] (*Midi*, France) New *AC* for an old section of the *Côtes du Roussillon-Villages*, close to the *Pyrenees*. ***Vignerons Catalans.***

*Carbonic Maceration* See *Macération Carbonique*.

🍷 **Ch. Carbonnieux** [kar-bon-nyeuh] (*Graves Cru Classé, Bordeaux*, France) Until recently, the whites here aged well, but lacked fresh appeal in their youth. Since 1991, however, they have greatly improved and the raspberryish reds are becoming some of the most reliable in the region. Red: 82 83 85 **86** 87 88 89 90 92 94 95 White: 87 88 89 90 92 93 94 95 ☆☆☆☆ **1992 Red £££**

🍷 **Carcavelos** [kar-kah-veh-losh] (Portugal) *DO* region producing usually disappointing fortified wines close to Lisbon. Vineyards are giving way to suburban sprawl.

🍷 **Cantina dei Produttori Nebbiolo Carema** [proh-doo-tohr-ree nay-bee-yoh-loh kah-ray-mah] (*Piedmont*, Italy) Wonderful, perfumed *Nebbiolo* produced in limited quantities.

🍇 **Carignan** [kah-ree-nyon] Prolific red grape making usually dull, coarse wine for blending, but classier fare in *Corbières* and *Fitou*. In Spain it is known as Cariñena and Mazuelo, while Italians call it Carignano. ☆☆☆☆☆ **1994 La Tour Boisee ££**; ☆☆☆☆☆ **1993 Terre Brune; Santadi £££**

**Louis Carillon & Fils** [ka-ree-yon] (*Burgundy*, France) Superlative modern *Puligny* estate. ☆☆☆☆ **1995 Puligny-Montrachet ££££**

**Cariñena** [kah-ree-nyeh-nah] (Spain) Important *DO* of Aragon for rustic reds, high in alcohol and, confusingly, made not from the *Cariñena* (or *Carignan)* grape, but mostly from the *Garnacha Tinta*. Also some whites. ☆☆☆☆ **1996 Bodegas San Valero Santero ££**

**Cariñena** [kah-ree-nyeh-nah] (Spain) The name for *Carignan*.

**Viña Carmen** [veen-yah kahr-men] (*Maipo*, Chile) Quietly developing a reputation as one of the best red wine producers in Chile. Seek out the *Grand Vidure Carmenère*. ☆☆☆☆ **1995 Cabernet Sauvignon Riserva ££**

**Carmenère** [kahr-meh-nehr] (Chile) Smoky-spicily distinctive grape that although almost extinct in Bordeaux is still a permitted variety for claret. Widely planted in Chile where it is usually sold as Merlot. Look for examples like the Santa Inès Carmenère or Carmen Grand Vidure.

**Carmenet Vineyard** [kahr-men-nay] (*Sonoma Valley*, California) Excellent and unusual winery tucked away in the hills and producing long-lived, very *Bordeaux*-like but approachable reds, and also (even more unusually for California) good *Semillon-Sauvignon* whites and *Cabernet Franc*. ☆☆☆☆ **1996 Sauvignon Semillon ££**

**Les Carmes-Haut-Brion** [lay kahrm oh bree-yon] (*Bordeaux*, France) Small property neighbouring *Ch. Haut-Brion* in the *Pessac-Leognan* area of the *Graves*.

**Carmignano** [kahr-mee-nyah-noh] (*Tuscany*, Italy) Exciting alternative to Chianti, in the same style but with the addition of *Cabernet* grapes. See *Villa di Capezzana*. **82** 85 88 90 91 93 94 95

**Carneros** [kahr-neh-ros] (California) Small, fog-cooled, high-quality region shared between the *Napa* and *Sonoma* Valleys. Producing top-class *Chardonnay* and *Pinot Noir*. Red: 84 **85** 86 87 **90 91** 92 93 95. White: **85 90 91** 92 95 ***Mondavi; Domaine Chandon Cuvee Napa; Saintsbury; Swanson.***

**Dom. Carneros** (*Napa Valley*, California) *Taittinger's* US fizz – produced in a perfect and thus ludicrously incongruous replica of their French HQ. The wine, however, is one of the best New World efforts by the Champenois.

**Carneros Creek** (*Carneros*, California) Producer of ambitious but disappointing *Pinot Noir* under this name and the far better (and cheaper) berryish Fleur de Carneros.

**Ch. Caronne-Ste-Gemme** [ka-ron sant jem] (*Haut-Médoc Grand Bourgeois Exceptionnel*, *Bordeaux*, France) A reliable but not overly showy *Cru Bourgeois*. 81 **82** 83 85 88 **89** 90 93 94 95. ☆☆☆☆**1982 ££££**

**Carr Taylor** (Sussex, England) One of England's more businesslike estates. ☆☆☆ **1994 Sparkling Wine.**

**Ch. Carras** [kar-ras] (*Macedonia*, Greece) Until recently the only internationally visible Hellenic effort at modern winemaking. Disappointing when compared with *Hatzimichalis*.

**Ch. Carruades de Lafite** [kah-roo-ahd-dur la-feet] (*Pauillac*, *Bordeaux*, France) The *Second Label* of *Ch. Lafite*. Rarely (quite) as good as its counterpart *les Forts de Latour*, nor Ch. Margaux's *Pavillon Rouge*.

**Ch. Carsin** [kahr-san] (*Entre-Deux-Mers, Bordeaux*, France) Finnish-owned, Aussie-style winery proving that this appellation is capable of producing wines of class and complexity. Australian Mandy Jones makes particularly tasty whites. **92** 93 94 95 ☆☆☆ **1995 Cuvee Blanc Sec ££**

*Casa* [kah-sah] (Italy, Spain, Portugal) Firm or company.

**Casablanca** [kas-sab-lan-ka] (*Aconcagua*, Chile) New region in *Aconcagua*; a magnet for quality conscious winemakers and producing especially impressive Sauvignons, Chardonnays and *Gewürztraminers*. ***Caliterra; Santa Carolina; Santa Emiliana; Villard and Casablanca; Santa Rita; Concha y Toro.***

**Viña Casablanca** [veen-yah kas-sab-lan-ka] (*Casablanca*, Chile) Go-ahead winery in the region of the same name, though also (confusingly) making wine from grapes grown elsewhere. A showcase for the talents of winemaker *Ignacio Recabarren*. ☆☆☆☆ **1997 Casablanca Valley White Label Sauvignon Blanc ££;** ☆☆☆☆ **1996 Santa Isabel Merlot ££**

**Caslot-Galbrun** [kah-loh gal-bruhn] (*Loire*, France) Top-class producer of serious, long-lived red *Loires*.

**Cassegrain** [kas-grayn] (*New South Wales*, Australia) Tucked away in the Hastings Valley on the East Coast, but also drawing grapes from elsewhere. The wines can be variable, but are often impressive. ☆☆☆☆ **1994 Semillon Hastings Valley ££**

**Cassis** [ka-sees] (*Provence*, France) Tiny coastal appellation producing (unreliable) red, (often dull) white and (good) rosé. ☆☆☆☆ **1994 Clos Ste Magdeleine Rouge ££**

**Castelgiocondo** [kas-tel-jee-yah-kon-doh] (*Tuscany*, Italy) High-quality *Brunello* estate owned by **Frescobaldi.**

**Castell'in Villa** [kas-tel-lin-veel-lah] (*Tuscany*, Italy) Producer of powerful *Chianti Classico Riserva* and a *Vino da Tavola* called Santa Croche.

**Castellare** [kas-tel-lah-ray] (*Tuscany*, Italy) Innovative small *Chianti Classico* estate whose Sangiovese-Malvasia blend, Nera I Sodi di San Niccoló, *Vino da Tavola*, is worth seeking out.

**Castellblanch** [kas-tel-blantch] (*Catalonia*, Spain) Producer of better-than-most *Cava*, provided you catch it very young. ☆☆☆ **Cava Brut Zero ££**

**Casteller** [kas-teh-ler] (*Trentino-Alto-Adige*, Italy) Pale red, creamy-fruity wines for early drinking, made from Schiava. See *Ca'Vit*

*Cat's pee* Describes the tangy smell frequently found in typical – and often delicious – *Müller-Thurgau* and *Sauvignon*.

**Vignerons Catalans** [veen-yehr-ron kah-tak-lon] (*Midi*, France) Dynamic cooperative with decent, inexpensive wines. ☆☆☆ **1995 Bon Verre Corbières £**

**Catalonia** [kat-tal-loh-nee-yah] (Spain) The semi-autonomous region in which are found the *Penedés, Priorato, Conca de Barberá, Terra Alta* and *Costers del Segre.*

**Catena Estate** [kat-tay-nah] (Argentina) Quality-focused part of the giant Catena-Esmeralda concern, helped by the expertise of ex *Simi* winemaker Californian, Paul Hobbs. ☆☆☆☆ **1995 Alta Chardonnay ££**

**Dom. Cauhapé** [koh-ap-pay] (South West France) Extraordinary *Jurançon* producer of excellent *Vendange Tardive* and dry wines from the *Manseng* grape. ☆☆☆☆ **1996 Jurançon Sec Chant des Vignes ££**

*Cava* [kah-vah] (*Catalonia*, Spain) Fizz produced in *Penedés* by the *Methode Champenoise*, but handicapped by innately dull local grapes and ageing, which deprives it of freshness. Avoid vintage versions and look instead for Ana de *Cordoniu* and *Raimat* Cava – both made from *Chardonnay* – or such well-made exceptions to the earthy rule as *Juve i Camps, Conde de Caralt, Cava Chandon* and *Segura Viudas.*

*Cava* (Greece) Legal term for wood and bottle-aged wine.

*Cave* (France) Cellar.

**Caymus Vineyards** [kay-muhs] (*Napa Valley*, California) Traditional producer of concentrated, Italianate reds (including a forceful *Zinfandel)* and a characterful *Cabernet Franc*. Liberty School is the *Second Label*.

**Dom. Cazes** [kahrs] (*Midi*, France) Maker of great *Muscat de Rivesaltes*, rich marmaladey stuff which makes most *Beaumes de Venise* seem very dull. ☆☆☆☆ **1996 Muscat de Rivesaltes ££**

**Cellier le Brun** [sel-yay luh-bruhn] (*Marlborough*, New Zealand) Specialist producer of *Méthode Champenoise* sparkling wine under the expert supervision of Daniel Le Brun, an expatriate Frenchman. ☆☆☆ **Brut NV £££**

**Cencibel** [sen-thee-bel] (*Valdepeñas*, Spain) An alternative name for *Tempranillo*.

**Central Coast** (California) Increasingly interesting, varied set of regions south of San Francisco, including *Santa Barbara*, *Monterey, Santa Cruz* and *San Luis Obispo*. Red: 84 **85** 86 87 **90 91** 92 93 94 95 96 White: **85 90 91** 92 95 96

**Central Valley** (California) Huge, irrigated region controlled by wine-making giants who annually make nearly three-quarters of the state's wines without, so far, producing much to compete with the fruit of similar regions Down Under. Newly planted vineyards and a concentration on the most climatically advantaged parts of the region are beginning to pay off for grape varieties like the Sauvignon Blanc. Better, smaller-scale winemaking would probably help too (this is wine-factory country). *Quady*'s fortified and sweet wines are still by far the best wines here. Red: 84 **85** 86 87 **90 91** 92 93 95 96 White: **85 90 91** 92 95 96

**Central Valley** (Chile) The region in which most of *Chile*'s wines are made. It includes *Maipo, Rapel, Maule* and *Curico,* but not the new cool-climate region of *Casablanca,* which is in *Aconcagua,* further north.

***Cépage*** [say-pahzh] (France) Grape variety.

**Cepparello** [chep-par-rel-loh] (*Tuscany*, Italy) The brilliant, pure *Sangiovese Vino da Tavola* made by Paolo de Marchi of *Isole e Olena*. ☆☆☆☆ **1994 £££**

**Ceretto** [cher-ret-toh] (*Piedmont*, Italy) Big producer of mid-quality *Barolos* and more impressive single-vineyard examples. ☆☆☆☆ **1990 Barbaresco Bricco Asili Faset ££££**

**Ch. de Cérons** [say-ron] (*Bordeaux*, France) One of the best properties in *Cérons*. White: 83 86 **88** 89 **90** ☆☆☆☆ **1990 Château de Cerons.**

**Ch. Certan de May** [sehr-ton dur may] (*Pomerol*, *Bordeaux*, France) Top-class *Pomerol* estate with subtly plummy wine. Red: 70 75 78 **79 81 82 83 85 86** 87 88 89 90 94 95 96 ☆☆☆☆☆ **1990 ££££**

**Ch. Certan-Giraud** [sehr-ton zhee-roh] (*Pomerol*, *Bordeaux*, France) *Pomerol* at its most overtly plummy. Good vintages last well. 75 82 **83** 85 86 87 88 89 90 93 94 95

**César** [say-zahr] (*Burgundy*, France) The forgotten plummy-raspberryish red grape of *Burgundy*, still vinified in tiny quantities near Chablis by Simonnet-Fèvre. ☆☆☆☆ **1988 Cuvée César ££**

**L A Cetto** [chet-toh] (*Baja California*, Mexico) With wines like LA Cetto's tasty *Cabernet* and spicy-soft *Petite Sirah,* it's hardly surprising that *Baja California* is now beginning to compete with a more northerly region across the US frontier. ☆☆☆ **1993 Nebbiolo ££**

**Chablais** [shab-lay] (*Vaud*, Switzerland) A good place to find Pinot Noir rosé and young *Chasselas* (sold as *Dorin*).

**Chablis** [shab-lee] (*Burgundy*, France) When not overpriced *Chablis* offers a steely European finesse that New World *Chardonnays* rarely capture. Grands Crus should show extra complexity. 85 **86** 88 89 **90** 92 94 95 96 ***Laroche; Raveneau; La Chablisienne; Louis Michel; Jean-Marc Brocard; René Dauvissat.***

**La Chablisienne** [shab-lees-yen] (*Burgundy*, France) Cooperative selling everything from *Petit Chablis* to *Grands Crus* under a host of labels. Rivals the best estates in the *Appellation*. ☆☆☆☆ **1992 Chablis Premier Cru Mont de Milieu £££**

***Chai*** [shay] (France) Cellar/winery.

**Ch. Chalon** [shal-lon] (*Jura*, France) Speciality *Jura AC* for a *Vin Jaune* which should keep almost indefinitely. **1949 Arbois £££££**

**Chalone** [shal-lohn] (*Monterey*, California) Under the same ownership as *Acacia, Edna Valley* and *Carmenet*, this 25-year old winery is one of the big names for *Pinot Noir* and *Chardonnay*. Unusually Burgundian, long-lived. ☆☆☆☆ **1991 Chardonnay Estate Reserve £££**

**Chalonnais/Côte Chalonnaise** [shal-lohn-nay] (*Burgundy*, France) Source of lesser-known, less complex Burgundies – *Givry, Montagny, Rully* and *Mercurey*. Potentially (rather than always actually) good-value. Red: **78 85** 87 **88** 89 90 92 95 96 White: **85 86** 87 **88** 89 **90 92** 95 96

**Chambers Rosewood** (*Rutherglen*, Australia) Competes with *Morris* for the crown of best *Liqueur Muscat* maker. The Rosewood is worth seeking out. ☆☆☆☆ **Old Vine Muscadelle. ££**

**Ch. Chambert-Marbuzet** [shom-behr mahr-boo-zay] (*St. Estèphe Cru Bourgeois, Bordeaux*, France) Characterful *Cabernet*-based *St. Estèphe*. 70 76 78 79 81 82 83 85 86 87 88 89 90 91 94 95

**Chambertin** [shom-behr-tan] (*Burgundy*, France) Ultra-cherryish, damsony *Grand Cru* whose name was adopted by the village of Gevrey. Famous in the 14th century, and Napoleon's favourite. Chambertin Clos-de-Bèze, Charmes-Chambertin, Griottes-Chambertin, Latricières-Chambertin, Mazis-Chambertin and Ruchottes-Chambertin are neighbouring Grands Crus. Red: 76 **78** 79 **80** 82 83 **85** 86 87 **88 89 90** 92 95 ***Armand Rousseau; B Clair; Dujac; J Roty; A Burguet; A Rousseau; Engel; Pierre Amiot; Bernard Meaume; B Dugat-Py.***

**Chambolle-Musigny** [shom-bol moo-see-nyee] (*Burgundy*, France) *Côte de Nuits* village whose wines are sometimes more like perfumed examples from the *Côte de Beaune*. Criticism of quality drove producers to tighten up the *Appellation* tastings in 1993. Others may follow. *Georges Roumier* is the local star, and *Drouhin, Dujac* and *Ponsot* are all reliable. Red: 76 78 79 **80** 82 83 **85** 86 87 **88 89 90** 92 95 96

**Champagne** [sham-payn] (France) Source of potentially the greatest sparkling wines, from *Pinot Noir*, *Pinot Meunier* and *Chardonnay* grapes. See individual listings. **81** 82 83 85 86 88 89 90 91 92

**Didier Champalou** [dee-dee-yay shom-pah-loo] (*Loire*, France) Young estate with serious sweet, dry and sparkling *Vouvray*. ☆☆☆☆ **1995 Vouvray Sec ££**

**Champigny** [shom-pee-nyee] (*Loire*, France) See *Saumur*.

**Champy** [shom-pee] (*Burgundy*, France) Long-established, much-improved *négociant*. ☆☆☆☆**1993 Volnay Premier Cru Les Caillerets ££££**

**Dom. Chandon** [doh-mayn shahn-dahn] (*Napa Valley*, California) *Moët & Chandon*'s Californian winery, until recently under-performing, has finally been allowed to compete with its counterpart at *Dom. Chandon* in Australia. Wines are sold in the UK as Shadow Creek.

**Dom. Chandon** [doh-mihn shon-don] (*Yarra Valley*, Australia) Sold as *Green Point* in the UK. Winemaker Tony Jordan proved to its owners, *Moët & Chandon*, that Aussie grapes, grown in a variety of cool climates, compete with *Champagne*. Now joined by a creditable, *Chablis*-like, still Colonades *Chardonnay*. ☆☆☆☆ **1993 Green Point Blanc de Blancs £££**

**Dom. Chandon de Briailles** [shon-don dur bree-iy] (*Burgundy*, France) Good *Savigny-lès-Beaune* estate whose owner is related to the original *Chandon* of *Champagne*. ☆☆☆☆ **1993 Corton Clos du Roi ££££**

**Chanson** [shon-son] (*Burgundy*, France) Slowly improving merchant.

**Ch. de Chantegrive** [shont-greev] (*Graves, Bordeaux*, France) Large, modern *Graves* estate with excellent modern reds and whites. Red: 82 83 85 87 88 93 94 95 White: 89 90 92 93 94 95 ☆☆☆☆☆ **1994 Cuvée Caroline (Blanc).**

**Chapel Down** (Kent, England) David Cowdroy's impressive winery-only operation uses grapes sourced from vineyards throughout southern England.☆☆☆ **Century Extra Dry Sparkling ££** ☆☆☆☆ **1995 Epoch Reserve £££**

**Chapel Hill Winery** (*McLaren Vale*, Australia) Pam Dunsford's impressively rich – some say too rich – reds and whites have recently been joined by a similarly leaner, unoaked Chardonnay. ☆☆☆☆☆ **1994 The Vicar £££**

**Chapoutier** [shah-poo-tyay] (*Rhône*, France) Family-owned merchant rescued from its faded laurels by a new generation who are using more or less organic methods. Not all wines live up to their early promise. ☆☆☆☆ **1995 Muscat de Rivesaltes ££**

***Chaptalisation*** [shap-tal-lih-zay-shuhn] The legal (in some regions) addition of sugar during fermentation to boost a wine's alcohol content.

**Charbono** [shar-boh-noh] (California) Obscure grape variety grown in California but thought to come from France. Makes interesting, very spicy, full-bodied reds at *Inglenook, Duxoup* and Bonny Doon. ☆☆☆☆ **1994 Duxoup £££**

**Chardonnay** [shar-don-nay] The great white grape of *Burgundy, Champagne* and now the New World. Capable of fresh simple charm in *Bulgaria* and buttery, hazelnutty richness in *Meursault*. See producers.

***Charmat*** [shar-mat] The inventor of the *Cuve Close* method of producing cheap sparkling wines. See *Cuve Close*.

**Ch. des Charmes** [day sharm] (Canada) One of Ontario's best producers of Chardonnay, Pinot and Ice Wine. ☆☆☆☆ **1994 Paul Bosc Estate Icewine ££££**

***Charta*** [kahr-tah] (*Rheingau*, Germany) *Rheingau* Syndicate using an arch as a symbol to indicate dry (*Trocken*) styles designed to be suitable for drinking with food – although often apparently acidic enough to remove enamel from teeth. *Spätlese* and preferably *Auslese* versions are made from riper grapes. *Kabinetts* are for keen lemon-suckers.

**Chartron & Trébuchet** [shar-tron ay tray-boo-shay] (*Burgundy*, France) Good small merchant specialising in white Burgundies. ☆☆☆☆ **1994 Meursault ££££**

**Chassagne-Montrachet** [shah-san mon-rash-shay] (*Burgundy*, France) *Côte de Beaune* commune making grassy, biscuity, fresh yet rich whites and mid-weight, often rustic tasting wild fruit reds. Pricy but sometimes less so than neighbouring *Puligny* and as recommendable. White: 79 84 **85 86** 87 **88** 89 **90 92** 95. Red: 78 80 83 **85** 86 87 **88 89 90** 92 95 ***Michel Niellon; Marc Colin; Jean-Noel Gagnard; M Morey; Colin-Déleger; L Carillon; Roux; Ramonet; J Pillot.***

**Ch. Chasse-Spleen** [shas spleen] (*Moulis Cru Bourgeois, Bordeaux*, France) *Cru Bourgeois* château whose wines can, in good years, rival those of many a *Cru Classé*, but which have shone a little less brightly of late. **70 78** 79 **81** 82 **83 85 86** 87 88 89 90 94 95 96 ☆☆☆ **1990 £££**

**Chasselas** [shas-slah] Widely grown, prolific white grape making light, often dull wine principally in Switzerland, eastern France and Germany. Good examples are rare. ☆☆☆☆ **1995 Vieilles Vignes, Reserve Pierre Sparr ££**

**Dom. du Chasseloir** [shas-slwah] (*Loire*, France) Makers of good domaine *Muscadets*. ☆☆☆ **1995 Cuvée de Ceps Centenaires ££**

***Château*** [sha-toh] (*Bordeaux*, France) Literally means 'castle'. Some châteaux are extremely grand, many are merely farmhouses. A building is not required; the term just applies to a vineyard or wine estate. Château names cannot be invented, but there are plenty of defunct titles that are used unashamedly by large cooperative wineries to market their members' wines.

**Châteauneuf-du-Pape** [shah-toh-nurf-doo-pap] (*Rhône*, France) Traditionally the best reds (rich and spicy) and whites (rich and floral) of the southern Rhône. Thirteen varieties can be used for the red, though purists still favour *Grenache*. 78 81 **82 83 85 88** 89 90 95 96 ***Ch. de Beaucastel; Chapoutier; Font de Michelle; Guigal; Rayas. Clos des Papes; Clos des Mont-Olivet; Lucien & André Brunel; Les Bosquet des Papes; Dom de Beaurenard; Pierre André; Henri Bonneau; Ch. La Nerthe; Vieux Télégraphe.***

**Gérard Chave** [sharv] (*Rhône*, France) The best estate in *Hermitage*, but the wines demand patience. NB: labels read JL Chave; the eldest son in alternate generations is thus named, so it is thought unnecessary to print anything else in between times. ☆☆☆☆☆ **1991 Hermitage ££££**

**Chavignol** [sha-veen_yol] (*Loire*, France) Village within the commune of *Sancerre*.

**Dom Gérard Chavy** [Shah-Vee] (*Burgundy*, France) High-quality estate. ☆☆☆ **1994 Puligny-Montrachet ££**

**Chénas** [shay-nass] (*Burgundy*, France) Good but least well-known of the *Beaujolais Crus*. Daniel Robin and *Duboeuf* are worthy examples.

**Dom du Chêne** [doo-shehn] (*Rhône*, France) Small estate producing rich ripe *Condrieu* and top class *St. Joseph*, the best cuvée of which is sold as 'Anais'.

***Chêne*** [shehn] (France) Oak, as in *Fûts de Chêne* (oak barrels).

**Chenin Blanc** [shur-nan-blon *for France*, shen nin blonk *for elsewhere*] Honeyed white grape of the *Loire*. Wines vary from bone-dry to sweet and long-lived. High acidity makes it ideal for fizz, while sweet versions benefit from *Noble Rot*. French examples are often marred by green unripe flavours and heavy handedness with *Sulphur Dioxide*. Grown successfully in South Africa (where it is known as *Steen*) and, though less frequently, New Zealand and Australia. It is generally disappointing in California. See *Vouvray, Quarts de Chaumes, Bonnezeaux, Saumur*.

**Ch. Cheval Blanc** [shuh-vahl blon] (*St. Emilion Premier Grand Cru Classé, Bordeaux*, France) Supreme *St. Emilion* property, unusual in using more *Cabernet Franc* than *Merlot*. **75** 76 78 79 80 **81 82 83 85 86** 87 88 89 90 91 93 94 95 96 ☆☆☆☆ **1995 ££££**

**Dom. de Chevalier** [shuh-val-yay] (*Graves Cru Classé, Bordeaux*, France) Great *Pessac-Léognan* estate which proves itself in difficult years. for both red and white. Red: **70 78** 79 **81** 82 **83** 84 85 86 87 88 89 90 92 93 94 95 96 White: 81 82 **83 85 87** 88 89 90 92 93 94 95 96 ☆☆☆☆☆ **1992 Blanc, Pessac-Léognan ££££**

*Chevaliers de Tastevin* [shuh-val-yay duh tat-van] (*Burgundy*, France) A *confrèrie* based in *Clos de Vougeot*, famed for grand dinners and fancy robes. Wines approved at an annual tasting may carry a special *'tasteviné'* label.

**Cheverny** [shuh-vehr-nee] (*Loire*, France) Light, floral whites from *Sauvignon* and *Chenin Blanc* and now, under the new 'Cour Cheverny' *Appellation*, wines made from the limey local *Romarantin* grape. 83 **85 86 88 89 90 94** 95 96 ☆☆☆ **1996 Dom. de la Desoucherie, Christian Tessier ££**

**Robert Chevillon** [roh-behr shuh-vee-yon] (France) Consistent producer with long-lived wines. ☆☆☆ **1993 Nuits St. Georges £££**

**Chianti** [kee-an-tee] (*Tuscany*, Italy) (Classico/Putto/Rufina) *Sangiovese*-dominant *DOCG*. Generally better than pre-1984, when it was customary to add wine from further south, and mandatory to put dull white grapes into the vat with the black ones. Wines labelled with the insignia of the *Classico, Putto* or the *Rufina* areas are supposed to be better too. Trusting good producers, however, is a far safer bet. 79 **82 85 88 90 94** 95 96 ***Antinori, Isole e Olena; Castello di Ama; Castell'in Villa; Castellare; Ruffino; Castello dei Rampolla; Castello di Volpaia; Frescobaldi; Selvapiana; Rocca di Castagnoli.***

**Chiaretto di Bardolino** [kee-ahr-reh-toh dee bahr-doh-lee-noh] (*Lombardy*, Italy) Potentially refreshing, berryish light reds and rosés from around Lake Garda. Rarely exported.

**Chile** Rising source of juicy, blackcurranty *Cabernet* and (potentially even better) *Merlot, Semillon, Chardonnay* and *Sauvignon*. ***Santa Rita; Casablanca; Concha y Toro; Errazuriz; Caliterra; Casa Lapostolle; Montes.***

**Chiltern Valley Vineyards** (Oxfordshire, England) Excellent Oxfordshire estate with a growing reputation, especially for its *Late Harvest* wines. ☆☆☆ **1993 Medium Dry ££**

**Chimney Rock** (*Stag's Leap District*, California) Producer of serious *Cabernet*. ☆☆☆☆ **1992 Reserve Stag's Leap District £££**

**Chinon** [shee-non] (*Loire*, France) An *AC* within *Touraine* for (mostly) red wines from the *Cabernet Franc* grape. Excellent in ripe years; otherwise potentially thin and green. *Olga Raffault* makes one of the best, or try *Couly-Dutheil*. Red: 78 83 **85** 86 **88 89 90** 95 96 ☆☆☆☆ **1995 Chinon Clos de L'Echo ££**

**Chiroubles** [shee-roo-bl] (*Burgundy*, France) Fragrant and early-maturing Beaujolais Cru, best expressed by the likes of Bernard Méziat. 85 87 **88 89** 90 **91** 93 94 95 ☆☆☆☆ **1995 Dom. Emile Cheyson ££**

**Chivite** [shee-vee-tay] (*Navarra*, Spain) Innovative producer whose reds and rosés easily outclass many of those from big name *Rioja Bodegas*. ☆☆☆☆ **1990 £££**

**Chorey-lès-Beaune** [shaw-ray lay bohn] (*Burgundy*, France) Modest raspberry and damson reds once sold as *Côte de Beaune* Villages, and now appreciated in their own right. Red: **78** 80 83 **85** 86 87 **88 89 90** 92 95 96 ***Tollot-Beaut; Ch. de Chorey*** ☆☆☆☆ **1994 Tollot-Beaut £££**

**Churchill** (*Douro*, Portugal) Small, dynamic young firm founded by Johnny Graham, whose family once owned a rather bigger port house. 82 **85** 91 94 ☆☆☆☆☆ **1985 Vintage ££££**

🍷 **Chusclan** [shoos-klon] (*Rhône*, France) Named village of *Côtes du Rhône* with maybe the best rosé of the area ☆☆☆☆☆ **Caves de Chusclan Roux-Laithwaite S5 ££**

🍇 **Cinsaut/Cinsault** [san-soh] Fruity-spicy, red grape with high acidity, often blended with *Grenache*. One of 13 permitted varieties of *Châteauneuf-du-Pape*, and also in the blend of *Ch. Musar* in the *Lebanon*. Widely grown in South Africa and Australia.

🍷 **Ch. Cissac** [see-sak] (*Haut-Médoc Cru Bourgeois*, *Bordeaux*, France) Traditional *Cru Bourgeois*, close to *St. Estèphe*, making tough wines that last. Those who dislike tannin should stick to ripe vintages. **70 75** 76 **78** 79 81 **82** 83 85 86 88 89 90 94 95 96 ☆☆☆☆ **1990 £££**

🍷 **Ch. Citran** [see-tron] (*Haut-Médoc Cru Bourgeois Bordeaux*, France) Improving – though still not dazzling – *Cru Bourgeois*, thanks to major investment by the Japanese. 82 85 86 87 88 **89 90** 91 92 93 **94 95 96** ☆☆☆ **1993 £££**

🍷 **Bruno Clair** [klehr] (*Burgundy*, France) *Marsannay* estate with good *Fixin*, *Gevrey Chambertin*, *Morey-St-Denis* and *Savigny*. ☆☆☆☆ **1991 Gevrey Chambertin Clos de Bèze £££**

***Clairet*** [klehr-ray] (*Bordeaux*, France) The word from which we derived claret – originally a very pale-coloured red from *Bordeaux*. Seldom used now. ☆☆☆ **1995 Ch La Freynelle Bordeaux Clairet Rosé £££**

🍇 **Clairette** [klehr-ret] (*Midi*, France) Dull white grape of southern France.

🍷 **Clairette de Die** [klehr-rheht duh dee] (*Rhône*, France) Unexciting sparkling wine normally but the Cuvée Tradition, however, made with *Muscat* is invariably far better; grapey and fresh – like a top-class French *Asti Spumante*. ☆☆☆ **Clairette de Die Tradition, Cave Diose ££**

🍷 **Auguste Clape** [klap] (*Rhône*, France) Probably the supreme master of *Cornas*. Great, intense, long-lived wines. ☆☆☆☆☆ **1995 Cornas ££££**

🍷 **La Clape** [la klap] (*Languedoc-Roussillon*, France) Little-known *cru* within the *Coteaux de Languedoc* with tasty *Carignan* reds and soft, creamy whites.

**Clare Valley** [klehr] (South Australia) Well-established, slatey soil region enjoying a renaissance with high-quality *Rieslings* that age well, and deep-flavoured *Shiraz*, *Cabernet* and *Malbec*. ***Petaluma; Penfolds; Mitchells; Leasingham; Tim Adams; Tim Knappstein; Pikes; Lindemans.***

***Claret*** [klar-ret] English term for red *Bordeaux*.

***Clarete*** [klah-reh-Tay] (Spain) Term for light red – frowned on by the EU.

***Classed Growth*** (France) Literal translation of *Cru Classé*, commonly used when referring to the status of *Bordeaux* Châteaux.

***Classico*** [kla-sih-koh] (Italy) A defined area within a *DOC* identifying what are supposed to be the best vineyards, eg *Chianti* Classico, *Valpolicella* Classico.

🍷 **Ch. Clerc-Milon** [klehr mee-lon] (*Pauillac 5th Growth*, *Bordeaux*, France) Juicy member of the *Mouton Rothschild* stable. **78** 81 **82** 83 85 **86** 87 88 89 90 92 93 94 95 ☆☆☆☆ **1993 £££**

🍷 **Domenico Clerico** [doh-meh-nee-koh Klay-ree-koh] (*Piedmont*, Italy) Makes great *Barolo* and *Dolcetto*, and Arte, a *Nebbiolo*, *Barbera* blend ☆☆☆☆ **1994 Arte £££**

***Climat*** [klee-mah] (*Burgundy*, France) An individual vineyard.

🍷 **Ch. Climens** [klee-mons] (*Barsac Premier Cru Classé Bordeaux*, France) Gorgeous, quite delicate *Barsac* which often easily outlasts many heftier *sauternes*. **71 75** 76 78 79 **80** 81 82 **83 85 86** 88 89 90 95 96 ☆☆☆☆☆ **1990 ££££**

🍷 **Ch. Clinet** [klee-nay] (*Pomerol Bordeaux*, France) Starry property with lovely, complex, intense wines. 82 83 85 **86** 87 88 89 90 91 92 93 95 96

*Clone* [klohn] Specific strain of a given grape variety. For example, more than 300 clones of *Pinot Noir* have been identified.

*Clos* [kloh] (France) Literally, a walled vineyard – and often a finer wine.

🍷 **Clos de la Roche** [kloh duh lah rosh] (*Burgundy*, France) One of the most reliable *Côte d'Or Grands Crus*. ☆☆☆☆ **1993 Ponsot ££££**

🍷 **Clos de Mesnil** [kloh duh may-neel] (*Champagne*, France) *Krug's* single vineyard *Champagne* made entirely from *Chardonnay* grown in the Clos de Mesnil vineyard. ☆☆☆☆☆ **1985 ££££**

🍷 **Clos de Tart** [kloh duh tahr] (*Burgundy*, France) *Grand Cru* vineyard in *Morey St. Denis*, exclusive to Mommessin. Others might make the wine better, but it does age well. ☆☆☆☆ **1990 ££££**

🍷 **Clos de Vougeot** [kloh duh voo-joh] (*Burgundy*, France) *Grand Cru* vineyard divided among more than 70 owners, some of whom are decidedly uncommitted to quality. ***Dom. Rion; Joseph Drouhin; Jean Gros; Leroy; Méo Camuzet; Faiveley; Arnoux; Confuron***.

🍷 **Ch. Clos des Jacobins** [kloh day zha-koh-Ban] (*St. Emilion Grand Cru Classé Bordeaux*, France) Generally rich, ripe, if not always the most complex of wines. **75** 78 79 81 **82 83** 85 86 87 88 89 90 92 93 ☆☆☆☆ **1990 ££££**

🍷 **Clos des Mont-Olivet** [kloh mon-to-lee-ray] (*Rhône*, France ) *Chateauneuf du Pape* estate with a rare mastery of white wine. The top red is called 'Cuvée du Papet'.

🍷 **Clos des Papes** [kloh day pap] (*Rhône*, France) Producer of serious *Chateauneuf du Pape* which – in top vintages – rewards at least a few years cellaring.

🍷 **Clos du Bois** [kloh doo bwah] (*Sonoma Valley*, California) Top-flight producer whose 'Calcaire' *Chardonnay* and Marlstone *Cabernet Merlot* are particularly fine. ☆☆☆☆ **1994 Sonoma County Merlot £££**

🍷 **Clos du Ciel** [kloh doo see-yel] (*Stellenbosch*, South Africa) Inspiring Chardonnay from South African wine critic John Platter.

🍷 **Clos du Clocher** [kloh doo klosh-shay] (*Pomerol*, *Bordeaux*, France) Reliably rich, plummy wine. 92 93 94 95 96 ☆☆☆☆ **1993 £££**

🍷 **Clos du Marquis** [kloh doo mahr-kee] (*St. Julien*, *Bordeaux*, France) The *Second Label* of *Léoville-Las-Cases*.

🍷 **Clos du Roi** [kloh doo rwah] (*Burgundy*, France) *Beaune Premier Cru* that is also part of *Corton Grand Cru*.

🍷 **Clos du Val** [kloh doo vahl] (*Napa Valley*, California) Bernard Portet, brother of Dominique, who runs *Taltarni* in Australia, makes generally good, if sometimes disappointing *Stag's Leap* reds – including *Cabernet* and *Merlot*. They develop with time. ☆☆☆ **1994 Cabernet £££**

🍷 **Clos l'Eglise** [klos lay-gleez] (*Pomerol*, *Bordeaux*, France) Attractive, spicy wines from a consistent small *Pomerol* Estate. 75 81 83 85 86 88 89 90 93 94 95 96

🍷 **Clos Floridène** [kloh floh-ree-dehn] (*Graves*, *Bordeaux*, France) Classy, oaked white *Graves* made by superstar *Denis Dubourdieu*. 88 **89 90** 92 93 **94** 95 96 ☆☆☆☆☆ **1994 White £££**

🍷 **Clos Fourtet** [kloh foor-tay] (*St. Emilion Premier Grand Cru*, *Bordeaux*, France) Traditional *St. Emilion* for those who don't like too much fruit. 78 79 81 **82** 83 85 86 88 89 90 92 93 95 96 ☆☆☆ **1993 £££**

🍷 **Clos René** [kloh ruh-nay] (*Pomerol*, *Bordeaux*, France) Estate making increasingly concentrated, though approachable wines. **82 83** 85 86 87 88 89 90 93 94 95 96

**Clos St-Landelin** [kloh San lon-duhr-lan] (*Alsace*, France) Long-lived wines; the sister label to *Muré*.

**Ch. La Clotte** [lah klot] (*St. Emilion Grand Cru Classé*, *Bordeaux*, France) Variable; potentially very good 82 **83** 85 86 88 89 90 92 93 94 95 96

**Cloudy Bay** (*Marlborough*, New Zealand) Under the same French ownership as *Cape Mentelle*, this ten-year-old cult winery proved how classily the *Sauvignon* can perform in *Marlborough*. The *Chardonnay* is equally impressive, as are the rare *Late Harvest* wines. The *Pelorus* fizz, made by an American winemaker, is too much of a buttery mouthful for some. Buy the *Sauvignon* if you see it; there's a waiting list for every vintage.

**Clusel-Roch** [kloo-se rosh] (*Rhône*, France) Well regarded Côte Rôtie producer. Quite traditional in style. ☆☆☆☆ **1993 Côte Rôtie Les Grandes Places £££**

***Cave Co-operative*** (France) Cooperative winery.

**J F Coche-Dury** [kosh doo-ree] (*Burgundy*, France) A superstar *Meursault* producer whose basic reds and whites outclass his neighbours' supposedly classier fare. ☆☆☆☆☆ **1993 Meursault £££**

**Cockburn-Smithes** [koh burn] (*Douro*, Portugal) Unexceptional Special Reserve but producer of great *Vintage* and superlative *Tawny* port. **55** 60 **63** 67 **70** 75 83 **85** ☆☆☆☆ **10 Year Old Tawny £££**

**Codorníu** [kod-dor-nyoo] (*Catalonia*, Spain) Humungous fizz maker whose Anna de Codorniu is a good *Chardonnay*-based *Cava*. The Californian effort tastes, well, *Cava*-ish, despite using *Champagne* varieties. ☆☆☆ **1992 Anna de Codorníu Brut Vintage ££**

**Colchagua Valley** [kohl-shah-gwah] (*Central Valley*, Chile) Up-and-coming sub-region. ***Los Vascos; Lapostolle; Undurraga***.

**Coldstream Hills** (*Yarra Valley*, Australia) Founded by lawyer-turned winemaker and wine writer *James Halliday* and recently bought by Penfolds, this is the source of stunning *Pinot Noir*, great *Chardonnay* and increasingly impressive *Cabernets and Merlots*. Proof that critics can make as well as break a wine! ☆☆☆☆ **1996 Pinot Noir £££**

***Colheita*** [kol-yay-tah] (Portugal) Harvest or Vintage – particularly used to describe Tawny port of a specific year.

**Marc Colin** [mahrk koh-lan] (*Burgundy*, France) Family estate with a small chunk of *Le Montrachet*. A class act. ☆☆☆☆ **1995 Santenay Vielles Vignes £££**

**Collards** [kol-lards] (*Auckland*, New Zealand) Small producer of lovely, pineappley *Chardonnay* and appley *Chenin Blanc*.

**Collegiata** [koh-lay-jee jah-tah] (*Toro* Spain) Rich red wine from the *Tempranillo* in a little known region.

***Colle/colli*** [kol-lay/kol-lee] (Italy) Hill/hills.

**Colli Berici** [kol-lee bay-ree-chee] (*Veneto*, Italy) Red and white *DOC*.

**Colli Orientali del Friuli** [kol-lee oh-ree yehn-tah-lee del free-yoo-lee] (*Friuli-Venezia Giulia*, Italy) Lively single-variety whites and reds from near the *Slovenian* border. Subtle, honeyed and very pricy *Picolit*, too.

**Collio** [kol-lee-yoh] (*Friuli-Venezia Giulia*, Italy) High-altitude region with a basketful of white varieties, plus those of *Bordeaux* and red *Burgundy*. Refreshing and often unshowy. ☆☆☆ **1995 Pinot Grigio ££**

**Collioure** [kol-yoor] (*Midi*, France) Intense *Rhône*-style red from *Languedoc-Roussillon*, often marked by the *Mourvèdre* in the blend. ☆☆☆☆ **1994 Clos de Paulilles ££**

**Colombard** [kol-om-bahrd] White grape grown in south-west France for making into Armagnac and good, light, modern whites by *Yves Grassa* and *Plaimont*. Also planted in Australia (*Primo Estate* and *Best's*) and the US, where it is known as French Colombard.

**Jean-Luc Colombo** [kol-lom-boh] (*Rhône*, France) Oenologist guru to an impressive number of *Rhône* estates – and producer of his own good, modern *Côtes du Rhône* and *Cornas*. People who feel new oak has no home in the *Rhône* may prefer to buy elsewhere; I like these wines. ☆☆☆☆ **1994 Cornas La Louvée ££££**

**Columbia Crest** (*Washington State*, USA) *Second Label* of *Ch. Ste Michelle*. ☆☆☆ **1995 Chardonnay £££**

**Columbia Winery** (*Washington State*, USA) Producer of good, *Chablis* – style *Chardonnay* and *Graves*-like *Semillon*; subtle single-vineyard Cabernet, especially good Merlot, Syrah and Burgundian Pinot Noir. ☆☆☆☆ **1991 Red Willow Vineyard £££**

***Commandaria*** [com-man-dah-ree-yah] (Cyprus) Traditional dessert wine with rich raisiny fruit.

***Commune*** [kom-moon] (France) Small demarcated plot of land named after its principal town or village. Equivalent to an English parish.

**Conca de Barberà** [kon-kah deh bahr-beh-rah] (*Catalonia*, Spain) Cool region where *Torres*'s impressive but pricy *Milmanda* is produced, as is *Hugh Ryman*'s rather cheaper Santara. ☆☆☆☆ **1995 Santara Chabonell Cabernet Sauvignon ££**

**Viña Concha y Toro** [veen-yah kon-chah ee tohr-roh] (*Maipo*, Chile) Steadily improving, thanks to the efforts of winemaker *Ignacio Rebabaren* and investment in *Casablanca*. Best wines are sold under Don Melchior, Marques de Casa Concha, Trio and Casillero del Diablo labels. ☆☆☆☆☆ **1996 Trio Chardonnay ££**

**Conde de Caralt** [kon-day day kah-ralt] (*Catalonia*, Spain) One of the best names in *Cava*. Catch it young.

**Conde de Valdemar** [kon-day day val-day-mahr] (Rioja, Spain) Label used by the excellent *Martinez Bujanda*. ☆☆☆☆ **1990 Rioja Gran Resérve £££**

**Condrieu** [kon-dree-yuhh] (*Rhône*, France) Fabulous, pricy pure *Viognier*. A cross between dry white wine and perfume. Far better than the hyped and high-priced *Ch. Grillet* next door. 82 85 87 **88 89 90** 91 94 95 96 ***Georges Vernay; Ettienne Guigal; Yves Cuilleron; Patrick & Cristophe Bonneford; Antoine Montez; Robert Niero; Alain Parent & Gerard Depardieu; Phillipe & Christophe Pichon; Hervé Richard; Francois Villand; Gerard Villano.*** ☆☆☆☆ **1995 Coteau de Chery, Perret £££**

***Confrèries*** [kon-fray-ree] (France) Promotional brotherhoods of those with some link to a particular wine or a specific area. Many, however, are nowadays more about pomp and pageantry, kudos and backslapping, than active promotion.

**Conn Creek** (*Napa Valley*, California) Maker of attractively fruity Cabernet blends and rich Chardonnay. ☆☆☆☆ **1988 Cabernet Sauvignon £££**

**Cono Sur** [kon-noh soor] (Chile) Concha y Toro subsidiary with a range of stunning varietals including a classy Pinot Noir. ☆☆☆ **1995 20 Barrels Pinot Noir ££**

**Ch. la Conseillante** [lah kon-say-yont] (*Pomerol*, *Bordeaux*, France) Brilliant property with lovely, complex, perfumed wines. **70 75** 76 79 **81 82** 83 84 **85** 86 87 88 89 90 91 93 94 95 96

***Consejo Regulador*** [kon-say-hoh ray-goo-lah-dohr] (Spain) Administrative body responible for *DO* laws.

***Consorzio*** [kon-sohr-zee-yoh] (Italy) Producers' syndicate, often with its own seal of quality.

**Constantia** [kon-stan-tee-yah] (South Africa) The first wine region in the New World. Until recently, the big name here was *Groot Constantia*. Now *Klein Constantia, Buitenverwachting* and *Steenberg* go much further to explain this region's enduring reputation. Red: **82 84** 86 **87** 89 **91 92** 93 94 95 White: **87 91** 92 93 94 95 96

🍷 **Aldo Conterno** [al-doh kon-tehr-noh] (*Piedmont*, Italy) Truly top-class *Barolo* estate with similarly top-class *Barbera*. Nobody does it better. ☆☆☆☆☆ **1990 Barolo Bricco Bussia Soprana ££££**

🍷 **Viñedos del Contino** [veen-yay-dos del con-tee-no] (*Rioja*, Spain) *CVNE*-owned *Rioja* Alavesa estate whose wines can have more fruit and structure than most. ☆☆☆☆ **1989 Rioja Reserva ££**

**Coonawarra** [koon-nah-wah-rah] (South Australia) Australia's only internationally acknowledged top-class mini-region. Stuck in the middle of nowhere, with cool(ish) climate and terra rossa soil. Great blackcurranty-minty *Cabernet*, underrated *Shiraz*, big *Chardonnays* and full-bodied *Riesling*. ***Petaluma; Penfolds; Wynns; Rouge Homme; Parker Estate; Lindemans; Katnook.***

🍷 **Coopers Creek** (*Auckland*, New Zealand) Good, individualistic whites including a *Chenin-Semillon* blend, *Chardonnay, Sauvignon* and *Riesling*.

🍷 **Copertino** [kop-per-tee-noh] (*Apulia*, Italy) Richly fascinating, intensely berryish wine made from the *Negroamaro* grape. ☆☆☆☆ **1993 Riserva, Cantina Sociale di Copertino.** ☆☆☆☆ **1992 Copertino Colucci £**

🍷 **Corbans** (*Henderson*, New Zealand) Big winery (encompassing *Cooks*). Good rich *Merlot* reds (even, occasionally, from *Marlborough*). ☆☆☆☆ **1994 Private Bin Gisborne Chardonnay ££**

🍷 **Corbières** [kawr-byayr] (*Languedoc-Roussillon*, France) Region where a growing number of small estates are now making tasty red wines, despite the shortcomings of the *Carignan*. ***Ch. Lastours; Mont Tauch.***

🍷 **Cordon Negro** [kawr-don nay-groh] (*Catalonia*, Spain) Brand name for *Freixenet's* successful *Cava*. Better than in the past but still dull.

🍷 **Coriole** [koh-ree-ohl] (*McLaren Vale*, Australia) *Shiraz* specialist that has diversified into *Sangiovese*. The *Semillons* and *Rieslings* are pretty good too.

🍷 **Corison** [kaw-ree-son] (*Napa*, California) Winery specialising in juicy Cabernet. ☆☆☆☆ **1994 Cabernet Sauvignon Napa Valley £££**

***Corked*** Unpleasant, musty smell and flavour, caused by fungus attacking the cork. Almost always gets worse on contact with oxygen.

🍷 **Cornas** [kawr-nas] (*Rhône*, France) Smoky, spicy *Syrah*; tannic when young but worth keeping. **76 78 82 83 85 88** 89 90 91 95 ***Clape; Tain Cooperative; Juge; de Barjac; Colombo: Thierry Allemand; Durvieu Serette; Jacques Lemercier; Robert Michel; Noel Verset; Alain Voge.***

**Corsica** (France) Mediterranean island making robust reds, whites and rosés under a raft of *Appellations* (doled out to assuage rebellious islanders). *Vins de Pays* (*de l'Ile de Beauté*) are often more interesting. ☆☆☆ **1995 Dom. du Mont St. Jean Oak Aged Chardonnay ££**

🍷 **Dom. Corsin** [kawr-san] (*Burgundy*, France) Reliable *Pouilly Fuissé* and *St. Véran* estate. ☆☆☆ **1995 St. Véran ££**

🍇 **Cortese** [Kawr-Tay-Seh] (*Piedmont*, Italy) Herby grape used in *Piedmont* and to make *Gavi*. Drink young.

**Corton** [kawr-ton] (*Burgundy*, France) *Grand Cru* hill potentially making great, intense, long-lived reds and – as Corton Charlemagne – whites. The supposed uniformly great vineyards seem to run a suspiciously long way round the hill. Reds can be very difficult to taste young; many never develop. White: **79** 84 **85 86** 87 **88** 89 **90 92** 95 Red: **78** 80 83 **85** 86 87 **88 89 90** 92 95 96 ***Chandon de Briailles; Dubreuil-Fontaine; A Nudant; Faiveley; Laleur-Piot; Tollot-Beaut.***

**Corvo** [kawr-voh] (Sicily, Italy) Ubiquitous producer of pleasant reds and whites. ☆☆☆ **1994 Corvo, Duca di Salaparuta ££**

**Ch. Cos d'Estournel** [koss-des-tawr-nel] (*St. Estèphe 2nd Growth Bordeaux*, France) In *St. Estèphe*, but making wines with *Pauillac* richness and fruit, this is top-class *Bordeaux*. Spice is the hallmark. **61** 70 **75 76 78** 79 **81 82 83** 84 **85** 86 87 88 **89** 90 91 92 93 94 95 96 ☆☆☆☆☆ **1990 ££££**

**Ch. Cos Labory** [koss la-baw-ree] (*St. Estèphe 5th Growth*, *Bordeaux*, France) Good, traditional, if tough wines. **82** 83 **85** 86 87 88 89 90 92 93 94 95 96 ☆☆☆ **1988 ££**

***Cosecha*** [coh-seh-chah] (Spain) Harvest or vintage.

**Cossart Gordon** (*Madeira*, Portugal) High-quality brand used by the Madeira Wine Co. ☆☆☆☆☆ **5 year Old Sercial £££**

**Costers del Segre** [kos-tehrs del say-greh] (*Catalonia*, Spain) *DO* created for *Raimat*,. which unlike their competitors elsewhere in Spain, is allowed to irrigate its vineyards. ☆☆☆ **1992 Gran Calesa ££**

**Costières de Nimes** [kos-tee-yehr duh neem] (*Midi*, France) An up-and-coming region which can make reds to match the northern *Rhône*. ☆☆☆☆ **1994 Cellier du Bondavin ££**

**Costières du Gard** [kos-tee-yehr doo gahr] (South West France) Fruity reds, rarer whites and rosés. ☆☆☆ **1993 Mas de Bressades Cabernet/Syrah ££**

**Cot** [koh] (France) The grape of *Cahors* and the *Loire* (aka *Malbec*). ☆☆☆ **1994 Ch. St. Didier Parnac ££**

**Côte d'Or** [koht dor] (*Burgundy*, France) Geographical designation for the finest slopes, encompassing the *Côte de Nuits* and *Côte de Beaune*.

**Côte de Beaune (Villages)** [koht duh bohn] (*Burgundy*, France) The southern half of the Côte d'Or. With the suffix '*Villages*', indicates red wines from one or more of the specified villages. Confusingly, wine labelled simply 'Côte de Beaune' comes from a small area around *Beaune* itself and often tastes like wines of that *Appellation*. White: **82 85 86** 87 **88** 89 **90 92** 95 **96** Red: **78** 83 **85** 86 87 **88 89 90 91** 92 95 **96**

**Côte de Brouilly** [koht duh broo-yee] (*Burgundy*, France) *Beaujolais Cru:* distinct from *Brouilly* – often finer. Floral and ripely fruity; will keep for a few years. **88 89** 90 **91** 94 95 96 **Bernillon; Ch. Thivin.**

**Côte de Nuits (Villages)** [koht duh nwee] (*Burgundy*, France) Northern, and principally 'red' end of the *Côte d'Or*. The suffix '*Villages*' indicates wine from one or more specified *communes*. **78 80** 82 83 **85** 86 87 **88 89 90** 92 95 96

**Côte des Blancs** [koht day blon] (*Champagne*, France) Principal *Chardonnay*-growing area.

**Côte Rôtie** [koh troh tee] (*Rhône*, France) Powerful, smoky yet refined *Syrah* (possibly with a touch of white *Viognier*) from the northern Rhône, divided into two principal hillsides, the 'Brune' and 'Blonde'. Most need at least six years. **76 78 82 83 85 88** 89 90 91 95 ***Barge; Burgaud; Champet; Clusel-Roch; Gallet; Gasse; Gentaz-Dervieuz; Gerin; Guigal; Jamet; Jasmin,Ogier; Rostaing; Saugère; L.de Vallouit***.

***Côte(s), Coteaux*** [koht] (France) Hillsides.

**Coteaux Champenois** [koh-toh shom-puh-nwah] (*Champagne*, France) Madly over-priced, mostly thin, light and acidic, still wine of the area. *Laurent Perrier's* is better than most, but it's still only worth buying in the ripest vintages. 82 83 85 86 88 89 90 91 92 ☆☆☆ **Laurent Perrier £££**

**Coteaux d'Aix-en-Provence** [koh-toh dayks on prov vons] (France) A recent *AC* region producing light, floral whites, and fruity reds and dry rosés using *Bordeaux* and Rhône varieties. ☆☆☆ **1992 Château Pigoudet Rouge Grand Reserve ££**

**Coteaux d'Ancenis** [koh-toh don-suh-nee] (*Loire*, France) So far, only *VDQS* status for this region near Nantes, producing light reds and deep pinks from the *Cabernet Franc* and *Gamay*, and *Muscadet*-style whites. Red: 78 83 **85** 86 **88 89 90** 95 96 White: **88 89 90** 94 95 96

**Coteaux d'Ardèche** [koh-toh dahr-desh] (*Rhône*, France) Light, country wines, mainly from the *Syrah* and *Chardonnay*. A popular place with Burgundians who need to produce affordable alternatives to their own region's white wine. ☆☆☆ **1994 Ardêche Merlot-Syrah ££**

**Coteaux de l'Aubance** [koh-toh duh loh bons] (*Loire*, France) Light wines (often semi-sweet) grown on the banks of a *Loire* tributary. Quite rare outside the region. White: 83 **85 86 88 89 90** 94 95 96

**Coteaux des Baux-en-Provence** [koh-toh day boh on pro-vonss] (*Provence*, France) Inexpensive fruity reds, whites and rosé, plus the cult *Dom. de Trévallon*, which impressively demonstrates what can be done round here.

**Coteaux du Languedoc** [koh-toh doo long-dok] (*Midi*, France) A big *Appellation*, and a popular source of fast-improving rich reds from *Rhône* and southern grapes. 78 81 **82 83 85 88** 89 90 95 96 ☆☆☆☆ **1994 Domaine de L'Hortus, Pic St. Loup ££**

**Coteaux du Layon** [koh-toh doo lay-yon] (*Loire*, France) Whites from the *Chenin Blanc* grape which are slow to develop and long lived. Lots of lean, dry wine but the sweet *Bonnezeaux* and *Quarts de Chaume* are superior. The wines of *Moulin Touchais* or Clos Ste. Catherine are worth seeking out. Sweet white: **76** 83 **85** 86 **88 89** 90 94 95 96

**Coteaux du Loir** [koh-toh doo lwahr] (*Loire*, France) Clean vigorous whites from a *Loire* tributary. White: 83 **85 86 88 89 90** 94 95 96

**Coteaux du Lyonnais** [koh-toh doo lee-ohn-nay] (*Rhône*, France) Just to the south of *Beaujolais*, making some very acceptable good-value wines from the same grapes. ***Descottes; Duboeuf; Fayolle.***

**Coteaux du Tricastin** [koh-toh doo tris-kass-tan] (*Rhône*, France) Southern *Rhône Appellation*, emerging as a source of good value, soft, peppery/blackcurranty reds. Red: **78 83 85 88** 89 90 95 96

**Côtes de Bourg** [koht duh boor] (*Bordeaux*, France) Clay-soil region just across the water from the *Médoc* and an increasingly reliable source of good value, if somewhat fast-maturing, *Merlot*-dominated plummy reds. Whites are much less impressive. 82 83 85 86 **88 89** 90 94 95

**Côtes de Buzet** [koht duh boo-zay] (*Bordeaux*, France) *AC* region adjoining *Bordeaux*, producing light clarety reds, and duller whites from *Sauvignon*. **Les Vignerons de Buzet.**

**Côtes de Castillon** [koht duh kass-tee-yon] (*Bordeaux*, France) A region worth knowing where the *Merlot* is often more lovingly handled than in nearby *St. Emilion*. ☆☆☆**1990 Ch La Chapelle Baradis £**

**Côtes de Duras** [koht duh doo-rahs] (*Bordeaux*, France) Inexpensive whites from the *Sauvignon*, often better value than basic *Bordeaux* Blanc (but that's not saying much).

**Côtes de Francs** [koht duh fron] (*Bordeaux*, France) Up-and-coming region close to *St. Emilion* where pioneering producers such as *Ch. de Francs* and *Puygeraud* are making increasingly good reds.

**Côtes de Montravel** [koht duh mon-Rah-vel] (South West France) Source of dry and sweet whites and reds which are comparable to neighbouring *Bergerac*. ☆☆☆☆ **1993 K de Krevel Montravel vin Blanc Sec.**

**Côtes de/Premières Côtes de Blaye** [koht duh/pruh-myerh koht duh blih] (*Bordeaux*, France) A ferry-ride across the river from *St. Julien*, the limestone soils found here make for good *Merlot* and white wines. Sadly, so far, poor winemaking has prevented many estates from living up to this potential. 82 83 85 86 **88 89** 90 94 95 **Jean-pierre Lymas; Grand Barail; Vignobles Germain.**

**Côtes de Provence** [koht dur prov-vonss] (France) Improving, good value fresh, fruity, whites and ripe, spicy reds. However, the rosés, for which the region is best known, are often carelessly made and stored, before being served to holidaymakers who rarely notice that the so-called pink wine is a deep shade of bronze and decidedly unrefreshing. A region, incidentally, with as much appeal to organic winemakers as to fans of Mr Mayle's rural tales. ☆☆☆☆ **1990 Dom. Terres Blanches ££**

🍷 **Côtes de Quenelle** [koht duh kuhr-nel] (South West, France) Unpredictable fare that is popular north of the border. Suzanne Brochet's famous *'Cauchemar-Parfois-Supportable' Cuvée* demands patience.

🍷 **Côtes de St. Mont** [koht duh san-mon] (South West, France) Large *VDQS* area encompassing the whole of the Armagnac region. *Plaimont* is the largest and best-known producer.

🍷 **Côtes du Frontonnais** [koht doo fron-ton-nay] (South West France) Up-and-coming inexpensive red (and some rosé); fruitily characterful.

🍷 **Côtes du Marmandais** [koht doo mahr-mon-day] (South West France) Uses the *Bordeaux* red grapes plus *Gamay, Syrah* and others to make pleasant, fruity, inexpensive, wines. ☆☆☆ **1995 Les Vignerons de Beaupuy £**

🍷 **Côtes du Rhône (Villages)** [koht doo rohn] (*Rhône*, France) Spicy reds produced mostly in the southern part of the *Rhône* Valley. The best supposedly come from a set of better *Villages* (and are sold as *CdR Villages*), though some single domaine 'simple' *Côtes du Rhônes* outclass many *Villages* wines. *Grenache* is the key red wine grape. Whites which can include new-wave *Viogniers* are improving. Red: 85 88 89 90 93 94 95 96 ☆☆☆☆ **1996 Domaine de la Grande Bellane Valreas ££**

🍷 **Côtes du Roussillon** [koht doo roo-see-yon] (*Midi*, France) Up-and-coming for red, white and rosé, though not always worthy of its *AC*. *Côtes du Roussillon Villages* is better. ☆☆☆ **1995 Ch. Dena Biassaso ££**

🍷 **Côtes du Ventoux** [koht doo von-too] (*Rhône*, France) Improving everyday country reds that are similar to *Côtes du Rhône*. 85 88 89 90 94 95 96 ☆☆☆ **1994 Les Cailloux £**

🍷 **Côtes du Vivarais** [koht doo vee-vah-ray] (*Provence*, France) Light southern *Rhône*-like reds, fruity rosé and fragrant, light whites.

**Cotesti** [kot tesh-tee] (Romania) Easterly vineyards growing varieties such as *Pinot Noir*, *Blanc*, *Gris* and *Merlot*.

🍷 **Cotnari** [kot nah-ree] (Romania) Traditional and now very rare, white dessert wine. Has potential.

🍷 **Bodegas El Coto** [el kot-toh] (*Rioja*, Spain) Small estate producing good, medium-bodied El Coto and Coto Imaz reds. ☆☆☆☆☆ **1987 Rioja Coto de Imaz Gran Réserva.**

🍷 **Quinta da Côtto** [kin-tah dah kot-toh] (*Douro*, Portugal) Small estate producing so-so port and flavoursome table reds.

🍷 **Ch. Coufran** [koo-fron] (*Haut-Médoc Cru Bourgeois*, *Bordeaux*, France) Maker of soft, often rather dull, wine. **82** 83 85 **86** 88 **89** 90 94 95 96

🍷 **Coulée de Serrant** [koo-lay duh seh-ron] (*Loire*, France) Great dry *Chenin* from a top property in *Savennières*. ☆☆☆☆ **1992 ££££**

***Coulure*** [koo-loor] Climate-related wine disorder which causes reduced yields (and possibly higher quality) as grapes shrivel and fall off the vine.

🍷 **Couly-Dutheil** [koo-lee doo-tay] (*Loire*, France) High-quality *Chinon* estate with vines just behind the château in which Henry II imprisoned his wife, Eleanor of Aquitaine. ☆☆☆ **1995 Clos de L'Echo ££**

🍷 **Pierre Coursodon** [koor-soh-don] (*Rhône*, France) One of the best producers in *St. Joseph*. ☆☆☆☆ **1994 St. Joseph L'Olivaire ££**

🍷 **Viña Cousiño Macul** [koo-sin-yoh mah-kool] (*Maipo*, Chile) The most traditional producer in Chile. Reds are more successful than whites. ☆☆☆ **1993 Finis Terrae ££**

🍷 **Ch. Coutet** [koo-tay] (*Barsac Premier Cru Classé*, *Bordeaux*, France) Delicate neighbour to *Ch. Climens*, often making comparable wines: Cuvée Madame is top flight. **71 75** 76 **81** 82 **83** 85 **86** 87 **88 89** 90 95 ☆☆☆ **1993 ££££**

🍷 **Ch. Couvent-des-Jacobins** [koo-von day zhah-koh-ban] (*St. Emilion Grand Cru Classé*, *Bordeaux*, France) Producer of juicy, plummy-spicy wines. 78 **79 82** 83 85 86 88 89 90 **92 93** 94 95 96 ☆☆☆ **1993 £££**

**Cowra** [kow-rah] (*New South Wales*, Australia) Up-and-coming region, making a name for itself with *Chardonnay*, for which it will one day eclipse its better known but less viticulturally ideal neighbour, the *Hunter Valley*.

🍷 **Dom. de Coyeux** [duh cwah-yuh] (*Rhône*, France) One of the best producers of Muscat de Beaumes de Venise. ☆☆☆☆ **1993 £££**

🍷 **Cranswick Estate** (South East, Australia) Successful *Riverina* producer making reliable, inexpensive wines, widely available under the Barramundi label. ☆☆☆☆ **1995 Shiraz ££**

🍷 **Quinta do Crasto** [kwin-tah doh cras-toh] (*Douro*, Portugal) An up-and-coming small port producer with lovely red table wines made by Australian-born *David Baverstock*, who is also reponsible for *Esperão* and *Quinta de la Rosa*. ☆☆☆☆ **1996 Douro Red ££**

🍷 **Cream Sherry** (*Jerez*, Spain) Popular style (though not in Spain) produced by sweetening an *Oloroso*. A visitor to *Harvey's* apparently preferred one of the company's sherries to the then popular 'Bristol Milk'. 'If that's the milk', she joked, 'this must be the Cream'.

***Crémant*** [kray-mon] (France) Term used in *Champagne*, denoting a slightly sparkling style due to a lower pressure of gas in the bottle. Elsewhere, a term to indicate sparkling wine, eg Crémant de *Bourgogne*, de *Loire* and d'*Alsace*.

***Créme de Cassis*** [kraym duh kas-seess] (*Burgundy*, France) Fortified fruit essence perfected in *Burgundy* using blackcurrants from around Dijon. Commonly drunk mixed with sharp local *Aligoté* as *Kir*, or sparkling wine, as *Kir* Royale. Crème de Mûre (blackberries), Framboise (raspberries), Fraise (strawberries) and Pèche (peaches) are also delicious.

🍷 **Crépy** [kray-pee] (*Savoie*, France) Crisp, floral white from *Savoie*.

***Criado y Embotellado (por)*** [kree-yah-doh ee em-bot-tay-yah-doh] (Spain) Grown and bottled (by).

***Crianza*** [kree-yan-thah] (Spain) Literally keeping 'con Crianza' means aged in wood – often preferable to the *Reservas* and *Gran Reservas*, which are highly prized by Spaniards but to Britons can taste dull and dried-out.

🍷 **Crichton Hall** [krih-ton] (*Rutherford*, California) Small winery specialising in top class Chardonnay. ☆☆☆☆ **1995 Chardonnay £££**

***Crisp*** Fresh, with good *acidity*.

🍷 **Ch. le Crock** [lur krok] (*St. Estèphe Cru Bourgeois*, *Bordeaux*, France) Traditional property which like *Léoville Poyferré*, its stablemate, has shown great recent improvement 82 85 86 88 **89** 90 91 92 93 95 96 ☆☆☆ **1991 ££**

🍷 **Croft** (Spain/Portugal) *Port* and *Sherry* producer making highly commercial but rarely memorable wines. The vintage port is back on form. 55 60 **63** 66 67 **70** 75 77 82 85 94 ☆☆☆☆ **1990 LBV £££**

🍷 **Ch. La Croix** [la crwah] (*Pomerol*, *Bordeaux*, France) Producer of long-lasting traditional wines. **75** 76 **79** 81 82 83 **85** 86 88 89 90 92 94 95 96 ☆☆☆☆ **1992 ££££**

**Ch. la Croix de Gay** [la crwah duh gay] (*Pomerol*, *Bordeaux*, France) Classy estate whose complex wines have good, blackcurranty-plummy fruit. 81 **82 83** 85 86 **88** 89 90 91 **92** 93 94 95 96

**Ch. Croizet-Bages** [krwah-zay bahzh] (*Pauillac 5th Growth*, *Bordeaux*, France) Underperformer showing some signs of improvement. **82** 83 85 86 87 88 **90** 94 95 96

**Croser** [kroh-sur] (*Adelaide Hills*, Australia) Made by *Brian Croser* of *Petaluma* in the Piccadilly Valley, this is one of the New World's most *Champagne*-like fizzes. Has become less lean as the proportion of *Pinot Noir* has increased. ☆☆☆☆ **1993 Brut £££**

**Crouchen** [kroo-shen] (France) Obscure white grape known as Clare Riesling in Australia and Paarl Riesling in South Africa.

**Crozes-Hermitage** [krohz ehr-mee-tahzh] (*Rhône*, France) Up-and-coming *Appellation* on the hills behind supposedly greater *Hermitage*. Smoky, blackberryish reds are pure *Syrah*. Whites (made from *Marsanne* and *Roussanne)* are creamy but less impressive. And they rarely keep. Red: **76 78 82 83 85 88** 89 90 91 95 White: **88 89 90** 91 94 95 ***Alain Graillot; Dom Combier; Paul Jaboulet Aine; Dom.du Pavilion-Mercure.***

*Cru Bourgeois* [kroo boor-zhwah] (*Bordeaux*, France) Wines beneath the *Crus Classés*, satisfying certain requirements, which can be good value for money and, in certain cases, better than more prestigious classed growths.

*Cru Classé* [kroo klas-say] (*Bordeaux*, France) The best wines of the *Médoc* are crus classés, split into five categories from first (top) to fifth growth (or cru) for the Great Exhibition in 1855. The *Graves, St. Emilion* and *Sauternes* have their own classifications.

*Cru Grand Bourgeois/Exceptionnel* [kroo gron boor-jwah/ek-sep-see-yoh-nel] (*Bordeaux*, France) An estate-bottled *Haut-Médoc Cru Bourgeois*, which is supposedly aged in oak barrels. Term is the same as Cru Bourgeois *Supérieur*, though *Exceptionnel* wines must come from the area encompassing the *Crus Classés*. Future vintages will not bear this designation as it has fallen foul of the EU.

**Weingut Hans Crusius** [hans skroos-yuhs] (*Nahe*, Germany) Family-run estate prized for the qulaity of it's highly traditional wines. Some of the best, ripest *trocken* wines around.

*Crusted Port* (*Douro*, Portugal) An affordable alternative to vintage port – a blend of different years, bottled young and allowed to throw a deposit. ***Churchill's, Grahams; Dows.***

**Cullen** (*Margaret River*, Australia) Brilliant pioneering estate run by mother-and-daughter team of Di and Vanya Cullen. Source of stunning *Sauvignon-Semilllon* blends, claret-like reds, a highly individual *Pinot Noir* and a Burgundian *Chardonnay*. ☆☆☆☆ **1996 Sauvignon Blanc ££**

*Cultivar* [kul-tee-vahr] (South Africa) South African for grape variety.

**Ch. Curé-Bon-la-Madelaine** [koo-ray bon lah mad-layn] (*St. Emilion Grand Cru Classé*, *Bordeaux*, France) Very small *St. Emilion* estate next to *Ausone*. 75 78 81 **82** 83 85 86 88 89 90 94 95 96

**Curico** [koo-ree-koh] (Chile) Region in which *Torres, San Pedro* and *Caliterra* have vineyards. Being eclipsed by *Casablanca* as a source for cool-climate whites, but still one of Chile's best wine areas for red and white.

**Cuvaison Winery** [koo-vay-san] (*Napa Valley*, California) Swiss-owned winery with high-quality *Carneros Chardonnay*, increasingly approachable *Merlot* and now good *Pinot Noir.* Calistoga Vineyards is a *Second Label*.

*Cuve close* [koov klohs] The third-best way of making sparkling wine, in which the wine undergoes secondary fermentation in a tank and is then bottled. Also called the *Charmat* or *Tank method*.

*Cuvée (de Prestige)* [koo-vay] Most frequently a blend put together in a process called *Assemblage*. *Prestige Cuvées* are (particularly in *Champagne*) supposed to be the cream of a producer's production.

**Cuvée Napa** (*Napa*, California) the Californian venture by *Mumm Champagne*, and still offering better quality and value for money than the mother-ship back in France.

**CVNE** [koo-nay] (*Rioja*, Spain) Compania Vinicola del Norte de Espana, a large, high-quality operation by the owners of *Contino*, producing the excellent Viña Real in *Crianza, Reserva, Imperial* or *Gran Reserva* in the best years, and a light CVNE *Tinto*. Some recent releases have been slightly less dazzling. ☆☆☆☆ **1994 Monopole Rioja Blanco ££**

**Cyprus** Shifting its focus away from making ersatz 'sherry'. Even so, the best wine is still the fortified *Commandaria*.

**Czech Republic** A region to watch for is *St. Laurents*. The best wines are *Pinot Blanc* and the local *Irsay Oliver*. Try also the funky sparkling reds.

# D

**Didier Dagueneau** [dee-dee-yay dag-guhn-noh] (*Loire*, France) The iconoclastic producer of some of the best, steeliest *Pouilly Fumé*, and even the occasional *Late Harvest* effort that upsets the authorities. Prices are high, but often decidedly worth paying.

**Ch. Dalem** [dah-lem] (*Fronsac, Bordeaux*, France) Maker of rich, full-bodied *Fronsac*. 82 83 **85** 86 88 89 90 94 95 96

**Dalwhinnie** [dal-win-nee] (*Pyrenees, Victoria*, Australia) Quietly classy producer close to *Taltarni*. Reds made to last. ☆☆☆☆ **1992 Chardonnay £££**

**Dão** [downg] (Portugal) Once Portugal's best-known region – despite the dullness of its wines. Thanks to a few pioneering producers like *Sogrape*, both reds and whites are improving. Red: **80 85 88 90 91 93** 94 95 96 ☆☆☆ **1996 Caves Aliança £**

**Ch. Dassault** [das-soh] (*St. Emilion Grand Cru Classé, Bordeaux*, France) Good, juicy *St. Emilion*. 82 83 **85** 86 88 89 **90** 92 93 94 95

**Kurt Darting** [koort dahr-ting] (*Pfalz*, Germany) New-wave producer who cares more about ripe flavour than making excessive quantities of tooth-scouringly dry wine. ☆☆☆☆ **1994 Dürkheimer Fronhof Schurebe Trockenbeerenauslese ££££**

**Ch. de la Dauphine** [duh lah doh-feen] (*Fronsac, Bordeaux*, France) Proof that *Fronsac* deserved its reputation in the days when it was better-regarded than *St. Emilion*. 85 86 87 88 89 90 93 94 95

**Réné and Vincent Dauvissat** [doh-vee-sah] (*Burgundy*, France) One of the best estates in *Chablis*. Watch out for other Dauvissats – the name is also one of several used by the *La Chablisienne* Co-op. ☆☆☆☆ **1995 Cuvée la Chablisenne ££**

**Ch. Dauzac** [doh-zak] (*Margaux 5th Growth, Bordeaux*, France) Rejuvenated, following its purchase in 1993 by Andre Lurton of *Ch. la Louvière*. That year's wine was unusually successful for the vintage. **82 83 85** 86 **88 89 90** 93 94 95

**Dealul Mare** [day-al-ool mah-ray] (Romania) Carpathian region once known for whites, now producing surprisingly good *Pinot Noir*. ☆☆☆☆ **1996 Idlerock Pinot Noir £**

**Etienne & Daniel Defaix** [duh-fay] (*Burgundy*, France) Classy, traditional *Chablis* producer, making long-lived wines with a steely bite. ☆☆☆ **1994 Chablis 1er Cru 'Vieilles Vignes' Clos de Lechet £££**

***Dégorgée (dégorgement)*** [day-gor-jay] The removal of the deposit of inert yeasts from *Champagne* after maturation.

**Deidesheim** [di-dess-hime] (*Pfalz*, Germany) Distinguished wine town noted for flavoursome *Rieslings*. QbA/Kab/Spät: **85 86 88 89 90** 91 92 93 94 95 96 Aus/Beeren/TBA: **83 85** 88 89 90 91 92 93 94 95

**Deinhard** [dine-hard] (*Mosel*, Germany) See *Wegeler Deinhard*.

**Marcel Deiss** [dise] (*Alsace*, France) A tiny property producing some of the best wine in the region. ☆☆☆☆☆ **1994 Gewurztraminer Grand Cru Allenburg ££££**

**Delaforce** [del-lah-forss] (*Douro*, Portugal) Small port house with lightish but good Vintage and *Tawny*. 55 58 60 **63 66** 70 74 75 77 85 94 ☆☆☆ **His Eminence's Choice £££**

**Delas Frères** [del-las] (*Rhône*, France) Often underrated *négoçiant* whose red, individual vineyard wines can sometimes rival those of *Guigal* and the reconstructed *Chapoutier*. ☆☆☆☆ **1994 Hermitage Les Bessards £££**

**Delatite** [del-la-tite] (*Victoria*, Australia) Producer of lean-structured, long-lived wines. ☆☆☆☆ **1995 Limited Release Chardonnay ££**

**Delegats** [del-leg-gats] (*Auckland*, New Zealand) Family firm which has hit its stride recently with impressively (for New Zealand) ripe reds, especially plummy *Merlots*. The *Second Label* is '*Oyster Bay*'. ☆☆☆☆ **1995 Reserve Chardonnay £££**

**Delheim Wines** [del-hihm] (*Stellenbosch*, South Africa) A commercial estate with generally improving wines and a few stars.

***Demi-sec*** [duh-mee sek] (France) Medium-dry.

**Demoiselle** [duh-mwah-zel] (*Champagne*, France). A new *Champagne* name to watch, with attractive, light, creamy wines.

**Denbies Wine Estate** [den-bees] (Surrey, England) Part tourist attraction, part winery, the largest wine estate in England has so far produced good dry wines and far better sweet ones. ☆☆☆☆ **1995 Special Late-Harvested ££**

**Peter Dennis** (*McLaren Vale*, Australia) Reliable producer with unusually good Merlot. ☆☆☆☆ **1996 Chardonnay ££**

***Deutsches Weinsiegel*** [doyt-shur vihn-see-gel] (Germany) Seals of various colours – usually neck labels – awarded for merit to German wines. Treat with circumspection.

***Deutscher Tafelwein*** [doyt-shur tah-fuhl-vihn] (Germany) Table wine, guaranteed German as opposed to Germanic-style EC *Tafelwein*.

**Deutz** [duhtz] (*Champagne*, France, and also Spain, New Zealand, California) Reliable small but dynamic producer at home and abroad. The Cuvée William Deutz is top class. ☆☆☆☆☆ **1989 Blanc de Blanc ££££** ☆☆☆☆ **1995 Marlborough Cuvée Brut £££**

**Maison Deutz** [may-zon duhtz] (Arroyo Grande, California) A 150-acre, cool-climate vineyard joint venture between Nestlé and *Deutz Champagne* and, unusually, a bit of *Pinot Blanc* in the – generally – excellent blend.

**Devaux** [duh-voh] (*Champagne*, France) Small producer with a knack of producing unusually good rosé. ☆☆☆ **Champagne Oeil de Perdrix Brut Rosé £££**

***Diabetiker Wein*** [dee-ah-beh-ti-ker vihn] (Germany) Indicates a very dry wine with most of the sugar fermented out (as in a Diat lager), thus suitable for diabetics.

**Diamond Creek** (*Napa Valley*, California) Big Name producer with very good vineyards (Gravelly Meadow, Red Rock Terrace and Volcanic Hill) but produces tough wine which demands, but does not always repay, patience. ☆☆☆☆ **1993 Diamond Creek Volcanic Hill Cabernet ££££**

**Schlossgut Diel** [Shlos-sgoot deel] (*Nahe*, Germany) Serious commentator and winemaker producing luscious wines with ripe intensity.

**Dieu Donné Vineyards** [dyur don-nay] (*Franschhoek*, South Africa) Variable producer of quality varietals in the *Franschhoek* valley. The 1992 *Chardonnay* was legendary. ☆☆☆ **1994 Cabernet Sauvignon**

**Dom. Disznókó** [diss-noh-koh] (*Tokaji*, Hungary) Newly-constituted estate run by Jean Michel Cazes of *Ch. Lynch Bages*. Top-class modern sweet *Tokaji* and dry, lemony *Fürmint*. ☆☆☆☆ **1995 Tokaji Dry Furmint £££** ☆☆☆☆☆ **1992 Tokaji Aszu 5 Puttonyos £££**

***DLG (Deutsche Landwirtschaft Gesellschaft)*** (Germany) Body awarding medals for excellence to German wines – far too generously.

***DO Denominac/ion/ão de Origen*** (Spain, Portugal) Demarcated quality area, guaranteeing origin, grape varieties and production standards.

***DOC*** (Spain) Denominacion de Origen Califacada. Ludicrously, and confusingly, Spain's newly launched higher quality equivalent to Italy's *DOCG* shares the same initials as Italy's lower quality *DOC* wines. So far, restricted to Rioja – good, bad and indifferent.

***DOC(G) Denominazione di Origine Controllata (e Garantita)*** (Italy) Quality control designation based on grape variety and/or origin. 'Garantita' is supposed to imply a higher quality level, in much the same way that Italy's politicians and businessmen are supposed to be incorruptible.

**Ch. Doisy-Daëne** [dwah-zee di-yen] (*Barsac Deuxième Cru Classé*, *Bordeaux*, France) Fine *Barsac* property whose wines can be more restrained than those of some of its neighbours. The top wine is L'Extravagance. **76** 78 79 81 82 83 85 86 **88 89** 90 91 94 95 96 ☆☆☆☆ **1989 ££££**

**Ch. Doisy-Dubroca** [dwah-zee doo-brohkah] (*Barsac Deuxième Cru Classé*, *Bordeaux*, France) Underrated *Sauternes* estate producing ultra-rich wines at often attractively low prices. **75** 76 78 79 **81 83** 85 86 87 88 89 90 95 96.

**Ch. Doisy-Védrines** [dwah-zee vay-dreen] (*Barsac Deuxième Cru Classé*, *Bordeaux*, France) Reliable *Barsac* property which made a stunningly concentrated 1989 (and a less impressive 1990). 70 **75 76** 78 79 81 **82 83** 85 86 **88** 89 90 92 93 95 96. ☆☆☆☆ **1990 Ch. Doisy-Védrines, Barsac ££££**

**Dolcetto (d'Alba, di Ovada)** [dohl-cheh-toh] (*Piedmont*, Italy) Grape making anything from soft, everyday red to robust and long-lasting examples. Generally worth catching young. See *Aldo Conterno*, *Bava* or *Vajra*. ☆☆☆☆ **1993 Settimo Dolcetto d'Alba £** ☆☆☆☆ **1994 Best's Great Western ££**

**Dôle** [Dohl] (Switzerland) Appellation of *Valais* producing attractive reds from the *Pinot Noir* and/or *Gamay* grapes. Best bought by people who have plenty of Swiss currency and who like light wines to knock back after a day on the piste.

**Dom Pérignon** [dom peh-reen-yon] (*Champagne*, France) *Moët et Chandon's Prestige Cuvée,* named after the cellarmaster who is erroneously said to have invented the *Champagne* method. Impeccable. (Moët will disgorge older vintages to order. Write and ask). ☆☆☆☆☆ **1985 ££££**

***Domaine (Dom.)*** [doh-mayn] (France) Wine estate.

**Domecq** [doh-mek] (*Jerez/Rioja*, Spain) Producer of La Ina *Fino* and the rare, wonderful 511A *Amontillado*.

**Ch. la Dominique** [lah doh-mee-neek] (*St. Emilion Grand Cru Classé*, *Bordeaux*, France) High-flying property; one of the finest in St. Emilion. 70 **71** 78 79 81 **82** 83 **86** 87 88 89 90 93 94 95 96

**Dominus** [dahm-ih-nuhs] (*Napa Valley*, California) *Christian Moueix* of *Ch. Petrus's* modestly named competitor to *Opus One* has always been a heftily tannic *Cabernet*. Since 1989 that *Tannin* has been matched by fruit, making for wine in which it is easier to believe. Even so, wines like the 1987 still need to be left to themselves for a few years. ☆☆☆☆☆ **1991 Napa Valley Napanook Vineyard ££££**

**Doonkuna** [doon-koo-nah] (*New South Wales*, Australia) Small winery making decent wine close to the capital. ☆☆☆☆ 1992 Shiraz ££

**Dopff 'Au Moulin'** [dop-foh-moo-lan] (*Alsace*, France) Underrated *négoçiant* whose *Grand Cru* wines are among the most concentrated around. ☆☆☆ ☆ Riesling Grand Cru Schoenenbourg Sélection de Grains Nobles ££££

**Dopff & Irion** [dop-fay-ee-ree-yon] (*Alsace*, France) Not to be confused with Dopff 'Au Moulin', its more recommendable namesake. ☆☆☆ 1994 Riesling Les Murailles ££

**Dorin** [doh-ran] (*Vaud*, Switzerland) The Swiss name for *Chasselas* in the *Vaud* region.

**Dornfelder** [dorn-fel-duh] (Germany) Juicy, berryish grape; needs careful handling. ☆☆☆☆ 1995 Lingenfelder Grosskarlbacher ££

***Dosage*** [doh-sazh] The addition of sweetening syrup to naturally dry *Champagne* after *dégorgement* to replace the wine lost with the yeast, and to set the sugar to the desired level (even *Brut Champagne* requires up to 4 grammes per litre of sugar to make it palatable).

**Douro** [doo-roh] (Portugal) The *port* region and river, producing increasingly good table wines thanks partly to Australians *David Baverstock* (at *Quinta de la Rosa* and *Crasto)* and *Peter Bright*. ***Barca Velha; Sogrape.***

***Doux*** [doo] (France) Sweet.

**Dow's** [dows] (*Douro*, Portugal) One of the big two (with *Taylors*) and under the same family ownership as *Warres, Smith Woodhouse* and *Graham's*. Great *Vintage* port and similarly impressive *Tawny*. The Quinta do Bomfim wines offer a chance to taste the Dow's style affordably. 55 60 **63 66 70** 72 75 77 85 94 96 ☆☆☆☆ 10 Year Old Tawny ££

**Drappier** [drap-pee-yay] (*Champagne*, France) Small, recommendable producer. ☆☆☆☆☆ Champagne Rosé Brut £££

**Jean-Paul Droin** [drwan] (*Burgundy*, France) Good, small *Chablis* producer with approachable, 'modern' wines ☆☆☆☆ 1994 Grand Cru Grenouilles ££££

**Dromana Estate** [droh-mah-nah] (*Mornington Peninsula*, Australia) Ace viticulturalist Gary Crittenden has pioneered this region, with good *Chardonnay* and raspberryish *Pinot Noir*, which might benefit from less of the viticultural expertise Mr C. unashamedly uses to achieve high yields per vine. ☆☆☆☆ 1988 Cabernet Merlot £££

**Dom. Drouhin** [droo-an] (*Oregon*, USA) Top *Burgundy* producer's highly expensive investment in the US that's increasingly producing world-beating reds - thanks to Veronique Drouhin's skill and commitment and some of *Oregon's* best vineyards. ☆☆☆☆ 1993 Pinot Noir ££££

**Joseph Drouhin** [droo-an] (*Burgundy*, France) Probably *Burgundy's* best *négoçiant* with a range of first class red and white wines that are unusually representative of their particular appellations. Also look out for the rare white *Beaune* from its own Clos des Mouches, top-class *Clos de Vougeot* and unusually (for a *négoçiant* ) high-quality *Chablis*. The Marquis de Laguiche *Montrachet* is sublime. ☆☆☆☆☆ 1995 Beaune Clos des Mouches ££££

**Pierre-Jacques Druet** [droo-ay] (*Loire*, France) Most reliable *Bourgueil* producer making characterful individual cuvées. ☆☆☆☆ 1990 Vaunoveau £££

**Dry Creek** (*Sonoma*, California) A rare example of a Californian *AVA* region whose wines have an identifiable quality and style. Look out for *Sauvignon Blanc* and *Zinfandel* – from wineries like *Dry Creek, Duxoup*, Quivira, Nalle and *Rafanelli*. Red: 84 **85** 86 87 **90 91** 92 93 95 96 White: **85 90 91** 92 95 96

**Dry Creek Vineyard** (*Sonoma*, California) Eponymous vineyard within the Dry Creek *AVA* making well-known *Fumé Blanc* and a great *Chenin Blanc*. ☆☆☆ 1996 Fumé Blanc ££

**Dry River** (*Martinborough*, New Zealand) Small estate with a particularly impressive *Pinot Gris*. ☆☆☆ 1995 Sauvignon Blanc £££

**Duboeuf** [doo-burf] (*Burgundy*, France) The 'king of *Beaujolais*', who introduced the world to the boiled sweet flavour of young *Gamay* at a time when most versions tasted like *Châteauneuf-du-Pape*. A wide range of good examples from individual growers, vineyards and villages. Reliable *Nouveau*, good straightforward *Mâconnais* white, single domaine *Rhônes* and now the biggest plantation of *Viognier* in the world. ☆☆☆ 1995 Morgon ££

**Denis Dubordieu** [doo-bor-dyuh] *Bordeaux* white wine guru.

**Duc de Magenta** [ma-zhen-tah] (*Burgundy*, France) Classy estate managed by *Jadot*.

**Duckhorn** (*Napa Valley*, California) Vaunted producer now moving away from the intentionally impenetrable style of his highly priced *Merlot*. This may dismay collectors and wine snobs who presumably derive similar pleasure from cold showers and being beaten with birch twigs. I'll open a bottle to celebrate. ☆☆☆☆ 1993 Napa Valley Merlot £££

**Ch. Ducru-Beaucaillou** [doo-kroo boh-ki-yoo] (*St Julien 2nd Growth*, *Bordeaux*, France) *Super Second* with a less obvious style than peers such as *Léoville-Las-Cases* and *Pichon Lalande*. Second wine is Croix-Beaucaillou. **70 75** 76 **78** 79 80 **81** 82 **83 85** 86 87 88 89 90 91 92 93 94 95 96 ☆☆☆☆ 1993 ££££

**Ch. Duhart-Milon-Rothschild** [doo-ahr mee-lon rot-sheeld] (*Pauillac 4th Growth*, *Bordeaux*, France) Under the same management as *Lafite* and benefiting from heavy investment. 78 79 80 81 **82** 83 **85** 86 87 88 89 90 91 92 93 95 ☆☆☆ 1990 ££££

**Dom. Dujac** [doo-zhak] (*Burgundy*, France) Cult *Burgundy* producer with fine, long-lived, if sometimes rather pallid, wines from *Morey St. Denis*, including *Clos de la Roche*. Now helped by Gary Farr of the excellent *Bannockburn* in Australia and busily investing time and effort into vineyards in Southern France. ☆☆☆☆ 1989 Echezeaux ££££

**Dumazet** [doo-mah-zay] (*Rhône*, France) Top flight Northern *Rhône* producer making fewer than 200 cases of perfumed *Condrieu* per year from his one acre plot of steeply sloping vineyards. Buy this instead of *Ch. Grillet*. ☆☆☆☆ 1993 Condrieu £££

***Dumb*** As in dumb nose, meaning without smell.

**Dumien-Serette** [doo-mee-yen seh-ret] (*Rhône* France) Fantastic, full-bodied rich wines from this tiny 3.2-acre plot. ☆☆☆☆ 1991 Cornas £££

**Dunn Vineyards** (*Napa Valley*, California) Tough, forbidding *Cabernets* from *Howell Mountain* for the very, very patient collectors who've run out of *Duckhorn Merlot* and *Dominus*. ☆☆☆☆ 1991 Cabernet Sauvignon Howell Mountain

**Durbach** [door-bahk] (*Baden*, Germany) Top vineyard area of this *Anbaugebiet*.

**Durif** [dyoor-if] See *Petite Sirah*.

**Jean Durup** [doo-roop] (*Burgundy*, France) Modern, high-quality estate whose owner controversially believes in extending vineyards of *Chablis* into what some claim to be less distinguished soil, and not using new oak. The best wines are sold as Ch. de Maligny. ☆☆☆☆ 1995 Château de Maligny ££

**Dusty Miller** (England) Local name for *Pinot Meunier*.

**Duxoup Wine Works** [duk-soop] (*Sonoma Valley*, California) Inspired winery-in-a-shed, producing very good characterful *Charbono* and fine *Syrah* from bought-in grapes. The curious name – which is incidentally not one to drop among US collectors who prefer tougher fare from château-like edifices – has nothing to do with the Marx Brothers movie. It refers to the owners' belief that starting a winery and planting a vineyard would – in the American expression – be as 'easy as duck soup'. ☆☆☆ 1993 Charbono £££

# E

**Echézeaux** [ay-shuh-zoh] (*Burgundy*, France) *Grand Cru* vineyard between *Clos de Vougeot* and *Vosne Romanée* and more or less an extension of the latter commune. *Flagey-Echézeaux*, a village on the relatively vine-less side of the Route Nationale, takes its name from the 'flagellation' used by the peasants to gather corn in the 6th century. Stars are *Dom. de la Romanée-Conti, Henri Jayer, Dom. Dujac and Dom. Thierry Vigst*. Grands-Echézeaux should be finer.

**L' Ecole No. 41** [ay-kohl] (*Washington State*, USA) Stylish producer of classy Chardonnay and Merlot. Also supplies rich Semillon. ☆☆☆☆ **1991 Cabernet Sauvignon ££££**

***Edelfäule*** [ay-den-fow-luh] (Germany) *Botrytis Cinerea*, or '*Noble rot*'.

***Edelzwicker*** [ay-del-zwik-kur] (*Alsace*, France) Generic name for a blend of grape varieties. The idea of blends is coming back – but not the name (see *Hugel*).

**Eden Ridge** (South Australia) Organic wines made by *Mountadam*. ☆☆☆☆ **1996 Dry White Adelaide Hills ££**

**Edna Valley Vineyard** (California) Long-standing maker of rich, buttery Chardonnay in the *AVA* of the same name. In the same stable as *Chalone, Carmenet* and *Acacia*. ☆☆☆ **1993 Chardonnay ££**

**Eger** [eg-gur] (Hungary) Region of Hungary where *Bull's Blood* is made.

**Dom. de l' Eglise** [duh lay glees] (*Pomerol*, *Bordeaux*, France) Fairly priced, middle-of-the-range, wines. **79 82** 83 85 86 88 89 90 94 95 96 ☆☆☆☆ **1993 ££££**

**Ch. l' Église-Clinet** [Lay gleez klee-nay] (*Pomerol*, *Bordeaux*, France) A terrific château that's fast getting even better. 70 **71** 75 76 81 **82 83 85** 86 **88** 89 **90** 93 94 95 96 ☆☆☆☆☆ **1993 ££££**

**Egri Bikaver** [eh-grih bih-kah vehr] (*Eger*, Hungary) See *Bull's Blood*.

***Einzellage/n*** [ine-tseh-lah-gur/gehn] (Germany) Single vineyard; most precise and often the last part of a wine name, finer by definition than a *Grosslage*.

***Eiswein*** [ihs-vihn] (Germany/Austria) The ultimate, ultra-concentrated *Late Harvest* wine, made from grapes naturally frozen on the vine. Rare and hard to make (and consequently very pricy) in Germany, but more affordable in Austria and, increasingly, Canada. Intensely delicious but often with worryingly high levels of *acidity*. ☆☆☆☆ **1988 Niersteiner Olberg Riesling ££££**

**Eitelsbach** [ih-tel-sbahk] (*Mosel*, Germany) One of the top two *Ruwer* wine towns, and the site of the famed Karthäuserhofberg vineyard. ☆☆☆ **1993 Eitelsbacher Karthauser Hofberg Riesling Kabinett ££**

***Elaborado y Anejado Por*** [ay-lah-boh-rah-doh ee anay-hahdo pohr] (Spain) 'Made and aged for'.

**Elba** [el-bah] (Italy) Island off the Tuscan coast where they make full dry reds and whites.

**Elbling** [el-bling] Inferior Germanic white grape.

**Elderton** (*Barossa Valley*, Australia) Maker of big competition-winning reds, especially *Cabernet*. ☆☆☆☆ **1994 Shiraz Barossa Valley £££**

***Eléver/éléveur*** [ay-leh-vay/vay-leh-vuhr] To mature or 'nurture' wine, especially in the cellars of the *Burgundy négoçiants*, who act as éléveurs, after traditionally buying in wine made by small estates.

**Elgin** [el-gin] (South Africa) Coolish – *Burgundy*-like – apple-growing country which is rapidly attracting the interest of big producers. Watch out for the Paul Cluver reds and whites from *Neil Ellis*. May eventually overshadow all but the best parts of *Stellenbosch* and *Paarl*.

**Neil Ellis** (*Stellenbosch*, South Africa) One of the Cape's best new wave winemakers and a pioneer of the new region of *Elgin*. ☆☆☆☆ **1996 Sauvignon Blanc ££**

**Eltville** [elt-vil] (*Rheingau*, Germany) Town housing the *Rheingau* state cellars and the German Wine Academy, producing good *Riesling* with backbone. QbA/Kab/Spät: **85** 86 **88 89 90** 91 92 93 94 95 96 Aus/Beeren/TBA: **83 85** 88 89 90 91 92 93 94 95 96 ☆☆☆ **1994 Eltville ££**

**Emerald Riesling** [rees-ling] (California) Bottom of the range white cross grape (*Riesling* x *Muscadelle*). At its best it is fresh and fruity but decidedly undistinguished.

**Emilia-Romagna** [eh-mee-lee-yah roh-ma-nya] (Italy) Region around Bologna best known for *Lambrusco;* also the source of *Albana, Sangiovese* di Romagna and *Pagadebit*.

***En primeur*** [on pree-muh] New wine, usually *Bordeaux*. Specialist merchants buy and offer wine *en primeur* before it has been released; customers rely on their merchant's judgement to make a good buy. In the US and Australia, where producers like *Mondavi* and *Petaluma* are selling their wine in this way, the process is known as buying 'futures'.

**Ch. l' Enclos** [lon kloh] (*Pomerol*, *Bordeaux*, France) Gorgeously rich, fairly priced wines. 70 75 79 **82** 83 85 86 88 **89** 90 95 96 ☆☆☆☆ **1990 £££**

***English wine*** Produced from grapes grown in England (or Wales), as opposed to the now-to-be-phased-out *British Wine,* which is made from imported concentrate. Quality has improved in recent years, as winemakers have developed their own personality, changing from semi-sweet, mock-Germanic to dry mock-*Loire* and now, increasingly, to aromatic-but-dry and *Late Harvest*. Best wines are being made by *Breaky Bottom, Thames Valley Vineyards, Bruisyard, Three Choirs, Carr Taylor, Chiltern Valley* and *Denbies*.

***Enoteca*** [ee-noh-teh-kah] (Italy) Literally wine library or, nowadays, wine shop.

**Entre-Deux-Mers** [on-truh duh mehr] (*Bordeaux*, France) Once a region of appalling sweet wine from vineyards between the cities of *Bordeaux* and Libourne. Now a source of basic *Bordeaux* Blanc and principally dry *Sauvignon*. Reds are sold as *Bordeaux* Rouge. Both reds and whites suffer from the difficulty grapes can have in ripening here in cool years. *Ch. Bonnet* is the star.

**Erbach** [ayr-bahkh] (*Rheingau*, Germany) Town noted for fine, full Riesling, particularly from the Marcobrunn vineyard. QbA/Kab/Spät: **85** 86 **88 89 90** 91 92 93 94 95 96 Aus/Beeren/TBA: **83 85** 88 89 90 91 92 93 94 95 96. ☆☆☆☆ **1994 Erbacher Marcobrunn Riesling Spätlese, Von Simmern £££**

**Erbaluce** [ehr-bah-loo-chay] (*Piedmont*, Italy) White grape responsible for the light, dry wines of the *Caluso,* and also the sweet, sun-dried Caluso Passito. **Boratto.**

**Erbaluce di Caluso** [ehr-bah-loo-chay dee kah-loo-soh] (*Piedmont*, Italy) Dry, quite herby, white wine made from the Erbaluce grape (*Bava* makes a good one, blending in a little *Chardonnay*). ☆☆☆ **1996 Ferrando £**

**Erden** [ehr-durn] (*Mosel-Saar-Ruwer*, Germany) In the *Bernkastel Bereich*, this northerly village produces full, crisp, dry *Riesling*. and includes the famous Treppchen vineyard. QbA/Kab/Spät: **85** 86 **88 89 90** 91 **92 93 94 95 96** Aus/Beeren/TBA: **83 85 88 89 90** 91 **92 93 94 95 96** ☆☆☆☆ **1996 Erdener Pralat Riesling Kabinett, Dr Loosen ££££**

**Errazuriz** [ehr-raz-zoo-riz] (*Aconcagua Valley*, Chile) One of Chile's big name producers and owner of *Caliterra*. Wines have been improved by input from Mondavi. ☆☆☆☆ **1995 Don Maximo Cabernet Sauvignon £££**

***Erzeugerabfüllung*** [ayr-tsoy-guhr-ab-foo-loong] (Germany) Bottled by the grower/estate.

**August Eser** [ay-zur] (*Rheingau* Germany) Crisp, easy-drinking wines with elegant floral character. ☆☆☆ **1992 Rauenthaler Rothenburg Riesling Spatlese £££**

**H.H. Eser-Johannishof** [ay-sur-joh-hah-nihs-hof] (*Rheingau* Germany) Wines of intense flavour, plenty of fruit and a rich finish. ☆☆☆ **1990 Johannisberger Riesling Auslese ££££**

**Esk Valley** (*Hawkes Bay*, New Zealand) Under the same ownership as *Vidal* and *Villa Maria*. Successful with *Bordeaux*-style reds and juicy rosé. ☆☆☆☆ **1996 Chardonnay ££**

**Esparão** [esp-per-row] (*Alentejo*, Portugal) Revolutionary wines made by Australian-born *David Baverstock*. *Alentejo*.

***Espum/oso/ante*** [es-poom-mo-soh/san-tay] (Spain/Portugal) Sparkling.

***Esters*** Chemical components in wine responsible for all those extraordinary odours of fruits, vegetables, hamster cages and trainers.

***Estufa*** [esh-too-fah] (*Madeira*, Portugal) The vats in which *Madeira* is heated, speeding maturity and imparting its familiar 'cooked' flavour.

**Eszencia** [es-sen-tsee-yah] (*Tokaji*, Hungary) Incredibly sweet and concentrated syrup made by piling around 100kg of *late-harvested*, *botrytised* grapes into *puttonyos* and letting as little as three litres of incredibly sticky treacle dribble out of the bottom. This will only ferment up to about 4% alcohol, over several weeks, before stopping completely. It is then stored and used periodically to sweeten normal *Aszu* wines. The Tzars of Russia discovered the joys of Eszencia, and it has long been prized for its effects on the male libido. It is incredibly hard to find, even by those who can see the point in doing anything with the outrageously expensive syrup other than pouring it on ice-cream. The easier to find *Aszu Essencia* (one step sweeter than *Aszu* 6 *puttonyos*) is far better value.

**Arnaldo Etchart** [et-shaht] (*Cafayate*, Argentina) Dynamic producer, benefiting from advice by *Michel Rolland* of *Pomerol* fame, and also investment by its new owners Pernod Ricard. The key wine here, though, is the grapey white *Torrontes*. ☆☆☆ **1994 Tinto £** ☆☆☆☆ **1995 Cabernet Sauvignon £**

**Etna** [eht-nuh] (*Sicily*, Italy) From the Sicilian volcanic slopes; hot-climate, soft, fruity *DOC* reds, whites and rosés. Can be flabby.

**Etude** [ay-tewd] (*Napa*, California) Well-respected consultant Tony Soter experiments by marrying specific sites and clones of Pinot Noir. Apart from these wines there are good rich *Napa* reds and *Carneros* Chardonnay. ☆☆☆☆☆ **1992 Pinot Noir Napa Valley £££**

**Ch. l' Évangile** [lay-van-zheel] (*Pomerol*, *Bordeaux*, France) A classy and increasingly sought-after property that can, in great vintages like 1988, 1989 and 1990, sometimes rival its neighbour *Pétrus*, but in a more tannic style. **61 64 75** 78 79 **82 83 85** 86 87 **88 89 90** 92 93 **95 96** ☆☆☆☆ **1990 ££££**

**Evans Family** (*Hunter Valley*, Australia) Len Evans' (founder, ex-Chairman of Rothbury Vineyards) own estate. Good rich *Chardonnay* and *Semillon* as characterful and generous as their maker. Set for expansion following the sale of Rothbury to *Mildara-Blass*. ☆☆☆☆ 1995 Chardonnay, Hunter Valley ££

**Evans & Tate** (*Margaret River*, Australia) Much improved producer following its move from the hot *Swan Valley* into the cooler *Margaret River*. ☆☆☆☆ 1995 Margaret River Chardonnay £££

**Eventail de Vignerons Producteurs** [ay-van-tih] (*Burgundy*, France) Reliable source of *Beaujolais*.

**Eyrie Vineyards** [ih-ree] (*Oregon*, USA) Pioneering *Pinot Noir* producer in the *Willamette Valley*, whose success in a blind tasting of Burgundies helped to attract *Joseph Drouhin* to invest his francs in a vineyard here. ☆☆☆☆ 1988 Pinot Meunier ££££

# F

**Fairview Estate** (*Paarl*, South Africa) Go-ahead estate where Charles Back makes a range of good-value wines more open-mindedly than some of his neighbours, and is one of the few South Africans responsible for genuine innovation. ☆☆☆☆☆ 1995 Merlot.

**Joseph Faiveley** [fay-vlay] (*Burgundy*, France) Modern *négoçiant* with particular strength in his backyard vineyards in the *Côte de Nuits* and *Nuits St. Georges*. ☆☆☆☆ 1992 Chambertin-Clos-de Bèze ££££

**Far Niente** [fah nee-yen-tay] (*Napa Valley*, California) Well regarded, but sometimes over-showy maker of *Chardonnays* and *Cabernet*. ☆☆☆☆☆ 1988 Chardonnay £££

**Ch. de Fargues** [duh fahrg] (*Sauternes*, *Bordeaux*, France) Elegant wines made by the winemaker at *Ch. d'Yquem* – and a good alternative. 70 71 75 76 83 85 86 88 89 90 95 96 ☆☆☆☆ 1990 ££££

***Fat*** Has a silky texture which fills the mouth. More fleshy than meaty.

***Fattoria*** [fah-tor-ree-ah] (Italy) Estate, particularly in *Tuscany*.

**Faugères** [foh-zhehr] (*Midi*, France) With neighbouring *St. Chinian*, this gently hilly region is a major cut above the surrounding *Coteaux du Languedoc*, and potentially the source of really exciting red, whites and rosés. For the moment, however, most still taste pretty rustic. ☆☆☆☆ 1992 Ch. de Grézan ££

**Bernard Faurie** [fow-ree] (*Rhône*, France) Based in Tournon, he makes intense perfumed wines with longevity of life. ☆☆☆☆ 1994 Hermitage ££££

**Bodegas Faustino Martinez** [fows-tee-noh mahr-tee-nehth] (*Rioja*, Spain) Dependable *Rioja* producer with excellent (Gran) *Reservas*, fair whites and a decent *Cava*. ☆☆☆☆ 1988 Tinto Gran Reserva £££

**Dom du Fauturie** [foh-too-ree] (*Rhône* France) Producer of impeccable Syrah-based reds of superb quality. ☆☆☆ 1990 St Joseph ££££

**Favorita** [fahvoh-ree-tah] (*Piedmont*, Italy) Traditional variety from *Piedmont* transformed by modern winemaking into delicate floral whites. *Conterno; Villa Lanata; Bava.*

**Weingut Feiler-Artinger** [fih-luh arh-ting-guh] (*Rust*, Austria) Superlative producer of dry and, especially, *Late Harvest* wines. ☆☆☆ 1995 Traminer £££

**Fattoria di Felsina Berardenga** [fah-toh-ree-ah dee fehl-see-nah beh-rah-den-gah] (*Tuscany*, Italy) High quality *Chianti* estate. ☆☆☆☆ 1994 Chianti Riserva £££

**Fendant** [fon-don] (Switzerland) See *Chasselas*.

**Fer** [fehr] (South West France) Grape used to make *Marcillac*.

***Fermentazione naturale*** [fehr-men-tat-zee-oh-nay] (Italy) 'Naturally sparkling' but, in fact, indicates the *Cuve Close* method.

**Fernão Pires** [fehr-now pee-rehsh] (Portugal) Muscatty grape, used to great effect by *Peter Bright* of the *Joao Pires* winery.

**Ch. Ferrand Lartique** [feh-ron lah-teek] (*St. Emilion Grand Cru Bordeaux*, France) Tiny 5-acre estate producing full-bodied rich wines from 40-year-old vines. ☆☆☆☆ **1994 £££**

**Luigi Ferrando** (*Piedmont* Italy) Producer in the Carema Doc of good Nebbiolo-based wines that are surprisingly light and elegant in style.

**Ferrari-Carano** [fuh-rah-ree kah-rah-noh] (*Sonoma*, California) Some US critics take these wines seriously; I find the Chardonnays too sweet. ☆☆☆☆ **1994 Fumé Blanc Sonoma County Reserve £££**

**A. A. Ferreira** [feh-ray-rah] (*Douro*, Portugal) Traditional Portuguese port producer, equally famous for its excellent tawnies as for its *Barca Velha*, Portugal's best traditional unfortified red. ☆☆☆☆ **Duque de Braganca 20 Year Old Tawny ££££** ☆☆☆ **1995 Estera £**

**Ch. Ferrière** [feh-ree-yehr] (*Margaux 3rd Growth*, *Bordeaux*, France) Once tiny, now rather bigger, thanks to the convenience of belonging to the same owners as the *Margaux Cru Bourgeois, Ch. la Gurgue*. 93 94 95 96 ☆☆☆ **1994 £££**

**Sylvain Fessy** [seel-van fes-see] (*Burgundy*, France) Reliable small *Beaujolais* producer with wide range of *crus*.

**Henry Fessy** [on-ree fes-see] (*Burgundy*, France) Reliable *négoçiant*, vineyard owner and producer of *Beaujolais*. ☆☆☆ **1996 Cote-de-Brouilly Dom. de l'Heronde ££**

***Fête des Fleurs*** [fayt day fluh] (*Bordeaux*, France) Annual social event where the Bordelais gather to party, and the *Château* chosen to host the affair tries to outdo the previous year's extravaganza.

**Fetzer** [fet-zuh] (*Mendocino*, California) The best of the bigger Californian wineries, one of the few which really tries to make good wine at (relatively) lower prices, and a laudable pioneering producer of organic wines. Recently taken over but still run by the family. ☆☆☆☆ **1993 Barrel Select Merlot ££** ☆☆☆☆ **1995 Bonterra Chardonnay ££**

**Nicolas Feuillatte** [fuh-yet] (*Champagne*, France) Quietly rising star with good value wine. ☆☆☆ **1989 Cuvée Speciale.**

**William Fèvre** [weel-yum feh-vr] (*Burgundy*, France) Quality *Chablis* producer who has been a revolutionary in his use of new oak. His efforts in Chile have been improving with each vintage. ☆☆☆ **1993 Chablis Grand Cru Bougros ££££**

**Ch. Feytit-Clinet** [fay-tee klee-nay] (*Pomerol*, *Bordeaux*, France) A Moueix property with good, delicate wines. 79 81 **82** 83 **85** 86 87 88 89 90 94 95 96

**Les Fiefs-de-Lagrange** [fee-ef duh lag-ronzh] (*St Julien*, *Bordeaux*, France) Recommendable *Second Label* of *Ch. Lagrange*.

**Ch. de Fieuzal** [duh fyuh-zahl] (*Pessac-Léognan Grand Cru Classé*, *Bordeaux*, France) *Pessac-Léognan* property which has made great whites and lovely raspberryish reds. Abeille de Fieuzal is the (excellent) *Second Label*. Red: 75 79 81 **82** 83 **85** 86 87 88 89 90 91 92 93 94 95 96 White: **85 88 89** 90 91 92 93 **96** ☆☆☆☆ **1993 Blanc** ☆☆☆☆ **1990 Rouge ££££**

**Ch. Figeac** [fee-zhak] (*St. Emilion Premier Grand Cru*, *Bordeaux*, France) Forever in the shadow of its neighbour, *Cheval Blanc*, but still one of the most characterful and best-made *St. Emilions*. 64 **70** 78 81 **82** 83 84 **85 86** 87 88 89 90 92 93 94 95 96 ☆☆☆☆ **1994 ££££**

**Finger Lakes** (*New York State*, USA) Cold region whose producers struggle (sometimes effectively) to produce good *vinifera*, including *Late Harvest Riesling*. *Hybrids* such as *Seyval Blanc* are more reliable. **Wagner.**

***Fining*** The clarifying of young wine before bottling to remove impurities, using a number of agents including *Isinglass* and *Bentonite*.

***Finish*** What you can still taste after swallowing.

🍷 ***Fino*** [fee-noh] (*Jerez*, Spain) Dry, delicate sherry which gains its distinctive flavour from the *flor* or yeast which grows on the surface of the wine during maturation. Drink chilled, with tapas, preferably within two weeks of opening. **Lustau; Barbadillo; Hidalgo; Gonzalez Byass.**

🍷 **Firestone** (*Santa Ynez*, California) Good producer – particularly of good value *Merlot* and *Sauvignon* and *Late Harvest Riesling* – in Southern California. ☆☆☆☆ **1995 Chardonnay ££**

🍷 **Fitou** [fee-too] (*Midi*, France) Long considered to be an up-market *Corbières* and still a quite reliable southern *AC*, making reds largely from the *Carignan* grape. Formerly dark and stubborn, the wines have become more refined, with a woody warmth, though they never quite shake off their rustic air. **Mont Tauch.**

**Fixin** [fee-san] (*Burgundy*, France) Northerly village of the *Côte de Nuits*, producing lean, tough, uncommercial reds which can mature well. *Faiveley* makes a good one. 76 **78** 79 **80** 82 83 **85** 86 87 **88 89 90** 92 95 96 ☆☆☆☆ **Les Hervelets, Gelin £££**

***Flabby*** Lacking balancing *acidity*.

**Flagey-Echézeaux** [flah-jay ay-shuh-zoh] (*Burgundy*, France) Village on the wrong (non-vine) side of the Route National 74 that lends its name to the appellations of *Echézeaux* and *Grands Echézeaux*.

🍷 **Ch. La Fleur** [flur] (*St. Emilion*, *Bordeaux*, France) Small *St. Emilion* property producing softly fruity wines. **82** 83 85 86 88 **89** 90 92 94 95 96 ☆☆☆ **1992 £££**

🍷 **Ch. la Fleur-de Gay** [flur duh gay] (*Pomerol*, *Bordeaux*, France) Ch. Croix de Gay's best wine and thus heavily sought after. Not always worth the extra money. 82 **86** 87 88 89 90 94 95 96

🍷 **Ch. la Fleur-Pétrus** [flur pay-trooss] (*Pomerol*, *Bordeaux*, France) For those who find *Pétrus* a touch too hefty, not to mention a touch unaffordable, this next-door neighbour offers gorgeously accessible *Pomerol* flavour for (in *Pétrus* terms) a bargain price. 70 **75** 78 79 **81** 82 **83** 85 86 87 88 89 90 92 93 95 96 ☆☆☆☆ **1993 ££££**

🍷 **Fleurie** [fluh-ree] (*Burgundy*, France) One of the 10 *Beaujolais Crus*, ideally fresh and fragrant, as its name suggests. Best vineyards include La Madonne and Pointe du Jour. Dom. Bachelard and Guy Depardon are names to watch. **85 87 88 89** 90 **91** 93 94 95 96. ☆☆☆☆ **Ch. de Fleurie Loron ££**

***Flor*** [flawr] Yeast which grows naturally on the surface of some maturing sherries, making them potential *Finos*.

🍇 **Flora** [flor-rah] A cross between *Semillon* and *Gewürztraminer*, best known in *Brown Brothers* Orange Muscat and Flora.

🍷 **Flora Springs** (*Napa Valley*, California) Good, unusual *Sauvignon Blanc* (Soliloquy) and (toughish) *Merlot, Cabernet Sauvignon* & *Cabernet Franc* blend (Trilogy). ☆☆☆☆ **1991 Chardonnay £££**

🍷 **Emile Florentin** [floh-ron-tan] (*Rhône*, France) Maker of ultra-traditional, ultra-tannic chewy *St. Joseph*. ☆☆☆☆ **1993 Clos de L' Arbalestrier £££**

***Flying Winemakers*** Young (usually) Antipodeans who have, since the 1980s, been despatched like vinous mercenaries to wineries worldwide to make better and more reliable wine than the home teams can manage. Often, as they have proved, all it has taken to improve the standards of a European cooperative has been a more scrupulous attitude towards picking ripe grapes (rather than impatiently harvesting unripe ones) and keeping tanks and pipes clean. The best-known include *Jacques Lurton*, *Hugh Ryman, Kym Milne*, *Peter Bright*, John Worontschak and Nick Butler.

**Folle Noir** [fol nwah] (France) Traditional grape used to make *Bellet*.

**Ch. Fombrauge** [fom-brohzh] (*St. Emilion*, *Bordeaux*, France) Middling St. Emilion. **82** 83 85 86 88 89 90 92 93 94 95 96 ☆☆☆ **1994 £££**

**Ch. Fonplégade** [fon-pleh-gahd] (*St. Emilion Grand Cru Classé*, *Bordeaux*, France) If you like your *St. Emilion* tough, this is for you. 78 **82** 83 85 86 87 88 89 90 94 95 96 ☆☆☆ **1989 ££££**

**Ch. Fonroque** [fon-rok] (*St. Emilion Grand Cru Classé*, *Bordeaux*, France) Property with concentrated wines, but not always one of *Moueix's* finest. 70 **75** 78 79 81 82 **83 85** 86 88 89 90 94 95 96 ☆☆☆ **1993 £££**

**Fonseca Guimaraens** [fon-say-ka gih-mah-rans] (*Douro*, Portugal) Now a subsidiary of *Taylors* but still independently making great port; in blind tastings the 1976 and 1978 beat supposedly classier houses' supposedly finer vintages. See also *Guimaraens*. Fonseca: 60 **63 66 70** 75 **77** 85 95 Fonseca Guimaraens: **76 78** 92 94 ☆☆☆☆☆ **1984 Fonseca Vintage Port.**

**J M da Fonseca Internacional** [fon-say-ka in-tuhr-nah-soh-nahl] (*Setúbal* Peninsula, Portugal) Highly commercial firm whose wines include Lancers, the *Mateus*-lookalike, semi-fizzy, semi-sweet pinks, whites sold in mock-crocks and fairly basic fizz made by a process known as the *Russian Continuous*.

**J M da Fonseca Successores** [fon-say-ka suk-ses-saw-rays] (*Estremadura*, Portugal) Unrelated to the port house of the same name and no longer connected to *JM da Fonseca Internacional*. Family-run firm, with *Aliança* and *Sogrape*, one of Portugal's big three dynamic wine companies. Top reds include Pasmados, *Periquita* (from the grape of the same name), *Quinta da Camarate*, Terras Altas Dão and the Cabernet-influenced 'TE' *Garrafeiras*. Dry whites are less impressive, but the sweet old *Moscatel de Setúbals* are luscious classics. ☆☆☆ **1996 Quinta do Azerado ££** ☆☆☆ **1995 Villa Regia Douro £**

**Dom. Font de Michelle** [fon-duh-mee-shel] (*Rhône*, France) Reliable producer of medium-bodied red *Châteauneuf-du-Pape* and tiny quantities of brilliant, almost unobtainable, white.

**Fontana Candida** [fon-tah-nah kan-dee-dah] (*Lazio*, Italy) Good producer, especially for *Frascati*. The top wine is Colle Gaio which is good enough to prove the disappointing nature of most other wines from this area. ☆☆☆ **1995 Santa Teresa Frascati Superiore ££**

**Fontanafredda** [fon-tah-nah-freh-dah] (*Piedmont*, Italy) Big producer with impressive *Asti Spumante* and very approachable (especially single-vineyard) *Barolo*. ☆☆☆☆ **1990 Barolo Vigna La Rosa ££££**

**Domaine de Font Sane** [fon-sen] (*Rhône*, France) Producer of fine Gigondas in a very underrated AC. Very traditional and full-bodied. ☆☆☆ **1995 ££**

**Forst** [Fawrst] (*Pfalz*, Germany) Wine town producing great, concentrated Riesling. Famous for the *Jesuitengarten* vineyard. QbA/Kab/Spät: **85** 86 **88 89 90** 91 92 93 94 95 Aus/Beeren/TBA: **83 85** 88 89 90 91 92 93 94 95 ☆☆☆☆ **1991 Forster Kirchenstuck, Dr V Basserman-Jordan £££**

**Fortant de France** [faw-tan duh frons] (*Languedoc-Roussillon*, France) Good-quality, revolutionary brand owned by *Skalli* and specialising in varietal *Vin de Pays d'Oc*. ☆☆☆ **1996 Grenache Rouge £**

**Les Forts de Latour** [lay faw duh lah-toor] (*Pauillac*, *Bordeaux*, France) *Second Label* of *Ch. Latour*. Not, as is often suggested, made exclusively from the fruit of young vines and wine which might otherwise have ended up in *Ch. Latour* – there are vineyards whose grapes are grown specially for Les Forts – but still often better than other classed growth châteaux. **70** 75 **78 82** 83 85 **86** 88 90 91 92 93 94 95 96 ☆☆☆☆ **1992 ££££**

**Ch. Fourcas-Dupré** [faw-kass doo-pray] (*Listrac Cru Bourgeois*, *Bordeaux*, France) Tough, very traditional Listrac. **70** 75 **78** 79 81 **82 83** 85 **86** 87 88 89 90 91 92 95 96 ☆☆☆ **1990 £££**

🍷 **Ch. Fourcas-Hosten** [faw-kass hos-ten] (*Listrac Cru Bourgeois, Bordeaux*, France) Firm, old-fashioned wine with plenty of 'grip' for *Tannin* fans. 70 75 **78** 79 81 **82 83** 85 86 87 88 89 90 91 92 95 96 ☆☆☆ **1993 ££**

🍷 **Ch. Franc-Mayne** [fron-mayn] (*St. Emilion Grand Cru Classé, Bordeaux*, France) Dry, austere traditional wines for those who like them that way. 85 86 87 88 **89 90** 94 95 96 ☆☆☆ **1990 £££**

**Franciacorta** [fran-chee yah-kor-tah] (*Lombardy*, Italy) *DOC* for good, light, French-influenced reds but better noted for sparklers made to sell at the same price as *Champagne*, if not more than. See *Ca Del Bosco*.

🍷 **Franciscan Vineyards** [fran-sis-kan] (*Napa Valley*, California) Reliable *Napa* winery whose Chilean owner, Agustin Huneeus, has pioneered natural yeast wines with his *Burgundy*-like 'Cuvée Sauvage' *Chardonnay* and has punctured the pretentious balloons of some of his neighbours – including those who tried to create a *'Rutherford Bench' Appellation*. Now taking another bite at Chile (following an earlier joint venture at *Caliterra*). ☆☆☆☆ **1994 Chardonnay Sauvage.**

🍷 **Ch. de Francs** [day fron] (*Côtes de Francs, Bordeaux*, France) Well-run estate which makes great-value crunchy, blackcurranty wine and, with *Ch. Puygeraud*, helps to prove the worth of this little-known region ☆☆☆ **1994 ££**

**Franken** [FRAN-ken] (Germany) *Anbaugebiet* making characterful, sometimes earthy, dry whites, traditionally presented in the squat flagon-shaped '*bocksbeutel*' on which the *Mateus* bottle was modelled. One of the key varieties is the *Sylvaner* which helps explain the earthiness of many of the wines. The weather here does make it easier to make dry wine than in many other regions, however.

**Franschhoek** [fran-shook] (South Africa) Valley leading into the mountains away from *Paarl* (and thus cooler). The soil is a little suspect however, and the best producers are mostly clustered at the top of the valley, around the picturesque town. Red: **84** 86 **87** 89 **91 92** 93 94 95 96 White: **87 91** 92 93 94 95 96

**Frascati** [fras-kah-tee] (*Latium*, Italy) Clichéd dry or semi-dry white from *Latium*. At its it is best soft and clean and with a fascinating 'sour cream' flavour. Drink within 12 months of vintage. **Fontana Candida, Colli di Catone.**

🍷 **Ca' dei Frati** [kah day-yee frah-tee] (*Lombardy*, Italy) Fine producers, both of *Lugana* and *Chardonnay*-based fizz. ☆☆☆ **1995 Lugana Vigna I Frati ££**

🍷 **Frei Weingartener Wachau** [fri-vine-gahrt-nur vah-kow] (*Wachau*, Austria) Fine cooperative with great vineyards and an inspired young winemaker who is performing miracles with dry and sweet versions of the indigenous *Grüner Veltliner*, and making concentrated *Rieslings* that outclass the efforts of many a big-name estate in Germany. This is the kind of producer Austria needs. ☆☆☆☆☆ **1979 Burgstadt Dürnstein Beerenauslese £££**

🍷 **Freixenet** [fresh-net] (*Catalonia*, Spain) Giant in the *Cava* field and proponent of traditional *Catalonian* grapes in fizz. Its dull, big-selling *Cordon Negro* is a perfect justification for adding *Chardonnay* to the blend.

🍷 **Marchesi de' Frescobaldi** [fmah-kay-see day fres-koh-bal-dee] (*Tuscany*, Italy) Family estate with classy wines including *Castelgiocondo*, Mormoreto, a *Cabernet Sauvignon* based wine, the rich white Pomino Il Benefizio *Chardonnay*, Pomino Rosso using Merlot and Cabernet Sauvignon, and Nippozano in Chianti. ☆☆☆☆ **1993 Chianti Montesodi £££**

**Freycinet** [fres-sih-net] (*Tasmania*, Australia) Small East Coast winery with some of Australia's best *Pinot Noir*. ☆☆☆☆ 1995 Pinot Noir.

**Friuli-Venezia Giulia** [free-yoo-lee veh-neht-zee-yah zhee-yoo-lee-yah] (Italy) Northerly region containing a number of *DOCs* which focus on single-variety wines like *Merlot, Cabernet Franc Pinot Bianco, Pinot Grigio* and *Tocai*. Jermann; Bidoli; Puiatti; Zonin.

***Frizzante*** [freet-zan-tay] (Italy) Semi-sparkling especially *Lambrusco*.

**Frog's Leap** (*Napa Valley*, California) Winery whose owners combine organic winemaking skill with a fine sense of humour (their slogan is 'Time's fun when you're having flies'). Tasty *Zinfandel*, 'wild yeast' *Chardonnay* and unusually good *Sauvignon Blanc*. ☆☆☆ 1994 Chardonnay £££

**Fronsac/Canon Fronsac** [fron-sak] (*Bordeaux*, France) *Pomerol* neighbours, who regularly produce rich, intense, affordable wines. They are rarely subtle; however, with some good winemaking from men like *Christian Moueix* of *Ch. Pétrus* (he is a great believer in these regions), they can often represent some of the best buys in *Bordeaux*. Canon Fronsac is supposedly the better of the pair. **70 75** 78 79 81 **82 83 85** 86 **88 89** 90 94 95 96 Ch. Canon; Fontenil.

**Ch. de Fuissé** [duh fwee-say] (*Burgundy*, France) Jean-Jacques Vincent is probably the best producer in this *commune*, making wines comparable to some of the best of the *Côte D'Or*. The *Vieilles Vignes* has the distinction of lasting as long as a good *Chassagne-Montrachet*, but the other cuvées run it a very close race.

***Fumé Blanc*** [fyoo-may blahnk] The name originally adapted from *Pouilly Blanc Fumé* by *Robert Mondavi* to describe his Californian oaked *Sauvignon*. Now widely used for this style.

**Fürmint** [foor-mint] (*Tokaji*, Hungary) Lemony white grape, used in Hungary for *Tokaji* and, given modern winemaking, good dry wines. See *Royal Tokay Wine Co* and *Disznoko*. ☆☆☆ 1995 Disznoko Furmint £

**Fürstlich Castell'sches Domanenamt** [foorst-likh kas-tel-shes doh-man-nehn-nahmt] (*Franken*, Germany) Prestigious producer of typically full-bodied dry whites from the German *Anbaugebiet* of *Franken*.

***Fûts de Chêne (élévé en)*** [foo duh shayne] (France) Oak barrels (matured in).

# G

**Dom de Gachon-Pascal Perrier** [ga-shon pas-kahl pay-ree-yay] (*Rhône*, France) Superb unfiltered reds from the often underrated appellation of St. Joseph, which could easily pass 'blind' for wines from supposedly smarter (and pricier) appellations. ☆☆☆☆ 1991 St Joseph £££

**Ch. la Gaffelière** [gaf-fuh-lyehr] (*St. Emilion Premier Grand Cru*, *Bordeaux*, France) Lightish-bodied but well-made wines. Not to be confused with *Ch. Canon la Gaffelière*. **82 83** 85 **86** 87 88 89 90 91 92 93 94 96 ☆☆☆☆ 1992 ££££

**Dom. Jean-Noël Gagnard** [jon noh-wel gan-yahr] (*Burgundy*, France) A reliable domaine with vineyards which spread across *Chassagne-Montrachet*. There is also some *Santenay*. ☆☆☆☆ 1994 Chassagne Mont Les Champs 1er Cru ££££

**Jacques Gagnard-Delagrange** [gan-yahr duh lag-ronzh] (*Burgundy*, France) A top-class producer to follow for those traditionalists who like their white Burgundies delicately oaked. ☆☆☆☆ 1992 Chassagne-Montrachet ££££

**Gaillac** [gih-yak] (South West France) Light, fresh, good-value reds and (sweet, dry and slightly sparkling) whites, produced using *Gamay* and Sauvignon grapes, as well as the indigenous *Mauzac*. The reds can rival *Beaujolais*. ☆☆☆ **1992 Ch. Clement Ternes £**

**Pierre Gaillard** [gi-yahr] (*Rhône*, France) A good producer of *Côte Rôtie*, *St. Joseph* and *Condrieu*. ☆☆☆☆ **1993 Condrieu ££££**

**Gainey Vineyard** [gay-nee] (*Santa Barbara*, California) Classy reds and whites, especially *Pinot* and *Chardonnay*. ☆☆☆☆ **1992 Sauvignon Blanc Limited Selection.**

**Gaja** [gi-yah] (*Piedmont*, Italy) The man who proved that wines from the previously modest region of *Barbaresco* could sell for higher prices than top-class clarets, let alone the supposedly classier neighbours *Barolo*. Individual vineyard reds are of great quality and the *Chardonnay* is the best in Italy. Asking whether they're worth these prices is like questioning the cost of a Ferrari.

***Galestro*** [gah-less-troh] (*Tuscany*, Italy) There is no such thing as *Chianti* Bianco – the light, grapey stuff that is made in the *Chianti* region is sold as Galestro. ☆☆☆ **1995 Marchesi Antinori ££**

**E & J Gallo** [gal-loh] (*Central Valley*, California) The world's biggest wine producer; annual production is around 60 per cent of the total Californian harvest and more than the whole of Australia or *Champagne*. At the top end, there is now some pretty good but pricy *Cabernet* and *Chardonnay* from Gallo's own huge 'Northern *Sonoma* Estate', a piece of land which was physically re-contoured by their bulldozers. The new Turning Leaf wines are good too, at their level; with the exception of the *French Colombard*, the rest of the basic range, though much improved and very widely stocked, is still pretty ordinary. ☆☆☆☆☆ **1993 Frei Ranch Cabernet Sauvignon £££** ☆☆☆☆ **1993 Sonoma County Chardonnay £££** ☆☆☆☆ **1992 Northern Sonoma Estate Cabernet ££££**

**Gamay** [ga-may] (*Beaujolais*, France) Light-skinned grape traditional to *Beaujolais* where it is used to make fresh and fruity reds for early drinking, usually by the *Carbonic Maceration* method, and more serious *Cru* wines that resemble light *Burgundy*. Also successful in California (*J Lohr*), Australia (*Brown Bros.*) and South Africa (*Fairview*).

***Gamey*** Smell or taste reminiscent of hung game. Particularly associated with old *Pinot Noirs* and *Syrahs*. Possibly at least partly attributable to the combination of those grapes' natural characteristics with overly generous doses of *Sulphur Dioxide* by winemakers. Modern examples of both styles seem to be distinctly less gamey than in the past.

**Gancia** [gan-chee-yah] (*Piedmont*, Italy) Reliable producer of *Asti Spumante* and good, dry Pinot di Pinot, as well as *Pinot Blanc* fizz. ☆☆☆ **Asti ££**

**Garnacha Blanca** [gahr-na-cha blan-ka] (Spain) The *Grenache* Blanc, with which *Miguel Torres* has chosen to make his white Coronas. Peppery but sometimes short of fruit.

**Garnacha Tinta** [gahr-na-cha tin-ta] (Spain) The Spanish name for *Grenache*. Rarely as intense as in France, but can be attractively peppery **1996 Gran Fueda Rosado, Chivite Navarra.**

***Garrafeira*** [gah-rah-fay-rah] (Portugal) Indicates a producer's 'reserve' wine, which has been selected and given extra time in cask (minimum 2 years) and bottle (minimum 1 year). ***C.R.& F; Caves Velhas.***

**Vincent Gasse** [gass] (*Rhône*, France) Next to La Landonne. Tiny production of superb concentrated inky black wines. ☆☆☆☆ **1991 Cote Rotie Brune.**

**Gattinara** [Gat-tee-nah-rah] (*Piedmont*, Italy) Red *DOC* from the *Nebbiolo* – varying in quality but generally full-flavoured and dry. 78 79 82 **85 88** 89 90 93 94 95 96 **Travaglini.**

**Gavi** [gah-vee] (*Piedmont*, Italy) Generally unexceptional dry white wine from the *Cortese* grape. Compared by Italians to white *Burgundy* with which it and the creamily pleasant Gavi di Gavi share a propensity for high prices.

**Ch. le Gay** [luh gay] (*Pomerol*, *Bordeaux*, France) Good *Moueix* property with intense, complex wine. 70 **75 76** 78 79 **82 83 85** 86 88 89 90 94 95 96 ☆☆☆☆ **1990 £££**

**Ch. Gazin** [Ga-zan] (*Pomerol*, *Bordeaux*, France) Has become far more polished since the mid 1980s. 85 86 **87** 88 89 90 92 93 94 95 96 ☆☆☆☆ **1994 ££££**

**Geelong** [zhee-long] (*Victoria*, Australia) Cool region pioneered by Idyll Vineyards (makers of old-fashioned reds) and rapidly attracting notice with *Bannockburn's* and Scotchman Hill's *Pinot Noirs*.

**Geisenheim** [gi-zen-hime] (*Rheingau*, Germany) Home of the German Wine Institute wine school, once one of the best in the world, but long overtaken by more go-ahead seats of learning in France, California and Australia. Qba/Kab/Spät: **85** 86 **88 89 90** 91 92 93 94 95 96 Aus/Beeren/Tba: **83 85** 88 89 90 91 92 93 94 95 96

***Generoso*** [zheh-neh-roh-soh] (Spain) Fortified or dessert wine.

**Gentaz-Dervieux** [jon-tahz dehr-vee-yur] (*Rhône* France) Top-class small estate with great vineyards, producing excellent wines. ☆☆☆☆ **1991 Côte Rôtie Brune ££££**

**Gentilini** [zhen-tee-lee-nee] (*Cephalonia*, Greece) Nick Cosmetatos's modern white wines, made using classic Greek grapes and French varieties, should be an example to all his countrymen who are still happily making and drinking stuff which tastes as fresh as an old election manifesto.

**J.M.Gerin** [ger-an] (*Rhône*, France) A producer of good Côte Rotie and Condrieu; uses new oak to make powerful, long-lived wines. ☆☆☆☆ **1991 Cote Rotie Les Grandes Places ££££**

**Gevrey-Chambertin** [zheh-vray shom-behr-tan] (*Burgundy*, France) Best-known big red *Côte de Nuits* commune; very variable, but still capable of superb, plummy cherryish wine. The top *Grand Cru* is Le *Chambertin* but, in the right hands, *Premiers Crus* like Les Cazetiers can beat this and the other *Grands Crus*. **78** 79 **80** 82 83 **85** 86 87 **88 89 90** 92 95 96 **Vallet Frères; Alain Burguet; Denis Bachelet; Roty; Rossignol-Trapet; Armand Rousseau; Dujac.**

**Gewürztraminer** [geh-VOORT-strah-mee-nehr] White (well, slightly pink) grape, making dry-to-sweet, full, oily-textured, spicy wine. Best in *Alsace*, but also grown in Australasia, Italy, the US and Eastern Europe. Instantly recogniseable by its parma violets-and-lychees character. **Zind Humbrecht; Scherer; Schoffit (in Alsace): Casablanca (in Chile): Stonecroft (in New Zealand).**

**Geyser Peak** [Gih-Suhr] (*Alexander Valley*, California) Australian winemaker Darryl Groom revolutionised Californian thinking in this once Australian-owned winery with his *Semillon Chardonnay* blend ('You mean *Chardonnay's* not the only white grape?'), and with reds which show an Aussie attitude towards ripe *tannin*. A name to watch. Canyon Creek is the second label. ☆☆☆☆ **1994 Marietta Cellars Shiraz ££**

**Ghiaie della Furba** [gee-yah del-lah foor-bah] (*Tuscany*, Italy) Great *Cabernet*-based *Super Tuscan* from Villa di Capezzana.

**Giaconda** [zhee-ya-kon-dah] (*Victoria*, Australia) Small producer hidden away high in the hills. Impressive *Pinot Noir* and *Chardonnay*. ☆☆☆☆ **1993 Chardonnay £££**

**Bruno Giacosa** [zhee-yah-koh-sah] (*Piedmont*, Italy) Stunning wine maker with a large range, including *Barolos* (Vigna Rionda in best years) and *Barbarescos* (Santo Stefano, again in best years). Recent success with whites, including a *Spumante*. ☆☆☆☆ **1990 Barbera d'Alba Maria Gioana £££**

**Gie les Rameaux** [lay ram-moh] (*Corsica*, France) One of this island's top producers.

**Giesen** [gee-sen] (*Canterbury*, New Zealand) Small estate, with particularly appley *Riesling* from *Canterbury*, and *Sauvignon* from *Marlborough*. ☆☆☆☆ **1996 Marlborough Sauvignon Blanc ££**

**Gigondas** [zhee gon-dass] (*Rhône*, France) *Côtes du Rhône commune*, with good-value, spicy/peppery, blackcurranty reds which show the *Grenache* at its best. A good competitor for nearby *Châteauneuf*. **82 83 85 88** 89 90 92 95 96 **Font-Sane; Guigal.**

**Ch. Gilette** [gil-lette] (*Sauternes*, *Bordeaux*, France) Eccentric, unclassified but of classed-growth quality *Sauternes* kept in tank (rather than cask) for 20 or 30 years. Rare, expensive, worth it. **61 62 67 70 75 76** ☆☆☆☆ **1970 ££££**

**Gippsland** [gip-sland] (*Victoria*, Australia) Up-and-coming coastal region where *Bass Philip* and *Nicholson River* are producing fascinating and quite European-style wines. Watch out for some of Australia's finest *Pinot Noirs*.

**Vincent Girardin** [van-son zhee-rahr-dan] (*Burgundy*, France) Reliable *Santenay* producer with vines in several other *communes*. ☆☆☆ **1990 Pommard Les Epenots ££££**

**Casa Girelli** [zhee-reh-lee] (*Veneto*, Italy) Big, but generally uneven, producer.

***Giropalette*** [zhee-roh-pal-let] Large machine which, in *Méthode Champenoise*, automatically and highly efficiently replaces the human beings who used to perform the task of *Remuage*. Used by almost all the bigger *Champagne* houses which, needless to say, prefer to conceal them from visiting tourists.

**Camille Giroud** [kah-mee zhee-roo] (*Burgundy*, France) Laudably old-fashioned family-owned *negoçiant* with no love of new oak and small stocks of great mature wine that go a long way to prove that good *Burgundy* really doesn't need it to taste good. ☆☆☆☆ **1993 Santenay ££££**

**Gisborne** [giz-bawn] (New Zealand) North Island vine-growing area since the 1920s. Cool, wettish climate, mainly used for New Zealand's best *Chardonnay*. An ideal partner for *Marlborough* in blends. White: **89 91** 92 94 95 96 **Coopers Creek; Matawhero; Millton; Corbans; Montana; Judd.**

**Ch. Giscours** [zhees-koor] (*Margaux 3rd Growth*, *Bordeaux*, France) *Margaux* property which, despite the lovely blackcurranty wines it produced in the late 1970s and early 1980s today remains on the threshold of competition with the best. **71 75** 76 **78 79 81** 82 85 86 88 89 90 91 92 96 ☆☆☆ **1982 ££££**

**Givry** [zheev-ree] (*Burgundy*, France) *Côte Chalonnaise* commune, making typical and affordable, if rather jammily rustic, reds and creamy whites. French wine snobs recall that this was one of King Henri IV's favourite wines, forgetting the fact that a) he had many such favourites dotted all over France and b) his mistress – of whom he also probably had several – happened to live here. **78** 80 **85** 86 87 88 89 90 92 95 96 **Steinmaier; Joblot; Thénard; Mouton.**

**Glen Carlou** [kah-loo] (*Paarl*, South Africa) Small-scale winery with rich, oily, oaky *Chardonnay* and less convincing reds. ☆☆☆ **1996 Chardonnay ££**

**Glen Ellen** (*Sonoma Valley*, California) Recently-purchased dynamic family firm producing large amounts of good commercial *Chardonnay* under its 'Proprietor's Reserve' label for Californiaphiles who like tropical fruit juice. Reds are approachable and good value. The *Benziger* range is better. ☆☆☆ **1996 Proprietors Reserve Chardonnay.**

**Glenrowan** [glen-roh-wan] (*Victoria*, Australia) Area near *Rutherglen* with a similar range of excellent *Liqueur Muscats* and *Tokays*.

**Ch. Gloria** [glaw-ree-yah] (*St. Julien Cru Bourgeois*, *Bordeaux*, France) One of the first of the super *Crus Bourgeois*. Went through a disappointing patch but now back on form. **70 71 75 82** 83 85 86 88 89 90 92 93 94 95 96. ☆☆☆ **1990 ££££**

**Golan Heights Winery** [goh-lan] (Israel) Until recently almost the only non-sacramental wines in Israel were made by *Carmel*, who produced one of the least palatable *Sauvignons* I have ever encountered. Today, *Carmel* wines are greatly improved, thanks to competition from this enterprise at which Californian expertise is used to produce good *Kosher Cabernet* and *Muscat*. ☆☆☆ **1994 Chardonnay.**

**Goldwater Estate** (*Auckland*, New Zealand) *Bordeaux*-like red wine specialist on Waiheke Island whose wines are expensive but every bit as good as many similarly-priced French offerings. ☆☆☆☆ **1996 Chardonnay £££**

**Gonzalez Byass** [gon-zah-lez bih-yas] (*Jerez*, Spain) If sherry is beginning to enjoy a long awaited comeback, this is the company that should take much of the credit. While competitors were scurrying around telling people to add ice to their sherry, or inventing spurious styles like 'pale cream', Gonzalez Byass stuck to its guns making the world's best-selling *Fino*, *Tío Pepe* – and a supporting cast of the finest, most complex, traditional sherries available to mankind. ☆☆☆☆ **Tío Pepe Muy Seco ££** ☆☆☆☆☆ **Matusalem Oloroso ££££**

**Gosset** [gos-say] (*Champagne*, France) The oldest house in *Champagne* producing some marvellous cuvées, particularly the Grand Millésime. ☆☆☆☆ **Brut Excellence NV ££££**

**Goulburn Valley** [gohl-boorn] (*Victoria*, Australia) Small, long-established region reigned over by the respectively ancient and modern *Ch. Tahbilk* and *Mitchelton*, both of whom make great *Marsanne*, though in very different styles.

**Gould Campbell** [goold] (*Douro*, Portugal) Underrated member of the same stable as *Dows, Grahams and Warres*. 60 63 66 70 75 80 83 85 94 ☆☆☆ **1985 Vintage Port £££**

**Goundrey** [gown-dree] (Western Australia) Young winery in the up-and-coming region of *Mount Barker*, bought by an American millionaire who has continued the founder's policy of making impressively fruity but not overstated *Chardonnay* and *Cabernet*. ☆☆☆☆ **1995 Reserve Chardonnay £££**

**Graach** [grahkh] (*Mosel-Saar-Ruwer*, Germany) *Mittelmosel* village producing fine wines. Best known for its *Himmelreich* vineyard. QbA/Kab/Spät: **85** 86 **88 89 90** 91 92 93 94 95 96 Aus/Beeren/TBA: **83 85** 88 89 90 91 92 93 94 95 96 ***Deinhard; JJ Prum; Max Ferd Richter; Friedrich-Wilhelm-Gymnasium; Von Kesselstadt.***

**Graham's** [gray-yams] (*Douro*, Portugal) Sweetly delicate wines, sometimes outclassing the same stable's supposedly finer but heftier *Dows*. Malvedos is the Single *Quinta*. 55 60 **63 66 70** 75 77 85 94 ☆☆☆ **1977 Vintage ££££**

🍷 **Alain Graillot** [al-lan grih-yoh] (*Rhône*, France) Producer who should be applauded for shaking up the sleepy, largely undistinguished *Appellation* of *Crozes-Hermitage*, using grapes from rented vineyards. All the reds are excellent, and La Guiraude is the wine from the top vineyard. ☆☆☆☆ **1995 Crozes Hermitage £££**

***Gran Reserva*** [gran rays-sehr-vah] (Spain) Quality wine aged for a designated number of years in wood and, in theory, only produced in the best vintages. Can be dried out and less worthwhile than *Crianza* or *Reserva*.

***Grand Cru*** [gron kroo] (France) The finest vineyards and – supposedly – the equally fine wine made in them. Official designation in *Bordeaux*, *Burgundy* and *Alsace*. Vague in *Bordeaux* and somewhat unreliable in *Alsace*. In *Burgundy* single vineyards with their own *ACs*, eg *Montrachet*, do not need to carry the name of the village (eg *Chassagne-Montrachet*) on their label.

🍷 **Ch. du Grand Moulas** [gron moo-lahs] (*Rhône*, France) Classy *Côtes du Rhône* property with unusually complex wines. ☆☆☆☆ **1995 ££**

***Grand Vin*** [gron van] (*Bordeaux*, France) The first (quality) wine of an estate – as opposed to its *Second Label*.

🍷 **Ch. Grand-Mayne** [gron mayn] (*St. Emilion Grand Cru Classé*, *Bordeaux*, France) An over-achiever who should be due for promotion to Premier *Grand Cru* status. 82 83 85 86 87 88 89 90 92 93 94 95 96 ☆☆☆☆ **1992 £££**

🍷 **Ch. Grand-Pontet** [gron pon-tay] (*St. Emilion Grand Cru Classé*, *Bordeaux*, France) Rising star with showy wines. **82** 83 85 **86** 87 88 89 90 92 93 94 95 ☆☆☆ **1992 £££**

🍷 **Ch. Grand-Puy-Ducasse** [gron pwee doo-kass] (*Pauillac 5th Growth*, *Bordeaux*, France) Excellent wines from fifth-growth *Pauillac* property. 79 81 **82** 83 85 86 87 88 89 90 91 92 93 94 95 96 ☆☆☆☆ **1992 ££££**

🍷 **Ch. Grand-Puy-Lacoste** [gron pwee lah-kost] (*Pauillac 5th Growth*, *Bordeaux*, France) Top-class Fifth Growth owned by the Borie family of *Ducru-Beaucaillou* and right up there among the *Super Seconds*. One of the best-value wines in the region. **61 70** 75 **78 79 81 82** 83 **85** 86 87 88 89 90 91 92 93 94 95 96 ☆☆☆ **1990 ££££**

🍷 **Grande Rue** [grond-roo] (*Burgundy*, France) Recently promoted *Grand Cru* in *Vosne-Romanée*, across the way from *Romanée-Conti* (hence the promotion). Sadly, the Dom. Lamarche to which this *Monopole* belongs is a long-term under-performer.

***Grandes Marques*** [grond mahrk] (*Champagne*, France) Supposedly significant syndicate of the major *Champagne* merchants cast in aspic and including firms which exist in no more than name.

**Grands-Echézeaux** [grons AY-sheh-zoh] (*Burgundy*, France) One of the best *Grand Crus* in *Burgundy; see Echézeaux*.

🍷 **Grange** [graynzh] (South Australia) Penfolds' and Australia's greatest wine – 'The Southern Hemisphere's only First Growth' – pioneered by Max Schubert in the early '50s, and made from *Shiraz* produced by 70-year-old vines sited in several South Australian regions. Recently discovered in the US and thus a collector's item that sells out as soon as each vintage hits the streets. ☆☆☆☆☆ **1990 ££££**

🍷 **Grangehurst** [graynzh-huhrst] (*Stellenbosch*, South Africa) Exceptionally concentrated modern reds from a tiny winery converted from the family squash court! Expanding. Good *Cabernet* and *Pinotage*. ☆☆☆☆ **1994 Pinotage ££**

🍷 **Ch. Grangeneuve de Figeac** [gronzh-nuhv duh fee-zhak] (*St. Emilion*, *Bordeaux*, France) *Second Label* of *Ch. Figeac*.

🍷 **Weingut Grans-Fassian** [grans-fass-yan] (*Mosel*, Germany) Improving estate with some really fine, classic wine. ☆☆☆☆ **1992 Piesporter Goldtröpfen Riesling ££**

🍷 **Yves Grassa** [gras-sah] (South West France) Pioneering producer of VDP de *Côtes de Gasçogne* ☆☆☆ **1996 Ch. Tariquet Cuvée Bois ££**

🍷 **Alfred Gratien** [gras-see-yen] (*Champagne*, France) Good *Champagne* house, using traditional methods. Also owner of *Loire* sparkling winemaker, Gratien et Meyer, based in *Saumur.* ☆☆☆☆ 1988 Vintage Champagne ££££

🍇 **Grauerburgunder** [grow-urh-buhr-goon-duhr] (Germany) Another name for *Pinot Gris.* Muller Cattoir.

🍷 **Dom. la Grave** [lah grahv] (*Graves*, *Bordeaux*, France) Small property in the Graves with a growing reputation for 100 per cent *Sémillon* whites. Red: **89 90** 91 94 95 White: **89** 91 93 96

**Grave del Friuli** [grah-veh del free-yoo-lee] (*Friuli-Venezia Giulia*, Italy) *DOC* for young-drinking reds and whites. *Cabernet*, *Merlot* and *Chardonnay* are increasingly successful.

**Graves** [grahv] (*Bordeaux*, France) Large region producing vast quantities of white, from good to indifferent. The best whites come from the northern part of the Graves and are sold as *Pessac-Léognan*. Reds can have a lovely raspberryish character. Red: **70** 75 78 79 81 82 83 85 86 88 89 90 94 95 96 White: 70 71 75 76 78 79 82 **83 85 86** 87 88 **89 90** 93 94 95 96 Haut-Brion; Dom. de Chevalier; Smith Haut Lafitte; Clos Floridène.

**Great Western** (*Victoria*, Australia) Region noted for *Seppelt's* fizzes including the astonishing 'Sparkling *Burgundy*' *Shirazes* for *Best's* and for the wines of *Mount Langi Ghiran*.

🍷 **Greco di Tufo** [greh-koh dee too-foh] (*Campania*, Italy) From *Campania*, best-known white from the ancient Greco grape; dry, characterfully herby southern wine. Librandi; Botomagno.

**Greece** Finally, if belatedly, beginning to modernise its wine industry – and to exploit the potential of a set of grapes grown nowhere else. Unfortunately, as Greece begins to rid itself of its taste for the stewed, oxidised styles of the past, the modern wines are so popular in the smart restaurants in Athens that they appear to be both expensive and hard to find overseas. Boutari; Ch. Carras; Gentilini; Hatzimichalis; Lazarides.

🍷 **Green Point** (*Yarra Valley*, Australia) See *Dom. Chandon*. ☆☆☆☆ 1993 Blanc de Blancs Brut £££

🍷 **Green & Red** (*Napa Valley*, California) Fast-rising star with impressive *Zinfandel*. ☆☆☆☆ 1993 Chiles Mill Vineyard Unfiltered Zinfandel.

🍇 **Grenache** [greh-nash] Red grape of the *Rhône* (aka *Garnacha* in Spain) making spicy, peppery, full-bodied wine, provided yields are kept low. Also increasingly used to make rosés across Southern France and California. Fortant de France; Eldredge; Yaldara.

🍷 **Marchesi de Gresy** [mah-kay-see day greh-see] (*Piedmont*, Italy) Good producer of single vineyard *Barbaresco*. ☆☆☆☆ 1990 Martinenga Camp Gros ££££

🍷 **Grgich Hills** [guhr-gich] (*Napa Valley*, California) Pioneering producer of *Cabernet Sauvignon*, *Chardonnay* and *Fumé Blanc*. The name is a concatenation of the two founders – Mike Grgich and Austin Hills, rather than a topographical feature.

🍇 **Grignolino** [green-yoh-lee-noh] (*Piedmont*, Italy) Red grape and modest but refreshing, cherryish wine, eg the *DOC* Grignolino d'Asti. Drink young.

🍷 **Ch. Grillet** [gree-yay] (*Rhône*, France) *Appellation* consisting of a single estate and producer of slowly improving *Viognier* white. Neighbouring *Condrieu* is better value. ☆☆☆ 1993 Ch. Grillet ££££

🍷 **Marqués de Griñon** [green-yon] (*La Mancha, Rioja, Ribera del Duero*, Spain) Dynamic exception to the dull *La Mancha* rule, making wines with the help of *Michel Rolland* which can outclass *Rioja*. The juicy *Cabernet Merlot* and fresh white *Rueda* have been joined by Durius, a blend from *Ribera del Duero*, an exceptional new *Syrah* and an extraordinary *Petit Verdot*. ☆☆☆☆ 1995 Syrah ££

🍷 **Bernard Gripa** [gree-pah] (*Rhône*, France) Maker of top-notch St. Joseph ripe, thick, tarry wine that could age forever. ☆☆☆☆ 1994 St. Joseph Le Berceau £££

🍷 **Jean-Louis Grippat** [gree-pah] (*Rhône*, France) An unusually great white *Rhône* producer in *Hermitage* and *St. Joseph*. His reds in both *Appellations* are less stunning, but still worth buying in their subtler-than-most way. Look out too for his ultra-rare Cuvée des Hospices *St. Joseph* Rouge. ☆☆☆☆ 1993 Hermitage Rouge ££££ ☆☆☆☆ 1994 Hermitage Blanc ££££

🍷 **Dom. Jean Grivot** [gree-voh] (*Burgundy*, France) Top-class *Vosne Romanée* estate whose winemaker Etienne has recently escaped from the spell of Lebanese guru oenologist Guy Accad, whose advice made for some curious wines in the 1980s. ☆☆☆☆ 1992 Vosne Romanée Beaux Monts ££££

🍷 **Groot Constantia** [khroot-kon-stan-tee-yah] (*Constantia*, South Africa) Government-run, 300-year-old wine estate and national monument – consistently underperforming until recent signs of stirring. ☆☆☆ 1994 Governer's Reserve.

🍷 **Dom Anne Gros** [groh] (*Burgundy* France) Unfortunately for one's wallet, the best wines from this domaine are delicious but expensive. ☆☆☆☆ 1993 Richebourg ££££

🍷 **Jean Gros** [groh] (*Burgundy*, France) Great *Vosne Romanée* producer, with unusually reliable *Clos Vougeots*. ☆☆☆☆☆ 1990 Clos du Vougeot ££££

🍇 **Gros Lot/Grolleau** [groh-loh] (*Loire*, France) The workhorse black grape of the *Loire*, particularly in *Anjou*, used to make white, rosé and sparkling *Saumur*.

🍇 **Gros Plant (du Pays Nantais)** [groh-plon doo pay-yee non-tay] (*Loire*, France) Light, sharp white *VDQS* wine from the western *Loire*. In all but the best hands, serves to make even a poor Muscadet look good.

🍷 **Grosset** [gros-set] (South Australia) Terrific white wine (*Chardonnay, Riesling, Semillon*) specialist in the *Clare* Valley. Give them time to develop. Also try the Gaia red *Bordeaux*-blend. ☆☆☆☆ 1994 Jeremy Grosset Piccadilly Chardonnay £££

***Grosslage*** [gross-lah-guh] (Germany) Wine district, the third subdivision after *Anbaugebiet* (eg *Rheingau*) and *Bereich* (eg *Nierstein*). For example, *Michelsberg* is a *Grosslage* of the *Bereich Piesport*.

🍷 **Groth** [grahth] (*Napa Valley*, California) Serious producer of quality *Cabernet* and *Chardonnay*. ☆☆☆☆ 1992 Cabernet Sauvignon Napa Valley £££

🍷 **Grove Mill** (New Zealand) Relatively new winery specialising in more aromatic styles such as Riesling. ☆☆☆ 1994 Sauvignon ££

🍷 **Ch. Gruaud-Larose** [groo-oh lah-rohz] (*St. Julien 2nd Growth, Bordeaux*, France) One of the stars of the *Cordier* stable. Rich but potentially slightly unsubtle. The second wine is 'Le Sarget'. **61** 70 75 76 **78** 79 81 **82 83 85 86** 87 88 89 90 91 92 93 94 95 96 ☆☆☆☆ 1990 £££

🍇 **Grüner Veltliner** [groo-nuhr felt-lee-nuhr] Spicy white grape of Austria and Eastern Europe, producing light, fresh, aromatic wine – and for *Willi Opitz* an extraordinary *Late Harvest* version. Kracher; Lang; Schuster; Steininger.

🍷 **Bodegas Guelbenzu** [guhl-bent-zoo] (*Navarra*, Spain) Starry new-wave producer of rich, red wines using local grapes and *Cabernet*. ☆☆☆☆ 1994 Merlot ££ ☆☆☆ 1994 Guelbenzu Evo ££

🍷 **Guenoc** [gwen-nahk] (*Lake County*, California) Lillie Langtry's winery. Sadly, not a source of starry wines. ☆☆☆☆ 1993 Chardonnay Genevieve Magoon Vineyard ££££

**Guerrieri-Rizzardi** [gwer-reh-ree rit-zar-dee] (*Veneto*, Italy) Solid organic producer, with good *Amarone* and single vineyard *Soave Classico*. ☆☆☆☆ **1995 Fontis Vineale Minus £££**

**E Guigal** [gee-gahl] (*Rhône*, France) Still the yardstick for *Rhône* reds, despite increased competition from *Chapoutier*. His extraordinarily pricy single-vineyard La Mouline, La Landonne and La Turque wines are still ahead of the young turks. The basic *Côtes du Rhône* is also well worth looking out for. ☆☆☆☆ **1994 Gigondas £££** ☆☆☆ **1995 Côtes du Rhône Blanc ££**

**Guimaraens** [gee-mah-rens] (*Douro*, Portugal) Associated with *Fonseca*; under-rated port-house making good wines. ☆☆☆☆ **1984 Fonseca Guimaraens £££**

**Ch. Guiraud** [gee-roh] (*Sauternes Premier Cru Classé, Bordeaux*, France) *Sauternes* classed-growth, recently restored to original quality and now back in the pack trailing in the wake of *Yquem*. 67 79 80 81 82 **83** 84 85 **86** 87 88 89 90 92 93 94 95 96. ☆☆☆☆ **1990 ££££**

**Weingut Gunderloch** [goon-duhr-lokh] (*Rheinhessen*, Germany) One of the few estates to make *Rheinhessen* wines of truly reliable quality. ☆☆☆ **1992 Niersteiner Pettenthal Kabinett ££**

**Gundlach-Bundschu** [guhnd-lakh buhnd-shoo] (*Sonoma Valley*, California) Good, well-made, juicy *Merlot* and spicy *Zinfandel*. ☆☆☆☆ **1991 Rhinefarm Vineyard Zinfandel £££**

**Louis Guntrum** [goon-troom] (*Rheinhessen*, Germany) Family-run estate with a penchant for *Sylvaner*. ☆☆☆☆ **1991 Oppenheimer Herrenberg Silvaner Eiswein ££££**

**Ch. la Gurgue** [lah guhrg] (*Margaux Cru Bourgeois, Bordeaux*, France) Reliable *Cru Bourgeois* across the track from *Ch. Margaux*. Seems less impressive recently, while the same owner's classed *Ch. Ferrière* has both improved and increased its production. Coincidence presumably. 81 82 **83 85** 86 88 89 90 94 95 ☆☆☆☆ **1990 £££**

**Gutedel** [goot-edel] (Germany) German name for the *Chasselas* grape.

**Friedrich-Wilhelm Gymnasium** [free-drikh vil-helm-gim-nahz-yuhm] (*Mosel*, Germany) Big-name estate that ought to be making better wine. ☆☆☆☆ **1990 Graacher Himmelreich Riesling Spätlese £££**

**Gyöngyös Estate** [zhon-zhosh] (*Eger*, Hungary) Ground-breaking winery in which *Hugh Ryman* first produced drinkable Eastern European *Sauvignon* and *Chardonnay*. ☆☆☆ **1996 Oak Aged Sauvignon £**

# H

**Weingut Fritz Haag** [hahg] (*Mosel-Saar-Ruwer*, Germany) Top-class small estate with classic *Rieslings*. ☆☆☆☆ **1992 Brauneberger Jutter Sonnenuhr Riesling Auslese 18 ££££**

**Weingut Willi Haag** [hahg] (*Mosel*, Germany) Steep-sloping slate vineyards producing crisp wines with fruity acidity. ☆☆☆☆ **1993 Brauneberger Jutter Riesling Kabinett ££**

**Weingut Reinhold Haart** [rihn-hohld hahrt] (*Mosel*, Germany) Fast rising Piesport star. ☆☆☆☆ **1992 Piesporter Goldtröpfchen Riesling Auslese £££**

***Halbtrocken*** [hahlb-trok-en] (Germany) Off-dry. Usually a safer buy than *Trocken* in regions like the *Mosel, Rheingau* and *Rheinhessen*, but still often aggressively acidic. Look for *QbA* or *Auslese* versions.

**Hallgarten** [hal-gahr-ten] (*Rheingau*, Germany) Important town near *Hattenheim* producing robust wines including the (in Germany) well-regarded produce from *Schloss Vollrads*. QbA/Kab/Spät: **85** 86 **88 89 90** 91 92 93 94 95 Aus/Beeren/TBA: **83 85** 88 89 90 91 92 93 94 95 96

**Hamilton Russell Vineyards** (*Walker Bay*, South Africa) Pioneer of impressive *Pinot Noir* and *Chardonnay* at a winery in Hermanus at the southernmost tip of the Cape. Now expanded to include a *second label* – Southern Right – to produce a varietal *Pinotage*, and a *Chenin*-based white. ☆☆☆ **1995 Pinot Noir £££**

**Hanging Rock** (*Victoria*, Australia) As in the movie, 'Picnic at...' this winery makes Australia's biggest, butteriest fizz. ☆☆☆ **Jim Jim Sauvignon ££**

**Hardy's** (South Australia) Or more properly BRL Hardy, as the merged Berri-Renmano/Hardy's is now known. The second biggest wine producer in Australia, encompassing *Houghton* and *Moondah Brook* in Western Australia, *Leasingham* in the *Clare Valley,* the improved but still under-performing *Redman* in *Coonawarra,* Hardy's itself and *Ch. Reynella.* Hardy's range is reliable throughout, including the commercial Nottage Hill, new Bankside, and multi-regional blends, though the wines to look for are the top-of-the-range Eileen and Thomas Hardy. The *Ch. Reynella* wines made from *McLaren Vale* fruit (and, in the case of the reds, using basket presses) are good, quite lean examples of the region. ☆☆☆☆ **1994 Eileen Hardy Shiraz £££** ☆☆☆☆ **1995 Bankside Shiraz ££** ☆☆☆☆☆ **1993 Thomas Hardy Cabernet Sauvignon £££**

**Hárslevelü** [harsh-leh-veh-loo] (Hungary) White grape used in *Tokaji* and for light table wines.

**Harveys** (*Jerez*, Spain) Maker of the ubiquitous *Bristol Cream*. Other styles are improving. ☆☆☆ **Bristol Cream ££**

**Hattenheim** [hat-ten-hihm] (*Rheingau*, Germany) One of the greatest *Johannisberg* Villages, producing some of the best German *Rieslings*. QbA/Kab/Spät: **85** 86 **88 89 90** 91 92 93 94 95 96 Aus/Beeren/TBA: **83 85** 88 89 90 91 92 93 94 95 96

**Hatzimichalis** [hat-zee-mikh-ahlis] (Atalanti, Greece) The face of future Greek winemaking? Hopefully. This small estate produces top-notch *Cabernet Sauvignon, Merlot* and fresh, dry Atalanti white. ☆☆☆ **1995 Dom. Hatzimichalis Cabernet Sauvignon ££**

**Ch. Haut-Bages-Averous** [oh-bahj-aveh-roo] (*Pauillac Cru Bourgeois, Bordeaux*, France) *Second Label* of *Ch. Lynch Bages*. Good-value black-curranty *Pauillac*. **82** 83 **85** 86 87 88 89 90 93 94 95 96 ☆☆☆☆ **1992 £££** ☆☆☆☆ **1993 £££**

**Ch. Haut-Bages-Libéral** [oh-bahj-lib-ay-ral] (*Pauillac 5th Growth, Bordeaux*, France) Classy small property in the same stable as *Chasse-Spleen*. **75** 78 **82** 83 85 **86** 87 88 89 90 91 93 94 95 96 ☆☆☆☆ **1990 ££££**

**Ch. Haut-Bailly** [oh bih-yee] (*Pessac Léognan Cru Classé, Bordeaux*, France) Brilliant *Pessac-Léognan* property consistently making, reliable, excellent quality, long-lived red wines, including an unusually good 1994. **61** 64 **70** 78 **79 81** 83 **85** 86 87 88 89 90 92 93 94 95 ☆☆☆☆☆ **1990 ££££**

**Ch. Haut-Batailley** [oh-ba-tih-yee] (*Pauillac 5th Growth, Bordeaux*, France) Subtly-styled from the same stable as *Ducru Beaucaillou* and *Grand Puy Lacoste*. **70 75** 78 79 81 **82** 83 85 86 87 88 89 90 91 92 93 94 95 96 ☆☆☆☆ **1994 £££**

**Ch. Haut-Brion** [oh bree-yon] (*Pessac-Léognan 1st Growth, Bordeaux*, France) Pepys' favourite and still the only non-*Médoc* First Growth. Situated in the *Graves* on the outskirts of *Bordeaux* in the shadow of the gasworks, and within easy reach of the airport. Wines can be tough and hard to judge when young but, at their best they develop a rich, fruity perfumed character which sets them apart from their peers. 1989and 1996 were both especially good, as – comparatively – were 1993, 1994 and 1995.The white is rare and often sublime. Red: **61 70 71 75** 76 **78 79** 80 81 **82 83** 84 85 86 87 88 89 90 91 92 93 94 95 96 White: 78 81 82 83 85 87 88 89 90 91 92 93 94 95 96 ☆☆☆☆☆ **1990 Ch. Haut Brion ££££**

🍷 **Ch. Haut-Marbuzet** [oh-mahr-boo-zay] (*St. Estèphe Cru Bourgeois*, *Bordeaux*, France) A *Cru Bourgeois* which thinks it's a *Cru Classé*. Well-made, immediately imposing wine with bags of oak. Decidedly new-wave *St. Estèphe*. 70 75 76 **78** 81 **82 83 85** 86 87 88 89 90 92 93 94 95 ☆☆☆☆ **1993 £££**

**Haut-Médoc** [oh-may-dok] (*Bordeaux*, France) Large *Appellation* which includes nearly all of the well-known *Crus Classés*. The basic Haut-Médoc should be better than the plain *Médoc*. 70 75 76 **78** 79 81 **82** 83 **85 86** 88 89 90 94 95

🍷 **Caves de Haut-Poitou** [oh-pwa-too] (*Loire*, France) Often boring yet (quite) good value *Sauvignon* and *Chardonnay* whites and less exciting reds. ☆☆☆ **1995 Sauvignon £**

**Haut-Poitou** [oh-pwa-too] (*Loire*, France) Once a useful source of inexpensive *Sauvignon* – in the days before the variety was planted in *Languedoc Roussillon*. An Australian team from *BRL Hardy* has recently shown that better winemaking could pay dividends here, though.

**Hautes Côtes de Beaune** [oht coht duh bohn] (*Burgundy*, France) Sound, soft, strawberry *Pinot Noir* hailing from a group of villages situated in the hills above the big-name *communes*. Worth buying in good vintages; in poorer ones the grapes have problems ripening. Much of the wine seen outside the region is made by one of *Burgundy*'s improving cooperatives. Red: 80 83 **85** 86 87 **88 89 90** 92 95 96 White: **85 86** 87 **88** 89 **90 92** 95 96

**Hautes Côtes de Nuits** [oht coht duh nwee] (*Burgundy*, France) Slightly tougher than *Hautes Côtes de Beaune*, particularly when young. White wines are very rare. White: **79** 84 **85 86** 87 **88** 89 **90 92** 95 96 Red: 76 **78** 79 **80** 82 83 **85** 86 87 **88 89 90** 92 95 96

**Hawkes Bay** (New Zealand) Major North Island vineyard area which is finally beginning to live up to the promise of producing top-class reds. Whites can be fine too, though rarely achieving the bite of *Marlborough*. White: 88 **89 91 92** 93 **94** 95 96 Red: **83 85 87 89** 90 **91 92** 93 94 95 **Te Mata; Delegats; Morton Estate, Esk Valley; Vidal; Ngatarawa; Montana Church Road; Babich.**

🍷 **Freiherr von Heddesdorff** [fri-hehr fon hed-des-dawf] (*Mosel*, Germany) Producer of classic steely *Riesling* with crisp acidity and floral flavour. ☆☆☆ **1991 Winninger Uhlen Riesling Halbtroken ££**

🍷 **Heemskerk** [heems-kuhrk] (*Tasmania*, Australia) Until recently associated with *Roederer* in the making of *Jansz*, this is a producer of (good) Aussie fizz and also the source of some sturdy reds. ☆☆☆ **1992 Chardonnay £££**

🍷 **Heggies** [heg-gees] (South Australia) Impressive estate in the Adelaide Hills, making good *Riesling* and improving *Viognier* and *Pinot Noir*. Also marvellous Botrytis affected stickies associated with *Yalumba*. ☆☆☆ **1996 Botrytis Riesling ££**

🍷 **HehnerKiltz** [hay-nur-kiltz] (*Nahe*, Germany) Classy estate with dry, elegant examples of *Riesling* ☆☆☆☆ **Brut Réserve £££**

🍷 **Charles Heidsieck** [hihd-seek] (*Champagne*, France) The non-vintage is amongst the best value around, eclipsed only by the *Blanc de Blancs*. ☆☆☆☆ **1985 Blanc des Millenaires ££££**

🍷 **Heidsieck Dry Monopole** [hihd-seek] (*Champagne*, France) A subsidiary of Mumm and thus now controlled by Seagrams. Wines have greatly improved of late. ☆☆☆ **Diamont Bleu ££££**

**Heitz Cellars** [hihtz] (*Napa Valley*, California) One of the great names of California and the source of stunning reds in the 1970s. Current releases of the flagship Martha's Vineyard *Cabernet* taste unacceptably musty, however, as do the traditionally almost-as-good Bella Oaks. In the US, such criticisms are treated as lèse-majesté. ☆☆☆☆ 1990 Cabernet Sauvignon Napa Valley £££

**Henderson** (New Zealand) A town a couple of hours from Auckland with a growing number of wine estates springing up. White: **89 91 92** 93 **94** 95 Red: **83 85 87 89** 90 **91 92** 93 94 95

**Joseph Henriot** [on-ree-yoh] (*Champagne*, France) Modern *Champagne* house producing soft, rich wines. ☆☆☆☆ 1985 Cuvée des Enchanteleurs Brut ££££

**Henriques & Henriques** [hen-reeks] (*Madeira*, Portugal) One of the few independent producers still active in Madeira. Top quality. ☆☆☆☆☆ 15 Year Old Verdelho Madeira £££

**Henschke** [hench-kee] (*Adelaide Hills*, Australia) One of the world's best. From the long-established Hill of Grace with its 130-year-old vines and (slightly less intense) Mount Edelstone *Shirazes* to the new Abbott's Prayer *Merlot-Cabernet* from *Lenswood*, the *Riesling* and Tilly's Vineyard white blend, there's not a duff wine in the cellar, and the reds last forever. Compare and contrast with *Heitz*. ☆☆☆☆☆ 1992 Mount Edelstone Keyneton Shiraz ££££

**Hermitage** [ayr-mee-tazh] (*Rhône*, France) Supreme Northern *Rhône* appellation for long-lived pure *Syrah*. Whites are less reliable. Red: **76 78 82 83 85 88** 89 90 91 95 White: **82 85** 87 **88 89 90** 91 94 95 Chave; Guiga; Jaboulet Aîné; Delas; Bernard Faurie; Chapoutier.

**The Hess Collection** (*Napa Valley*, California) High-class *Cabernet* producer, high in the *Mount Veeder* hills. The lower-priced *Monterey* wines are worth buying too. ☆☆☆☆☆ 1992 Cabernet Sauvignon Napa Valley £££

**Hessische Bergstrasse** [hess-ishuh behrg-strah-suh] (Germany) Smallest *Anbaugebiet* capable of fine *Eisweins* and dry *Sylvaners* which can surpass those of nearby *Franken*. QbA/Kab/Spät: **85** 86 **88 89 90** 91 92 93 94 95 96 Aus/Beeren/TBA: **83 85** 88 89 90 91 92 93 94 95

**Vinicola Hidalgo y Cia** [hid-algoh] (*Jerez*, Spain) Specialist producer of impeccable dry 'La Gitana' Sherry and a great many own-label offerings. ☆☆☆☆ Mariscal Manzanilla ££

**Hill Smith Wines** (South Australia) A classy firm, under the same family ownership as *Yalumba* and *Heggies* Vineyard, and now active in New Zealand and California (where its Voss wines are made). ☆☆☆☆ Eden Valley Riesling ££ ☆☆☆☆ Pewsey Vale Cabernet ££

**Hillstowe** [hil-stoh] (South Australia) Up-and-coming producer in the *McLaren Vale*, using grapes from various parts of the region to produce unusually stylish *Chardonnay*, *Sauvignon* and *Cabernet-Merlot*. ☆☆☆☆ 1994 Buxton Cabernet Merlot ££

**Himmelreich** [him-mel-rihkh] (*Mosel*, Germany) One of the finest vineyards in *Graach*. QbA/Kab/Spät: **85 86 88 89** 90 **91** 92 93 94 95 Aus/Beeren/TBA: **83** 85 88 89 90 91 92 93 94 95 Robert Eymael.

**Serge Hochar** [hosh-ah] see *Ch. Musar*.

***Hochfeinste*** [hokh-fihn-stuh] (Germany) 'Very finest'.

***Hochgewächs QbA*** [hokh-geh-fex] (Germany) Recent official designation for Rieslings which are as ripe as a *QmP* but can still only call themselves *QbA*. This from a nation supposedly dedicated to simplifying what are acknowledged to be the most complicated labels in the world.

**Hochheim** [hokh-hihm] (*Rheingau*, Germany) Village whose fine *Rieslings* gave the English the word *'Hock'*. QbA/Kab/Spät: **85** 86 **88 89 90** 91 92 93 94 95 96 Aus/Beeren/TBA: **83 85** 88 89 90 91 92 93 94 95 96 **Geh'rat Aschrott; KonigenVictoria Berg.**

**Hogue Cellars** [hohg] (*Washington State*, USA) Dynamic *Yakima Valley* producer of good *Chardonnay*, *Riesling*, *Merlot* and *Cabernet*. ☆☆☆☆ **1992 Merlot Washington Reserve £££**

**Hollick** (*Coonawarra*, Australia) A good, traditional producer; the Ravenswood is particularly worth seeking out. ☆☆☆☆ **1993 Coonawarra Cabernet £££**

**Ch. Hortevie** [awt-uhr-vee] (*St. Julien*, *Bordeaux*, France) Not really a Château at all – the wine (which is excellent) is made at *Ch. Terrey-Gros-Caillou*. 81 82 83 **85** 86 87 88 89 90 92 94 ☆☆☆☆ **1990 ££££**

**Hospices de Beaune** [os-peess duh bohn] (*Burgundy*, France) Hospital, whose wines (often *Cuvées* or blends of different vineyards), are sold at an annual charity auction, the prices of which are erroneously thought to set the tone for the *Côte d'Or* year. In the early 1990s, wines were generally sub-standard, improving instantly in 1994 with the welcome return of winemaker Andre Porcheret. Even so, be aware that although price lists often merely indicate 'Hospices de Beaune' as a producer, all of the wines bought at the auction are matured and bottled by local merchants, some of whom are more scrupulous than others.

**Houghton** [haw-ton] (*Swan Valley*, Australia) Long-established subsidiary of *Hardy*'s. Best known for its *Chenin*-based rich white blend traditionally sold Down Under as 'White *Burgundy*' and sold in the UK as 'HWB'. The wines to watch though are the ones from the *Moondah Brook* vineyard. ☆☆☆ **1995 Wildflower Ridge Chardonnay ££** ☆☆☆ **1995 Wildflower Ridge Chenin Blanc £**

**Weingut von Hovel** [fon huh-vel] (*Mosel-Saar-Ruwer*, Germany) A 200-year-old estate with fine *Rieslings* from great vineyards. These repay the patience that they demand. ☆☆☆☆ **1991 Oberemmel Hutte Riesling Spätlese ££**

**Howard Park** (Western Australia) One of the best producers in Western Australia. ☆☆☆☆ **1993 Margaret River Cabernet Merlot £££**

**Howell Mountains** [how-wel] (*Napa Valley*, California) Hillside region to the north of *Napa*, capable of fine whites and reds. Red: **85** 86 87 **90 91** 92 93 95 96 White: **85 90 91** 92 95 96. **La Jota; Dunn.**

**Alain Hudelot-Noellat** [ood-uh-loh noh-el-lah] (*Burgundy*, France) A great winemaker whose generosity with oak is matched, especially in his *Grand Cru Richebourg* and *Romanée St Vivant* by intense fruit flavours. ☆☆☆☆☆ **Chambolle Musigny Les Charmes ££££**

**Huelva** [wel-vah] (*Extramadura*, Spain) *DO* of the *Extremadura* region, producing rather heavy whites and fortified wines.

**Gaston Huët** [oo-wet] (*Loire*, France) Long-time mayor of *Vouvray* and one of the very few producers who has consistently produced top-quality individual vineyard examples of *Sec*, *Demi-Sec* and *Moëlleux* wines. His non-vintage fizz, though only made occasionally, is top class too. ☆☆☆☆ **1990 Vouvray Moëlleux Le Haut Lieu ££££**

**Hugel et Fils** [oo-gel] (*Alsace*, France) Reliable *négoçiant*. Best are the *Late Harvest* and Jubilee wines. The wine 'Gentil' revives the tradition of blending different grape varieties. ☆☆☆☆ **1993 Riesling 'Jubilee' £££**

**Hungary** Country too long known for its infamous *Bull's Blood*, and *Olasz Rizling* rather than the far more interesting **Tokaji. Hugh Ryman; Kym Milne; Disznoko; Egervin; Nagyrede; Nezmely.**

**Hunter Valley** (*New South Wales*, Australia) The best-known wine region in Australia is ironically one of the least suitable parts in which to make wine. When the vines are not dying of heat and thirst they are drowning beneath the torrential rains which like to fall at harvest time. Even so, the *Shirazes* and *Semillons* – traditionally sold as 'Hermitage', 'Claret', '*Burgundy*', 'Chablis' and 'Hunter Valley Riesling' – develop remarkably. ***Lake's Folly; Brokenwood; Rothbury Estate; Rosemount; Tyrrells; McWillliams; Lindemans; Reynolds; Evans Family; Petersons.***

**Hunter's** (*Marlborough*, New Zealand) One of *Marlborough*'s most consistent producers of ripe fruity *Sauvignon Blancs* and now a quality fizz. ☆☆☆☆ **1995 Miru Miru Brut £££**

**Huxelrebe** [huk-sel-ray-buh] Minor white grape, often grown in England but proving what it can do when harvested late in Germany. **Anselmann (Germany) Nutbourne Manor; Barkham Manor (England).**

***Hybrid*** [hih-brid] Cross-bred grape Vitis *vinifera* (European) x Vitis *labrusca* (North American) – an example is *Seyval Blanc*.

***Hydrogen sulphide*** Naturally occurring gas produced by certain yeasts as a by-product of fermentation, or by *reductive* conditions, resulting in a smell of rotten eggs. (If you suspect a wine of having this, you may be able to remove it by adding a copper coin). Also caused by insufficient racking. If left untreated, hydrogen sulphide will react with other components in the wine to form *mercaptans* which smell unpleasant and cannot be removed.

# I

***Icewine*** Increasingly popular Anglification of the German term *Eiswein*, used particularly by Canadian producers making luscious, spicily exotic wines from the frozen grapes of varieties like *Vidal*.

**Il Podere dell'Olivos** [eel poh-deh-reh del-oh-lee-vohs] (California) Pioneering producer of Italian varietals. ☆☆☆ **1995 Tocai Fruiliano ££**

***Imbottigliato nel'origine*** [im-bot-til-yah-toh neh-loh-ree-zhee-nay] (Italy) Estate-bottled.

**Immich Batterieberg** [Ih-mikh bat-teh-ree-burg] (*Mosel*, Germany) Makes long lasting wines with some botrytis character. ☆☆☆☆ **1992 Enkircher Zeppwingert Riesling Spätlese £££**

***Imperiale*** [am-pay-ray-ahl] (*Bordeaux*, France) Bottle containing almost six and a half litres of wine (eight and a half bottles). Cherished by collectors partly through rarity, partly through the greater longevity that large bottles are supposed to give their contents.

**India** Source of generally execrable table wine and surprisingly reliable fizz, labelled as Marquis de Pompadour or *Omar Khayam*.

**Inferno** [een-fehr-noh] (*Lombardy*, Italy) *Lombardy DOC*. Chiefly red from the *Nebbiolo*, needing ageing for at least five years. ☆☆☆ **1992 Nino Negri ££**

**Inglenook Vineyards** [ing-gel-nook] (*Napa Valley*, California) Once-great winery which, like *Beaulieu*, fell into the hands of the giant Grand Metropolitan. The Gothic building and vineyards now belong appropriately to Francis Ford Coppola. The brand has been sold to a firm with little evident love of fine wine.

**Inniskillin** (*Ontario*, Canada) Long-established, pioneering winery with good *Icewines* (from the *Vidal* grape), highly successful *Chardonnay* and a rare example of a good *Maréchal Foch*. ☆☆☆ **1995 Icewine ££££**

***Institut National des Appellations d'Origine (INAO)*** (France) French official body which designates and (half-heartedly) polices quality, and outlaws sensible techniques like irrigation and the blending of vintages which are permitted elsewhere. Maybe this is why *Appellation Contrôlée* wines are often inferior to the newer *Vins de Pays* over which this body has no authority.

***International Wine Challenge*** (England) International wine competition, held each May in London. (The author is founder chairman).

**Irancy** [ee-ron-see] (*Burgundy*, France) Little-known, light reds and rosés made near *Chablis* from a blend of grapes including the *Pinot Noir* and the little-known *César.* Curiously, Irancy has *AC* status whereas *Sauvignon de St. Bris,* a nearby source of superior whites, is merely a *VDQS* region.

**Iron Horse Vineyards** (*Sonoma Valley*, California) One of the best sparkling wine producers in the New World, thanks to cool climate vineyards. Reds and still whites are increasingly impressive too. ☆☆☆ **1993 Chardonnay Estate Cuvée Joy £££**

**Irouléguy** [ee-roo-lay-gee] (South West France) Earthy, spicy reds and rosés, improving whites. The local Co-op makes the best wines.

***Isinglass*** [Ih-sing-glahs] Fining agent derived from sturgeon bladders.

**Isole e Olena** [ee-soh-lay ay oh-lay-nah] (*Tuscany*, Italy) Brilliant, small *Chianti* estate with a pure *Sangiovese Super-Tuscan, Cepparello* and Italy's first (technically illegal) *Syrah.* ☆☆☆☆ **1994 Cepparello.**

**Israel** Once the source of appalling stuff, but the new-style varietal wines are improving. *Golan Heights; Carmel.*

**Ch. d'Issan** [dee-son] (*Margaux 3rd Growth*, *Bordeaux*, France) Recently revived *Margaux* third growth with recognisable blackcurranty *Cabernet Sauvignon* intensity. 70 **75** 78 79 81 **82 83** 85 86 87 88 89 90 93 94 95 ☆☆☆☆ **1993 £££**

**Italian Riesling/Riesling Italico** [ee-tah-lee-koh] Not the great Rhine Riesling, but another name for an unrelated variety, which also goes by the names Welschriesling, Lutomer and Laski Rizling, and is widely grown in Northern and Eastern Europe. At its best in Austria.

**Italy** Tantalising, seductive, infuriating. In many ways the most exciting wine nation in the world, though, as ever, in a state of change as it reorganises its wine laws. See individual regions.

# J

**Paul Jaboulet Aîné** [zha-boo-lay ay-nay] (*Rhône*, France) *Négoçiant*-owner of the illustrious *Hermitage* La Chapelle and producer of good *Côtes du Rhône* and *Châteauneuf-du-Pape*. Reliable but now overshadowed by *Guigal*. Even so, on its day, the La Chapelle can blow everything else out of the water. Look for white Hermitage and a chunky St. Joseph. ☆☆☆ **1995 Crozes Hermitage Dom. de Thalabert ££**

**Jackson Estate** (*Marlborough*, New Zealand) Next-door neighbour to *Cloudy Bay* and producer of *Sauvignon,* which is giving that superstar estate a run for its money. The sparkling wine is good too. ☆☆☆☆ **1996 Sauvignon Blanc ££**

**Jacob's Creek** (Australia) Brilliantly commercial South Australian wines made by *Orlando*.

**Jacquart** [zha-kahr] (*Champagne*, France) Large cooperative with some very passable wines. ☆☆☆☆ **1990 Vintage Brut ££££**

**Jacqère** [zha-kehr] The slightly citrusy grape of *Savoie*.

**Jacquesson et Fils** [jak-son] (*Champagne*, France) A small Champagne house that deserves to be better known, particularly for its exceptional, delicately stylish *Blanc de Blancs*. ☆☆☆☆ **1990 Blanc de Blancs ££££**

**Louis Jadot** [zha-doh] (*Burgundy*, France) Good, sometimes great, *Beaune négoçiant* with top-class vineyards in *Beaune, Chassagne* and *Puligny-Montrachet*. Jadot has also been a pioneering producer of Rully in the Côte Châlonnais. Whites are most impressive. ☆☆☆☆ **1994 Auxey Duresses red ££££**

**Jaffelin** [zhaf-lan] (*Burgundy*, France) Small *négoçiant* recently bought from *Drouhin* by *Boisset*. Particularly good at supposedly 'lesser' *Appellations*. *Rully Blanc* and *Monthélie* are particularly good. ☆☆☆☆ **1990 Corton Grand Cru ££££**

**E Jackoby-Mathy** [yah-koh-ee mah-tee] (*Mosel* Germany) Estate producing elegant *Late Harvest* wines with honeyed fruit flavours. ☆☆☆☆ **1992 Kinheimer Rosenburg Riesling Eiswein ££££**

**Joseph Jamet** [zha-may] (*Rhône*, France) Top-class *Côte Rôtie* estate. ☆☆☆☆ **1994 ££££**

**Jamiesons Run** (*Coonawarra*, Australia) *Mildara's* pair of prize winning, good-value red and white wines. ☆☆☆☆ **1995 Jamiesons Run Red ££**

**Jansz** [yantz] (*Tasmania*, Australia) Starry fizz originally made as a joint venture with Roederer. ☆☆☆☆ **1993 £££**

**Robert Jasmin** [zhas-man] (*Rhône*, France) Traditionalist *Côte Rotie* estate, eschewing new oak. ☆☆☆☆☆ **1994 Côte Rôtie ££££**

**Jasnières** [zhan-yehr] (*Loire*, France) On rare occasions bone-dry and – even rarer – *Moëlleux*, sweet *Chenin Blanc* wines from *Touraine*. Buy carefully. Poorly made, over-sulphured efforts offer a pricy chance to taste the *Chenin* at its worst. White: **86 88 89 90** 94 95 Sweet White: **76** 83 **85** 86 **88 89** 90 94 95 96

**Jasper Hill** (*Bendigo*, Australia) Winery in Heathcote with a cult following for both reds and whites – especially those from the Georgia's Paddock vineyard. ☆☆☆☆ **1995 Georgia's Paddock Riesling, Heathcote ££**

**Jaume Serra** [how-may seh-rah] (*Penedès*, Spain) Privately owned company which recently relocated from *Alella* to *Penedès*, and is doing good things with *Xarel-lo*.

**Patrick Javillier** [zha-vil-yay] (*Burgundy*, France) Reliable, small merchant making meticulous village Meursault and good reds. ☆☆☆☆ **1994 Meursault Clos Cronin ££££**

**Henri Jayer** [zha-yay] (*Burgundy*, France) Cult winemaker whose top *Côte de Nuits* reds rival those of the *Dom. de la Romanée Conti*. Now retired but still represented on labels referring to Georges et Henri. Also an influence on the wines of *Meo Camuzet*. ☆☆☆ **1993 Vosne-Romanee Les Beaux Monts ££££**

**Robert Jayer-Gilles** [zhah-yay-zheel] (*Burgundy*, France) *Henri Jayer's* cousin, whose top wines – including an *Echézeaux* – bear comparison with those of his more famous relative. (His whites – particularly the *Aligoté* are good, too). ☆☆☆ **1994 Hautes Cotes de Nuits Rouge £££**

**Jekel Vineyards** [zheh-kel] (Arroyo Seco, California) After a spell under other owners, and a more recent takeover taking it into the same camp as *Fetzer* – it is once again run by its founder Bill Jekel, a famous critic of *terroir*. *Cabernets* and *Chardonnays* are better nowadays than the very commercial *Riesling* and are worth following if you accept their slightly herbaceous style. ☆☆☆☆ **1995 Chardonnay ££**

**Jerez (de la Frontera)** [hay-rez] (Spain) Centre of the *Sherry* trade, giving its name to entire *DO* area. ***Gonzalez Byass; Lustau; Hidalgo; Barbadillo.***

🍷 **Jermann** [zhehr-man] (*Friuli-Venezia Giulia*, Italy) Brilliant winemaker who gets outrageous flavours – and prices – out of every white grape variety he touches. Look out for the Vintage Tunina blend of *Tocai*, *Picolit* and *Malvasia*, and the 'Where the Dreams have no End' white blend plus the single-vineyard Capo Martino. Also good at *Chardonnay*, *Pinot Gris* and *Pinot Blanc*. ☆☆☆☆ **1996 Vinnae £££**

***Jeroboam*** [zhe-roh-bohm] Large bottle; in *Champagne* holding three litres (four bottles); in *Bordeaux*, four and a half (six bottles). Best to check before writing your cheque.

**Jesuitengarten** [zhes-yoo-wi-ten-gahr-ten] (*Rheingau*, Germany) One of Germany's top vineyards – well-handled by *Bassermann-Jordan*. QbA/Kab/Spät: **85** 86 **88 89 90** 91 92 93 94 95 96 Aus/Beeren/TBA: **83 85** 88 89 90 91 92 93 94 95 96

***Jeunes Vignes*** [zhuhn veen] Denotes vines too young for their crop to be sold as an *Appellation Controlée* wine.

🍷 **Dom. François Jobard** [fron-swah joh-bahr] (*Burgundy*, France) Great small white wine estate in Meursault. ☆☆☆☆ **1994 Meursault Genevrières £££**

🍷 **Dom Joblot** [zhob-loh] (*Burgundy*, France) One of the top domaines in *Givry*. ☆☆☆ **1995 Cellier Aux Moines ££££**

🍷 **Charles Joguet** [zho-gay] (*Loire*, France) One of the finest producers of red *Loire*, making wines that can last. ☆☆☆☆ **1996 Chinon, Jeunes Vignes ££**

**Johannisberg** [zho-han-is-buhrg.] (*Rheingau*, Germany) Village making superb *Riesling*, which has lent its name to a *Bereich* covering all the *Rheingau*. QbA/Kab/Spät: **85** 86 **88 89 90** 91 92 93 94 95 96 Aus/Beeren/TBA: **83 85** 88 89 90 91 92 93 94 95 96 ☆☆☆ **1992 Winkeler Hasensprung ££**

🍇 **Johannisberg Riesling** [rees-ling] Californian name for *Rhine Riesling*.

🍷 **Weingut Karl-Heinz Johner** [karl-hihntz yoh-nuh] (*Baden*, Germany) Former winemaker at *Lamberhurst*, now making good oaky *Pinot Noir* in southern Germany.

🍷 **Jordan** (*Stellenbosch*, South Africa) Young winery whose Californian-trained winemakers are hitting the mark with their *Sauvignon* and *Chardonnay*.

🍷 **Jordan** (*Sonoma Valley*, California) *Sonoma* winery surrounded by the kind of hype more usually associated with *Napa*. Table wines – from the *Alexander Valley* – are good rather than great, though the fizz is of *Champagne* quality. ☆☆☆☆☆ **1991 'J', Sonoma County ££££**

🍷 **Joseph** (*South Australia*) Label used by *Primo Estate* for its wines, including a great red fizz.

🍷 **Josmeyer** [jos-mi-yur] (*Alsace* France) Estate producing wines that are more delicate and restrained than those of some of its neighbours. ☆☆☆☆ **1992 Riesling Le Kottabe ££**

🍷 **Weingut Toni Jost** [toh-nee yohst] (*Mittelrhein*, Germany) A new-wave producer with (well-sited) vines in Bacharach and a penchant for experimenting (successfully) with new oak barrels. ☆☆☆☆☆ **1993 Bacharacher Hahn Riesling Auslese £££**

🍷 **Judd's Hill** (*Napa Valley*, California) Young winery with dazzling *Cabernets*. ☆☆☆☆ **1992 Cabernet Sauvignon Napa Valley.**

**Juffer** [yoof-fuh] (*Mosel*, Germany) Famous vineyard in the village of *Brauneberg*. QbA/Kab/Spät: **85** 86 **88 89 90** 91 92 93 94 95 96 Aus/Beeren/TBA: **83 85** 88 89 90 91 92 93 94 95 96 ***Max Ferd. Richter.***

***Jug wine*** (California) American term for quaffable *Vin Ordinaire*, mainly originating from the *Central Valley* in California.

🍷 **Marcel Juge** [zhoozh] (*Rhône*, France) Producer of one of the subtlest, classiest examples of *Cornas*. ☆☆☆☆ **1993 Cornas £££**

🍷 **Juliénas** [joo-lee-yay-nas] (*Burgundy*, France) One of the ten *Beaujolais Crus*, producing classic, vigorous wine which often benefits from a few years in bottle. **85 87 88 89** 90 **91** 93 94 95 96 ***Ch. de Juliénas; Georges Duboeuf.***

🍷 **Weingut Juliusspital** [yoo-lee-yoos-shpit-ahl] (*Franken*, Germany) Top-class estate whose profits benefit the poor and sick. A good source of *Riesling* and *Sylvaner*.

**Jumilla** [hoo-mee-yah] (Spain) Improving *DO* region, traditionally known for heavy, high-alcohol wines but increasingly making lighter *Beaujolais*-style ones. **87** 89 90 **91 94** 95 96

**Côtes de Jura** [koht duh zhoo-rah] (Eastern France) Region containing *Arbois* and *Savoie*, home of the *Savagnin* (not *Sauvignon*) grape and best known for specialities such as *Vin Gris, Vin Jaune* and *Vin de Paille*.

🍷 **Cave de Jurançon** [kahv duh zhoo-*ron*-son] (South West France) Good co-operative cellar making rich, dry apricotty white and excellent long-living sweet wines. ☆☆☆☆ **1995 Jurançon Grains Sauvage ££**

**Jurançon** [zhoo-*ron*-son] (South West France) Rich, dry apricotty white and excellent sweet wines made from the *Gros* and *Petit Manseng* found almost nowhere else. **83** 85 86 **89 90** 92 93 95 96 ***Dom Cauhapé*** ☆☆☆ **Domaine Castera £££**

🍷 **Justin** (*San Luis Obispo*, California) A winery to watch, with stunning reds, including a great *Cabernet Franc* and Isosceles, a *Bordeaux* blend. ☆☆☆☆ **1992 Isosceles San Luis Obispo County Reserve.**

🍷 **Juvé y Camps** [hoo-vay ee kamps] (*Catalonia*, Spain) The exception which proves the rule – by making and maturing decent *Cava* from traditional grapes and excellent vintage Brut.

# K

***Kabinett*** (Germany) First step in German quality ladder, for wines which achieve a certain natural sweetness.

**Kaiserstuhl-Tuniberg** [kih-sehr shtool too-nee-burg] (*Baden*, Germany) Supposedly finest *Baden Bereich* (actually it covers a third of Baden's vineyards) with top villages producing rich, spicy *Riesling* and *Sylvaner* from volcanic slopes. QbA/Kab/Spät: **85** 86 **88 89 90** 91 92 93 94 95 96 Aus/Beeren/TBA: **83 85** 88 89 90 91 92 93 94 95 96 **Von Gleichenstein; Badischer Winzerkellerei**

**Kallstadt** [kahl-shtaht] (*Pfalz*, Germany) Village containing the best-known and finest vineyard of Annaberg, making luscious, full Riesling. QbA/Kab/Spät: **85** 86 **88 89 90** 91 92 93 94 95 96 Aus/Beeren/TBA: **83 85** 88 89 90 91 92 93 94 95 **Stump Fitz'sches Weingut Annaberg**

🍷 **Kanonkop Estate** [ka-NON-kop] (*Stellenbosch*, South Africa) Estate with largely traditional equipment, but a modern approach to its unusually classy *Pinotage*. The light red blend, 'Kadette', is good too, and *Bordeaux*-style 'Paul Sauer' is one of the Cape's best. ☆☆☆☆ **1994 Pinotage ££**

**Katnook Estate** (*Coonawarra*, Australia) Small estate making the highly commercial Deakin Estate wines as well as plenty of such innovative stuff as a *Late Harvest Coonawarra Chardonnay* and top-class *Coonawarra Merlot* and *Cabernet*. ☆☆☆☆ 1996 Riddoch Sauvignon Blanc £

***Kellerei/kellerabfüllung*** [kel-luh-rih/kel-luh-rab-foo-loong] (Germany) Cellar/producer/estate-bottled.

**Kendall-Jackson** (*Clear Lake*, California) High-profile producer with supposedly classy *Chardonnay* and *Sauvignon* which are decidedly off-dry. ☆☆☆☆ 1995 Chardonnay Vintners Reserve ££

**Kenwood Vineyards** (*Sonoma Valley*, California) Classy *Sonoma* winery with good single vineyard *Chardonnays* and impressive, if tough, *Cabernets* (including one made from the author Jack London's vineyard). The star is the brilliant *Zinfandel*. ☆☆☆☆☆ 1994 Zinfandel ££

**Kerner** [kuh-nuh] A white grape variety. A *Riesling*-cross that is grown in Germany and also widely in England. *Anselmann.*

**Weingut Reichsgraf von Kesselstatt** [rihkh-sgraf fon kes-sel-shtat] (*Mosel-Saar-Ruwer*, Germany) Large, though much improved, collection of four *Riesling* estates spread between the *Mosel*, *Saar* and *Ruwer*. ☆☆☆☆ Weingut Steinger Grüner Veltliner ££

**Kiedrich** [kee-drikh] (*Rheingau*, Germany) Top village high in the hills whose vineyards can produce great, intense *Rieslings*. QbA/Kab/Spät: **85** 86 **88 89 90** 91 92 93 94 95 96 Aus/Beeren/TBA: **83 85** 88 89 90 91 92 93 94 95 96

**Kientzheim** [keents-him] (*Alsace*, France) Village noted for its *Riesling*. **71** 75 **76 83 85 86** 88 **89 90** 92 93 95 96

**André Kientzler** [keent-zluh] (*Alsace*, France) Classy producer with better-than average *Pinot Blanc*. ☆☆☆ 1993 Pinot Blanc d'Alsace ££

**J.F. Kimich** [kih-mikh] (*Pfalz* Germany) Fast-rising star making rich spicy wines typical of the *Pfalz*. Gewürztraminers are as good as Rieslings ☆☆☆☆ 1992 Foster Elster Riesling Kabinett ££££

**Kiona** [kih-yoh-nah] (*Washington State*, US) Small producer in the middle of nowhere with a penchant for intensely flavoured *Late Harvest* wines. ☆☆☆☆ 1993 Riesling ££

***Kir*** (*Burgundy*, France) A mixture of sweet, fortified *Crème de Cassis* (regional speciality of *Burgundy*) with simple and often rather acidic local white wine (*Aligoté*, or basic *Bourgogne* Blanc) to produce a delicious summertime drink. Try it with Crème de Mûre or Crème de Framboise instead.

**Ch. Kirwan** [keer-wahn] (*Margaux 3rd Growth*, *Bordeaux*, France) Rejuvenated property belatedly coming out of prolonged doldrums. Still doesn't warrant its third growth status. 70 78 81 **82 83** 85 86 87 88 89 90 92 93 94 95 96 ☆☆☆☆ 1990 ££££

**Kistler** [kist-luh] (*Sonoma Valley*, California) Probably California's top *Chardonnay* producer, with a really dazzling range of uncompromising, complex single-vineyard wines and fast-improving *Pinot Noirs*. *Burgundy* quality at *Burgundy* prices. ☆☆☆☆☆ 1993 Chardonnay Kistler Estate.

**Klein Constantia** [klihn kon-stan-tee-yah] (*Constantia*, South Africa) Small, go-ahead estate on the site of the great 17th-century *Constantia* vineyard. Wines, especially the *Sauvignon*, are not quite living up to the hype the estate has received, nor the prestige of the *Constantia* estate. Even so, they're light years ahead of *Groot Constantia*. ☆☆☆☆ 1995 Estate Chardonnay ££

**Klusserath** [kloo-seh-raht] (*Mosel-Saar-Ruwer*, Germany) Small village best known in UK for *Sonnenuhr* and Konigsberg vineyards. QbA/Kab/Spät: **85** 86 **88 89 90** 91 92 93 94 95 96 Aus/Beeren/TBA: **83 85** 88 89 90 91 92 93 94 95 96

🍷 **Tim Knappstein** [nap-steen] (*Clare Valley, Lenswood*, Australia) Long-time master of *Riesling* from the *Clare Valley*. Apart from *Clare* wines, look out for the brilliant *Sauvignon* and promising *Pinot Noirs* sold under the *Lenswood* label. ☆☆☆☆ **1994 Cabernet Merlot ££**

🍷 **Knudsen-Erath** [noos-den ee-rath] (*Oregon*, USA) One of the better pioneers of this region, but still far from earth-shattering.

🍷 **Konocti Cellars** [ko-nok-tih] (*Lake County*, California) Dynamic producer with recommendable straightforward wines. ☆☆☆

***Kosher*** (Israel) Wine made under complex rules. Every seventh vintage is left unharvested and non-Jews are barred from the winemaking process.

🍷 **Kourtakis** [koor-tah-kis] (Greece) One of Greece's most dynamic companies with unusually recommendable white. ☆☆☆ **1996 Vin de Crète Red £**

🍷 **Weinlaubenhof Weingut Alois Kracher** [Ah-loys krah-kuh] (*Neusiedlersee*, Austria) Source of great (very) *Late Harvest* wines including a very unusual effort with *Chardonnay*. ☆☆☆☆☆ **1991 Scheurebe No4 Zwischen Den Seen ££££**

**Krems** [krems] (*Wachau*, Austria) Town and *Wachau* vineyard area producing Austria's most stylish *Rieslings* from terraced vineyards.

**Kreuznach** [kroyt-znahkh] (*Nahe*, Germany) Northern *Bereich*, boasting fine vineyards situated around the town of *Bad Kreuznach*. QbA/Kab/Spät: **85** 86 **88** **89** **90** 91 92 93 94 95 Aus/Beeren/TBA: **83** **85** 88 89 90 91 92 93 94 95 96 ***Paul Anheuser***

🍷 **Dom. Kreydenweiss** [krih-den-vihs] (*Alsace*, France) Top-class organic producer with particularly good *Pinot Gris* and *Riesling*.

🍷 **Krondorf** [kron-dorf] (*Barossa Valley*, Australia) Winery specialising in traditional, big *Barossa* styles wines. ☆☆☆☆ **1993 Chardonnay Show Reserve £££**

🍷 **Krug** [kroog] (*Champagne*, France) The *Ch. Latour* of *Champagne*. Great vintage wine, extraordinary rosé and pure *Chardonnay* from the *Clos de Mesnil* vineyard. Theoretically the best non-vintage, thanks to the greater proportions of aged Reserve wine. ☆☆☆☆☆ **1985 Vintage ££££**

🍷 **Kruger-Rumpf** [kroo-gur roompf] (*Nahe* Germany) Nahe estate, demonstrating the potential of varieties like the *Scheurebe*. ☆☆☆☆☆ **1992 Munsterer Dautenflanzer Scheurebe Spatlëse ££££**

🍷 **Kuentz-Bas** [koontz bah] (*Alsace*, France) Reliable producer, for *Pinot Gris* and *Gewürztraminer*. ☆☆☆ **1992 Pinot Blanc, Cuvée Tradition ££**

🍷 **Kuhling-Gillot** [koo-ling gil-lot] (*Rheinhessen*, Germany) Hither to a little-known producer, now fast developing a reputation for his rich concentrated wines. ☆☆☆☆ **1992 Oppenheimer Kreuzkerner Riesling Auslese ££££**

🍷 **Kumeu River** [koo-myoo] (*Auckland*, New Zealand) Michael Brajkovich is successful with a wide range of wines, including a very unusual dry *Botrytis Sauvignon* which easily outclasses many a dry wine from *Sauternes*. ☆☆☆☆☆ **1995 Chardonnay £££**

🍷 **Weingut Franz Künstler** [koont-sluh] (*Rheingau*, Germany) A new superstar producer who is showing the big name estates of the *Rheingau* what they ought to be doing with their *Riesling*. ☆☆☆☆ **1992 Hochheimer Holle Riesling Auslese ££**

🍷 **KWV** (*Cape*, South Africa) Huge cooperative formed by the South African government at a time when surplus wine seemed set to flood the industry, and maintained by the National Party when it needed to keep the members of the big wine cooperatives, well, cooperative. Now facing privatisation and accusations of having been involved in the sale of fake *Champagne*, the KWV is a fascinating example of the way in which old Afrikaans establishment is having to come to terms with the advent of a free market at home and an outside world whose taste in wine has little in common with many of the traditional favourites in the Cape. ☆☆☆☆ **1996 Chenin Blanc £**

# L

**Ch. Labégorce** [la-bay-gors] (*Bordeaux*, France) Good, traditional Margaux. **82 83 85** 86 88 **89** 90 94 95 96 ☆☆☆☆ **1989 £££**

**Ch. Labégorce-Zédé** [la-bay-gors zay-day] (*Margaux Cru Bourgeois, Bordeaux*, France). A name to remember for wine beyond its Bourgeois class. 80 82 **83 85 86** 88 89 90 94 92 95 96 ☆☆☆ **1993 ££**

**Labouré-Roi** [la-boo-ray rwah] (*Burgundy*, France) A highly successful and very commercial *négoçiant*, responsible for some quite impressive wines. ☆☆☆☆ **1995 Meursault Clos de la Baronne £££**

***Labrusca*** [la-broo-skah] *Vitis labrusca*, the North American species of vine, making wine which is often referred to as 'foxy'. All *vinifera* vine stocks are grafted on to *Phylloxera*-resistant labrusca roots, though the vine itself is banned in Europe and its wines, thankfully, are almost unfindable.

**Ch. Lacoste-Borie** [la-cost-bo-ree] (*Pauillac, Bordeaux*, France) The reliable *Second Label* of *Grand-Puy-Lacoste*. ☆☆☆ **1993 Ch. Lacoste-Borie £££**

***Lacryma Christi*** [la-kree-mah kris-tee] (*Campania*, Italy) Literally, 'tears of Christ', the melancholy name for some amiable, light, rather rustic reds and whites. Those from Vesuvio are *DOC*. ☆☆☆ **1993 Mastroberardino Rosso £££**

**Ladoix-Serrigny** [la-dwah-seh-reen-yee] (*Burgundy*, France) Village including parts of *Corton* and Corton Charlemagne. The village wines are not well known and some bargains are still to be found. White: 79 84 **85 86** 87 **88** 89 **90 92** 95 96 Red: 78 80 83 **85** 86 87 **88 89 90** 92 95 96 **Capitain-Gagnerot**

**Patrick de Ladoucette** [duh la-doo-set] (*Loire*, France) Fine, intense, *Pouilly Fumé*, sold as 'Baron de L'. Other wines are less exciting. ☆☆☆☆ **1996 Baron De 'L' ££££**

**Michel Lafarge** [la-farzh] (*Burgundy*, France) One of the very best producers in *Volnay* – and indeed *Burgundy*. Fine, long-lived modern wine. ☆☆☆☆ **1994 Volnay Clos des Chênes £££**

**Ch. Lafaurie-Peyraguey** [la-foh-ree pay-rah-gee] (*Sauternes Premier Cru Classé, Bordeaux*, France) Much-improved *Sauternes* estate that has produced creamy, long-lived wines in the '80s and in 1990. 78 80 **81** 82 **83** 85 **86 88** 89 90 96 ☆☆☆☆ **1990 ££££**

**Ch. Lafite-Rothschild** [la-feet roh-chihld] (*Pauillac 1st Growth, Bordeaux*, France) Often almost impossible to taste young, this *Pauillac* First Growth is still one of the monuments of the wine world – especially since the early '80s. **61 75 76** 78 79 **81 82** 83 84 85 86 87 88 89 90 91 92 93 94 95 96 ☆☆☆☆ **1994 ££££**

**Ch. Lafleur** [la-flur] (*Pomerol, Bordeaux*, France) *Christian Moueix*'s pet *Pomerol*, often on a par with the wine *Moueix* makes at *Petrus*. **61 62 66** 70 75 78 79 81 **82 83 85** 86 88 89 90 92 93 94 95 96 ☆☆☆☆ **1994 ££££**

**Ch. Lafleur-Gazin** [la-flur-ga-zan] (*Pomerol, Bordeaux*, France) Another good member of the Moueix team. **82** 83 **85** 86 87 88 89 90 92 93 94 95

**Dom. des Comtes Lafon** [day comt la-fon] (*Burgundy*, France) The best domaine in *Meursault*, with great vineyards in *Volnay* and a small slice of *Montrachet*. Wines last forever. ☆☆☆☆ **1994 Meursault Les Charmes ££££**

**Ch. Lafon-Rochet** [la-fon-ro-shay] (*St. Estèphe 4th Growth, Bordeaux*, France) An increasingly modern *St. Estèphe*. One to follow. **70** 79 81 82 **83** 85 86 87 88 89 90 91 92 93 94 95 96 ☆☆☆☆ **1994 £££**

**Alois Lageder** [la-GAY-duh] (*Trentino-Alto-Adige*, Italy) New-wave producer of the kind of wine the *Alto-Adige* ought to make.

**Lago di Caldaro** [LA-goh dah KAHL-deh-roh] (*Trentino-Alto-Adige*, Italy) Also known as the *Kalterersee*, using the local *Schiava* grape to make cool, light reds with slightly unripe, though pleasant fruit.

**Ch. Lagrange** [la-gronzh] (*St. Julien 3rd Growth, Bordeaux*, France) A once under-performing third growth rejuvenated by Japanese cash and local know-how (from Michel Delon of *Léoville-Lascases*). Look out for *Les Fiefs de Lagrange*, the impressive *Second Label*. 70 82 83 84 **85 86** 87 88 89 90 91 92 93 94 95 96

**Ch. Lagrange** [la-gronzh] (*Pomerol, Bordeaux*, France) Yet another *Moueix* property – and yet another good wine. **70 75** 78 81 **82** 83 **85** 86 87 88 89 90 92 93 94 96 ☆☆☆ **1993 £££**

**Lagrein** [la-grayn] (Italy) Cherryish red grape of north east Italy.

**Ch. la Lagune** [la-goon] (*Haut-Médoc 3rd Growth, Bordeaux*, France) Lovely, accessible wines which last well and are worth buying even in poorer years. **70 75 76 78** 79 81 **82 83** 85 86 87 88 89 90 91 92 93 94 95 96 ☆☆☆☆ **1991 ££££**

**Lake County** (California) Vineyard district salvaged by improved irrigation techniques and now capable of some fine wines as well as *Kendall Jackson's* highly commercial efforts. Red: 84 **85** 86 87 **90 91** 92 93 95 White: **85 90 91** 92 95 96 ***Guenoc***.

**Lake's Folly** (*Hunter Valley*, Australia) Meet Max Lake, surgeon-turned-winemaker-cum writer/researcher who has great theories about the sexual effects of sniffing various kinds of wine. He is also a leading Australian pioneer of *Chardonnay*, with an unusually successful *Hunter Valley Cabernet Sauvignon*. Wines now made by Max's son, Stephen. ☆☆☆☆ **1994 Cabernet Sauvignon, Hunter Valley £££**

**Lalande de Pomerol** [la-LOND duh po-meh-rol] (*Bordeaux*, France) Bordering on *Pomerol* with similar, but less fine wines. Still generally better than similarly priced *St. Emilions*. Some good-value *Petits-Châteaux*. **70 75** 78 79 81 **82 83 85** 86 **88 89** 90 94 95 96

**Ch. Lalande-Borie** [la-LOND bo-ree] (*St. Julien, Bordeaux*, France) In the same stable as *Ch. Ducru Beaucaillou*. Reliable wines. 81 82 83 85 86 87 88 89 90 91 92 93 94 95 96 ☆☆☆☆ **1989 £££**

**Ch. Lamarque** [la-mahrk] (*Haut-Médoc Cru Bourgeois, Bordeaux*, France) Spectacular château with good, traditional wines. 82 **83** 85 **86** 87 88 89 90 91 92 93 94 95 96 ☆☆☆ **1992 £££** ☆☆☆ **1993 ££**

**Lamberhurst** (Kent, England) One of the first English vineyards and still one of the more reliable, though rarely the most innovative. ☆☆☆ **1996 Bacchus ££**

**Lambrusco** [lam-broos-koh] (*Emilia-Romagna*, Italy) Famous/infamous low-strength (7.5 per cent) sweet, fizzy UK and North American version of the fizzy dry red wine favoured in Italy. The real thing – fascinating with its dry, unripe, cherry flavour – comes with a cork rather than a screw-cap. ☆☆☆ **Secco Sorbara Cavicchioli £**

**Ch. de Landiras** [lon-dee-ras] (*Bordeaux*, France) An out-of-the-way corner of the *Graves* that has been reclaimed from the forest by Peter Vinding-Diers and also serves as the winery for the *Dom. La Grave* property a few miles away. Red: 88 89 **90** 94 95 96 White: 90 91 **93** 95 96

**Landskroon Estate** [land-skroon] (*Paarl*, South Africa) Good traditional *'Port'*, *Shiraz* and a rare solo outing for *Cabernet Franc*. ☆☆☆ **1991 'Port'.**

***Landwein*** [land-vihn] (Germany) The equivalent of a French *Vin De Pays* from one of 11 named regions (*Anbaugebiet*). Often dry.

**Ch. Lanessan** [la-neh-son] (*Haut-Médoc Cru Bourgeois, Bordeaux*, France) Old-fashioned *Cru Bourgeois* largely untouched by new oak. A long-lived argument for the way things used to be done. **79 82 83 85 86** 88 89 90 **93** 94 95 96 ☆☆☆☆ **1993 ££££**

**Langhe** [lang-gay] (*Piedmont*, Italy) A range of hills; when preceded by '*Nebbiolo* delle', indicates declassified *Barolo* and *Barbaresco*. Ascheri; Conterno.

**Ch. Langoa-Barton** [lon-goh-wah-bahr-ton] (*St. Julien 3rd Growth*, *Bordeaux*, France) *Léoville Barton's* (slightly) less complex kid brother. Often one of the best bargain classed growths in *Bordeaux*. Well made in poor years. **70 75** 76 **78** 79 81 **82** 83 85 **86** 88 89 90 91 92 93 94 95 96 ☆☆☆☆ 1993 ££££

**Languedoc-Roussillon** [long-dok roo-see-yon] (*Midi*, France) One of the world's largest wine regions and, until recently, a major source of the wine lake. But a combination of government-sponsored up-rooting and keen activity by *Flying Winemakers* and (a few) dynamic producers is beginning to turn this into a worrying competitor for the New World. The region includes *Appellations* like *Fitou*, *Corbières* and *Minervois*, and a torrent of *Vin De Pays d'Oc*.

**Lanson** [lon-son] (*Champagne*, France) Much improved Champagne house with decent non-vintage 'Black Label', good *Demi-Sec* and sublime *Vintage* fizz. ☆☆☆☆ 1988 Noble Cuvée Vintage ££££

**Casa Lapostolle** [la-pos-tol] (*Colchagua Valley*, Chile) One of Chile's newest stars. Belongs to the owners of Grand Marnier and benefiting from the expertise of *Michel Rolland*. Classy *Merlot* reds; whites need more work. ☆☆☆☆ 1996 Merlot Alexandre ££

**Ch. Larcis-Ducasse** [lahr-see doo-kass] (*St. Emilion Grand Cru Classé*, *Bordeaux*, France) Property whose lightish wines rarely live up to the potential of its hillside site. 66 78 79 81 **82** 83 84 85 86 87 88 89 90 94 95 96 ☆☆☆☆ 1990 £££

**Ch. Larmande** [lahr-mond] (*St. Emilion*, *Grand Cru Classé*, *Bordeaux*, France) A property to watch for well-made, ripe-tasting wines. 85 86 **88** **89** 90 92 93 94 95 96

**Dom. Laroche** [la-rosh] (*Burgundy*, France) Good *Chablis négoçiant* with some enviable vineyards of its own, including *Premiers* and *Grands Crus*. Reliable southern French *Chardonnay Vin De Pays d'Oc* and innovative wines from *Corsica*. ☆☆☆☆ 1993 Chablis 1er Cru Les Fourchaumes £££

**Ch. Lascombes** [las-komb] (*Margaux 2nd Growth*, *Bordeaux*, France) Much improved, subtle, second growth *Margaux* which often exemplifies the perfumed character of this *Appellation*. **70 75** 82 83 85 **86** 87 **88** 89 90 91 92 93 94 95 96 ☆☆☆☆ 1994 ££££

**Laski Riesling/Rizling** [lash-kee riz-ling] (Former Yugoslavia) Yugoslav name for white grape, unrelated to the *Rhine Riesling*, aka *Welsch*, *Olasz* and *Italico*. Jeruzalem Ormoz.

**Ch. de Lastours** [duh las-toor] (*Languedoc-Roussillon*, France) Combined winery and home for the mentally handicapped, and proof that *Corbières* can rival *Bordeaux*. Look out for the Cuvée Simone Descamps. ☆☆☆ 1993 Corbières ££

***Late Harvest*** Made from (riper) grapes picked after the main vintage. Should have at least some *Botrytis*.

***Late-Bottled Vintage (port) (LBV)*** (*Douro*, Portugal) Officially, bottled four or six years after a specific (usually non-declared) vintage. Until the late 1970s, this made for a *Vintage Port*-style wine that matured earlier, was a little lighter and easier to drink, but still needed to be decanted. *Warres* and *Smith Woodhouse* both still produce delicious examples of this style. Almost every other LBV around, however, is of the filtered, 'modern' style pioneered by *Taylors*. These taste pretty much like up-market *Ruby* and *Vintage Character*, need no decanting and bear very little resemblance to real *Vintage* or even *Crusted Port*. Under their self-imposed laws, the port shippers allow themselves to use the same name for these two very different styles of wine. Confused? I don't blame you.

**Latium/Lazio** [**Lah-Tyum**] [lah-tee-yoom] (Italy) The vineyard area surrounding Rome, including frascati and Marino. **Fontana Candida; Colli di Cantone.**

🍷 **Louis Latour** [loo-wee lah-toor] (*Burgundy*, France) Underperforming *négoçiant* who still pasteurises his – consequently muddy-tasting – reds, treating them in a way no quality-conscious New World producer would contemplate. Some whites, including *Corton Charlemagne,* can be sublime. ☆☆☆☆ **1993 Montrachet** ☆☆☆☆ **1992 Corton-Charlemagne ££££**

🍷 **Ch. Latour** [lah-toor] (*Pauillac 1st Growth*, *Bordeaux*, France) First Growth *Pauillac* which can be very tricky to judge when young, but which develops majestically. Recently bought (by a Frenchman) from its British owners, Allied Domecq. *Les Forts de Latour* is the – often worthwhile – *Second Label*. **61** 62 64 **66** 67 **70** 73 **75** 76 **78** 79 80 81 82 83 84 85 86 87 88 89 90 91 92 93 94 95 96 ☆☆☆☆ **1994 ££££**

🍷 **Ch. Latour-à-Pomerol** [lah-toor ah po-meh-rol] (*Pomerol*, *Bordeaux*, France) A great value, tiny (3,500-case) *Pomerol* under the same ownership as *Ch. Petrus* and the same *Moueix* winemaking team. It is a little less concentrated than its big brother, but then it is around a quarter of the price, too. 76 78 79 81 **82** 83 **85** 86 87 88 89 90 92 93 94 95 96 ☆☆☆☆ **1990 ££££**

🍷 **Ch. Latour-Martillac** [la-toor mah-tee-yak] (*Graves Cru Classé*, *Bordeaux*, France) Good, if sometimes overlooked reds and whites. Red: **82** 83 **85** 86 87 88 89 90 91 92 93 94 95 96 White: 86 87 88 **89** 90 91 **92** 93 94 94 96 ☆☆☆☆ **1992 £££**

**Laudun** [loh-duhn] (*Rhône*, France) Named village of *Côtes du Rhône,* with some atypical fresh, light wines and attractive rosés.

🍷 **Laurel Glen** (*Sonoma* Mountain, California) Small, hillside-estate with ripe-flavoured, *Bordeaux*-style reds that are well respected by true Californian wine lovers. Terra Rosa is the accessible *Second Label*. ☆☆☆☆ **1994 Terra Rosa Cabernet Merlot ££**

🍷 **Laurent-Perrier** [law-ron pay-ree-yay] (*Champagne*, France) One of the more reliable larger houses with particularly recommendable rosé. ☆☆☆☆ **1990 Vintage Brut ££££**

🍷 **Ch. Laville-Haut-Brion** [la-veel oh-bree-yon] (*Graves Cru Classé*, *Bordeaux*, France) Exquisite white *Graves* that lasts for 20 years or more. 62 **66** **75** 82 **83** **85** 86 **87** 88 89 90 92 93 94 95 96

**Lazio** [lat-zee-yoh] (Italy) See *Latium*.

***LBV*** (*Douro*, Portugal) See *Late Bottled Vintage*.

***Lean*** Lacking body.

🍷 **Leasingham** (South Australia) BRL Hardy subsidiary in the Clare Valley that makes top flight Shiraz. ☆☆☆☆☆ **1994 Classic Clare Cabernet Sauvignon £££**

**Lebanon** Best known for the remarkable *Ch. Musar* from the *Bekaa Valley,* made in *Bordeaux* style from *Cabernet Sauvignon, Cinsault* and *Syrah*.

🍷 **Leconfield** [leh-kon-feeld] (South Australia) Reliable producer of highly impressive, intense *Coonawarra* reds that improve with every vintage. ☆☆☆☆☆ **1994 Shiraz £££**

***Lees or lie(s)*** The sediment of dead yeasts that fall in the barrel or vat as a wine develops. See *Sur Lie*.

🍷 **Leeuwin Estate** [loo-win] (*Margaret River*, Western Australia) Showcase winery (and concert venue) whose genuinely world-class ('art label') *Chardonnay* is one of Australia's priciest and longest-lived. Other wines are less dazzling. ☆☆☆☆☆ **1994 Art Series Chardonnay £££**

**Dom. Leflaive** [luh-flayv] (*Burgundy*, France) A new generation of Leflaives is using organic methods – and making better wines than ever. ☆☆☆☆☆ **1994 Chevalier Montrachet ££££**

**Olivier Leflaive** [luh-flayv] (*Burgundy*, France) The *négoçiant* business launched by Vincent Leflaive's nephew. High-class white wines. ☆☆☆☆ **1994 Bourgogne Aligote ££** ☆☆☆☆ **1993 Chassagne-Montrachet 1er Cru Morgeot £££**

**Peter Lehmann** [lee-man] (*Barossa Valley*, Australia) The grand (not so) old man of the *Barossa Valley,* Peter Lehmann and his son Doug make intensely concentrated *Shirazes*, *Cabernet*s, *Semillon*s and *Chardonnay*s which make up in character (and value for money) what they lack in subtlety. Stonewell is the best red. ☆☆☆☆☆ **1995 Semillon £££**

***Length*** How long the taste lingers in the mouth.

**Lenswood** (South Australia) New high-altitude region near Adelaide, proving its potential with *Sauvignon*, *Chardonnay*, *Pinot Noir* and even (in the case of *Henschke*'s Abbott's Prayer), *Merlot* and *Cabernet Sauvignon*. Pioneers include *Stafford Ridge* and *Knappstein's* Lenswood who also makes good Pinot Noir. White: **86 87** 88 **90 91 94 95** Red: **80 82 84 85 86 87** 88 **90 91 94** 95 ***Tim Knappstein; Stafford Ridge.***

**Léognan** [lay-ohn-yon] (*Bordeaux*, France) Leading village of *Graves* with its own *AC, Pessac-Léognan.* ***Lurton.***

**Leon** [lay-on] (Spain) North-western region producing acceptable dry, fruity reds and whites.

**Jean León** [zhon lay-ON] (*Catalonia*, Spain) American pioneer of *Chardonnay* and *Cabernet*, recently bought by *Torres.* ☆☆☆ **1990 Cabernet Sauvignon £££**

**Leonetti Cellars** [lee-oh-net-tee] (*Washington State*, US) One of the best red wine producers in the US. ☆☆☆☆ **1992 Cabernet Sauvignon Columbia Valley.**

**Ch. Léoville-Barton** [lay-oh-veel bahr-ton] (*St. Julien 2nd Growth*, *Bordeaux*, France) One of the classiest bargains in *Bordeaux.* A fairly priced, reliably stylish *St. Julien* second growth, whose wines are among the best in the *Médoc,* especially in 1994. *Langoa Barton* is the sister property. **61 70 75** 7687 **78** 81 **82** 83 85 86 87 88 89 90 91 92 93 94 95 ☆☆☆☆☆ **1993 ££££**

**Ch. Léoville-Las-Cases** [lay-oh-veel kas-kahz] (*St. Julien 2nd Growth*, *Bordeaux*, France) Impeccably made *St. Julien Super-Second* which often – as in 1996 – matches its neighbour *Ch. Latour.* The *Second Label, Clos du Marquis*, is worth buying too. 76 **78** 81 **82 83 85** 86 87 88 89 90 91 92 93 94 95 96 ☆☆☆☆☆ **1994 ££££**

**Ch. Léoville-Poyferré** [lay-pwah-feh-ray] (*St. Julien 2nd Growth*, *Bordeaux*, France) 1995 and 1996 showed the touch of *Michel Rolland* here. A rising star. The *Second Label* is Moulin Riche. **82 83** 84 85 86 87 88 89 90 91 93 94 95 96. ☆☆☆☆ **1991 ££££**

**Dom. Leroy** [luh-rwah] (*Burgundy*, France) Organic domaine in *Vosne-Romanée* founded by the former co-owner of the *Dom. de la Romanée-Conti* making wines as good as those of that estate. ☆☆☆☆☆ **1990 Corton Charlemagne ££££**

**Lexia** [lex-ee-yah] See *Muscat d'Alexandrie*

***Lie(s)*** See *Lees/Sur Lie.*

***Liebfraumilch*** [leeb-frow-mihlkh] (Germany) Seditious exploitation of the *QbA* system. Good examples are pleasant; most are alcoholic sugar-water bought on price alone.

**Lievland** [leev-land] (*Stellenbosch*, South Africa) Estate which has emerged as a high quality specialist producer of *Shiraz* and *Late Harvest* wines. ☆☆☆☆ **1995 Shiraz. ££**

🍷 **Ch. Lilian-Ladouys** [la-dwees] (*St. Estèphe Cru Bourgeois, Bordeaux*, France) New estate with creditably approachable wines. A far more creamy style with early drinking potential. 89 90 91 92 93 94 95 96 ☆☆☆☆ **1991 ££££**

🍷 **Limestone Ridge** (South Australia) *Lindemans'* variable *Coonawarra* red. ☆☆☆☆ **1993 Shiraz Cabernet £££**

***Limousin*** [lee-moo-zan] (France) Oak forest that provides barrels that are high in wood *tannin*. Better, therefore, for red wine than for white.

**Limoux** [lee-moo] (*Midi*, France) New *Appellation* for *Chardonnays* which were previously sold as *Vin De Pays d'Oc*. See *Blanquette*.

🍷 **Lindauer** [lin-dowr] (*Marlborough*, New Zealand) Good-value *Montana* fizz. ☆☆☆ **Brut and rosé ££** ☆☆☆☆ **Special Reserve ££**

🍷 **Lindemans** (South Australia) Once *Penfolds'* greatest rival, now its subsidiary (aren't they all?). Noted for long-lived *Hunter Valley Semillon* and *Shiraz*, *Coonawarra* reds and good-value multi-region blends, such as the internationally successful Bin 65 Chardonnay and Bin 45 Cabernet.

🍷 **Weingut Karl Lingenfelder** [lin-gen-fel-duh] (*Pfalz*, Germany) Great new-wave *Rheinpfalz* producer of a special *Riesling, Dornfelder, Scheurebe* and an unusually successful *Pinot Noir.* ☆☆☆☆ **1994 Freisenheimer Riesling Halbtroken Spätlese ££**

🍷 **Jean Lionnet** [lee-oh-nay] (*Rhône*, France) Classy *Cornas* producer whose Rochepertius is a worthwhile buy. ☆☆☆☆ **1990 Cornas Dom. de Rochepertuis £££**

🍷 **Ch. Liot** [lee-yoh] (*Barsac, Bordeaux*, France) Good light and elegant *Barsac*. 75 76 82 83 86 88 89 90 92 94☆☆☆☆ **1992 £££**

***Liqueur Muscat*** (*Rutherglen*, Australia) A wine style unique to Australia. Other countries make fortified *Muscats*, but none achieve the caramelised marmalade and Christmas pudding flavours that *Rutherglen* can achieve. **Mick Morris; Campbell's.**

***Liqueur d'Expedition*** [lee-kuhr dex-pay-dees-see-yon] (*Champagne*, France) Sweetening syrup for *Dosage*.

***Liqueur de Tirage*** [lee-kuhr duh tee-rahzh] (*Champagne*, France) The yeast and sugar added to base wine to induce secondary fermentation (and hence the bubbles) in bottle.

***Liquoreux*** [lee-koh-ruh] (France) Rich and sweet.

***Liquoroso*** [lee-koh-roh-soh] (Italy) Rich and sweet.

🍷 **Lirac** [lee-rak] (*Rhône*, France) Peppery, *Tavel*-like rosés, and increasingly impressive deep, berry-fruit reds. Red: **82 83 85 88** 89 90 95 96 **Perrin; Delorme; Ch. D'Aqueria; André Méjan.**

🍷 **Listel** [lees-tel] (*Languedoc-Roussillon*, France) Recently taken over, now improving pioneer with vineyards on beaches close to Sète. Best wines: rosé ('Grain de Gris') and low-alcohol sparkling *Muscat* (Petillant de Raisin).

**Listrac** [lees-trak] (*Bordeaux*, France) Small *commune* in the *Haut-Médoc*, near *Moulis*, though quite different in style. Clay makes this *Merlot* country, though this isn't always reflected in the vineyards. Far too many wines are toughly unripe. 70 75 76 **78** 79 81 **82** 83 **85 86** 88 89 90 94 95 96 **Ch. Fourcas-Hosten; Ch. Poujeaux.**

**Livermore (Valley)** [liv-uhr-mohr] (California) Warm climate vineyard area with fertile soil producing full, rounded whites, including increasingly fine *Chardonnay.* Red: 84 **85** 86 87 **90 91** 92 93 95 White: **85 90 91** 92 95.96.**Wente; Concannon; Livermore Cellars.**

🍷 **Los Llanos** [los yah-nos] (*Valdepeñas*, Spain) Commendable modern exception to the tradition of dull *Valdepeñas*, with quality mature reds.

🍷 **De Loach** [duh lohch] (Sonoma, California) Look for the letters O.F.S. – Our Finest Selection – on the *Chardonnay* and *Cabernet*. But even these rarely surpass the stunning individual vineyard Zinfandels.

🍷 **J Lohr** [lohr] (Santa Clara, California) Winery noted for its well-made, affordable wines, particularly the Wildflower: and now more classic noble styles. ☆☆☆☆ **1995 Riverstone Chardonnay ££**

**Loire** [lwahr] (France) An extraordinary variety of wines come from this area – dry whites such as *Muscadet* and the classier *Savennières, Sancerre* and *Pouilly Fumé*; grassy, summery reds; *Chinon* and *Bourgeuil*, buckets of rosé – some good, most dreadful; glorious sweet whites – *Vouvray*, etc – and very acceptable sparkling wines (also *Vouvray* plus *Crémant de Loire*). Stick to growers and domaines. White: 83 **85 86 88 89 90** 94 95 Sweet White: **76** 83 **85** 86 **88 89** 90 94 95 **96.** Red: **78** 81 83 **85** 86 **88 89 90** 95 **96**

**Lombardy** [lom-bahr-dee] (Italy) Region (and vineyards) around Milan, known mostly for sparkling wine but also for increasingly interesting reds, such as *Valcalepio* and *Oltrepo Pavese* and the whites of *Lugana*. Red: **78** 79 81 **82 85 88 90** 94 95 **96**

**Long Island** (*New York State*, US) A unique micro-climate where fields once full of potatoes are now yielding classy *Merlot* and *Chardonnay*. See *Bridgehampton, Hargrave and Palmer Vineyards.*

🍷 **Longridge** (*Stellenbosch*, South Africa) Designer winery tailoring three ranges (Longridge, Bay View and Capelands) to the export market. ☆☆☆☆ **1996 Chardonnay £**

**Lontue** [lon-too-way] (Chile) Region where some of Chile's best *Merlots* are being made. *Santa Carolina; Valdevieso; Torcornal; San Pedro.*

🍷 **Weingut Dr Loosen** [loh-sen] (*Mosel-Saar-Ruwer*, Germany) New Wave *Riesling* producer. Probably the best and most reliable in the *Mosel*. ☆☆☆☆ **1996 Erdener Pralat Auslese ££££**

🍷 **Lopez de Heredia** [loh-peth day hay-ray-dee-yah] (*Rioja*, Spain) Ultra-traditional winery producing old-fashioned Viña Tondonia white and *Gran Reserva* reds. ☆☆☆ **1993 Vina Tondonia Tinto Crianza £££**

🍷 **Louisvale** [loo-wis-vayl] (*Stellenbosch*, South Africa) Once avowed *Chardonnay* specialists, Louisvale's range has expanded to include some *Cabernet*-based reds. ☆☆☆ **1995 Cabernet Merlot ££**

**Loupiac** [loo-peeyak] (*Bordeaux*, France) *Sauternes* neighbour with similar but less fine wines. **83 85 86 88** 89 90 95 *Ch. Loupiac-Gaudiet*.

🍷 **Ch. Loupiac-Gaudiet** [loo-pee-yak goh-dee-yay] (*Loupiac, Bordeaux*, France) A good producer of *Loupiac*. **83** 85 **86 88** 89 90 95 **96**

🍷 **Ch. la Louvière** [lah loo-vee-yehr] (*Graves, Bordeaux*, France) André Lurton's best known *Graves* property. Reliable, rich, modern whites and reds.. The second wine is called 'L' de Louvière. Red: 81 **82** 83 **85 86** 87 88 89 90 91 92 93 94 95 White: 86 88 **89 90** 91 92 93 94 95 96 ☆☆☆☆ **1993 Red £££**

🍷 **Van Loveren** [van loh-veh-ren] (*Robertson*, South Africa) Large family owned estate producing excellent value for money wine. Contrasting primarily on classic fresh whites and also soft reds ☆☆☆ **1996 Late Harvest Gewürztraminer £**

**Côtes du Lubéron** [koht doo LOO-bay-*ron*] (*Rhône*, France) Reds like light *Côtes du Rhône*, pink and sparkling wines and *Chardonnay*-influenced whites. A new *Appellation* and still good value.

**Lugana** [loo-gah-nah] (*Lombardy*, Italy) Potentially appley, almondy whites made from the *Trebbiano*, grown on the shores of Lake Garda. ☆☆☆ **1995 Vigna Brolettino Dal Cero ££**

**Lugny** [loo-nee] (*Burgundy*, France) See *Mâcon*.

🍷 **Pierre Luneau** [loo-noh] (*Loire*, France) A rare beast: a top-class *Muscadet* producer. M. Luneau likes to try out wacky ideas with his wines like keeping juice under nitrogen for a few yearsto see what happens. ☆☆☆ **1996 Muscadet Sur Lie 'L' d'Or ££**

🍷 **Cantine Lungarotti** [kan-tee-nah loon-gah-roh-tee] (*Umbria*, Italy) Innovative producer who more or less created the *Torgiano* denomination. ☆☆☆☆ **1987 Rubesco Riserva £££**

🍷 **Jacques Lurton** [loor-ton] Son of the owner of *Ch. la Louvière* and *Ch. Bonnet* in *Entre-Deux-Mers* who, having made a success there (especially with his whites), now makes wine all over the world. Look out for Hermanos Lurton wines from Spain. ☆☆☆☆ **1994 Belongrade y Lurton white ££**

🍷 **Ch. de Lussac** [loo-sak] (*Lussac St. Émilion*, *Bordeaux*, France) A name to watch out for in *Lussac St. Emilion*. 86 **89** 90 94 95 ☆☆☆ **1994 ££**

**Lussac-St. Emilion** [loo-sak sant-ay-mee-yon] (*Bordeaux*, France) A potentially worthwhile satellite of *St. Emilion*. **82** 83 **85** 86 **88** 89 90 94 95

🍷 **Emilio Lustau** [loos-tow] (*Jerez*, Spain) Great *Sherry* producer, particularly noted for individual *Almacanista* wines. ☆☆☆☆ **Almacanista Dry Oloroso ££**

**Lutomer** [loo-toh-muh] (Slovenia) Wine-producing area still known mostly for its (very basic) Lutomer *Laski Riesling*. Now doing better things with *Chardonnay*.

**Luxembourg** [luk-sehm-burg] Source of some pleasant, fresh, white wines from Alsace-like grape varieties, and generally dire fizz.

🍷 **Ch. Lynch-Bages** [lansh bazh] (*Pauillac 5th Growth*, *Bordeaux*, France) Reliably over-performing Fifth Growth *Pauillac* which belongs to Jean-Michel Cazes, of *Ch. Pichon Longueville*. The (very rare) white is worth seeking out too. **61** 62 66 **70** 75 78 79 81 **82 83 85** 86 87 88 89 90 91 92 93 94 95 ☆☆☆☆☆ **1990 ££££**

🍷 **Ch. Lynch-Moussas** [lansh moo-sahs] (*Pauillac 5th Growth*, *Bordeaux*, France) Slowly improving. **85** 86 88 89 90 91 94 ☆☆☆ **1994 £££**

***Macération carbonique*** [ma-say-ra-see-yon kahr-bon-eek] Technique of fermenting uncrushed grapes under pressure of a blanket of carbon dioxide gas to produce fresh, fruity wine. Used in *Beaujolais*, Southern France and, increasingly, the New World.

🍷 **Machard de Gramant** [ma-shahr duh gra-mon] (*Burgundy*, France) Producer of superb *Nuits-St-Georges* and *Savigny-Lès Beaune*. ☆☆☆☆ **1993 Nuits St. Georges. Les Allots £££**

**Mâcon/Mâconnais** [ma-kon/nay] (*Burgundy*, France) Avoid unidentified 'rouge' or 'blanc' on wine lists. Mâcons with the suffix *Villages*, *Superieur* or Prissé, *Viré*, *Lugny* or Clessé should be better and can afford some pleasant, good-value *Chardonnay*. The region contains the appellations *St-Véran* and *Pouilly Fuissé*. For straight Mâcon try *Jadot* or *Duboeuf*, but the *Dom Thevenet Dom de la Bongran* from Clessé is of *Côte d'Or* quality. Red: **78** 80 **85** 86 87 88 89 90 92 95 96 White: 84 **85 86** 87 **88** 89 **90 92** 95 96 **Caves de Lugny; Cave de Prissé; Roger Lasserat; Deux Roches.**

**Maculan** [mah-koo-lahn] (*Veneto*, Italy) A superstar producer of black-curranty *Cabernet* Breganze, an oaked *Pinot Bianco-Pinot Grigio-Chardonnay* blend called Prato di Canzio and the lusciously sweet *Torcolato*. ☆☆☆☆ **1990 Cabernet Palazzotto £££** ☆☆☆☆ **1992 Acini Nobile ££££**

**Madeira** [ma-dee-ruh] (Portugal) Atlantic island producing fortified wines, usually identified by style: *Bual, Sercial, Verdelho* or *Malmsey*. Most is ordinary stuff for use by mainland European cooks and, more rarely, finer fare for those who appreciate the unique marmaladey character of good Madeira. Also home to the *Madeira Wine Company*, owners of the *Rutherford & Miles, Blandy*, Leacock and *Cossart Gordon* labels. This well-run quasi-monopolistic company now belongs to the Symingtons who, with *Dows, Grahams, Warres*, etc, have a similar role in the *Douro*. Other producers to look out for include *Henriques & Henriques* and Barros e Souza.

***Maderisation*** [mad-uhr-ih-zay-shon] Deliberate procedure in *Madeira*, produced by the warming of wine in *Estufas*. Otherwise undesired effect, commonly produced by high temperatures during storage, resulting in a dull, flat flavour tinged with a *Sherry* taste and colour.

**Madiran** [ma-dee-ron] (South West France) Robust country reds made from the *Tannat* grape; tannic when young, but worth ageing. ☆☆☆ **1994 Producteurs de Plaimont ££**

**Ch. Magdelaine** [Mag-duh-layn] (*St. Emilion Premier Grand Cru*, *Bordeaux*, France) *St. Emilion* estate owned by JP *Moueix* and neighbour to *Ch. Ausone*, producing reliable, rich wines. **61 70 71** 75 78 79 81 **82 83** 85 86 88 89 90 92 93 94 95 96 ☆☆☆☆ **1993 £££**

***Magnum*** Large bottle containing the equivalent of two bottles of wine (one and a half litres in capacity).

**Maipo** [mih-poh] (Chile) Historic region in which are found many good-producers. Reds are most successful, especially *Cabernet*, *Merlot* and softer *Chardonnays*.Watch out for new varieties and enterprising organic vineyards. **Canepa; Cousino Macul; Peteroa; Santa Carolina; Santa Rita; Undurraga; Viña Carmen.**

***Maître de Chai*** [may-tr duh chay] (France) Cellar master.

**Malaga** [ma-la-gah] (Spain) A semi-moribund Andalusian *DO* producing raisiny dessert wines of varying degrees of sweetness, immensely popular in the 19th century. *Lopez Hermanos*.

**Ch. Malartic-Lagravière** [mah-lahr-teek lah-gra-vee-yehr] (*Pessac-Léognan Cru Classé, Bordeaux*, France) Previously slumbering estate, bought in 1994 by *Laurent Perrier*, improving new-wave whites; reds need time. Red: 81 **82** 83 85 **86** 87 88 89 90 94 95 96 White: 85 **87** 88 89 90 91 92 94 95 96 ☆☆☆ **1992 Red £££**

**Malbec** [mal-bek] Red grape, now rare in *Bordeaux* but widely planted in Argentina, the *Loire* ( where it is known as the *Côt*),*Cahors* and also in Australia. Producing rich plummy silky wines.

**Ch. Malescasse** [ma-les-kas] (*Haut-Médoc Cru Bourgeois, Bordeaux*, France) Watch this space; since 1993, wines have been made by the former cellarmaster of *Pichon-Lalande*. 82 83 85 86 88 89 90 93 94 95 96

**Ch. Malescot-St-Exupéry** [ma-les-koh san tek-soo-peh-ree] (*Margaux 3rd Growth, Bordeaux*, France) Understated but often very classy wines. **61** 70 **82** 83 86 87 88 89 90 91 92 94 95 96 ☆☆☆ **1993 £££**

**Ch. de Malle** [duh mal] (*Sauternes Deuxième Cru Classé, Bordeaux*, France) Wonderful *Sauternes* property near Preignac famous for its beautiful *Château*. 76 **81** 82 **83** 85 **86** 88 89 90 94 95 ☆☆☆☆ **1990 ££££**

**Mallorca** [ma-yor-kah] (Spain) See *Binnisalem*.

***Malolactic Fermentation*** [ma-loh-lak-tik] Secondary 'fermentation' in which appley malic acid is converted into the 'softer', creamier *lactic* acid by naturally present or added strains of bacteria. Almost all red wines undergo a malolactic fermentation. For whites, it is common practice in *Burgundy*. It is varyingly used in the New World, where natural acid levels are often low. Recognisable in excess in wine, as a buttermilky flavour.

**Ch. de la Maltroye** [mal-trwah] (*Burgundy*, France) Classy modern *Chassagne*-based estate with fingers in 14 *AC* pies around *Burgundy*, all of whose wines are made by *Dom. Parent*.☆☆☆☆ **1994 Chassagne Montrachet Clos du Château ££££**

**Malvasia** [mal-vah-see-ah] Muscatty white grape vinified dry in Italy (as a component in *Frascati* for example), but far more successfully as good, sweet traditional *Madeira*, where it is known as *Malmsey*. It is not the same grape as *Malvoisie* (see below).

**Malvoisie** (*Loire*, France) Local name for the *Pinot Gris;* used in dessert wines.

**La Mancha** [lah man-cha] (Spain) Huge region known for mostly dull and old-fashioned wines, but in recent times producing increasingly clean, modern examples. Also the place where the *Marques de Griñon* is succeeding in his experiments with new vine growing-techniques and grapes, especially Syrah.

**Albert Mann** (*Alsace*, France) Top grower who always manages to express true varietal character without over blown alcohol flavours. ☆☆☆ **1995 Cuvée Albert £££**

**Manseng (Gros M. & Petit M.)** [man-seng] (South West France) Two varieties of white grape grown in South Western France, the Gros M. is a flavoursome workhorse for much of the dry white of the Armagnac region, whereas Petit M. is capable of extraordinary apricot-and-cream concentration in the great *Vendange Tardive* wines of *Jurançon*. The Manseng is one of the few noble varieties not to have found wide favour across the globe, possibly because it is low-yielding and hard to grow. **Dom. Cauhapé; Grassa; Producteurs de Plaimont.**

***Manzanilla*** [man-zah-nee-yah] (*Jerez*, Spain) Dry, tangy *sherry* – a *fino* style widely (though possibly mistakenly) thought to take on a salty tang from the coastal *Bodegas* of Sanlucar de Barrameda. **Don Zoilo; Barbadillo; Hidalgo.**

**Maranges** [mah-ronzh] (*Burgundy*, France) A new hillside *Appellation* promising potentially affordable, if a little rustic *Côte d'Or* wines. White: **90 92** 95 96 Red: **90** 92 95 96

**Ch. de Marbuzet** [MAHR-boo-zay] (*St. Estèphe Cru Bourgeois*, *Bordeaux*, France) *Second Wine* of Ch. *Cos d'Estournel*. 82 85 86 88 89 90 91 95 96 ☆☆☆ **1991 £££**

***Marc*** [mahr] The residue of pips, stalks and skins left after the grapes are pressed – and often distilled into a fiery brandy of the same name, eg Marc de Bourgogne.

**Marches** [MAHR-kay] (Italy) Central wine region on the Adriatic coast, below Venice. Best known for *Rosso Conero* and good, dry, fruity **Verdicchio whites. Umani Ronchi; Garofoli; Fazi Battaglia.**

**Marcillac** [mah-see-yak] (South West France) Full-flavoured country reds, made principally from the *Fer* grape – they may also contain some *Cabernet* and *Gamay*.

**Maréchal Foch** [mah-ray-shahl fohsh] A hybrid vine producing red grapes in Canada and Eastern North America. *Inniskillin*.

**Margaret River** (Western Australia) Cool(ish) vineyard area on the coast of Western Australia, gaining notice for *Cabernet Sauvignon* and *Chardonnay*. Also Australia's only *Zinfandel*. White: **85 86 87** 88 90 91 93 94 95 Red: **80 82 83 85 86 87** 88 **90** 91 92 93 94 95 **Cape Mentelle; Moss Wood; Cape Mentelle; Leeuwin; Cullen; Pierro; Vasse Felix; Ch. Xanadu.**

**Margaux** [mahr-goh] (*Bordeaux*, France) Large *commune* with a concentration of *Crus Classés* including *Ch. Margaux, Palmer, Lascombes*. Sadly, other wines which should be deliciously blackberryish are variable, partly thanks to the diverse nature of the soil, and partly through the producers' readiness to sacrifice quality for the sake of yields. Curiously, though, if you want a good 1983, this vintage succeeded better here than elsewhere in the *Médoc*; 1995s look good too. Also worth hunting out are generic *Margaux from reputable négociants*. 70 75 **78** 81 **82 83 85 86** 88 89 90 94 95

**Ch. Margaux** [mahr-goh] (*Margaux 1st Growth*, *Bordeaux*, France) Peerless First Growth, back on form since the dull 1970s, and producing intense wines with cedary perfume and velvet softness when mature. The second wine, *Pavillon Rouge* (red and matching white) is worth buying too. **61 78 79 81** 82 83 84 85 86 87 88 89 90 91 **92** 93 94 95 96 ☆☆☆☆☆ **1990 ££££**

**Markham** (*Napa Valley*, California) A *Cabernet* and *Chardonnay* producer who looks like being one to watch. ☆☆☆☆ **1995 Barrel Fermented Napa Valley Chardonnay £££**

**Marlborough** [morl-buh-ruh] (New Zealand) An important wine area with cool climate in the South Island producing excellent *Sauvignon*, *Chardonnay* and improving *Merlot* and *Pinot Noir*, as well as a growing number of impressive sparkling wines. White: **89 91** 92 96 **Cloudy Bay, Hunter's, Vavasour, Jackson Estate, Cellier le Brun; Montana.**

**Marne et Champagne** [mahr-nay-shom-pan-y] (*Champagne*, France) A huge Cooperative which prefer to focus on those companies with more active public relations departments. Owns Besserat de Bellefon, *Lanson* and Alfred Rothschild labels, and seems to be able to provide really good own-label wines for U.K. merchant and supermaket buyers who are prepared to pay the price!

**Ch. Marquis-de-Terme** [mahr-kee duh tehrm] (*Margaux 4th Growth*, *Bordeaux*, France) Traditional property with quite tough wines. **81** 82 **83** 85 **86** 87 88 89 90 93.☆☆☆ **1990 £££**

**Marsala** [mahr-sah-lah] (*Sicily*, Italy) Dark, rich, fortified wine from *Sicily* essential for use in recipes such as Zabaglione. **De Bartoli; Pellegrino; Cantine Florio.**

**Marsannay** [mahr-sah-nay] (*Burgundy*, France) Northernmost village of the *Côte de Nuits* with a range of largely undistinguished but, for *Burgundy*, affordable *Chardonnay* and *Pinot Noir* (red and rosé). White: **79** 84 **85 86** 87 **88** 89 **90 92** 95 Red: 76 **78** 79 **80** 83 **85** 86 87 **88 89 90** 92 95 96 **Bruno Clair Louis Jadot.**

**Marsanne** [mahr-san] (*Rhône*, France) The grape usually responsible (in blends with *Roussanne*) for most of the northern *Rhône* white wines. Also successful in the *Goulburn Valley* in Victoria for *Ch. Tahbilk* and *Mitchelton* and in California for *Bonny Doon*. It has a delicate perfumed intensity when young and fattens out with age. Look out for un-oaked versions from Australia. **Tahbilk; Mitchelton; Bonny Doon; Guigal.**

**Martinborough** (New Zealand) Up-and-coming North Island region for *Pinot Noir* and *Chardonnay*. White: 87 88 **89 91** 92 **94** 96 Red: **83 85 87** 89 90 **91** 92 93 94 95 96 **Dry River; Ata Rangi; Palliser Estate.**

**Martinborough Vineyard** (*Martinborough*, New Zealand) Producer of the best Kiwi *Pinot Noir* and one of the best *Chardonnays*. Wines can be so Burgundian in style that the 1991 *Pinot Noir* was refused an export licence for being untypically "farmyardy" until a delegation of wine-loving politicians intervened. ☆☆☆☆ **1995 Chardonnay £££1996 Late Harvest Riesling £££**

**Bodegas Martinez Bujanda** [mahr-tee-neth boo-han-dah] (*Rioja*, Spain) New-wave producer of fruit-driven wines sold as *Conde de Valdemar*. Probably the most consistently recommendable producer in *Rioja*. ☆☆☆**1992 Milenio Rioja Reserva £££**

**Martini** (*Piedmont*, Italy) Good *Asti Spumante* from the producer of the vermouth house which invented 'lifestyle' advertising – still we're all guilty of something. ☆☆☆ **1996 Asti Fratelli Martini ££**

**Louis Martini** (*Napa Valley*, California) Grand old name with superlative long-lived *Cabernet* from the Monte Rosso vineyard.

**Martini & Rossi** (Italy) Good fizz to drink as an alternative to vermouth.

**Marzemino** [mahrt-zeh-mee-noh] (Italy) Spicy red grape producing black yet plummy wines from this now rarely used varietal. ☆☆☆☆ **1995 Letrari Trentino Marzemino ££**

**Mas Amiel** [mahs ah-mee-yel] (*Provence*, France) The producer of wonderful rich almost port-like wine, hailing from *Bandol* in the west of Provence. ☆☆☆ **1994 Maury ££**

**Mas de Daumas Gassac** [mas duh doh-mas gas-sac] (*Midi*, France) Ground-breaking *Vin De Pays* from *Herault*. Compared by some to top claret: its flavours come from an eclectic blend and its unique 'terroir'. Half a dozen varieties (including *Pinot Noir*, Syrah, Mourvedre and *Cabernet*) and a white blend including *Viognier*. Strangely approachable when young, then lasts for ages. ☆☆☆☆ **1995 Blanc ££££** ☆☆☆ **1992 Rouge £££**

**Bartolo Mascarello** [mas-kah-reh-loh] (*Piedmont*, Italy) Great ultra-traditional *Barolo* specialist whose rose-petally wine proves that the old ways can compete with the new.

**Giuseppe Mascarello** [mas-kah-reh-loh] (*Piedmont*, Italy) Top-class *Barolo* estate (unconnected with that of *Bartolo Mascarello*), producing characterful wine from individual vineyards. Great *Dolcetto*. ☆☆☆☆ **1993 Monprivato Falletto ££££**

**Masi** [mah-see] (*Veneto*, Italy) Producer with reliable, affordable reds and whites and single-vineyard wines which serve as a justification for *Valpolicella's* denomination. ☆☆☆☆ **1993 Amarone Valpolicella £££**

**Massandra** [mahsan-drah] (Crimea, CIS) Producer of good but not great *Cabernet* and source of great, historic, dessert wines which were sold at a memorable Sotheby's auction.

***Master of Wine (MW)*** One of a small number of people (around 250) internationally who have passed a gruelling set of trade exams.

**Mastroberadino** [maas tro be rah dino] (Campania, Italy) Top producer of great full wines from Italy's south ☆☆☆ **1993 £££**

**Matanzas Creek** [muh-tan-zuhs] (*Sonoma Valley*, California) Top-class complex *Chardonnay*, good *Sauvignon* and high-quality accessible *Merlot*. ☆☆☆☆ **1995 Sauvignon Blanc. ££££**

**Mataro** [muh-tah-roh] See *Mourvèdre*.

**Mateus** [ma-tay-oos] (Portugal) Highly commercial pink and white off-dry, *frizzante* wine made by *Sogrape*, sold in bottles traditional in *Franken*, Germany, and with a label depicting a palace with which the wine has no connection. A 50-year-old marketing masterpiece. ☆☆☆ **Mateus Rosé £**

**Thierry Matrot** [tee-yer-ree ma-troh] (*Burgundy*, France) Top-class white producer with great white and recommendable red *Blagny*. ☆☆☆☆ **1992 Meursault Les Charmes ££££**

**Matua Valley** [ma-tyoo-wah] (*Auckland*, New Zealand) Reliable maker of great (*Marlborough*) *Sauvignon*, (Judd Estate) *Chardonnay* and *Merlot*. Also producer of the even better *Ararimu* red and white. ☆☆☆☆ 1996 Hawkes Bay unoaked Chardonnay ££

**Yvon Mau** [ee-von moh] (*Bordeaux* & South West France) Highly commercial producer of *Bordeaux* and other, mostly white, wines from South-Western France. Occasionally good. ☆☆☆ 1996 Sauvignon Gris ££

**Ch. Maucaillou** [mow-kih-yoo] (*Moulis Cru Bourgeois, Bordeaux*, France) *Cru Bourgeois* in the *commune* of *Moulis* producing approachable wines to beat some *Crus Classés*. 75 82 83 85 86 88 89 90 92 93 94 95 ☆☆☆ 1992 £££

**Maule** [mow-lay] (Chile) Up-and-coming *Central Valley* region especially for white wines (Sauvignon in particular) but warm enough for red Santa Carolina; Carta Vieja

**Bodegas Mauro** [mow-roh] (Spain) Just outside the *Ribera del Duero DO*, but making very similar rich, red wines.

**Mauzac** [moh-zak] (France) White grape used in southern France for *Vin De Pays* and *Gaillac*. Can be characterful, wild, floral or dull and earthy.

**Mavrodaphne** [mav-roh-daf-nee] (Greece) Greek red grape and the wine made from it. Dark and strong, it needs ageing to be truly worth drinking. ☆☆☆ Mavrodaphne of Patras £

**Mavrud** [mah-vrood] (Bulgaria) Traditional red grape and the characterful, if rustic, wine made from it.

**Maximin Grünhaus** [mak-siee min groon-hows] (*Mosel-Saar-Ruwer*, Germany) 1,000-year-old estate with intense *Rieslings*. ☆☆☆☆ 1992 Abtsberg Riesling Spätlese, von Schubert £££

**Maxwell** (*McLaren Vale*, Australia) Reliable producer of intense *Shiraz* and Semillon. ☆☆☆☆ 1993 Semillon McLaren Vale ££

**Mayacamas** [mih-yah-kah-mas] (*Napa Valley*, California) Long-established winery on *Mount Veeder* with tannic but good *Cabernet* and long-lived, rich *Chardonnay*. ☆☆☆☆ 1994 Cabernet Sauvignon ££££

**McGuigan Brothers** (*Hunter Valley*, Australia) Commercial stuff from the former owners of *Wyndham Estate*. ☆☆☆☆ 1993 Bin 2000 Shiraz ££

**McLaren Vale** (South Australia) Region close to Adelaide renowned for European-style wines, but possibly too varied in topography, soil and climate to create its own identity. White: 86 87 88 90 91 94 95 Red: 80 82 84 85 86 87 88 90 91 94 95 See individual entries.

**McWilliams** (*Hunter Valley*, Australia) *Hunter Valley*-based, evidently non-republican firm with great, traditional ('Elizabeth') *Semillon* and ('Philip') *Shiraz* which are now sold younger than previously and so may need time. Fortified wines can be good, too, as are the pioneering *Barwang* and improved *Brand's* wines. Surprisinglly good at 'Bag-in-box' wines! ☆☆☆☆ 1994 Brand's Laira Cabernet Merlot £££

**Médoc** [may-dok] (*Bordeaux*, France) Area encompassing the region of *Bordeaux* south of the *Gironde* and north of the town of *Bordeaux* in which the *Cru Classés* as well as far more ordinary fare are made. Should be better than basic *Bordeaux* and less good than *Haut-Médoc*, which tend to have more flavour: experience however suggests that this is not always the case. 70 75 76 78 79 81 82 83 85 86 88 89 90 94 95

**Meerlust Estate** [meer-loost] (*Stellenbosch*, South Africa) One of the Cape's best estates. Classy *Merlots* and a highly rated *Bordeaux*-blend called 'Rubicon', both of which will hopefully one day benefit from being bottled on the estate rather than by the *Bergkelder* some time in the future. ☆☆☆☆ 1993 Pinot Noir £££

**Gabriel Meffre** [mef-fr] (*Rhône*, France) Sound, commercial *Rhône* and, now, southern French producer under the Galet Vineyards label. However still maintains a tradition of producing reliable more classy wines. ☆☆☆ **1995 Châteauneuf-du-Pape Laurus ££**

**Ch. Megyer** [meg-yer] (*Tokaji*, Hungary) French-owned pioneer of *Tokaji* and *Fürmint*.

**Melon de Bourgogne** [muh-lon duh boor-goyn] (France) Tricky grape imported from *Burgundy* (where it is no longer grown) to *Muscadet*, where some producers are still trying to comprehend why it can be so difficult to work with!

**Charles Melton** (*Barossa Valley*, Australia) Small-scale producer of lovely still and sparkling *Shiraz* and world-class rosé called 'Rosé of Virginia', as well as Nine Popes, a wine based on, and mistakenly named after, *Châteauneuf du Pape*. ☆☆☆☆ **1995 Shiraz Barossa Valley £££**

**Mendocino** [men-doh-see-noh] (California) Northern, coastal wine county successfully exploiting cool microclimates to make 'European-style' wines. Red: 84 **85** 86 87 **90 91** 92 93 95 White: **85 90 91** 92 95. **Fetzer; Scharffenberger**

**Mendoza** [men-doh-zah] (Argentina) Capital of a now up and coming-principal wine region. Source of good rich reds from firms producing traditional style reds but with more uplifting fruit. **Trapiche; Catena; St. Felicien; Finca Flichman; San Telmo.**

**Ménétou-Salon** [men-too sah-lon] · (*Loire*, France) Bordering on *Sancerre*, making similar if earthier, less pricy *Sauvignon*, as well as some decent *Pinot Noir. Henri Pellé* makes the best. White: 83 **85 86 88 89 90** 94 95 Red: **78** 81 83 **85** 86 **88 89 90** 95 ☆☆☆☆ **1996 Menetou Salon Blanc, Morogues Clos Ratiero ££**

**Dom. Méo-Camuzet** [may-oh-ka-moo-zay] (*Burgundy*, France) Brilliant *Côte de Nuits* estate with top-class vineyards and intense, oaky wines, made, until his retirement, by the great *Henri Jayer*. ☆☆☆☆ **1990 Nuits St. Georges Aux Boudots ££££**

***Mercaptans*** [mehr-kap-ton] See *Hydrogen Sulphide*.

**Mercier** [mehr-see-yay] (*Champagne*, France) Subsidiary or is it sister company of, *Moët & Chandon* and producer of improving but pretty commercial fizz. ☆☆☆ **Champagne Mercier Brut £££** ☆☆☆☆ **Champagne Mercier Demi-Sec £££**

**Mercurey** [mehr-koo-ray] (*Burgundy*, France) Village in the *Côte Chalonnaise*, where *Faiveley* makes high quality wine. Red: **78** 80 **85** 86 87 88 89 90 92 95 White: 84 **85 86** 87 **88** 89 **90 92** 95 ☆☆☆ **1993 Ch. de Mercey Premier Cru £££**

**Merlot** [mehr-loh] Red grape making soft, honeyed, even toffee-ish wine with plummy fruit, especially when planted in clay soil. Used to balance the more tannic *Cabernet Sauvignon* throughout the *Médoc*, where it is actually the most widely planted grape; as it is in *Pomerol* and *St. Emilion*, where clay also prevails. Also increasingly successful in the *Languedoc* in southern France as well as in California, especially for *Newton*, and in *Washington State*, *Chile* and Australia.

**Merricks Estate** (*Mornington Peninsula*, Australia). Small estate specialising in *Shiraz*. ☆☆☆☆ **1994 Shiraz**

**Geoff Merrill** (*McLaren Vale*, Australia) The ebullient mustachioed winemaker who has nicknamed himself 'The Wizard of Oz'. Impressive if restrained *Semillon, Chardonnay* and *Cabernet* in *McLaren Vale* under his own label, plus easier-going Mount Hurtle wines (especially the rosé). ☆☆☆☆ **1994 Mount Hurtle Shiraz ££**

🍷 **Merryvale** (*Napa Valley*, California) Starry winery with especially good Reserve and Silhouette *Chardonnay* and Profile *Cabernet*. ☆☆☆☆ **1992 Cabernet Sauvignon Napa Valley Profile**

***Méthode Champenoise*** [may-tohd shom-puh-nwahz] Term restricted to *Champagne* – and method used for all quality sparkling wines. Labour-intensive, because bubbles are made by secondary fermentation in bottle, rather than in a vat or by the introduction of gas. Bottles are individually given the '*dégorgémont process*' topped up and recorked!

***Methuselah*** Same size bottle as an *Imperiale* (six litres). Used in *Champagne*.

**Meursault** [muhr-soh] (*Burgundy*, France) Superb white *Burgundy*; the *Chardonnay* ideally showing off its nutty, buttery richness in full-bodied dry wine. Like *Nuits St. Georges* and *Beaune* it has no *Grands Crus* but great *Premiers Crus* such as Charmes, Perrières and Génévrières. There is a little red here too, some of which is sold as *Volnay-Santenots*. White: **79 85 86** 87 **88** 89 **90 92** 95 96 **Comte Lafon; Coche-Dury; Drouhin; Michelot; Ampeau; Jobard and Roulot.**

🍷 **Ch. de Meursault** [muhr-soh] (*Burgundy*, France) If on a trip to *Beaune worth a visit*. See *Patriarche*. ☆☆☆☆☆ **1994 Beaune Premier Cru £££**

**Mexico** See *Baja California*.

🍷 **Ch. Meyney** [may-nay] (*St. Estèphe Cru Bourgeois*, *Bordeaux*, France) Improving *St. Estèphe* property, with wines that are richer in flavour than some of its neighbours. **75 78** 79 81 **82** 83 85 86 87 88 89 90 94 95 96 ☆☆☆ **1993 ££££**

🍷 **Peter Michael** (*Sonoma*, California) UK-born Sir Peter Michael produces stunning *Sonoma* and California *Chardonnays*, *Sauvignons* and *Cabernets*. ☆☆☆☆ **1993 Cabernet Sauvignon 'Les Pavots', Knights Valley £££**

🍷 **Louis Michel et Fils** [mee-shel] (*Burgundy*, France) Top-class *Chablis* producer. ☆☆☆ **1993 Chablis Grand Cru Vaudésir ££££**

🍷 **Robert Michel** (*Rhône*, France) Produces softer *Cornas* than most from this sometimes tough '*Appellation*': beautiful strong yet silky wines. ☆☆☆☆ **1993 Cornas £££**

🍷 **Alain Michelot** [mee-shloh] (*Burgundy*, France) Producer of excep tionally perfumed, elegant *Nuits St. Georges*. These wines tend to drink earlier than some of their neighbours never mind less time to wait. ☆☆☆☆ **1993 Nuits-St-Georges Les Chaignots ££££** ☆☆☆☆ **1993 Nuits St. Georges Richemone ££££**

🍷 **Dom. Michelot-Buisson** [mee-shloh bwee-son] (*Burgundy*, France) One of the great old *Meursault* properties. A pioneer of estate bottling – and of the use of new oak. Wines are rarely subtle, but then they never lack typical *Meursault* flavour either. ☆☆☆☆ **1993 Meursault Les Genévrieres ££££**

**Michelsberg** [mikh-kels-buhrg] (*Mosel*, Germany) One of the largest *Grosslage*, known for the quantity of its production rather than the quality. A great deal of dull *Müller Thurgau* is sold as *Piesporter Michelsberg*. QbA/Kab/Spät; **85** 86 **88 89 90** 91 92 93 94 95 Aus/Beeren/TBA; **83 85** 88 89 90 91 92 93 94 95

🍷 **Mildara Blass** [mil-dah-rah] (South Australia) A highly dynamic company that recently bought *Rothbury*, having been itself acquired by *Fosters*. *Coonawarra* wines, including the very commercial Jamieson's Run, are best. Sometimes labels seem to resemble those of competitors' wines. Other subsidiaries include *Wolf Blass*, *Yellowglen* and *Balgownie*. .All in all an enormous varied portfolio of styles.☆☆☆☆ **1995 Wolf Blass Yellow Label Cabernet Sauvignon**

🍷 **Millton Estate** (*Auckland*, New Zealand) James Millton is an obsessive, not to say a masochist. He loves the hard-to-make *Chenin Blanc* and uses it to make first-class organic wine in *Gisborne*. Sadly it seems, most people would rather buy his *Chardonnay*. ☆☆☆☆ **1995 Semillon ££**

🍷 **Milmanda** [mil-man-dah] (*Conca de Barbera*, Spain) Torres' top label *Chardonnay*. Classy by any standards. ☆☆☆☆☆ **1995 £££**

🍷 **Kym Milne** Antipodean *Flying Winemaker* who has been quietly expanding his empire with great success, particularly with Vinfruco in *South Africa*; at Le Trulle in southern *Italy* and at *Nagyrede* in *Hungary*. ☆☆☆☆**1996 Vignetti di Caremia Chardonnay ££**

**Minervois** [mee-nehr-vwah] (South West France) Firm, fruity and improving suppertime reds – *Corbières*' sometimes (slightly) classier cousin.

***Mis en Bouteille au Ch./Dom.*** [mee on boo-tay] (France) Bottled at the estate.

🍷 **Ch. la Mission-Haut-Brion** [lah mee-see-yon oh-bree-yon] (*Pessac-Léognan Cru Classé*, *Bordeaux*, France) Tough but rich reds which rival, and in 1982 overtake, its supposedly classier neighbour *Haut-Brion*. **61 64 66 70 75 78 79** 80 **81 82 83** 84 **85** 86 87 88 89 90 91 92 93 94 95 96 ☆☆☆☆ **1992 ££££**

🍷 **Mitchell** (*Clare Valley*, Australia) Good producer of *Riesling* and of the Peppertree *Shiraz*, one of the *Clare Valley's* best reds. Also good for *Semillon* and one of those very Australian style wines a sparkling *Shiraz*. ☆☆☆☆ **1995 Shiraz Peppertree Vineyard ££**

🍷 **Mitchelton** (*Goulburn Valley*, Australia) A modern producer of *Marsanne* and *Semillon* which has recently been bought by *Petaluma*. *Late Harvest Rieslings* are also good, as is a *Beaujolais*-style red, known as Cab Mac. The Preece range – named after the former winemaker – is also well-worth seeking out. owing to their French style. ☆☆☆☆ **1994 Reserve Cabernet Sauvignon £££**

**Mittelhaardt** [mit-tel-hahrt] (*Pfalz*, Germany) Central and best *Bereich* of the *Rheinpfalz*. QbA/Kab/Spät: **85** 86 **88 89 90** 91 92 93 94 95 Aus/Beeren/TBA: **83 85** 88 89 90 91 92 93 94 95 96

**Mittelmosel** [mit-tel-moh-zuh] (*Mosel-Saar-Ruwer*, Germany) Middle and best section of the *Mosel*, including the *Bernkastel Bereich*. QbA/Kab/Spät: **85** 86 **88 89 90** 91 92 93 94 95 Aus/Beeren/TbA: **83 85** 88 89 90 91 92 93 94 95 96

**Mittelrhein** [mit-tel-rihne] (Germany) Small, northern section of the *Rhine*. Good *Rieslings* that are sadly rarely seen outside Germany. QbA/Kab/Spät: **85** 86 **88 89 90** 91 92 93 94 95 Aus/Beeren/TBA: **83 85** 88 89 90 91 92 93 94 95

🍷 **Mittnacht-Klack** [mit-nakt-clack] (*Alsace*, France) Seriously high-quality wines with particular accent on '*Vendage Tardive*' and *Late havest* wines. ☆☆☆☆ **1992 Gewuztraminer S.G.N. ££££**

***Moëlleux*** [mwah-luh] (France) Sweet.

🍷 **Moët & Chandon** [moh-wet ay shon-don] (*Champagne*, France) The biggest producer in *Champagne*. *Dom Pérignon*, the top wine, and *Vintage* Moët are reliably good and new *cuvées* of 'Brut Imperial Non-Vintage, show a welcome reaction to recent criticism of inconsistency. Watch out too for a good Brut Rosé. **Torre de Gall; Dom. Chandon; Green Point.** ☆☆☆☆ **1993 Torre del Gall Cava £££**

🍷 **Moillard** [mwah-yar] (*Burgundy*, France) Middle-of-the-road *négoçiant* whose best wines are sold under the 'Dom. Thomas Moillard' label. ☆☆☆ **1993 Côtes de Beaune Villages £££**

**Moldova** Young republic next to *Romania* whose vinous potential is being exploited by *Hugh Ryman* at the Hincesti winery.

**Monbazillac** [mon-ba-zee-yak] (South West France) *Bergerac AC* using the grapes of sweet *Bordeaux* to make improving alternatives to *Sauternes*. 88 89 90 95

🍷 **Ch. Monbousquet** [mon-boo-skay] (*St. Emilion Grand Cru Classé*, *Bordeaux*, France) Newly taken over and now producing rich, concentrated wines. The 1994 was specially successful. 78 79 82 **85** 86 88 89 90 92 93 94 95 ☆☆☆ **1993 Ch. Monbousquet, St. Emilion £££**

🍷 **Ch. Monbrison** [mon-bree-son] (*Margaux*, *Bordeaux*, France) Reliable, frequent over-performer. **78** 79 82 **85** 86 88 89 90 92 94 95 ☆☆☆☆ **1990 ££££**

🍷 **Mönchof** [moon-chof] (*Mosel*, Germany) Top *Mosel* producer with vineyards in *Urzig*.

🍷 **Ch. de Moncontour** [mon-con-toor] (*Loire*, France) One of the more recommendable – and affordable – sources of still and sparkling Vouvray. ☆☆☆ **1993 Vouvray Demi-Sec ££**

🍷 **Robert Mondavi** [mawn-dah-vee] (*Napa Valley*, California) Pioneering producer of great Reserve *Cabernet* and *Pinot Noir*, and back-on-form *Chardonnay*, and inventor of oaky *Blanc Fumé Sauvignon*. The Woodbridge wines – apart from the *Zinfandel* – are pleasant but less interesting. Co-owner of *Opus One* and now in a joint venture with *Caliterra* in Chile. ☆☆☆☆ **1993 Oakville District Cabernet Sauvignon £££**

🍷 **Mongeard-Mugneret** [mon-zhahr moon-yeh-ray] (*Burgundy*, France) A source of invariably excellent and sometimes stunningly exotic red *Burgundy*. ☆☆☆☆ **1993 Vosne-Romanée Suchots ££££**

🍇 **Monica (di Cagliari/Sardegna)** [moh-nee-kah] (*Sardinia*, Italy) Red grape and wine of Sardinia producing drily tasty and fortified spicy wine.

🍷 **Marqués de Monistrol** [moh-nee-strol] (*Catalonia*, Spain) Single-estate *Cava*. Also producing noble varietals.☆☆☆ **1993 Merlot £**

***Monopole*** [mo-noh-pohl] (France) Literally, exclusive – in *Burgundy* denotes single ownership of an entire vineyard.

🍷 **Mont Grasl** [mon gra] (*Rapel*,Chile) Relatively new outfit producing solidly reliable wines. ☆☆☆☆ **1996 Cabernet Merlot Reserve ££**

🍷 **Les Producteurs du Mont Tauch** [mon-tohsh] (*Midi*, France) Good southern cooperative with surprisingly good, top-of-the-range wines. ☆☆☆ **Rivesaltes Vin Doux Naturel NV ££**

**Montagne St. Emilion** [mon-tan-yuh san tay-mee-yon] (*Bordeaux*, France) A 'satellite' of *St. Emilion*. Often good-value reds which can outclass supposedly finer fare from *St. Emilion* itself. Drink young. **82 83 85** 86 **88 89** 90 94 95

**Montagny** [mon-tan-yee] (*Burgundy*, France) Tiny hillside *Côte Chalonnaise* commune producing good, lean *Chardonnay* that can be a match for many *Pouilly Fuissés*. *Premier Crus* are not from better vineyards; they're just made from riper grapes. White: 84 **85 86** 87 **88** 89 **90 92** 95 ***Antonin Rodet; Olivier Leflaivre; Caves de Buxy.***

**Montalcino** [mon-tal-chee-noh] (*Tuscany*, Italy) Village near Sienna known for *Brunello di Montalcino, Chianti's* big brother, whose reputation was largely created by the *Biondi Santi* estate whose wines no longer deserve the prices they command. *Rosso di Montalcino* is lighter. **78 79** 81 **82 85 88 90** 94 95.***Altesino; Frescobaldi; Banfi.***

🍷 **Montana** (*Marlborough*, New Zealand) Huge firm with tremendous *Sauvignons*, improving *Chardonnays* and good-value *Lindauer* and *Deutz Marlborough Cuvée* fizz. Reds still tend to be on the green side. Look out for the smartly packaged, single-estate wines such as the Brancott Sauvignon. ☆☆☆☆☆ **1996 Montana Reserve Chardonnay ££**

🍷 **Monte Real** [mon-tay ray-al] (*Rioja*, Spain) Made by Bodegas *Rioja*nos; generally decent, richly flavoured and tannic *Rioja*.

🍷 **Bodegas Montecillo** [mon-tay-thee-yoh] (*Rioja*, Spain) Classy wines including the oddly named Viña Monty. The Cumbrero Blanco white is good, too. ☆☆☆☆ **1987 Viña Monty Gran Reserva ££**

**Montée de Tonnerre** [mon-tay duh ton-nehr] (*Burgundy*, France) Excellent *Chablis Premier Cru*.

**Montefalco Sagrantino** [mon-teh-fal-koh sag-ran-tee-noh] (*Umbria*, Italy) Intense cherryish red made from the local Sagrantino grape.

🍷 **Ch. Montelena** [mon-teh-lay-nah] (*Napa Valley*, California) Its two long-lived *Chardonnays* (from *Napa* and the rather better *Alexander Valley*) make this one of the more impressive producers in the state. The vanilla-and-blackcurranty *Cabernet* is too impenetrable, however.

🍇 **Montepulciano** [mon-tay-pool-chee-yah-noh] (Italy) Confusingly, both a red grape used to make red wines in central and South-east Italy (Montepulciano *d'Abruzzi*, etc) and the name of a town in *Tuscany* (see *Vino Nobile di Montepulciano*).**Poliziano.**

**Monterey** [mon-teh-ray] (California) Underrated region south of San Francisco, producing potentially good if sometimes rather grassy wines. Red: 84 **85** 86 87 **90 91** 92 93 95 White: **85 90 91** 92 95 ***Jekel; Sterling Redwood Trail; Franciscan.***

🍷 **The Monterey Vineyard** (*Monterey*, California) Reliable, inexpensive varietal wines now under the Redwood Trail label. Go for the 'Classic' range. Beware of wines, the small print of whose labels reveal them to have been made in the 'Languedoc Region' in France. ☆☆☆ **1996 Pinot Noir ££**

🍷 **Viña Montes** [mon-tehs] (*Curico*, Chile) Go-ahead winery with improving reds (including the flagship Alpha) and improved *Sauvignon*. ☆☆☆☆ **1993 Montes Alpha Cabernet Sauvignon ££** ☆☆☆ **1996 Special Cuvée Chardonnay ££**

🍷 **Montevĩna** [mon-tay-veen-yah] (*Amador County*, California) Exceptionally good *Zinfandel* from *Amador County*, reliable *Cabernet*, *Chardonnay* and a *Fumé Blanc* to make *Robert Mondavi* weep. ☆☆☆ **1994 Napa Valley Chardonnay ££**

**Monthélie** [mon-tay-lee] (*Burgundy*, France) Often overlooked *Côte de Beaune* village producing potentially stylish reds and whites. The appropriately named Dom. Monthélie-Douhairet is the most reliable estate. White: **79** 84 **85 86** 87 **88** 89 **90 92** 95 Red: **78** 80 83 **85** 86 87 **88 89 90** 92 95 ***Dom.Monthélie-Douhairet; Jaffelin.***

**Montilla-Moriles** [mon-tee-yah maw-ree-lehs] (Spain) *DO* region producing Sherry-type wines in *Solera* systems, often so high in alcohol that fortification is unnecessary. Good examples easily match rather basic Sherry, offering better value for money.

🍷 **Dom. de Montille** [duh mon-tee] (*Burgundy*, France) A lawyer-cum-winemaker whose *Volnays* and *Pommards* are unusually fine and long-lived. Tend to be rather tough and astringent when young.☆☆☆☆ **1993 Volnay 1er Cru £££**

**Montlouis** [mon-lwee] (*Loire*, France) Neighbour of *Vouvray* making similar, lighter-bodied, dry, sweet and sparkling wines. 83 **85** **86** **88** **89** **90** 94 95 Sweet White: **76** 83 **85** 86 **88** **89** 90 94 95 ☆☆☆☆ **1996 Ch. Boulay de Cray ££**

**Le Montrachet** [luh mon-ra-shay] (*Burgundy*, France) Shared between the villages of *Chassagne* and *Puligny Montrachet*, with its equally good neighbours Bâtard-M, Chevalier-M, Bienvenue-Bâtard-M, Criots-Bâtard-M, potentially the greatest, biscuitiest white *Burgundy* – and thus dry white wine – in the world. Stars: *Drouhin*-Marquis de Laguiche, *Domaine de la Romanée-Conti*, *Sauzet*, *Comtes Lafon*. ☆☆☆☆☆ **1993 Etienne Sauzet ££££** ☆☆☆☆☆ **1993 Domaine Leflaive ££££** ☆☆☆☆☆ **1993 Domaine Comtes Lafon ££££**

**Ch. Montrose** [mon-rohz] (*St. Estèphe 2nd Growth*, *Bordeaux*, France) Back-on-form *St. Estèphe* renowned for its longevity. More typical of the *Appellation* than *Cos d'Estournel* but often less approachable in its youth. however, still maintains a rich tarry inky style. Especially good in 1994, though less so in 1995. **61** **64** 66 **70** **75** 76 78 79 81 **82** 83 84 85 86 87 88 89 90 91 92 93 94 95 ☆☆☆☆ **1993 ££££**

**Ch. Montus** [mon-toos] (South West France) Ambitious producer in *Madiran* with carefully oaked examples of *Tannat* and *Pacherenc de Vic Bilh*. Bouscassé is a cheaper, more approachable label. ☆☆☆ **1994 Madiran £££**

**Moondah Brook** (*Swan Valley*, Australia) An untypically (for the baking *Swan*) cool vineyard belonging to *Houghtons* (and thus *Hardys*). The stars are the wonderful, tangy *Verdelho* and richly oaky *Chenin Blanc*. The *Chardonnay* and reds are less impressive. ☆☆☆☆ **1996 Verdelho ££**

**Moorilla Estate** [moo-rillah] (*Tasmania*, Australia) Long-established, recently reconstituted estate with particularly good Riesling.

**Mór** [mohr] (Hungary) Hungarian town making clean, aromatic white wines from a blend including the *Traminer*.

**Morellino di Scansano** [moh-ray-lee-noh dee skan-sah-noh] (*Tuscany*, Italy) Amazing cherry and raspberry, young-drinking red made from a clone of *Sangiovese*. **Le Pupile**.

**Dom. Pierre Morey** [maw-ray] (*Burgundy*, France) Top-class producer known for concentrated wines.in good vintages. ☆☆☆☆ **1994 Meursault Les Narvaux £££**

**Bernard Morey et Fils** [maw-ray] (*Burgundy*, France) Top-class producer in *Chassagne Montrachet* with good individual vineyard wines here and in *St. Aubin*. ☆☆☆☆ **1993 Chassagne Montrachet 1er Cru Morgeots ££££**

**Morey St. Denis** [maw-ray san duh-nee] (*Burgundy*, France) Côtes de Nuits village which produces deeply fruity, richly smooth reds, especially the Grand Cru 'Clos de la Roche'. Best producer is Domaine Dujac, which virtually makes this '*Appellation*' it's own. Red: 76 **78** 79 **80** 82 83 **85** 86 87 **88** **89** **90** 92 95

**Morgon** [mohr-gon] (*Burgundy*, France) One of the ten *Beaujolais Crus*. Worth maturing, as it can take on a delightful chocolate/cherry character. **88** **89** 90 **91** 93 94 95 96 ***Sylvain Fessy, Georges Duboeuf (aka Marc Dudet) Jean Descombes.***

**Morio Muskat** [maw-ree-yoh moos-kat] White grape grown in Germany and Eastern Europe and making simple, grapey wine.

**Mornington Peninsula** (*Victoria*, Australia) Some of Australia's newest and most southerly vineyards on a perpetual upward crescent. Close to Melbourne and under threat from housing developers. Good *Pinot Noir*, minty *Cabernet* and juicy *Chardonnay*, though the innovative T'Galant is leading the way with other varieties. **T'Galant Stoniers Dromana.**

**Morris of Rutherglen** (*Rutherglen*, Australia) Extraordinarily successful producer of delicious *Liqueur Muscat* and *Tokay* (seek out the Show Reserve) and intense *Durif*,along with a sparkling version *Shiraz*. ☆☆☆☆ **1990 Morris Durif ££**

**Morton Estate** (Waikato, New Zealand) Top-class producer of *Sauvignon*, *Chardonnay* and *Loire*.and *Bordeaux*-style s. The wines accross the board are now reaching a far more appreciative audience. ☆☆☆☆ **1995 Black Label Chardonnay Reserve £££**

**Moscatel de Setúbal** [mos-kah-tel day say-too-bahl] (Portugal) see *Setúbal*. ☆☆☆☆ **1970 Setúbal Moscatel Superior ££££**

**Moscato** [mos-kah-toh] (Italy) The Italian name for *Muscat*, widely used across Italy in all styles of white wine from *Moscato d'Asti*, through the more serious *Asti Spumante*, to dessert wines like Moscato di Pantelleria.

**Moscato d'Asti** [mos-kah-toh das-tee] (Italy) Delightfully grapey, sweet and fizzy low alcohol wine from the *Muscat*, or *Moscato* grape. Far better (and cheaper) than designer alcoholic lemonade; it's more flavoursome. ☆☆☆ **Moscato d'Asti Bava £**

**Mosel-Saar-Ruwer** [moh-zuhl sahr roo-vuhr] (Germany) Region surrounding the rivers of its name.

**Mosel/Moselle** [moh-zuhl] (Germany) River and loose term for *Mosel-Saar-Ruwer* wines, equivalent to the '*Hock*' of the Rhine. Not to be confused with the uninspiring *Vins de Moselle* produced on the French side of the river. The wines tend have flavours of green fruits when young but develop a wonderful ripeness as they fill out with age. Arguably, the best wine region in Germany today. QbA/Kab/Spät: **85** 86 **88 89 90** 91 92 93 94 95 96 Aus/Beeren/TBA: **83 85** 88 89 90 91 92 93 94 95 96 ***Dr Loosen; J. J. Chriastobel; E. Jakoby-Mathy; Freiher von Heddesdorff; Willi Haag; Heribert Kerpen; Weingut Karlsmuhle; Karp-Schreiber; Immich Batterieberg.***

**Moselblumchen** [moh-sel-bloom-chen] (*Mosel*, Germany) *Mosel-Saar-Ruwer* equivalent to the Rhine's *Liebfraumilch*. Basic stuff, but. there can be some exceptions.

**Vins de Moselle** [van duh moh-zell] (Eastern France) Neighbouring *Alsace*; once full of vines and generally dull wine. There are now a mere 70 hectares planted.

**Lenz Moser** [lents moh-zur] (Austria) Big producer with a range including crisp dry whites and luscious dessert wines. Once very famous but blighted by the glycol scandel from which Austria has taken some time to recover: the wines are right back on top form. ☆☆☆ **1996 Blauer Zweigelt ££**

**Moss Wood** (*Margaret River*, Australia) Pioneer producer of *Pinot Noir* and *Cabernet* and *Semillon*. The wines have long cellaring potential and have a very French feel to them. The *Semillon* is reliably good in both its oaked and un oaked form; while the *Chardonnay* is big and forward but in a slightly less blousy way than normal. ☆☆☆☆ **1995 Cabernet Sauvignon Reserve £££**

**La Motte Estate** [la mot] (*Franschhoek*, South Africa) Best known for top *Shiraz*. ☆☆☆ **1996 Sauvignon Blanc ££**

**JP Moueix** [mwex] (*Bordeaux*, France) Top-class *négoçiant*/producer, Christian *Moueix*, specialises in *Pomerol* and *St. Emilion* and is responsible for *Pétrus, La Fleur-Pétrus, Bel Air,* Richotey and *Dominus* in California.

**Moulin Touchais** [moo-lan too-shay] (*Loire*, France) Producer of intensely honeyed, long-lasting, sweet white from *Coteaux du Layon*.

**Moulin-à-Vent** [moo-lan-na-von] (*Burgundy*, France) One of the ten *Beaujolais Crus* – big and rich at its best and, like *Morgon,* can benefit from a few years' ageing. **85 87 88 89** 90 **91** 93 94 95 ***Duboeuf; Degrange; Paul Janin.***

**Ch. Moulin-à-Vent** [moo-lan-na-von] (*Moulis Cru Bourgeois*, *Bordeaux*, France) Leading *Moulis* property. **82** 83 **85** 86 89 90 94

**Moulis** [moo-lees] (*Bordeaux*, France) Red wine village of the *Haut-Médoc*; often paired with *Listrac,* but making far more approachable, good-value *Crus Bourgeois*. 76 **78** 79 81 **82** 83 **85 86** 88 89 90 **94** 95 **Ch. Chasse-Spleen, Ch. Maucaillou.**

**Mount Barker** (Western Australia) Cooler climate southern region with great *Riesling, Verdelho,* impressive *Chardonnay* and restrained *Shiraz*. White: **87** 88 90 91 93 94 95 Red: **80 82 83 85 86 87** 88 **90** 91 92 93 94 95 96 **Plantagenet, Goundrey, Howard Park.**

**Mount Hurtle** (*McLaren Vale*, South Australia) See Geoff Merrill.

**Mount Langi Ghiran** [lan-gee gee-ran] (*Victoria*, Australia) A maker of excellent cool-climate *Riesling*, peppery *Shiraz* and very good *Cabernet*. ☆☆☆☆☆ **1995 Shiraz, Grampians £££**

**Mount Mary** (*Yarra Valley*, Australia) Dr Middleton makes *Pinot Noir* and *Chardonnay* that are astonishingly and unpredictably *Burgundy*-like in the best and worst sense of the term. The clarety Quintet blend is more reliable.

**Mount Veeder** (*Napa Valley*, California) Convincing hillside *Appellation* where Mount Veeder Winery, Ch. Potelle, *Hess Collection* and *Mayacamas* all produce impressive reds. Red: 84 **85** 86 87 **90 91** 92 93 95 White: **85 90 91** 92 95 96

**Mountadam** (*Eden Valley*, Australia) Son of *David Wynn*; Adam makes classy Burgundian *Chardonnay* and *Pinot Noir* (both still and sparkling) and an impressive blend called 'The Red'. Also worth seeking out are the *Eden Ridge* organic wines and the fruity *David Wynn* range, especially the unoaked *Chardonnay*. ☆☆☆☆ **1995 Mountadam Riesling ££**

**Mourvèdre** [mor-veh-dr] (*Rhône*, France) Floral-spicy *Rhône* grape usually found in blends. Increasingly popular in France and California where, as in Australia, it is called *Mataro*. ***Bandol; Jade Mountain; Penfolds; Ridge.***

***Mousse*** [mooss] The bubbles in *Champagne* and sparkling wines.

***Mousseux*** [moo-sur] (France) Sparkling – generally cheap and unremarkable.

**Mouton Cadet** [moo-ton ka-day] (*Bordeaux*, France) A brilliant commercial invention by Philippe de Rothschild who used it to profit handsomely from the name of *Mouton Rothschild,* with which it has no discernible connection. The white, though better than in the past, has even less of a raison d'être. ☆☆☆ **1994 Bordeaux Rouge ££**

**Ch. Mouton-Baronne-Philippe** [moo-ton ba-ron-fee-leep] (*Pauillac 5th Growth*, *Bordeaux*, France) *Pauillac* fifth growth now renamed *Ch. Armailhac*.

**Ch. Mouton-Rothschild** [moo-ton roth-child] (*Pauillac 1st Growth, Bordeaux*, France) Brilliant First Growth *Pauillac* with gloriously complex flavours of roast coffee and blackcurrant. Since the early 1980s, equal to the best in the *Médoc*, though some prefer the less obvious, less oaky style of *Lafite*. **61 62 66 70 75** 76 78 79 81 82 83 85 86 87 88 89 90 91 92 93 94 95 ☆☆☆☆☆ 1990 ££££

**Mudgee** [mud-zhee] (*New South Wales*, Australia) Australia's first *Appellation* region, though heaven knows why. Although now, this high-altitude, isolated area is making far better wines than the robust, often clumsy stuff it used to. Rothbury; Botobolar.

**Bodegas Muga** [moo-gah] (*Rioja*, Spain) Producer of good old-fashioned *Riojas*, of which Prado Enea is the best. ☆☆☆ 1991 Rioja Tinto ££

**Mulderbosch** [mool-duh-bosh] (*Stellenbosch*, South Africa) South Africa's answer to *Cloudy Bay*: exciting *Sauvignon* and *Meursault*-like *Chardonnay*, not to mention a delicious red blend called Faithful Hound. ☆☆☆☆ 1996 Sauvignon Blanc.

**Weingut Müller-Catoir** [moo-luh kah-twah] (*Pfalz*, Germany) Great, new-wave producer using new-wave grapes as well as *Riesling*. Wines of all styles are impeccable and packed with flavour. Search out powerful Grauburgunder, Rieslaner and Scheurebe wines. ☆☆☆☆☆ 1993 Haardter Herrenletten Riesling Spätlese ££

**Egon Müller-Scharzhof** [moo-luh shahtz-hof] (*Mosel-Saar-Ruwer*, Germany) Top-class *Saar* producer. ☆☆☆☆ 1993 Scharzhofberger Riesling Kabinett £££

**Müller-Thurgau** [moo-lur-toor-gow] (Germany) Workhorse white grape, a *Riesling* x *Sylvaner* cross – also known as *Rivaner* – making much unremarkable wine in Germany, but yielding some gems for producers like *Muller Catoir*. Very successful in England.

**Mumm/Mumm Napa** [murm] (*Champagne*, France) Maker of slightly improved Cordon Rouge *Champagne* and far better *Cuvée Napa* from California. ☆☆☆ 1991 Cuvée Napa Vintage £££

**Réné Muré** [moo-ray] (*Alsace*, France) Producer of full-bodied wines, especially from the Clos St. Landelin vineyard. ☆☆☆☆ Crémant d'Alsace Cuvée Prestige ££

**Murfatlar** [moor-fat-lah] (Romania) Major vineyard and research area that is having increasing success with *Chardonnay*.

**Murphy-Goode** (*Alexander Valley*, California) Excellent *Chardonnays*. Classy producer of quite Burgundian style whites which sell at – for California – affordable prices. ☆☆☆☆ 1995 Fumé Blanc ££

**Murray River Valley** (Australia) The area ranging between Victoria and New South Wales producing much of the Antipodes' cheapest wine – a great deal of which is to be found in UK retailers' own-label bottles.

**Bodegas Marqués de Murrieta** [mar-kays day moo-ree-eh-tah] (*Rioja*, Spain) Until recently the best old-style oaky white (sold as Castillo Ygay), though recent efforts have been disappointing. The red, at its best, is one of the most long-lived elegant *Riojas* – look out for the old Castillo Ygays from the 1960s with their distinctive old-stlye labels. ☆☆☆☆ 1989 Ygay Reserva £££

**Murrumbidgee** [muh-rum-bid-zhee] (New South Wales, Australia) Area formerly known for bulk dessert wines, now improving irrigation and vinification techniques to make good table wines and some stunning *Botrytis*-affected sweet wines. De Bortol; Kingston Estate; Lindemans.

**Ch. Musar** [moo-sahr] (Ghazir, Lebanon) *Serge Hochar* makes a different red every year, varying the blend of *Cabernet*, *Cinsault* and *Syrah*. The style veers wildly between *Bordeaux*, the *Rhône* and Italy, but there's never a risk of becoming bored. Good vintages easily keep for a decade. The *Chardonnay*-based whites are less than dazzling, though. **70 75** 77 78 **79 82** 83 85 **86** 88 89

**Muscadelle** [mus-kah-del] Spicy ingredient in white *Bordeaux*, aka *Tokay* in Australia.

**Muscadet** [moos-kah-day] (*Loire*, France) Often dull. When good, (which, sadly, is rare) they are clean, yeasty, slightly sparkling and fresh. New legislation and a new 'Côtes de Grandlieu' *Appellation* may improve matters. *Sur Lie* should be better. See also *Sèvre-et-Maine*. 94 95 96 ***Dom. de Chasseloir; Pierre Luneau.***

**Muscat** [mus-kat] Generic name for a species of white grape (aka *Moscato* in Italy) of which there are a number of different sub-species.

**Muscat à Petits Grains** [moos-kah ah puh-tee gran] Aka *Frontignan*, the best variety of Muscat and the grape responsible for *Muscat de Beaumes de Venise, Muscat de Rivesaltes, Asti Spumante, Muscat of Samos, Rutherglen* Muscats and dry *Alsace* Muscats.

**Muscat of Alexandria** [moos-kah] Grape responsible for *Moscatel de Setúbal, Moscatel de Valencia* and sweet South Australians. Also known as *Lexia*, and in South Africa it satisfies the sweet tooth of much of the Afrikaner population as *Hanepoot*.

**Muscat Ottonel** [moos-kah ot-oh-NEL] Muscat variety grown in Middle and Eastern Europe.

**Musigny** [moo-zee-nyee] (*Burgundy*, France) Potentially wonderful but more often disappointing *Grand Cru* from which *Chambolle Musigny* takes its name. 76 **78** 79 **80** 82 83 **85** 86 87 **88 89 90** 92 95 ***De Vogüé***

**Dom. Mussy** [moos-see] (*Burgundy*, France) Top-class, tiny *Pommard* estate with concentrated wines from that village, *Beaune* and *Volnay*. ☆☆☆☆ **1992 Beaune Les Montrevenots £££**

***Must*** Unfermented grape juice.

**MW** See *Master of Wine*.

# N

**Nackenheim** [nahk-ehn-hime] (*Rheinhessen*, Germany) Village in the *Nierstein Bereich*, sadly best known for its debased *Grosslage*, Gütes Domtal. QbA/Kab/Spät: **85** 86 **88 89 90** 91 92 93 94 95 96 Aus/Beeren/TBA: **83 85** 88 89 90 91 92 93 94 95 96. **Gunderloch; Heinrich Seip; Kürfurstenhof.**

**Nahe** [nah-huh] (Germany) *Anbaugebiet* producing wines which can combine delicate flavour with full body. QbA/Kab/Spät: **85** 86 **88 89 90** 91 92 93 94 95 Aus/Beeren/TBA: **83 85** 88 89 90 91 92 93 94 95 96 **Kruger-Rumpf; Schlossgut; Diel; Hermann Donnhoff; Hehner Kiltz.**

**Ch. Nairac** [nay-rak] (*Sauternes Deuxième Cru Classé, Bordeaux*, France) Delicious, long-lasting *Sauternes* from a classed growth estate. 75 **76** 80 81 **83** 85 86 88 89 90 95 96 ☆☆☆☆ **1990 ££££**

**Naoussa** [nah-oosa] (Greece) Region producing dry red wines, often from the Xynomavro grape.

**Napa** [na-pa] (California) Named after the American-Indian word for 'plenty', this is a region with plentiful wines ranging from ordinary to sublime. Too many are hyped; none is cheap. In the future, *Appellations* within *Napa*, such as *Carneros, Stag's Leap* and *Mt Veeder*, and other nearby regions (like *Sonoma*) will take greater prominence when it is realised that parts of the county will never make spectacular wine. Red: 84 **85** 86 87 **90 91** 92 93 94 95 96 White: **85 90 91** 92 95 96. **Atlas Peak; Sutter Home; Geyser Peak; Montevina; Mumm; Sebastiani.**

**Nautilus Estate** [naw-tih-luhs] (*Marlborough*, New Zealand) *Yalumba's* New Zealand offshoot. Great fizz and *Sauvignon*. ☆☆☆☆☆ **Cuvée Marlborough Brut £££**

**Navajas** [na-VA-khas] (*Rioja*, Spain) Small producer making reds and oaky whites worth keeping. ☆☆☆ **1992 Tinto Crianza ££**

**Navarra** [na-VAH-rah] (Spain) Northern *DO*, traditionally renowned for rosés and heavy reds but now producing wines to rival those from neighbouring *Rioja*, where prices are often higher. Look for innovative *Cabernet Sauvignon* and *Tempranillo* blends. **81** 82 **83 85 87** 89 90 91 92 94 95 96 **Ochoa; Guelbenzu; Senorio de Sarria; Chivite; Nekeas; Palacio de la Vega.**

**Nebbiolo** [neh-bee-oh-loh] (*Piedmont*, Italy) Grape of *Piedmont*, producing wines with tarry, cherryish, spicy flavours that are slow to mature but become richly complex – epitomised by *Barolo* and *Barbaresco*. Quality and style vary enormously depending on soil. Aka *Spanna*. **Mascarello; Gaja; Vajra; Fontanafredda; Conterno.**

**Nederburg** [neh-dur-burg] (*Paarl*, South Africa) Huge commercial producer. Edelrood is a fair red blend; but the Edelkeur *Late Harvest* wines are the gems of the cellar. Sadly, the best wines are only sold at the annual Nederburg Auction, one of the major events of the South African social calendar. ☆☆☆☆ **1995 Pinotage ££**

**Neethlingshof Estate** [neet-lihngs-hof] (*Stellenbosch*, South Africa) *Late Harvest* wines are impressive. Others need work. ☆☆☆☆ **1993 Shiraz ££**

***Négociant*** [nay-goh-see-yon] (France) (Eléveur) Merchant who buys (matures) and bottles wine.

***Négociant-manipulant (NM)*** [ma-nih-pyoo-lon] (*Champagne*, France) Buyer and blender of wines for *Champagne*, identifiable by the NM number which is mandatory on the label.

**Negroamaro** [nay-groh-ah-mah-roh] (*Puglia*, Italy) A Puglian grape that produces warm, gamey reds. Found in *Salice Salentino* and *Copertino*. ☆☆☆ **1988 Rosso del Salento Notarpanaro ££**

**Bodegas Nekeas** [nek-ay-as] (*Navarra*, Spain) Producers of top-class French-style *Merlot* and *Chardonnay*. ☆☆☆ **1996 Barrel Fermented Chardonnay ££**

**Nelson** (New Zealand) Small region, a glorious bus-ride to the north-west of *Marlborough*. *Neudorf* and *Redwood Valley* are the stars. White: **89 91** 94 96 Red: **87 89** 90 **91 92** 94 95

**Nemea** [nur-may-yah] (Peleponnese, Greece) Improving cool(ish) climate region for reds made from the Agiorgitiko grape. **Tsantalis; Kouros; Boutari.**

**Ch. La Nerthe** [nurf] (*Rhône*, France) One of the most exciting estates in *Châteauneuf-du-Pape* producing rich wines with seductive dark fruit. ☆☆☆☆ **1992 Cuvée Les Cadettes £££**

**Ch. Nenin** [nay-nan] (*Pomerol, Bordeaux*, France) A rising star since 1993. 82 83 **85** 86 87 88 89 90 93 94 95 ☆☆☆☆☆ **1993 £££**

**Neuchâtel** [nur-sha-tel] (Switzerland) Lakeside region. Together with Les Trois Lacs a source of good red and rosé, *Pinot Noir* and *Chasselas* and *Chardonnay* whites. Ch. d'Auvernier and Porret.

🍷 **Neudorf** [noy-dorf] (*Nelson*, New Zealand) Pioneering small-scale producer of beautifully made *Chardonnay*, *Semillon*, *Riesling* and *Pinot Noir*. ☆☆☆☆☆ 1993 Moutere Pinot Noir £££

**Neusiedlersee** [noy-zeed-lur-zay] (Austria) *Burgenland* region on the Hungarian border. Great *Late Harvest* and improving whites and reds. *Willi Opitz*.

***Nevers*** [nur-vehr] (France) Subtlest oak – from a forest in *Burgundy*.

**New South Wales** (Australia) Major wine-producing state which is home to the famous *Hunter Valley*, along with the *Cowra, Mudgee, Orange* and *Murrumbidgee* regions. White: **85 86 87 88** 90 **91** 94 95 96 Red: **82** 83 **85 86 87 88** 90 91 93 94 95 96

**New York State** (USA) See *Finger Lakes* and *Long Island*.

**New Zealand** Superstar nation with proven *Sauvignon Blanc* and *Chardonnay* and increasingly successful reds. See *Marlborough, Martinborough, Hawkes Bay, Gisborne, Auckland*. White: **89 91** 94 96 Red: **87 89** 90 **91 92** 94 95

🍷 **Newton Vineyards** (*Napa Valley*, California) High-altitude vineyards with top-class *Chardonnay, Merlot* and *Cabernet*, now being made with help from *Michel Rolland*. ☆☆☆☆ 1993 Unfiltered Merlot £££

🍷 **Ngatarawa** [na-TA-ra-wah] (*Hawkes Bay*, New Zealand) Small superstar winery with impressive reds and even better *Chardonnays* and *Late Harvest* whites. ☆☆☆☆ 1994 Ngatarawa Alwyn Chardonnay £££

🍷 **Nicholson River** (Gippsland, Australia) The temperamental *Gippsland* climate ensures that this estate has a frustratingly small production, however its efforts have been repaid over and over by stunning *Chardonnays* ☆☆☆☆ 1993 Chardonnay £££

🍷 **Niebaum-Coppola** [nee-bowm coh-po-la] (*Napa Valley*, California) You've seen the movie. Now taste the wine. The 'Dracula' and 'Godfather' director's own estate now includes the appropriately Gothic *Inglenook* winery, has some of the oldest vines around and makes intensely concentrated *Cabernets* to suit the patient. ☆☆☆☆ 1991 Rubicon Napa Valley £££

🍷 **Niederhausen Schlossböckelheim** [nee-dur-how sen shlos-bok-ehl-hime] (*Nahe*, Germany) State-owned estate producing highly concentrated *Riesling* from great vineyards.

🍷 **Dom. Michel Niellon** [nee-el-lon] (*Burgundy*, France) Estate ranking consistently among the top five white *Burgundy* producers and making elegant and amazingly concentrated wines. ☆☆☆☆ 1993 Chassagne-Montrachet £££

🍷 **Niepoort** [nee-poort] (*Douro*, Portugal) Small, independent, port house making subtle *Vintage* and particularly impressive *Colheita* tawnies. A name to watch. ☆☆☆ 1991 Redoma £££

**Nierstein** [neer-stine] (*Rheinhessen*, Germany) Village and (with *Piesport*) *Bereich* best known in the UK. Some fine wines, obscured by the notoriety of the reliably dull Niersteiner Gütes Domtal. QbA/Kab/Spät: **85** 86 **88 89 90** 91 92 93 94 95 Aus/Beeren/TBA: **83 85** 88 89 90 91 92 93 94 95 96 *Balbach; Gunderloch*.

🍷 **Weingut Nikolaihof** [nih-koh-li-hof] (*Niederösterreich*, Austria) One of the producers of some of the best *Grüner Veltliners* and *Rieslings* in Austria. ☆☆☆☆ **1992 Riesling Smaragd Wachau Von Stein.**

🍷 **Nipozzano** [nip ots zano] (*Tuscany*, Italy) Chianti estate. ☆☆☆☆ **1993 Reserva ££**

**Nitra** [neet-ra] (Slovakia) Promising hilly region, especially for *Pinots Blanc, Gris* and *Noir.*

🍷 **Nobilo** [nob-ih-loh] (Huapai, New Zealand) Family-owned firm making good oaky *Chardonnay* from *Gisborne* and a pleasant commercial off-dry *White Cloud* blend.

***Noble rot*** Popular term for *Botrytis Cinerea.*

🍷 **Normans** (*McLaren Vale*, Australia) Well-established *Cabernet* and *Shiraz* specialist. ☆☆☆☆ **1993 Clarenden Shiraz £££**

**North-East Victoria** (Australia) The region is split between rich *liqueur Muscat* producers of *Rutherglen* and *Glenrowan* and the cooler climate viticulture region as seen used by Brown Bros. Grapes range from Cabernet, Riesling, Chardonnay to Muscat. White: **86 87 88 90 91 92 94 95** 96 Red: 80 **82** 84 **85 86 87 88 90 91 92** 94 95 96 **Morris; Chambers; Baileys; Brown Bros.**

🍷 **Bodega Norton** [naw-ton] (Argentina) One of Argentina's most recommendable producers, producing a wide range of varietal wines ☆☆☆☆ **1994 Malbec ££**

🍷 **Ch. Notton** [not-ton] (*Margaux*, *Bordeaux*, France) The *Second Label* of *Ch. Brane-Cantenac*

***Nouveau*** [noo-voh] New wine, most popularly used of *Beaujolais.*

🍷 **Quinta do Noval** (*Douro*, Portugal) Fine and potentially finer estate.The ultra-rare Nacional *Vintage* ports are the jewel, made from ungrafted vines. ☆☆☆☆ **1982 Colheita Port ££**

🍷 **Albet i Noya** [al-bet-ee-noy-ya] (Spain) Innovative producer with red and white traditional and imported varieties. A future Spanish superstar? ☆☆☆ **1993 Col Leccio Macabeu ££**

**Nuits-St.-Georges** [noo-wee san zhawzh] (*Burgundy*, France) *Commune* producing the most claret-like of red Burgundies, properly tough and lean when young but glorious in age. Whites are good but ultra-rare. 76 78 79 **80** 82 83 **85** 86 87 **88 89 90** 92 95 96 **Dom. de l'Arlot; Daniel Rion; Jean Grivot or Alain Michelot.**

🍷 **Nuragus di Cagliari** [noo-rah-goos dee ka-lee-yah-ree] (*Sardinia*, Italy) Good-value, tangy, floral wine from the Nuragus grape.

***NV*** Non-vintage, meaning a blend of wines from different years.

# O

🍷 **Oakville Ranch** (*Napa Valley*, California) Potentially one of the Napa's most exciting red wine producers, but wines have so far been a little too tough. ☆☆☆☆ **1992 Cabernet Sauvignon Napa Valley.**

***Oaky*** Flavour imparted by oak casks which will vary depending on the source of the oak (American is more obviously sweet than French). Woody is usually less complimentary.

🍷 **Bodegas Ochoa** [och-OH-wah] (*Navarra*, Spain) New-wave producer of creamy, fruitily fresh *Cabernet*, *Tempranillo* and *Viura.* ☆☆☆☆ **1990 Navarra Tinto Reserva ££**

**Ockfen** [ok-fehn] (*Mosel-Saar-Ruwer*, Germany) Village producing some of the best, steeliest wines of the *Saar-Ruwer Bereich*, especially *Rieslings* from the *Bockstein* vineyard. QbA/Kab/Spät: **85** 86 **88 89 90** 91 92 93 94 95 Aus/Beeren/TBA: **83 85** 88 89 90 91 92 93 94 95 ☆☆☆ **1992 Ockfener Bockstein Kabinett, Reichsgraf von Kesselstadt ££**

***Oechsle*** [urk-slur] (Germany) Scale used to indicate the sugar levels in grapes or wine.

***Oenology/ist*** The science of wine/one who advises winemakers.

**Oeste** [wes-teh] (Portugal) Western region in which a growing number of fresh, light, commercial wines are being made, of which the most successful has undoubtedly been *Arruda*. **80 85 88 90 91 92 93** 94 95

**Oesterich** [ur-strihckh] (*Rheingau*, Germany) Source of good *Riesling*. QbA/Kab/Spät: **85** 86 **88 89 90** 91 92 93 94 95 Aus/Beeren/TBA: **83 85** 88 89 90 91 92 93 94 95 **Wegeler Deinhar; Balthazar Ress.**

🍷 **Michel Ogier** [ogee-yay] (*Rhône*, France) Less muscular wines from this excellent Côte Rôtie producer. ☆☆☆☆ **1991 *Côte Rôtie* ££**

***Oïdium*** [oh-id-ee-yum] Fungal grape infection, shriveling them and turning them grey.

🍷 **Bodegas Olarra** [oh-lah-rah] (*Rioja*, Spain) Unexceptional producer whose whites are reliably and pleasantly adequate. ☆☆☆ **1990 Añares £**

***Olasz Rizling*** [oh-lash-riz-ling] (Hungary) Local term for the inferior *Welschriesling*.

🍷 **Ch. d'Olivier** [oh-liv-ee-yay] (*Pessac-Léognan Cru Classé*, *Bordeaux*, France) An underperformer which has yet to join the *Graves* revolution. Red: 82 83 85 86 88 89 90 91 94 95 White: 90 92 93 94 96 ☆☆☆ **1991 Red £££**

***Oloroso*** [ol-oh-roh-soh] (*Jerez*, Spain) Style of full-bodied Sherry, that is either dry or Semi-sweet.

**Oltrepó Pavese** [ohl-tray-poh pa-vay-say] (*Lombardy*, Italy) *Lombardy DOC* made from local grapes including the characterfully spicy red Gutturnio and white Ortrugo. Fugazza is the big name. **Vinocurore.** ☆☆☆☆☆ **1995 Vinocurore La Botte no. 18 Selezzione Cabanon ££**

🍷 **Omar Khayyam (Champagne India)** [oh-mah-ki-yam] (Maharashtra, India) *Champagne*-method wine which, when drunk young, has more than novelty value. The producer's cheeky name, '*Champagne* India' is a source of considerable annoyance to the Champenois, but they, in the shape of *Piper Heidsieck*, were happy enough to sell the Indians their expertise. Besides, *Moët* and *Mumm* still shamelessly sell their South American wines as 'Champaña' and 'Champanha'.

**Ontario** (Canada) The best wine region in *Canada*, with over 80 per cent of Canada's wine being produced here. Look out for bottles with *VQA* stickers which guarantee quality and provenance. ☆☆☆☆ **1994 St. David's Bench Chardonnay ££** ☆☆☆☆ **1994 Paul Bosc Estate Icewine ££££ Pillitierri; *Inniskillin*.**

🍷 **Willi Opitz** [oh-pitz] (*Neusiedlersee*, Austria) Odd-ball pet food-manufacturer-turned-producer of a magical mystery tour of *Late Harvest* and straw-dried wines, including an extraordinary *Botrytis* red briefly labelled – to the discomfort of some Californians – 'Opitz One'. Opitz recently released a soothing CD of his wines fermenting in cask, presumably allowing fans to decide whether or not they reckon them to be 'sound'. ☆☆☆☆☆ **1995 Gewürztraminer Trockenbeerenauslese £££**

**Oppenheim** [op-en-hime] (*Rheinhessen*, Germany) Village in *Nierstein Bereich* best known – unfairly – for unexciting wines from the Krottenbrunnen. Elsewhere produces soft wines with concentrated flavour. QbA/Kab/Spät: **85** 86 **88 89 90** 91 92 93 94 95 Aus/Beeren/TBA: **83 85** 88 89 90 91 92 93 94 95 96

**Opus One** (*Napa Valley*, California) Co-production between *Mouton Rothschild* and *Robert Mondavi*. Classy and very claret-like wine; decidedly more successful so far than *Dominus*, but it will have to be so to justify the price. The Opus One winery, excavated into land to the side of the main road through Napa, has been described as the world's most expensive hole in the ground. Mind you, they never suspected they'd hit water down there. ☆☆☆☆☆ **1993 ££££**

**Orange** (*New South Wales*, Australia) Recently developed coolish region which, with *Cowra*, is likely to eclipse the *Hunter Valley* as a major quality wine region of this state. For a taste of things to come, try the classy Orange *Chardonnay* made by Philip Shaw of *Rosemount* from vineyards of which he is the proud co-owner. White: **85 86 87 88** 90 **91** 94 95 ☆☆☆☆ **1994 Rosemount Orange Vineyard Chardonnay ££**

**Orange Muscat** Another highly eccentric member of the Muscat family, best known for dessert wines in California by *Quady* and in Australia for the delicious *Brown Brothers Late Harvest* Orange Muscat and *Flora*.

**Oregon** (US) Fashionable, cool-climate, American wine-producing state whose bearded, be-sandled winemakers, have been known to grow marijuana as keenly as their speciality, *Pinot Noir*. The *Chardonnays* are even less successful, thanks to the planting of a late-ripening clone as recommended by experts from California. Red: 85 88 **89 90** 91 92 94 95 White: **85 88 89 90 91 92 94** 95 **Drouhin; Argyle.**

**Oriachovitza** [oh-ree-ak-hoh-vit-sah] (Bulgaria) Major source of reliable *Cabernet Sauvignon* and *Merlot*. ☆☆☆ **1992 Special Reserve Cabernet £**

**Orlando** (South Australia) Huge, French-owned (Pernod-Ricard) producer of the world-beating and surprisingly reliable *Jacob's Creek* wines. The RF range is good but the harder-to-find Gramps and Flaxmans wines are more exciting, as are the 'Saints' series. **Lawsons, Jacaranda Ridge** ☆☆☆☆☆ **1991 Jacaranda Ridge Cabernet Sauvignon £££**

**Orléanais** [aw-lay-yo-nay] (*Loire*, France) A vineyard area around Orléans in the Central Vineyards region of the *Loire*, specialising in unusual white blends of *Chardonnay* and *Pinot Gris*, and reds of *Pinot Noir* and *Cabernet Franc*. White: 83 **85 86 88 89 90** 94 95 Red: 81 83 **85** 86 **88 89 90** 95

**L' Ormarins Estate** [aw-mur-rins] (*Franschhoek*, South Africa) One of South Africa's should-do-better properties – only the *Shiraz* and the *Bordeaux* blend – Optima – consistently impress. ☆☆☆☆ **1989 Optima.**

**Ch. Les Ormes-de-Pez** [awm dur-pay] (*St. Estèphe Cru Bourgeois*, *Bordeaux*, France) Often underrated stable-mate of *Lynch Bages* and made with similar skill. **75** 78 79 **81 82 83** 85 86 87 88 89 90 92 93 94 95. ☆☆☆☆ **1990 ££££**

**Tenuta dell'Ornellaia** [teh-noo-tah del-aw-nel-li-ya] (*Tuscany*, Italy) *Bordeaux*-blend *Super-Tuscan* from the brother of *Pierro Antinori*. This is serious wine that is worth maturing. ☆☆☆☆ **1993 Ornellaia ££££**

**Ortega** [aw-tay-gah] Recently developed variety, and grown in Germany and England, though rarely to tasty advantage. *Biddenden* makes a good one, however, as does *Denbies*, which uses it to produce *Late Harvest* wine. ☆☆☆ **1995 Denbies Noble Harvest £££**

**Orvieto** [ohr-vee-yet-toh] (*Umbria*, Italy) White Umbrian *DOC* responsible for a quantity of dull wine. Orvieto *Classico* is better. Look out for *Secco* if you like your white wine dry; *Amabile* if you have a sweet tooth. **Antinori; Bigi; Covio Cardetto.**

**Osbourne** [os-sbaw-nay] (*Jerez*, Spain) Producer of a good range of sherries including a brilliant *Pedro Ximenez*.

**Dom. Ostertag** [os-tur-tahg] (*Alsace*, France) Poet and philosopher Andre Ostertag presides over this superb Alsace domaine. **1994 Fronshol Riesling ££**

***Oxidation*** The effect (usually detrimental, occasionally – as in Sherry – intentional) of oxygen on wine.

***Oxidative*** The opposite to *reductive*. Certain wines – most reds, and whites like *Chardonnay* – benefit from limited exposure to oxygen during their fermentation and maturation, such as barrel ageing.

**Oyster Bay** (*Marlborough*, New Zealand) See entry for *Delegats*. ☆☆☆ **1996 Sauvignon Blanc ££**

# P

**Paarl** [pahl] (South Africa) Warm region in which *Backsberg* and *Boschendal* make a wide range of appealing wines. Hotter and drier than neighbouring *Stellenbosch*. Red: **82 84** 86 **87** 89 **91 92** 93 94 95 White: **87 91** 92 93 94 95 **Charles Back; KWV; Backsberg.**

**Pacherenc du Vic-Bilh** [pa-shur-renk doo vik beel] (South West France) Dry or fairly sweet white wine made from the *Petit* and *Gros Manseng*. A speciality of *Madiran* growers. Very rarely seen, worth trying. ☆☆☆☆☆ **1995 Brumaire, Alain Brumont ££**

**Padthaway** [pad-thah-way] (South Australia) Vineyard area just north of *Coonawarra* specialising in *Chardonnay* and *Sauvignon*, though reds work well here too. White: **90 91 94** 95 96 Red: **86 87** 88 **90 91** 94 95 96 **Penfolds; Lindemans; Hardys.**

**Pagadebit di Romagna** [pah-gah-deh-bit dee roh-man-ya] (*Emilia-Romagna*, Italy) Dry, sweet and fizzy whites from the Pagadebit grape.

**Bodegas Palacio** [pa-las-see-yoh] (*Rioja*, Spain) Underrated *Bodega* with stylish fruit-driven reds and distinctively oaky whites, Also helped by wine guru *Michel Rolland*. ☆☆☆☆ **1995 Cosme Palacio Rioja Red ££**

***Palate*** The taste of a wine.

**Palatinate** [pa-lah-tih-nayt] (Germany) Obsolete term for the *Pfalz*. QbA/Kab/Spät: **89 90** 92 93 94 95 Aus/Beeren/TBA: 89 90 91 92 93 94

**Palazzo Altesi** [pah-lat-see-yoh al-tay-see] (*Tuscany*, Italy) Oaky, pure *Sangiovese Super-Tuscan* by *Altesino*.

**Palette** [pa-let] (*Provence*, France) *AC* rosé and creamy white, well liked by holidaymakers in St. Tropez who are so used to extortionate prices for cups of coffee that they don't notice paying more for a pink wine than for a serious claret. The white, which can be very perfumed, is better value.

🍷 **Palliser Estate** [pa-lih-sur] (*Martinborough*, New Zealand) Source of classy *Sauvignon Blanc* and *Chardonnay* from *Martinborough*. ☆☆☆☆ **1996 Martinborough Sauvignon Blanc ££**

🍷 **Ch. Palmer** [pahl-mur] (*Margaux 3rd Growth*, *Bordeaux*, France) Wonderfully perfumed Third Growth *Margaux* which stands alongside the best of the *Médoc* and often outclasses its more highly ranked neighbours. The 1983s are a good buy – more than can be said for most *Médocs* of that vintage. **61** 62 **66 70 71 75** 76 **78 79** 80 82 **83** 84 85 86 87 **88 89** 90 91 92 93 94 95 ☆☆☆☆ **1993 ££££**

🍷 **Palo Cortado** [pah-loh kaw-tah doh] (*Jerez*, Spain) A rare Sherry pitched between an *Amontillado* and an *Oloroso*. ☆☆☆☆ **Valdespino Palo Cortado del Carascal ££**

🍇 **Palomino** [pa-loh-mee-noh] (*Jerez*, Spain) White grape responsible for virtually all fine sherries – and almost invariably dull white wine, when unfortified. Also widely grown in South Africa as a workhorse white grape.

🍷 **Ch. Pape-Clément** [pap klay-mon] (*Pessac-Léognan Cru Classé*, *Bordeaux*, France) Great source of rich reds since the mid 1980s and, more recently, small quantities of peach-oaky white. Red: **61** 70 **75** 83 85 **86** 88 89 90 93 94 95 ☆☆☆☆ **1993 Rouge ££££**

🍷 **Parducci** [pah-doo-chee] (*Mendocino*, California) Steady producer whose *Petite Sirah* is a terrific bargain. ☆☆☆☆☆ **1994 Petite Sirah.**

🍇 **Parellada** [pa-ray-yah-dah] (*Catalonia*, Spain) Essentially dull grape used for *Cava*. At its best in *Torres*' Viña Sol, but more thanks to winemaking than to any innate quality.

🍷 **Dom. Parent** [pa-ron] (*Burgundy*, France) *Pommard*-based grower/*négociant,* which includes Thomas Jefferson among its former clients. Wines are quite old-fashioned too, but attractively so in their fruit-packed way.

🍷 **Dom. Alain Paret** [pa-ray] (*Rhône*, France) Producer of a great Condrieu, in partnership with one of the world's best-known wine makers. (Though, to be fair, Gérard Dépardieu does owe his fame to the cinema rather than his efforts among the vines). ☆☆☆ **1995 Lys de Volan ££££**

🍷 **Parker Estate** (Coonawarra, Australia) A small producer sharing its name with the US guru ,and calling its red 'First Growth'. Marks for cheek and good wine. ☆☆☆☆ **1991 Terra Rossa Cabernet ££**

***Pasado/Pasada*** [pa-sah-doh/dah] (Spain) Term applied to old or fine *Fino* an *Amontillado* sherries. Worth seeking out.

🍷 **C J Pask** [pask] (*Hawkes Bay*, New Zealand) *Cabernet* pioneer with excellent *Chardonnay* and *Sauvignon*. One of New Zealand's very best. ☆☆☆☆☆ **1995 Cabernet Hawkes Bay £££**

**Paso Robles** [pa-soh roh-blays] (*San Luis Obispo*, California) Warmish, long-established region, good for *Zinfandel* (especially *Ridge*), *Rhône* and Italian varieties. Plus increasingly successful *Chardonnays* and *Pinots*. Red: **85** 86 87 **90 91** 92 93 95 White: **85 90 91** 92 95 96

🍷 **Pasqua** [pas-kwah] (*Veneto*, Italy) Producer of fairly priced, reliable, wines. ☆☆☆ **1994 Valpolicella Vigneti Casterna £**

***Passetoutgrains*** [pas-stoo-gran] (*Burgundy*, France) Wine supposedly made from two-thirds *Gamay*, one third *Pinot Noir* – though few producers respect these proportions. Once the Burgundians' daily red – until they decided to sell it and drink cheaper wine from other regions.

🍷 **Passing Clouds** (*Bendigo*, Australia) 'We get clouds here, but it never rains ...' Despite a fairly hideous label, this is one of Australia's most serious red blends. Worth keeping. ☆☆☆☆ **1992 Ben's Shiraz-Cabernet £££**

***Passito*** [pa-see-toh] (Italy) Sweet, raisiny wine, usually made from sun-dried Erbaluce grapes in Italy. This technique is now used in Australia by *Primo Estate*.

🍷 **Ch. Patache d'Aux** [pa-tash-doh] (*Médoc Cru Bourgeois*, *Bordeaux*, France) Traditional, toughish stuff. **83** 85 88 **89** 90 93 95 ☆☆☆ **1993 £££**

🍷 **Frederico Paternina** [pa-tur-nee-na] (*Rioja*, Spain) Ernest Hemingway's favourite *Bodega* – which is probably the only reason to buy its wine nowadays. ☆☆☆ **1995 Banda Azul Rioja Tinto ££**

🍷 **Luis Pato** [lweesh-pah-toh] (*Bairrada*, Portugal) One of Portugal's rare superstar winemakers, proving, amongst other things, that the *Baga* grape can make first-class spicy, berryish red wines. ☆☆☆ **1995 Quinta do Riberinho ££**

🍷 **Patriarche** [pa-tree-arsh] (*Burgundy*, France) Huge merchant whose name is not a watchword for great *Burgundy*. The *Ch. de Meursault* domaine, however, produces good *Meursault*, *Bourgogne* Blanc, *Volnay* and *Beaune*. Has a particular interest in the Marché du Vin in *Beaune*, a show-piece excuse to taste and make your own mind up about the various nuances of the taste of *Burgundy*.

🍷 **Patz & Hall** (*Napa Valley*, California) The maker of delicious, unashamedly full-flavoured *Chardonnays*. ☆☆☆☆ **1994 Chardonnay Napa Valley £££**

🍷 **Pauillac** [poh-yak] (*Bordeaux*, France) One of the four famous '*communes*' of the *Médoc*, Pauillac is the home of Châteaux *Latour*, *Lafite* and *Mouton Rothschild*, as well as the two *Pichons* and *Lynch Bages*. The epitome of full-flavoured, blackcurranty *Bordeaux*; very classy (and pricy) wine. 70 75 76 **78** 79 81 **82** 83 **85 86** 88 89 90 94 95 96

🍷 **Neil Paulett** [paw-let] (South Australia) Small, top-flight *Clare Valley Riesling* producer. ☆☆☆☆ **1995 Polish Hill River Riesling ££**

🍷 **Dr Pauly-Bergweiler** [pur-gwi-lur] (*Mosel-Saar-Ruwer*, Germany) Ultra-modern winery with good, modern *Riesling*. ☆☆☆☆ **1995 Beerenauslese Mosel-Saar-Ruwer Bernkasteler Lay.**

🍷 **Ch. Pavie** [pa-vee] (*St-Emilion Premier Grand Cru Classé*, *Bordeaux*, France) Classy, impeccably made, plummily rich but complex *St. Emilion* wines. 70 78 **79** 81 **82 83** 85 **86** 87 **88 89 90** 91 93 94 95 96 ☆☆☆☆☆ **1990 ££££**

🍷 **Ch. Pavie-Decesse** [pa-vee dur-ses] (*St. Emilion Grand Cru Classé*, *Bordeaux*, France) Neighbour to *Ch. Pavie*, but a shade less impressive. 82 83 85 86 88 89 90 92 94 95 96 ☆☆☆ **1993 £££**

🍷 **Le Pavillon Blanc de Ch. Margaux** [pa-vee-yon blon] (*Bordeaux*, France) The (rare) *Sauvignon*-dominated white wine of *Ch. Margaux* which still acts as the yardstick for the growing number of *Médoc* white wines. 85 86 89 90 92 95 ☆☆☆☆ **1993 Pavillon Blanc ££££**

🍷 **Ca' del Pazzo** [kah-del-pat-soh] (*Tuscany*, Italy) Ultra-classy oaky *Super-Tuscan* with loads of ripe fruit and oak.

**Pécharmant** [pay-shar-mon] (South West France) In the *Bergerac* area, producing light, *Bordeaux*-like reds. Worth trying.

🍇 **Pedro Ximénez (PX)** [peh-droh khee-MEH-nes] (*Jerez*, Spain) White grape, dried in the sun to create a sweet, curranty wine, which is used in the blending of the sweeter Sherry styles, and in its own right by *Osbourne*, and by *Gonzalez Byass* for its brilliant Noe. Also produces a very unusual wine at *De Bortoli* in Australia. ☆☆☆☆☆ **Hildago Pedro Ximénez Viejo ££**

🍷 **Viña Pedrosa** [veen-ya pay-droh-sah] (*Ribera del Duero*, Spain) Modern wine showing what the *Tempranillo* can do when blended with the classic *Bordelais* varieties. The Spanish equivalent of a *Super-Tuscan*.

🍷 **Clos Pegase** [kloh-pay-gas] (*Napa Valley*, California) Showcase winery with generally overpraised wines. ☆☆☆ **1992 Merlot Napa Valley £££**

🍷 **Dom. Henry Pellé** [on-ree pel-lay] (*Loire*, France) Reliable producer of fruitier-than-usual *Ménetou-Salon*. ☆☆☆ **1994 Menetou-Salon £££**

🍷 **Pelorus** [pe-law-rus] (*Marlborough*, New Zealand) Showy, big, buttery, yeasty, almost Champagnois-style New Zealand fizz from *Cloudy Bay* – the top exponents, according to some, for quality Sauvignon Blanc in this part of the world. ☆☆☆☆ **1992 £££**

***Pelure d'Oignon*** [pur-loor don-yon] (France) 'Onion skin': orangey-brown tint of some rosé – including ones that have lost their freshness.

**Pemberton** (Western Australia) Up-and-coming cooler climate region for more restrained styles of *Chardonnay* and *Pinot Noir;* one to watch out for in the future.

**Penedés** [peh-neh-dehs] (*Catalonia*, Spain) Largest *DOC* of *Catalonia* with varying altitudes, climates and styles ranging from *Cava* to still wines pioneered by *Torres* and others, though some not as successfully. The use of noble varietals such as *Cabernet Sauvignon*, *Merlot* and *Chardonnay* allows a far more French expression of winemaking without losing intrinsic Spanish Character. Belatedly beginning to live up to some of its early promise. White: **91** 94 95 Red: **85 87** 88 89 90 **91** 93 94 95 96 **Torres; Leon; Freixenet.**

**Penfolds** (South Australia) The world's biggest premium wine company with a high quality from Bin 2 to *Grange*. Previously a red wine specialist but now becoming a rapidly skilful producer of still white wines, and classy sparklers. See *Wynns, Seaview, Rouge Homme, Lindemans, Tullochs, Leo Buring, Seppelt,* and now James Halliday's *Coldstream Hills* and *Devil's Lair* in the *Margaret River.* ☆☆☆☆ **1992 Bin 28 Kalimna Shiraz ££** ☆☆☆☆ **Bin 707 Cabernet Sauvignon £££**

**Penley Estate** (*Coonawarra*, Australia) High-quality *Coonawarra* estate with rich *Chardonnay* and very blackcurranty *Cabernet*. ☆☆☆☆ **1991 Cabernet Sauvignon £££**

**Comte Peraldi** [peh-ral-dee] (*Corsica*, France) High-class *Corsican* wine producer, now also making good wine in Romania. ☆☆☆☆ **1993 Dom. Comte Peraldi, Ajaccio ££**

**Le Pergole Torte** [pur-goh-leh taw-teh] (*Tuscany*, Italy) Long-established pure *Sangiovese*, oaky *Super Tuscan*. ☆☆☆☆☆ **1987 Montevertine ££**

**Periquita** [peh-ree-kee-tah] (Portugal) Spicy, tobaccoey grape – and the wine *J M da Fonseca* makes from it.

***Perlé/Perlant*** [pehr-lay/lon] (France) Lightly sparkling.

***Perlwein*** [pehrl-vine] (Germany) Sparkling wine.

**Pernand-Vergelesses** [pehr-non vehr-zhur-less] (*Burgundy*, France) *Commune* producing rather jammy reds but fine whites, including some *Côte d'Or* best buys. White: **85 86** 87 **88** 89 **90 92** 95 Red: **78** 83 **85** 87 **88 89 90** 92 95 **Jadot; Pavelot; Rapet Dom. Rollin.**

**André Perret** (*Rhône*, France) Producer of notable *Condrieu* and decent *St. Joseph*. ☆☆☆☆☆ **1995 Vintage £££**

**Joseph Perrier** [payh-ree-yay] (*Champagne*, France) Long-lasting, elegant *Champagnes* with a heavy *Pinot Noir* influence. ☆☆☆☆**1989 Cuvée Royale Brut ££££**

**Perrier-Jouët** [payh-ree-yay zhoo-way] (*Champagne*, France) Sometime underperforming *Champagne* house which, like Mumm, curiously enough belongs to Canadian distillers, Seagram. Sidestep the non-vintage for the genuinely worthwhile – and brilliantly packaged – Belle Epoque prestige fizz. ☆☆☆☆ **1989 Belle Epoque ££££**

**Pesquera** [peh-SKEH-ra] (*Ribera del Duero*, Spain) *Robert Parker* dubbed this the *Ch. Pétrus* of Spain. Well, maybe. I'd say it''s a top-class *Tempranillo* often equal to *Vega Sicilia* and the best of *Rioja*. ☆☆☆☆ **1993 Tinto ££**

**Pessac-Léognan** [peh-sak LAY-on-yon] (*Bordeaux*, France) *Graves commune* containing most of the finest châteaux. **Ch. Fieuzal, Domaine de Chevalier, La Louvière, Haut Brion, Smith Haut Laffite.**

**Petaluma** [peh-ta-loo-ma] (*Adelaide Hills*, Australia) High-tech creation of *Brian Croser*. Classy *Chardonnays* from Piccadilly in the *Adelaide Hills, Clare Rieslings* (particularly good *Late Harvest*) and *Coonawarra* reds. ☆☆☆☆☆ **1995 Piccadilly Valley Chardonnay £££**

***Pétillant*** [pur-tee-yon] Lightly sparkling.

**Petit Chablis** [pur-tee shab-lee] (*Burgundy*, France) (Theoretically) less fine than plain *Chablis* – though plenty of vineyards that were previously designated as Petit Chablis can now produce wines sold as *Chablis*. Often poor value. **90** 92 94 95 96 **La Chablisienne.**

***Petit Château*** [pur-tee sha-toh] (*Bordeaux*, France) Loose term for minor property.

**Petit Verdot** [pur-tee vehr-doh] (*Bordeaux*, France) Spicy, tannic variety used in small proportions in red *Bordeaux*, California (rarely) and now Italy, and Spain. **Marquès de Griñon**.

**Ch. Petit Village** [pur-tee vee-lahzh] (*Pomerol*, *Bordeaux*, France) Classy, intense, blackcurranty-plummy *Pomerol*. Worth keeping. **75** 78 79 81 **82** 83 **85** 86 87 88 89 90 93 94 95 96 ☆☆☆☆ **1989 ££££**

**Petite Sirah** [peh-TEET sih-RAH] Red grape grown in California and Mexico and as *Durif* in the *Midi* and Australia. Nothing to do with the *Syrah* but can produce lovely, spicy red. **Ridge, Fetzer, Morris, Parducci**

***Petrolly*** A not unpleasant overtone often found in mature *Riesling*.

**Ch. Pétrus** [pay-trooss] (*Pomerol*, *Bordeaux*, France) Until recently the priciest of all *clarets* (until *Le Pin* came along). Ultra-voluptuous *Pomerol*, which hits the target especially well in the US, and is finding a growing market in the Far East. **61** 62 **64** 66 **67 70 71 75** 76 78 **79** 81 82 83 84 85 86 **87** 88 89 90 92 93 94 95 96 ☆☆☆☆☆ **1989 ££££**

**Pewsey Vale** [pyoo-zee vayl] (*Adelaide Hills*, Australia) Classy cool-climate wines from winery associated with *Yalumba* and *Hill-Smith* and *Heggies*. ☆☆☆☆ **1994 Cabernet Sauvignon ££**

**Ch. de Pez** [dur pez] (*St. Estèphe Cru Bourgeois*, *Bordeaux*, France) Good, rather than great, traditional *St. Estèphe*. **78** 81 **82** 83 85 86 88 89 90 93 94 95 ☆☆☆ **£££**

**Pfalz** [*Pfaltz*] (Germany) Formerly known as the *Rheinfalz*, and before that as the *Palatinate*. Warm, southerly *Anbaugebiet* noted for riper, spicier *Riesling*. Currently the best of Germany's wine regions. QbA/Kab/Spät: **85** 86 **88 89 90** 91 92 93 94 95 96 Aus/Beeren/TBA: **83 85** 88 89 90 91 92 93 94 95 ***Lingenfelder; Müller-Cattoir.***

**Pfeffingen** [pfef-fing-gen] (*Pfalz*, Germany) Good place to find impeccably made *Riesling* and *Scheurebe*. QbA/Kab/Spät: **88 89 90** 91 92 93 94 95 96 Aus/Beeren/TBA: **83 85 88 89 90** 91 92 93 94 95 96

**Ch. Phélan-Ségur** [fay-lon say-goor] (*St. Estèphe Cru Bourgeois*, *Bordeaux*, France) A good-value property since the mid-1980s, with ripe, well-made wines. **82** 85 86 87 88 89 90 92 93 94 95. ☆☆☆ **1993 ££**

**Joseph Phelps** (*Napa Valley*, California) Pioneer Napa user of *Rhône* varieties (*Syrah* and *Viognier*), and a rare source of *Late Harvest Riesling*. *Cabernet* is a strength. ☆☆☆☆ **1993 Insignia Napa Valley ££££**

**Philipponnat** [fee-lee-poh-nah] (*Champagne*, France) Small producer famous for Clos des Goisses, but also notable for *Vintage* and rosé.

***Phylloxera Vastatrix*** [fih-lok-seh-rah] Root-eating louse that wiped out Europe's vines in the 19th century. Foiled by grafting *vinifera* vines onto resistant American *labrusca* rootstock. Pockets of pre-Phylloxera and/or ungrafted vines still exist in France (in a *Bollinger* vineyard and on the south coast – the louse hates sand), Portugal (in *Quinta da Noval*'s 'Nacional' vineyard), Australia and Chile. Elsewhere, a (supposedly) new breed – 'Phylloxera B' – has devastated *Napa Valley vines* planted on insufficiently resistant rootstock.

**Piave** [pee-yah-vay] (*Veneto*, Italy) *DOC* in *Veneto* region, including reds made from a *Bordeaux*-like mix of grapes.

**Ch. Pibarnon** [pee-bah-non] (*Bandol*, France) Top-class producer of modern Bandol. 88 **89** 90 92 93 ☆☆☆☆☆ **1993 £££**

**Ch. Pibran** [pee-bron] (*Pauillac Cru Bourgeois, Bordeaux*, France) Small but high quality and classically *Pauillac* property. 88 **89** 90 92 94 95 ☆☆☆☆ **1990 £££**

**Ch. Pichon-Lalande** [pee-shon la-lond] (*Pauillac 2nd Growth, Bordeaux*, France) The new name for Pichon Longueville-Lalande. Famed *Super Second* and tremendous success story, thanks to top-class wine-making and the immediate appeal of its unusually high *Merlot* content. A great 1996. **61** 62 66 **70 75** 76 **78 79 81 82 83** 84 **85** 86 87 88 89 90 91 92 93 94 95 ☆☆☆☆ **1989 ££££**

**Ch. Pichon-Longueville/Pichon Baron** [pee-shon long-veel/ba-ron] (*Pauillac 2nd Growth, Bordeaux*, France) New name for Pichon-Longueville-Baron. An under-performing Second Growth *Pauillac* until its purchase by *AXA* in 1988. Now level with, and sometimes ahead of, *Ch. Pichon-Lalande*, once the other half of the estate. Wines are intense and complex. Les Tourelles, the *Second Label*, is a good value alternative. **82** 83 85 86 87 88 89 90 91 92 93 94 95 ☆☆☆☆ **1992 ££££**

**Picolit** [pee-koh-leet] (*Friuli*, Italy) Grape, used to make both sweet and dry white wine. *Jermann* makes a good one. ☆☆☆☆ **1988 Di Capriva, Pighin ££££**

**Piedmont/Piemonte** [pee-yed-mont/pee-yeh-mon-tay] (Italy) Ancient and modern north-western region producing old-fashioned, tough *Barolo* and *Barbaresco* and brilliant modern fruit-packed wines. Also *Oltrepo Pavese, Asti Spumante* and *Dolcetto d'Alba.* See *Nebbiolo, Gaja, Altare, Mascarello, Conterno, Vajra, Bava.* Red: 78 79 82 **85 88** 89 90 93 94 95 96 White: 94 95 96

**Pieropan** [pee-yehr-oh-pan] (*Veneto*, Italy) *Soave*'s top producer, which more or less invented single vineyard wines here and is still a great exception to the dull Soave rule. ☆☆☆☆ **1995 Soave Classico Superiore Vigneto La Rocca ££**

**Pierro** [pee-yehr-roh] (*Margaret River*, Australia) Small estate producing an unusually rich, buttery, *Meursault*-like *Chardonnay.* ☆☆☆☆ **1995 Chardonnay £££**

**Piesport** [pees-sport] (*Mosel-Saar-Ruwer*, Germany) Produced in the *Grosslage – Michelsberg*, a region infamous for dull German wine and bought by people who think themselves above *Liebfraumilch.* Try a single vineyard – Gunterslay or Goldtröpchen – for something more memorable. QbA/Kab/Spät: **85** 86 **88 89 90** 91 92 93 94 95 96 Aus/Beeren/TBA: **83** 85 88 89 90 91 92 93 94 95 96 **Reichsgraf von Kesselstadt.**

**Pikes** (South Australia) Top-class *Clare* estate with especially good *Riesling* and *Shiraz*, and unusually successful *Sauvignon*. ☆☆☆☆ **1992 Shiraz**

**Ch. Le Pin** [lur pan] (*Pomerol, Bordeaux*, France) Ultra-hyped, tiny, recently formed estate whose – admittedly delicious – wines sell at increasingly silly prices to 'collectors' in the US and the Far East. The fore-runner of a string of other similar honey-traps (see *Ch. Valandraud* and *la Mondotte*), and one of the wines that is helping to create a burgeoning trade in forged bottles. **81 82 83 85** 86 87 88 89 90 92 93 94 95 95 ☆☆☆☆☆ **1990 ££££**

**Pineau de la Loire** [pee-noh dur la lwah] (*Loire*, France) Local name for the *Chenin Blanc*

**Pinot Bianco** [pee-noh-bee-yan-koh] (Italy) Aka *Pinot Blanc*. Found mostly in Northern Italy, it is sometimes misleadingly sold as *Chardonnay*.

**Pinot Blanc** [pee-noh blon] Rather like *Chardonnay* without all that fruit, and rarely as classy or complex. Fresh, creamy and adaptable. At its best in *Alsace* (*Pinot d'Alsace*), the *Alto-Adige* in Italy (as Pinot Bianco), and in Germany and Austria (as *Weissburgunder*). In California, a synonym for *Melon de Bourgogne* and quite widely planted in Eastern Europe. Zind-Humbrecht

**Pinot Chardonnay** (Australia) Misleading name for *Chardonnay*, still used by *Tyrrells*. Don't confuse with *Pinot Noir/Chardonnay* fizz blends.

**Pinot Gris** [pee-noh gree] (*Alsace*, France) White grape of uncertain origins, making full, rather heady, spicy wine. Best in *Alsace* (also known as *Tokay d'Alsace*), Italy (as *Pinot Grigio*) and Germany (as *Rülander* or *Grauburgunder*). Zind–Humbrecht; Cave de Turckheim.

**Pinot Meunier** [pee-noh-mur-nee-yay] (*Champagne*, France) Dark pink-skinned grape. Plays an unsung but major role in *Champagne*. Can also be used to produce a still varietal wine. Bests; Randall Grahm; Bonny Doon; William Wheeler .

**Pinot Noir** [pee-noh nwahr] Black grape responsible for all red *Burgundy* and in part for white *Champagne*. Also grown in the New World with increasing success in sites whose climate is neither too warm nor too cold. Winemakers need the dedication which might otherwise have destined them for a career in nursing. Buying is like Russian Roulette, once you've got a taste for that complex, raspberryish flavour, you'll go on pulling the expensive trigger. See *Oregon, Carneros, Yarra, Santa Barbara, Tasmania Burgundy.*

**Pinotage** [pee-noh-tazh] (South Africa) *Pinot Noir* x *Cinsault* cross with a spicy, plummy character, used in *South Africa* and (now very rarely) *New Zealand*. Good old examples are brilliant but rare; most taste muddy and rubbery. New winemaking and international demand are making for more exciting wines. Clos Malverne; Kanonkop; Warwick; Simonsig; Saxenberg; Grangehurst.

**Piper Heidsieck** [pi-pur hide-sehk] (*Champagne*, France) Greatly improved *Champagne*, though the ultra-dry *Brut* Sauvage is an acquired taste and the US Piper Sonoma decidedly undistinguished.

**Pipers Brook Vineyards** (*Tasmania*, Australia) The best-known producer in Tasmania, Dr Andrew Pirie is a pioneering producer of fine Burgundian *Chardonnay, Pinot Noir* and *Pinot Gris*. Ninth Island, the *Second Label*, includes an excellent unoaked *Chablis*-like *Chardonnay*. ☆☆☆☆ 1995 Chardonnay £££

**Ch. de Pitray** [pee-tray] (*Côtes de Castillon*, *Bordeaux*, France) Good value wine to buy in ripe vintages. 82 83 85 86 87 88 89 90 93 94 95 ☆☆☆ 1990 ££

**Producteurs Plaimont** [play-mon] (South-West France) Reliable co-operative in *Côtes de St. Mont* producing *Bordeaux*-lookalike reds and whites with some use of local grapes. ☆☆☆ 1995 Côtes de St. Mont £

**Plaisir de Merle** [play-zeer dur mehrl] (*Paarl*, South Africa) Paul Pontallier of *Ch. Margaux* is helping to make ripe, soft reds and New World style whites for *Stellenbosch Farmers Winery* in this new showcase winery. ☆☆☆☆ 1995 Chardonnay ££

**Plantagenet** (Mount Barker, Australia) Good producer of *Chardonnay, Riesling, Cabernet* and lean *Shiraz* in this increasingly successful region in the South West corner of Australia. ☆☆☆☆☆ 1994 Mount Barker Shiraz £££.

**Plovdiv** [plov-div] Bulgaria) Region for *Mavrud, Cabernet* and *Merlot*.

**Poggio Antico** [pod-zhee-yoh an-tee-koh] (*Tuscany*, Italy) Ultra-reliable *Brunello* producer. ☆☆☆☆ 1992 Brunello di Montalcino ££££

**Pol Roger** [pol rod-zhay] (*Champagne*, France) Consistently fine producer, with an unusually subtle *Non-Vintage* that improves with keeping. The Cuvée Winston Churchill (named in honour of one of this wine's most faithful fans) is spectacular, and the *Demi-Sec* is a rare treat. ☆☆☆☆☆ 1990 Vintage ££££

**Pomerol** [pom-meh-rohl] (*Bordeaux*, France) With *St. Emilion*, the *Bordeaux* for lovers of the *Merlot*, which predominates in its rich, soft, plummy wines. *Ch. Pétrus* and *Le Pin* are the big names but wines like *Petit Village* and *Clos René* abound. None are cheap because production is often limited to a few thousand cases (in the *Médoc*, 20–40,000 is more common). Quality is far more consistent than in *St. Emilion*. See *Pétrus*, *Moueix* and individual châteaux. **70 75** 78 79 81 **82 83 85** 86 **88 89** 90 94 95 94

**Pomino** [poh-mee-noh] (*Tuscany*, Italy) Small *DOC* within *Chianti Rufina*; virtually a monopoly for *Frescobaldi* who make a buttery unwooded white *Pinot Bianco/Chardonnay*, the oaky-rich Il Benefizio and a tasty *Sangiovese/Cabernet*. ☆☆☆ **1993 Pomino Rosso ££**

**Pommard** [pom-mahr] (*Burgundy*, France) Very variable quality *commune*, theoretically with a higher proportion of old vines, making slow-to-mature, then solid and complex reds. 78 80 83 **85** 86 87 **88 89 90** 92 95 ***Comte Armand; de Montille; Mussy; Château de Meursault; Dom. de Pousse d'Or.***

**Ch. de Pommard** (*Burgundy*, France) Good rather than great property specialising in selling directly to visitors.

**Pommery** [pom-meh-ree] (*Champagne*, France) Returned-to-form big-name with rich, full-flavoured style. The top label, Louise Pommery white and rosé are tremendous. ☆☆☆☆☆ **1988 Cuvée Louise ££££**

**Pongràcz** [pon-gratz] (South Africa) Brand name for the *Bergkelder*'s (excellent) *Cap Classique*. ☆☆☆☆ **Cap Classique ££**

**Dom. Ponsot** [pon-soh] (*Burgundy*, France) Top-class estate noted for *Clos de la Roche* and (rare) white *Morey St. Denis*. At a more affordable level, the *Gevrey* is good too. ☆☆☆☆ **1993 Gevrey Chambertin Cuvée de l'Abeille £££**

**Ch. Pontet-Canet** [pon-tay ka-nay] (*Pauillac 5th Growth*, *Bordeaux*, France) Rich, concentrated up-and-coming *Pauillac*, benefitting from the dedicated ambition of its owners. **61** 70 71 78 81 **82** 83 85 **86** 87 88 89 90 91 92 93 94 95 96 ☆☆☆☆ **1990 ££££**

**Ponzi** [pon-zee] (*Oregon*, USA) The ideal combination: a maker of good *Pinot Noir*, *Chardonnay* and even better beer. ☆☆☆ **1995 Pinot Noir, Willamette Valley £££**

**Port** (*Douro*, Portugal) Fortified wine made in the upper *Douro* valley. Comes in several styles; see *Tawny*, *Ruby*, *LBV*, *Vintage*, *Crusted* and *White Port*.

**Ch. Potensac** [po-ton-sak] (*Médoc Cru Bourgeois*, *Bordeaux*, France) Under the same ownership as the great *Léoville-Las-Cases*, and offering a more affordable taste of the winemaking that goes into that wine. **78 81** 82 83 **85** 86 87 88 **89** 90 94 95 ☆☆☆☆ **1990 £££**

**Pouilly Fuissé** [poo-yee fwee-say] (*Burgundy*, France) Variable white often sold at vastly inflated prices. Pouilly Vinzelles, Pouilly Loché and other *Mâconnais* wines are often better value, though top-class Pouilly Fuissé from producers like *Ch. Fuissé* Dom Noblet, or Dom. Ferret can compete with the best of the *Côte d'Or*. White: 85 86 87 **88** 89 **90 92** 95 96 ☆☆☆☆ **Ch. Fuissé; Barraud; Corsin; Ferret; Lapierre; Noblet; Philibert.**

**Pouilly Fumé** [poo-yee foo-may] (*Loire*, France) Potentially ultra-elegant *Sauvignon Blanc* with classic gooseberry fruit and 'smoky' overtones derived from flint ('*Silex*') sub-soil. Like *Sancerre*, rarely repays cellaring. See *Ladoucette* or the enfant terrible of Pouilly Fumé – *Didier Dagueneau*. **94** 95 96

🍷 **Ch. Poujeaux** [poo-joh] (*Moulis Cru Bourgeois, Bordeaux*, France) Up-and-coming plummy-blackcurranty wine from *Moulis*. 70 75 76 78 79 81 **82 83 85** 86 87 88 89 90 93 94 95 96 ☆☆☆ **1993 £££**

***Pourriture noble*** [poo-ree-toor nohbl] (France) See *Botrytis Cinerea* or *Noble Rot*.

🍷 **Dom. de la Pousse d'Or** [poos-daw] (*Burgundy*, France) Top red wine producer from Volnay. ☆☆☆☆ **1993 Pommard Les Jarollières ££££**

***Prädikat*** [pray-dee-ket] (Germany) As in Qualitatswein mit Pradikat (*QmP*), the higher quality level for German wines, indicating a greater degree of ripeness.

***Precipitation*** The creation of a harmless deposit, usually of *tartrate* crystals, in white wine, which the Germans romantically call 'diamonds'.

***Premier Cru*** [prur-mee-yay kroo] In *Burgundy*, indicates wines that are better than village level and second only to *Grand Cru*. In communes which have no *Grand Cru*, such as *Meursault, Beaune* and *Nuits St. Georges*, the top Premiers Cru can outclass many a poorly made *Grand Cru*.

**Premières Côtes de Bordeaux** [prur-mee-yay koht dur bohr-doh] (*Bordeaux*, France) Up-and-coming riverside *Appellation* for reds and (often less interestingly) Sweet whites: 76 **83** 85 **86** 88 89 90 95

***Prestige Cuvée*** [koo-vay] (*Champagne*, France) The top wine of a *Champagne* house, usually from a vintage year. Fearsomely expensive and elaborately packaged. Some, like *Dom Perignon*, are brilliant; others less so. Other best-known examples include: *Veuve Cliquot's* Grand Dame and *Roederer's* Cristal.

🍷 **Dom. Jacques Prieur** [pree-yur] (*Burgundy*, France) Reliable estate, improved since takeover by *Antonin Rodet*.

🍷 **Ch. Prieuré-Lichine** [pree-yur-ray lih-sheen] (*Margaux 4th Growth, Bordeaux*, France) Reliable wine with improving, blackcurranty fruit, thanks partly to the input by *Michel Rolland*. 70 75 78 **82 83** 85 86 87 88 89 90 91 92 93 94 95 96 ☆☆☆☆ **1995 £££**

***Primeur*** [pree-mur] (France) New wine, eg Beaujolais Primeur (the same as Beaujolais Nouveau) or, as in *en primeur*, wine which is sold while still in barrel.

🍇 **Primitivo di Mandura** [pree-mih-tee-voh dee man-doo-ra] (*Puglia*, Italy) Spicy, red made from the Primitivo, supposedly another name for the *Zinfandel*.

🍷 **Primo Estate** [pree-moh] (South, Australia) Extraordinarily imaginative venture among the fruit farms of the Adelaide Plains. Passion-fruity *Colombard*, sparkling *Shiraz* and *Bordeaux*-blends made *Passito*-style, using grapes partially dried in the sun. ☆☆☆☆ **1994 Adelaide Shiraz ££** ☆☆☆☆ **Joseph Sparkling Shiraz £££**

**Priorato** [pree-yaw-rah-toh] (*Catalonia*, Spain) Heftily alcoholic reds and (rare) whites from *Carinena* and *Garnacha* grapes grown in a very warm region. New wave producers are bringing a touch of class with lighter, more modern reds like Clos Mogador. ☆☆☆ **1994 Priorato Scala Dei £** ☆☆☆☆ **1992 Clos Mogador £££**

***Propriétaire (Récoltant)*** [pro-pree-yeh-tehr ray-kohl-ton] (France) Vineyard owner-manager.

**Prosecco di Conegliano** [proh-sek-koh dee coh-nay-lya-noh] (*Veneto*, Italy) Soft, slightly earthy, dry and sweet fizz made from the *Prosecco* grape, often served from bottles containing the yeast which has made them fizz. Less boisterous than *Asti Spumante*. A taste of the past.

🍷 **Prosper-Maufoux** [pros-pehr moh-foo] (*Burgundy*, France) Large *négoçiant* based in *Santenay* and producing a large range of *Beaujolais, Mâconnais* and *Bourgogne*. ☆☆☆☆ **1985 Volnay, Clos des Anges ££££**

**Provence** [proh-vons] (France) Southern region producing fast improving wine with a number of minor *ACs*. Rosé de Provence should be dry and fruity with a hint of peppery spice. **Ch. Routas**

**J J Prüm** [proom] (*Mosel-Saar-Ruwer*, Germany) Top *Riesling* producer with fine *Wehlen*er vineyards. ☆☆☆☆ **1994 Riesling Kabinett ££**

**Dom. Michel Prunier** [proo-nee-yay] (*Burgundy*, France) Reliable, traditional estate. ☆☆☆ **1993 Auxey-Duresses 1er Cru Clos du Val £££**

**Alfredo Prunotto** [proo-not-toh] (*Piedmont*, Italy) Good Barolo producer recently bought by Antinori. ☆☆☆☆ **1994 Nebbiolo d'Alba Ochetti ££**

**Puglia** [poo-lee-yah] (Italy) Hot region, now making pretty cool wines thanks partly to *Flying Winemakers* like *Kym Milne*. Also see *Salice Salentino* and *Copertino*.

**Puisseguin St. Emilion** [pwees-gan san tay-mee-lee-yon] (*Bordeaux*, France) Satellite of *St. Emilion* making similar, *Merlot*-dominant wines which are often far better value. 78 79 81 **82 83 85** 86 **88 89** 90 94 95

**Puligny-Montrachet** [poo-lee-nee mon-ra-shay] (*Burgundy*, France) Aristocratic white *Côte d'Or commune* that shares the *Montrachet* vineyard with *Chassagne*. Should be complex buttery *Chardonnay* with a touch more elegance than *Meursault*. *Carrillon, Sauzet, Ramonet, Drouhin* and *Dom. Leflaive* are all worth their money. **85 86** 87 **88** 89 **90 92** 95

***Putto*** [poot-toh] (Italy) As in *Chianti* Putto: wine from a consortium of growers who use the cherub (putto) as their symbol. Taken very seriously in Italy.

***Puttonyos*** [poot-TOH-nyos] (*Tokaji*, Hungary) The measure of sweetness (from 1 to 6) of *Tokaji*. The number indicates the number of Puttonyos (baskets) of sweet *aszu* paste that are added to the base wine.

**Ch. Puygeraud** [Pwee-gay-roh] (*Bordeaux*, France) Perhaps the best property on the *Côtes de Francs*. 85 86 88 **89** 90 93 94 95

**PX** (Jerez, Spain) See *Pedro Ximénez*.

**Pyrénées** (*Victoria*, Australia) One of the classiest regions in Victoria, thanks to the efforts of *Taltarni* and *Dalwhinnie*. White: **86 87 88 90 91 92 94 95** 96 Red: 80 **82** 84 **85 86 87 88 90 91 92** 94 95

**Pyrénées Orientales** [pee-reh-nay oh-ree-yon-tahl] (*Midi*, France) Big region including *Roussillon* and *Rivesaltes*.

**Pyrus** [pi-rus] (Australia) see *Lindemans*. ☆☆☆☆ **1992 Pyrus £££**

# Q

***QbA*** (Germany) Qualitätswein bestimmter Anbaugebiet: [Kvah-Lih-Tayts-Vine Behr-Shtihmt-Tuhr Ahn-Bow-Geh-Beet] Basic quality German wine from one of the 11 *Anbaugebiet*, eg *Rheinhessen*.

***QmP*** (Germany) Qualitätswein mit Pradikat: [Pray-Dee-Kaht] *QbA* wine (supposedly) with 'special qualities'. The QmP blanket designation is broken into five sweetness rungs, from *Kabinett* to *Trockenbeerenauslesen* plus *Eiswein*.

**Quady** [kwo-dee] (*Central Valley*, California) Quirky producer of the wittily named 'Starboard' (hint: serve it in a decanter), the *Orange Muscat* Essencia (great with chocolate), *Black Muscat* Elysium, and Electra, low-alcohol. ☆☆☆☆ **Quady's Starboard Batch 88 ££**

**Quarles Harris** [kwahrls] (*Douro*, Portugal) Underrated producer with a fine 1980 and 1983. ☆☆☆☆ **1983 Vintage Port £££**

**Quarts de Chaume** [kahr dur shohm] (*Loire*, France) Luscious but light sweet wines, uncloying, ageing beautifully, from the *Coteaux du Layon*. The Dom. de Baumard is exceptional. Sweet white: **76** 83 **85** 86 **88 89** 90 94 95 96 **Dom des Baumard; Pierre Soulez.**

**Queensland** (Australia) The Granite Belt produces *Hunter Valley*-style *Shiraz* and *Semillon* from (relatively) cool vineyards.

**Quilceda Creek** [kwil-see-dah] (*Washington State*, USA) Producer of one of the best, most blackcurranty *Cabernets* in the north-west.

**Quincy** [kan-see] (*Loire*, France) Dry *Sauvignon*, lesser-known and sometimes good value alternative to *Sancerre* or *Pouilly Fumé*. **Joseph Mellot.**

***Quinta*** [keen-ta] (Portugal) Vineyard or estate, particularly in the *Douro*, where 'single Quinta' vintage ports are increasingly being taken as seriously as the big-name blends. See *Crasto, Vesuvio* and *De la Rosa*.

**Guiseppe Quintarelli** [keen-ta-reh-lee] (*Veneto*, Italy) Wonderful old-fashioned *Recioto*-maker producing some of the quirkiest, most sublime (and most expensive) *Valpolicella*. Try the more affordable Molinara. ☆☆☆☆☆ **1995 Molinara ££**

**Qupé** [kyoo-pay] (*Central Coast*, California) Run by one of the founders of *Au Bon Climat*, this *Santa Barbara* winery produces brilliant *Syrah*. ☆☆☆☆ **1994 Syrah ££**

# R

**Ch. Rabaud-Promis** [rrah-boh prraw-mee] (*Sauternes Premier Cru Classé, Bordeaux*, France) Underperforming until 1986; now making top class wines. **83** 85 **86** 87 88 89 90 95 ☆☆☆☆☆ **1990 £££**

***Racking*** The drawing off of wine from its *Lees* into a clean cask or vat.

**A Rafanelli** [ra-fur-nel-lee] (*Sonoma*, California) One of the few non-*Beaujolais* wineries making a success of *Gamay*; the *Zinfandel* is also highly rated. ☆☆☆☆ **1994 ZinfandelUnfiltered.**

**Olga Raffault** [ra-foh] (*Loire*, France) There are several Raffaults in *Chinon*; Olga's is the best estate – and the best source of some of the longest-lived examples of this *Appellation*. ☆☆☆☆ **1994 Chinon les Barnabés ££**

**Raïmat** [ri-mat] (*Catalonia*, Spain) Innovative winery founded by *Codorníu*, in the dry *Costers del Segre* region, and unusual in being allowed to use irrigation. *Merlot*, a *Cabernet Merlot* blend called Abadia and *Tempranillo* are interesting and *Chardonnay* – both still and sparkling – has been good. ☆☆☆☆ **1991 Merlot ££**

**Rainwater** (*Madeira*, Portugal) Light, dry style of *Madeira* popular in the US. ☆☆☆ **Berry Bros & Rudd's Selected Rainwater ££**

**Ch. Ramage-la-Batisse** [ra-mazh la ba-teess] (*Haut-Médoc Cru Bourgeois, Bordeaux*, France) Good *Cru Bourgeois* from St. Laurent, close to *Pauillac* 82 **83** 85 86 88 89 90 91 92 93 94 95 ☆☆☆ **1993 ££**

**Ramitello** [ra-mee-tel-loh] (*Molise*, Italy) Spicy-fruity reds and creamy, citric whites produced by di Majo Norante in Biferno on the Adriatic coast.

**Dom. Ramonet** [ra-moh-nay] (*Burgundy*, France) Mecca for *Burgundy* lovers the world over, who queue to buy top flight wines like the *Bâtard-Montrachet*. Pure class; worth waiting for too. ☆☆☆☆☆ **1995 Bâtard Montrachet ££££**

**Adriano Ramos Pinto** [rah-mosh pin-toh] (*Douro*, Portugal) Family-run winery that belongs to *Roederer.* Vintage-dated *Colheita* tawnies are a speciality, but the *Vintage wines* are good too. ☆☆☆☆ **1994 Vintage £££**

**Castello dei Rampolla** [kas-teh-lohday-ee ram-poh-la] (*Tuscany*, Italy) Good *Chianti*-producer whose wines need time to soften.

***Rancio*** [ran-see-yoh] Term for the peculiar yet prized *oxidised* flavour of certain fortified wines, particularly in France (eg *Banyuls*) and Spain.

**Rapel** [ra-pel] (*Central Valley*, Chile) Important sub-region of the *Central Valley*, especially for reds.

**Rapitalà** [ra-pih-tah-la] (*Sicily*, Italy) Estate producing a fresh, peary white wine from a blend of local grapes.

**Rasteau** [ras-stoh] (*Rhône*, France) Southern village producing peppery reds with rich berry fruit. The fortified *Muscat* can be good too. Red: 78 81 82 83 85 88 89 90 95. **La Soumade; Bressy-Masson.**

**Ch. Rauzan-Ségla** [roh-zon say-glah] (*Margaux 2nd Growth*, *Bordeaux*, France) For a long time an under-performing *Margaux* Second Growth. Now one of the best buys in *Bordeaux*. 70 82 83 85 86 88 89 90 91 92 93 94 95 96 ☆☆☆☆☆ **1990 ££££**

**Ch. Rauzan-Gassies** [roh-zon ga-sees] (*Margaux 2nd Growth*, *Bordeaux*, France) Despite recent improvements, compared to Rauzan Ségla this property is still underperforming magnificently. The 1983 was a recommendable exception to the rule. 75 82 83 85 89 90 94 95

**Ravenswood** (*Sonoma Valley*, California) Brilliant Zinfandel-maker whose Merlots are good too. ☆☆☆☆ **1994 Zinfandel Wood Road, £££**

**Ravenswood** (South, Australia) Label confusingly adopted by Hollick for its top Coonawarra reds (no relation to the above entry). ☆☆☆☆ **1993 ££££**

**Raventos i Blanc** [ra-vayn-tos ee blank] (*Catalonia*, Spain) Josep Raventos' ambition is to produce the best fizz in Spain, adding *Chardonnay* to local varieties.

**Ch. Raymond-Lafon** [ray-mon la-fon] (*Sauternes*, *Bordeaux*, France) Great small producer whose wines deserve keeping. 75 80 82 83 85 86 89 90 94 95 ☆☆☆☆☆ **1990 ££££**

**Ch. de Rayne-Vigneau** [rayn VEEN-yoh] (*Sauternes Premier Cru Classé*, *Bordeaux*, France) *Sauternes* estate, located at *Bommes*, producing a rich, complex wine. 76 83 85 86 88 89 90 92 94 ☆☆☆☆ **1990 ££££**

***RD*** (*Champagne*, France) Récemment Dégorgée – a term invented by *Bollinger* to describe their delicious *Vintage Champagne*, which has been allowed a longer-than-usual period (as much as fifteen years) on its *Lees*. ☆☆☆☆☆ **1982 ££££**

**Ignacio Recabarren** [ig-na-see-yoh reh-ka-ba-ren] (Chile) Superstar winemaker and *Casablanca* pioneer.

***Recioto*** [ray-chee-yo-toh] (*Veneto*, Italy) Sweet or dry alcoholic wine made from semi-dried, ripe grapes. Most usually associated with *Valpolicella* and *Soave*.

***Récoltant-manipulant (RM)*** [ray-kohl-ton ma-nih-poo-lon] (*Champagne*, France) Individual winegrower and blender, identified by mandatory RM number on label.

***Récolte*** [ray-kohlt] (France) Vintage, literally 'harvest'.

**Redman** (South Australia) Improved Coonawarra estate with intense reds. ☆☆☆☆ **1992 Cabernet Sauvignon.**

***Reductive*** Indicates that everything has been done to minimise the contact of the wine with oxygen, to preserve the freshness of its fruit.

**Redwood Valley Estate** (Nelson, New Zealand) Starry specialist in *Late Harvest* Rieslings. ☆☆☆☆ **1995 Chardonnay ££**

**Refosco** [re-fos-koh] [(*Friuli-Venezia Giulia*, Italy) Red grape and its dry and full-bodied *DOC* wine. Benefits from ageing.

**Regaleali** [ray-ga-lay-ah-lee] (*Sicily*, Italy) Ambitious aristocratic estate, using local varieties to produce *Sicily*'s most serious wines. ☆☆☆☆ **1992 Rosso del Conte Tasca d'Almerita £££**

***Régisseur*** [rey-jee-sur] (*Bordeaux*, France) In *Bordeaux*, the cellar-master.

**Régnié** [ray-nyay] (*Burgundy*, France) The wines of Regnié were once perfectly respectable *Beaujolais Villages*, now they have to compete with *Chiroubles, Chénas* and the other *Crus*. They're mostly like amateurs competing against pros. Fortunately for *Régnié*, those pros often aren't on great form. *Duboeuf* makes a typical example. **85 88 89** 90 **91** 93 94 95 96 **Dubost; Trichard.**

**Reichensteiner** [rike-en-sti-ner] Recently developed white grape, popular in England (and Wales).

**Reif Estate Winery** [reef] (*Ontario*, Canada) Impressive icewine specialist. ☆☆☆☆ **1994 Icewine Riesling ££££**

**Remelluri** [ray-may-yoo-ree] (*Rioja*, Spain) For most modernists, this is the nearest *Rioja* has got to a top-class, small-scale organic estate. Wines are more serious (and *tannic*) than most, but they're fuller of flavour too and they're built to last. ☆☆☆☆ **1994 Rioja ££**

***Remuage*** [reh-moo-wazh] (*Champagne*, France) Part of the *Méthode Champenoise*, the gradual turning and tilting of bottles so that the yeast deposit collects in the neck ready for *Dégorgement*.

***Reserva*** [ray-sehr-vah] (Spain) Indicates the wine has been aged for a number of years specified by the relevant *DO*: usually one year for reds and six months for reds and pinks.

***Réserve*** [rur-surv] (France) Legally meaningless, as in 'Réserve Personelle', but implying a wine selected and given more age.

***Residual sugar*** Term for wines which have retained grape sugar not converted to alcohol by yeasts during fermentation. In France 4 grammes per litre is the threshold. In the US, the figure is 5 and many so-called 'dry' white wines contain as much as 10. New Zealand *Sauvignons* are rarely bone dry, but their *acidity* balances and conceals any residual sugar.

**Weingut Balthasar Ress** [bul-ta-zah rress] (*Rheingau*, Germany) Classy producer in *Hattenheim*, blending delicacy with concentration. ☆☆☆☆ **1992 Schloss Reichhartshousener Riesling Kabinett £££**

***Retsina*** [ret-see-nah] (Greece) Wine made the way the ancient Greeks used to make it – resinating it with pine to keep it from going off. Today, it's an acquired taste for non-holidaying, non-Greeks. Pick the freshest examples you can (not easy when there's no vintage on the bottle).

**Reuilly** [rur-yee] (*Loire*, France) (Mostly) white *AC* for dry *Sauvignons*, good value, if sometimes rather earthy alternatives to nearby *Sancerre* and *Pouilly Fumé*. Search out some spicy *Pinot* rosé from some of the best producers. White: 94 95 96 Red: **89 90** 95 **Henri Beurdin.**

**Rex Hill Vineyards** (*Oregon*, USA) Greatly improved *Pinot* specialist.

**Chateau Reynella** [ray-nel-la] (McLaren Vale, Australia) BRL Hardy subsidiary, mastering both reds and whites. ☆☆☆☆ **1995 Chardonnay.**

**Ch. Reynon** [ray-non] (*Premier Côtes de Bordeaux*, France) Fine red and especially recommendable white wines from *Denis Dubourdieu*. White: 92 **93** 94 95 96 ☆☆☆☆ **1994 Vieilles Vignes ££££**

**Rheingau** [rine-gow] (Germany) Should produce the finest *Rieslings* of the 11 *Anbaugebiete*, but sadly hijacked by producers who prefer quantity to quality and the *Charta* campaign for dry wines. There are still great things to be found, however. QbA/Kab/Spät: **85** 86 **88 89 90** 91 92 93 94 95 96 Aus/Beeren/TBA: **83 85** 88 89 90 91 92 93 94 95 96 **Künstler; Balthasar Ress; Domdechant Werner'sches; HH Eser.**

**Rheinhessen** [rine-hehs-sen] (Germany) Largest of the 11 *Anbaugebiete*, now well known for *Liebfraumilch* and *Niersteiner*. Fewer than one vine in 20 is now *Riesling*; throughout the region, easier-to-grow varieties and lazy cooperative wineries prevail. Pick and choose to get the good stuff. QbA/Kab/Spät: **85** 86 **88 89 90** 91 92 93 94 95 96 Aus/Beeren/TBA: **83 85** 88 89 90 91 92 93 94 95 96. **Gunderloch; Balbach.**

**Rheinpfalz/Pfalz** [rine-fahlts] (Germany) See *Pfalz*.

**Rhine Riesling/Rhein Riesling** Widely used – though frowned-on by the EU – name for the noble *Riesling* grape.

**Rhône** [rohn] (France) Fast-improving, exciting, packed with the newly sexy *Grenache, Syrah* and *Viognier* varietal wines. See *St. Joseph, Crozes-Hermitage, Hermitage, Condrieu, Côtes du Rhône, Châteauneuf du Pape, Tavel, Lirac, Gigondas, Ch. Grillet, Beaumes de Venise*. White: **82 85** 87 **88 89 90** 91 94 95 Northern Rhône Red: **76 78 82 83 85 88** 89 90 91 95 96 Southern Rhône Red: **78 82 83 85 88** 89 90 95 96

**Rias Baixas** [ree-yahs bi-shahs] (Galicia, Spain) The place to find Spain's spicy, apricotty *Albariño*. **Lagar de Cervera; Santiago Ruiz.**

**Ribatejo** [ree-bah-tay-joh] (Portugal) *DO* area north of Lisbon where Peter Bright is very active these days. The cooperatives are fast learning how to make highly commercial white and red wine, but traditional *Garrafeiras* are worth watching out for too. Red: **85 88 90 91 92 93** 94 95 96

**Ribeira Sacra** [ree-bay-rah sak-rah] (Spain) Newly acknowledged terraced region in the north-west. Good well-made *Albariño*.

**Ribera del Duero** [ree-bay-rah del doo-way-roh] (Spain) This is potentially the region to watch in Spain for good reds (whites are forbidden, despite what might be ideal conditions for them). Unfortunately, despite the established success of *Vega Sicilia* and, more recently, that of producers like *Pesquera Arroyo* and *Alion*, and despite high-tech 'smart card' technology in the cooperatives to check the quality of the grapes, there is still too much poor winemaking. 82 **83 85 87** 89 90 91 92 94 95 96 **Pago de Carraovejas; Valduero Reserva; Pesquera; Balbas, Pedrosa.**

**Dom. Richeaume** [ree-shohm] (*Provence*, France) One of the leading lights in the new wave of quality, conscious Southern French estates, and a dynamic producer of good, earthy, long-lived, organic *Cabernet* and *Syrah*. Sadly, as with many other smaller organic wineries, quality can vary from bottle to bottle. Recommendable, nonetheless. ☆☆☆ **1993 Cuvée Tradition ££**

**Richebourg** [reesh-boor] (*Burgundy*, France) Top-class *Grand Cru* vineyard just outside *Vosne Romanée* with a recognisable floral-plummy style. 76 **78** 79 **80** 82 83 **85** 86 87 **88 89 90** 92 95 96 **Domaine de la Romanée-Conti; A&F Gros; Jayer; Leroy; D&D Mugneret.**

**Weingut Max Ferd Richter** [rikh-tur] (*Mosel-Saar-Ruwer*, Germany) Excellent producer of long-lived concentrated-yet-elegant *Mosel Rieslings* from high quality vineyards. ☆☆☆☆☆ **1989 Graacher Himmelreich Riesling Spätlese ££**

🍷 **John Riddoch** (South, Australia) Classic *Wynn's Coonawarra* red. One of Australia's best and longest-lasting wines. (Not to be confused with the wines that *Katnook Estate* sells under its own 'Riddoch' label.

🍷 **Ridge Vineyards** (Santa Cruz, California) Paul Draper, and Ridge's hilltop *Santa Cruz* and *Sonoma* vineyards produce some of California's very finest *Zinfandel, Cabernet, Mataro* and *Chardonnay*. ☆☆☆☆☆ **1992 Geyserville Sonoma County ££££**

🍇 **Riesling** [reez-ling] The noble grape responsible for Germany's finest offerings, ranging from light, floral everyday wines, to the delights of *Botrytis*-affected sweet wines which retain their freshness for decades. Reaching its zenith in the superbly balanced racy wines of the *Mosel*, and the richer offerings from the ***Rheingau***, it also performs well in *Alsace*, California, South Africa and Australia. Watch out for the emergence of the *Wachau* region as a leader of the Austrian Riesling pack.

🍇 **Riesling Italico** see *Italian Riesling*, etc.

🍷 **Ch. Rieussec** [ree-yur-sek] (*Sauternes Premier Cru Classé, Bordeaux*, France) Fantastically rich and concentrated *Sauternes*, often deep in colour and generally at the head of the pack chasing Yquem. Now owned by the Rothschilds of *Lafite*. R de Rieussec is the dry white wine. **67 71** 75 79 82 **83 85 86** 88 89 90 92 93 94 95 ☆☆☆☆ **1993 ££££**

**Rioja** [ree-ok-hah] (Spain) (Alavesa/Alta/Baja), Spain's best-known wine region is split into three parts. The Alta produces the best wines, followed by the Alavesa, while the Baja is by far the largest. Most Riojas are blends made by large *Bodegas* using grapes grown in two or three of the regions. Small *Bordeaux* and *Burgundy*-style estates are rare, thanks to restrictive Spanish rules which require wineries to store unnecessarily large quantities of wine. Things are happening in the vineyards, however, including plantings of 'experimental' *Cabernet* alongside the traditional *Tempranillo* and lesser quality *Garnacha*. Such behaviour breaks all sorts of local rules – as does the irrigation which is also now in evidence – but is already paying off for producers like Martinez Bujanda. With luck, this kind of innovative thinking will help the region as a whole to live up to its reputation. **79 80 81** 82 **83 85 87** 89 90 91 92 94 95 **Remelluri; Campillo; La Rioja Alta; Contino; Riscal, Amezola de la Mora; Baron de Ley; Martinez Bujanda.**

🍷 **Dom. Daniel Rion** [ree-yon] (*Burgundy*, France) Patrice Rion, head of this family estate, produces impeccably made *Nuits St. Georges* and *Vosne Romanées*. ☆☆☆☆ **1993 Nuits St. Georges Hauts Pruliers £££**

***Ripasso*** [ree-pas-soh] (*Veneto*, Italy) Method whereby newly made *Valpolicella* is partially refermented in vessels recently vacated by *Recioto* and *Amarone*. *Ripasso* wines made in this way are richer, alcoholic and raisiny. Increases the alcohol and body of the wine. **Tedeschi; Quintarelli; Masi.**

**Riquewihr** [reek-veer] (*Alsace*, France) *Commune* noted for *Riesling*.

🍷 **Marqués de Riscal** [ris-KAHL] (*Rioja*, Spain) Famous, but for a long time flawed, property that has got its act together at last. The whites are already impressive thanks to the help of *Hugh Ryman*, and a comparison of the 1991 Reserva with the 1981 Gran Reserva reveals the benefits of more modern winemaking for the reds.

***Riserva*** [ree-ZEHR-vah] (Italy) *DOC* wines aged for a specified number of years – often an unwelcome term on labels of wines like *Bardolino*, which are usually far better drunk young.

🍇 **Rivaner** [rih-VAH-nur] (Germany) The name used for *Müller-Thurgau* (a cross between *Riesling* and *Sylvaner*) in parts of Germany and *Luxembourg*.

**Riverina** [rih-vur-ee-na] (*New South Wales*, Australia) Irrigated *New South Wales* region which produces basic-to-good wine, much of which ends up in '*South-East Australian*' blends. *Late Harvest Semillons* can, however, be surprisingly spectacular. **Cranswick Estate.**

**Riverland** (Australia) Generic name for major irrigated wine-growing regions.

🍷 **Rivesaltes** [reev-zalt] (*Midi*, France) Fortified dessert wine of both colours. The white, which is made from the *Muscat*, is lighter and more lemony than that of *Beaumes de Venise*, while the red made from *Grenache* is almost like liquid Christmas pudding and can age wonderfully. **Cazes; Ch de Jau.**

🍷 **Ch. de la Rivière** [rih-vee-yehr] (*Fronsac*, *Bordeaux*, France) Picture-book *Fronsac* property producing instantly accessible, *Merlot*-dominant red wines. Not the classiest of fare, but a lot more fun to drink than many a duller *St. Emilion* or more 'serious' (and pricier) wine from the *Médoc*. 82 83 **85 88** 89 90 94 95 ☆☆☆ **1986 £££**

**Robertson** (South Africa) Up-and-coming area where the Cape's new wave of *Chardonnays* and *Sauvignons* are grabbing the spotlight from the *Muscats* previously the region's pride. Red: 82 84 86 **87** 89 **91 92** 93 94 95 White: 87 **91** 92 93 94 95

🍷 **Robertson's Well** (South Australia) Good commercial label. ☆☆☆☆ **1993 Cabernet Sauvignon, Coonawarra. ££**

🍷 **Rocca delle Macie** [ro-ka del leh mah-chee-yay] (*Tuscany*, Italy) Reliable if unspectacular *Chianti* producer. ☆☆☆ **1990 Chianti Classico Fizzano ££**

🍷 **La Roche aux Moines** [rosh oh mwahn] (*Loire*, France) A superstar producer of *Savennières*, perhaps as good as dry *Chenin* gets. ☆☆☆☆☆ **1995 Savennières £££**

🍷 **Joe Rochioli** [roh-kee-yoh-lee] (*Sonoma*, California) Brilliant *Pinot Noir* producer. ☆☆☆☆☆ **1994 Pinot Noir £££**

🍷 **Rockford** (*Barossa Valley*, Australia) Robert, 'Rocky' O'Calaghan makes great, intense *Barossa Shiraz* using 100-year-old vines and 50-year-old equipment. There's a mouthfilling *Semillon*, a wonderful Black *Shiraz* fizz and a magical *Alicante Bouschet* rose. Only to be found at the winery. ☆☆☆☆ **1992 Basket Press Shiraz, Barossa Valley £££**

🍷 **Antonin Rodet** [on-toh-nan roh-day] (*Burgundy*, France) Good *Mercurey*-based *Négoçiant*, which has also improved the wines of the Jacques Prieur Domaine in *Meursault*.

🍷 **Louis Roederer** [roh-dur-rehr] (*Champagne*, France) Family-owned, and still one of the most reliable *Champagne* houses. No longer involved with the Jansz sparkling wine in Tasmania but making good fizz – sold as 'Quartet' at the Roederer Estate in *Mendocino*, California. ☆☆☆☆ **Champagne Brut ££££**

**Michel Rolland** [ROH-lon] Based in *Pomerol*, St. Emilion, and now increasingly international guru-oenologist, whose taste for ripe fruit flavours is influencing wines from Ch. *Ausone* to Argentina and beyond.

🍷 **Rolly-Gassmann** [rroh-lee gas-sman] (*Alsace*, France) Fine producer of subtle, long-lasting wines which are sometimes slightly marred by an excess of *Sulphur Dioxide*. ☆☆☆ **1991 Riesling ££**

🍷 **Dom. de la Romanée-Conti** [rroh-ma-nay kon-tee] (*Burgundy*, France) Aka 'DRC'. Small *Grand Cru* estate. The jewel in the crown is the Romanée-Conti vineyard itself, though *La Tâche* runs it a close second. Both can be extraordinary, ultra-concentrated spicy wine, as can the Romanée-St-Vivant. The *Richebourg*, *Echézeaux* and *Grands Echézeaux* and *Montrachet* are comparable to those produced by other estates – and sold by them for less kingly ransoms. ☆☆☆☆☆ **1992 La Tâche ££££**

**Castelli Romani** [kas-steh-lee roh-mah-nee] (*Latium*, Italy) *Frascati*-like whites and dull reds produced close to Rome.

**Romania** Traditional source of sweet reds and whites, now developing drier styles from classic European varieties. *Flying winemakers* are helping, as is the owner of the Comte Peraldi estate in Corsica, but progress is slow. Note that Romania's well-praised Pinot Noirs may be made from a different variety which has been mistaken for the Pinot.

**Romarantin** [roh-ma-ron-ta*n*] (*Loire*, France) Interesting limey grape found in obscure white blends in the *Loire*. See *Cheverny*.

**Romerlay** [*r*roh-mehr-lay] (*Mosel*, Germany) One of the *Grosslage* in the *Ruwer* river valley. QbA/Kab/Spät: **85** 86 **88 89 90** 91 92 93 94 95 96 Aus/Beeren/TBA: **83 85** 88 89 90 91 92 93 94 95 96

**Rongopai** [ron-goh-pi] (Te Kauwhata, New Zealand) Estate in a region of the North Island pioneered by *Cooks*, but which has fallen out of favour with that company and with other producers. The speciality here is *Botrytis* wines, but the dry *Sauvignons* are good too.

**La Rosa** (Chile) One of the fastest-growing wineries in Chile, with new vineyards and great winemaking from Ignacio Recabaren. Las Palmeras is a second label.

**Quinta de la Rosa** (*Douro*, Portugal) Recently established estate producing excellent port and exemplary dry red wine,under guidance from David Baverstock, Australian-born former winemaker at *Dow's* and now filling a similar rôle at the nearby *Quinta do Crasto*. ☆☆☆ **1995 Red ££**

***Rosato*** (Italy) Rosé.

**Rosé d'Anjou** [roh-zay don-joo] (*Loire*, France) Widely exported, usually dull semi-sweet pink from the *Malbec, Groslot* and *Cabernet Franc*.

**Rosé de Riceys** [roh-zay dur ree-say] (*Champagne*, France) Rare and occasionally delicious still rosé from the *Pinot Noir*. Pricy.

**Rosemount Estate** (*Hunter Valley*, Australia) The ultra-dynamic company which introduced the world to oaky Hunter *Chardonnay*, including the benchmark Show Reserve. Since then, reliably good-value blends from other areas have followed, including impressive *Syrah*s and *Chardonnays* from the newly developed region of *Orange*. Not the Rolls Royce of Aussie wines; more the B.M.W.☆☆☆☆☆ **1994 Balmoral Syrah £££**

**Dom. Rossignol-Trapet** [ros-seen-yol tra-pay] (*Burgundy*, France) Once old-fashioned, now highly recommendable, up-to-the-minute estate in *Gevrey Chambertin*. ☆☆☆☆ **1989 Gevrey Chambertin £££**

**Rosso Conero** [ros-doh kon-neh-roh] (*Marches*, Italy) Big *Montepulciano* and *Sangiovese* red, with a rich, herby flavour. Good value characterful stuff. ☆☆☆☆ **1994 Vigneto San Lorenzo, Umani Ronchi ££**

**Rosso di Montalcino** [ros-soh dee mon-tal-chee-noh] (*Tuscany*, Italy) *DO* for lighter, earlier-drinking versions of the more famous *Brunello di Montalcino*. Often better – and better value – than that wine. **82** 85 88 90 91 93 94 95 **Altesino; Caparzo; Fattoria dei Barbi.**

**René Rostaing** [ros-tang] (*Rhône*, France) Producer of serious Northern *Rhône* reds. ☆☆☆☆ **1991 Côte Rôtie la Landonne ££££**

**Rothbury Estate** (*Hunter Valley*, Australia) Founded by Len Evans, Svengali of the Australian wine industry and now – via *Mildara* – a subsidiary of Fosters, this is a great source of *Shiraz, Semillon* and *Chardonnay* from the *Hunter Valley*. There are also wines from nearby *Cowra* and first class *Sauvignon* from the bit of the estate which surfaces in *Marlborough, New Zealand*. ☆☆☆☆ **1994 Hunter Valley Reserve Shiraz ££**

🍷 **Alfred Rothschild** (*Champagne*, France) Brand name used in France by the huge *Marne & Champagne* company and nothing to do with the family of the same name.

🍷 **Joseph Roty** [roh-tee] (*Burgundy*, France) Inconsistent superstar producer of intensely concentrated but unsubtle *Gevrey Chambertin*. ☆☆☆☆ **1992 Mazis Chambertin ££££**

🍷 **Rouge Homme** (*Coonawarra*, Australia) Founded by the linguistically talented Mr Redman, but now part of the huge *Penfolds* empire. This is one of the most reliable producers in *Coonawarra*. Reds are more successful than whites. ☆☆☆☆ **1993 Richardson's Red Block, Coonawarra £££**

🍷 **Dom. Guy Roulot** [roo-loh] (*Burgundy*, France) One of the greatest Domaines in *Meursault*. ☆☆☆ **1993 Meursault les Vireuils ££££**

🍷 **Georges Roumier** [roo-me-yay] (*Burgundy*, France) Blue-chip winery with great quality at every level, from village *Chambolle-Musigny* to the *Grand Cru*, Bonnes Mares and (more rarely seen) white Corton Charlemagne. ☆☆☆☆ **1992 Chambolle Musigny les Amoureuses ££££**

🍷 **Round Hill** (*Napa*, California) A name to remember for anyone looking for Californian bargains. Large-production, inexpensive Merlots and Chardonnays that outclass many a pricier offering from smart boutique wineries.

🍇 **Roussanne** [roos-sahn] (*Rhône*, France) With the *Marsanne*, one of the key white grapes of the northern *Rhône*. Producers argue over their relative merits.

🍷 **Armand Rousseau** [roos-soh] (*Burgundy*, France) *Gevrey Chambertin* estate on top form with a range of *Premiers* and *Grands Crus*. Well-made, long-lasting wines. ☆☆☆☆ **1995 Charmes-Chambertin ££££**

**Roussillon** [roos-see-yon] (*Languedoc-Roussillon*, France) Vibrant up-and-coming region, redefining traditional varieties, especially *Muscat*.

🍷 **Ch. Routas** [roo-tahs] (*Provence*, France) Impressive little producer of intense reds and whites in the Coteaux Varois. **1994 Pyramus Coteaux Varois ££**

🍷 **Royal Oporto Wine Co.** (*Douro*, Portugal) Occasionally successful, large producer.

🍷 **The Royal Tokaji Wine Co.** (*Tokaji*, Hungary) Recently-founded company helping to drag *Tokaji* into the late 20th century. ☆☆☆☆ **1991 Royal Tokaji Aszú 5 Puttonyos £££**

🍷 **Rozendal Farm** [roh-zen-dahl] (*Stellenbosch*, South Africa) Eccentric small producer with richly flavoured and quirkily old-fashioned *Bordeaux* blends.

**Rubesco di Torgiano** [roo-bes-koh dee taw-jee-yah-noh] (*Umbria*, Italy) Modern red *DOCG*; more or less the exclusive creation of *Lungarotti*. ☆☆☆ **1986 Rubesco Riserva £££**

***Ruby*** (*Douro*, Portugal) Cheapest, basic *port*; young, blended, sweetly fruity.

🍇 **Ruby Cabernet** [roo-bee k-behr-nay] (California) A *Cabernet Sauvignon* and *Carignan* cross producing unsubtly fruity wines in California, Australia and South Africa.

🍇 **Ruche** [roo-kay] (*Piedmont*, Italy) Raspberryish red grape from Northern Italy producing early-drinking wines. Best from *Bava*.

**Rüdesheim** [rroo-des-hime] (*Rheingau*, Germany) Tourist town producing powerful *Rieslings*. QbA/Kab/Spät: **85** 86 **88 89 90** 91 92 93 94 95 96 Aus/Beeren/TBA: **83 85** 88 89 90 91 92 93 94 95 96 **Georg Breuer.**

**Rueda** [roo-way-dah] (Spain) *DO* in North-West Spain for clean, dry whites from the local *Verdejo*. Progress is being led most particularly by the *Lurtons* and the *Marqués de Riscal*.

🍷 **Ruffino** [roof-fee-noh] (*Tuscany*, Italy) Big *Chianti* producer with good top-of-the-range wines, including the reliable Cabreo *Vino da Tavola*. 85 88 90 91 93 94 ☆☆☆ **1990 Riserva Ducale 'Gold' ££**

**Rufina** [roo-fee-na] (*Tuscany*, Italy) A sub-region within *Chianti*, producing supposedly classier wine. **78 79** 81 **82 85 88 90** 94 95

🍷 **Ruinart** [roo-wee-nahr] (*Champagne*, France) High-quality sister to *Moët & Chandon*, with the superlative *Blanc De Blancs*. ☆☆☆☆☆ **1990 R. de Ruinart ££££**

🍇 **Rülander** [roo-len-dur] (Germany) German name for *Pinot Gris*.

**Rully** [roo-yee] (*Burgundy*, France) *Côte Chalonnaise* commune producing rich white and a red that's been called the 'poor man's' *Volnay*. See *Jadot* and *Olivier Leflaive*. Red: **78** 80 **85** 86 87 88 89 90 92 95 White: 84 **85 86** 87 **88** 89 **90 92** 95 **Faiveley; Jadot; Olivier Leflaive; Antonin Rodet.**

**Ruppertsberg** [roo-purt-sbehrg] (*Pfalz*, Germany) Top-ranking village with a number of excellent vineyards making vigorous, fruity Riesling. QbA/Kab/Spät: **85** 86 **88 89 90** 91 92 93 94 95 96 Aus/Beeren/TBA: **83 85** 88 89 90 91 92 93 94 95 96 ☆☆☆☆ **1993 Bürkllin-Wolf; Kimich; Werlé.**

**Russe** [rooss] (Bulgaria) Danube town best known in Britain for its reliable red blends but vaunted in *Bulgaria* as a source of modern whites.

**Russian River Valley** (California) Cool area north of *Sonoma* and west of *Napa*. Ideal for apples and good fizz, as is proven by the excellent *Iron Horse*, which also makes impressive table wines. Great Pinot Noir country. Red: 84 **85** 86 87 **90 91 92** 93 95 96 White: **85 90 91** 92 95 96 **Joseph Swan; Marimar Torres.**

**Rust** [roost] (*Burgenland*, Austria) Wine centre of *Burgenland*, famous for Ruster *Ausbruch* sweet white wine.

🍷 **Rust-en-Vrede** (*Stellenbosch*, South Africa) Well-regarded producer, but needs to improve. ☆☆☆ **1994 Tinta Barocca ££**

🍷 **Rustenberg** (*Stellenbosch*, South Africa) New winemaking brooms are sweeping through this well-regarded estate. And not before time. We'll see.

**Rutherford** (California) *Napa* region in which some producers believe sufficiently to propose it – and its geological 'bench' – as an *Appellation*. Red: **85** 86 87 **90 91** 92 93 95 White: **90 91** 92 95

**Rutherglen** (*Victoria*, Australia) Hot area on the *Murray River* pioneered by gold miners. Today noted for rich, *Muscat* and *Tokay* dessert and port-style wines, incredibly tough reds and attempts at *Chardonnay* which are used by cool-region winemakers to demonstrate why port and light dry whites cannot be successful in the same climate. See *Morris, All Saints, Campbells* ☆☆☆☆ **Campbell's Old Rutherglen Muscat £££**

**Ruwer** [roo-vur] (*Mosel-Saar-Ruwer*, Germany) *Mosel* tributary alongside which is to be found the *Romerlay Grosslage*, and includes Kasel, *Eitelsbach* and the great *Maximin Grunhaus* estate. QbA/Kab/Spät: **85** 86 **88 89 90** 92 93 94 95 96 Aus/Beeren/TBA: 83 **85** 88 89 90 92 93 94 95 96

**Hugh Ryman** [ri-man] Peripatetic *Flying Winemaker* whose team annually and reliably turns grapes into wine under contract (usually for UK retailers) in *Bordeaux, Burgundy*, Southern France, Spain, Germany, Moldavia, Chile, California, South Africa and Hungary. The give-away sign of a Ryman wine is the initials HDR at the foot of the label. ☆☆☆☆ **1995 Jacana Reserve South African Pinotage ££**

**Rymill** [ri-mil] (South Australia) One of several *Coonawarra* wineries to mention Riddoch on its label (in its Riddoch Run). Rymill at least has the legitimacy of a family link to John Riddoch, the region's founder. The *Shiraz* and *Cabernet* are first class. ☆☆☆☆ **1993 Shiraz, Coonawarra £££**

# S

**Saar** [zahr] (*Mosel-Saar-Ruwer*, Germany) The other *Mosel* tributary associated with lean, slatey *Riesling*. Villages include *Ayl, Ockfen,* Saarburg, Serrig and *Wiltingen.* QbA/Kab/Spät: **85 88 89 90** 91 92 93 94 95 96 Aus/Beeren/TBA: **83 85** 88 89 90 91 92 93 94 95 96

**Sablet** (*Rhône*, France) Good *Côtes du Rhône* village. Red: **78** 81 **82 83 85 88** 89 90 95 96

**Sachsen** [zah-khen] (Germany) Remember East Germany? Well, this is where poor wines used to be made there in the bad old days and good ones are being produced today by producers like Ulrich.

**Villa Sachsen** [za-shehn] (*Rheinhessen*, Germany) Estate with good, low-yielding vineyards in *Bingen*.

**Saintsbury** (*Carneros*, California) Superstar *Carneros* producer of unfiltered *Chardonnay* and – more specially – *Pinot Noir.* The slogan: 'Beaune in the USA' refers to the winery's Burgundian aspirations! The Reserve Pinot is a world-beater, while the easy-going Garnet is the good *Second Label*. ☆☆☆☆ **1994 Carneros Pinot Noir £££**

**Sakar** [sa-kah] (Bulgaria) Long-time source of much of the best *Cabernet Sauvignon* to come from *Bulgaria.*

**Castello della Sala** [kas-tel-loh del-la sah-lah] (*Umbria*, Italy) *Antinori's* over-priced but sound *Chardonnay, Sauvignon* and good *Sauvignon* and Procanico blend. ☆☆☆☆☆ **1996 Sauvignon Umbria della Sala ££**

**Salice Salentino** [sa-lee-chay sah-len-tee-noh] (*Puglia*, Italy) Spicy intense red made from the characterful *Negroamaro.* Great value, especially when mature. **Candido; Taurino.**

**Salon le Mesnil** [sah-lon lur may-neel] (*Champagne*, France) Small traditional subsidiary of *Laurent Perrier* with cult following for pure, long-lived *Chardonnay* fizz.

**Saltram** [sawl-tram] (South Australia) Greatly improved since coming under the *Rothbury* umbrella. Good, fairly priced *Barossa* reds and whites and top-flight ports. ☆☆☆ **1996 Classic Chardonnay ££**

**Samos** [sah-mos] (Greece) Aegean island producing sweet, fragrant, golden *Muscat* once called 'the wine of the Gods'. ☆☆☆☆ **Samos, Unione delle Cooperative Viticole £**

**Cellier des Samsons** [sel-yay day som-son] (*Burgundy*, France) Source of better-than-average *Beaujolais*. ☆☆☆☆ **1989 Moulin à Vent Cuvée Musique ££**

**San Luis Obispo** [san loo-wis oh-bis-poh] (California) Californian region gaining a reputation for *Chardonnay* and *Pinot Noir*. Try *Edna Valley*. Red: 84 **85** 86 87 **90 91** 92 93 95 96 White: **85 90 91** 92 95 96

**Viña San Pedro** [veen-ya san-pay-droh] (*Curico*, Chile) Huge *Curico* firm whose wines are quietly improving thanks to the efforts of consultant *Jacques Lurton*. ☆☆☆☆ **1994 Castillo de Molina Cabernet Sauvignon ££**

**Sancerre** [son-sehr] (*Loire*, France) At its best, the epitome of elegant, steely dry *Sauvignon;* at its worst, over-sulphured, fruitless dry wine. Reds and rosés, though well regarded-and highly priced-by French restaurants, are generally little better than quaffable *Pinot Noir*. **88 89 90** 94 95 **Jean-Max Roger; Bourgeois; Pierre Dézat; Crochet; Vacheron; Natter; Mellot; Vincent Pinard; Vatan.**

**Sandeman** (Spain/Portugal) North American-owned, generally underperforming but occasionally dazzling port and sherry producer. Port: **55** 57 58 **60 62 63** 65 66 67 68 **70** 72 75 80 94 ☆☆☆☆☆ **Royal Corregidor Rare Old Oloroso Sherry ££££**

**Sanford Winery** (*Santa Barbara*, California) *Santa Barbara* superstar producer of *Chardonnay* and especially distinctive, slightly horseradishy *Pinot Noir*. ☆☆☆☆ **1994 Pinot Noir £££**

**Sangiovese** [san-jee-yoh vay-seh] (Italy) The tobaccoey, herby-flavoured red grape of *Chianti* and *Montepulciano*, now being used increasingly in *Vino da Tavola* and in California where wineries like Atlas Peak see it as a lucrative alternative to *Cabernet Sauvignon*. **Atlas Peak; Antinori; Isole e Olena; Bonny Doon.**

**Santa Barbara** (California) Successful southern, cool-climate region for *Pinot Noir* and *Chardonnay*. See *Au Bon Climat* and *Sanford, Qupé* and Ojai. Red: 84 **85** 86 87 **90 91** 92 93 95 White: **85 90 91** 92 95

**Viña Santa Carolina** [ka-roh-lee-na] (Chile) Greatly improved producer, thanks to *Ignacio Recabarren* and vineyards in Casablanca. Still some way to go. Good reds. ☆☆☆☆ **1996 Chardonnay Gran Reserva ££**

**Santa Cruz Mountains** [krooz] (California) Exciting region to the south of San Francisco. See *Ridge* and *Bonny Doon*. Red: 84 **85** 86 87 **90 91** 92 93 95 White: **85 90 91** 92 95

**Santa Emiliana** (*Aconcagua*, Chile) Large producer with good Andes Peak offerings from *Casablanca*, and wines from the new southern region of Mulchen. ☆☆☆☆ **1995 Casablanca Chardonnay.**

**Santa Maddalena** [mad-dah-lay-nah] (*Trentino-Alto-Adige*, Italy) High-altitude region whose often lederhosen-clad winemakers use the local *Schiava* to make tangy red wine. **Vitticoltori Alto Adige.**

**Santa Rita** [ree-ta] (*Maipo*, Chile) Back on track after a slightly bumpy patch. The Casa Real is not only Chile's best red; it is also truly world class.☆☆☆☆☆ **1994 Casa Real £££**

**Santenay** [sont-nay] (*Burgundy*, France) Southern *Côte d'Or* village, producing pretty whites and good, though occasionally rather rustic reds. Look for *Girardin* and *Pousse d'Or*. White: 85 86 87 **88** 89 **90 92** 95 Red: 76 78 79 **80** 82 83 **85** 86 87 **88 89 90** 92 95

**Caves São João** [sow-jwow] (*Bairrada*, Portugal) Small company which produces high-quality *Bairrada*.

**Sardinia** (Italy) Traditionally the source of powerful reds (try *Santadi*) and whites, increasingly interesting *DOC* fortified wines, and new-wave modern reds to match the best *Super Tuscans*. **Sella & Mosca.**

**Sarget de Gruaud-Larose** [sahr-jay dur groowoh lah-rohs] (*St. Julien*, *Bordeaux*, France) *Second Label* of *Ch. Gruaud-Larose*.

**Sassicaia** [sas-see-ki-ya] (*Tuscany*, Italy) World-class *Cabernet*-based *Super Tuscan* with more of an Italian than a claret taste. No longer a mere *Vino da Tavola* since the *DOC* Bolgheri was introduced in 1994. ☆☆☆☆☆ **1992 ££££**

**Saumur** [soh-moor] (*Loire*, France) Heartland of variable *Chenin*-based fizz and still white, and the potentially more interesting *Saumur Champigny* reds which show what the *Cabernet Franc* can do here. See *Bouvet Ladubay*. Red: 83 **85** 86 **88 89 90 95** 96 White: 83 **85 86 88 89 90** 94 95 96 Sweet white: **76** 83 **85** 86 **88 89** 90 94 95 **Langlois-Chateau; Cave des Vignerons de Saumur.**

**Saumur Champigny** [soh-moor shom-pee-nyee] (*Loire*, France) Crisp, refreshing *Cabernet Franc* red; like *Beaujolais*, best served slightly chilled. Good examples are worth keeping for a few years. See *Bouvet-Ladubay*. 83 **85** 86 **88 89 90** 95 96 **Ch. du Hureau; Ch. de Targé. Ch de Vileneuve.**

**Sauternes** [soh-turn] (*Bordeaux*, France) Rich, honeyed dessert wines from *Sauvignon* and *Sémillon* (and possibly *Muscadelle*) blends. Should be affected by *Botrytis* but the climate does not always allow this. That's one explanation for disappointing Sauternes; the other is careless winemaking, and, in particular, a tendency to be heavy-handed with the *sulphor dioxide*. **70 71 75 76** 83 85 86 88 89 90 95 ***Barsac, Yquem, Rieussec, Climens, Suduiraut, Bastor-Lamontagne.***

**Sauvignon Blanc** [SOH-vin-yon-BLON] 'Grassy', 'catty', 'asparagussy', 'gooseberryish' grape grown the world over, but rarely really loved, so often blended, oaked or made sweet. In France at home in the *Loire* and *Bordeaux*. New Zealand gets it right – especially in *Marlborough*. In Australia, *Knappstein, Cullens, Stafford Ridge, Amberley* and *Shaw & Smith* are right on target. *Mondavi's* oaked *Fumé Blanc* and *Kendall Jackson's* sweet versions are successful but, *Monteviña*, Quivira, *Dry Creek, Simi* and – in blends with the *Semillon* – from *Guenoc* and *Carmenet* are the stars. Chile is making better versions every year, despite starting out with a lesser variety. See *Caliterra, Cánepa, Villiard*. In South Africa, see *Thelema, Mulderbosch* and *Neil Ellis*.

**Sauvignon de St. Bris** [SOH-vin-yon-dur san BREE] (*Burgundy*, France) *Burgundy's* only *VDQS*. An affordable and often worthwhile alternative to *Sancerre*, produced in vineyards near *Chablis*. **95** 96 **Brocard; Moreau.**

**Etienne Sauzet** [SOH-zay] (*Burgundy*, France) First-rank estate whose white wines are almost unfindable outside collectors' cellars and Michelin-starred restaurants. ☆☆☆☆ **1993 Bienvenues-Bâtard-Montrachet ££££**

**Savagnin** [sa-van-yan] (*Jura*, France) No relation of the *Sauvignon*; a white *Jura* variety used for *Vin Jaune* and blended with *Chardonnay* for *Arbois*. Also, confusingly, the Swiss name for the *Gewürztraminer*. ☆☆☆ **1990 Arbois, Fruitière Vinicole d'Arbois £££**

**Savennières** [sa-ven-yehr] (*Loire*, France) Fine, if sometimes aggressively dry *Chenin Blanc* whites, very long-lived *Coulée de Serrant* and *La Roche aux Moines* are the top names. White: 83 **85 86 88 89 90** 94 95 96

**Savigny-lès-Beaune** [sa-veen-yee lay bohn] (*Burgundy*, France) Distinctive whites (sometimes made from *Pinot Blanc*) and plummy raspberry reds. At their best can compare with neighbouring *Beaune*. Look for *Simon Bize, Bruno Clair* or *Machard de Gramont*. White: **79 85 86** 87 **88** 89 **90 92** 95 96 Red: **78** 80 83 **85** 86 87 **88 89 90** 92 95 96

**Savoie** [sav-wah] (Eastern France) Mountainous region near Geneva best known for crisp, floral whites such as Abymes, *Apremont, Seyssel* and *Crépy*.

**Scharffenberger** [shah-fen-bur-gur] (*Mendocino*, California) *Pommery*-owned, independently-run producer of top-class, top-value fizz. ☆☆☆☆ **Scharffenberger Brut £££**

**Scharzhofberg** [shahts-hof-behrg] (*Mosel-Saar-Ruwer*, Germany) Top-class *Saar* vineyard, producing great *Riesling*. QbA/Kab/Spät: **85** 86 **88 89 90** 91 92 93 94 95 96 Aus/Beeren/TBA: **83 85 88 89** 90 91 92 93 94 95 96 **Reichsgraf von Kesselstadt £££**

***Schaumwein*** [showm-vine] (Germany) Low-priced sparkling wine.

**Scheurebe** [shoy-ray-bur] (Germany) *Riesling/Sylvaner* cross, grown in Germany and in England. Tastes deliciously and recogniseably like pink grapefruit. In Austria, where it is used to make brilliant sweet wines, they sometimes know it as Samling 88. **Lingenfelder; Alois Kracher.**

**Schiava** [skee yah-vah] (Alto-Adige, Italy) Grape used in *Lago di Caldaro* to make light reds.

***Schilfwein*** [shilf-vine] (Austria) Luscious 'reed wine' – Austrian *Vin de Paille* pioneered by *Willi Opitz*.

***Schloss*** [shloss] (Germany) Literally 'castle', vineyard or estate.

**Schloss Böckelheim** [shloss boh-kell-hime] (*Nahe*, Germany) Varied Southern part of the *Nahe*. Wines from the Kupfergrübe vineyard and the State Wine Domaine are worth buying. QbA/Kab/Spät: **85** 86 **88 89 90** 91 92 93 94 95 96 Aus/Beeren/TBA: **83 85 88 89** 90 91 92 93 94 95 96 ☆☆☆☆ **Staat. Weinb. Neiderhäuser-Schlossböckelheim ££**

**Schloss Groenesteyn** [shloss groon-shtine] (*Rheingau*, Germany) Once successful, now a woeful under-performer.

**Schloss Reinhartshausen** [shloss rine-harts-how-zehn] (*Rheingau*, Germany) Innovative estate successful with *Pinot Blanc* and *Chardonnay* (the latter introduced following a suggestion by *Robert Mondavi*). The *Rieslings* are good too. QbA/Kab/Spät: **85 88 89 90** 91 92 93 94 95 96 Aus/Beeren/TBA: **83 85 88 89** 90 91 92 93 94 95 96

**Schloss Saarstein** [shloss sahr-stine] (*Mosel-Saar-Ruwer*, Germany) High-quality *Riesling* specialist in *Serrig*. QbA/Kab/Spät: **85** 86 **88 89 90** 91 92 93 94 95 96 Aus/Beeren/TBA: **83 85 88** 89 90 91 92 93 94 95 96 ☆☆☆☆ **1990 Serriger Riesling Auslese, Christian Eber £££**

**Schloss Vollrads** [shloss fol-rahts] (*Rheingau*, Germany) Under-performing *Charta* pioneer and devout believer in German dry wines.

**Schlossbockelheim** [shloss bok-el-hime] (*Nahe*, Germany) Village which gives its name to a large *Nahe Bereich*, producing elegant *Riesling*. QbA/Kab/Spät: **85** 86 **88 89 90** 91 92 93 94 95 Aus/Beeren/TBA: **83 85 88** 89 90 91 92 93 94 95 **Staatsweingut Niederhausen.**

🍷 **Dom. Schlumberger** [shloom-behr-jay] (*Alsace*, France) Great estate owner whose subtle top level wines can rival those of the somewhat more showy *Zind Humbrecht*. ☆☆☆☆ 1991 Gewürztraminer Christine Vendanges Tardives £££

🍷 **Scholl & Hillebrand** [shohl oont hil-brahnt] (*Rheingau*, Germany) Reliable merchant belonging to *Bernhard Breuer* who markets his estate wines under the *Georg Breuer* label. A sensible *Charta* producer.

🍷 **Scholtz Hermanos** [sholts hehr-mah-nohs] (Malaga, Spain) The only serious *Malaga* producer, though sadly with an uncertain future. ☆☆☆☆ Malaga Virgen ££

🍷 **Schramsberg** [shram-sberg] (*Napa Valley*, California) Old winery with cellars built into a hillside. This is the one that single-handedly put Californian fizz on the quality trail. Wines used to be too big for their boots, possibly because too many of the grapes were from warm vineyards in *Napa*. The J Schram is aimed at *Dom Perignon* and gets pretty close to the target. ☆☆☆☆ 1989 J Schram ££££

🍷 **Seaview** (South Australia) Penfolds brand for (excellent) fizz and (less frequently) red table wines. Look out for the Edwards & Chaffey label too. ☆☆☆☆ 1993 Pinot Noir/Chardonnay £££

🍷 **Sebastiani** [seh-bas-tee-yan-nee] (*Sonoma Valley*, California) Despite the *Sonoma* address, the main activity here lies in producing inexpensive, unexceptional wine from *Central Valley* grapes. Quality is improving however. The *Zinfandel* is the strongest suit, but the *Chardonnay* is pleasant enough. ☆☆☆ 1995 Sebastiani Chardonnay £

***Sec/secco/seco*** [se-koh] (France/Italy/Spain) Dry.

***Second Label*** (*Bordeaux*, France) Wine from a *Bordeaux Château's* lesser vineyards, younger vines and/or lesser *Cuvées* of wine. Especially worth buying in good vintages. See *Les Forts de Latour.*

🍷 **Segura Viudas** [say-goo-rah vee-yoo-dass] (*Catalonia*, Spain) The quality end of the *Freixenet* giant. One of the better examples of traditional *Cava*. ☆☆☆☆ Heredad Brut Reserva £££

🍷 **Seifried Estate** [see-freed] (Nelson, New Zealand) Also known as *Redwood Valley Estate*. Hermann Seifried makes superb *Riesling* especially *Late Harvest* style, and very creditable *Sauvignon* and *Chardonnay,* in the up-and-coming region of *Nelson*.

***Sekt*** [zekt] (Germany) Very basic sparkling wine best won in rifle booths at carnivals. Watch out for anything that does not state that it is made from *Riesling* – other grape varieties almost invariably make highly unpleasant wines. Only the prefix 'Deutscher' guarantees German origin.

🍷 **Selaks** [see-lax] (*Auckland*, New Zealand) Large, successful company in Kumeu best known for the piercingly fruity *Sauvignon* first made a decade ago by a young man called Kevin Judd, who went on to produce a little-known wine called *Cloudy Bay*. ☆☆☆☆ 1996 Sauvignon Blanc, Marlborough ££

🍷 **Weingut Selbach-Oster** [zel-bahkh os-tehr] (*Mosel-Saar-Ruwer*, Germany) Archetypal *Mosel Riesling*. ☆☆☆☆

***Sélection de Grains Nobles (SGN)*** [say-lek-see-yon day gran nohbl] (*Alsace*, France) Equivalent to German *Beerenauslesen*; rich, sweet *Botrytised* wine from specially selected grapes.

🍷 **Sella e Mosca** [seh-la eh mos-kah] (Sardinia, Italy) Dynamic firm with a good *Cabernet* called Villamarina, the rich *Anghelu Ruju* and traditional *Cannonau*. ☆☆☆☆ 1992 Tanca Farra ££

🍷 **Fattoria Selvapiana** [fah-taw-ree-ya sel-va-pee-yah-nah ] (*Tuscany*, Italy) Benchmark *Chianti Rufina*, excellent *Vin Santo*, and olive oil. ☆☆☆☆ 1993 Chianti Rufina Riserva £££

🍇 **Sémillon** [*in France:* say-mee-yon; *in Australia:* seh-mil-lon and even seh-mih-lee-yon] Peachy grape generally blended with *Sauvignon* in *Bordeaux* to give fullness in both dry and sweet wines, notably *Sauternes*, vinified separately to great effect in Australia, where it is also sometimes blended with Chardonnay. Rarely as successful in other New World countries where many versions taste more like *Sauvignon*. Carmenet; Geyser Peak; Rothbury, McWilliams; Xanadu.

**Seppelt** (South Australia) *Penfolds* subsidiary and pioneer of the *Great Western* region where it makes good rich Shiraz. The Drumborg is still a great example of this variety but, perversely, the Seppelt Shiraz I'd go for is off-dry and is as fizzy as Champagne. Fizzy reds are admittedly an acquired taste, but the spicy richness of the 20-year old Show Reserve Sparkling Shiraz ought to change your mind. Other Seppelt fizzes are recommendable too, though the once-fine Sallinger seems to have lost its way recently. ☆☆☆☆ **1993 Sparkling Shiraz £££**

**Sequoia Grove** [seh-koy-yah grohv] (*Napa Valley*, California) Source of interesting spicy Cabernet and variable Chardonnay. ☆☆☆☆ **1992 Cabernet Sauvignon Napa Valley £££**

**Ch. la Serre** [la sehr] (*St. Emilion Grand Cru Classé*, *Bordeaux*, France) Up-and-coming property with approachable, well made wines. 75 82 83 85 88 89 90 93 94 95 96

***Servir frais*** (France) Serve chilled.

**Setúbal** [shtoo-bal] (Portugal) *DOC* on the *Setúbal Peninsula.*

**Setúbal Peninsula** (Portugal) Home of the *Setúbal DOC*, but now equally notable for the rise of two new wine regions, Arrabida and Palmela, where *J. M Fonseca Succs* and *J. P. Vinhos* are making some excellent wines from local and international grape varieties.The lusciously rich *Muscat de Setúbal* made here is, however, still the star of the show.

**Sèvre-et-Maine** [sayvr ray mayn] (*Loire*, France) (Muscadet de) Demarcated area that supposedly produces wines that are a cut above plain *Muscadet*. (Actually, it is worth noting that this 'higher quality' region produces the vast majority of each *Muscadet* harvest.) **Chéreau-Carré; Ch de la Ragotière; Ch de la Galissonnière; Luneau; Metaireau; Sauvion.**

**Seyssel** [say-sehl] (*Savoie*, France) *AC* region near Geneva producing light white wines that are usually enjoyed in après-ski mood when no-one is overly concerned about value for money. **Varichon et Clerc.**

**Seyval blanc** [aay-vahl blon] Hybrid grape – a cross between French and US vines – unpopular with EU authorities but successful in eastern US, Canada and England, especially at *Breaky Bottom*.

**Shafer** [shay-fur] (*Napa Valley*, California) Top *Cabernet* producer in the *Stag's Leap* district, and maker of some increasingly classy Chardonnay. ☆☆☆☆ **1994 Cabernet Sauvignon Stag's Leap District £££**

**Shaw & Smith** (*Adelaide Hills*, Australia) Recently founded winery producing one of Australia's best *Sauvignons* and a pair of increasingly Burgundian *Chardonnays* that demonstrate how good wines from this variety can taste with and without oak. ☆☆☆☆ **1996 Sauvignon Blanc £££**

***Sherry*** (*Jerez*, Spain) The fortified wine made in the area surrounding *Jerez*. Wines made elsewhere – Australia, England, South Africa, etc.– may now no longer use the name *Almecenista; Fino; Amontillado; Manzanilla; Cream Sherry Barbadillo; Lustau; Gonzalez Byass; Hidalgo.*

**Shiraz** [shee-raz] (Australia, South Africa) The *Syrah* grape in Australia and South Africa, taking its name from its supposed birthplace in Iran. South African versions are, incidentally, as different in style (lighter and generally greener) from the Australians as the Aussies are from the (less ripe and oaky) efforts of the *Rhône*. **Wolf Blass; Penfolds; Rothbury; St. Hallett; Rockford; Plantagenet; Rust-en-Vrede; Saxenberg; Lievland.**

**Sicily** (Italy) Historically best known for *Marsala* and sturdy 'southern' table wine. Now, however, there is an array of other unusual fortified wines and a fast-growing range of new-wave reds and whites, many of which are made from grapes grown nowhere else on earth. **Corvo, De Bartoli, Regaleali, Terre di Ginestra.**

**Siglo** [seeg-loh] (*Rioja*, Spain) Good brand of modern red (traditionally sold in a hessian 'sack') and old-fashioned whites.

***Silex*** [see-lex] (France) Term describing flinty soil, used by *Didier Dagueneau* for his oak-fermented *Pouilly Fumé*.

**Silver Oaks Cellars** (*Napa Valley*, California) Specialist *Cabernet* producers favouring fruitily accessible but still classy wines which benefit from long ageing in (American oak) barrels and bottle before release. Look out for older vintages of the single-vineyard Bonny's Vineyard wines, the last of which was made in 1991. ☆☆☆☆☆ **1993 Cabernet Sauvignon Alexander Valley ££££**

**Silverado** [sil-veh-rah-doh] (*Napa Valley*, California) Reliable *Cabernet* and *Chardonnay* winery that belongs to Walt Disney's widow. ☆☆☆☆ **1992 Limited Reserve Chardonnay, Napa Valley.£££**

**Simi Winery** [see-mee] (*Sonoma Valley*, California) *Moët & Chandon* subsidiary with complex, long-lived Burgundian *Chardonnay*, archetypical *Sauvignon* and lovely blackcurranty *Alexander Valley Cabernet*. ☆☆☆☆☆ **1991 Alexander Valley Reserve Cabernet Sauvignon £££**

**Bert Simon** (*Mosel-Saar-Ruwer*, Germany) Newish estate in the *Saar* river valley with super-soft *Rieslings* and elegant *Weissburgunder*.

**Simonsig Estate** [see-mon-sikh] (*Stellenbosch*, South Africa) A big estate with a very impressive commercial range, and the occasional gem – try the *Shiraz, Cabernet, Pinotage* and Kaapse Vonkel sparkler. ☆☆☆ **1993 Cabernet Sauvignon ££**

***Sin Crianza*** [sin cree-an-tha] (Spain) Not aged in wood.

**Ch. Siran** [see-ron] (*Margaux Cru Bourgeois, Bordeaux*, France) Beautiful *château* outperforming its classification and producing increasingly impressive and generally very fairly priced wines. 70 **75 78** 81 **82** 83 85 86 88 89 90 93 94 95 96

**Skillogalee** [kil-log-gah-lee] (South Australia) Well-respected *Clare* producer, specialising in *Riesling*, but also showing his skill with reds. ☆☆☆☆ **1995 Shiraz, Clare Valley.**

***Skin contact*** The longer the skins of black grapes are left in with the juice after the grapes have been crushed, the greater the *tannin* and the deeper the colour. Some non-aromatic white varieties (*Chardonnay* and *Sémillon* in particular) can also benefit from extended skin contact (usually between six and twenty-four hours) which increases flavour.

**Slovakia** Up-and-coming source of wines from grapes little seen elsewhere, such as the Muscatty Irsay Oliver.

**Slovenia** Former Yugoslavian region in which *Laski Rizling* is king. Other grapes show greater promise.

**Smith Woodhouse** (*Douro*, Portugal) Part of the same empire as *Dow's, Grahams* and *Warres* but often overlooked *Vintage* ports can be good, as is the house speciality: traditional *Late-Bottled Vintage Port*. 60 **63 66 70** 75 77 85 94 ☆☆☆☆ **1984 Traditional Late Bottled £££**

**Ch. Smith-Haut-Lafitte** [oh-lah-feet] (*Pessac-Léognan Cru Classé, Bordeaux*, France) Rejuvenated property with increasingly classy reds and (specially) whites. Red: **82** 85 86 **89 90** 91 92 93 94 95 White: 92 93 94 95 ☆☆☆☆ **1995 ££££**

**Smithbrook** (Western Australia) A winery specialising in Pinot Noirs in the new southerly region of Pemberton. ☆☆☆☆ **1993 Pinot Noir Pemberton £££**

**Soave** [swah-veh] (*Veneto*, Italy) Dull stuff for the most part, but Soave *Classico* is better; single vineyard versions are best. Sweet *Recioto* di Soave is delicious. *Pieropan* is almost uniformly excellent.

🍷 **Ch. Sociando-Mallet** [soh-see-yon-doh ma-lay] (*Haut-Médoc Cru Bourgeois, Bordeaux*, France) A *Cru Bourgeois* whose oaked, fruity red wines are way above its status. **82** 83 **85 86** 88 89 90 92 93 94 95 96

🍷 **Sogrape** [soh-grap] (Portugal) Big producer of *Mateus* Rosé and (relatively) modern *Dão, Douro* and *Bairrada*. ☆☆☆☆ **1992 Reserve Dão ££**

🍷 **Solaia** [soh-li-yah] (*Tuscany*, Italy) Yet another *Antinori Super Tuscan* phenomenonal blend of *Cabernet Sauvignon* and *Franc*, with a little *Sangiovese*. ☆☆☆☆☆ **1993 Solaia, Antinori ££££**

***Solera*** [soh-leh-rah] (*Jerez*, Spain) Ageing system involving older wine being continually 'refreshed' by slightly younger wine of the same style.

🍷 **Bodegas Felix Solís** [fay-leex soh-lees] (*Valdepeñas*, Spain) By far the biggest, most go-ahead winery in *Valdepeñas*.

**Somló** [som-loy] (Hungary) Ancient wine district, now source of top-class whites. See *Fürmint*.

**Somontano** [soh-mon-tah-noh] (Spain) *DO* Region in the foothills of the Pyrenees in Aragon, now experimenting with international grape varieties. **Viñas Del Vero; Enate.**

**Sonnenuhr** [soh-neh-noor] (*Mosel*, Germany) Vineyard site in the famous village of *Wehlen*. See *Dr Loosen*. QbA/Kab/Spät: **85** 86 **88 89 90** 91 92 93 94 95 96 Aus/Beeren/TBA: **83 85** 88 89 90 91 92 93 94 95 96

**Sonoma Valley** [so-NOH-ma] (California) Despite the *Napa* hype, this lesser-known region not only contains some of the state's top wineries; it is also home to *E&J Gallo's* super-premium vineyard. The region is subdivided into the *Sonoma, Alexander* and *Russian River Valleys* and *Dry Creek*. Red: **85** 86 87 **90 91** 92 93 95 96 White: **90 91** 92 95 96 **Simi; Clos du Bois; Iron Horse; Matanzas Creek; Sonoma Cutrer; Jordan; Laurel Glen; Kistler; Duxoup; Ravenswood; Kenwood; Quivira; Dry Creek; Gundlach Bundschu; Adler Fels; Arrowood; Carmenet.**

🍷 **Sonoma-Cutrer** [soh-noh-ma koo-trehr] (*Sonoma Valley*, California) Producer of world-class *Chardonnay* from specified single vineyards – whose wine can rival the best *Puligny-Montrachet*. ☆☆☆☆ **1992 Cutrer Vineyard Chardonnay ££££**

🍷 **Sonop Winery** [so-nop] (*Cape*, South Africa) Three ranges, Cape Levant, Cape Soleil and Kumala, are mostly quite basic. Diemersdal is better. ☆☆☆ 1996 Diemersdal Merlot **££**

🍷 **Henri Sorrel** [soh-rel] (*Rhône*, France) Long-established domaine with two good red *Hermitages* (Le Gréal is the top cuvée) and an attractively floral white fom the same *Appellation*. ☆☆☆☆ **1992 Le Gréal £££**

**South Africa** Three years after the return to democracy, South Africa remains the focus of interest for wine drinkers – and winemakers. Traditional reds which used to be left to dry out in big old casks are fast being supplanted by modern winemaking. Unfortunately, too many producers are still picking their grapes too early and making wines with an unripe, green flavour. Good, simple dry *Chenins, Late Harvest* wines and surprisingly good *Pinotages*; otherwise very patchy. Red: 86 **87** 89 **91 92** 93 94 95 White: 92 93 94 95 96 **Vergelegen' Plaisir de Merle; Kanonkop; Mulderbosch; Thelema.**

**South Australia** Home of almost all the biggest wine companies and still producing over 50 per cent of Australia's wine. The *Barossa Valley* is one of the country's oldest wine producing regions, but like its neighbours *Clare* and *McLaren Vale,* faces competition from cooler areas like the *Adelaide Hills, Padthaway* and *Coonawarra.* White: **87** 88 **90 91 94** 95 96 Red: **82 84 85 86 87** 88 **90 91** 94 95 96

**South-East Australia** A cleverly meaningless regional description which helps the Australians get round some of Europe's pettier appellation-focused rules. Technically, it covers around 85% of Australia's vineyards.

**South-West France** An unofficial umbrella term covering the areas between *Bordeaux* and the *Pyrenees, Bergerac, Madiran, Cahors, Jurançon* and the *Vins de Pays de Côtes de Gascogne.* A good source of very traditional wines.

**Spanna** [spah-nah] (*Piedmont*, Italy) The *Piedmont*ese name for the *Nebbiolo* grape and the more humble wines made from it.

**Pierre Sparr** (*Alsace*, France) Big producer; a rare chance to taste traditional *Chasselas*. ☆☆☆ **1994 Chasselas Vieilles Vignes ££**

***Spätlese*** [shpayt-lay-zeh] (Germany) Second step in the *QmP* scale, *Late-Harvested* grapes making wine a notch drier than *Auslese*.

**Spottswoode** (*Napa Valley*, California) Excellent small producer of complex reds. ☆☆☆☆ **1992 Cabernet Sauvignon Napa Valley.**

***Spritz/ig*** [shprit-zig] Slight sparkle or fizz. Also *Pétillance*.

***Spumante*** [spoo-man-tay] (Italy) Sparkling.

**St. Amour** [san ta-moor] (*Burgundy*, France) One of the ten *Beaujolais Crus* – usually light and fruity. Michel Tête makes a good one, as does *Georges Dubeouf*. **85 87 88 89** 90 **91** 93 94 95 96

**St. Aubin** [san toh-ban] (*Burgundy*, France) Underrated *Côte d'Or* village for (jammily rustic) reds and rich, nutty, rather classier white; affordable alternatives to *Meursault Olivier Leflaive* and *Gérard Thomas* are consistently excellent. White: **79** 84 **85 86** 87 **88** 89 **90 92** 95 Red: **78** 80 83 **85** 86 87 **88 89 90** 92 95

**St. Chinian** [san shee-nee-yon] (South-West France) Neighbour of *Faugères* and a fellow *AC* in the *Coteaux du Languedoc*, producing mid-weight, good-value wines from *Carignan* and other *Rhône* grapes. ☆☆☆ **Ch. Babeau; Ch. Quartironi de Sars; Mas Champart; Mas de la Tour.**

**St. Emilion** [san tay-mee-lee-yon] (*Bordeaux*, France) Large commune with very varied soils and wines. At best, sublime *Merlot*-dominated claret; at worst dull, earthy and fruitless. Supposedly 'lesser' satellite neighbours – *Lussac, Puisseguin, St. Georges* etc,– often make better value wine. **70 75** 78 79 81 **82 83 85** 86 **88 89** 90 94 95 **Pavie; Angelus; Ausone; Canon; Figeac; Cheval Blanc; Troplong Mondot.**

**St. Estèphe** [san teh-stef] (*Bordeaux*, France) Northernmost *Médoc* commune with clay soil and wines which can be a shade more rustic than those of neighbouring *Pauillac* and *St. Julien*. Tough when young but potentially very long-lived. 70 75 76 **78** 79 **82** 83 **85 86** 88 89 90 94 95 96 ***Calon Segur, Cos d'Estournel, Montrose***.

🍷 **St. Francis** (*Sonoma*, California) Innovative winery with great *Zinfandels*, and Reserve *Chardonnays* and *Cabernets*. The first Californian to introduce artificial corks in a laudable effort to protect wine drinkers from faulty bottles. ☆☆☆☆ **1992 Unfiltered Old Vine Zinfandel £££**

**St. Georges St. Emilion** [san jorrzh ay-mee-lee-yon] (*Bordeaux*, France) Satellite of *St. Emilion* with good *Merlot*-dominant reds, often better value than *St. Emilion* itself. **82 83 85** 86 **88 89** 90 94 95 96 **Ch. St. Georges; Maquin St. Georges.**

🍷 **St. Hallett** (*Barossa Valley*, Australia) Superstar *Barossa* winery specialising in wines from old ('old block') *Shiraz* vines. Rich, spicily intense ☆☆☆☆ **1993 Old Block Shiraz, Barossa Valley £££**

🍷 **St. Hubert's** (*Victoria*, Australia) Improving (since its purchase by *Rothbury*) pioneering *Yarra* winery with ultra-fruity *Cabernet* and mouth-filling whites. ☆☆☆☆ **1996 Sauvignon Blanc ££**

🍷 **Château St. Jean** [jeen] (*Sonoma*, California) Named after the founder's wife; now Japanese-owned and a source of good single-vineyard *Chardonnays, Late Harvest Rieslings* and Bordeaux-style reds. ☆☆☆☆ **1991 Cabernet Sauvignon Sonoma County Cinq Cépages £££**

**St. Joseph** [san joh-sef] (*Rhône*, France) Potentially vigorous, fruity *Syrah* from the northern *Rhône*. Whites range from flabby to fragrant *Marsannes*. Red: **76 78 82 83 85 88** 89 90 91 95 96 **Grippat; Trollo; Du Chênes; Gacho-Pascal; Perrier Fauturie.**

**St. Julien** [san-joo-lee-yen] (*Bordeaux*, France) Aristocratic *Médoc* commune producing classic rich wines, full of cedar and deep, ripe fruit. 70 75 76 **78** 79 81 **82** 83 **85 86** 88 89 90 94 95 96 **Léoville Barton; Léoville-Las-Cases; Ducru-Beaucaillou; Beychevelle.**

🍇 **St. Laurent** [sant loh-rent] (Austria) *Pinot Noir*-like berryish red grape, mastered, in particular, by *Umathum*.

**St. Nicolas de Bourgueil** [san nee-koh-lah duh boor-goy] (*Loire*, France) Lightly fruity *Cabernet Franc*; needs a warm year to ripen its raspberry fruit. Red: **85** 86 **88 89 90** 95 **Jamet; Mabileau; Vallée.**

**St. Péray** [san pay-reh] (*Rhône*, France) *AC* near Lyon for full-bodied, still white and *Methode Champenoise* sparkling wine, at risk from encroaching housing. **Auguste Clape; Alain Voge; Jean Lionnet.**

🍷 **Ch. St. Pierre** [san pee-yehr] (*St. Julien 4th Growth*, *Bordeaux*, France) Reliable *St. Julien* under the same ownership as *Ch. Gloria*. **70 78 82 83** 85 86 88 89 90 93 94 95 ☆☆☆☆ **1982 Ch. St. Pierre ££££**

**St-Pourçain-sur-Sioule** [san poor-san soor see-yool] (*Loire*, France) *Light* reds and rosés and white *Sauvignon, Chardonnay* and Trésallier.

**St. Romain** [san roh-man] (*Burgundy*, France) *Hautes Côtes de Beaune* village producing undervalued fine whites and rustic reds. White: **85 86** 87 **88** 89 **90 92** 95 Red: 83 **85** 86 87 **88 89 90** 92 95 **Alain Gras.**

**St. Véran** [san vay-ron] (*Burgundy*, France) Once sold as *Beaujolais* Blanc; affordable alternative to *Pouilly Fuissé*; better than most *Mâconnais* whites. Ch. Fuissé is worth keeping an eye out for.White: 84 **85 86** 87 **88** 89 **90 92** 95 **Dom des Deux Roches; Corsin; Luquet; Pacquet.**

***Staatsweingut*** [staht-svine-goot] (Germany) A state-owned wine estate such as Staatsweinguter Eltville (Rheingau), a major cellar in *Eltville*.

🍷 **Stafford Ridge** (*Adelaide Hills*, Australia) Fine *Chardonnay* and especially *Sauvignon* from *Lenswood* by the former chief winemaker of *Hardys*. ☆☆☆☆ **1995 Lenswood Sauvignon ££**

**Stag's Leap District** (*Napa Valley*, California) A long-established hillside region, specialising in blackcurranty *Cabernet Sauvignon*. See *Shafer, Clos du Val, Stag's Leap*. Red: 84 **85** 86 87 **90 91** 92 93 95 96

🍷 **Stag's Leap Wine Cellars** (*Napa Valley*, California) Pioneering supporter of the *Stag's Leap Appellation*, and one of finest wineries in California. The best wines are the Faye Vineyard, SLV and Cask 23 Cabernets. ☆☆☆☆☆ **1990 SLV-FAY Cabernet Sauvignon £££**

***Stalky or stemmy*** Flavour of the stem rather than of the juice.

🍷 **Stanton & Killeen** (Rutherglen, Australia) Reliable producer of Liqueur Muscat. ☆☆☆☆☆ **Rutherglen Liqueur Muscat ££**

**Ste. Croix-du-Mont** [sant crwah doo mon] (*Bordeaux*, France) *Sauternes* neighbour with less fine wines. 76 **83** 85 86 88 89 90 95 96 **Ch. Louhens; Ch. Lamarque.**

🍷 **Ch. Ste. Michelle** (*Washington State*, USA) Big winery producing increasingly impressive Merlot, Riesling and Sauvignon. ☆☆☆☆ **1994 Cabernet Sauvignon £££**

***Steely*** Refers to young wine with evident *acidity*. A compliment when paid to *Chablis* and dry *Sauvignons*.

🍇 **Steen** [steen] (South Africa) Local name for (and possibly odd *clone* of) *Chenin Blanc*. Widely planted (over 30% of the vineyard area). The best come from *Boschendal* and *Fairview*.

**Steiermark** [stehr-mark] (Austria) An Austrian wine region more commonly known in England as *Styria*. Generally expensive dry whites in a lean austere style. *Chardonnay* is confusingly sold here as Morillon.

**Stellenbosch** [stel-len-bosh] (South Africa) Centre of the Cape wine industry, and taken far too seriously as a regional appellation. Sub-regions like Helderberg make more sense. Red: 82 84 86 **87** 89 **91 92** 93 94 95 96 White: **87 91** 92 93 94 95 **Meerlust; Rustenberg; Thelema; Mulderbosch; Kanonkop; Bergkelder; Delheim.**

🍷 **Stellenbosch Farmers' Winery** (*Stellenbosch*, South Africa) South Africa's biggest wine producer; wines include Sable View, Libertas, *Nederburg* and, now, *Plaisir de Merl*, which is made by Paul Pontallier of *Ch. Margaux* ☆☆☆☆ **1994 Plaisir de Merle Cabernet ££**

🍷 **Stellenryck** [stel-len-rik] (South Africa) The *Bergkelder's* top red and white. The Cabernet is well thought of in South Africa but could be less lean. ☆☆☆ **1991 Cabernet ££**

🍷 **Stellenzicht Vineyards** [stel-len-zikht] (*Stellenbosch*, South Africa) The baby sister estate of *Neethlingshof*; a much more attractive proposition with an impressive *Sauvignon* and a *Shiraz* good enough (in 1994) to beat *Penfolds Grange* in a blind tasting. ☆☆☆ **1994 Shiraz ££**

🍷 **Sterling Vineyards** (*Napa Valley*, California) Founded by Peter Newton (now at *Newton* vineyards) and once the plaything of Coca-Cola, this showcase estate now belongs to Canadian liquor giant *Seagram*. Among the current successes are the fairly priced Redwood Trail wines. ☆☆☆☆ **1994 Cabernet Sauvignon ££**

🍷 **Weingut Georg Stiegelmar** [stee-gel-mahr] (*Burgenland*, Austria) Producer of pricy, highly acclaimed dry whites from *Chardonnay* and *Pinot Blanc* and some particularly good reds from *Pinot Noir* and *St. Laurent*. ☆☆☆☆☆ **1993 Juris St. Laurent £££**

**Stoneleigh** (*Marlborough*, New Zealand) Reliable Marlborough label used by *Cooks/Corbans*. ☆☆☆☆ **1996 Sauvignon Blanc ££**

**Stoniers** [stoh-nee-yurs] (Mornington Peninsula, Australia) Small *Mornington* winery, successful with impressive *Pinot Noir, Chardonnay* and *Merlot*. (Previously known as Stoniers-Merrick.) ☆☆☆☆ **1995 Chardonnay ££**

**Stratford** (California) British-born Tony Cartledge sells highly commercial blends under this and the Cartledge & Brown labels.

***Structure*** The 'structural' components of a wine include *tannin, acidity* and *alcohol*. They provide the skeleton or backbone that supports the 'flesh' of the fruit. A young wine with structure should age well.

**Ch. de Suduiraut** [soo-dee-rroh] (Sauternes Premier Cru Classé, *Bordeaux*, France) Producing greater things since its purchase by French insurance giant, *AXA*. Top wines: 'Cuvée Madame', 'Crème de Tête'. 75 **76** 78 **79** 81 **82 83** 84 85 86 88 89 90 94 ☆☆☆☆ **1988 ££££**

**Suhindol** [soo-win-dol] (Bulgaria) One of *Bulgaria's* best-known regions, the source of widely available, fairly-priced *Cabernet Sauvignon*.

***Sulfites*** US labelling requirement alerting those suffering from an (extremely rare) allergy to the presence of *sulphur dioxide*. Curiously, no such requirement is made of cans of baked beans and dried apricots, which contain twice as much of the chemical.

***Sulphur Dioxide/SO2*** Antiseptic routinely used by food packagers and winemakers to protect their produce from bacteria and oxidation.

**Suntory** (Japan) Japanese drinks conglomerate with substantial interests in various wineries around the world. See *Firestone* in California; *Ch. La Grange* in *St. Julien* and *Dr Weil* in Germany.

***Super Second*** (*Bordeaux*, France) A small gang of *Médoc* Second Growths: *Pichon Lalande, Pichon Longueville, Léoville-Las-Cases, Ducru Beaucaillou, Cos d'Estournel*; whose wines are thought to rival – and cost nearly as much as – the first growths. Other over-performers include: *Rauzan-Segla* and *Léoville Barton, Lynch Bages, Palmer, La Lagune, Montrose*.

***Super Tuscan*** (Italy) New-wave *Vino da Tavola* (usually red) wines pioneered by producers like *Antinori* which stand outside traditional *DOC* rules. Generally *Bordeaux*-style blends or *Sangiovese* or a mixture of both.

***Supérieur/Superiore*** [soo-pay-ree-ur/soo-pay-ree-ohr-ray] (France/Italy) Often meaningless in terms of discernible quality; denotes wine that has been made from riper grapes.

***Sur lie*** [soor-lee] (France) The ageing 'on its *Lees*' – or dead yeasts – most commonly associated with *Muscadet*, but now being used by pioneering producers to make other fresher and richer and sometimes slightly sparkling wines in southern France.

***Süssreserve*** [soos-sreh-zurv] (Germany) Unfermented grape juice used to bolster sweetness and fruit in German and English wines.

**Sutter Home Winery** (*Napa Valley*, California) Home of robust red *Zinfandel* in the 1970's, and responsible for the invention of successful sweet 'white' (or, as the non-colour-blind might say, pink) *Zinfandel*. ☆☆☆ **1991 Amador County Reserve Zinfandel ££**

**Swan Valley** (Western Australia) Well-established, hot vineyard area: good for fortified wines, and a source of fruit for *Houghton's* successful *HWB*. Houghton also produces cooler-climate wines in the microclimate of *Moondah Brook*.

**Swanson** [swon-son] (*Napa Valley*, California) Top-flight, innovative producer of *Cabernet, Chardonnay*, Sangiovese, Syrah and Late Harvest Semillon. ☆☆☆☆☆ **1992 Syrah £££**

**Switzerland** Produces mostly enjoyable but expensive; light, floral wines for early drinking. See *Dôle, Fendant, Chablais*.

🍇 **Sylvaner/Silvaner** [sihl-vah-nur] Relatively non-aromatic white grape, originally from *Austria* but adopted by other European areas, particularly *Alsace* and *Franken*. Elsewhere, wines are often young, dry and earthy, though there are some promising efforts with it in South Africa. ☆☆☆ **1993 Henry Fuchs Sylvaner d'Alsace ££**

🍇 **Syrah** [see-rah] (*Rhône*, France) The red *Rhône* grape, an exotic mix of ripe fruit and spicy, smoky, gamey, leathery flavours. Skilfully adopted by Australia, where it is called *Shiraz* and in southern France for *Vin de Pays d'Oc*. Increasingly popular in California, thanks to '*Rhône* Rangers' like *Bonny Doon* and *Phelps*. See *Qupé, Marqués de Griñon* in Spain and *Isole e Olena,* plus *Côte Rôtie, Hermitage, Shiraz.*

# T

🍷 **La Tâche** [la tash] (*Burgundy*, France) Wine from the La Tâche vineyard, exclusively owned by the *Dom. de la Romanée Conti.* Frequently as good as the rarer and more expensive 'La Romanée Conti'. ☆☆☆☆☆ **1992 La Tâche Grand Cru ££££**

***Tafelwein*** [tah-fel-vine] (Germany) Table wine. Only prefix 'Deutscher' guarantees German origin.

🍷 **Ch. Tahbilk** [tah-bilk] (*Victoria*, Australia) Old-fashioned winemaking in the *Goulbourn Valley.* Great, long-lived *Shiraz* from 130-year-old vines, surprisingly good, *Chardonnay* and lemony *Marsanne* which needs a decade. The second wine is Dalfarras. ☆☆☆☆ **1995 Marsanne ££**

🍷 **Ch. Taillefer** [tile-fehr] (*Pomerol*, *Bordeaux*, France) Good, rather than great wine. To buy in riper vintages. 82 83 85 86 88 89 90 93 94

🍷 **Cave de Tain L'Hermitage** (*Rhône*, France) Reliable cooperative with good *Crozes Hermitage* and *Hermitage.* ☆☆☆ **1993 Crozes-Hermitage.**

🍷 **Taittinger** [tat-tan-jehr] (*Champagne*, France) Producer of reliable non-vintage and superlative Comtes de *Champagne Blanc de Blancs*. ☆☆☆☆ **Taittinger Brut Reserve ££££**

🍷 **Ch. Talbot** [tal-boh] (*St. Julien 4th Growth*, *Bordeaux*, France) Reliable if sometimes slightly jammy wine. Connetable Talbot is the *Second Wine.* 75 **78** 79 81 **82 83** 84 **85** 86 87 88 89 90 92 93 94 95 ☆☆☆☆ **1990 ££££**

🍷 **Taltarni** [tal-tahr-nee] (*Victoria*, Australia) Run by Dominique Portet whose brother Bernard runs *Clos du Val*. Understated *Shiraz* and European-style *Cabernets* are the stars from this beautiful vineyard in the *Pyrenees*. The sparkling wines, including a recently launched effort from *Tasmania,* are impressive too.

***Tank Method*** See *Cuve Close.*

🍇 **Tannat** [ta-na] (France) Rustic French grape variety traditionally widely used in the blend of *Cahors* and in South America, principally *Uruguay.*

***Tannic*** See *Tannin.*

***Tannin*** *Astringent* component of red wine which comes from the skins, pips and stalks and helps the wine to age.

🍇 **Tarantino** [ta-ran-tee-noh] (California) Remarkable grape variety created by Emanuelle and Ilbe Beck in 1984 in the Casablanca Valley, by crossing the Barbarella Rosso with the Travolta-Peschita. The better examples enjoy a brief encounter of nine-and-a-half-weeks with oak barrels. The 1990 vintage should last from here to eternity – or at least until 2001.

🍷 **Tardy & Ange** [tahr-dee ay onzh] (*Rhône*, France) Partnership producing classy *Crozes-Hermitage* at the Dom. de Entrefaux.

**Tarragona** [ta-ra-GO-nah] (*Catalonia*, Spain) *DO* region south of *Penedés* and home to many cooperatives. Contains the better quality *Terra Alta.*

**Tarrango** [ta-RAN-goh] (Australia) Juicy grape pioneered by *Brown Brothers*. ☆☆☆☆ **1996 Brown Brothers £**

**Tarrawarra** [ta-ra-wa-ra] (*Yarra Valley*, Australia) Increasingly successful *Pinot* pioneer in the cool climate region of the *Yarra Valley*. *Second Label* is Tunnel Hill. ☆☆☆☆ **1995 Reserve Pinot Noir, Yarra Valley ££££**

***Tarry*** Red wines from hot countries often have an aroma and flavour reminiscent of tar. The *Syrah* and *Nebbiolo* grapes in particular exhibits this characteristic.

***Tartaric*** Type of acid found in grapes. Also the form in which acid is added to wine in hot countries whose legislation allows this.

***Tartrates*** [tar-trayts] Harmless white crystals often deposited by white wines in the bottle. In Germany, these are called 'diamonds'.

**Tasmania** (Australia) Cool-climate island, showing potential for sparkling wine, *Chardonnay, Riesling, Pinot Noir* and even (somewhat herbaceous) *Cabernet Sauvignon*. Questions remain, however, over which are the best parts of the island for growing vines. White: **92 94 95** 96 Red: **90 91 92** 94 95 96 **Heemskerk; Moorilla; Piper's Brook and Freycinet.**

***Tastevin*** [tat-van] The silver *Burgundy* tasting-cup proudly used as an insignia by vinous brotherhoods (*confréries*), as a badge of office by sommeliers and as ashtrays by the author. The *Chevaliers de Tastevin* organise an annual tasting, the successful wines are recogniseable by an ugly mock-mediaeval Tastevinage label. *Chevaliers de Tastevin* attend banquets, often wearing similarly mock-mediaeval clothes.

**Taurasi** [tow-rah-see] (Campania, Italy) Big, old-fashioned red from the *Aglianico* grape, needs years to soften and develop a characteristic burnt cherry taste. **Mastroberardino.**

**Tavel** [ta-vehl] (*Rhône*, France) Dry rosé. Often very disappointing. Seek out young versions and avoid the bronze colour revered by traditionalists. **Dom du Prieuré; Ch d'Aquéria; Dom de la Mordorée.**

***Tawny*** (*Douro*, Portugal) In theory, this should be pale browny-red port with a distinctly nutty flavour that acquires its mature appearance from long ageing in oak casks. Port houses can, however, perfectly legally produce stuff they call 'tawny' by mixing basic *ruby* with *white port* and skipping the tiresome business of barrel-ageing altogether. The real stuff comes with an indication of age, such as 10, or 20-year-old, but even these figures are approximate. A 10-year-old malt whisky has, by law, to be a decade old; a 10-year-old port only has to 'taste as though it is that old'. I wouldn't bother to make a point about this if it weren't for the fact that the port shippers get terribly aerated if anyone ever describes a similar fortified wine (such as an Australian, genuinely wood-aged tawny, as 'port-style'. Incidentally, I love real tawny port (and good port-style tawnies, from elsewhere!) – and heartily recommend them to anyone who gets a hangover from vintage port. **Noval; Taylors; Graham's; Cockburns; Dow's; Niepoort; Ramos Pinto; Calem.**

**Taylor (Fladgate & Yeatman)** (*Douro*, Portugal) With *Dows*, one of the 'First Growths' of the *Douro*. Outstanding *Vintage Port*, 'modern' *Late Bottled Vintage*. Also owns *Fonseca* and *Guimaraens*, and produces the excellent *Quinta de Vargellas* Single-*Quinta* port. **55 60 63 66 70** 75 77 83 85 92 94 ☆☆☆☆☆ **20 Year Old Tawny £££**

**Te Mata** [tay mah-tah] (*Hawkes Bay*, New Zealand) Pioneer John Buck proves what *New Zealand* could do with *Chardonnay* (in the Elston Vineyard) and pioneered reds with his Coleraine and (lighter) Awatea. ☆☆☆☆☆ **1996 Elston Chardonnay £££**

**Fratelli Tedeschi** [tay-dehs-kee] (*Veneto*, Italy) Reliable producer of rich and concentrated *Valpolicellas*. The *Amarones* are particularly impressive. ☆☆☆☆ **1993 Amarone Classico Monte Olmi £££**

**Dom. Tempier** [tom-pee-yay] (*Provence*, France) *Provence* superstar estate, producing impressive single-vineyard *Bandols* which support the claim that the *Mourvèdre* (from which they are largely made) ages well. ☆☆☆☆ 1993 Cabassaou £££

**Tempranillo** [tem-prah-nee-yoh] (Spain) The red grape of *Rioja* – and just about everywhere else in Spain, thanks to the way in which its strawberry fruit suits the vanilla/oak flavours of barrel-ageing. In *Navarra*; it is called *Cencibel*, in *Ribera del Duero;* Tinto Fino, in the Penedés; *Ull de Llebre*, in Toro; Tinto de Toro and, in Portugal; – where it is used for port – as *Tinto Roriz*. As yet it is rarely grown outside Spain.

***Tenuta*** [teh-noo-tah] (Italy) Estate or vineyard.

**Terlano/Terlaner** [tehr-lah-noh/tehr-lah-nur] (*Trentino-Alto-Adige*, Italy) Northern Italian village and its wine: usually fresh, crisp and carrying the name of the grape from which it was made.

**Teroldego** [teh-ROL-deh-goh] (*Trentino-Alto-Adige*, Italy) Dry reds, quite full-bodied, with lean, slightly bitter berry flavours which make them better accompaniments to food. Foradori.

**Terra Alta** [tay ruh al-ta] (*Catalonia*, Spain) Small *DO* within the much larger *Tarragona DO*, but producing wines of higher quality due to the difficult climate and resulting low yields. Pedro Rovira.

**Terre di Ginestra** [tay-reh dee jee-nehs-tra] (*Sicily*, Italy) New-wave Sicilian red and white wine with plenty of easy-going fruit. ☆☆☆ 1996 Rosso £

**Terret** [tehr-ret] (France) Suddenly fashionable, herby, grassy white grape. Possibly best in blends, but a welcome new arrival on the scene. Jacques Lurton is a particularly keen – and succesful – user.

**Ch. du Tertre** [doo tehr-tr] (*Margaux 5th Growth*, *Bordeaux*, France) Recently restored to former glory by the owners of *Calon Ségur*. **70 79 82 83** 85 86 88 89 90 94 95 96 ☆☆☆☆ 1990 ££££

**Ch. Tertre-Daugay** [tehr-tr doh-gay] (*St. Emilion Grand Cru Classé*, *Bordeaux*, France) An improving property with some way to go. **82 83** 85 86 88 89 90 92 94 95

**Ch. Tertre-Rôteboeuf** [Tehr-tr roht-burf] (*St. Emilion Grand Cru Classé*, *Bordeaux*, France) St. Emilion, good rich, concentrated wines. 85 86 87 88 89 90 91 93 94

***Téte de Cuvée*** [teht dur coo-vay] (France) An old expression still used by traditionalists to describe their finest wine.

**Thames Valley Vineyard** (Reading, England) Home winery of Australian-born roving 'enfant terrible', *John Worontschak – Flying Winemaker* and consultant to The Harvest Group, which is consistently at the cutting edge of English wine production. ☆☆☆☆ 1993 Fumé ££

**Weingut Dr H Thanisch** [tah-nish] (*Mosel-Saar-Ruwer*, Germany) Once illustrious producer, now, like so many others, often under-performing woefully, which is especially unfortunate given the fact that, with *Wegeler-Deinhard*, Thanisch is co-owner of the great *Bernkasteler* Doctor, one of the finest vineyards in Germany.

**Thelema Mountain Vineyards** [thur-lee-ma] (*Stellenbosch*, South Africa) One of the very best wineries in South Africa, thanks to Gyles Webb's skill as a winemaker and to stunningly situated hillside vineyards. *Chardonnay* and *Sauvignon* are the stars, though Webb is coming to terms with his reds too. ☆☆☆☆ 1996 Sauvignon Blanc ££

**Jean Thévenet** [tayv-nay] (*Burgundy*, France) Brilliant *Meursault*-quality *Mâcon* plus occasional *Late Harvest* extravagance. ☆☆☆☆ 1993 Mâcon Clessé Dom. de la Bon Gran £££

**Ch. Thieuley** [tee-yur-lay] (*Entre-Deux-Mers*, *Bordeaux*, France) Reliable property forging the way for concentrated *Sauvignon*-based, well-oaked whites, and silky affordable reds. White: **92** 93 94 95 96 ☆☆☆ 1994 Cuvée Francis Courselle ££

🍷 **Gérard Thomas** [toh-mah] (*Burgundy*, France) A small *St. Aubin* domaine producing exemplary, fairly priced whites and (as is frequently the case in this commune) generally rather less impressive reds. ☆☆☆☆ **1992 St. Aubin 1er Cru La Chatenière £££**

🍷 **Three Choirs Vineyard** (Gloucestershire, England) Named for the three cathedrals of Gloucester, Hereford and Worcester, this is one of England's most reliable estates. Try the wines that are being served on British Airways, and the annual 'New Release' *Nouveau*.

🍷 **Tiefenbrunner** [TEE-fen-broon-nehr] (*Trentino-Alto-Adige*, Italy) Consistent producer of fair-to-good varietal whites, most particularly *Chardonnay* and *Gewürztraminer.*

🍷 **Tignanello** [teen-yah-neh-loh] (*Tuscany*, Italy) *Antinori's* 80% *Sangiovese,* 20% *Cabernet Super-Tuscan* is one of Italy's original superstars. Should last for a decade. 82 83 **85** 88 **90** 93 **94** ☆☆☆☆ **1993 ££££**

🍇 **Tinta Negra Mole** [teen-tah nay-grah moh-lay] (Madeira) Versatile, widely-used *Madeira* grape traditionally found in cheap blends instead of one of the four 'noble' varieties. Convincingly said to be a distant cousin of the *Pinot Noir*, which could explain the way its flavour varies from one vineyard site to the next.

🍷 **Tio Pepe** [tee-yoh peh-peh] (Jerez, Spain) Ultra-reliable *Fino* sherry from *Gonzalez Byass*. ☆☆☆☆ **££**

🍇 **Tocai** [toh-kay] (Italy) Lightly herby Venetian white grape, confusingly unrelated to others of similar name. Drink young.

**Tokaji** [toh-ka-yee] (Hungary) Not to be confused with Australian *Liqueur Tokay,* Tocai Friulano or *Tokay d'Alsace, Tokaji Aszu* is a dessert wine made in a specific region of Eastern *Hungary* (and a tiny corner of *Slovakia*) by adding measured amounts (*Puttonyos*) of *Eszencia* (a paste made from individually-picked, over-ripe and/or Botrytis-affected grapes) to dry wine made from the local *Fürmint* and *Harslevelu* grapes. Sweetness levels, which depend on the amount of *Eszencia* added, range from one to six *Puttonyos,* anything beyond which is labelled *Aszu Eszencia.* This last is often confused with the pure syrup which is sold – at vast prices – as *Eszencia.* The heavy investment (principally by French companies and by *Vega Sicilia* of Spain) has raised quality, international interest, and local controversy over the way *Tokaji* is supposed to taste. Traditionalists like it oxidised like *Sherry.* The newcomers and some locals disagree. Names to look for include the *Royal Tokaji Wine Co* and *Disznoko.*

**Tokay** [*in France*: to-kay; *in Australia*: toh-ki ] Various different regions have used Tokay as a local name for other grape varities. In Australia it is the name of a fortified wine from *Rutherglen* made from the *Muscadelle*, in *Alsace* it is *Pinot Gris*, while the Italian *Tocai* is quite unrelated. Hungary's Tokay – now helpfully renamed *Tokaji* – is largely made from the *Furmint*.

🍇 **Tokay d'Alsace** [toh-ki dal-sas] (*Alsace*, France) See *Pinot Gris*.

🍷 **Tollana** [to-lah-nah] (South Australia) Yet another Penfolds brand – and a frequent source of good-value wine.

🍷 **Dom. Tollot-Beaut** [to-loh-boh] (*Burgundy*, France) Wonderful *Burgundy* domaine in *Chorey les Beaune*, with top-class Corton vineyards, and a mastery over modern techniques and new oak. Wines have lots of rich fruit flavour. ☆☆☆☆ **1995 Chorey les Beaune £££**

🍷 **Torcolato** [taw-ko-lah-toh] (Veneto, Italy) See *Maculan*.

**Torgiano** [taw-jee-yah-noh] (Umbria, Italy) Zone in *Umbria* and modern red wine made famous by *Lungarotti*. See *Rubesco*.

**Toro** [TO-roh] (Spain) Up-and-coming region on the *Douro,* close to Portugal, producing, richly intense red wines such as Farina's *Collegiata* from the *Tempranillo,* confusingly known here as the Tinto de Toro.

🍷 **Torre de Gall** [to-ray day-gahl] (*Catalonia*, Spain) *Moët & Chandon's* Spanish fizz. About as good as you can get using traditional *Cava* varieties, but still experimenting. ☆☆☆☆ **££**

🍷 **Torres** [TO-rehs] (*Catalonia*, Spain) Miguel Torres Jr. revolutionised Spain's wine industry with reliable wines like Viña Sol, Gran Viña Sol, Gran Sangre De Toro, Esmeralda and Gran Coronas, before moving on to perform the same trick in Chile. Torres is still a leading light in Spain with wines like the Milmanda Chardonnay and Mas Borras (the new name for the old 'Black Label' *Cabernet Sauvignon*). In Chile, where they were the first to introduce modern methods, the firm faces fierce competition from locals like *Ignacio Recabarren* and other outside investors. ☆☆☆☆☆ **1995 Milmanda £££**

🍷 **Marimar Torres** [TO-rehs] (*Sonoma*, California) Miguel Torres' sister is using the same wine-making techniques as her brother and is producing some of the most impressive Pinot Noir and Chardonnay from a spectacular little vineyard in Russian River. ☆☆☆☆☆ **1992 Don Miguel Vineyard Chardonnay £££**

🍇 **Torrontes** [to-ron-TEHS] (Argentina) Promisingly aromatic grape variety related to the *Muscat*, now rarely seen in Spain, but highly successful in *Argentina*. *Etchart* is a star producer. Recognisable by its odd propensity to smell as though it is going to taste sweet even when the wine is bone dry. ☆☆☆ **1996 Etchart £**

**Toscana** [tos-KAH-nah] (Italy) See *Tuscany*.

🍷 **Ch. la Tour Blanche** [lah toor blonsh] (*Sauternes Premier Cru Classé*, *Bordeaux*, France) Since the late 1980s, one of the finest, longest-lasting *Sauternes*. Also a well-run wine school. **81** 82 **83** 85 86 87 88 89 90 92 94 95 96 ☆☆☆☆☆ **1990 ££££**

🍷 **Ch. la Tour-Carnet** [lah toor kahr-nay] (*Haut-Médoc Fourth Growth*, *Bordeaux*, France) Picturesque but *Cru Bourgeois*-level fourth growth. 82 83 85 86 88 **89 90** 91 92 93 94 95 96

🍷 **Ch. la Tour-de-By** [lah toor dur bee] (*Médoc Cru Bourgeois*, *Bordeaux*, France) Reliable and, in ripe years, recommendable. **82** 83 **85** 86 88 89 90 94 95 96 ☆☆☆☆ **1990 £££**

🍷 **Ch. la Tour-de-Mons** [lah toor dur mons] (*Margaux*, *Bordeaux*, France) Yet another *Margaux château* which fails to exploit the potential of its situation. 79 82 83 85 86 88 89 90 93 94 95 96

🍷 **Ch. Tour-du-Haut-Moulin** [toor doo oh moo-lan] (*Haut-Médoc Cru Bourgeois*, *Bordeaux*, France) An under-appreciated producer of what often can be *Cru Classé* quality wine. 75 76 81 **82** 83 **85** 86 88 89 90 94 96 ☆☆☆☆ **1994 £££**

🍷 **Ch. la Tour-Haut-Brion** [lah toor oh bree-yon] (*Graves Cru Classé*, *Bordeaux*, France) A name to follow for reliably concentrated and often first-rate wines from very well-sited vineyards close to *Haut-Brion* itself – not to mention the gasworks. **61** 66 70 **75 78** 81 **82** 83 85 86 88 89 90 91 **92** 93 94 95 96

**Touraine** [too-rayn] (*Loire*, France) Area encompassing the *AC's Chinon*, *Vouvray* and *Bourgueil*. Also an increasing source of quaffable varietal wines – *Sauvignon*, *Gamay* de Touraine, etc. White: 85 86 **88 89 90** 94 95 96 Red: 85 86 **88 89 90** 95 96

🍷 **Les Tourelles de Longueville** [lay too-rel dur long-ur-veel] (*Pauillac*, *Bordeaux*, France) The *Second Label* of *Pichon Longueville Baron*.

🍇 **Touriga (Nacional/Francesa)** [too-ree-ga nah-see-yoh-nahl/fran-say-sa] (Portugal) Red port grape, also (though rarely) seen in the New World.

🍇 **Traminer** [tra-mee-nur; *in Australia*: trah-MEE-nah] A less aromatic variant of the *Gewürztraminer* grape widely grown in Eastern Europe and Italy, although the term is confusingly also used as a pronouncable, alternative name for the latter grape – particularly in Australia.

***Transfer Method*** A method of sparkling wine production, involving a second fermentation in the bottle, but differing from the *Méthode Champenoise* in that the wine is separated from the *lees* by pumping it out of the bottle into a pressurised tank for clarification before returning it to another bottle.

**Bodegas Trapiche** [tra-pee-chay] (Argentina) Big, go-ahead producer with note worthy barrel-fermented *Chardonnay* and *Cabernet/Malbec*. ☆☆☆ **1994 Oak Cask Cabernet £**

**Tras-os-Montes** [tras-ohsh-montsh] (*Douro*, Portugal) Wine region of the *Upper Douro*, right up by the Spanish border, source of *Barca Velha*. Red: **80 85 88 90 91 92 93** 94 95

**Trebbiano** [treh-bee-YAH-noh] (Italy) Ubiquitous white grape in Italy. Less vaunted in France, where it is called *Ugni Blanc*.

**Trebbiano d'Abruzzo** [treh-bee-YAH-noh dab-ROOT-zoh] (*Abbruzzo*, Italy) A *DOC* region within Italy where they grow a clone of *Trebbiano*, confusingly called Trebbiano di Toscana, and use it to make generally unexceptional dry whites.

**Trentino** [trehn-TEE-noh] (Italy) Northern *DOC* in Italy. *Trentino* specialities include crunchy red *Marzemino*, nutty white Nosiola and excellent *Vin Santo*. **Ferrari; Càvit; Roberto Zeni.**

**Trentino-Alto Adige** [trehn-tee-noh al-toh ah-dee-jay] (Italy) Northern wine region combining the two *DOC* areas *Trentino* and *Alto-Adige*.

**Dom. de Trévallon** [treh-vah-lo*n*] (*Provence*, France) Les Baux de Provence superstar blend of *Cabernet Sauvignon* and *Syrah* to prove that the Aussies aren't the only people to get this cocktail right ☆☆☆☆ **1995 £££**

**Dom. Frédéric-Emile Trimbach** [tram-bahkh] (*Alsace*, France) Distinguished grower and merchant. ☆☆☆☆☆ **1990 Riesling Alsace Cuvée Frédéric Emile £££**

**Trittenheim** [trit-ten-hime] (*Mosel-Saar-Ruwer*, Germany) Village whose vineyards are said to have been the first in Germany planted with *Riesling*, making honeyed wine. QbA/Kab/Spät: **85 88 89 90** 91 92 93 94 95 96 Aus/Beeren/TBA: **83 85** 88 89 90 91 92 93 94 95

***Trocken*** [trok-ken] (Germany) Dry, often aggressively so. Avoid Trocken *Kabinett* from such northern areas as the *Mosel*, *Rheingau* and *Rheinhessen QbA* (*Chaptalised*) and *Spatlese*. Trocken wines (made, by definition, from riper grapes) are better. See also *Halbtrocken*.

***Trockenbeerenauslese*** [trok-ken-beh-ren-ows-lay-zeh] (Austria/Germany) Fifth rung of the *QmP* ladder, wine from selected dried grapes which are usually *Botrytis*-affected and full of concentrated natural sugar. Only made in the best years, rare and expensive, though less so in Austria than Germany.

**Trollinger** [trroh-ling-gur] (Germany) The German name for the Black Hamburg grape, used in *Wurttemburg* to make light red wines.

***Tronçais*** [tron-say] (France) Forest producing some of the best oak for wine barrels.

**Ch. Tronquoy-Lalande** [trron-kwah-lah-lond] (*St. Estèphe Cru Bourgeois*, *Bordeaux*, France) Traditional producer to follow in ripe years. 79 **82** 83 85 86 88 **89** 90 93 94 ☆☆☆☆ **1990 £££**

**Ch. Troplong-Mondot** [trroh-lo*n* mo*n*doh] (*St. Emilion Grand Cru Classé*, *Bordeaux*, France) Top-class property (over)due for reclassification. **82** 83 **85** 86 88 89 90 91 92 93 94 95 96 ☆☆☆☆ **1992 ££££**

🍷 **Ch. Trotanoy** [trrot-teh-nwah] (*Pomerol*, *Bordeaux*, France) Never less than fine, and back on especially roaring form since the beginning of the 1990s to compete with *Pétrus*. Some may, however, prefer the lighter style of some of the 1980s. **61 64 67 70 71 75** 76 78 79 81 **82** 83 84 **85** 86 87 **88 89** 90 92 93 94 95 96 ☆☆☆☆ **1994 ££££**

🍷 **Ch. Trottevieille** [trrott-vee-yay] (*St. Emilion Premier Grand Cru*, *Bordeaux*, France) Improving but still middle-grade property. **79** 81 **82** 83 **85** 86 87 88 89 90 92 94 95 ☆☆☆☆ **1989 ££££**

**Trousseau** [trroh-soh] (Eastern France) Grape variety found in *Arbois*.

🍷 **Tsantalis** [tsan-tah-lis] (*Nemea*, Greece) Increasingly impressive producer, redefining traditional varieties.

**Tulbagh** [tool-bakh] (South Africa) Coolish valley north of *Paarl* where Nicky Krone of Twee Jongegezellen makes aromatic whites and impressive fizz. White: **87 91** 92 93 94 95 96

🍷 **Tulloch** [tul-lurk] (Hunter Valley, Australia) Underperforming backwater of the *Penfolds* empire.

**Tunisia** [Too-Nee-Shuh] Best known for dessert *Muscat* wines.

🍷 **Cave Vinicole de Turckheim** [turk-hime] (*Alsace*, France) Cooperative whose top wines can often rival those of some the region's best estates. ☆☆☆☆ **1993 Gewürztraminer Heim-bourg ££** ☆☆☆ **1994 Reserve Pinot Blanc £**

**Turkey** Now making clean, dry white, but still drowning in oxidised red.

🍷 **Turkey Flat** (South Australia) Tiny *Barossa* Shiraz maker. ☆☆☆☆☆ **1994 Grenache Noir, Barossa Valley £££**

**Tuscany** (Italy) Major region, the famous home of *Chianti* and reds such as *Brunello di Montalcino* and the new-wave of *Super Tuscan Vini da Tavola*. Red: **78 79** 81 **82 85 88 90** 94 95

🍷 **Tyrrell's** (*Hunter Valley*, Australia) *Chardonnay* (sold as *Pinot Chardonnay*) pioneer, and producer of old-fashioned *Shiraz* and *Semillon* and even older-fashioned *Pinot Noir*, which tastes like *Burgundy*. ☆☆☆☆ **1992 Vat 1 Semillon, Hunter Valley.**

# U

**Ugni Blanc** [oo-nee blo*n*] (France) Undistinguished white grape in France which needs modern winemaking to produce anything better than basic fare, although its relative neutrality renders it suitable as a base wine for distillation into Cognac and Armagnac. Curiously, in Italy, where it is known as the *Trebbiano*, it takes on a mantle of (spurious) nobility. For reasonable examples try *Vin De Pays des Côtes de Gascogne*.

**Ull de Llebre** [ool dur yay-bray] (Spain) Literally 'hare's eye'. See *Tempranillo*.

***Ullage*** Space between surface of wine and top of cask or, in a bottle, the cork. The wider the gap, the greater the danger of *oxidation*. Older wines almost always have some degree of ullage; the less the better.

🍷 **Umani Ronchi** [oo-MAH-nee RON-kee] (Marches, Italy) Innovative producer of both reds and whites, with wines like the extraordinary new Pelago proving that Tuscany is not the only exciting region in Italy. ☆☆☆☆☆ **1994 Pelago £££**

**Umathum** [oo-ma-toom] (*Neusiedlersee*, Austria) Producer of unusually good red wines including a brilliant *St. Laurent*. ☆☆☆☆ **1994 Umathum Junger Berg Pinot Noir ££**

**Umbria** [uhm-bree-ah] (Italy) Central wine region, best known for white *Orvieto* and *Torgiano*, but also producing the excellent red Rubesco. ☆☆☆ **1995 Peive Santa Lucia di Filippo ££**

**Viña Undurraga** [oon-dur-rah-ga] (*Central Valley*, Chile) Founded in 1882, greatly improved, independent, family-owned estate. Producing a range of single varietal wines from the classic grape varieties. ☆☆☆☆ **1995 Cabernet Sauvignon £**

***Unfiltered*** Filtering a wine can remove flavour; on the other hand, so can fining it with egg white or bentonite, and most winemakers would traditionally argue that both practices are necessary if the finished wine is going to be crystal-clear and free from bacteria that could turn it to vinegar. Many quality-conscious new wave winemakers, however, are now cutting back on fining and filtering, and some are even making a point of not doing either.

**Uruguay** Surprising new source of improving reds made from the *Cabernet Sauvignon* and *Tannat*. This, by the way, was where the world's top wine experts chose to hold a recent annual conference.

**Urzig** [oort-zig] (*Mosel-Saar-Ruwer*, Germany) Village on the *Mosel* with steeply sloping vineyards and some of the very best producers, including *Monchof* and *Dr Loosen*. QbA/Kab/Spät: **85** 86 **88 89 90** 91 92 93 94 95 Aus/Beeren/TBA: **83 85** 88 89 90 91 92 93 94 95

**Utiel-Requena** [oo-tee-yel reh-kay-nah] (Valencia, Spain) *DO* of *Valencia*, producing heavy red and good fresh rosé from the Bobal grape.

**Dom. Vacheron** [va-shur-ron] (*Loire*, France) Reliable, if unspectacular, producer of *Sancerre* – including a better-than-average red made from *Pinot Noir*. ☆☆☆☆ **1996 Sancerre Les Roches ££**

**Vacqueyras** [va-kay-ras] (*Rhône*, France) *Côtes du Rhône* village producing fine, full-bodied, peppery reds which can compete with (pricier) *Gigondas* and other more famous southern *Rhône* wines. Red: 78 81**82 83 85 88** 89 90 95 **Jaboulet Ainé; Vidal-Fleury; Ch. des Tours;Domaine de Mont Vac.**

**Cave de Vacqueyras** (*Rhône*, France) Reliable cooperative. ☆☆☆☆ **1995 Vacqueyras Cuvée du Marquis de Fonseguille ££**

**Aldo Vajra** [vi-rah] (*Piedmont*, Italy) Producer of serious reds, including rich, complex *Barolo* and the deliciously different, gamey Freisa delle Langhe.

**Val d'Aosta** [val-day-yos-tah] (Italy) Small, spectacularly beautiful area between *Piedmont* and the French/Swiss border. Great for tourism; less so for wine-lovers. Red: 78 79 82 **85 88** 89 90 93 94 95 White: 92 93 94 **95** 96

🍷 **Vignerons du Val d'Orbieu** [val-dor-byur] (*Midi*, France) The face of the future? An association of over 200 cooperatives and growers in southern France trying to compete with *Skalli* for the prize of most innovative producer in the south of France. Even so, apart from the excellent Cuvée Mythique, far too many wines – including the Laperouse co-production with *Penfolds* – leave plenty of scope for improvement. ☆☆☆☆ **1995 Cuvée Mythique.**

**Valais** [va-lay] (Switzerland) Vineyard area on the upper *Rhône*, making good *Fendant* (*Chasselas*) which surmount the usual innate dullness of that grape. There are also some reasonable – in all but price – light reds.

🍷 **Ch. Valandraud** [va-lon-droh] (*St. Emilion*, *Bordeaux*, France) An instant superstar launched in 1991 as competition for *le Pin*. Production is tiny (of *Pomerol* proportions) and the price astronomical. The 1995 *en primeur* price quintupled following demand from the US and Far East.

**Valdeorras** [bahl-day-ohr-ras] (*Galicia*, Spain) A barren and mountainous *DO* in *Galicia* beginning to exploit the *Cabernet Franc*-like local Mencia and the indigenous white Godello. ☆☆☆ **1995 Valderroa Mencia, Bodegas Senorio SAT, Corgomo ££**

**Valdepeñas** [bahl-deh-pay-nyass] (*La Mancha*, Spain) *La Mancha DO* striving to refine its rather hefty, strong reds and whites. Progress is being made, particularly with reds. **los Llanos; Felix Solis**.

🍷 **Valdespino** [bahl-deh-spee-noh] (*Jerez*, Spain) Old-fashioned Sherry company that uses wooden casks to ferment most of its wines. Makes a classic *Fino* Innocente and an excellent *Pedro Ximenez*.

🍷 **Valdevieso** [val-deh-vee-yay-soh] (*Curico*, Chile) Formerly family-owned, but now producing thoroughly modern styles of wine.

**Valençay** [va-lon-say] (*Loire*, France) *AC* within *Touraine*, near *Cheverny*, making comparable whites: light, clean if rather sharp. **85 86 88 89 90** 94 95

**Valencia** [bah-LEN-thee-yah] (Spain) Produces quite alcoholic red wines and also deliciously sweet, grapey *Moscatel de Valencia*.

🍷 **Vallet Frères** [va-lay frehr] (*Burgundy*, France) Good, small, traditional merchant, also known as Pierre Bourrée. ☆☆☆ **1991 Beaune Les Epenottes Premier Cru £££**

**Valpolicella** [val-poh-lee-cheh-lah] (*Veneto*, Italy) Over-commercialised, light, red wine which should – with rare exceptions – be drunk young to catch its interestingly bitter-cherryish flavour. Bottles labelled *Classico* are better; best are *Ripasso* versions, made by refermenting the wine on the *lees* of an earlier vat. For a different experience, buy *Amarone* or *Recioto*. 81 82 **85 86 88 90 91** 93 94 95 **Masi; Allegrini;, Boscaini; Tedeschi; Le Ragose; Serego Alighieri; Guerrieri-Rizardi; Quintarelli.**

**Valréas** [val-ray-yas] (*Rhône*, France) Peppery, inexpensive red *Côtes du Rhône* village. Red: 78 81 **82 83 85 88** 89 90 95

**Valtellina** [vat-teh-lee-na] [Vahl-Teh-Lee-Nah] (*Lombardy*, Italy) Red *DOC* from the *Nebbiolo* grape, of variable quality. Improves with age.

🍷 **Varichon et Clerc** [va-ree-shon ay klayr] (*Savoie*, France) Fair quality, sparkling wines.

***Varietal*** A wine made from and named after one or more grape variety, eg California *Chardonnay*. The French authorities would like to outlaw such references from the labels of most of their *Appellation Contrôlée* wines, however the world has left them little alternative but to comply.

🍷 **Viña Los Vascos** [los vas-kos] (*Colchagua Valley*, Chile) Estate belonging to Eric de Rothschild of *Ch. Lafite,* and shamelessly sold with a Lafite-like label. This ought to be a flagship for Chile. The Cabernet is generally uninspiring; the white, disappointing, not to say downright poor. ☆☆☆ **1992 Grande Reserve**

🍷 **Vasse Felix** [vas-fee-liks] (*Margaret River*, Australia) Very classy *Margaret River* winery belonging to the widow of millionaire Rupert Holmes à Court, specialising in juicy, high-quality reds. ☆☆☆ **1995 Cabernet Merlot ££**

**Vaucluse** [voh-klooz] (*Rhône*, France) *Côtes du Rhône* region producing good *Vin De Pays* and peppery reds and rosés from villages such as *Vacqueyras*. Red: 78 81 **82 83 85 88** 89 90 95 96

**Vaud** [voh] (Switzerland) Swiss wine area on the shores of Lake Geneva, famous for unusually tangy *Chasselas*.

**Vaudésir** [voh-day-zeer] (*Burgundy*, France) Possibly the best of the seven *Chablis Grands Crus*. ☆☆☆☆☆ **Domaine des Malandes £££**

🍷 **Vavasour** [va-va-soor] (*Marlborough*, New Zealand) Pioneers of the Awatere Valley sub-region of *Marlborough,* hitting high standards with *Bordeaux*-style reds, powerful *Sauvignons* and impressive *Chardonnays*. Dashwood is the *Second Label*. ☆☆☆☆ **1996 Hunters Chardonnay ££**

***VDQS*** (France) *Vin Délimitée de Qualité Supérieur*. Official, neither-fish-nor-fowl, designation for wines better than *Vin De Pays* but not fine enough for an *AC*. Enjoying a strange half-life (amid constant rumours of its imminent abolition), this includes such oddities as *Sauvignon de St. Bris*.

***Vecchio*** [veh-kee-yoh] (Italy) Old.

🍷 **Vecchio Samperi** [veh-kee-yoh sam-peh-ree] (*Sicily*, Italy) Best *Marsala* estate, belonging to *De Bartoli*. Although not *DOC*, a dry aperitif similar to an *Amontillado Sherry*.

🍷 **Vega Sicilia** [bay-gah sih-sih-lyah] (*Ribera del Duero*, Spain) *Tempranillo-Bordeaux* blend called Unico, and Spain's top wine with prices to match. For a cheaper, slightly fresher taste of the Vega Sicilia-style, try the supposedly lesser Valbuena. Alternatively, check out the wines from the new offshoot *Alion* bodega. 60 61 62 64 66 67 69 **70** 72 74 75 76 79 80 82 83 ☆☆☆☆☆ **1984 Valbuena ££££** ☆☆☆☆☆ **1985 Valbuena ££££** ☆☆☆☆☆ **1990 Valbuena ££££** ☆☆☆☆☆ **1983 Unico ££££**

***Vegetal*** Often used of *Sauvignon Blanc*: like 'grassy'. Can be complimentary – though not in California or Australia, where it is held to mean 'unripe'.

🍷 **Caves Velhas** [kah-vash-vay-yash] (Portugal) Large, traditional merchants who blend wine from all over the country to sell under their own label. Almost single-handedly saved the *Bucelas DO* from extinction. Wines are good, but rarely outstanding.

***Velho/velhas*** [vay-yoh/vay-yas] (Portugal) Old, as of red wine.

**Velletri** [veh-leh-tree] Italy) Town in the Alban hills (*Colli Albani*), producing mainly *Trebbiano* and *Malvasia*-based whites, similar to *Frascati*.

🍇 **Veltliner** See *Grüner Veltliner*.

***Vendange*** [Von-donzh] (France) Harvest or vintage.

***Vendange Tardive*** [von-donzh tahr-deev] (France) Particularly in *Alsace*, wine from *Late-Harvested* grapes, usually lusciously sweet.

***Vendemmia/Vendimia*** [ven-DEH-mee-yah/ven-DEE-mee-yah] (Italy/Spain) Harvest or vintage.

**Venegazzú** [veh-neh-GAHT-zoo] (*Veneto*, Italy) Good, quite understated claret-like *Vino da Tavola* from the *Cabernet Sauvignon*; a sort of 'Super-Veneto' to compete with those *Super Tuscans*. Needs five years. Look out, too, for the rather pricier black label.

**Veneto** [veh-neh-toh] (Italy) North-eastern wine region, the home of *Soave, Valpolicella* and *Bardolino*.

**de Venoge** [dur vur-nohzh] (*Champagne*, France) Up-and-coming producer of quality fizz.. ☆☆☆☆ **Brut Vintage 1990 £££**

**Veramonte** [vay-rah-mon-tay] (*Casablanca*, Chile) New venture by Agustin Huneeus, winemaker of Franciscan Vineyards in *California*, already producing impressive reds.

**Verdejo** [vehr-de-khoh] (Spain) Interestingly herby white grape; confusingly not the *Verdelho* of *Madeira* and Australia, but the variety used for new wave *Rueda*.

**Verdelho** [*in Madeira*: vehr-deh-yoh; *in Australia*: vur-DEL-loh] (Madeira/Australia) White grape used for fortified *Madeira* and *White Port* and for limey, dry, table wine in Australia. ☆☆☆ **1995 McGuigan Brothers Verdelho Bin 6000 ££**

**Verdicchio** [vehr-dee-kee-yoh] (*Marches*, Italy) Spicy white grape seen in a number of *DOCs* in its own right, the best of which – when made by Bucci – is *Verdicchio dei Castelli di Jesi*. In *Umbria*, a major component of *Orvieto*. ☆☆☆ **1995 Umani Ronchi Verdicchio Classico Villa Bianchi ££**

**Verdicchio dei Castelli di Jesi** [vehr-dee-kee-yoh day-ee kas-tay-lee dee yay-zee] (*Marches*, Italy) Light, clean and crisp wines to drink with seafood.

**Verduzzo** [vehr-doot-soh] (*Friuli-Venezia Giulia*, Italy) White grape making a dry and a fine *Amabile*-style wine in the *Colli Orientale*.

**Vergelegen** [vehr-kur-lek-hen] (Somerset West, South Africa) Hi-tech winery in which winemaker Martin Meinert is now beginning to show his true colours, hampered until recently by indifferent bought-in grapes.

**Vermentino** [vayr-men-tee-noh] (*Liguria*, Italy) The spicy, dry white wine of the Adriatic and, increasingly, in southern French *Vins de Table*.

**Vernaccia** [vayr-naht-chah] (*Tuscany*, Italy) White grape making the Tuscan *DOCG* Vernaccia di San Gimignano (where it's helped by a dash of *Chardonnay*) and Sardinian Vernaccia di Oristano. At best with a distinct nut 'n' spice flavour.

**Georges Vernay** [vayr-nay] (*Rhône*, France) The great master of *Condrieu* who can do things with *Viognier* that few seem able to match. ☆☆☆☆☆ **1995 Condrieu ££££**

**Noel Verset** [vayr-say] (*Rhône*, France) Top-class producer of Cornas, who owns some of the oldest vines in the *appellation*.

**Quinta do Vesuvio** [veh-soo-vee-yoh] (*Douro*, Portugal) Single *Quinta* port from the family that owns *Dow's, Graham's, Warre's*, etc. Proof that top-flight *vintage port* doesn't have to be (as members of that same family used to claim) a blend of wines from different estates. ☆☆☆☆☆ **1992 Vintage Port.**

**Veuve Clicquot-Ponsardin** [vurv klee-koh pon-sahr-dan] (*Champagne*, France) The distinctive orange label is back on form after a few years of producing a rather green, non-vintage *Brut*. The *prestige cuvée* is called Grand Dame after the famous Widow Cliquot. ☆☆☆☆☆ **1989 Vintage Reserva ££££** ☆☆☆☆ **White Label Demi-Sec NV ££££** ☆☆☆☆☆ **1989 Rose Reserve ££**

**Victoria** (Australia) Huge variety of wines from the *liqueur Muscats* of *Rutherglen* to the peppery *Shirazes* of *Bendigo* and the elegant *Chardonnays* and *Pinot Noirs* of the *Yarra Valley*. **Murray River; Mornington; Goulburn Valley; Geelong; Pyrenees.**

🍷 **Vidal** [vee-dahl] (*Hawkes Bay*, New Zealand) One of New Zealand's top four red wine producers. Associated with *Villa Maria* and *Esk Valley*. Chardonnays are the strongest suit. ☆☆☆☆ **Vidal Estates Cabernet Merlot £££**

🍇 **Vidal** [VI-dal] (Canada) A hybrid and highly frost-resistant variety looked down on by European authorities but widely and successfully grown in *Canada* for spicily exotic *Icewine*. ***Iniskillin; Rief Estate.***

🍷 **J. Vidal-Fleury** [vee-dahl flur-ree] (*Rhône*, France) Grower and shipper that belongs to *Guigal* and shares that firm's attitude towards quality. ☆☆☆☆ **1991 Côtes du Rhône Villages ££**

***VIDE*** [vee-day] (Italy) Marketing syndicate supposedly denoting finer estate wines. Look for VIDE stickers on labels.

🍷 **Ch. La Vieille Cure** [la-vee-yay koor] (*Fronsac*, *Bordeaux*, France) Rich, ripe *Merlot*-based wines. Fronsac at its best 90 92 93 94 95 96

***Vieilles Vignes*** [vee-yay veeñ] (France) Wine (supposedly) made from a producer's oldest vines. (In reality this could easily mean anything between 20 and 90 years of age.).

🍷 **Vieux Château Certan** [vee-yur-cha-toh-sehr-tan] (*Pomerol*, *Bordeaux*, France) Ultra-classy, small *Pomerol* property, known as 'VCC' to its fans, and producing reliable, concentrated, complex wine. **64** 70 78 81 **82 83** 85 86 87 88 89 90 93 94 95 ☆☆☆☆ **1994 ££££**

🍷 **Dom. du Vieux-Télégraphe** [vee-yor tay-lay-grahf] (*Rhône*, France) Modern *Châteauneuf-du-Pape* domaine which does not always live up to expectations. ☆☆☆☆ **1995 Châteauneuf-du-Pape £££**

🍷 **Ch. Vignelaure** [veen-yah-lawrr] (*Provence*, France) Founded by a refugee from *Bordeaux* in an attempt to show that top-quality wines could be made elsewhere, but went through a very dull patch under other owners, who continued the tradition of putting bad poems by Anthony Burgess on the labels. Back on form now following its purchase by David O'Brien, son of Vincent the Irish racehorse trainer, and the arrival of *Hugh Ryman* as winemaker, this is one of the best examples of *Coteaux d'Aix en Provence*. Juicy reds and bright, fresh rosés. Watch this space.

***Vignoble*** [veen-yohbl] (France) Vineyard; vineyard area.

🍷 **Villa Maria** (*Auckland*, New Zealand) One of New Zealand's biggest producers, and one which is unusual in coming close to hitting the target with its reds as well as its whites. ☆☆☆☆ **1996 Private Bin Chardonnay ££** ☆☆☆☆☆ **1996 Reserve Wairau Valley Sauvignon Blanc ££**

🍷 **Villa Mount Eden** [Vihl-Luh Mownt Ee-Dn] (California) Under the ownership of Ch. Ste Michelle and back on form after a dull patch. Wines, from Mendocino, Santa Barbara, *Napa* and *Carneros* are generally impressive and includes a good *Pinot Blanc*. ☆☆☆☆ **1994 Zinfandel ££**

***Villages*** (France) The suffix 'villages' eg *Côtes du Rhône* or *Mâcon* generally – like *Classico* in Italy – indicates a slightly superior wine from a smaller delimited area encompassing certain village vineyards.

**Villany** [vee-lah-nyee] (Hungary) Warm area of Hungary with a promising future for soft young drinking reds. ☆☆☆ **Villanyi Cabernet Sauvignon Barrique ££**

🍷 **Villard** [vee-yarr] (Hungary) Improving wines from French-born Thierry Villard, especially Chardonnays from Casablanca.

🍷 **Ch. Villemaurine** [veel-maw-reen] (*St. Emilion Grand Cru Classé*, *Bordeaux*, France) Often hard wines which are not helped by heavy-handedness with oak. **82** 83 **85** 86 88 **89** 90 92 94 96

🍷 **Villiera Estate** [vil-lee-yeh-rah] (*Paarl*, South Africa) Reliable range of affordable sparkling and still wines from the go-ahead Grier family. ☆☆☆☆ **1995 Villera Wine Estate Cru Monro £**

**Vin de Corse** [van dur kaws] (*Corsica*, France) *Appellation* within *Corsica*

***Vin de garde*** [van dur gahrd] (France) Wine to keep.

**Vin de l'Orléanais** [van dur low-lay-yon-nay] (*Loire*, France) Small *VDQS* in the *Central Vineyards* of the *Loire*. See *Orléannais*.

***Vin de Paille*** [van dur piy] (*Jura*, France) Now quite rare, regional speciality; sweet golden wine from grapes dried on straw mats.

***Vin de Pays*** [van dur pay-yee] (France) Lowest/broadest geographical designation; simple country wines with certain regional characteristics. Includes some of France's most exciting wines, as they don't have the same restrictions imposed on them as the AC and VDQS wines, allowing them much more room for experimentation. See *Côtes de Gascogne* and *Vin De Pays d'Oc*.

**Vin de Pays de l'Hérault** [dur lay-roh] (*Midi*, France) Largest vine-growing département, producing some 20% of France's wine, nearly all *Vin De Pays* or *VDQS*, of which *Coteaux du Languedoc* is the best known. Also the home of the extraordinary *Mas de Daumas Gassac*.

**Vin de Pays de l'Ile de Beauté** [dur leel dur boh-tay] (*Corsica*, France) Picturesque name for wines that are improving thanks to outsiders such as *Laroche*. Often better than this island's *Appellation* wines.

**Vin de Pays des Côtes de Gascogne** [day koht dur gas-koyñ] (South West, France) The region of the Three Musketeers – and a town called Condom – was once only known for Armagnac. Today, people like *Yves Grassa*, and *Hugh Ryman*, as well as the *Plaimont* cooperative are producing good, fresh, floral whites and light reds. Competition is now increasingly tough, however, from the warmer vineyards of *Languedoc-Roussillon*. ☆☆☆☆ **1994 Dom. du Tariquet Cuvée Bois £**

**Vin de Pays du Gard** [doo gahrr] (*Midi*, France) Huge area with one fair *VDQS*, *Costières du Gard*.

**Vin de Pays du Jardin de la France** [doo jar-dan dur-lah-fronss] (*Loire*, France) Marketing device to describe some 50 million bottles of *Vins de Pays* from the *Loire*.

***Vin de table*** [van dur tahbl] (France) Table wine from no particular area.

**Vin de Thouarsais** [twar-say] (*Loire*, France) *VDQS* for a soft, light red from the *Cabernet Franc*; whites from the *Chenin Blanc*. ☆☆☆ **1995 Dry White; Michel Gigon ££**

**Vin de Tursan** [toor-san] (South West France) *VDQS* whose big, country reds are now beginning to be seen outside France.

***Vin Doux naturel*** [doo nah-too-rrel] Van-Doo Nah-Tew-Rehl] (France) Fortified – so not really 'naturel' – dessert wines, particularly the sweet, liquorous *Muscats* of the south, eg *Beaumes de Venise* and *Rivesaltes*.

**Vin du Bugey** [boo-jay] (*Savoie*, France) Formerly thin, astringent whites of little merit, but becoming rather trendy in France as a source of fresh crisp *Chardonnay*.

***Vin Gris*** [van gree] (France) Chiefly from *Alsace* and the *Jura*, pale rosé from red grapes pressed straight after crushing or following a few hours of *skin contact*.

***Vin Jaune*** [van john] (Jura, France) Golden-coloured *Arbois* speciality; slightly oxidised – like *fino* sherry. See *Ch. Chalon*.

***Vin Ordinaire*** (France) A simple, local wine, usually served in carafes.

***Vin Santo*** [vin sahn-toh] (Italy) Powerful, highly traditional white dessert wine from bunches of grapes hung to dry in airy barns for up to six years, especially in *Tuscany* and *Trentino*. At its best, competes head-on with top-quality medium sherry. Best drunk with sweet almond ('Cantuccine') biscuits. ☆☆☆☆ **1990 Ca'Vit Vino Santo ££££**

***Vin vert*** [van vehrr] (*Midi*, France) Light, refreshing, acidic white wine, found in *Roussillon*.

***Vina de Mesa*** [vee-nah day may-sah] (Spain) Spanish for house wine.

**Vinho Verde** [veeñ-vayrd] (Portugal) Young, literally 'green' wine, confusingly red or pale white often tinged with green. At worst, dull and sweet (especially when over-aged; vintages being rarely printed on labels). At best delicious, refreshing, slightly fizzy. ☆☆☆ **1996 Azevedo £**

🍷 **Vinícola Navarra** [vee-NEE-koh-lah na-VAH-rah] (*Navarra*, Spain) Ultra-modern winemaking and newly-planted vineyards beginning to come on stream. Owned by *Bodegas y Bebida*.

***Vinifera*** [vih-nih-feh-ra] Properly *Vitis vinifera*: the species name for all European vines.

***Vino da Tavola*** [VEE-noh dah TAH-voh-lah] (Italy) Table wine, but the *DOC* quality designation net is so riddled with holes that producers of many superb – and pricy – wines have contented themselves with this 'modest' Appellation. Efforts to herd these quality wines into a new *IGT* – Vin de Pays-style – designation are being hampered by the fact that, this being Italy, no one knows how and when these new rules will be introduced.

***Vino de la Tierra*** [bee-noh day la tyay rah] (Spain) New Spanish wine designation similar to the French *Vin de Pays*, and worth looking out for if you like interesting, affordable, regional wines.

🍷 **Vino Nobile di Montepulciano** [vee-noh NOH-bee-lay dee mon-tay-POOL-chee-AH-noh] (*Tuscany*, Italy) *Chianti* in long trousers; potentially truly noble (though not often), and made from the same grapes. Can age well to produce a traditional full red. Rosso di Montepulciano is the lighter, more accessible version. The Montepulciano of the title is the Tuscan town, not the grape variety. *Avignonesi* is one of the stars. Red: 78 79 81 **82 85 88 90** 94 95 96

***Vino novello*** [vee-noh noh-vay-loh] (Italy) New wine; equivalent to French *Nouveau*.

***Vintage*** Year of production.

***Vintage Champagne*** (*Champagne*, France) Wine from one, 'declared' year.

***Vintage Character (port)*** (*Douro*, Portugal) Supposedly inexpensive alternative to *Vintage*, but really up-market *Ruby* made by blending various years' wines.

***Vintage (Port)*** (*Douro*, Portugal) Produced only in 'declared' years, aged in wood then in the bottle for many years. In 'off' years, port houses release wines from their top estates as single *Quinta* ports. This style of port must be decanted, as it throws a sediment ***Warre's; Dow's; Taylor's.***

**Viognier** [vee-YON-nee-yay] (*Rhône*, France) Infuriating white variety which, at its best, produces floral, peachy wines that startle with their intensity and originality. Once limited to the *Rhône – Condrieu* and *Ch. Grillet* – but now increasingly planted in southern France, California and Australia. Try *Andre Perret, Georges Vernay.* ☆☆☆☆ **1996 Yalumba Reserve Viognier ££** ☆☆☆☆☆ **1995 Condrieu Guigal ££££**

**Viré** [vee-ray] (*Burgundy*, France) Village of *Mâcon* famous for whites. White: 84 **85 86** 87 **88** 89 **90 92** 95 ☆☆☆☆ **Mâcon Viré "Cuvée Spèciale"; Dom. André Bonhomme ££**

**Virgin Hills** [*Victoria*, Australia] A single red blend that is unusually lean in style for Australia and repays keeping. ☆☆☆☆ **1992 £££**

**Dom. Virginie** [veer-jee-nee] (*Midi*, France) Dynamic estate whose Australian winemaker is performing Vin de Pays d'Oc wonders with local grapes such as the *Marsanne* and *Viognier*.

***Viticulteur (-Propriétaire)*** (France) Vine grower/vineyard owner.

**Viura** [vee-yoo-ra] (Spain) Dull, white grape of the *Rioja* region and elsewhere, now being used to greater effect.

**Viu Manent** [vee-oo ma-nayn] (Chile) Having decided to bottle their own juice only in the last ten years, great strides have been made in producing quality premium varietals. ☆☆☆ **1995 Cabernet ££**

**Dom. Michel Voarick** [vwah-rik] (*Burgundy*, France) Slow-maturing, old-fashioned wines that avoid the use of new oak. The *Corton* Charlemagne is particularly spectacular.

**Dom.Vocoret** [vok-ko-ray] (*Burgundy*, France) Classy *Chablis* producer known for making wines that age well. ☆☆☆☆☆ **1994 Chablis Blanchot £££**

**Roberto Voerzio** [vwayrt-zee-yoh] (*Piedmont*, Italy) One of the new-wave producers of juicy, spicy reds, including a first-rate *Barolo*. ☆☆☆ **1995 Dolcetto D'Alba ££**

**de Vogüé** [dur voh-gway] (*Burgundy*, France) Extraordinary Chambolle Musigny estate whose ultra-concentrated red wines last – and deserve to be kept – for ages. Not cheap, but nor are many of the life's true luxuries. ☆☆☆☆☆ **1993 Musigny Grand Cru ££££**

***Volatile Acidity (VA)*** Vinegary character found in wines which have been spoiled by bacteria – and also in subtler, and more acceptable measure in many Italian reds.

**Volnay** [vohl-nay] (*Burgundy*, France) Red wine village in the *Côte de Beaune* (the Caillerets vineyard, now a *Premier Cru,* was once ranked equal to *le Chambertin*). This is the home of fascinating plummy-violety reds. Top producers include *de Montille, Pousse d'Or* and *Lafarge*. **78** 80 83 **85** 86 87 **88 89 90** 92 95 96 ☆☆☆☆☆ **1992 Francois Buffet Volnay Clos de la Rougeotte £££**

**Castello di Volpaia** [vol-pi-yah] (*Tuscany*, Italy) High-quality *Chianti* estate with *Super-Tuscan* Coltassala. ☆☆☆☆ **1991 Coltassala ££££** ☆☆☆☆ **1993 Chianti Classico ££**

**Vosne Romanée** [vohn roh-ma-nay] (*Burgundy*, France) *Côte de Nuits* red wine village with *Romanée-Conti* among its many grand names, and many other potentially gorgeous, plummy-rich wines, froma variety of different producers . Red: 78 79 80 82 83 **85** 86 87 **88 89 90** 92 95 96 **Jayer; Hudelot-Noellat; Jean Gros.**

**Vougeot** [voo-joh] (*Burgundy*, France) *Côte de Nuits* commune comprising the famous *Grand Cru Clos de Vougeot* and a great number of growers of varying skill. *Drouhin, Leroy, Gros* and Chopin-Groffier are all outstanding. Red: 78 79 80 82 83 **85** 86 87 **88 89 90** 92 95 96

**Vouvray** [voov-ray] (*Loire*, France) White wines from the *Chenin Blanc*, ranging from clean, dry whites and refreshing sparklers to *Demi Secs* and honeyed, long-lived, sweet *Moelleux* wines. Often spoiled by massive doses of *sulphur dioxide*. See *Huët*. Sweet white: **76** 83 **85** 86 **88 89** 90 94 95 White: 83 **85 86 88 89 90** 94 95 ☆☆☆☆☆ **1990 Huët Vouvray Moelleux ££££** ☆☆☆ **1995 Vouvray Sec Champalou ££**

***VQA*** (Canada) Acronym for Vintners Quality Alliance, a group of Canadian producers with a self-styled quality designation.

**Vriesenhof** [free-zen-hof] (*Stellenbosch*, South Africa) Tough, occasionally classic reds and so-so *Chardonnay*. ☆☆☆ **1995 Kallista red ££**

**Wachau** [vak-kow] (Austria) Major wine region producing some superlative *Riesling* from steep, terraced vineyards. **Alzinger; Jamek; Pichler; Hirtzberger; Nikolaihof** ☆☆☆ **1994 Unger Chardonnay Spätlese Trocken £££**

**Freie Weingärtner Wachau** [fri vine-gahrt-nur vak-kow] (*Wachau*, Austria) Impressive cooperative with specially reliable *Grüner Veltliner*. Competes on level terms with some of Austria's best small estates.

**Wachenheim** [vahkh-en-hime] (*Pfalz*, Germany) Superior *Mittelhaardt* village which should produce full, rich, unctuous Riesling. QbA/Kab/Spät: **85** 86 **88 89 90** 91 92 93 94 95 96 Aus/Beeren/TBA: **83 85** 88 89 90 91 92 93 94 95 ☆☆☆ **1994 Wachenheimer Rechbachel, Dr Burklin-Wolf £££**

**Waipara Springs** [wi-pah-rah] (*Canterbury*, New Zealand) Tiny producer offering the opportunity to taste wines from this southern region at their best. ☆☆☆ **1995 Chardonnay ££** ☆☆☆ **1995 Riesling ££**

**Wairau River** [wi-row] (*Marlborough*, New Zealand) Classic Kiwi Chardonnays and Sauvignons with piercing fruit character. ☆☆☆☆ **1996 Sauvignon Blanc ££**

**Walker Bay** (South Africa) Promising southerly region for *Pinot Noir* and *Chardonnay*. Established vineyards include *Hamilton Russell* and *Bouchard Finlayson*. Red: **82 84** 86 **87** 89 **91 92** 93 94 95 96 White: 87 **91** 92 93 94 95.

**Warre** [waw] (*Douro*, Portugal) Oldest of the big seven *Port* houses and now a stablemate to *Dow's*, *Graham's* and *Smith Woodhouse*. Traditional *port* which is both rather sweeter and more tannic than most. The old-fashioned *Late-Bottled Vintage* is particularly worth seeking out too. **55** 58 60 **63 66** 70 75 77 85 94 ☆☆☆☆☆ **Warre's Warrior ££** ☆☆☆☆ **1989 Cavadinha** ☆☆☆☆ **1980 Vintage £££**

**Warwick Estate** [wo-rik] (*Stellenbosch*, South Africa) Source of some of South Africa's best reds, including a good *Bordeaux*-blend called Trilogy. The Cabernert Franc grows extremely well here. ☆☆☆ **1994 Cabernet Franc ££**

**Washington State** (USA) Underrated (especially in the US) state whose dusty, irrigated vineyards produce top class *Riesling*, *Sauvignon* and *Merlot*. Red: 85 88 **89** 91 92 94 95 White: **90 91 92 94** 95 **Leonetti Cellars; Woodward Canyon; Hogue.**

**Jimmy Watson Trophy** (*Victoria*, Australia) Coveted trophy given annually for the best young red at the Melbourne Wine Show. Critics complain about the giving of a prize to a wine that is still in barrel (and thus subject to further evolution); winners celebrate the fact that the trophy can bring in a million dollars-worth of sales. *Mildara's Jamieson's Run* was a notable winner.

**Geheimrat J Wegeler Deinhard** [vayg-lur-dine-hard] (*Rheingau*, Germany) Producers with estates all over Germany; they have also taken the innovative – and possibly very sensible – step of leaving out the vineyard name from most of their labels. A large range of acceptable dry *Rieslings* and some of the best German sparkling wine. ☆☆☆☆ **1994 Auslese Rheingau Winkeler Hasensprung** ☆☆☆☆ **NV Silver Ridge Brut ££**

**Wehlen** [VAY-lehn] (*Mosel-Saar-Ruwer*, Germany) *Mittelmosel* village making fresh, sweet, honeyed wines; look for the *Sonnenuhr* vineyard and wines from the great. QbA/Kab/Spät: **85** 86 **88 89 90** 91 92 93 94 95 Aus/Beeren/TBA: **83 85** 88 89 90 91 92 93 94 95 **Dr Loosen; Prum; Wegeler: Deinhard.**

**Weingut Dr Robert Weil** [vile] (*Rheingau*, Germany) *Suntory*-owned winery with stunning *Late-Harvest* wines. ☆☆☆☆☆ **1996 Rheingau Riesling Halbtrocken £££**

**Dom. Weinbach** [vine-bahkh] (*Alsace*, France) Madame Faller's Domaine regularly turns out wonderful, concentrated wines. ☆☆☆☆ **1995 Gewürtraminer Altenbourg Cuvée Laurence ££££**

**Bodegas y Cavas de Weinert** [vine-nurt] (Argentina) Excellent Cabernet Sauvignon specialist, whose soft, ripe wines last extra-ordinarily well. ☆☆☆☆ **1991 Weinert Malbec ££**

***Weingut*** [vine-goot] (Germany) Wine estate.

***Weinkellerei*** [vine-keh-lur-ri] (Germany) Cellar or winery.

**Weissburgunder** [vi-sbur-goon-dur] (Germany/Austria) The *Pinot Blanc* in Germany and Austria. Relatively rare, so often made with care.

**Welschriesling** [velsh-rreez-ling] Aka *Riesling Italico*, *Lutomer*, *Olasz*, *Laski Rizling*. Dull grape, unrelated to the Rhine Riesling, but with many synonyms. Comes into its own when affected by *Botrytis*.

**Weltevrede Estate** [fel-tur-fray-dur] (*Robertson*, South Africa) Pioneer of the *Robertson* area, successful with *Gewürztraminer* and fortified *Muscadel*. ☆☆☆ **1992 Thistle Hill Cabernet Sauvignon**

**Wendouree** [*Clare*, Australia] Small winery with a cult following for its often Malbec-influenced reds. Wines are hard to find outside Australia but well worth seeking out. ☆☆☆☆ 1992 **Cabernet Malbec £££**

**Wente Brothers** [Livermore, California] Improving family company which, despite such potentially distracting enterprises as producing cigars and entering into various kinds of joint venture in places as diverse as Mexico, Israel and Eastern Europe, is still trailing behind firms like Fetzer. The Murrieta's Well wines are the strongest card in the Wente pack. ☆☆☆☆ **1995 Estate Grown Chardonnay £** ☆☆☆☆ 1992 **Murrieta's Well Vendimia ££**

**Domdechant Werner'sches Weingut** [dom-dekh-ahnt vayr-nehr-ches vine-goot] (*Rheingau*, Germany) Excellent vineyard sites at *Hochheim* and *Riesling* grapes produce a number of traditional wines that age beautifully.

**Western Australia** Varied state whose climates range from the baking *Swan Valley* to the far cooler *Mount Barker, Margaret River and Pemberton* growing areas. **Cape Mentelle; Capel Vale; Cullens; Houghton Wines; Leeuwin Estate; Pierro.**

**De Wetshof Estate** [vets-hof] (*Robertson*, South Africa) *Chardonnay* pioneer Danie de Wet makes up to seven different styles of wine for different markets. ☆☆☆ **1994 Chardonnay d'Honneur ££**

**William Wheeler Winery** (*Sonoma*, California) Inventive producer, whose Quintet brings together such diverse grapes as the *Pinot Meunier*, the *Pinot Noir*, the *Grenache* and the *Cabernet Sauvignon*. ☆☆☆☆☆ **1993 Wheeler Quintet ££**

**White Cloud** (New Zealand) Commercial white made by *Nobilo*.

***White Port*** (*Douro*, Portugal) An increasingly popular semi-dry aperitif, though it's very hard to say why when Vermouth is far fresher and considerably cheaper. Port producers tend to drink it with tonic water and ice, which shows what they think of it. *Churchills* make the one worthwhile version. ☆☆☆☆ **Churchill's White Port ££**

**Whitehall Lane** (*Napa Valley*, California) Impressive Merlots and *Cabernets*. ☆☆☆☆☆ **1992 Cabernet Sauvignon Napa Valley Morisoli Vineyard.**

**Wild Horse** (San Luis Obispo) *Chardonnays*, *Pinot Blancs* and *Pinot Noirs* are all good, but the perfumed *Malvasia* Bianca is the real star.

***Wild yeast*** Fermentation in most European wines is traditionally kicked off by the natural yeasts that live on the skins of the grapes. In the New World, cultured yeasts are now generally preferred because of their predictability. New World reactionaries like *Franciscan* and *Frog's Leap*, however, are proving that the European way can make for greater complexity of flavour.

**Wildekrans** [fil-dur-krunss] (Bot River, South Africa) Pioneer of the Bot River area, with a light lemony *Chardonnay*, piercing *Sauvignon* and extraordinary smokey-bacon-and-strawberry *Pinotage*.

**Willamette Valley** [wil-AM-et] (*Oregon*, USA) The heart of *Oregon's Pinot Noir* vineyards. Red: 85 88 **89** 91 92 94 95 White: **90 91 92 94** 95 ☆☆☆ **1994 Willamette Valley Vineyards Oregon Pinot Noir Whole Berry Fermented**

**Williams Selyem** [sel-yem] (*Sonoma*, California) Eccentric producer of world class Burgundian-style *Chardonnay* and *Pinot Noir*.

**Wiltingen** [vihl-ting-gehn] (*Mosel-Saar-Ruwer*, Germany) Distinguished *Saar* village, making elegant, slatey wines. Well-known for the *Scharzhofberg* vineyard. QbA/Kab/Spät: **85** 86 **88 89 90** 91 92 93 94 95 Aus/Beeren/TBA: **83 85** 88 89 90 91 92 93 94 95

**Wing Canyon** (Mount Veeder, California) Small hillside Cabernet specialist, high in the hills of Mount Veeder. Great, intense, blackcurranty wines. ☆☆☆☆ **1994 Cabernet Sauvignon ££££**

**Winkel** [vin-kel] (*Rheingau*, Germany) Village with a reputation for complex, delicious wine, housing *Schloss Vollrads* estate. QbA/Kab/Spät: **85** 86 **88 89 90** 91 92 93 94 95 Aus/Beeren/TBA: **83 85** 88 89 90 91 92 93 94 95 96

***Winzerverein/Winzergenossenschaft*** [vint-zur-veh-RINE/vint-zur-geh-NOSH-en-shaft] (Germany) Cooperative.

**Wirra Wirra Vineyards** (*McLaren Vale*, Australia) Reliable producer, making first-class *Riesling* and *Cabernet* which, in best vintages is sold as The Angelus. ☆☆☆☆☆ **1993 R. S. W McLaren Vale Shiraz ££**

**Wolff-Metternich** [volf met-tur-nikh] (*Baden*, Germany) Good rich *Riesling* from the granite slopes of *Baden*.

**Woodward Canyon** (Washington State, USA) Small producer of characterful but subtle *Chardonnay* and *Bordeaux*-style reds that compete with the best of California. ☆☆☆☆ **1994 Cabernet Sauvignon £££**

**Wootton** (Somerset, England) Successful vineyard, noted for its *Schönberger* but more recently entering the commercial arena in a very un-English way with the highly marketable 'Trinity' blend of wines from three separate sources.

**Wurttemburg** [voo-thm-burg] (Germany) *Anbaugebiet* surrounding the Neckar region, producing more red than any other.

**Wyndham Estate** (*Hunter Valley*, Australia) Ultra-commercial winery which now belongs to Pernod Ricard. Quite what that firm's French customers would think of these jammy blockbusters is anybody's guess; they're certainly not like anything they'll have seen out of France. ☆☆☆☆ **1994 Oak Cask Chardonnay ££**

**Wynns** (Coonawarra, Australia) Well-established subsidiary of *Penfolds* and top-class producer of *Coonawarra Cabernets* (especially the John Riddoch) and buttery *Chardonnay*. The Ovens Valley *Shiraz* is another rich, spicy gem. ☆☆☆☆ **1996 Coonawarra Estate Chardonnay ££**

**Ch. Xanadu** [za-na-doo] (*Margaret River*, Australia) The reputation here was built on *Semillon*, but the *Cabernet* is good too. ☆☆☆☆☆ **1993 Semillon £££**

**Xarel-Lo** [sha-REHL-loh] (*Catalonia*, Spain) Fairly basic grape exclusive to *Catalonia*. Used for *Cava;* best in the hands of *Jaume Serra*.

**"Y" d'Yquem** [ee-grek dee-kem] (*Bordeaux*, France) Hideously expensive dry wine of *Ch. d'Yquem* which, like other such efforts by *Sauternes Châteaux*, is of greater academic than hedonistic interest.

**Yakima Valley** [YAK-ih-mah] (*Washington State*, USA) Principal region of *Washington State*. Good for *Merlot*, *Riesling* and *Sauvignon Columbia Crest, Columbia Winery, Ch. Ste Michelle*. Red: 85 88 **89** 91 92 94 95 White: **90 91 92 94** 95

**Ch. Yaldara Lakewood** [yal-DAH-ra] (*Barossa Valley*, Australia) Big *Barossa* producer with a creditable, if uncharacteristic, ultra-ripe *Merlot*.

**Yalumba** [ya-LUM-ba] (*Barossa Valley*, Australia) Associated with *Hill-Smith* and producer of good dry and sweet whites, serious reds, fortified wines (including *Rutherglen* Muscat) and some of Australia's most appealing fizz, including *Angas Brut* and the brilliant Cuvée One *Pinot Noir-Chardonnay*. Now also making wine in California under the Voss label. ☆☆☆☆ **Galway Pipe Port, Barossa Valley.**

**Yarra Valley** [ya-ra] (*Victoria*, Australia) Historic wine district whose 'boutiques' make top-class *Burgundy*-like *Pinot Noir* and *Chardonnay* (*Coldstream Hills* and *Tarrawarra*)*;* but has also produced stylish *Bordeaux*-style reds and, at *Yarra Yering*, a brilliant *Shiraz*. White: **90 91 92 94 95** 96 Red: **85 86 87 88 90 91 92** 94 95 96

**Yarra Yering** [ya-ra yeh-ring] (Yarra Valley, Australia) Bailey Carrodus proves that the *Yarra Valley* is not just *Pinot Noir* country by producing a complex *Cabernet* blend, including a little *Petit Verdot* (Dry Red No.1) and a *Shiraz* (Dry Red No.2) in which he puts a bit of *Viognier*. Underhill is the *Second Label*. ☆☆☆☆ **1991 Dry Red No.1 £££**

**Yecla** [yay-kla] (Spain) *DO* region of Spain near *Valencia* with alcoholic reds.

🍷 **Yellowglen** (South Australia) Producer of uninspiring basic fizz, and some really fine top-end fare, including the 'Y' which looks oddly reminiscent of a sparkling wine called 'J' from *Jordan* in California.

🍷 **Yonder Hill** (Stellenbosch, South Africa) New winery making waves with well-oaked reds. ☆☆☆☆ **1993 Merlot.**

**Yonne** [yon] (*Burgundy*, France) Northern *Burgundy* Département in which *Chablis* is to be found.

🍷 **Ch. d'Yquem** [dee-kem] (*Sauternes Premier Cru Supérieur*, *Bordeaux*, France) Sublime *Sauternes*. The grape pickers are sent out several times to select the best grapes. Not produced every year and not, it seems, particularly profitable, even at the horrendous prices it commands. Currently the subject of a legal tussle between its manager and part-owner Comte Alexandre de Lur Saluces and members of his family, who want to sell out to the giant Louis-Vuitton Moët Hennessy group which, in turn, wants to sell the wine through their duty-free shops in the Far East. Such is the wine world in 1998. **62 67 71** 73 **75 76** 77 78 79 **80 81 82** 83 84 85 86 87 88 89 90 ☆☆☆☆☆ **1989 ££££**

# Z

🍷 **Zaca Mesa** [za-ka may-sa] (*Santa Barbara*, California) Fast-improving winery with a focus on spicy *Rhône* varietals. ☆☆☆☆☆ **1993 Syrah Santa Barbara County.**

**Zell** [tzell] (*Mosel-Saar-Ruwer*, Germany) *Bereich* of lower *Mosel* and village, making pleasant, flowery *Riesling*. Famous for the *Schwarze Katz* (black cat) *Grosslage*. QbA/Kab/Spät: **85 88 89 90** 91 92 93 94 95 Aus/Beeren/TBA: **83 85** 88 89 90 91 92 93 94 95

***Zentralkellerei*** [tzen-trahl-keh-lur-ri] (Germany) Massive, central cellars for groups of cooperatives in six of the *Anbaugebiet* – the *Mosel-Saar-Ruwer* Zentralkellerei is Europe's largest cooperative.

**Zimbabwe** The industry here started during the days of sanctions and involved growing grapes in ex-tobacco fields. Now the quality is improving to a level of international adequacy.

🍷 **Dom. Zind-Humbrecht** [zind-hoom-brekht] (*Alsace*, France) Extraordinarily consistent producer of highly perfumed, ultra-concentrated, single-vineyard wines and good varietals that have won a shelf-ful of awards from the International Wine Challenge and helped to draw Alsace to the attention of a new generation of wine drinkers. ☆☆☆☆ **1993 Gewurztraminer Alsace Grand Cru Goldert £££**

🍇 **Zinfandel** [zin-fan-del] (California) Versatile, red grape, producing everything from dark, jammy, leathery reds, to pale pink, spicy 'blush' wines, and even a little fortified wine that bears comparison with port. The finest exponents are undoubtedly *Ridge*. Also grown by *Cape Mentelle* in Australia, and *Blauwklippen* in South Africa.

🍷 **Don Zoilo** [don zoy-loh] (Jerez, Spain) Classy sherry producer. ☆☆☆☆ **Don Zoilo Oloroso ££**

🍇 **Zweigelt** [zvi-gelt] (Austria) Distinctive, berryish red wine grape, more or less restricted to Austria and Hungary.

# UK Merchants

**3 D Wines** ☆☆☆☆ Holly Lodge, High Street, Swineshead, Lincolnshire, PE20 3LH. ☎ 01205 820 745. FAX 01205 821 042. By the case only, credit cards, delivery, tastings, *en primeur*, cellarage.
*A club offering exclusive wines and the option of renting your own vines; specialises in the Loire and Burgundy.*

**W.M. Addison** ☆☆☆☆ The Warehouse, Village Farm, Lilleshall, Newport, Shropshire, TF10 9HB. ☎ 01952 670 200. FAX 01952 677 309. Credit cards, delivery, *en primeur*, cellarage, glass hire, tastings.
*Good traditional French wines.*

**Addison-Bagot Vintners** ☆☆☆☆ 13 London Road, Alderley Edge, Cheshire, SK9 7JT. ☎ 01625 582 354. FAX 01625 586 404. Credit cards, delivery, tastings, glass loan.
*Good regional French and impressive wines from Italy and the New World.*

**Adnams Wine Merchants** ☆☆☆☆☆ The Crown, High Street, Southwold, Suffolk, IP18 6DP. ☎ 01502 727 222. FAX 01502 727 223. E-mail: wines.adnams@paston.co.uk Credit cards, delivery, tastings, *en primeur*, cellarage, glass hire/loan.
*Arguably Britain's best merchant, with an eclectic, stylish list. Brilliant throughout, but especially in the New World, Italy and Germany.*

**Allez Vins!** ☆☆☆☆ P O Box 278, Harrogate, N. Yorkshire, HG3 3AL. ☎+FAX 0385 264 445. E-mail: av@bigfoot.com Credit cards, tastings, glass hire/loan.
*Go-ahead family company specialising in French wines from small producers.*

**Amathus Wines Ltd** ☆☆☆☆ 377 Green Lanes, Palmers Green, London, N13 4JG. ☎ 0181 886 3787/1864. FAX 0181 882 1273. Credit cards, delivery, glass hire/loan.
*A wholesale price list with great whiskies and good French wines.*

**John Arkell Vintners** ☆☆☆ Arkells Brewery Ltd, Hyde Road, Stratton St. Margaret, Swindon, Wilts, SN2 6RU. ☎ 01793 823 026. FAX 01793 828 864. Credit cards, tasting, delivery, *en primeur*, cellarage, glass hire/loan.
*Reasonable Bordeaux, vintage ports and* négociant *Burgundies.*

**John Armit Wines Ltd** ☆☆☆☆☆ 5 Royalty Studios, 105 Lancaster Road, London, W11 1QF. ☎ 0171 727 6846. FAX 0171 727 7133. E-mail: info@jarmit.co.uk By the case only, credit cards, delivery, tastings, *en primeur*, cellarage.
*A stylish list – clarets galore and Domaine Burgundies from Leflaive.*

**Asda Stores** ☆☆☆☆ Asda House, Southbank, Great Wilson Street, Leeds, LS1 5AD. ☎ 0113 243 5435. FAX 0113 241 7766. Credit cards, tastings, glass hire/loan.
*Dynamic supermarket chain with wines presented by price and style rather than country.*

**Australian Wine Club** ☆☆☆☆☆ Freepost WC5500, Slough, Berks, SL3 9BY. ☎ 01753 594 925. Order line 0800 852 6004. FAX 01753 591 369. E-mail: sales@austwine.demon.co.uk Mail order only, by the case only, *en primeur*, credit cards, delivery.
*There are wines here Australians would give their eye-teeth for.*

**Averys of Bristol Ltd** ☆☆☆☆ Orchard House, Southfield Road, Nailsea, Bristol, BS19 1JD. ☎ 01275 811 100. FAX 01275 811 101. Credit cards, delivery, tastings, *en primeur*, cellarage, glass hire/loan.
*Traditional merchant where New World offerings are a speciality.*

**B.H.Wines** ☆☆☆☆☆ Boustead Hill House, Boustead Hill, Burgh-By-Sands, Carlisle, Cumbria, CA5 6AA. ☎+FAX 01228 576 711. By the case only, delivery, tastings, glass hire/loan.
*First class, innovative, wide range.*

**Ballantynes of Cowbridge** ☆☆☆☆ 3 Westgate, Cowbridge, Vale of Glamorgan, CF71 7AQ. ☎ 01446 774 840. FAX 01446 775 253. Credit cards, delivery, tastings, *en primeur*, cellarage, glass loan.
*Characterful wines from France, Italy and Germany.*

**Adam Bancroft Associates** ☆☆☆☆ The Mansion House, 57 South Lambeth Road, Vauxhall, London, SW8 1RJ. ☎ 0171 793 1902. FAX 0171 793 1897. By the case only, credit cards, tastings, delivery, glass hire/loan.
*Serious supporter of French wines, but with some great Australians too.*

**Georges Barbier** ☆☆☆☆
267 Lee High Road, London, SE12 8RU. ☎ 0181 852 5801. FAX 0181 463 0398. By the case only, delivery, *en primeur*, cellarage.
*Unusual Spanish wines, good Burgundy and brilliant old Armagnacs.*

**Barrels & Bottles** ☆☆☆☆☆
1 Walker Street, Wicker, Sheffield, S3 8G2. ☎ 0114 2769 666. FAX 0114 2799 182. E-mail: jmh6868@AOL
Credit cards, delivery, tastings, *en primeur*, cellarage, glass hire/loan.
*See* The Wine Schoppen.

**Benedict's** ☆☆☆ 28 Holyrood Street, Newport, Isle of Wight, PO30 5AU. ☎ 01983 529 596. FAX 01983 826 868. Credit cards, delivery, tastings, cellarage, glass hire/loan.
*Small firm with good traditional French and South African selections.*

**Bennetts Wines** ☆☆☆☆☆ High Street, Chipping Campden, Glos, GL55 6AG. ☎+FAX 01386 840 392. Credit cards, delivery, tastings, *en primeur*, cellarage, glass hire/loan.
*Old and New World class.*

**Berry Bros & Rudd** ☆☆☆☆☆
3 St. James's Street, London, SW1A 1EG. ☎ 0171 396 9666. FAX 0171 396 9611. E-mail: orders@bros.co.uk
Web Site: www.berry_bros.co.uk
Credit cards, delivery, *en primeur*, cellarage, tastings, glass hire/loan.
*Fast rejuvenating firm with great clarets and Germans and increasingly good New World wines. Also worth visiting at Heathrow – or on the Internet.*

**Bibendum Wine Limited** ☆☆☆☆☆
113 Regents Park Road, London, NW1 8UR. ☎ 0171 916 7706. FAX 0171 916 7705. By the case only, credit cards, delivery, tastings, *en primeur*, cellarage.
*Innovative firm: good across the board, with excellent* en primeur *clarets, Californians, Burgundies, Rhônes. Great tastings.*

**Booths of Stockport** ☆☆☆☆ 62 Heaton Moor Road, Heaton Moor, Stockport, SK4 4ND. ☎+FAX 0161 432 3309. Credit cards, delivery, tastings, glass hire/loan.
*A reliable range, with well-chosen examples throughout.*

**Booths Supermarkets** ☆☆☆☆☆
4–6 Fishergate, Preston, PR1 3LJ. ☎ 01772 251 701. FAX 01772 255 642. E-mail: 101475,1546@compuserve.com
Credit cards, glass hire/loan, tastings.
*Would probably be recognised as Britain's best supermarket if it were south of Watford.*

**Bordeaux Direct** ☆☆☆☆ New Aquitaine House, Paddock Road, Caversham, Berkshire, RG4 5JY. ☎ 0118 948 1711. FAX 0118 947 1928. E-mail: orders@bordeaux-direct.co.uk
Credit cards, delivery, tastings, *en primeur*, cellarage, glass hire/loan.
*Mixed cases, good wines, newsletters and an excellent tasting festival.*

**The Bottleneck** ☆☆☆ 7 & 9 Charlotte Street, Broadstairs, Kent, CT10 1LR. ☎+FAX 01843 861 095. Credit cards, delivery, tastings, glass hire/loan.
*Reliable local merchant with a good range of New World wines.*

**Bottoms Up** ☆☆☆☆ Sefton House, 42 Church Road, Welwyn Garden City, Herts, AL8 6PJ. ☎ 0151 449 4000. FAX 01707 371 398. Credit cards, delivery, tastings, glass hire/loan.
*Friendliest part of the Thresher empire. If you find a case cheaper elsewhere within seven days, they will refund the difference and give you an extra bottle of the same wine.*

**Andrew Bruce Wines** ☆☆☆☆
22 Hans Place, London, SW1X 0EP. ☎ 0171 591 1982. FAX 0171 225 0366. Mail order only, delivery.
*Expertly selected range of fine wines, continually updated.*

**The Burgundy Shuttle Ltd**
☆☆☆☆ 13 Mandeville Courtyard, 142 Battersea Park Road, London, SW11 4NB, ☎ 0171 498 0755. FAX 0171 498 0724. By the case only, cellarage, glass loan, delivery.
*As the name suggests, an excellent Burgundy specialist.*

**Bute Wines** ☆☆☆☆☆ 2 Cottesmore Gardens, London, W8 5PR. ☎ 0171 937 1629. FAX 0171 361 0061. By the case only, *en primeur*.
*Fine claret, Burgundy and Californian specialist. No longer associated with Goedhuis (qv).*

**The Butlers Wine Cellar** ☆☆☆☆ 247 Queens Park Road, Brighton, East Sussex, BN2 2XJ. ☎ 01273 698 724. FAX 01273 622 761. Credit cards, delivery, tastings, glass hire/loan.
*A wide selection of (often old) gems.*

**Anthony Byrne** ☆☆☆☆☆ Ramsey Business Park, Stocking Fen Road, Ramsey, Cambs, PE17 1UR. ☎ 01487 814 555. FAX 01487 814 962. Delivery, tastings, *en primeur*, cellarage.
*A major supplier to top restaurants, offering great wines from Alsace, the Loire and Burgundy; also good French country wines.*

**D. Byrne & Co** ☆☆☆☆☆ Victoria Buildings, 12 King Street, Clitheroe, Lancs, BB7 2EP. ☎ 01200 423 152. Delivery, tastings, *en primeur*, cellarage, glass hire/loan.
*One of the wine world's best-kept secrets. An Aladdin's cave of gems at reasonable prices.*

**Cairns & Hickey** ☆☆☆ 854/856 Leeds Road, Bramhope, Leeds, LS16 9ED. ☎ 0113 2673 746. FAX 0113 2613 826. Credit cards, delivery, *en primeur*, cellarage, glass hire/loan.
*A good broad-ranging, if sometimes rather unadventurous selection.*

**Cape Province Wines** ☆☆☆ 77 Laleham Road, Staines, Middlesex, TW18 2EA. ☎ 01784 451 860. FAX 01784 469 267. E-mail: capewines@msn.com Credit cards, delivery, tastings, glass hire/loan.
*The best place to find a representative range of modern South African wines.*

**A Case of Wine (Pigs 'n' Piglets)** ☆☆☆ Harford, Pumpsaint, Llanwrda, Dyfed, SA19 8DT. ☎+FAX 01558 650 671. By the case only, credit cards, delivery, tastings, glass hire/loan.
*Italian-owned merchant with a recommendable range of Italian (and non-Italian) wines.*

**Cave Cru Classé** ☆☆☆☆ 13 Leathermarket, Weston Street, London, SE1 3LR. ☎ 0171 378 8579. FAX 0171 378 8544. E-mail: ccc@mailbox.co.uk By the case only, credit cards, delivery, cellarage, *en primeur*.
*Specialists in top-of-the-range Bordeaux and Burgundy.*

**Cellars Direct Wine Club** ☆☆☆ Nest Road, Gateshead, NE10 0ES. ☎ 0191 495 5000. FAX 0191 438 6261. Mail order only, by the case only, credit cards, delivery, tastings, *en primeur*.
*Specialises in preselected, generally well-chosen, mixed cases, mostly under £55.*

**The Celtic Vintner** ☆☆☆☆ The Star Trading Estate, Ponthir Road, Caerleon, Newport, Gwent, NP6 1PQ. ☎ 01633 430 055. FAX 01633 430 154. By the case only, credit cards, delivery, *en primeur*, glass hire/loan.
*Some great Late Harvest wines, Welsh wines and plenty more besides.*

**Charterhouse Wine Emporium** ☆☆☆☆ 86 Goding Street, London, SE11 5AW. ☎ 0171 587 1302. FAX 0171 589 0982. Credit cards, delivery, *en primeur*, tastings, glass hire/loan.
*Good range of wines particularly from Australia and Chile.*

**Chateaux Wines** ☆☆☆ Paddock House, Upper Tockington Road, Tockington, Bristol, BS12 4LQ. ☎+FAX 01454 613 959. By the case only, credit cards, delivery, *en primeur*, cellarage, tastings.
*An attractive selection of wines including Burgundy estates.*

**Chippendale Fine Wines** ☆☆☆☆ 15 Manor Square, Otley, West Yorkshire, LS21 3AP. ☎+FAX 01943 850 633. Credit cards, delivery, tastings.
*A fascinatingly chatty list, packed with good quality and value.*

**Classic Wines and Spirits** ☆☆☆☆ Vintners House, Third Avenue, Deeside Industrial Park, Deeside, Chester, CH5 2LA.. ☎ 01244 288 444. FAX 01244 280 008. Credit cards, delivery, tastings, glass loan.
*Champagnes galore at sub-Oddbins prices.*

**Brian Coad Fine Wines** ☆☆☆☆ 66 Cole Lane, Stowford Park, Ivybridge, Devon, PL21 0PN. ☎ 01752 896 545. FAX 01752 691 160. By the case only, delivery, *en primeur*, tasting, glass hire/loan.
*Fine wine merchant, leaning towards the classic areas of Bordeaux, Burgundy and the Loire.*

**Cockburn & Co (Leith)** ☆☆☆☆
The Wine Emporium, 7 Devon Place, Edinburgh, EH12 5HJ. ☎ 0131 346 1113. FAX 0131 313 2607. Credit cards, delivery, tastings, *en primeur*, cellarage.
*A good range of reliable rather than exciting wines.*

**Connolly's Ltd** ☆☆☆☆ Arch 13, 220 Livery Street, Birmingham, B3 1EU. ☎ 0121 236 9269. FAX 0121 233 2339. Credit cards, delivery, tastings, *en primeur*, glass hire/loan.
*A mainly Old World range with excellent service and regular tastings.*

**Co-op** ☆☆☆ New Century House, P. O. Box 53, Manchester, M60 4ES. ☎ 0800 317 827. FAX 0161 827 5117. Credit cards, tastings.
*Can be an unexpected source of bargains.*

**Co-operative** ☆☆☆ Sandbrook Park, Sandbrook Way, Rochdale, OL11 1SA. ☎ 01706 731 000. FAX 01706 891 207. Credit cards, tastings.
*Separate to the Co-op. A mixed bag with some good buys.*

**Corkscrew Wines** ☆☆☆☆
Arch no. 5, Viaduct Estate, Carlisle, CA2 5BN. ☎ +FAX 01228 43033. Credit cards, delivery, tastings, *en primeur,* glass hire/loan.
*Excellent small merchant, continuing to impress.*

**Corney and Barrow Ltd** ☆☆☆☆
12 Helmet Row, London, EC1V 3QJ. ☎ 0171 251 4051. FAX 0171 608 1373. E-mail: (JAB)@corbar.co.uk Credit cards, delivery, *en primeur*, cellarage.
*Bordeaux, Burgundy and fine wine specialists.*

**Craven's** ☆☆☆☆ 15 Craven Road, Paddington, London, W2 3BP. ☎ 0171 723 0252. FAX 0171 262 5823. Credit cards, delivery, tastings, *en primeur*, cellarage.
*A small firm specialising in the Loire, Rhône and Languedoc-Roussillon.*

**Croque-en-Bouche** ☆☆☆☆☆
221 Wells Road, Malvern Wells, Worcester, WR14 4HF. ☎ +FAX 01684 565 612. E-mail: croque@globalnet.co.uk By the case only, delivery, tastings, cellarage, glass hire/loan.
*Restaurant-cum-wine merchants, offering an encyclopaedic range, especially Australian and French.*

**Davisons Direct** ☆☆☆☆
7 Aberdeen Road, Croydon, Surrey, CR0 1EQ. ☎ 0800 606 070. FAX 0181 760 0390. Credit cards, delivery, *en primeur*, cellarage, glass hire/loan.
*The remains of Davisons: a mail-order merchant offering delivery (within two days) to SW London.*

**Rodney Densem Wines** ☆☆☆☆
Stapeley Bank, London Road, Stapeley, Nantwich, Cheshire, CW5 7JW. ☎ 01270 623 665. FAX 01270 624 062. E-mail: 100705.1374@ com puserve.com. Credit cards, delivery, tastings, *en primeur*, cellarage, glass loan.
*Focuses neatly on France grand and humble. Good range of ports.*

**Direct Wine Shipments** ☆☆☆☆☆
5/7 Corporation Square, Belfast, N. Ireland, BT1 3AJ. ☎ 01232 243 906/ 238 700. FAX 01232 240 202. Credit cards, delivery, tastings, *en primeur*, cellarage, glass hire/loan.
*One of the best merchants in the UK, with good* en primeur, *plus unusual wines from the Old and New Worlds.*

**Domaine Direct** ☆☆☆☆☆
29 Wilmington Square, London, WC1X 0EG. ☎ 0171 837 1142. FAX 0171 837 8605. Mail order only, by the case only, credit cards, delivery, tastings, *en primeur*.
*A Burgundian heaven in which to find wines from the best growers.*

**Drinks Cabin** ☆☆☆ Sefton House, 42 Church Road, Welwyn Garden City, Herts, AL8 6PJ. ☎ 0151 449 4000. FAX 01707 371 398. Credit cards, delivery, glass hire/loan.
*Part of the Thresher empire selling lower-priced, larger-volume offerings.*

**Eckington Wines** ☆☆☆☆
2 Ravencar Road, Eckington, Sheffield, S21 4JZ. ☎ +FAX 01246 433 213. By the case only, *en primeur,* delivery, tastings, glass hire/loan.
*A fine range of big-name Australians heads a strong list.*

**Edencroft Fine Wines** ☆☆☆
8-10 Hospital Street, Nantwich, Cheshire, CW5 5RJ. ☎ +FAX 01270 625 302. Credit cards, *en primeur,* delivery, tastings, glass hire/loan.
*A small, enterprising range from Australia and Burgundy.*

**El Vino** ☆☆☆ Vintage House, 1 Hare Place, Fleet Street, London, EC4Y 1BJ. ☎ 0171 353 5384. FAX 0171 936 2367. Credit cards, delivery, tastings, *en primeur*, cellarage, glass hire/loan.
*Ultra-traditional merchant with four tasting-houses in the City and over 170 wines to purchase by the bottle.*

**Eldridge Pope & Co Plc** ☆☆☆☆ Weymouth Avenue, Dorchester, Dorset, DT1 1QT. ☎ 01305 258 347. FAX 01305 258 155. Credit cards, delivery, tastings, *en primeur*, cellarage, glass loan.
*One of England's finest country merchants with a dozen shops. Traditional but also innovative.*

**Ben Ellis Wines** ☆☆☆☆ The Brockham Wine Cellars, Wheelers Lane, Brockham, Surrey, RH3 7HJ. ☎ 01737 842160. FAX 01737 843 210. By the case only, credit cards, delivery, tastings, *en primeur*, cellarage, glass hire/loan.
*Importers of distinctive individual estate wines, especially from Burgundy and other French regions.*

**Philip Eyres Wine Merchant/ S. H. Jones** ☆☆☆ The Cellars, Coleshill, Amersham, Bucks, HP7 0LS. ☎ 01494 433 823. FAX 01494 431 349. By the case only, credit cards, delivery, *en primeur*. *See* S.H. Jones.

**Farr Vintners** ☆☆☆☆☆ 19 Sussex Street, Pimlico, London, SW1V 4RR. ☎ 0171 821 2000. FAX 0171 821 2020. By the case only, credit cards, delivery, *en primeur*, cellarage.
*Wall-to-wall fine wine, old and young. Known to every Oriental and American collector and investor.*

**Fernlea Vintners** ☆☆☆ 7 Fernlea Road, Balham, London, SW12 7RT. ☎ 0181 673 0053. FAX 0181 675 3360. By the case only, credit cards, delivery, cellarage.
*A range of small and unusual French domaines, most of which are recommendable.*

**Ferrers Le Mesurier** ☆☆☆ 'Turnslowe', North Street, Titchmarsh, Kettering, Northants, NN14 3DH. ☎+FAX 01832 732 660. By the case only, delivery, cellarage.
*A short, French-biased list but with some really appealing, unusual wines.*

**Findlater Mackie Todd** ☆☆☆☆ Deer Park Road, Merton Abbey, London, SW19 3TU. ☎ 0181 543 7528. FAX 0181 543 2415. Mail order only, by the case only, credit cards, delivery, *en primeur*, cellarage.
*Mail order division of Waitrose, offering good Bordeaux, solid Rhônes and some crackers from New Zealand.*

**Fine Wines of New Zealand/New Zealand Direct** ☆☆☆ P.O. Box 476, London, NW5 2NZ. ☎ 0171 482 0093 or 0171 916 8166. FAX 0171 267 8400. By the case only, tastings, credit cards, delivery.
*The name says it all.*

**Le Fleming Wines** ☆☆☆☆ 9 Longcroft Avenue, Harpenden, Herts, AL5 2RB. ☎+FAX 01582 760 125. By the case only, delivery, *en primeur*, tastings, glass hire/loan.
*Great one-woman band – aka Cherry Jenkins – with an excellent range.*

**Forth Wines Ltd** ☆☆☆☆ Crawford Place, Milnathort, KY13 7XF. ☎ 01577 863 668. FAX 01577 865 296. Credit cards, delivery, *en primeur*.
*Imports from good producers in countries such as France, Chile and South Africa.*

**Fortnum & Mason Plc** ☆☆☆☆☆ 181 Piccadilly, London, WIA IER. ☎ 0171 734 8040. FAX 0171 437 3278. Credit cards, delivery, tastings, *en primeur*, cellarage.
*One of the best ranges of wine in London, often at unexpectedly affordable prices.*

**Four Walls Wine Co** ☆☆☆☆☆ 1 High Street, Chilgrove, Nr Chichester, W. Sussex, PO18 9HX. ☎ 01243 535 219. FAX 01243 535 301. Credit cards, delivery.
*Extraordinary extensive list of blue-chip Bordeaux, Burgundies, Germans and Loire.*

**John Frazier Ltd** ☆☆☆ Stirling Road, Cranmore Industrial Estate, Shirley, Solihull, W. Midlands, B90 4NE. ☎ 0121 704 3415. FAX 0121 711 2710. Credit cards, delivery, cellarage, *en primeur*, glass hire/loan.
*A workaday list of wines by major producers.*

**Friarwood Ltd** ☆☆☆☆ 26 New Kings Road, London, SW6 4ST. ☎ 0171 736 2628. FAX 0171 731 0411. Credit cards, delivery, *en primeur*, tastings, cellarage, glass hire/loan.
*Smart Fulham corner shop offering blue-chip Burgundy and Bordeaux and good* en primeur.

**Fuller's** ☆☆☆☆☆ The Griffin Brewery, Chiswick Lane South, Chiswick, W4 2QB. ☎ 0181 996 2000. FAX 0181 996 2087. Credit cards, delivery, glass hire/loan.
*Excellent high street merchant with an interesting range concentrating on quality. Giving Oddbins a run for its money.*

**Gallery Wines** ☆☆☆ The Gomshall Gallery, Station Road, Gomshall, Surrey, GU5 9LB. ☎ 01483 203 795. FAX 01483 203 282. Credit cards, delivery, , tastings, cellarage, glass loan.
*French wine specialist, sourcing direct from smaller domaines.*

**Gauntleys of Nottingham** ☆☆☆☆☆ 4 High Street, Nottingham, NG1 2ET. ☎ 0115 911 0555. FAX 0115 911 0557. Credit cards, delivery, tastings, *en primeur*, glass hire/loan.
*One of the country's leading experts on the Rhône, the Loire and the South of France.*

**Gelston Castle Fine Wines** ☆☆☆☆ 45 Warwick Street, London, SW1V 2AJ. ☎ 0171 821 6841 / 01556 503 012. FAX 01556 504 183. Credit cards, delivery, tastings, *en primeur*, cellarage.
*Burgundy, the Rhône and some serious wines from Germany dominate the list.*

**The General Wine & Liquor Company** ☆☆☆ 25 Station Road, Liphook, Hampshire, GU30 7DW. ☎ 01428 722 201. FAX 01428 724 037. Credit cards, delivery, tastings, glass hire/loan.
*Covers the field reliably rather than innovatively.*

**Goedhuis & Co** ☆☆☆☆☆ 6 Rudolf Place, Miles Street, London, SW8 IRP. ☎ 0171 793 7900. FAX 0171 793 7170. By the case only, credit cards, delivery, *en primeur*, cellarage, glass hire/loan.
*A source of serious classic wines, and an inventive build-a-cellar scheme.*

**Gordon & MacPhail** ☆☆☆☆ George House, Boroughbriggs Road, Elgin, Moray, IV30 1JY. Shop: 58–60 South Street. ☎ 01343 545 111. FAX 01343 540 155. Credit cards, delivery, tastings, glass hire/loan.
*Malt from your birth year, old-fashioned clarets and New World.*

**Grape Ideas** ☆☆☆☆ 47 West Way, Botley, Oxford, OX2 0JR. ☎ 01865 263 303. FAX 01865 791 594. Credit cards, delivery, tastings, glass loan.
*Good South Americans, Burgundies, Alsaces, Italians and Iberians.*

**The Great Northern Wine Co** ☆☆☆☆ Unit 5, Granary Wharf, Leeds Canal Basin, Leeds, LS1 4BR. ☎ 0113 246 1200. FAX 0113 246 1209. Credit cards, delivery, *en primeur*, glass hire/loan.
*One of the best merchants between Scotland and Watford.*

**The Great Western Wine Co** ☆☆☆☆ The Wine Warehouse, Wells Road, Bath, BA2 3AP. ☎ 01225 446 009. FAX 01225 442 139. By the case only, credit cards, delivery, tastings, cellarage, glass hire/loan, *en primeur*.
*Especially good Burgundies.*

**Greek Wine Centre** ☆☆☆☆ 46-48 Underdale Road, Shrewsbury, Shrops. SY2 5DT. ☎ 01743 364 636 FAX 01743 367 960. E-mail: 100705.2453@compuserve.com By the case only.
*The best "new wave" wines from Greece.*

**Peter Green** ☆☆☆☆☆ 37 A/B Warrender Park Road, Edinburgh, EH9 1HJ. ☎+FAX 0131 229 5925. Credit cards, delivery, tastings, glass loan.
*Top class across-the-board.*

**H. & H. Fine Wine Ltd** ☆☆☆☆ 29 Roman Way Industrial Park, London Road, Godmanchester, Cambs, PE18 8LN. ☎ 01480 411 599. FAX 01480 411 833. By the case only, credit cards, delivery, *en primeur*, cellarage.
*Particularly fine on Burgundy and French regional wines.*

**Hall Batson** ☆☆☆☆ 168 Wroxham Road, Norwich, Norfolk, NR7 8DE. ☎ 01603 415 115. FAX 01603 484 096. E-mail: hbwine@paston.co.uk By the case, credit cards, delivery, tastings, glass loan.
*Classy Old and New World wines.*

**Halves Ltd** ☆☆☆☆ 5 Long Lane Industrial Estate, Craven Arms, Shropshire, SY7 8DU. ☎ 01588 673 040. FAX 01588 673 020. Credit cards, delivery.
*Everything is done by halves here – except the quality of the wine.*

**Roger Harris Wines** ☆☆☆☆ Loke Farm, Weston Longville, Norfolk, NR9 5LG. ☎ 01603 880 171/2. FAX 01603 880 291. By the case only, mail order only, credit cards, delivery.
*Nothing but the best of Beaujolais.*

**Harrods** ☆☆☆☆ Knightsbridge, London, SW1X 7XL. ☎ 0171 730 1234. FAX 0171 225 5823. Credit cards, delivery.
*Smart Knightsbridge one-stop shop.*

**Harvey Nichols** ☆☆☆☆☆ Knightsbridge, London, SW1X 7RJ. ☎ 0171 235 5000 ext 2348. FAX 0171 235 5020. Credit cards, delivery, tastings.
*Outclassing Harrods, with a great range of old and new classics.*

**John Harvey & Sons** ☆☆☆☆ 12 Denmark Street, Bristol, BS1 5DQ. ☎ 0117 927 5010. FAX 0117 927 5002. Credit cards, delivery, tastings, *en primeur*, cellarage, glass hire/loan.
*Focuses on long-established producers but getting better at the New World.*

**The Haslemere Cellar** ☆☆☆ Rear of 2 Lower Street, Haslemere, Surrey, GU27 2NX. ☎+FAX 01428 645 081. Credit cards, delivery, tastings, *en primeur*, cellarage, glass hire /loan.
*Skilfully chosen Old World wines.*

**Haynes Hanson & Clark** ☆☆☆☆ 25 Ecclestone Street, London, SW1W 9NP. ☎ 0171 259 0102. FAX 0171 259 0103. Credit cards, delivery, tastings, *en primeur*, glass hire/loan.
*Burgundy is the speciality here, and the general emphasis is on France.*

**Hedley Wright & Co Ltd** ☆☆☆☆ Twyford Business Centre, London Road, Bishops Stortford, Herts, CM23 3YT. ☎ 01279 506 512. FAX 01279 657 462. By the case only, credit cards, delivery, tastings, *en primeur*, cellarage, glass hire/loan.
*A good country merchant offering classy New Zealanders, Chileans and stars from the Old World.*

**Pierre Henck** ☆☆☆☆ 287 Tettenhall Road, Newbridge, Wolverhampton, WV6 OLE. ☎ 01902 751 022. FAX 01902 752 212. Credit cards, delivery, tastings, *en primeur*, glass loan.
*Affordable wines from Bordeaux, Alsace and New Zealand.*

**Charles Hennings Vintners Ltd** ☆☆☆ London House, Pulborough, Sussex, RH20 2BW. ☎ 01798 872 485/873 909. FAX 01798 873 163. Credit cards, delivery, tastings, glass loan.
*Offers a traditional list from Europe, featuring Bordeaux, and some interesting new wave wines.*

**Heyman Barwell Jones Ltd** ☆☆☆☆ 130 Ebury Street, London, SW1W 9QQ. ☎ 0171 730 0324. FAX 0171 730 0575. By the case only, credit cards, delivery, tastings, *en primeur*, cellarage.
*One for Burgundy-lovers especially, but also a range of affordable Bordeaux.*

**Hicks & Don** ☆☆☆☆ The Old Bakehouse, Westbury, Wilts, BA13 3DY. ☎ 01373 864 723. FAX 01373 858 250. By the case only, credit cards, delivery, *en primeur*, cellarage, tastings, glass hire.
*A traditional merchant which takes the trouble to give customers the best advice on when to pull the cork from their bottles.*

**High Breck Vintners** ☆☆☆ Bentworth House, Bentworth, Nr Alton, Hampshire, GU34 5RB. ☎ 01420 562 218. FAX 01420 563 827. By the case only, delivery, *en primeur*, cellarage, glass hire/loan.
*French classic and regional wines are the speciality of this well-established traditional merchant.*

**George Hill of Loughborough** ☆☆☆ 59 Wards End, Loughborough, Leics, LE11 3HB. ☎ 01509 212 717. FAX 01509 236 963. By the case only, credit cards, delivery, tastings, *en primeur*, cellarage.
*Across-the-board range at reasonable prices.*

**J.E. Hogg** ☆☆☆☆ 61 Cumberland Street, Edinburgh, EH3 6RA. ☎+FAX 0131 556 4025. Delivery, glass loan, tastings.
*Merchant with a wide and varied list. Areas of particular strength include France and Australia.*

**The Holland Park Wine Co** ☆☆☆☆ 12 Portland Road, London, W11 4LA. ☎ 0171 221 9614. FAX 0171 221 9613. Credit cards, delivery, tastings, *en primeur*, cellarage, glass hire/loan.
*Great place to learn about wine at classes and tastings held by the producers themselves. Shop has good wines from just about everywhere.*

**Hoults Wine Merchants** ☆☆☆ 10 Viaduct Street, Huddersfield, HD1 6AJ. ☎ 01484 510 700. FAX 01484 510 712. Credit cards, delivery, glass hire/loan.
*Bargain specialists with shops in Leeds and Huddersfield.*

**Howells of Bristol Ltd – The Bin Club** ☆☆☆ The Old Brewery, 61 Station Road, Wickwar, Glos, GL12 8NB. ☎ 01454 294 085. FAX 01454 294 090. *En primeur*, cellarage, delivery.
*Specialists in providing wines for laying down for future drinking.*

**Irma Fingal-Rock** ☆☆☆ 64 Monnow Street, Monmouth, NP5 3EN. ☎ 01600 712 372. Credit cards, delivery, tastings, glass loan.
*Specialists in red Burgundy and Welsh wines.*

**Jeroboams/Stones of Belgravia** ☆☆☆ 6 Clarendon Road, London, W11 3AA. ☎ 0171 727 9359. FAX 0171 792 3672. Credit cards, delivery, tastings, glass loan.
*The place to buy everything you need for a brilliant cheese and wine party.*

**Michael Jobling Wines Ltd** ☆☆☆ Baltic Chambers, 3–7 Broad Chare, Newcastle upon Tyne, NE1 3DQ. ☎ 0191 261 5298. FAX 0191 261 4543. By the case only, credit cards, delivery, *en primeur*, tastings, glass loan.
*Unusual French regionals rub shoulders with Alsace, Burgundy and New World stars.*

**S.H. Jones** ☆☆☆☆ 27 High Street, Banbury, Oxon, OX16 8EW. ☎ 01295 251 179. FAX 01295 272 352. Credit cards, delivery, tastings, *en primeur*, cellarage, glass hire/loan.
*Good tutored wine tastings are a regular feature. The list includes plenty of clarets, Rhônes from Grand Moulas, California's Opus One and some excellent malt whiskies.*

**Just-in-Case** ☆☆☆☆ 1 The High Street, Bishops Waltham, Southampton, Hants, SO32 1AB. ☎+FAX 01489 892 969 Credit cards, delivery, tastings, *en primeur*, cellarage, glass hire/loan.
*Good, unusual wines from Southern France, as well as serious Italians and Burgundies.*

**Justerini & Brooks Ltd** ☆☆☆☆☆ 61 St. James's Street, London, SW1A 1LZ. ☎ 0171 493 8721. FAX 0171 499 4653. E-mail: j-b.retail@dial,pipex.com Credit cards, delivery, tastings, *en primeur*, cellarage, glass hire/loan.
*One of Britain's best merchants in London and Edinburgh, with a bible-like list of enticing wines from around the globe.*

**King & Barnes Ltd** ☆☆☆☆ 16 Bishopric, Horsham, W. Sussex, RH12 1QP. ☎ 01403 270 870. FAX 01403 270 570. E-mail: king.barnes@btinternet.com Credit cards, delivery, tastings, glass loan.
*Sussex brewer/wine merchant. Good across-the-board and fairly priced range, particularly Australian.*

**Kwik Save Group Plc** ☆☆☆ Warren Drive, Prestatyn, Clwyd, LL19 7HU. ☎ 01745 887 111. FAX 01745 882 821. Credit cards.
*Source of remarkably cheap, well-chosen bargains.*

**Lay & Wheeler** ☆☆☆☆☆ 117 Gosbecks Road, Gosbecks Park, Colchester, Essex, CO2 9JT. ☎ 01206 764 446. FAX 01206 560 002. E-mail: Laywheeler@ndirect.co.uk Credit cards, delivery, tastings, *en primeur*, cellarage, glass hire/loan.
*Impeccable, extensive range and highly knowledgeable staff. Still one of the best regional and mail-order merchants for Old and New World classics. Holds great tastings.*

**Laymont & Shaw Ltd** ☆☆☆☆ The Old Chapel, Millpool, Truro, Cornwall, TR1 1EX. ☎ 01872 70545. FAX 01872 223 005. By the case only, delivery, tastings, cellarage, glass hire/loan.
*An Iberian wine-lover's paradise. This is just the right place to keep track of the quiet revolution occurring in the Spanish vineyards.*

**Laytons** ☆☆☆☆ 20 Midland Road, London, NW1 2AD. ☎ 0171 388 4567. FAX 0171 383 7419. E-mail: sales@laytons.co.uk Credit cards, delivery, *en primeur*, cellarage, glass hire/loan.
*The best own-label Champagne on the market. Also specialises in Bordeaux and Burgundy.*

**Lea & Sandeman** ☆☆☆☆☆ 301 Fulham Road, London, SW10 9QH. ☎ 0171 376 4767. FAX 0171 351 0275. E-mail: barnes@l-sandemann.netkonect.co.uk Credit cards, delivery, *en primeur*, cellarage, tastings, glass hire/loan.
*First class merchant with branches in Chelsea, Kensington and Barnes. Well-chosen wines across the board.*

**Lloyd Taylor Wines** ☆☆☆ P. O. Box 7281, Perth, PH1 3WD. ☎ 01738 840 494. FAX 01738 840 100. Credit cards, delivery, tastings, *en primeur*.
*One of Scotland's best traditional merchants.*

**O.W. Loeb** ☆☆☆☆ 64 Southwark Bridge Road, London, SE1 OAS. ☎ 0171 928 7750. FAX 0171 928 1855. By the case only, delivery, *en primeur*, credit cards, tastings, cellarage.
*A short list of some of the superstars of Burgundy and Germany. Bordeaux is also worth a look.*

**Magnum Fine Wines** ☆☆☆☆ 43 Pall Mall, London, SW1Y 5JG, ☎ 0171 839 5732. FAX 0171 321 0848. Credit cards, delivery, *en primeur*, tastings, cellarage.
*Excellent fine wines – at a price.*

**Majestic Wine Warehouses Ltd** ☆☆☆☆ Odhams Trading Estate, St. Albans Rd, Watford, Herts, WD2 5RE. ☎ 01923 816 999. FAX 01923 819 105. By the case only, credit cards, delivery, tastings, *en primeur*, glass hire/loan.
*A very good range of interesting wines, supplemented by one-off parcels sold at bargain prices. Great staff.*

**Marks & Spencer** ☆☆☆☆ Michael House, Baker Street, London, W1A 1DN. ☎ 0171 268 6478. FAX 0171 268 2674. M&S chargecard, tastings.
*Improved and enterprising chain, with a limited but generally reliable range. Strong in Southern France and has some classy wines from New Zealand.*

**Martinez Fine Wine** ☆☆☆☆ 36 The Grove, Ilkley, LS29 9EE. ☎ 01943 603 241. FAX 01943 816 489. Credit cards, delivery, tastings, *en primeur*, cellarage, glass loan.
*Enterprisingly chosen wines from around the world. Also stores in Halifax and Harrogate.*

**F. & E. May Ltd** ☆☆☆☆ 27 Brownlow Mews, Bloomsbury, London, WC1N 2LA. ☎ 0171 405 6249. FAX 0171 404 4472. By the case only, cellarage, tastings, *en primeur*.
*Lovers of serious German stop here; also a good range of Alsace, Bordeaux and Burgundy.*

**Mayor Sworder** ☆☆☆☆ 7 Aberdeen Road, Croydon, CRO 1EQ. ☎ 0181 686 1155. FAX 0181 760 0390. Credit cards, delivery, *en primeur*, cellarage, tastings, glass hire/loan.
*Classy Old World list and some unusual New World offerings.*

**Milton Sandford Wines Ltd** ☆☆☆☆ The Old Chalk Mine, Warre Row Road, Knowl Hill, Reading, Berks, RG10 8QS. ☎ 01628 829 449. FAX 01628 829 424. By the case only, delivery, cellarage.
*Any list with over a page of non-oaked Chardonnay gets our vote. Impeccable.*

**Mitchells Wine Merchants** ☆☆☆☆ 354 Meadowhead, Sheffield, S. Yorkshire, S8 7UJ. ☎ 0114 274 5587. FAX 0114 274 8481. Credit cards, delivery, tastings, *en primeur*, cellarage, glass hire/loan.
*Straight-talking characterful wines – from both the Old and New World.*

**Montrachet** ☆☆☆☆ 24 Cornwall Road, Waterloo, London, SE1 8TW. ☎ 0171 928 1990. FAX 0171 928 3415. Credit cards, mail order only, by the case only, delivery, tastings, *en primeur*, cellarage.
*Excellent French domaines with a bias towards Burgundy.*

**Moreno Wine Importers** ☆☆☆☆ 2 Norfolk Place, London, W2 1QN. ☎ 0171 723 6897. FAX 0171 724 3813. E-mail: morenowines@morenowines.co.uk Credit cards, delivery.
*Spanish and South American specialist. Monthly Spanish wine club.*

**Morris & Verdin Ltd** ☆☆☆☆☆ 10 The Leathermarket, Weston Street, London, SE1 3ER. ☎ 0171 357 8866. FAX 0171 357 8877. E-mail: 100072.263@compuserve.com By the case only, delivery, tastings, *en primeur*, cellarage, glass hire/loan.
*Burgundies, Californians like Bonny Doon, Jade Mountain and Ridge, and the Spanish superstar, Vega Sicilia.*

**Wm. Morrison Supermarkets PLC** ☆☆☆ Wakefield 41 Industrial Estate, Carr Gate, Wakefield, W. Yorks. WF2 0XF ☎ 01924 870000. FAX 01924 875120. Credit cards, tastings, glass hire/loan.
*Good-value mid-price wines.*

**Nadder** ☆☆☆ Hussars House, 2 Netherhampton Road, Harnham, Salisbury, Wilts, SP2 8HE. ☎ 01722 325 418. FAX 01722 421 617. By the case only, credit cards, delivery, tastings, glass loan.
*Serious wines including Jaffelin from Burgundy and Taltarni.*

**Le Nez Rouge** ☆☆☆☆☆ 12 Brewery Road, London, N7 9NH. ☎ 0171 609 4711. FAX 0171 607 0018. Credit cards, *en primeur*, cellarage.
*Burgundies are the stars, supported by plenty of other good French wines and noteworthy New World offerings.*

**James Nicholson** ☆☆☆☆☆ 27a Killyleagh Street, Crossgar, Co. Down, Northern Ireland, BT30 9DQ. ☎ 01396 830091. FAX 01396 830028. Credit cards, delivery, tastings, *en primeur*, free glass hire/loan.
*Impressive merchant with excellent New and Old World wines.*

**Nickolls and Perks Ltd** ☆☆☆☆ 37 High Street, Stourbridge, West Midlands, DY8 1TA. ☎ 01384 394 518. FAX 01384 440 786. Credit cards, delivery, tastings, *en primeur*, cellarage, glass hire/loan.
*Some excellent Champagnes, old Burgundies and New World classics. Big in* en primeur.

**Nicolas UK Ltd** ☆☆☆☆ 157 Great Portland Street, London, W1N 5FH. ☎ 0171 436 9338. FAX 0171 637 1691. Credit cards, delivery, tastings, glass hire/loan.
*Reliable source of top flight clarets and little-known French wines.*

**Noble Rot Wine Warehouses Ltd** ☆☆☆☆ 18 Market Street, Bromsgrove, Worcs, B61 8DA. ☎ 01527 575 606. FAX 01527 574 091. Credit cards, delivery, tastings, glass loan.
*Majestic-like warehouse emporium, offering a well-priced energetic list.*

**The Nobody Inn** ☆☆☆☆☆ Doddiscombsleigh, Nr Exeter, Devon, EX6 7PS. ☎ 01647 252 394. FAX 01647 252 978. Credit cards, delivery, tastings, glass hire/loan.
*Country pub with the best wine list imaginable – including top and lesser-known regions and producers.*

**Oddbins** ☆☆☆☆☆ 31–33 Weir Road, Wimbledon, London, SW19 8UG. ☎ 0181 944 4400. FAX 0181 944 4444. Credit cards, delivery, tastings, glass hire/loan.
*Simply the best. A great, ever-changing range and helpful wine-mad staff. Who could ask for more?*

**Pallant Wines Ltd** ☆☆☆ 17 High Street, Arundel, W. Sussex, BN18 9AD. ☎ 01903 882288. FAX 01903 882801. Credit cards, delivery, tastings, glass hire/loan.
*Focuses on top-class producers in Germany, France and Italy.*

**Parfrements Wine Merchants** ☆☆☆ 68 Cecily Road, Cheylesmore, Coventry, Warwickshire, CV3 5LA. ☎+FAX 01203 503 646. E-mail: parfrements@dial.pipex.com Web site www.parfrements.co.uk By the case only, delivery, tastings, *en primeur*.
*Convincing selections from most major regions.*

**Partridges of Sloane Street** ☆☆☆ 132-134 Sloane Street, Chelsea, London, SW1X 9AT. ☎ 0171 730 0651. FAX 0171 730 7104. Credit cards, delivery, tastings, glass hire/loan.
*Upmarket grocers whose wines are usually premium brands.*

**The Pavilion Wine Co** ☆☆☆ Finsbury Circus Gardens, Finsbury Circus, London, EC2M 7AB. ☎ 0171 628 8224. FAX 0171 628 6205. By the case only, credit cards, delivery, *en primeur*, cellarage.
*Mail order specialists in country wines from smaller producers.*

**Thos. Peatling Ltd** ☆☆☆☆☆
Westgate House, Westgate Street, Bury St. Edmunds, Suffolk, IP33 1QS. ☎ 01284 755 948. FAX 01284 705 795. Credit cards, delivery, tastings, cellarage, glass loan.
*As good as ever, despite a takeover by Victoria Wine. Peatlings Direct is the mail order business.*

**Penistone Court Wine Cellars**
☆☆☆ The Railway Station, Penistone, Sheffield, S30 6HG. ☎ 01226 766 037. FAX 01226 767 310. By the case only, delivery, tastings, glass loan.
*Worthy merchant carrying a good range of well-known brands.*

**Philglas & Swiggot** ☆☆☆☆ 21 Northcote Road, Battersea, London, SW11 1NG. ☎ 0171 924 4494 FAX 0171 642 1308. Credit cards, delivery, tastings, glass loan.
*Antipodean specialists* par excellence.

**Christopher Piper Wines Ltd**
☆☆☆☆ 1 Silver Street, Ottery St. Mary, Devon, EX11 1DB. ☎ 01404 814 139. FAX 01404 812 100. Credit cards, delivery, tastings, *en primeur*, cellarage, glass loan.
*A large, solid list of excellent quality across the board.*

**Terry Platt Wine Merchant**
☆☆☆☆☆ Ferndale Road, Llandudno Junction, Gwynedd, LL31 9NT. ☎ 01492 592 971. FAX 01492 592 196. Credit cards, delivery, tastings, cellarage, glass hire/loan.
*One of the most skilfully selected sets of wines from just about everywhere.*

**Le Pont de la Tour** ☆☆☆☆☆
The Butlers Wharf Building, 36d Shad Thames, Butlers Wharf, London, SE1 2YE. ☎ 0171 403 2403. FAX 0171 403 0267. Credit cards, delivery, tastings, glass hire/loan.
*Meticulous coverage of classic and emerging regions.*

**Portland Wine Company** ☆☆☆
152a Ashley Road, Hale, Altringham, Cheshire, WA15 9SA. ☎ 0161 962 8752. FAX 0161 905 1291. E-mail: portlandco@adl.com Credit cards, tastings, glass hire/loan.
*The Antipodes are covered in depth; gems from Chile and South Africa too.*

**Quellyn-Roberts** ☆☆☆☆☆
21 Watergate Street, Chester, Cheshire, CH1 2LB. ☎ 01244 310455. FAX 01244 346704. Credit cards, cellarage, tastings, *en primeur*, glass hire/loan.
*Traditional merchant specialising in Burgundy and Bordeaux, with some New World wines.*

**R.S.Wines** ☆☆☆☆ 32 Vicarage Road, Southville, Bristol, BS3 1PD. ☎ 0117 963 1780. FAX 0117 953 3797. By the case only, delivery, *en primeur*, cellarage, glass hire/loan.
*Sells difficult-to-find Californian wines and some affordable Bordeaux and Burgundy.*

**Raeburn Fine Wines** ☆☆☆☆☆
21/23 Comely Bank Road, Edinburgh, EH4 1DS. ☎ 0131 343 1159 FAX 0131 332 5166. E-mail: tmahmud@netcomuk.co.uk Credit cards, delivery, tastings, *en primeur*, cellarage, glass loan.
*Grocer-turned-merchant with a cult following among wine lovers. Very classy, often unusual, wines.*

**Ramsbottom Victuallers** ☆☆☆
18 Market Place, Ramsbottom, Bury, Lancs, BL0 9HT. ☎ 0170 682 5070. FAX 0170 682 2005. Credit cards, tastings.
*Serious beers, Burgundy and Bordeaux from an ace wine shop.*

**Reid Wines (1992) Ltd** ☆☆☆☆☆
The Mill, Marsh Lane, Hallatrow, Nr Bristol, BS18 5EB. ☎ 01761 452 645. FAX 01761 453 642. Credit cards, delivery, cellarage, tastings, glass hire/loan.
*An eccentric merchant with one of the most entertaining lists in the UK, packed with the classic and rare.*

**La Réserve** ☆☆☆☆☆ 56 Walton Street, London, SW3 1RB. ☎ 0171 589 2020. FAX 0171 581 0250. E-mail: mreynier@lareserve.netkonect.co.uk Credit cards, delivery, tastings, *en primeur*, cellarage, glass hire/loan.
*Top flight Burgundies, Italians and unusual New World offerings.*

**Howard Ripley** ☆☆☆☆☆
35 Eversley Crescent, London, N21 1EL. ☎ 0181 360 8904. FAX 0181 351 6564. By the case only, delivery, tastings, *en primeur*, glass loan.
*Specialist* par excellence. *Nothing but Burgundy at its best.*

**Roberson Wine Merchant** ☆☆☆☆☆ 348 Kensington High Street, London, W14 8NS. ☎ 0171 371 2121. FAX 0171 371 4010. New mail order service, credit cards, delivery, tastings, *en primeur*, cellarage, glass hire/loan.
*Old Bordeaux and Italian superstars are particular strengths, but attend the regular tastings and you are bound to find something unfamiliar.*

**The Rogers Wine Co** ☆☆☆ Rectory Cottage, 20 Lower Street, Sproughton, Ipswich, Suffolk, IP8 3AA. ☎ +FAX 01473 748 464. By the case only, delivery, *en primeur*, tastings, glass loan.
*The place to find Bunratty Poteen (illegal in Ireland) – and a commendable, if limited, range of wine.*

**The Rose Tree Wine Co** ☆☆☆ 15 Suffolk Parade, Cheltenham, Glos, GL50 2AE. ☎ 01242 583 732. FAX 01242 222 159. Credit cards, delivery, tastings, *en primeur*, cellarage, glass loan.
*Solid wines from Spain and France (especially the south).*

**Safeway** ☆☆☆☆ Safeway House, 6 Millington Road, Hayes, Middlesex, UB3 4BY. ☎ 0181 848 8744. FAX 0181 573 1865. Credit cards, tastings.
*Quietly innovative, with a redesigned wine department and (in 120 stores) DIY barcode scanning. Marks for trying to develop more informative labels and shelves.*

**J. Sainsbury plc** ☆☆☆☆ Stamford House, Stamford Steet, London, SE1 9LL. ☎ 0171 921 6000. FAX 0171 921 6988. Credit cards, glass loan.
*Now often overshadowed by Tesco, Asda and Safeway, but still a reliable place to buy wine.*

**Sandiway Wine Company** ☆☆☆☆☆ Chester Road, Sandiway, Cheshire, CW8 2NH. ☎ 01606 882 101. FAX 01606 888 407. Credit cards, delivery, tastings, glass loan.
*Wacky merchants with fairly priced wines from good producers.*

**Santat Wines Ltd** ☆☆☆ Cavendish House, Sydenham Road, Guildford, Surrey, GU1 3RX. ☎ 01483 450 494. FAX 01483 455 068. By the case only, credit cards, delivery, tastings, glass hire/loan.
*Good for French country wines.*

**Scatchard Ltd** ☆☆☆ 36 Exchange Street East, Liverpool, L2 2BA. ☎ 0151 236 6468. FAX 0151 236 7003. Credit cards, delivery, tastings, glass loan.
*Spain is the specialist subject, but good Southern French wines and unusual New World efforts.*

**Sebastopol Wines** ☆☆☆☆ Sebastopol Barn, London Road, Blewbury, Oxon, OX11 9HB. ☎ 01235 850 471. FAX 01235 850 776. By the case only, credit cards, delivery, *en primeur*, delivery, glass loan.
*Mouth-watering Burgundies, Italians, Bordeaux and Rhônes.*

**Seckford Wines Limited** ☆☆☆☆ 2 Betts Avenue, Martlesham Heath, Ipswich, IP5 3RH. ☎ 01473 626 072. FAX 01473 626 004. By the case only, credit cards, delivery, tastings, *en primeur*, cellarage, glass hire/loan.
*Good-value claret and some highly recommendable German, Italian and Australian wines.*

**Selfridges Ltd** ☆☆☆☆☆ 400 Oxford Street, London, W1A 1AB. ☎ 0171 318 3730. FAX 0171 491 1880. Credit cards, delivery, tastings, cellarage, glass hire/loan.
*Department store with a surprisingly fairly priced and highly comprehensive range of wine .*

**Shaws of Beaumaris** ☆☆☆☆ 17 Castle Street, Beaumaris, Anglesey, LL58 8AP. ☎ +FAX 01248 810 328. Credit cards, delivery, tastings, glass loan.
*A wine list from which you can pick at random.*

**Edward Sheldon Ltd** ☆☆☆☆ New Street, Shipston on Stour, Warks, CV36 4EN. ☎ 01608 661409 /661639 /662210. FAX 01608 663166. E-mail: Edward.sheldon@shipstonTelMe.com Credit cards, delivery, tastings, *en primeur*, cellarage, glass hire/loan.
*Claret is the strong point, but there are a few New World stars too. Good, regular tastings.*

**Sherston Wine Company** ☆☆☆☆ 97 Victoria Street, St. Albans, Hertfordshire, AL1 3TJ. ☎ 01727 858841. Credit cards, delivery, tastings, glass hire/loan.
*A bias towards Spain, balanced by very well-chosen wines from Italy.*

**Smedley Vintners** ☆☆☆☆☆
Rectory Cottage, Lilley, Luton, LU2 8LU. ☎ 01462 768 214. FAX 01462 768 332. By the case only, delivery, *en primeur*, cellarage, tastings, glass hire/loan.
*One of Britain's best and friendliest small independent merchants.*

**Somerfield Stores Ltd** ☆☆☆
Somerfield House, Whitchurch Lane, Bristol, BS14 OTJ. ☎ 0117 9359 359. FAX 0117 9780 629. Credit cards.
*Keenly priced wines, some far more recommendable than others.*

**Sommelier Wine Co Ltd** ☆☆☆☆
The Grapevine, 23 St. George's Esplanade, St. Peter Port, Guernsey, Channel Islands, GY1 2BG. ☎ 01481 721 677. FAX 01481 716 818. Credit cards, delivery, cellarage, tastings, glass loan.
*Impeccably chosen New and Old World wines; VAT free.*

**Spar (UK) Ltd** ☆☆☆ 32–40 Headstone Drive, Harrow, Middlesex, HA3 5QT. ☎ 0181 863 5511. FAX 0181 863 0603. Credit cards.
*Good in parts.*

**Frank E Stainton Wines** ☆☆☆
3 Berrys Yard, Finkle Street, Kendal, Cumbria, LA9 4AB. ☎ 01539 731 886. FAX 01539 730 396. Credit cards, delivery, tastings.
*Particularly good Rieslings and decent Southern French wines.*

**John Stephenson & Sons** ☆☆☆
254 Manchester Road, Nelson, Lancashire, BB9 7DE. ☎ 01282 698 827. FAX 01282 601 161. Credit cards, delivery, tastings, *en primeur*, glass hire/loan.
*You have to pick and choose here but the best wines repay your efforts.*

**Stewarts World of Wine** ☆☆☆
224 Castlereagh Road, Belfast, N. Ireland, BT5 5HZ. ☎ 01232 704 434 FAX 01232 799 008. Credit cards, delivery, tastings, glass hire/loan.
*Big name wines from the New and Old World – a great place to buy South African wines.*

**Stones of Belgravia** ☆☆☆ 6 Pont Street, London, SW1X 9EL. ☎ 0171 235 1612. FAX 0171 235 7246. Credit cards, delivery, *en primeur*.
*See* Jeroboams

**Stratford's Wine Shippers**
☆☆☆☆ High St, Cookham-on-Thames, Berks, SL6 9SQ. ☎ 01628 810 606. FAX 01628 810 605. Credit cards, delivery, tastings, glass hire/loan.
*Stratfords have an admirable set of Old and New World producers.*

**The Sunday Times Wine Club**
*See* Bordeaux Direct

**T. & W. Wines** ☆☆☆☆☆
51 King Street, Thetford, Norfolk, IP24 2AU. ☎ 01842 765646. FAX 01842 766407. Credit cards, delivery, tastings, *en primeur*, cellarage, glass hire/loan.
*California specialists, with great Burgundies and Bordeaux.*

**Tanners Wines Ltd** ☆☆☆☆ 26 Wyle Cop, Shrewsbury, Shropshire, SY1 1XD. ☎ 01743 232 400. FAX 01743 344 401. Credit cards, delivery, tastings, *en primeur*, glass hire/loan.
*Friendly country merchant with wide range; ever-willing to hold tastings.*

**Tesco Stores Ltd** ☆☆☆☆ Delamare Road, Cheshunt, Herts, EN8 9SL. ☎ 01992 632 222. FAX 01992 658 225. Credit cards, tastings, glass loan.
*Leaving Sainsbury standing these days, with all sorts of bright initiatives such as the "Great With" range to serve with particular foods.*

**Thresher Wine Shop** ☆☆☆☆
Sefton House, 42 Church Rd, Welwyn Garden City, Herts, AL8 6PJ. ☎ 0151 449 4000. FAX 01707 371398. Credit cards, delivery, tastings, glass hire/loan.
*Middle-of-the-road off-licences with reasonably well-chosen wines.*

**House of Townend** ☆☆☆
Red Duster House, York Street, Hull, E. Yorkshire, HU2 OQX. ☎ 01482 326 891. FAX 01482 587 042. E–mail: 101332,1720@compuserve.com Credit cards, delivery, *en primeur*, cellarage, tastings, glass hire/loan.
*An improving list with strong areas in Bordeaux and Burgundy.*

**Trout Wines** ☆☆☆☆ The Trout, Nether Wallop, Stockbridge, SO20 8EW. ☎+FAX 01264 781 472. Credit cards, delivery, tastings, glass hire/loan.
*A short but good and affordable list. Also source hard-to-find wines.*

**Turville Valley Wines** ☆☆☆☆☆
The Firs, Potter Row, Great Missenden, Bucks, HP16 9LT. ☎ 01494 868818. FAX 01494 868832. By the case only, delivery, *en primeur*, cellarage.
*Bordeaux from 1942–1995, and Burgundy from as far back as 1919. Get the picture?*

**The Ubiquitous Chip Ltd** ☆☆☆☆☆
12 Ashton Lane, Glasgow, G12 8FA. ☎ 0141 384 7109. FAX 0141 337 1302. Credit cards, delivery, tastings, cellarage, glass hire/loan.
*Glasgow's top merchant with stars from both hemispheres.*

**Unwins Wine Merchants** ☆☆☆
Birchwood House, Victoria Road, Dartford, Kent, DA1 5AJ. ☎ 01322 272 711. FAX 01322 294 469. Credit cards, delivery, tastings, glass hire.
*South-east England chain which has just taken over Davisons. Once dull, now improving shops and range.*

**Valvona & Crolla Ltd** ☆☆☆☆☆
19 Elm Row, Edinburgh, EH7 4AA. ☎ 0131 556 6066. FAX 0131 556 1668. Credit cards, delivery, tastings, glass loan.
*A stunning specialist in Italian wines. Eat and drink at the restaurant above the shop, or order by mail.*

**VCA Vintners** ☆☆☆☆ 11 Berkley Street, Mayfair, London, W1X 6BU. ☎ 0171 355 5049, FAX 0171 355 5050. Cellarage, delivery, mail order.
*Fine wine specialists – mainly for investment purposes.*

**Helen Verdcourt** ☆☆☆☆☆ Spring Cottage, Kimbers Lane, Maidenhead, Berks, SL6 2QP. ☎ 01628 25577. By the case only, delivery, tastings, glass hire/loan.
*This one-woman band selects and buys one of the best little wine ranges in the country.*

**The Victoria Wine / V.W. Cellars**
☆☆☆ Dukes Court, Duke Street, Woking, Surrey, GU21 5XL. ☎ 01483 715 066. FAX 01483 755 234. Internet: http://www.itl.net/go/to /victoria wine Credit cards, delivery, glass loan.
*Still in the shadow of Thresher and Wine Cellar, which both look better than the basic V.W. shops. But there are often better wines on offer here. Also visit the store in Calais.*

**La Vigneronne** ☆☆☆☆☆
105 Old Brompton Road, London, SW7 3LE. ☎ 0171 589 6113. FAX 0171 581 2983. Credit cards, delivery, tastings, *en primeur*.
*Fantastic wines from just about everywhere.*

**Village Wines** ☆☆☆ 6 Mill Row, High Street, Bexley, Kent, DA5 1LA. ☎+FAX 01322 558 772. By the case only, credit cards, delivery, tastings, *en primeur*, glass loan.
*Italy and Burgundy are the strongest suits from a firm begun by a group of enthusiasts.*

**Villeneuve Wines Ltd** ☆☆☆☆
1 Venlaw Court, Peebles, Scotland, EH45 8AE. ☎ 01721 722 500. FAX 01721 729 922. E-mail: wines@villeneuvewines.com By the case only, credit cards, delivery, tastings, *en primeur*, cellarage, glass hire/loan.
*Enterprising list across the board, including otherwise unfindable wines from Utah.*

**Vin du Van** ☆☆☆☆ Colthups, The Street, Appledore, Kent, TN26 2BX. ☎ 01233 758 727. FAX 01233 758 389. Delivery, credit cards, glass hire/loan.
*Extraordinary list with tempting wines from the New World. Mail order and local delivery only.*

**Vinceremos Wines and Spirits**
☆☆☆ 261 Upper Town Street, Leeds, LS13 3 JT. ☎ 0113 257 7545. FAX 0133 257 6906. E-mail: vinceremos@aol.com By the case only, credit cards, delivery, cellarage, glass hire/loan.
*Organic specialists who take the trouble to choose good examples.*

**Vine Trail** ☆☆☆ 5 Surrey Road, Bishopston, Bristol, BS7 9DJ. ☎+FAX 0117 942 3946. By the case only, delivery, cellarage, glass hire/loan.
*Regional French wine from small domaines.*

**Vintage Roots** ☆☆☆☆ Sheeplands Farm, Wargrave, Berks, RG10 8DT. ☎ 0118 940 1222. FAX 0118 940 4814. E-mail: roots@ptop.demon.co.uk By the case only, credit cards, delivery, tastings, glass hire/loan.
*Organic specialist with particularly good offerings from Italy. Also features Vouvray from Huët.*

**The Vintry** ☆☆☆ Park Farm, Milland, Liphook, Hampshire, GU30 7JT. ☎ 01428 741 389. FAX 01428 741 368. By the case only, delivery, glass hire/loan.
*Four individual outlets offering a selection including good British-made French wines such as Ch. Méaume.*

**Waitrose Wine Direct** ☆☆☆☆ Deer Park Road, Merton Abbey, London, SW19 3TU. ☎ 0800 188 881. FAX 0800 188 888. Mail order only, by the case only, credit cards, delivery, *en primeur*, cellarage.
*see* Findlater Mackie Todd.

**Waitrose Ltd** ☆☆☆☆ Southern Industrial Area, Bracknell, Berkshire, RG12 8YA. ☎ 01344 424 680. FAX 01344 305 662. Credit cards.
*Range is always good on traditional wines, but there are plenty of innovative wines to look out for.*

**Waterloo Wine Company** ☆☆☆☆ 59–61 Lant Street, London, SE1 1QN. ☎ 0171 403 7967. FAX 0171 357 6976. Credit cards, delivery, tastings, glass hire/loan.
*Emphasis on French wines, especially the Loire. Otherwise starry efforts from New Zealand – Mark Rattray Vineyard, Waipara West and Springs.*

**Waters of Coventry** ☆☆☆ Collins Road, Heathcote, Warwick, CV34 6TF. ☎ 01926 888 889. FAX 01926 887 416. E-mail: rob.caldicott@dial.pipex.com By the case only, credit cards, delivery, *en primeur*.
*Interesting and eclectic wine list. Top class Rhônes and Burgundies.*

**Weavers of Nottingham** ☆☆☆ 1 Castle Gate, Nottingham, NE1 7AQ. ☎ 0115 958 0922. FAX 0115 950 8076. Credit cards, delivery, tastings, *en primeur*, glass hire/loan.
*A plethora of malts and some well-chosen wines from Spain, Alsace and Bordeaux.*

**Wessex Wines** ☆☆☆☆ 88 St Michael's Estate, Bridport, Dorset, DT6 3RR. ☎ 01308 427177. FAX 01308 424343. By the case only, delivery, tastings, glass loan.
*Fine little merchant in the heart of Hardy country. Encourages tasting before buying.*

**Whiteside's of Clitheroe** ☆☆☆☆ Shawbridge Street, Clitheroe, Lancashire, BB7 INA. ☎ 01200 422281. FAX 01200 427129. Credit cards, delivery, tastings, glass hire.
*Good on France in general, Bordeaux in particular. Also excellent New World.*

**Whittalls Wines** ☆☆☆ Darlaston Road, Walsall, West Midlands, WS2 9SQ. ☎ 01922 361 61. FAX 01922 361 67. By the case only, delivery, tastings, *en primeur*, cellarage.
*Good Rhônes and Burgundies.*

**The Wine Bureau** ☆☆☆☆ 5 Raglan Street, Harrogate, N. Yorks, HG1 1LE. ☎ 01423 527772. FAX 01423 563077. Credit cards, delivery, tastings, *en primeur*, cellarage, glass loan.
*Interesting finds from both New and Old World.*

**Wine Cellar** ☆☆☆☆ PO Box 476, Loushers Lane, Warrington, Cheshire, WA4 6RR. ☎ 01925 444 555. FAX 01925 415 474. Credit cards, delivery, *en primeur*, glass hire/loan.
*Innovative with cafés in some of the shops and a zappy, interactive internet site: http://www.winecellar.co.uk*

**The Wine Cellar** ☆☆☆☆ 10 Station Parade, Sanderstead Road, South Croydon, Surrey, CR2 OPH. ☎ +FAX 0181 657 6936. Credit cards, delivery, tastings, *en primeur*, cellarage, glass hire/loan.
*This independent single outlet offers a commendable selection of wines from Bordeaux.*

**Wine Finds** ☆☆☆☆ Cellar-Select Ltd, Dinton Business Park, Dinton, Near Salisbury, Wiltshire SP3 5SR. ☎ 01722 716 100. FAX 01722 716 103. Mail order only, by the case only, credit cards, delivery.
*An inventive idea here: a range of wines (well) chosen 'blind' by a team of independent tasters.*

**The Wine Press** ☆☆☆ Grange Lane, Lye, Stourbridge, DY9 7HH. ☎ 01384 892941. FAX 01384 422913. Credit cards, delivery, tastings, *en primeur*, cellarage, glass hire/loan.
*Burgundy is very well represented, while the wines of New Zealand and Argentina also feature strongly.*

**Wine Rack** ☆☆☆☆ Sefton House, 42 Church Rd, Welwyn Garden City, Herts, AL8 6PJ. ☎ 0151 449 4000. FAX 01707 371 398. Credit cards, delivery, tastings, glass hire/loan.
*The up-market face of Thresher with a good range and friendly staff.*

**Wine Raks (Scotland) Ltd** ☆☆☆ 21 Springfield Rd, Aberdeen, AB15 7RJ. ☎ 01224 311 460. FAX 01224 312 186. E-mail: 101646.261 Credit cards, delivery, tastings, *en primeur*, cellarage, glass hire/loan.
*A good little merchant with Bordeaux dating back to the 1940s.*

**The Wine Schoppen Ltd** ☆☆☆☆ 3 Oak Street, Heeley, Sheffield, S8 9UB. ☎ 0114 255 3301. FAX 0114 255 1010. E-mail: jmh6868@aol.com Credit cards, delivery, tastings, *en primeur*, cellarage, glass hire/loan.
*Top Germans and specialist beers.*

**The Wine Society** ☆☆☆☆☆ Gunnels Wood Road, Stevenage, Hertfordshire, SG1 2BG. ☎ 01438 741177. FAX 01438 761167. E-mail: winesociety@dial.pipex.com Mail order only, credit cards, delivery, tastings, *en primeur*, cellarage.
*Great mail order merchant. French classics,* en primeur, *mixed case offers, trips, newsletters, Duty Free shop.*

**The Wine Treasury** ☆☆☆☆ 69-71 Bondway, London, SW8 1SQ. ☎ 0171 793 9999. FAX 0171 793 8080. Mail order only, by case only, credit cards, delivery, tastings.
*French classics and rare Californians.*

**Wine World** ☆☆☆ "Owlet", Templepan Lane, Chandlers Cross, Rickmansworth, Herts, WD3 4NH. ☎+FAX 01923 264 718. By the case only, credit cards, delivery, tastings, glass hire/loan.
*Short, but good quality range.*

**Winemark** ☆☆☆ 3 Duncrue Place, Belfast, N. Ireland, BT3 9BU. ☎ 01232 746 274. FAX 01232 748 022. Credit cards, delivery, tastings, glass hire/loan.
*Good mid-range wines.*

**The Winery** ☆☆☆ 4 Clifton Road, Maida Vale, London, W9 1SS. ☎ 0171 286 6475. FAX 0171 286 2733. Credit cards, delivery, tastings, glass hire/loan.
*Good Italian and Californian wines.*

**Wines of Westhorpe Ltd** ☆☆☆ Marchington, Staffs., ST14 8NX. ☎ 01283 820 285. FAX 01283 820 631. By the case only, mail order only, delivery, tastings credit cards.
*Eastern European specialist.*

**Woodhouse Wines** ☆☆☆☆ The Brewery, Blandford St. Mary, Dorset, DT11 9LS. ☎ 01258 452 141. FAX 01258 450 147. Credit cards, delivery, tastings, glass hire/loan.
*Good French regional wines and interesting bin ends.*

**The Wright Wine Co** ☆☆☆ The Old Smithy, Raikes Road, Skipton, N. Yorks, BD23 1NP. ☎ 01756 700 886. FAX 01756 798 580. Credit cards, delivery, cellarage, glass loan.
*Recommendable classics and wines from the Cape and Australia.*

**Wrightson & Company** ☆☆☆☆ Manfield Grange, Manfield, Darlington, N. Yorks, DL2 2RE. ☎ 01325 374 134. FAX 01325 374 135. By the case only, credit cards, delivery, tastings, *en primeur*, cellarage, glass hire/loan.
*Elegant list with good tasting notes.*

**Peter Wylie Fine Wines** ☆☆☆☆☆ Plymtree Manor, Plymtree, Cullompton, Devon, EX5 4NW ☎ 01884 277 555. FAX 01884 277 557. Delivery, *en primeur*, cellarage.
*Treasure trove of rare and fine wines.*

**Yapp Brothers Limited** ☆☆☆☆☆ The Old Brewery, Mere, Wiltshire, BA12 6DY. ☎ 01747 860 423. FAX 01747 860 929. Credit cards, delivery, tastings, *en primeur*, cellarage, glass hire/loan.
*Britain's most faithful – and best – Loire and Rhône specialists.*

**York Wines** ☆☆☆ Wellington House, Sheriff Hutton, York, YO6 1QY. ☎ 01347 878 716. FAX 01347 878 546. Credit cards, delivery, *en primeur*, tastings, glass hire/loan.
*Traditional merchant, with a well-chosen, if quite limited, range.*

**Noel Young Wines** ☆☆☆☆☆ 56 High Street, Trumpington, Cambridge, CB2 2LS. ☎ 01223 844 744. FAX 01223 844 736. Credit cards, mail order, delivery, tastings, glass hire/loan.
*Great, broad range. Brilliant Austrians.*

# WHERE TO BUY

The following section has been conceived in order to help you to find almost everything – short of a congenial companion – that you are likely to need to enjoy wine. If you are looking for a wine from a specific region, or perhaps glasses, corkscrews, courses, holidays, auctioneers, cellars or wine books, this is the place.

# WINE SPECIALISTS

*Corney and Barrow (see Page 243)*
*Direct Wine Shipments (see Page 243)*
*Eckington Wines (see Page 243)*
*Farr Vintners (see Page 244)*
*Fortnum & Mason (see Page 244)*
*Four Walls (see Page 44)*
*Friarwood (see Page 245)*
*Gallery Wines (see Page 245)*
*Goedhuis & Co (see Page 245)*
*Justerini & Brooks (see Page 247)*
*Laytons (see Page 248)*
*Lea & Sandeman (see Page 248)*
*Nickolls & Perks (see Page 249)*
*Nicolas (see Page 249)*
*Oddbins (see Page 249)*
*Thos. Peatlings (see Page 250)*
*La Reserve (see Page 250)*
*Roberson (see Page 251)*
*Edward Sheldon Ltd (see Page 251)*
*Smedley Vintners (see Page 252)*
*Tanners Wines (see Page 252)*
*Turville Valley (see Page 253)*
*The Wine Society (see Page 255)*
*Peter Wylie (see Page 255)*

BURGUNDY
*John Armit Wines (see Page 240)*
*Adam Bancroft (see Page 240)*
*Bibendum (see Page 241)*
*The Burgundy Shuttle (see Page 241)*
*Bute Wines (see Page 241)*
*Anthony Byrne (see Page 242)*
*Cave Cru Classé (see Page 242)*
*Corney & Barrow (see Page 243)*
*Croque en Bouche (see Page 243)*
*Direct Wine Shipments (see Page 243)*
*Domaine Direct (see Page 243)*
*Farr Vintners (see Page 244)*
*Fernlea Vintners (see Page 244)*
*Fortnum & Mason (see Page 244)*
*Four Walls Wine Co (see Page 244)*
*Gelston Castle (see Page 245)*
*Goedhuis & Co (see Page 245)*
*Gordon & MacPhail (see Page 245)*
*Haynes Hanson & Clark (see Page 246)*
*Laytons (see Page 248)*
*Montrachet (see Page 248)*
*Morris & Verdin (see Page 249)*
*Le Nez Rouge (see Page 249)*
*Oddbins Fine Wine (see Page 249)*
*La Reserve (see Page 250)*
*Howard Ripley (see Page 250)*
*T.&W. Wines (see Page 252)*
*Turville Valley (see Page 253)*
*The Wine Society (see Page 255)*
*Peter Wylie (see Page 250)*

CHAMPAGNE
*Bute Wines (see Page 241)*
*Classic Wines & Spirits (see Page 242)*
*Farr Vintners (see Page 244)*
*Fortnum & Mason (see Page 244)*
*Majestic (see Page 248)*
*Oddbins (see Page 249)*

COUNTRY WINES
*Allez Vins (see Page 240)*
*Adam Bancroft (see Page 240)*
*Craven's (see Page 243)*
*Croque en Bouche (see Page 234)*
*Davisons Direct (see Page 243)*
*Fernlea Vintners (see Page 244)*
*Just in Case (Page 247)*
*Laytons (see Page 248)*
*Nadder (see Page 249)*
*Nicolas (see Page 249)*
*Santat Wines (see Page 251)*
*Smedley Vintners (see Page 252)*
*Victoria Wine /VW Cellars (see Page 253)*
*La Vigneronne (see Page 253)*
*Vine Trail (see Page 253)*
*The Wine Society (see Page 255)*
*Yapp Brothers (see Page 255)*

LOIRE
*Adam Bancroft (see Page 240)*
*Anthony Byrne (see Page 242)*
*Brian Coad (see Page 242)*
*Craven's (see Page 243)*
*Croque en Bouche (see Page 243)*
*Eldridge Pope & Co (see Page 244)*
*Four Walls Wine Co (see Page 244)*
*Gauntleys (see Page 245)*
*Montrachet (see Page 248)*
*The Nobody Inn (see Page 249)*
*Pavilion (see Page 249)*
*Tanners (see Page 252)*
*Waterloo Wine Co (see Page 254)*
*Yapp Brothers (see Page 255)*

RHONE
*Adam Bancroft (see Page 240)*
*Bibendum (see Page 241)*
*Cave Cru Classé Ltd (see Page 242)*
*Croque en Bouche (see Page 243)*
*Farr Vintners (see Page 244)*
*Findlater Mackie Todd (see Page 244)*
*Gauntleys (see Page 245)*
*Gelston Castle (see Page 245)*
*Great Northern Wine (see Page 245)*
*Great Western (see Page 245)*
*Oddbins (see Page 249)*
*Pavilion (see Page 249)*
*Tanners Wines (see Page 252)*
*Helen Verdcourt (see Page 253)*
*La Vigneronne (see Page 253)*
*Yapp Brothers (see Page 255)*

## GERMANY

*Adnams (see Page 240)*
*Berry Bros (see Page 241)*
*Four Walls Wine Co (see Page 244)*
*Gelston Castle (see Page 245)*

### FINE AND RARE WINES

*John Armit (see Page 240)*
*Berry Bros & Rudd (see Page 241)*
*Bibendum Wine Ltd (see Page 241)*
*Bute Wines (see Page 241)*
*Anthony Byrne (see Page 242)*
*Cave Cru Classé Ltd (see Page 242)*
*Corney and Barrow Ltd (see Page 243)*
*Eckington Wines (see Page 243)*
*Farr Vintners (see Page 244)*
*Fortnum & Mason (see Page 244)*
*Four Walls Wine Co (see Page 244)*
*Goedhuis & Co (see Page 245)*
*Harrods (see Page 246)*
*Nickolls & Perks (see Page 249)*
*Nicolas (see Page 249)*
*Oddbins Fine Wine (see Page 249)*
*Thos. Peatlings (see Page 250)*
*Reid Wines (see Page 250)*
*La Reserve (see Page 250)*
*Roberson (see Page 251)*
*T.&W. Wines (see Page 252)*
*Tanners Wines (see Page 252)*
*Turville Valley (see Page 253)*
*VCA Vintners (see Page 253)*
*Peter Wylie (see Page 255)*
*Noel Young Wines (see Page 255)*

## AUCTIONEERS

**Bigwood Auctioneers** 01789 269 415 FAX 01789 294 168
**Christies Auction House** 0171 581 7611 FAX 0171 321 3321
**Lacy Scott** 01284 763 531 FAX 01284 704 713
**Lithgow** 01642 710 158 FAX 01642 712 641
**Phillips** 01865 723 524 FAX 01865 791 064
**Sotheby's** +FAX 0171 924 3287

## LEARNING ABOUT WINE

### LECTURERS

Tim Atkin, Liz Berry MW, Michael Broadbent MW, Nick Clarke MW, Oz Clarke, Clive Coates, David Gleave MW, Anthony Hanson MW, Richard Harvey MW, Richard Hobson MW, Jane Hunt MW, Tony Keys, Patrick McGrath MW, Maggie McNie MW, Charles Metcalfe, David Molyneux-Berry MW, Jasper Morris MW, Angela Muir MW, David Peppercorn MW, Anthony Rose, Michael Schuster, Steven Spurrier, Serena Sutcliffe MW, Pamela Vandyke Price, John Vaughan Hughes MW, Roger Voss.

### WINE COURSES

**Association of Wine Educators** 0181 995 2277 FAX 0171 371 1626
**Challenge Educational Services** 01273 220 261 FAX 01273 220 376
**Christie's** 0171 581 3933 FAX 0171 589 0383
**Ecole du Vin, Château Loudenne** 01279 626 801 FAX 01279 633 333
**German Wine Academy** 0171 376 3329 FAX 0171 351 7563
**Justerini & Brooks** 0131 226 4202 FAX 0131 225 2351
**Kensington & Chelsea College** 0181 964 1311 FAX 0181 960 2693
**Leicestershire Wine School** 0116 254 2702 FAX 0116 254 2702
**Leith's** 0171 229 0177 FAX 0171 937 5257
**Maurice Mason** 0181 841 8732 FAX 0181 841 8732
**North West Wine and Spirit Assoc** +FAX 01244 678 624
**Notts, Arnold & Carlton College** 0115 953 1222 FAX 0115 953 1210
**Plumpton College** 01273 890 454 FAX 01273 890 071
**Scala School** +FAX 0171 637 9077
**Sotheby's** 0171 408 5051 FAX 0171 408 5961
**Vinform** 0181 876 0110
**Wensum Lodge** 01603 666 021 FAX 01603 765 633
**West Suffolk College** 01284 701301 FAX 01284 750 561
**Wine & Spirit Education Trust** 0171 236 3551 FAX 0171 329 8712
**Winecraft** +FAX 01727 845136
**Wine Education Service** 0181 886 0304
**Wine Wise** 0171 254 9734
**Wink Lorch** 0181 670 6885 FAX 0181 670 6885
**York** 01904 612 107 FAX 01904 612 107

## Wine Holidays

**Accompanied Cape** ☎ 01531 660 210
**Allez France** ☎ 01903 745 319/ 742 345
**Alternative Travel** ☎ 01865 513 333 FAX 01865 310 299
**Arblaster & Clarke Wine Tours** ☎ 01730 893 344 FAX 01730 892 888
**Backroads** ☎ 01425 655 022 FAX 01425 655177
**The Cape Vine** ☎ 01604 648 768 FAX 01604 644 013
**Connoisseur** FAX 0171 376 7966
**DER Travel** ☎ 0171 290 1111 FAX 0171 629 7442
**Edwin Doran Travel** ☎ 0181 744 1212 FAX 0181 744 1169
**Eurocamp Canute Court** ☎ 01565 626 262 FAX 01565 755 352
**Francophiles Discover France** ☎ 0117 962 1975 FAX 0117 9622642
**French Alps** ☎ 0181 670 6885 FAX 0181 670 6885
**Friendship Travel** ☎ 01483 273 355 FAX 01483 268621
**Grenadier Travel** ☎ 01206 549 585 FAX 01206 561 337
**HGP Wine Tours** ☎ 01803 299 292 FAX 01803 292 008
**KD River Cruises Europe** ☎ 01372 742 033 FAX 01372 724 871
**Millers House Hotel** ☎ 01969 622 630 FAX 01969 623 570
**Moswin Tours** ☎ 0116 271 4982 FAX 0116 271 6016
**Page & Moy** ☎ 0116 254 2000 FAX 0116 254 9949
**Tanglewood Wine Tours** ☎ 01932 348720 FAX 01932 350 861
**Travel Club of Upminster** ☎ 01708 227 260 FAX 01708 229 678
**Ski Morgins** ☎ 01746 783 005 FAX 01746 783 005
**Walker's France** ☎ 01734 402 153 FAX 01734 404 815
**Wessex Continental Travel** ☎+FAX 01752 846 880
**Wine Club Tours** ☎ 01730 895 353 FAX 01730 892 888
**Winetrails** ☎ 01306 712 111 FAX 01306 713 504

## Wine Accessories

### GLASSES

**Bibendum (Riedel Glass Range)** (see Page 241)
**Conran Shop (Riedel Glass Range)** ☎ 0171 589 7401
**Dartington Crystal** ☎ 01805 622 321 FAX 01805 623 469
**Roberson** (seePage 251)
**Schott UK** ☎ 01785 223 688
**The Wine Glass Company** ☎ 01234 721 300 FAX 01234 721 311

### CORKSCREWS

**Screwpull** (The Kitchenware Merchants) ☎ 01264 353 912

### STORAGE

**Abacus** ☎ 0181 991 9717 FAX 0181 991 9611
**Consort Wine Care Systems** ☎ 01635 33993 FAX 01635 41733
**Euro-cave** ☎ 0181 343 4888 FAX 0181 343 3422
**Octavian** ☎ 01992 470 694 FAX 01992 451 1187
**Smith & Taylor** ☎ 0171 627 5070 FAX 0171 622 8235
**Sowesco** ☎ 01935 826 333 FAX 01935 826 310
**Vin-Garde (Storage Cabinets) Ltd** ☎ 01926 811376

### WINE RACKS

**A.&W. Moore** ☎ 0115 944 1434 FAX 0115 932 0735
**RTA Wine Racks** ☎ 01328 829 666 FAX 01328 829 667
**Spiral Cellars** ☎ 01372 372 181 FAX 01372 360 142
**The Wine Rack Company** ☎+FAX 01243 543 253

### ANTIQUES

**Richard Kihl** ☎+FAX 0171 493 0602

### GENERAL WINE ACCESSORIES

**Birchgrove Products Ltd** ☎ 01483 33400 FAX 01483 33700
**The Hugh Johnson Collection** ☎ 0171 491 4912 FAX 0171 493 0602

### WINE PRESERVATION

**Vacu Products (Vacuvin)** ☎ 01264 339 821 FAX 01264 356 777
**Winesaver** ☎ 01264 339 821 FAX 01264 356 777

### CHILLING DEVICES

**Chilla** ☎ 0850 264 582
**Vacu Products** (Rapid Ice, Champagne Rapid Ice) ☎ 01264 339 821 FAX 01264 356 777
**Coolbags & Boxes UK** ☎ 01734 333 331

### BOOKS

**Richard Stanford** ☎ 0171 836 1321
**Adnams** ☎ 01502 727 220 FAX 01502 727 223
**Bibendum** (see Page 241)
**Cooking The Books** ☎+FAX 01633 400 150

## WINE CLUBS

*Alston Wine Club* ☎ *01434 381 034*
*Amersham* ☎ *01494 771 983*
*Association of Wine Cellarmen* ☎ *0181 871 3092*
*Birmingham* ☎ *0121 415 5227*
*Cambridge* ☎ *01954 780 438*
*Central London* ☎ *01634 848 345*
*Chandlers Cross* ☎ *01923 264 718*
*Charlemagne* ☎ *0181 423 6338*
*Chiswick* ☎ *0171 481 1242*
*Cirencester* ☎ *01285 641 126*
*Civil Service* ☎ *01634 848 345*
*Cleveland* ☎ *01287 624 459*
*Confrèrie Internationale de St Vincent* ☎ *0113 267 9258*
*Cornwall* ☎ *01872 73856*
*Eastbourne* ☎ *01323 725528*
*Edinburgh* ☎ *0131 332 5332*
*Fine Wine Dining* ☎ *01895 632 053*
*Garforth* ☎ *0113 266 6322*
*Goring & Streatley* ☎ *01491 872 930*
*Grimsby & Cleethorpes* ☎ *01472 826 307*
*Guild of Sommeliers* ☎ *0161 928 0852*
*Harrogate Medical* ☎ *01423 503 129*
*Herefordshire* ☎ *01432 275 656*
*Hextable Wine Club* ☎ *01732 823 345*
*Hollingworth* ☎ *01706 374 765*
*Ightham Wine Club* ☎ *01732 885 557*
*Institute of Wines & Spirits* ☎ *01324 554 162*
*International Wine and Food Society* ☎ *0171 4954191* FAX *0171 4954172*
*L' Academie du Vin* ☎ *01803 299 292*
*Lay & Wheeler* ☎ *01206 764 446* FAX *01206 560 002*
*Leicester Evington* ☎ *0116 231 4760*
*Leicester Grand Union* ☎ *0116 287 1662*
*Lincoln Wine Society* ☎ *01522 680388*
*London* ☎ *0181 349 2260*
*Maidenhead* ☎ *01628 25577*
*Manchester* ☎ *01706 824 283*
*Moreno* ☎ *0171 286 0678*
*Myster Wine Club* ☎ *01633 893 485*
*North Hampshire* ☎ *01256 473 503*
*Petersham* ☎ *01932 348 720* FAX *01932 350 861*
*Preston* ☎ *01772 254 251*
*Rochester* ☎ *01634 848 345*
*Scottish* ☎ *01368 864 892*
*Sevenoaks* ☎ *01732 460 789*
*Sittingbourne* ☎ *01795 478 818*
*South African* ☎ *01708 743 808*
*Wessex Wine Society* ☎ *01985 214 578*
*West Hampstead* ☎ *0171 794 3926*
*West Suffolk* ☎ *01284 787 598*
*Whitewater Valley* ☎ *01256 769 726*
*Windsor and Eton* ☎ *01753 790 188*
*Wine and Dine* ☎ *0181 673 4439*
*Wine Collectors'* ☎ *01306 742 164*
*Wine Schoppen* ☎ *0114 255 3301* FAX *0114 255 1010*
*Winetasters* ☎ *0181 997 1252*
*York* ☎ *01904 691 628*

## CROSS-CHANNEL SHOPPING

**Centre Leclerc** Route Oudalle, Gonfrevill L'Orchère, Le Havre. ☎ (33) 2 35 49 02 22
**EastEnders Bulk Beer Warehouse** Rue Garennes, Zone Ind. des Dunes, 62100 Calais. ☎ (33) 3 21 34 53 33
**La Maison du Vin** 71 Avenue Carnot 50100 Cherbourg. ☎ (33) 2 33 43 39 79
**Sainsbury's** CC Calais Ouest, Fort Nieulay, Route de Boulogne, 62100 Calais. ☎ (33) 3 21 82 38 48
**Le Tastevin** 9 rue Val 35400 St-Malo. ☎ (33) 2 99 82 46 56
**Tesco Vin Plus** Espace 122 Cité d'Europe, 62231 Coquelles, Calais. ☎ (33) 3 21 46 02 70
**Victoria Wine** Unit 139 Cité d'Europe, 62231 Coquelles, Calais. ☎ (33) 3 21 82 07 32
**The Wine Society** 1 rue de la Paroisse, 62140 Hesdin. ☎ (33) 3 21 86 52 07
**The Wine & Beer Company** CC Quais de l'Entrepôt, 50100 Cherbourg. ☎ (33) 2 33 22 23 22

# INDEX

A list of recommended wines to be be used as a supplement to the A–Z (see Page 83) and UK Merchants section. (see Page 239)

## A



## B

# C

# D



# E



# F

# G



# H

# I



# J



# K



# L

# M



# N

# O



# P



# Q



# R

# S



# T

# U



# V



# W

# Y



# Z

# Wine on the Web

If you enjoy

*The Sunday Telegraph Good Wine Guide*

visit Robert Joseph's

*Good Wine Guide*

site on the World Wide Web

at

**http://www.goodwineguide.com**

for news, competitions,

an electronic Wine Atlas, comment and links to over 200 wineries and merchants throughout the world.

Visit

**http://www.wineschool.com**

**http://www.robertjoseph.com**

for a daily interactive food and wine updates

and

**http://www.dk.com**

for details of other Dorling Kindersley titles